Social Security Handbook

Overview of Social Security Programs

2024

Social Security Handbook

Overview of Social Security Programs

2024

Lanham • Boulder • New York • London

Published by Bernan Press
An imprint of The Rowman & Littlefield Publishing Group, Inc.
4501 Forbes Boulevard, Suite 200, Lanham, Maryland 20706
www.rowman.com
800-462-6420

86-90 Paul Street, London EC2A 4NE, United Kingdom

Copyright © 2024 by The Rowman & Littlefield Publishing Group, Inc.

All rights reserved. No part of this book may be reproduced in any form or by any electronic or mechanical means, including information storage and retrieval systems, without written permission from the publisher, except by a reviewer who may quote passages in a review. The Rowman & Littlefield Publishing Group, Inc. does not claim copyright in U.S. government information.

ISBN: 979-8-89205-000-5

∞™ The paper used in this publication meets the minimum requirements of American National Standard for Information Sciences—Permanence of Paper for Printed Library Materials, ANSI/NISO Z39.48-1992.

Contents

Preface vii

1. Overview of the Social Security System 1
2. Becoming Insured 37
3. Cash Retirement and Auxiliary Benefits;
   Special Age 72 Payments 57
4. Survivors Benefits 93
5. Cash Disability Benefits and Related Disability Protection 121
6. Factors in Evaluating Disability 153
7. Figuring the Cash Benefit Rate 175
8. Who Are Employees? 215
9. Special Coverage Provisions 231
10. State and Local Employment 275
11. Are You Self-Employed? 293
12. Net Earnings From Self-Employment 317
13. Wages 345
14. Earnings Records and Tax Reports 361
15. Filing a Claim 383
16. Representative Payees 399
17. Evidence Required to Establish Right to Benefits 419
18. Reduction or Nonpayment of Social Security Benefits 443
19. Underpayments and Overpayments 493
20. Determinations and the Administrative Review Process 511
21. Supplemental Security Income 537
22. Black Lung Benefits 617
23. Other Benefit Programs 619
24. Health Insurance Protection (Medicare) 621
25. Medicare Income-Related Monthly Adjustment Amount 623
26. Extra Help with Medicare Prescription Drug Costs 631
27. Special Veterans Benefits 645

Index 661

Preface

The Bernan Press edition of the *Social Security Handbook: Overview of Social Security Programs, 2024* contains information about the benefit programs administered by the Social Security Administration. The *Handbook* includes the provisions of the Social Security Act (the Act), regulations issued under the Act, and precedential case decisions (rulings).

The Social Security programs are so complex it is impossible to include information about every topic. The *Handbook* includes the most common and helpful information. In case of a conflict between the contents of the *Handbook* and the Act, Regulations, and Rulings, the latter take precedence.

The completely updated *Handbook*, organized by section number, is a readable, easy-to-understand resource for the very complex Social Security programs and services. It contains information on:

- How Social Security programs are administered
- Who is and is not covered under retirement, survivors, disability, and hospital insurance programs
- Who is responsible for submitting the necessary evidence to support a claim
- How claims are processed by the Social Security office
- What Social Security benefits are owed to you
- How to obtain information about your rights under Social Security policy

In developing the Bernan Press edition of the *Handbook*, every effort has been made to include information that is accurate, meaningful, and useful. The responsibility of the publisher of this volume is limited to reasonable care in the reproduction and presentation of public domain data from the Social Security programs and the Social Security Administration. Please visit https://www.ssa.gov/.

CHAPTER 1
Overview of the Social Security System

TABLE OF CONTENTS

INTRODUCTION
100. Purposes of Social Security
101. Obtaining A Social Security Card
102. Checking Individual Earnings Records
103. Application for Social Security Benefits, Medicare Coverage, or Medicare Protection
104. Who is responsible for proving a claim?
105. How are claims processed by the Social Security office?
106. Duty to Report Certain Events
107. Totalization Agreements
108. Who is NOT covered under retirement, survivors, disability, and hospital insurance programs?

ORGANIZATIONAL STRUCTURE OF THE SOCIAL SECURITY ADMINISTRATION (SSA)
109. How is the Social Security Administration (SSA) structured?
110. The Function of the Social Security Office
111. Program Service Center Functions
112. Where are earnings records maintained?
113. Recording Earnings Credits
114. SSI Claimants Residing Abroad
115. Determinations of Disability

SERVICES OF SSA
116. Information Program of the Social Security Office
117. Information Required by Law to be Made Available to the Public
118. Does the Social Security office make referrals to other government or community agencies?

DISBURSEMENT OF BENEFIT PAYMENTS
119. Social Security Benefits Payable
120. Who issues Social Security benefits and SSI payments?
121. Payment Dates
122. Direct Deposit of Benefits
123. Checks
124. How do you endorse your check if you cannot sign your name?
125. Entitlement To Retirement, Survivors, And Disability Insurance Benefits
126. Supplemental Security Income Benefits
127. Hospital and Medical Insurance Benefits Provided
128. Prescription Drug Benefits Provided
129. Benefits Not Transferable
130. Special Request For Expedited Benefit Payment
131. Checks to Husband and Wife
132. Are separate Social Security benefit checks mailed to each child in a family?

BENEFICIARY'S OBLIGATIONS
133. Reporting to Social Security
134. Returning Checks To The Social Security Office
135. What is done if you receive more money than you are entitled?

FUNDING THE PROGRAMS
136. Sources of Funds for Social Security and Supplemental Security Income Benefits
137. How are hospital insurance benefits funded?
138. How are medical insurance benefits funded?
139. How are prescription drug benefits funded?
140. Where are money gifts to Social Security deposited?

TRUST FUNDS
141. Trust Funds Available For Benefits

FRAUD
142. What investigative responsibilities does SSA have in administering the Social Security program?
143. Fraud In Connection With Benefit Claims And Earnings Records
144. Social Security Cost-Of-Living Adjustment And Other Automatic Increases

100. PURPOSES OF SOCIAL SECURITY

100.1 What are the purposes of Social Security?

The Social Security Act and related laws establish a number of programs that have the following basic purposes:
A. To provide for the material needs of individuals and families;
B. To protect aged and disabled persons against the expenses of illnesses that may otherwise use up their savings;
C. To keep families together; and
D. To give children the chance to grow up healthy and secure.

100.2 What programs are included under the Social Security Act and related laws?

The following programs are included:
A. Retirement insurance;
B. Survivors insurance;
C. Disability insurance;
D. Hospital and medical insurance for the aged, the disabled, and those with end-stage renal disease;
E. Prescription Drug Benefit;
F. Extra Help with Medicare Prescription Drug Costs;
G. Supplemental security income;
H. Special Veterans Benefits;
I. Unemployment insurance; and
J. Public assistance and welfare services, including:
    1. Temporary assistance for needy families;
    2. Medical assistance;
    3. Maternal and child health services;
    4. Child support enforcement;
    5. Family and child welfare services;
    6. Food stamps; and
    7. Energy assistance.

101. OBTAINING A SOCIAL SECURITY CARD

101.1 What is a Social Security Number?

A Social Security Number (SSN) is a nine digit number SSA assigns to individuals to identify their records of earnings in employment or self-employment covered by Social Security and to pay benefits.

101.2 How can you obtain a Social Security Number?

To obtain an SSN, you need to complete an application for a Social Security card at your local Social Security office and submit certain documents. If you visit a Social Security office you can file your application electronically. If you prefer to mail in your application and documents, Form SS-5 (Application for a Social Security Card) is available for download at: https://www.ssa.gov/forms/ss-5.pdf, or by calling 1-800-772-1213. These services are free.

101.3 What documents do you need?

To apply for an SSN, you need to provide at least two documents to prove your age, identity, and United States (U.S.) citizenship or lawful employment-authorized immigration status. We can only accept original documents or documents certified by the custodian of the original record. Notarized copies or photocopies which have not been certified by the custodian of the record are not acceptable.

Additional documents may be required:

A. If you are a non-citizen lawfully in the U.S. without Department of Homeland Security (DHS) employment-authorization, you must also provide a document from the government agency requiring your SSN that explains why you need a number and that you meet all of the requirements for the benefit or service except for the number. A State or local agency requirement must conform to Federal law.
B. If you are a non-citizen in the U.S. without employment-authorization or are not a U.S. lawful permanent resident and reside outside the U.S., you need to provide proof you are entitled to a federally funded benefit for which an SSN is required for you to receive payment.
C. If you are applying for an SSN on behalf of someone else, you must provide evidence of your authority to sign the application on behalf of the person to whom the card will be issued and evidence of your own identity.

101.4 Is it necessary to apply in person?

If you are 12 or older and have never been assigned an SSN, you must apply in person for a Social Security card. It is important for you to provide complete and correct personal information so your earnings are credited properly and to prevent the unlawful use of your number by someone else. There are penalties for falsely obtaining or improperly using an SSN.

101.5 When is a Taxpayer Identification Number needed?

You need a Taxpayer Identification Number (TIN) if you:

A. Have income that is reported to the Internal Revenue Service (IRS); or

B. You are claimed as a dependent on someone's Federal income tax return.

The IRS uses your SSN as your TIN if you have been assigned one. If you are not eligible for an SSN, you may apply for an Individual Taxpayer Identification Number (ITIN) from IRS. If you have any questions about use of TINs, contact the nearest IRS office.

101.6 How should you protect your Social Security number and card?

Protect your Social Security card and number from loss and potential identity theft. *DO NOT* routinely carry your card or any document that shows your Social Security number with you. Keep it in a secure location and only take it with you when you must show the card to obtain a new job, open a new bank account, or obtain benefits or services from certain government agencies. Additionally, do not allow others to use your SSN as their own.

101.7 What should you do if you lose your Social Security card?

You may not need to replace your lost Social Security card. Knowing your Social Security number is what is important. However, if you wish to do so, you need to apply for a replacement card by visiting a Social Security office or completing Form SS-5. The new card will have the same number as the lost card. You must present evidence of your identity when requesting a replacement card. If you were born outside the U.S., you must also provide evidence of your U.S. citizenship (if not already shown on our records) or current employment-authorized immigration status. If you are not a U.S. citizen or do not have current employment-authorized immigration status, you must prove that you have a valid nonwork reason for a replacement card.

101.8 How do you update information on your Social Security record?

If you want to correct or update information that you gave on the original, or your most recent application for an SSN, you must complete a new application for a Social Security card and submit certain supporting documents that show the corrected information (e.g., your birth certificate or other acceptable evidence of your age if the date of birth provided is incorrect). To change your name, you must show evidence of a legal name change, for example, a marriage document or court order for a name change. The evidence of a legal name change should identify you by both your old and new names and contain information about you that we can compare to our records (i.e., your date of birth, age, parents' names). If the evidence of the legal name change does not provide sufficient information to properly identify you, we will request additional evidence. If you were born outside the U.S., you must also provide evidence of your U.S. citizenship (if not already shown in our records) or current lawful immigration status.

101.9 Limits on Replacement SSN Cards

The number of replacement SSN cards you may receive is limited to 3 per year and 10 in a lifetime. In determining these limits, SSA will not count changes in legal name (i.e., first name or surname), or changes to a restrictive legend (i.e., Valid for Work with DHS Authorization, Not Valid for Employment) shown on the SSN card. In addition, we may grant exceptions on a case-by-case basis if you can provide evidence to establish a need for an SSN card beyond these limits (e.g., a letter from a social services agency stating that you must show the SSN card in order to get benefits).

102. CHECKING INDIVIDUAL EARNINGS RECORDS

102.1 How can you check your Social Security earnings record?

To create an account and check your earnings records, please go to https://www.ssa.gov/myaccount.

102.2 What should you do if your earnings record is inaccurate?

If you find that your earnings have not been credited correctly, contact any convenient Social Security office and ask us how to go about correcting your records. There are specific time limits for correcting an earnings record. (See §§1423-1427.)

103. APPLICATION FOR SOCIAL SECURITY BENEFITS, MEDICARE COVERAGE, OR MEDICARE PROTECTION

103.1 Where do you file applications for Social Security benefits and applications for Medicare?

You may file applications for Social Security benefits (Retirement, Spouse's and Disability benefits), Supplemental Security Income (SSI), Medicare coverage, or apply for Medicare protection and Extra Help with Medicare prescription drug costs, through the Internet, https://www.ssa.gov, by telephone (1-800-772-1213) or in person at any Social Security office. (See §2601 for information about the Extra Help with Medicare prescription drug costs.)

We provide you with the proper application and enrollment forms. If you need assistance, our employees will help you fill out the forms. If you need an interpreter to communicate with us, we will provide one upon request, free of charge. SSA has a nationwide contract for telephone interpreter services in more than 150 languages and dialects. In some cases, you may file an application for food stamps at any Social Security office if you are applying for or are receiving SSI. (See §2108)

103.2 Where do you file your claims if you live outside the United States?

For information on how to obtain services when you are outside the United States, see: https://www.ssa.gov/foreign/.

104. WHO IS RESPONSIBLE FOR PROVING A CLAIM?

You are responsible for submitting the necessary evidence to support a claim. We assist you by explaining the evidence that is required to establish your claim. If you are unable to collect the evidence, we offer special assistance to ensure the proper outcome of your claim. In addition, we maintain cooperative relationships with many groups and organizations that provide assistance with the application process.

105. HOW ARE CLAIMS PROCESSED BY THE SOCIAL SECURITY OFFICE?

We make most decisions on the non-disability issues. We send completed retirement and survivors insurance claims to the appropriate program service center for spot review and, in some cases, for final processing. We keep Supplemental Security Income (SSI) claims paper files (if the claim was not electronically processed) in our field offices and later ship them to the Folder Staging Operations Center at the Wilkes-Barre Data Operations Center.

If a disability decision is involved, we forward the claim in accordance with the procedure in §115.

106. DUTY TO REPORT CERTAIN EVENTS

106.1 Who is responsible for reporting events affecting benefits?

You are responsible for reporting any event(s) that may affect your Social Security or Supplemental Security benefits. We explain this responsibility when you apply for benefits. (See §133 and Chapter 18.)

107. TOTALIZATION AGREEMENTS

107.1 What are Totalization agreements?

The Social Security Act allows the President to enter into international agreements to coordinate the U.S. Social Security Act's title II (old age, survivors and disability) insurance programs with the social security programs of other countries. These agreements are known as "Totalization agreements."

107.2 With what countries does the U.S. have Totalization agreements?

The United States currently has social security agreements in effect with 30 countries - Australia (2002), Austria (1991), Belgium (1984), Brazil (2018), Canada (1984), Chile (2001), Czech Republic (2009), Denmark (2008), Finland (1992), France (1988), Germany (1979), Greece (1994), Hungary (2016), Iceland (2019), Ireland (1993), Italy (1978), Japan (2005), Luxembourg (1993), the Netherlands (1990), Norway (1984), Poland (2009), Portugal (1989), Slovak Republic (2014), Slovenia (2019), South Korea (2001), Spain (1988), Sweden (1987), Switzerland (1980), the United Kingdom (1985), and Uruguay (2018).

107.3 What are the purposes of Totalization agreements?

Totalization agreements have three main purposes:
A. To eliminate dual social security coverage and taxation. This situation occurs when a person from one country works in the other country and is required to pay social security taxes to both countries for the same work;
B. To avoid situations in which workers lose benefit rights because they have divided their careers between two countries. Under an

agreement, such workers may qualify for partial U.S. or foreign benefits based on combined work credits from both countries.

C. To increase benefit portability by guaranteeing that neither country will impose restrictions on benefit payments based solely on residence or presence in the other country.

107.4 Totalization Agreements - Other Resources

For additional information on "Totalization agreements" see: https://www.ssa.gov/international/agreements_overview.html.

108. WHO IS NOT COVERED UNDER RETIREMENT, SURVIVORS, DISABILITY, AND HOSPITAL INSURANCE PROGRAMS?

Nine out of 10 workers in the U.S. are in employment or self-employment covered by the retirement, survivors, disability, and hospital insurance programs. You are *not* covered if you are:

A. A Federal civilian employee hired before 1984 unless you later changed to the Federal Employee Retirement System. However, all Federal civilian employees are covered by the hospital insurance program.

B. An employee of a State or local government who is:
   1. A member of your employer's retirement system; and
   2. Not covered by a voluntary Federal/State Social Security agreement.

C. A certain agricultural and domestic worker.

109. HOW IS THE SOCIAL SECURITY ADMINISTRATION (SSA) STRUCTURED?

SSA is headed by a Commissioner. Our central office is located in Baltimore, Maryland. Our administrative offices and the computer operations are also located there. Individual claims services are provided by our local Social Security offices.

110. THE FUNCTION OF THE SOCIAL SECURITY OFFICE

110.1 What services can your local Social Security Office provide?

Your local Social Security office is the place where you can:

A. Apply for a Social Security number;
B. Check on your earnings record;
C. Apply for Social Security benefits, SSI, hospital insurance protection, and Extra Help with Medicare prescription drug costs;
D. Enroll for medical insurance;

E. Receive assistance in applying for food stamps; and
F. Get full information about individual and family rights and obligations under the law. There is no charge for the services of the office staff.

110.2 How can you obtain Social Security services?

You can call our toll-free telephone number, 1-800-772-1213, to receive the services listed in (A) - (F) above. This toll-free telephone number service is available from 7 a.m. to 7 p.m. any business day. All calls are confidential. The toll-free telephone number is not accessible from outside the United States. For information on how to obtain services when you are outside the United States, see: https://www.ssa.gov/foreign/.

110.3 Are there other places you can meet Social Security office staff other than the local offices?

If you live far away from the city or town in which the local office is located, our staff makes regular visits to outlying areas. We make visits to locations called contact stations. You can obtain a schedule of these visits from the nearest Social Security office. You can also telephone the nearest Social Security office or call our toll-free number, 1-800-772-1213, to obtain prompt answers to questions or to apply for benefits.

If necessary, a representative from our office will make a personal visit to your home if you are unable to visit the office or contact station because of illness or infirmity. (See §1512.)

110.4 Where can you find contact information for the nearest Social Security office?

For the telephone number or address of the nearest Social Security office, look in the telephone directory in the blue pages for Social Security Administration under "United States Government." You can also call our toll-free number, 1-800-772-1213 or access the SSA website (https://www.ssa.gov), for assistance.

110.5 Where are SSA's regional offices located?

We have regional offices headed by Regional Commissioners who are directly responsible for the Social Security offices located within a specified area. There are approximately 1,300 Social Security offices throughout the U.S., the U.S. Virgin Islands, Puerto Rico, Guam, and American Samoa that deal directly with the public as described throughout this Chapter. Each region also has a number of teleservice centers located primarily in metropolitan areas. These offices handle telephone inquiries and refer callers appropriately.

110.6 Where are SSA's program service centers located?

Program service centers are located in Birmingham, Alabama; Chicago, Illinois; Kansas City, Missouri; New York, New York; Philadelphia, Pennsylvania; and Richmond, California. These offices, along with the Office of International Operations and the Office of Disability Operations in Baltimore, Maryland, house and service the records of individuals who are receiving Social Security benefits.

110.7 What is the purpose of the Office of Disability Adjudication and Review?

The Office of Disability Adjudication and Review oversees the nationwide hearings and appeals program for the Social Security Administration. Administrative law judges hold hearings and make decisions when a claimant or organization appeals a decision affecting rights to benefits or participation in Social Security programs.

110.8 Where are administrative law judges located?

Administrative law judges are located in or travel to major cities throughout the U.S., Puerto Rico, the U.S. Virgin Islands, Guam, the Northern Mariana Islands, and American Samoa. The Appeals Council, located in Falls Church, Virginia, also may review hearing decisions. (See Chapter 20.)

110.9 What is the purpose of the Office of Central Operations?

The Office of Central Operations maintains records of individuals' earnings and prepares benefit computations.

110.10 Where is the Office of Central Operations located?

The major operations are located in Salinas, California; and Wilkes-Barre, Pennsylvania. (See §113 and §114.) Data processing is the responsibility of the Office of Systems located in Baltimore, Maryland.

111. PROGRAM SERVICE CENTER FUNCTIONS

111.1 What functions do the program service centers perform?

Program service centers act as processing centers. They make formal decisions as to entitlement on many claims for Social Security benefits

(See §110). (See §116 regarding disability insurance benefits; Chapter 24 regarding payment of hospital and medical insurance benefits; Chapter 21 regarding SSI claims; and §115 regarding claims from beneficiaries residing abroad.)

At the program service center, a permanent claims folder is set up for the claims material. It may be reviewed for the following:

A. To see that the necessary applications and forms have been properly completed;
B. To make sure all the evidence needed for the claim has been obtained;
C. To ensure all requirements set by law have been met; and
D. To check that all benefit amounts have been figured correctly.

111.2 How are you notified by the program service center when it makes a decision on your claim?

If the program service center finds that you are entitled to benefits, your claim is approved and the U.S. Treasury Department is notified that payment should be made. If you are entitled to hospital or medical insurance protection, the program service center advises you of the decision and sends you a health insurance identification card. If you are not entitled to monthly benefits or to hospital or medical insurance protection, your claim is denied.

The program service center prepares and mails the notice of award or denial to you. This notice shows the type and amount of benefit awarded; or explains why the claim was not approved and how you may appeal.

112. WHERE ARE EARNINGS RECORDS MAINTAINED?

If you are assigned a Social Security number, your earnings record is maintained at the Office of Central Operations of the Social Security Administration in Baltimore, Maryland. The earnings record is kept so that when it is time to decide on your eligibility for Social Security benefits and benefit amount, your earnings history is available.

113. RECORDING EARNINGS CREDITS

113.1 Where are earnings reports processed?

We send earnings reports of employees and self-employed persons to the Office of Central Operations. Employer reports of earnings are received in the central office and in our facility at Wilkes-Barre, Pennsylvania. Each person's earnings amounts are credited to his or her record.

113.2 What happens if there is an error in your earnings report?

If there is any error in your earnings report, or if your Social Security number or name is reported incorrectly, the Office of Central Operations investigates so that it can correct the error. It also decides if your reported earnings are covered by Social Security.

The Office of Central Operations may write directly to you or your employer to get information needed to clarify your earnings report. If necessary, it may ask a Social Security office to get directly in touch with you to resolve any problem or obtain information needed to determine if your work is covered by Social Security.

114. SSI CLAIMANTS RESIDING ABROAD

114.1 Where is your case handled if you live overseas?

If you live overseas, your SSI payments are handled by one of the following:

A. If you are a *blind or disabled child of military parents stationed overseas*, your case is handled by the Social Security office in Cumberland, Maryland;

B. If you are a *temporarily abroad student*, your case is handled by any Social Security office; or

C. If you are *any other claimant living abroad*, your case is handled in the Office of International Operations of the Office of Disability and International Operations (ODIO).

114.2 What is the Office of Disability and International Operations?

ODIO receives, develops, and settles Social Security claims of persons residing outside the U.S. This office also acts on requests for reconsideration. ODIO receives assistance from the State Department's Foreign Service posts around the world, the American Institute in Taipei (Taiwan), and the Veterans Affairs Regional Office in the Philippines to carry out this mission.

114.3 When are you considered outside the U.S. for claims settlement purposes?

For claims settlement purposes, you are considered outside the U.S. if you are physically outside the 50 States, the District of Columbia, Puerto Rico, the U.S. Virgin Islands, Guam, the Northern Mariana Islands, and American Samoa.

114.4 Where do you report events that could affect your benefits if you live abroad?

If you are a beneficiary living in a foreign country, report the events described in §133 to one of the following:

A. The nearest Social Security office;
B. One of the offices listed above; or
C. The Social Security Administration, Post Office Box 17769, Baltimore, Maryland 21235-7769.

114.5 Where do disabled children of military parents stationed overseas report events that could affect their benefits?

Blind or disabled children of military parents stationed overseas should report the events in §133 to one of the following:

A. The U.S. Embassy;
B. The nearest U.S. Consular Office; or
C. Social Security Administration, ATTN: SSI Military Children Overseas Coordinator, 1 Frederick Street, Suite 100, Cumberland, MD 21502.

114.6 Where do you send correspondence concerning totalization claims?

The Office of International Operations is responsible for all claims under the international totalization agreements described in §107. This is true even if you live in the U.S. Send any correspondence concerning totalization claims to the Social Security Administration, Post Office Box 17049, Baltimore, Maryland 21235.

115. DETERMINATIONS OF DISABILITY

115.1 How does SSA determine disability cases?

State Disability Determination Services (DDS) generally make decisions on disability cases. DDSs are state agencies in every state that SSA funds and administers for the purpose of making disability determinations. SSA makes disability insurance determinations for persons living outside the U.S., and for a few other applicants whose cases are not covered under the Federal-State regulations. Generally, an evaluation team composed of a medical or psychological consultant and a lay disability evaluation specialist is responsible for making the disability determination. The evaluation team makes every reasonable effort to obtain medical evidence from your treatment sources.

115.2 Who checks to make sure that determinations made on disability cases are correct?

Our Office of Quality Assurance and Performance Assessment reviews a continuing sample of DDS determinations in the Disability Quality Branches (DQB) in our ten regions. These DQBs ensure that DDS determinations are correct, consistent, and in line with national policies and standards. As a result of a Quality Assurance review, a DDS's findings may be reversed.

115.3 What can you do if you do not agree with our determination about your claim?

If you are not satisfied with the determination made on your claim, you may appeal. In most states, you may request reconsideration and submit new evidence if it is available. A reconsideration determination for disability claims is made by a different decision maker, not connected with the initial determination in the DDS where the original determination was made. Again, the DQBs review the DDS reconsideration determinations. If you appeal your case further, an administrative law judge (ALJ) may hear your case in a face-to-face or video teleconference hearing, unless you indicate in writing that you do not wish to appear before an ALJ at an in-person hearing. If the ALJ's decision is not favorable to you, you may request review of the decision by the the Appeals Council of the Office of Disability Adjudication and Review. (See Chapter 20.)

116. INFORMATION PROGRAM OF THE SOCIAL SECURITY OFFICE

116.1 Where can you obtain information about your rights under Social Security?

Social Security offices conduct an Information Program to keep you informed of your rights and obligations under the Social Security law. Our offices also conduct outreach programs to locate and assist people who are potentially eligible for benefits.

116.2 What do offices participating in the Information Program do?

The offices keep on hand supplies of publications, exhibit posters, and videos. The office staff:

A. Makes presentations before civic, labor, medical, farm, management, school, and other groups and organizations interested in our programs;
B. Prepares or provides articles about Social Security for local newspapers and magazines;
C. Develops special exhibits illustrating features of the Social Security program; and
D. Prepares and presents radio and television programs about Social Security and SSI.

You may make arrangements with a participating Social Security office to obtain any of the informational materials listed above, to view a video, to have an exhibit set up, or to have a member of the office staff speak before a group or organization.

The Social Security offices also participate in community programs and activities in the fields of aging, blindness, disabilities (including AIDS/HIV, mental health, and substance abuse), child welfare, and economic opportunity.

117. INFORMATION REQUIRED BY LAW TO BE MADE AVAILABLE TO THE PUBLIC

117.1 What laws require SSA to release information?

We are required, along with all Federal agencies, to comply with the Freedom of Information Act and the Privacy Act. These laws control the type and scope of information that may be released and to whom it may be released.

117.2 What information is made available to the public under the Freedom of Information Act?

The Freedom of Information Act makes the following types of information available to the public:
A. Statement of organization;
B. Administrative procedures;
C. Policies;
D. Interpretations of law; and
E. Precedent decisions that affect the public.

The type of information above is available unless it falls within one of the law's specific exceptions. Generally, information on your earnings may be disclosed only to you, or for purposes of administering Social Security programs. Revealing earnings information is generally governed by Section 6103 of the Internal Revenue Code, as amended (26 U.S.C. 6103).

117.3 When can additional information be made available under the Freedom of Information Act?

Under the Freedom of Information Act, information about your Social Security record, other than items (A) - (E) above, may not be revealed to "the public" without your permission. "The public" generally includes any requester other than a Federal agency or a Federal, State, or local court.

Additional information is only made available if the requesting party can demonstrate that revealing information would shed light on how the Federal Government operates to a degree that outweighs your rights and expectations of privacy.

117.4 What information is made available to the public under the Privacy Act?

The Privacy Act requires Federal agencies to publish notices of systems of records they maintain that contain personal information about individuals. This information is published in the *Federal Register*. Under the Privacy Act, information about you is generally not disclosed without your permission, except as provided by that law.

117.5 Can you access information maintained under the Privacy Act?

You have the right to gain access to information pertaining to you. You may have a copy made of your own record, request a correction to your record, or amend your record. There are special procedures for accessing medical records. Direct your request for information from these systems of records to the local Social Security office or the manager of the pertinent system of records. There is generally no charge to obtain information contained in your file.

117.6 What are Informational Facilities?

We have "Informational Facilities" that contain various legal publications, informational publications about us, and several manuals of instructions used in processing Social Security and SSI claims. This information is available to the public.

117.7 What type of information can you access at Informational Facilities?

The following is a partial list of the materials available to you at our Informational Facilities:

A. Compilation of the Social Security Laws;
B. Social Security Administration Regulations Nos. 1, 4, 10, 16, and 22;
C. Social Security Rulings;
D. Acquiescence Rulings;
E. Program Operations Manual System;
F. Social Security Handbook;
G. Handbook for State Social Security Administrators;
H. Part A Intermediary Manual;
I. Medicare Carrier's Manual;
J. Hearing Appeals and Litigations Manual; and
K. Hospital Manual.

Our case decisions that set precedence, policy interpretations of the law, and regulations are published as Social Security Rulings. The Social Security Regulations contain the rules and policies of general applicability used in administering the Social Security Act.

117.8 Is there a charge for using information provided by the Informational Facilities?

Generally, there is no charge for information needed for program purposes. If information is provided for non-program purposes, a charge is made, subject to some exceptions.

118. DOES THE SOCIAL SECURITY OFFICE MAKE REFERRALS TO OTHER GOVERNMENT OR COMMUNITY AGENCIES?

If you need health or human services that are not available under Social Security, the Social Security office refers you to a government or community agency. Each Social Security office maintains a list of the types of services provided by the agencies (both public and private) in your community. The Social Security office can immediately refer you to the agency providing the services you need.

119. SOCIAL SECURITY BENEFITS PAYABLE

119.1 Are you eligible for monthly Social Security benefits?

You may be eligible for monthly Social Security benefits if you are any of the following:

A. A disabled insured worker who has not reached full retirement age;
B. A retired insured worker age 62 or over;
C. The spouse of a retired or disabled worker entitled to benefits who:

1. Is age 62 or over; or
2. Has in care a child who is either under age 16, or over age 16 and disabled, who is entitled to benefits on the worker's Social Security record.

D. The divorced spouse of a retired or disabled worker entitled to benefits if you are at least 62 and married to the worker for at least 10 years;

E. The divorced spouse of a fully insured worker (see §203) who:
   1. Has not yet filed a claim for benefits if both you and your ex-spouse are at least 62;
   2. Was married for at least 10 years; and
   3. Has been finally divorced for at least two years in a row.

F. The dependent, who is an unmarried child of a wage earner who is retired, disabled, or a deceased insured worker is entitled to benefits if he or she is:
   1. Under age 18;
   2. Under age 19 and a full-time elementary or secondary school student; or
   3. Age 18 or older but under a disability which began before age 22.

G. The surviving spouse (including a surviving divorced spouse) of a deceased insured worker if you are age 60 or older;

H. The disabled surviving spouse (including a surviving divorced spouse in some cases) of a deceased insured worker if you are age 50-59 and become disabled within the period specified in §513;

I. The surviving spouse (including a surviving divorced spouse) of a deceased insured worker, regardless of age, if you are caring for an entitled child of the deceased who is either under age 16 or disabled before age 22; or

J. The dependent parents of a deceased insured worker age 62 or over.

Note: In addition to monthly survivors benefits, a lump-sum death payment is payable upon the death of an insured worker. (See §§428-433.)

120. WHO ISSUES SOCIAL SECURITY BENEFITS AND SSI PAYMENTS?

Social Security benefits and SSI payments are issued by the U.S. Treasury Department, not by SSA's processing centers. However, if you have any questions about your direct deposit or check, get in touch with a Social Security office.

121. PAYMENT DATES

121.1 When are your payment days if you filed for benefits before May 1, 1997?

Social Security payments are usually dated and delivered on the third day of the month following the month for which the payment is due. For example, payments for January are delivered on February 3. If the third of the month is a Saturday, Sunday or Federal holiday, payments are dated and delivered on the first day preceding the third of the month which is not a Saturday, Sunday, or Federal holiday. For example, if the third is a Saturday or Sunday, payments are delivered on the preceding Friday.

121.2 When are your payment days if you filed for benefits on or after May 1, 1997?

If you file for Social Security benefits May 1, 1997, or later, you are assigned one of three new payment days based on the date of birth of the person on whose record your entitlement is established (the insured individual):

A. The payment day for insured individuals *born on the 1st through the 10th* of the month is the second Wednesday of each month;

B. The payment day for insured individuals *born on the 11th through the 20th* of the month is the third Wednesday of each month; and

C. The payment day for insured individuals *born after the 20th* of the month is the fourth Wednesday of each month.

If the scheduled Wednesday payment day is a Federal holiday, payment is made on the preceding day that is not a Federal holiday.

121.3 When are you paid on the 3rd of the month, even if you file for benefits on or after May 1, 1997?

You will receive your Social Security payment on the third of the month if you are any of the following:

A. A beneficiary who also receives SSI payment;

B. A beneficiary whose income is deemed to an SSI recipient;

C. A beneficiary whose Medicare premiums are paid for by the state in which you live;

D. A beneficiary living in a foreign country;

E. A beneficiary entitled to payments on the third of the month, who later became entitled on another record, as long as there is no break in your entitlement;

F. A recipient of garnished payments, tax levy case payments, or payments made via the critical payment system; or

G. A beneficiary entitled on the same record as one of the above.

121.4 Can payment days be changed?

If you are paid on the third of the month, you can volunteer to change your payment day as long as all beneficiaries receiving benefits on your record agree. The date-of-birth formula determines the payment cycle for beneficiaries. The decision to change to a cycled payment day is permanent.

121.5 When are the payment days for SSI?

SSI payments are usually dated and delivered on the first day of the month that they are due. However, if the first falls on a Saturday, Sunday, or Federal holiday, they are dated and delivered on the first day preceding the first of the month that is not a Saturday, Sunday, or Federal holiday.

122. DIRECT DEPOSIT OF BENEFITS

122.1 What is direct deposit?

A "direct deposit" is a payment sent electronically to an account in a financial institution. The financial institution can be a bank, trust company, savings and loan association, or credit union.

122.2 Do you have to receive your Social Security and SSI benefits by direct deposit?

Direct deposit is now the standard way to receive Social Security and SSI benefits. The law requires that after December 1998, with limited exceptions, all Federal benefits must be paid through some form of direct deposit.

122.3 How do you sign up for direct deposit?

You can sign up for direct deposit through your financial institution or by calling Social Security's toll free number, 1-800-772-1213 or by logging into your mySocialSecurity account at https://www.socialsecurity.gov/myaccount.

122.4 How can you get direct deposit if you live outside the U.S.?

We have an international direct deposit (IDD) program in certain countries outside the U.S. If you live in a country that has an IDD program, you must participate in the program. If you live in a country where no IDD program exists, you are exempt until such a program is available. However, you may have direct deposit to an account in the U.S. or any

IDD country. For more information on direct deposit, see https://www.ssa.gov/pubs/EN-05-10137.pdf.

122.5 What information do you report to Social Security if you have direct deposit?

A. If you have direct deposit, you must advise us if you change your account. You must also tell us if you change your address or residence. This is important so we can communicate with you and mail necessary forms, etc. when necessary.

B. If you do not receive your payment in your account on the payment date, you should check with your bank and then call SSA's toll free number, 1-800-772-1213. It is important to have your claim number ready. (See §133.)

123. CHECKS

123.1 What is your time limit for cashing Social Security checks?

Checks are issued with the words "VOID AFTER ONE YEAR" printed across the face of the check. If you have a check that you have not cashed past the one-year time limit, you will not be able to cash it. Contact a Social Security office to have the check reissued.

123.2 How are checks sent to beneficiaries living outside of the U.S.?

If you live outside the U.S., your check is mailed either from the U.S. Treasury Department or from a U.S. diplomatic or consular office in the country where you are living. In a few countries, special arrangements are made for check delivery. Because of the distance and additional handling involved, your checks are generally delivered somewhat later than if you were living in the U.S.

123.3 What should you do if you do not receive your check?

If you are living in the U.S. and you do not receive your check within three business days after it is usually mailed, contact the Social Security office right away. Also call the Social Security office if your check has been stolen, lost, destroyed, or forged. Be prepared to provide the Social Security office with the following information:

A. The claim number (see §133) on which the benefit is being paid;
B. The period of payment covered by the missing check (or checks); and
C. The name and address which should be shown on the check.

123.4 How do you report a change of address?

If your address changes, report the change to Social Security right away. You can make your report by telephone, in writing, in person or on the SSA web-site. Provide your Social Security claim number and your old address, including the ZIP code, so that any check already printed can be found and sent to your new address. Also, notify the post office of your change of address to ensure prompt delivery of your check.

Note: If there is any doubt as to the authenticity of a telephone report, the Social Security office requests written confirmation from you.

124. HOW DO YOU ENDORSE YOUR CHECK IF YOU CANNOT SIGN YOUR NAME?

If you are unable to sign your name, signature by mark is acceptable. Two individuals who sign their own names and show their complete addresses must witness your signature by mark.

125. ENTITLEMENT TO RETIREMENT, SURVIVORS, AND DISABILITY INSURANCE BENEFITS

125.1 What are Social Security benefits?

Social Security benefits are payments made under a social insurance program administered by the Social Security Administration. They are paid monthly by check or direct deposit to the beneficiary or to a representative payee if the beneficiary is incapable of managing his or her own funds (see Chapter 16).

125.2 How can you receive retirement, survivors, and disability insurance benefits?

Retirement, survivors, and disability insurance benefits are Social Security benefits. In order to receive these benefits, you must file an application with us. You must also meet certain eligibility requirements.

125.3 Are your Social Security benefits subject to taxes?

If you have substantial income in addition to your Social Security benefits, up to 85 percent of your annual benefits may be subject to Federal income tax.

If you:
- **file a federal tax return as an "individual"** and your *combined income** is
  - between $25,000 and $34,000, you may have to pay income tax on up to 50 percent of your benefits.

- more than $34,000, up to 85 percent of your benefits may be taxable.
- **file a joint return**, and you and your spouse have a *combined income**
that is
  - between $32,000 and $44,000, you may have to pay income tax on up to 50 percent of your benefits.
  - more than $44,000, up to 85 percent of your benefits may be taxable.
- **are married and file a separate tax return**, you probably will pay taxes on your benefits.

$$\begin{array}{r}\text{Your adjusted gross income}\\ +\text{ Nontaxable interest}\\ \underline{+\text{ ½ of your Social Security benefits}}\\ =\text{Your "}combined\ income\text{"}\end{array}$$

In January, we send you a Form 1099 (*Social Security Benefit Statement*), showing the amount of benefits you received in the prior calendar year. You can use this when you complete your federal income tax return to find out if your benefits are subject to income tax.

125.4 What is your tax rate if you are a non-U.S. citizen?

If you are not a U.S. citizen or resident, Federal income taxes are withheld from your benefits. The tax is 30 percent of 85 percent of your benefit (an effective tax rate of 25.5 percent).

This tax rate is withheld from the benefits of all nonresident aliens, unless you live in a country with which the United States has a tax treaty. Tax treaties do not permit taxing of U.S. Social Security benefits (or provide for a lower tax rate).

125.5 With what countries does the U.S. have tax treaties?

The United States has tax treaties with numerous countries including but not limited to Canada, Egypt, Germany, Ireland, Israel, Italy, Japan, Romania, Switzerland, and the United Kingdom (defined as England, Scotland, Wales, and Northern Ireland). In addition, if you live in and are a citizen of India, your Social Security benefits are exempt from Federal taxes to the extent that your benefits are based on Federal, State or local government employment. For a complete list of countries please go to https://www.irs.gov/businesses/international-businesses/united-states-income-tax-treaties-a-to-z.

125.6 How do you know the amount of taxes withheld from your benefits?

At the end of each year, we send a Form 1042S (*Social Security Benefit Statement*) to each beneficiary. This statement shows the amount of taxes withheld from your Social Security benefits.

126. SUPPLEMENTAL SECURITY INCOME BENEFITS

126.1 What is Supplemental Security Income (SSI)?

Supplemental Security Income (SSI) is a Federal program administered by SSA. The SSI program was established to provide cash assistance to individuals who:

A. Have limited income and resources;
B. Are age 65 or older;
C. Are blind; or
D. Are disabled.

Disability and blind children are also included in the SSI program.

126.2 Who receives SSI payments?

SSI checks (see §123) or direct deposits (see §122) are paid either directly to the eligible person or to a representative payee (see Chapter 16) if the person is incapable of managing benefits. Chapter 21 explains the SSI program in more detail.

127. HOSPITAL AND MEDICAL INSURANCE BENEFITS PROVIDED

127.1 What is Medicare?

The Health Insurance Program, commonly known as "Medicare," provides comprehensive health insurance protection to the aged, disabled, and those with end-stage kidney disease.

127.2 What are the parts of the Medicare program?

There are four parts to the Medicare program. (See Chapter 24.) *Medicare hospital insurance (Part A)* helps pay for inpatient hospital care, inpatient care in a skilled nursing facility, home health care, and hospice care. *Medicare medical insurance (Part B)* helps pay for physician services, outpatient hospital services, outpatient physical therapy, other medical services, and supplies and equipment that are not covered by Part A. *Medicare Advantage Plans (Part C)* are plans offered by private companies that contract with Medicare to provide all Medicare Part A and Part B benefits. Medicare Advantage Plans are HMOs, PPOs, or Private

Fee-for-Service Plans. Some plans also offer prescription drug coverage. The *Medicare Prescription Drug Benefit (Part D)* provides outpatient prescription drug coverage for the aged and disabled.

127.3 Who administers the Medicare program?

The Centers for Medicare & Medicaid Services (CMS) administers the Medicare program. It sets the standards for hospitals, skilled nursing facilities, home health agencies, hospices, and other providers and suppliers of services in order to receive payment for Medicare-covered services and items. CMS sets the standards used by Utilization and Quality Peer Review Organizations, intermediaries, and carriers in making payment and coverage decisions for health care furnished to individuals who have hospital or medical insurance.

127.4 What role does SSA have in the Medicare program?

We provide beneficiary services for the Medicare program. Social Security offices accept and process applications for enrollment in Part A and B. Social Security also responds to beneficiary and public inquiries. We also perform some data processing support and premium billing and collection activities.

127.5 How are Medicare premiums paid?

Medicare Part B premiums must be deducted from Social Security benefits if the monthly benefit covers the deduction. If the monthly benefit does not cover the full deduction, the beneficiary is billed. Beneficiaries may elect deduction of Medicare Part C (Medicare Advantage) from their Social Security benefit. Some Medicare Advantage plans include a reduction in the Part B premium. Social Security takes that reduction into account, as soon as we are notified of the reduction by CMS. Beneficiaries may also elect deduction of their prescription drug plan premium from their Social Security benefit.

For more information about Medicare premiums, go to Medicare & You 2024 at: www.medicare.gov/pubs/pdf/10050-Medicare-and-you.pdf

128. PRESCRIPTION DRUG BENEFITS PROVIDED

128.1 What is the Prescription Drug Benefit?

The Prescription Drug Benefit provides outpatient prescription drugs to the aged and disabled.

128.2 Who administers the Prescription Drug Benefit program?

The Centers for Medicare & Medicaid Services administers the Prescription Drug Benefit program.

128.3 What role does SSA have in the Prescription Drug Benefit program?

SSA and the Centers for Medicare & Medicaid Services (CMS) are working together to provide persons with limited income and resources Extra Help paying for their prescription drugs. SSA's role in this partnership is to provide general information to the public about the Prescription Drug Benefit and the Extra Help with prescription drug costs. SSA supplies applications for the Extra Help with prescription drug costs and assists the public with filing the applications. SSA processes the applications and appeals for Extra Help with Medicare prescription drug costs. SSA also performs some collection activities.

To learn more about the Prescription Drug Benefit, go to: https://www.medicare.gov.

129. BENEFITS NOT TRANSFERABLE

129.1 Can you transfer future Social Security benefits?

No, you cannot transfer your future Social Security benefits and SSI payments to someone else.

129.2 Can your Social Security benefits be levied or garnished?

If you have any unpaid Federal taxes, the Internal Revenue Service can levy your Social Security benefits. Your benefits can also be garnished in order to collect unpaid child support and/or alimony. Your benefits may also be garnished in response to Court Ordered Victims Restitution. SSI payments cannot be levied or garnished. The Treasury's Financial Management Service can also offset, or reduce, your Social Security benefits to collect delinquent debts owed to other Federal agencies, such as student loans owed to the Department of Education.

129.3 Can you voluntarily withhold money to meet your tax liability (voluntary tax withholding)?

You may ask to have a percentage of your monthly payment amount withheld and paid each month to the Internal Revenue Service to help meet your Federal income tax liability.

129.4 What types of payments are not subject to voluntary tax withholding?

The following types of payments *are not* subject to voluntary tax withholding:
A. SSI payments;
B. Black Lung payments;
C. Medicare premium refunds;
D. Lump-sum Death Payments; and
E. Returned check re-issuances.

130. SPECIAL REQUEST FOR EXPEDITED BENEFIT PAYMENT

130.1 Can you ask to expedite your benefit payment if it was not received on time?

If you did not receive your Social Security benefit for a particular month, you may file a written request for prompt payment. Your request is considered filed at the end of the period if you file your request before the end of:
A. 90 days after the date that you provided all the evidence requested to support the claim;
B. If later, 90 days after the date on which payment is supposed to have been due; or
C. If you received a regular monthly benefit in the prior month, 30 days after the 15th day of the month in which payment is supposed to have been due.

If you file your request under condition (A), (B), or (C) above, benefits are due and you will be paid within 15 days after the end of the period. If it appears that benefits are probably due, preliminary payment may be made without regard to these time limits, even if additional evidence is needed for a final decision.

130.2 What types of benefit payments can be expedited?

Expedited payment procedures apply to disability insurance benefits and SSI benefits, which primarily involves dire needs, terminal illness, or presumptive cases meeting SSA guidelines. However, expedited payments do not apply in cases where a check was issued and the U.S. Treasury Department records show the check was cashed. In these instances, check investigation is conducted by the U.S. Treasury Department rather than us. In both situations, the delays are reported to us.

131. CHECKS TO HUSBAND AND WIFE

131.1 Are separate Social Security benefit checks mailed to husbands and wives?

Separate payments for Social Security benefits are made to a husband and wife by either direct deposit or check.

131.2 Are separate Supplemental Security Income benefit checks mailed to husbands and wives?

If you and your spouse receive SSI payments, you will receive separate direct deposit payments or checks, even if you live in the same household. If your spouse dies, return any checks not cashed to the Social Security office. Any payments due your spouse will be paid to you if you were living together within six months before the death of your spouse, even if you are not eligible for SSI.

132. ARE SEPARATE SOCIAL SECURITY BENEFIT CHECKS MAILED TO EACH CHILD IN A FAMILY?

Separate Social Security benefit payments are paid to each child by either direct deposit or check.

133. REPORTING TO SOCIAL SECURITY

You must notify the Social Security Administration of any event affecting your eligibility for, or amount of, benefit payment (See §133.2 and §133.1). The office or telephone service center that you notify will make the change to your record or forward the information to the program service center. We will ask for your Social Security claim number. You must report any change affecting SSI benefits within 10 calendar days after the month the change occurred. (See §2126.)

133.1 What is the claim number?

The claim number is the social security number under which a claim is filed or benefits are paid. If you are an SSI beneficiary, your claim number is your nine-digit Social Security Number (SSN) (000-00-0000) followed by two letters such as EI, DI, DS, DC.

If you are a Social Security beneficiary, your claim number is the nine-digit SSN followed by one or more letters such as A, B, C, HA.

133.2 What events must you report immediately under Social Security?

If you receive Social Security benefits on behalf of yourself or another person you must immediately report any of the following events to us:

A. A beneficiary (other than a disabled individual) is working and has, or expects to have, more earnings than the amount exempted under the earnings test explained in Chapter 18;

B. The marriage of a person who is entitled to child's, widow(er)'s, mother's, father's, parent's, or divorced spouse's insurance benefits;

C. A beneficiary under age 62 entitled to spouse's, mother's, or father's insurance benefits no longer has in care a child under age 16 or disabled that is entitled to benefits;

D. A person entitled to benefits because of disability has either (1) returned to work; or (2) the person's condition has improved so that he or she is able to work;

E. A non-disabled child beneficiary age 18 or over no longer attending elementary or secondary school full-time;

F. The death of a beneficiary;

G. A beneficiary works outside the U.S. for more than 45 hours in a calendar month;

H. A person under age 65 who is entitled because of disability becomes entitled to workers' compensation benefits; or there is a change in the public disability payment rate;

I. Imprisonment for a conviction of a criminal offense that carries a sentence of more than one year;

J. Confinement by court order to an institution at public expense following a verdict or finding that an individual has been found guilty by reason of insanity or similar verdict;

K. A person begins to receive a governmental pension or annuity; or there is a change in a present pension amount and the person receives a spouse's Social Security benefit;

L. A beneficiary leaves the U.S.;

M. A beneficiary's citizenship or alien status changes; or

N. A retirement or disability beneficiary is divorced from the parent of an entitled stepchild.

133.3 What events must the recipient or the representative payee report immediately under Supplemental Security Income (SSI)?

Any of the following events must be reported immediately to us on behalf of persons receiving SSI payments:

A. A change in living arrangements, including a change in residence, mailing address, marital status, or amount of earned or unearned income;
B. The death of the recipient or anyone with whom he or she lives;
C. A disabled or blind recipient goes to work or has improvement in his or her condition;
D. A change in ownership or value of real or personal property (including those belonging to a living-with spouse or parent);
E. A change in the amount of earned or unearned income of a living-with spouse or parent, or of the sponsor of an alien;
F. A recipient enters or leaves an institution;
G. A recipient leaves the U.S. for more than 30 days;
H. A recipient under age 22 is no longer attending school full-time;
I. A recipient's citizenship or alien status changes;
J. A recipient is fleeing to avoid criminal prosecution;
K. A recipient is taken into custody or confinement after conviction of a crime that is a felony;
L. A recipient is violating a condition of probation or parole imposed under Federal or State law; or
M. A recipient becomes eligible for other benefits.

133.4 What happens after you notify SSA of a reportable event?

Based on the information provided, the Social Security office or the program service center adjusts benefit payments and notifies the beneficiary of the action.

133.5 What are the consequences if you do not notify SSA of a reportable event?

If you fail to make reports promptly, there may be monetary penalties. (See Chapter 18 and §2126.)

134. RETURNING CHECKS TO THE SOCIAL SECURITY OFFICE

134.1 When must you return checks to the Social Security Administration?

If you received a check from us and you are not entitled to the payment, you must return the check. Returning checks helps permit prompt payment when you become entitled and may save you from the possible penalties described in §§1820, 1828, and 1831.

134.2 How do you return Social Security checks?

Return the check to the Regional Financial Center (RFC), U.S. Treasury Department, using the address on the check envelope. If you prefer, you may return the check to the Social Security office. That office will give you a receipt for the check and will return the check to the U.S. Treasury Department. When returning a check, give the reason why it is being returned.

135. WHAT IS DONE IF YOU RECEIVE MORE MONEY THAN YOU ARE ENTITLED?

If you cash a check to which you are not entitled, a refund is ordinarily required. Often the program service center withholds later checks to make up for the overpayment. However, if this is not done you must refund the money.

Contact any convenient Social Security office to find out if a refund is necessary. If so, make the refund to the Social Security office, or program service center that handled the claim. Refunds may be made by check, money order, or other draft payable to the Social Security Administration. Be sure to show your Social Security claim number so that it can be associated with the proper claims folder.

136. SOURCES OF FUNDS FOR SOCIAL SECURITY AND SUPPLEMENTAL SECURITY INCOME BENEFITS

136.1 How are Social Security benefits funded?

To pay for Retirement, Survivors, Disability Insurance, and Hospital Insurance Benefits, taxes are collected from employers, employees, and the self-employed who are working in jobs and businesses covered by Social Security.

136.2 How are SSI payments funded?

SSI payments are paid from the general revenues of the U.S. and in States which supplement the Federal benefits from State funds.

137. HOW ARE HOSPITAL INSURANCE BENEFITS FUNDED?

Hospital Insurance Benefits are either paid from the FICA/SECA taxes or by monthly premium payments. Funding depends on the circumstances of eligibility.

138. HOW ARE MEDICAL INSURANCE BENEFITS FUNDED?

To pay for Medical Insurance Benefits, the law provides for the collection of monthly premiums. The people enrolled in the program (or in some cases, the State) pay these premiums. (See §2400.) Since the premiums cover only about one-fourth of the cost of the program, the Government pays the remaining amount from general revenues.

Starting in January 2007, people enrolled in Medicare Part B with modified adjusted gross incomes over a set threshold are required to pay a higher percentage of their total Part B premium costs. Increases in Part B premiums for these individuals were phased in from 2007 to 2009.

For more information on the Medicare Part B premium amounts, see §2400.

139. HOW ARE PRESCRIPTION DRUG BENEFITS FUNDED?

Prescription drug benefits are funded by general revenues of the U.S., monthly beneficiary premiums, and state payments.

140. WHERE ARE MONEY GIFTS TO SOCIAL SECURITY DEPOSITED?

Unconditional money gifts to Social Security may be accepted and deposited in whatever Social Security trust fund is designated by the donor. If no specific fund is designated, the gift is deposited in the Federal Old-Age and Survivors Insurance Trust Fund.

141. TRUST FUNDS AVAILABLE FOR BENEFITS

141.1 Where are Social Security tax amounts deposited?

Amounts equivalent to the Social Security taxes are deposited in three separate trust funds:

A. The Federal Old-Age and Survivors Insurance Trust Fund;
B. The Federal Disability Insurance Trust Fund; and
C. The Federal Hospital Insurance Trust Fund.

The Federal Hospital Insurance Trust Fund also receives the amounts appropriated from general revenues on account of "uninsured" persons age 65 and over (see §137).

141.2 What is the Federal Supplementary Medical Insurance Trust Fund?

The Federal Supplementary Medical Insurance Trust Fund receives the amounts collected as premiums for medical insurance coverage and the amounts appropriated from general U.S. revenues. This trust fund covers the Government's share of the cost of the program.

141.3 Who is responsible for managing the trust funds?

A Board of Trustees holds the funds for the Social Security Trust Funds. By law, the Board of Trustees is composed of the Secretary of the Treasury, the Secretary of Labor, the Secretary of Health and Human Services, and two members of the public appointed by the President and confirmed by the Senate. The Commissioner of Social Security serves as the Secretary of the Board of Trustees for the Federal Old-Age and Survivors Insurance Trust Fund and the Federal Disability Insurance Trust Fund. The Administrator of the Centers for Medicare & Medicaid Services serves as Secretary of the Board of Trustees for the Federal Hospital Insurance Trust Fund and the Federal Supplementary Medical Insurance Trust Fund.

141.4 Where is the money in the trust funds spent?

The deposits in the four trust funds are used for the retirement, survivors, disability, hospital, and medical insurance programs. The trust funds also cover administrative expenses associated with these programs. Excess funds are invested in interest-bearing Federal securities.

142. WHAT INVESTIGATIVE RESPONSIBILITIES DOES SSA HAVE IN ADMINISTERING THE SOCIAL SECURITY PROGRAM?

In administering the retirement, survivors, disability insurance, and the SSI programs, we must:

A. *Provide benefits to people who are entitled to them* under the provisions of the Social Security Act; and

B. *Protect the Social Security trust funds and the general revenues* by denying benefits when not due.

In carrying out these responsibilities, we investigate all questionable actions and statements made in connection with claims for benefits or earnings records. If there is adequate evidence that a criminal provision was violated, the case may be referred to the Department of Justice for prosecution.

143. FRAUD IN CONNECTION WITH BENEFIT CLAIMS AND EARNINGS RECORDS

143.1 When can you be prosecuted for Social Security fraud?

You may be prosecuted as a criminal for fraud if you knowingly:

A. Furnish false information as to your identity in connection with the establishment and maintenance of Social Security records;

B. For the purpose of increasing your payment under Social Security or any other Federally funded program; or for the purpose of obtaining such payment:
   1. Use a Social Security number obtained on the basis of false information; or
   2. Falsely represent a number to be your Social Security number;
C. Make or cause to be made a false statement or misrepresentation of a material fact for use in determining your rights to Social Security or SSI benefits;
D. Make or cause to be made any false statement or representation as to:
   1. Whether wages were paid to you, the period during which wages were paid, or the amount of your wages; or
   2. Whether you have net earnings from self-employment, the amount of your earnings, or the period during which you earned the money;
E. Conceal or fail to report any event affecting the initial or continued right to payment received or to be received by you personally or on behalf of another; or
F. Use payment received on behalf of another for any purpose other than the use for the benefit of that person.

Other penal provisions contained in the Social Security Act or in the Federal Criminal Code may also apply to offenses affecting the Social Security program.

We will prosecute even if a fraudulent act is discovered before wrongful payments are made by the Government.

143.2 What is the penalty for conviction?

The penalty upon conviction for violation of the penal provisions of the Social Security Act, or one of the related provisions of the Federal Criminal Code may be a fine, imprisonment, or both. The penalty ranges from a fine of not more than $500, imprisonment of one year, or both, to a fine of not more than $10,000, imprisonment of not more than 15 years, or both. The penalty depends upon the specific law violated.

144. SOCIAL SECURITY COST-OF-LIVING ADJUSTMENT AND OTHER AUTOMATIC INCREASES

For information on the Social Security Cost-of-Living Adjustment (COLA) and other automatic increases see: https://www.ssa.gov/OACT/COLA/autoAdj.html.

Chapter 2
Becoming Insured

TABLE OF CONTENTS

INSURED STATUS
- 200. Insured Status Requirements
- 201. Determining Insured Status
- 202. If you have fully insured status, can you receive all types of benefits?
- 203. Fully Insured Status Defined
- 204. Chart of Credits Required to Be Fully Insured
- 205. Deemed Fully Insured Status
- 206. Currently Insured Status Defined

DISABILITY INSURED STATUS
- 207. When do you have disability insured status?
- 208. Special Insured Status-Disabled Before Age 31
- 209. Periods of Disability and Insured Status
- 210. Do your credits based on military service before 1957 count toward disability?

SUMMARY CHART
- 211. Summary Chart of Requirements for Insured Status

SOCIAL SECURITY CREDITS
212. Earning Social Security Credits
213. When are calendar quarters NOT counted for determining Social Security credits?
214. Social Security Credits Based On Wages Earned After 1936
215. Social Security Credits Based On Self-employment

TOTALIZATION AGREEMENT
216. Totalization-Coordination of Social Security Systems of the United States and a Foreign Country

200. INSURED STATUS REQUIREMENTS

200.1 Why is insured status important?

You must be insured under the Social Security program before retirement, survivors, or disability insurance benefits can be paid to you or your family.

200.2 Are Social Security credits used to determine insured status?

We consider the number of Social Security credits you earned to determine if you have:

A. Fully insured status;
B. Currently insured status; or
C. Insured status for establishing a period of disability.

You earn Social Security credits (previously called quarters of coverage) for a certain amount of work covered under Social Security. (See §§211-215.)

Note: Under Section 211 of the Social Security Protection Act of 2004 ("SSPA," or Public Law 108-203), certain alien workers must meet additional requirements to be fully or currently insured and to establish entitlement to benefits based on the alien's earnings. (See §201.)

201. DETERMINING INSURED STATUS

201.1 How does SSA determine insured status?

We use your lifetime earnings record reported under your Social Security Number (SSN). The number of quarters you have covered credits determine if you have enough credits for insured status. (See §212.6.)

201.2 How do the requirements of the Social Security Protection Act of 2004 (SSPA) affect insured status determinations?

Under Section 211 of the SSPA, an alien worker whose Social Security Number (SSN) was originally assigned on or after January 1, 2004, must meet *one* of the following additional requirements to be fully or currently insured and in order to establish entitlement to any retirement, survivors or disability Social Security benefit or Medicare based on End Stage Renal Disease (ESRD). These additional requirements also affect entitlement of any family members of the alien worker who may otherwise be entitled to benefits based on the alien worker's earnings:

A. The alien worker must have been issued an SSN for work purposes at any time on or after January 1, 2004; OR
B. The alien worker must have been admitted to the U.S. at any time as a nonimmigrant visitor for business (B-1) or as an alien crewman (D-1 or D-2).

If an alien worker whose SSN was originally assigned January 1, 2004 or later does not meet either of these additional requirements, then the worker *is not fully or currently insured*. This is true even if the alien worker appears to have the required number of Social Security credits to meet the insured status provisions.

201.3 Who is an "alien worker" under the SSPA?

For purposes of the SSPA requirements, an "alien worker" is a worker who is not a U.S. citizen or national of the U.S.

202. IF YOU HAVE FULLY INSURED STATUS, CAN YOU RECEIVE ALL TYPES OF BENEFITS?

Insured status is required before you can receive any type of benefit. "Fully insured status" is only one requirement for determining whether you receive a particular type of benefit. However, it does *not* mean that you can receive all types of benefits on your Social Security record, nor does it have anything to do with the amount of benefits that are paid. (See §211.)

203. FULLY INSURED STATUS DEFINED

203.1 When are you fully insured?

You are fully insured if:
A. You have at least one credit for each calendar year after 1950; or
B. If you turn 21 after 1950, you have at least one credit for each calendar year after you turned 21 and the earliest of the following:
  1. The year before you turn 62;
  2. The year before you die; or
  3. The year before you become disabled.

You can obtain covered credits and count them in any year. (See §201.2 for additional requirements if you are an alien worker and you were assigned an original Social Security number on or after January 1, 2004.)

203.2 Are there any exceptions to determining fully insured status (as above)?

The following individuals are also fully insured:

A. *Males born before January 2, 1911*, need one credit for each year after 1950 up to the year before the year below that occurs first:
   1. They turn 65;
   2. They die; or
   3. They become disabled; and

B. *Males born from January 2, 1911, through January 1, 1913*, need one credit for each year after 1950 up to the year before the year below that occurs first:
   1. 1975;
   2. They die; or
   3. They become disabled.

203.3 Are years included in a period of disability counted to determine credits?

In determining the number of years to be used in computing your credits, any year (all or part of a year) that was included in a period of disability is not counted. (For exception, see §209.2.)

203.4 Do you need a minimum number of credits in order to be fully insured?

In order to be considered for fully insured status, you need at least six credits. No more than 40 credits are required, regardless of your date of birth.

203.5 Are there special benefits if you turned 72 before 1972?

If you turned 72 before 1972, you may be entitled to a special cash monthly payment. This is true even if you are not fully insured (see §211 and §346).

204. CHART OF CREDITS REQUIRED TO BE FULLY INSURED

204.1 How many credits do you need if you were born on or before January 1, 1913, to be fully insured?

For people born before January 1, 1913, the number of credits needed to be fully insured is different for men and women. The following chart shows the number of credits you need if you were born before January 1, 1913.

If your date of birth is...	Then you need the following number of credits...	
	Men	Women
1/1/1893 or earlier	6	6
1/2/1893-1/1/1894	7	6
1/2/1894-1/1/1895	8	6
1/2/1895-1/1/1896	9	6
1/2/1896-1/1/1897	10	7
1/2/1897-1/1/1898	11	8
1/2/1898-1/1/1899	12	9
1/2/1899-1/1/1900	13	10
1/2/1900-1/1/1901	14	11
1/2/1901-1/1/1902	15	12
1/2/1902-1/1/1903	16	13
1/2/1903-1/1/1904	17	14
1/2/1904-1/1/1905	18	15
1/2/1905-1/1/1906	19	16
1/2/1906-1/1/1907	20	17
1/2/1907-1/1/1908	21	18
1/2/1908-1/1/1909	22	19
1/2/1909-1/1/1910	23	20
1/2/1910-1/1/1911	24	21
1/2/1911-1/1/1912	24	22
1/2/1912-1/1/1913	24	23

204.2 How many credits do you need if you were born on or after January 2, 1913, to be fully insured?

For people born on or after January 2, 1913, the number of credits needed to be fully insured is the same for men and women. The chart below shows the number of credits you need if you were born on or after January 2, 1913.

If your date of birth is...	Then you need the following number of credits...
1/2/13-1/1/14	24
1/2/14-1/1/15	25
1/2/15-1/1/16	26
1/2/16-1/1/17	27
1/2/17-1/1/18	28
1/2/18-1/1/19	29
1/2/19-1/1/20	30
1/2/20-1/1/21	31
1/2/21-1/1/22	32
1/2/22-1/1/23	33
1/2/23-1/1/24	34
1/2/24-1/1/25	35
1/2/25-1/1/26	36
1/2/26-1/1/27	37
1/2/27-1/1/28	38
1/2/28-1/1/29	39
1/2/29 or later	40

Note: If you are a male who turned 62 before 1975, see §203.

205. DEEMED FULLY INSURED STATUS

205.1 When are you deemed fully insured?

You are deemed fully insured if you meet the following conditions:
A. You were at least 55 on January 1, 1984;
B. You were an employee of a nonprofit (non-covered) employer (see §931) on January 1, 1984; and
C. Your employer did not have a waiver certificate (under section 3121(k) of the Internal Revenue Code) in effect on January 1, 1984.

205.2 How do the 1983 amendments affect fully insured status?

You can obtain *deemed fully insured status* with fewer credits if you were extended Social Security coverage effective January 1, 1984, provided:
A. Your coverage was extended solely by reason of the 1983 amendments;
B. Your credits are earned after 1983; and
C. You meet the requirements in §205.1 above.

Note: This provision does not apply if you declined the option to elect coverage, even though a waiver certificate was in effect on January 1, 1984. This condition also does not apply if you are a member of a religious order who has taken a vow of poverty.

205.3 How many credits do you need to be deemed fully insured?

The age and number of credits required for deemed fully insured status is provided in the chart below.

If you were the following age on January 1, 1984,…	Then you need the following number of credits…
60 or over	6
59 or over, but less than 60	8
58 or over, but less than 59	12
57 or over, but less than 58	16
55 or over, but less than 57	20

Note: You may not use credits earned before January 1, 1984, for deemed fully insured status. You may use them in addition to credits earned after 1983 to establish regular fully insured status.

205.4 What World War II veterans are considered to have died fully insured?

Certain World War II veterans who separated from active military service before July 27, 1951, and died within three years of their separation are considered to have died fully insured (see §960).

206. CURRENTLY INSURED STATUS DEFINED

206.1 When do you have currently insured status?

"Currently insured status" may be all that is needed for you to receive some types of benefits (see §211).

A person is currently insured if he or she has at least six Social Security credits during the full 13-quarter period ending with the calendar quarter in which he or she:

A. Died;

B. Most recently became entitled to disability benefits; or

C. Became entitled to retirement insurance benefits.

(See §201.2 for additional requirements if you are an alien worker and you were assigned an original Social Security number on or after January 1, 2004.)

206.2 How is the 13-quarter period determined?

Calendar quarters, all or part of which are in an established prior period of disability, are generally not counted. However, the first or last quarter of the prior period of disability may be counted if the quarter is used as a credit. (For exception, see §209.)

207. WHEN DO YOU HAVE DISABILITY INSURED STATUS?

You have disability insured status if you:

A. Have at least 20 credits during a 40-calendar quarter period (the 20/40 rule);

B. The 40-calendar quarter period ends with the quarter that you are determined to be disabled; and

C. You are fully insured in that calendar quarter as explained in §203

208. SPECIAL INSURED STATUS-DISABLED BEFORE AGE 31

208.1 What is special insured status?

"Special insured status" allows an option to the "20 credits in 40 quarters" provision (20/40 rule - See §207). Individuals disabled before age 31 can qualify for disability insurance benefits or establish a period of disability. (See §201.2 for additional requirements if you are an alien worker and you were assigned an original Social Security number on or after January 1, 2004.)

208.2 When do you have special insured status?

You meet the special insured status requirements if, in the quarter your disability is determined to have begun or in a later quarter, you:

A. Have not yet turned 31;

B. Are fully insured as explained in §203; and

C. Have credits in at least one-half of the calendar quarters:

1. During the period beginning with the quarter after the quarter you turned 21; and

2. Ending with the quarter that you became disabled.

The credits *must* be earned in this period. If the number of elapsing calendar quarters is an odd number, the next lower even number is used.

208.3 What is the minimum number of credits you need for special insured status?

You need at least six credits in order to have special insured status. If you became disabled before the quarter you turned 24, you must have six credits in the 12-quarter period ending with the quarter your disability began. In this case, the quarters counted will go back before the quarter in which you turned age 21.

208.4 Can you obtain special insured status if you become disabled again at age 31 or older?

If you are age 31 or older and become disabled again, you may obtain special insured status if you meet the following conditions:

A. You had a previous period of disability established before you turned 31;

B. You met and currently meet the special insured requirements (as set out above);

C. You do not meet the 20/40 rule in the quarter your current period of disability begins;

D. You are fully insured as explained in §203.

(See §201.2 for additional requirements if you are an alien worker and you were assigned an original Social Security number on or after January 1, 2004.)

208.5 Are there any special provisions for the blind?

A person disabled because of blindness may qualify for entitlement to disability benefits if he or she is fully insured as explained in §203. Blind workers are not required to meet "20 credits in 40 quarters" or "special insured status" tests.

(See §201.2 for additional requirements if you are an alien worker and you were assigned an original Social Security number on or after January 1, 2004.)

209. PERIODS OF DISABILITY AND INSURED STATUS

209.1 When is your period of disability NOT counted in determining credits for insured status?

If you have an established period of disability, it is not counted in determining the number of credits you need to be fully or currently insured. It is also not counted when computing your benefit amount.

(See §510 for definition of when a period of disability begins and §511 for when it ends.)

209.2 When is your period of disability counted in determining credits for insured status?

Your period of disability is not excluded in computing your (or your survivors') Social Security benefits if including it would be more beneficial for you. For example, your period of disability is counted if you have potential credits in your disability period and if the potential credits would qualify you for another benefit formula that would increase your benefit rate or would give you insured status.

210. DO YOUR CREDITS BASED ON MILITARY SERVICE BEFORE 1957 COUNT TOWARD DISABILITY?

Your Social Security credits based on military service before 1957, and certain railroad compensation, may be used to establish a period of disability. However, these credits may or may not be used to pay monthly Social Security benefits. (See §948.)

211. SUMMARY CHART OF REQUIREMENTS FOR INSURED STATUS

211.1 What are the requirements for monthly Social Security benefits?

The following chart shows the requirements for receiving the various types of monthly Social Security benefits.

Monthly Social Security benefits can be paid to...	If the worker...
A retired worker age 62 or over.	Is fully insured.
A disabled worker under full retirement age.	Would have been fully insured had he or she turned 62 in the month the disability began. The worker also needs 20 credits out of the 40 calendar quarters ending with the quarter that the disability began (20/40). *Note:* This does not apply in the case of a person disabled because of blindness as described in §507.

Monthly Social Security benefits can be paid to…	If the worker…
A worker disabled before age 31 who does not have sufficient credits to meet 20/40 requirement. *Note:* Special insured status may apply to a worker who becomes disabled after age 31, provided the individual had a period of disability prior to age 31. See §208.	Has credits in one-half of the quarters elapsing in the period after the quarter of reaching age 21 and up to and including the quarter of becoming disabled. The worker needs at least six credits (see §208); or if disabled in a quarter before turning 24, he or she needs six credits in the 12 calendar-quarter period, including the quarter in which the disability began and immediately before becoming disabled.
Worker disabled due to blindness.	Has at least one credit for each year after reaching age 21 (or 1950, if later) up to the year the qualifying credit is earned. Must have a minimum of six credits.
The spouse of a person entitled to disability or retirement insurance benefits, if he or she is: (A) Age 62 or over (may be divorced spouse in certain circumstances; see §311); or (B) Caring for a child who is under age 16; or a child under a disability which began before the child reached age 22 and entitled to benefits (see Chapter 3).	Is fully insured or insured for disability benefits, whichever is applicable as shown above.

Monthly Social Security benefits can be paid to...	If the worker...
A dependent, unmarried child of a person entitled to disability or retirement insurance benefits if the child is: (A) Under 18; (B) Under 19 and a full-time elementary or secondary school student; or (C) Age 18 or over and under a disability which began before the child reached age 22.	Is insured for retirement or disability benefits, whichever is applicable, as shown above.
A widow(er) (may be surviving divorced spouse in certain circumstances; see §403) age 60 or over.	Is fully insured.
A widow(er) and, under certain conditions, a surviving divorced spouse, if the widow(er), or divorced spouse is caring for a child entitled to benefits if the child is under 16 or disabled.	Is either fully or currently insured.
A disabled widow(er) (may be surviving divorced spouse in certain circumstances; see §403) age 50 or over but under age 60 whose disability began within a certain period (see §513).	Is fully insured.

Monthly Social Security benefits can be paid to...	If the worker...
A dependent, unmarried child of a deceased worker if the child is: (A) Under 18; (B) Under 19 and a full-time elementary or secondary school student; or (C) Age 18 or over and under a disability which began before the child reached age 22.	Is either fully or currently insured.
The dependent parents age 62 or over of the deceased worker (see §421).	Is fully insured.

211.2 What are the requirements for a special monthly cash benefit?

You can receive a special monthly cash payment if you meet the following requirements:

A. You are at least 72 years old;
B. You are not insured for regular Social Security benefits; and
C. You turned 72 either;
   1. Before 1968; or
   2. Between 1968 and 1971 and you have at least three credits for each calendar year elapsing after 1966 and before the year you turn 72.

Note: This benefit is not available if you turn 72 after 1971.

211.3 What are the requirements for a lump-sum death payment?

The worker must be either fully or currently insured for a beneficiary to receive a lump-sum death payment. The lump-sum death payment is paid in the following order of priority:

A. First, to the widow(er) of the deceased worker who was living in the same household as the deceased worker at the time of death;
B. Second, to the widow(er) (excluding a divorced spouse) who is eligible for or entitled to benefits based on the deceased worker's record for the month of death; and

C. Third, to children who are eligible for or entitled to benefits based on the deceased worker's record for the month of death.

Note: If there is no surviving widow(er) or child as defined above, no lump-sum is payable.

212. EARNING SOCIAL SECURITY CREDITS

212.1 How do you earn Social Security credits?

You earn Social Security credits by working at a job covered by Social Security.

212.2 How were credits earned for years before 1978?

To earn credits for the years before 1978, you must have:

A. Earned at least $50 in wages for employment covered under the law in any calendar quarter beginning January 1, April 1, July 1, or October 1;

B. Earned at least $100 in annual wages paid for agricultural labor for years after 1954 and before 1978; or $50 in wages paid for agricultural labor in any calendar quarter in 1951 through 1954. (See §214);

C. Earned at least $400 in annual net earnings from self-employment in taxable years 1951 through 1977 (see §215); or

D. Earned the maximum taxable wages for that year. For maximum taxable wages, (see §1301).

212.3 How do you earn credits for years after 1977?

For the years after 1977, the Commissioner of the Social Security Administration determines the amount of earnings that will equal a credit for each year. The amount of earnings is determined by using a formula in the Social Security Act that reflects a national percentage increase in average wages. The amount the Commissioner determines is published in the *Federal Register* on or before November 1 of the preceding year.

The table below shows the amount of wages or self-employment income needed to obtain a quarter of coverage:

Year	Amount of wages or self-employment income necessary to obtain a quarter of coverage
1985	$410
1986	$440
1987	$460
1988	$470
1989	$500
1990	$520
1991	$540
1992	$570
1993	$590
1994	$620
1995	$630
1996	$640
1997	$670
1998	$700
1999	$740
2000	$780
2001	$830
2002	$870
2003	$890
2004	$900
2005	$920
2006	$970
2007	$1,000
2008	$1,050
2009	$1,090
2010	$1,120
2011	$1,120
2012	$1,130
2013	$1,160
2014	$1,200
2015	$1,220
2016	$1,260
2017	$1,300
2018	$1,320
2019	$1,360
2020	$1,410
2021	$1,470
2022	$1,510
2023	$1,640
2024	$1,730

212.4 What is the maximum number of credits you can earn per year?

You may earn a maximum of four credits each year. The credits are based on your total earnings. Total earnings may consist of non-agricultural wages, military wages, railroad compensation, agricultural wages, and self-employment income.

212.5 How is self-employment income assigned?

If self-employment income is not reported on a calendar year basis, it is assigned to each of the calendar quarters in the taxable year. This is done in proportion to the number of months completely included in each calendar year which are included completely in the taxable year. The month that the taxable year ends is considered to be completely within the taxable year.

212.6 What does calendar quarter mean?

The term "calendar quarter" means a period of three calendar months ending March 31, June 30, September 30, or December 31 of any year.

212.7 What do wages and self-employment income include?

The terms "wages" and "self-employment income" do not necessarily include all of your income from employment or self-employment. They may also include pay for work that is ordinarily covered by the Railroad Retirement Act, and special wage credits for military service. Wages and self-employment income are defined and discussed in Chapter 13 and Chapter 12, respectively.

213. WHEN ARE CALENDAR QUARTERS NOT COUNTED FOR DETERMINING SOCIAL SECURITY CREDITS?

Even if the worker meets the earnings requirement for Social Security credits, he or she cannot earn a credit for a calendar quarter if the calendar quarter:

A. Begins after the quarter that the worker died;
B. Has not started yet; or
C. Is within a prior period of disability that is excluded in figuring benefit rights. (However, the beginning and ending quarters of the prior disability period may be counted as credits if the earnings requirements in §212 are met in these quarters.)

Note: A calendar quarter can only be counted once as a credit.

214. SOCIAL SECURITY CREDITS BASED ON WAGES EARNED AFTER 1936

214.1 How are credits assigned for work before 1978?

Credits earned are based on wages earned after 1936 and up to and including the calendar quarter that the worker dies. Before 1978, credit was obtained as of the first day of that quarter. As long as the total wages paid to the worker in that quarter amounted to at least $50, it does not matter on which date the $50 total was first reached.

214.2 How are credits assigned for work after 1977?

Under the revised definition of credit in effect after 1977, the number of credits assigned to a calendar year depends on the amount or earnings credited to that year. This is true regardless of the type of earnings credited. If your total earnings for the calendar year equals four times the designated amount reflected on the chart in §212.3, each quarter is a credit.

214.3 How are credits assigned for years after 1977 if you earn less than four in a year?

If you earn less than four credits in a year after 1977, the credits are assigned to a specific quarter when needed to meet insured status or increase the amount payable. Credit is effective on the first day of the quarter that it is assigned.

214.4 How are credits assigned for agricultural work?

Credit for agricultural wages was obtained in the same manner as non-agricultural wages from 1951 through 1954. From 1955 through 1977, a farm employee acquired credits based on total covered wages paid to him or her for farm work during a calendar year. A farm employee earned one credit for each $100 in cash wages paid during the year. After 1977, a *farm employee* earns a credit for each designated amount in cash wages paid during the year. (See §212.3.)

Note: Not all cash pay for farm work is "wages" to qualify for credits. (See §901.)

215. SOCIAL SECURITY CREDITS BASED ON SELF-EMPLOYMENT

215.1 Can you earn credits on self-employment income?

Beginning after 1950, you can earn credits based on self-employment income earned in taxable years.

215.2 How are credits assigned on self-employment income earned before 1978?

Before 1978, four credits were acquired for every taxable year at least $400 was earned in self-employment income.

Note: A self-employed person with actual net earnings of less than $400 may still be given credits if gross earnings were at least $600. He or she also must be eligible to use the "optional method" of reporting earnings. An individual that is not fully insured is considered to have a credit for each $400 of total wages during 1937-1950 if the person is fully insured based on credits derived under this method plus the credits earned after 1950.

Self-employment income, net earnings from self-employment, and the optional method available to figure net earnings are discussed in Chapter 12.

215.3 How are credits assigned on self-employment income earned after 1977?

After 1977, you acquire one credit for each designated amount of self-employment income (or self-employment income plus wages) wholly or partly in a taxable year. If you earn less than four credits, they will be assigned to your benefit. Self-employment income earned during any taxable year is assigned to calendar quarters in that taxable year as explained in §212.

216. TOTALIZATION-COORDINATION OF SOCIAL SECURITY SYSTEMS OF THE UNITED STATES AND A FOREIGN COUNTRY

216.1 Is your work performed in a foreign country taken into account for determining U.S. Social Security benefit eligibility?

If you worked under the social security system of a foreign country, the periods of work may be taken into account toward meeting U.S. insured status requirements for the U.S. Social Security Act's title II retirement, survivors, and disability insurance programs if:

A. A social security agreement between the U.S. and the foreign country (Totalization agreement) (see §107) provides for counting the foreign periods of coverage;
B. You have at least six credits earned under the U.S. program; and
C. You would not be insured for benefits without taking the foreign periods into account.

216.2 What happens if you qualify for benefits based on combined coverage?

If you qualify for benefits using combined coverage, the amount payable is based on a U.S. primary insurance amount (see Chapter 7). This is pro rated to reflect the fact that although foreign coverage helped you acquire insured status, the benefit payable is based on your U.S. coverage only.

216.3 Totalization-Coordination of Social Security Systems of the United States and A Foreign Country - Other Resources

https://www.ssa.gov/international/agreement_descriptions.html

Chapter 3
Cash Retirement and Auxiliary Benefits; Special Age 72 Payments

TABLE OF CONTENTS

RETIREMENT INSURANCE BENEFITS
- 300. Retirement Insurance Benefits
- 301. Entitlement to Retirement Insurance Benefit
- 302. Amount of Retirement Insurance Benefit
- 303. When are retirement benefits NOT payable (or only partly payable)?
- 304. Do your retirement insurance benefits end when you die?

SPOUSE'S INSURANCE BENEFIT
- 305. When is a spouse entitled to spouse's insurance benefits on the worker's Social Security record?
- 306. Spouse Defined
- 307. Common-Law Marriage
- 308. How does a divorce affect your marital status?
- 309. What is the effect of violating State-imposed restrictions on remarriage?
- 310. If there are several conflicting marriages, which one is valid?
- 311. When are you entitled to divorced spouse's insurance benefits?

CHILD IN-CARE

312. What does having a "child in care" mean?
313. What does "parental control and responsibility" mean?
314. What does "personal services" mean?
315. When does a parent NOT meet the in-care requirements?
316. Can a parent meet the in-care requirements while temporarily separated from a child?
317. Can a parent meet the in-care requirements during a separation from a child because of employment?
318. Separation Due to Child's School Attendance
319. Can a parent meet the in-care requirements when separated from a child because of illness?

SPOUSE'S INSURANCE BENEFIT PAYMENT

320. Spouse's Insurance Benefit
321. When are spouse's insurance benefits not payable?
322. When do spouse's and divorced spouse's insurance benefits end?

CHILD'S INSURANCE BENEFIT

323. Who is entitled to child's insurance benefits?
324. Who is a "child" for Social Security purposes?
325. When can a dependent grandchild or step-grandchild be considered the grandparent's "child"?
326. Legitimacy of a Child
327. Legitimated Children
328. Can a child NOT meeting the State law test in section 326 or 327 be considered the child of the worker?
329. Legally Adopted Children
330. Inheritance Rights of 'Equitably Adopted' Children
331. Stepchild-Stepparent Relationship
332. Can a child qualify as the stepchild of an invalid marriage?

CHILD'S DEPENDENCY REQUIREMENTS
333. Does a child have to be dependent on the worker to qualify for benefits?
334. When is a child presumed "dependent"?
335. When is a child dependent upon a stepparent?
336. When is a child dependent upon a grandparent or step-grandparent?
337. When A Child Must Be Dependent Upon Insured Parent

CHILD'S INSURANCE BENEFIT PAYMENT
338. Amount of Child's Insurance Benefit
339. When are child's insurance benefits NOT payable (or only partly payable)?
340. Termination of Child's Insurance Benefits
341. Can a child be re-entitled to benefits?
342. When do benefits end for a child who is attending elementary or secondary school?
343. What is an "educational institution"?
344. What does "full-time" mean?
345. When are benefits paid to a child who is not attending school?

SPECIAL MONTHLY CASH PAYMENT
346. Special Monthly Payment at 72
347. Can special monthly payments be made for the months before the application was filed?
348. Special Payments and Government Pensions

300. RETIREMENT INSURANCE BENEFITS

300.1 When do monthly cash retirement benefits begin?

You are eligible for monthly cash retirement insurance benefits (also called old-age insurance benefits) when you are age 62 or older and meet the conditions described in §301.

300.2 What additional benefits are available?

Additional monthly benefits, called auxiliary benefits, may be payable to other persons based on your earnings record as follows:

A. Monthly spouse's insurance benefits (see §§305-322); or
B. Monthly child's insurance benefits (see §§323-345).

These auxiliary benefits may also be payable on your earnings record if you are entitled to a disability insurance benefit. (See Chapter 5.)

301. ENTITLEMENT TO RETIREMENT INSURANCE BENEFIT

301.1 When are you entitled to retirement insurance benefits?

You are entitled to retirement insurance benefits if you:

A. Are at least age 62 throughout your first month of entitlement and are fully insured; and
B. Have filed an application for retirement insurance benefits.

If you met the requirements in (A) above before the month you filed the application, you may be entitled to retirement insurance benefits back to the first month in which you met those requirements. There are certain limitations, as explained in §1513.

301.2 When Is It NOT Necessary to File an Application?

You do not need to file an application if you are entitled to disability insurance benefits the month before the month you reach retirement age. The disability insurance benefit ends and the retirement insurance benefit begins automatically.

(See §346 for a special monthly cash payment for certain uninsured persons age 72 or older.)

302. AMOUNT OF RETIREMENT INSURANCE BENEFIT

302.1 How is your retirement insurance benefit amount computed?

The retirement insurance benefit rate is equal to the primary insurance amount, which is the basis for all benefits. In some cases, a special minimum benefit is provided for some individuals as explained in §717. These amounts may be increased by a cost-of-living benefit increase.

(See Chapter 7 for the methods of determining your primary insurance amount and for the effect of delayed retirement credits.)

302.2 Can you receive a reduced benefit before you reach retirement age?

If you wait until retirement age, you will receive the full retirement insurance benefit rate. However, if you are a worker age 62 to retirement age and otherwise eligible for retirement insurance benefits, you can choose to receive a reduced benefit. If you choose to receive and do receive benefits for one or more months before retirement age:

A. The benefit rate ordinarily received at retirement age is reduced by a certain percentage for each month you were under retirement age when the benefit began, as explained in §§723-724; and

B. A reduced benefit rate will continue to be paid after you reach retirement age.

303. WHEN ARE RETIREMENT BENEFITS NOT PAYABLE (OR ONLY PARTLY PAYABLE)?

Retirement benefits may *not* be payable or may be payable only in part if you meet any of the conditions below:

A. You are under retirement age and earn more than the exempt amount (see §1803);

B. You are under full retirement age and work outside the U.S. for more than 45 hours in a month (see §1823);

C. You are in the U.S. and are neither a citizen nor an alien lawfully present;

D. You have been deported or removed from the U.S. (see §1841);

E. You are an alien who is outside the U.S. for more than six full calendar months in a row and you do not meet an exception to the alien nonpayment provisions (see 1843-1846). For information on payments while you are outside the U.S., see "Your Payments While You Are Outside the United States" at https://ssa.gov/pubs/EN-05-10137.pdf and the *Payments Abroad Screening Tool* at https://www.ssa.gov/international/payments_outsideUS.html;

F. You are in a U.S. Treasury restricted country where we cannot send U.S. Government payments (see 1847-1849). For information on payments while you are outside the U.S., see "Your Payments While You Are Outside the United States" at https://www.ssa.gov/pubs/EN-05-10137.pdf;

G. You are in an SSA restricted country and do not meet an exception (see 1847-1849). For information on payments while you are outside the U.S., see "Your Payments While You Are Outside the United States" at https://www.ssa.gov/pubs/EN-05-10137.pdf;

H. You have waived the right to benefits because you are a member of a recognized religious group that is opposed to insurance. In this situation, you must have been granted exemption from paying the self-employment tax (see §§1128-1129); or

I. You are confined within the U.S. in a jail, prison, or other penal institution or correctional facility because you have been convicted of a felony.

(The conditions regarding nonpayment of benefits are explained in Chapter 18.)

304. DO YOUR RETIREMENT INSURANCE BENEFITS END WHEN YOU DIE?

Yes, your benefits end with your death. No retirement insurance benefit is paid for the month of your death. However, survivor benefits may be payable to your survivors beginning with the month of your death unless:

A. You or your survivor waived the right to benefits because of religious conviction (see §1128); or

B. You or your survivor has been convicted of certain crimes and sentenced accordingly (see §1837).

305. WHEN IS A SPOUSE ENTITLED TO SPOUSE'S INSURANCE BENEFITS ON THE WORKER'S SOCIAL SECURITY RECORD?

As the spouse of an insured worker, you are entitled to spouse's insurance benefits if you meet the conditions below:

A. The worker is entitled to retirement or disability insurance benefits;

B. You have filed an application for spouse's benefits;

C. You are not entitled to a retirement or disability insurance benefit based on a primary insurance amount which equals or exceeds one-half the worker's primary insurance amount;

D. You either:
   1. Are age 62 or over; or
   2. Have in care (as defined in §312) a child under age 16 or disabled who is entitled to benefits on the worker's Social Security record; and
E. You meet one of the following conditions:
   1. You have been married to the worker for at least one continuous year just before he or she filed the application for benefits;
   2. You are the mother or father of the worker's biological son or daughter (as defined in §324). This requirement is met if a live child was born to you and the worker. The child need not be living when you apply for benefits;
   3. You were entitled or "potentially" entitled to spouse's (including deemed or divorced spouse's), widow(er)'s (including deemed widow(er)'s or surviving divorced spouse's), parent's, or childhood disability benefits based on the record of a fully insured individual under the Social Security Act in the month before the month you married the worker. You are "potentially entitled" if you meet all the requirements for entitlement other than filing of an application, and (in the case of spouse's, widow(er)'s, or parent's benefits) attaining the required age; or
   4. You were entitled or potentially entitled to a widow(er)'s, parent's, or child's (age 18 or over) annuity under the Railroad Retirement Act in the month before the month you married the worker.

306. SPOUSE DEFINED

306.1 What is the definition of spouse for Social Security purposes?

You are considered a spouse for Social Security purposes if you meet the conditions in either (A) or (B) below at the time you apply for benefits:

A. Under applicable law:
   1. You and the worker were validly married; or
   2. You would have the status of a husband or a wife with respect to the taking of intestate personal property;
B. You entered into a ceremonial marriage with the worker that was invalid under applicable law because of an impediment resulting from a prior marriage or its dissolution; or a defect in the procedure followed in connection with the alleged marriage, provided:

1. You married the worker in good faith, not knowing of any defect at the time of the marriage;
2. You were living with the worker in the same household when he or she applied for benefits (unless you were divorced from the worker at the time); and
3. For benefits payable prior to January 1991, there is no other person who is or was entitled to monthly insurance benefits on the worker's earnings record as his or her spouse and who still has status as the worker's spouse.

306.2 What is applicable law?

Applicable law is the law that would be applied by the courts of:
A. The State where the insured worker was domiciled when you filed for benefits; or
B. The law applied by the District of Columbia if the insured worker was not domiciled in any State when you filed for benefits.

See §306.1 A. footnote.[1]

307. COMMON-LAW MARRIAGE

307.1 What is a common-law marriage?

A "common-law marriage" is one in which neither a religious nor civil ceremony was held. In certain States, a common-law marriage may be entered into if a man and a woman agree to be married for the rest of their lives. Most States (even those in which a man and woman cannot enter into a valid common-law marriage) generally recognize a common-law marriage that has been validly entered into in another State.

307.2 What are the requirements for a valid common-law marriage?

The basic requirements for a valid common-law marriage (in addition to other requirements in some States) are that both parties must:
A. Be legally capable of contracting a valid marriage with each other;
B. Contract the marriage in a State that recognizes common-law marriages;
C. Have the intent to be married;

---

1. On June 26, 2013, the Supreme Court ruled Section 3 of the Defense of Marriage Act (DOMA) unconstitutional. Therefore, Social Security no longer is prevented from recognizing same-sex marriages to determine entitlement or payment amount.

D. Consider themselves husband and wife; and
E. Mutually agree to become husband and wife from that time on.

308. HOW DOES A DIVORCE AFFECT YOUR MARITAL STATUS?

A divorce decree has one of three possible effects:

A. In some States, divorce immediately returns your status to that of a single person, without restriction as to remarriage;
B. In other States, while you are no longer a husband or wife after the judgment of divorce, State law or the divorce decree prohibits you from remarrying for a certain period; e.g., during a stated waiting period; or
C. In still other States, the dissolution of your marriage is postponed for a stated period following the judgment of divorce. Sometimes, the parties to the divorce or the court must take additional action to make a divorce final and thereby dissolve the marriage.

309. WHAT IS THE EFFECT OF VIOLATING STATE-IMPOSED RESTRICTIONS ON REMARRIAGE?

The status of your remarriage following a divorce is affected under the following conditions:

A. If you remarry before a judgment or an interlocutory divorce decree that dissolves your prior marriage becomes final, your remarriage is generally void in all States;
B. If a State imposes a restriction against remarriage after a final divorce and you remarry in that State in violation of its restriction, generally that State considers your remarriage void; or
C. If you remarry in another State, your remarriage is generally considered valid in all States unless:
   1. The State where you either obtained the divorce or got remarried denies recognition of a marriage by a party who goes to another State in order to avoid the restrictions; or
   2. The State where you got remarried prohibits marriages of residents of other States that would be void if the marriage took place in the your home State.

310. IF THERE ARE SEVERAL CONFLICTING MARRIAGES, WHICH ONE IS VALID?

Your last (most recent) of several conflicting marriages is the one most States presume to be valid. This is provided there is no evidence that your marriage is not valid. This does not mean that evidence of your most recent marriage is enough to establish the end of your last marriage(s). You must make reasonable efforts to provide enough information which would enable the Social Security Administration to provide assistance in obtaining evidence concerning the continuation or dissolution of a former marriage(s). Such evidence will permit a determination to be made on the facts. If all the information and evidence supplied still leaves doubt as to whether your last marriage(s) ended, then your most recent marriage will be presumed the valid one.

311. WHEN ARE YOU ENTITLED TO DIVORCED SPOUSE'S INSURANCE BENEFITS?

You are entitled to a divorced spouse's insurance benefits on the worker's Social Security record if:

A. The worker is entitled to retirement or disability insurance benefits;
B. You have filed an application for divorced spouse's benefits;
C. You are not entitled to a retirement or disability insurance benefit based on a primary insurance amount which equals or exceeds one-half the worker's primary insurance amount;
D. You are age 62 or over;
E. You are not married; and
F. You were married to the worker for at least 10 years before the date the divorce became final.

Note: You are not entitled before age 62 even if you have an entitled child in care.

The divorced spouse of a worker who is not entitled to retirement or disability insurance benefits, but has reached age 62 and is fully insured, can become independently entitled to benefits on the worker's earnings record. To do so, however, the divorced spouse must meet the requirements in (B)-(F) above and have been divorced from the worker for not less than two continuous years.

312. WHAT DOES HAVING A "CHILD IN CARE" MEAN?

Having a "child in care" is a basic requirement for some benefits, including spouse's benefits for a spouse under age 62 and for mother's and father's benefits (see §415). "In care" means:

A. Exercising parental control and responsibility for the welfare and care of a child under age 16 or a mentally disabled child age 16 or over; or

B. Performing personal services for a physically disabled child age 16 or over.

The mother or father may exercise parental control and responsibility or perform personal services alone or together. When the child in care turns 16, the parent may continue to receive benefits if the child is disabled and the parent meets the requirements for having a disabled child in care.

313. WHAT DOES "PAPENTAL CONTROL AND RESPONSIBILITY" MEAN?

Exercising "parental control and responsibility" means that you:

A. Display a strong interest in the proper rearing of the child;
B. Supervise the child's activities;
C. Participate in the important decisions about the child's physical needs and mental development; and
D. Measurably control the child's upbringing and development.

This parental responsibility can be exercised directly or indirectly. You may exercise direct control when you and the child are living together. You may exercise indirect control when you instruct the child's custodian (whether an individual or institution) and ensure that the instructions are carried out. In any case, you must be doing more than just providing for the child's food and shelter.

314. WHAT DOES "PERSONAL SERVICES" MEAN?

You are considered to be performing "personal services" for a child age 16 and over when:

A. You perform services regularly; and
B. The services you perform for the child are in addition to any routine household services normally done by you or any other adult in the household.

Examples of personal services:
- You provide nursing care;
- You feed or dress a physically disabled child;
- You direct or supervise the activities of a physically disabled child who is unable to mange funds or can do so only with help and guidance; and
- Your presence is required by the nature of the child's disability, e.g., epilepsy.

315. WHEN DOES A PARENT NOT MEET THE IN-CARE REQUIREMENTS?

You do not meet the in-care requirements (see §312) (whether based on "parental control and responsibility" (see §313) or "personal services" (see §314)) if:

A. The child is age 16 or over (unless the child is disabled); or

B. You and the child are not living together and any of the following conditions are met:
1. You and your spouse are separated or divorced and you have lost or given up your right to control the child;
2. You are mentally disabled;
3. The child was removed from your custody and control by court order;
4. You have given up the right to custody and control of the child to some other person or agency;
5. The separation is for a period of more than six months and the child is age 16 or over and physically disabled; or
6. The child is under the jurisdiction of a court appointed guardian (of the child's person) other than the claimant.

316. CAN A PARENT MEET THE IN-CARE REQUIREMENTS WHILE TEMPORARILY SEPARATED FROM A CHILD?

You can still meet the in-care requirements (see §312) during a temporary separation if:

A. The child was in care when you were living together;
B. The child normally lives with you; and
C. None of the factors in §315 exists.

317. CAN A PARENT MEET THE IN-CARE REQUIREMENTS DURING A SEPARATION FROM A CHILD BECAUSE OF EMPLOYMENT?

When your employment is the reason for separation from a child under age 16 and the separation is indefinite or is not expected to end within six months, you may have the child in care if:

A. You exercise parental responsibility (see §313); and

B. You make regular and substantial contributions to the child's support (see §1724).

318. SEPARATION DUE TO CHILD'S SCHOOL ATTENDANCE

318.1 Can a parent meet the in-care requirements when separated from a child because of the child's school attendance?

When the child's school attendance is the reason for your separation from a child under age 16, you may have a child in care if:

A. The child is not under the sole control and jurisdiction of the school; and

B. The child spends an annual vacation of at least 30 days with you (unless it is not possible for the child to return home during vacation).

318.2 Which parent is considered to have the child in care in the case of a separation?

If you are separated from the child's other parent, you may be found to have a child in care if:

A. The child normally returns to you during vacations; and

B. The school authorities look to you when they have a question concerning the child's welfare.

319. CAN A PARENT MEET THE IN-CARE REQUIREMENTS WHEN SEPARATED FROM A CHILD BECAUSE OF ILLNESS?

If your physical illness or disability causes you to be separated from a child under age 16, you may have a child in care if you are:

A. Supervising the child's activities; and

B. Participating in the important decisions about the child's physical and mental needs.

320. SPOUSE'S INSURANCE BENEFIT

320.1 What is your spouse's insurance benefit amount?

As a spouse, your insurance benefit is one-half of the worker's primary insurance amount (see §302). The benefit paid to you may be less than one-half of the worker's primary insurance amount if:

A. The "family maximum" applies (see §§731-732 for an explanation of reduction in benefit rates because of this provision);

B. You are entitled to a retirement, disability, or widow(er)'s insurance benefit that is smaller than your spouse's benefit rate (only the difference between the retirement, disability, or widow(er)'s benefit and the spouse's benefit rate is paid as a spouse's insurance benefit); or

C. You qualified for a reduced spouse's benefit before retirement age. (See §§723-724 for an explanation of how the reduced rate is figured.)

Note: If you have in care the worker's child under age 16 or disabled, who is entitled to child's insurance benefits, your benefits are not reduced. (See §312 for an explanation of "in care".)

320.2 What is the effect of receiving reduced spouse's benefits prior to full retirement age?

If you choose to receive, and are paid, a reduced spouse's benefit for months before full retirement age, you are not entitled to the full spouse's benefit rate upon reaching full retirement age. A reduced benefit rate is payable for as long as you remain entitled to spouse's benefits. (For possible adjustment at retirement age, see §728.)

320.3 What do you need to know about divorced spouse's benefits?

If you are a divorced spouse, your spouse's benefit is not reduced under (A) above.

If you do not have the worker's entitled child in your care in the first month of your entitlement before full retirement age, your benefit is reduced under (C) above. However, if you have such a child in care in that month, your benefit is not reduced. It remains unreduced even for later months before full retirement age in which no child is in your care.

321. WHEN ARE SPOUSE'S INSURANCE BENEFITS NOT PAYABLE?

321.1 When are spouse's insurance benefits NOT payable (or only partly payable)?

Your spouse's insurance benefits may not be payable or may be payable only in part if:

A. Some or all of the worker's retirement insurance benefits are not payable because:
   1. The worker is under full retirement age (FRA) (as defined in §723.1), works, and earns more than the exempt amount (see §1803);
   2. The worker works outside the United States (U.S.) for more than 45 hours in a month (see §1823);

   If you and the worker have been divorced for at least two continuous years, your monthly benefit is paid without regard to work deductions of the worker. However, effective January 1, 1991, if the worker was entitled to a retirement insurance benefit, in the month before the month of divorce, you are exempt from the two-year waiting period;

B. You are under FRA, working, and earning more than the exempt amount (see §1803); or you are working outside the U.S. for more than 45 hours in a month (see §1823);

C. You are in the U.S. for a full calendar month and you are not a U.S. citizen, U.S. national or alien lawfully present in the U.S.;

D. You are an alien who is outside the U.S. for more than six full calendar months in a row and you do not meet an exception to the alien non-payment provisions or do not meet the additional U.S. residency requirements for dependents or survivors. (see §1843-1846). For information on payments while you are outside the U.S., see "Your Payments While You Are Outside the United States" at https://www.ssa.gov/pubs/EN-05-10137.pdf and the *Payments Abroad Screening Tool* at www.ssa.gov/international/payments_outsideUS.html;

E. You are in a U.S. Treasury restricted country where we cannot send U.S. Government payments (see §1847-1849). For information on payments while you are outside the U.S., see "Your Payments While You Are Outside the United States" at https://www.ssa.gov/pubs/EN-05-10137.pdf;

F. You are in an SSA restricted country and do not meet an exception (see §1847-1849). For information on payments while you are outside the U.S. see "Your Payments While You Are Outside the United States" at https://www.ssa.gov/pubs/EN-05-10137.pdf;

G. The worker has been deported or removed from the U.S. and you are an alien who is outside the U.S. (see §1842);

H. You or the worker was granted a tax exemption as a member of a religious group opposed to insurance (see §§1128-1129);

I. The worker is receiving disability insurance benefits that are subject to offset because of the worker's compensation payments (This deduction does not apply to an independently entitled divorced spouse; see §311.) You are subject to deductions if the worker is receiving disability insurance benefits, is entitled to workers compensation benefits, and you have not been divorced for two years. If the worker was entitled to the current disability insurance benefit in the month before the month of the divorce, the two-year waiting period is waived; or

J. You are under age 62 and do not have in your care a child of the worker under age 16 or disabled who is entitled to child's benefits (see §312 and §1829.1);

K. You are entitled, on the basis of your own employment, to a governmental pension (Federal, State, or a political subdivision of a State) not covered by Social Security. Your pension must require offset against the Social Security payment and the exceptions in §1836 do not apply;

L. You were convicted of unruly activities and a court imposed an additional penalty (see §1837);

M. You do not have a social security number and refuse to apply for one; or

N. You are confined within the U.S. to a correctional institution for more than 30 continuous days, as a result of a conviction of a criminal offense or a court of competent jurisdiction issues a verdict, finding or a ruling that declares you are:

- guilty but insane with respect to a criminal offense;
- not guilty of such a criminal offense by reason of insanity;
- incompetent to stand trial under an allegation of a criminal offense;
- determined to have a similar verdict or finding, with respect to a criminal offense based on similar factors (such as mental disease,

mental defect or mental incompetence) *and* you are confined to an institution at public expense for more than 30 continuous days; or
- Immediately upon completion of confinement in a correctional institution (confinement in the correctional institution was based on a crime; an element of which was sexual activity), you are confined by court order to an institution for more than 30 continuous days at public expense because you were determined to be a sexually dangerous person or a sexual predator or similar finding.

O. You have an unsatisfied Federal, State or international law enforcement warrant for more than 30 continuous days for:
- A crime, or attempted crime, that is a felony or, in jurisdictions that do not classify crimes as felonies, a crime that is punishable by death or imprisonment for more than one year (regardless of the actual sentence imposed); or
- Violation of a condition of probation/parole imposed under Federal or State law (see §1854).

P. The worker requested voluntary suspension of his or her retirement benefits on or after April 30, 2016. The conditions regarding nonpayment of benefits are explained in more detail in Chapter 18.

321.2 Do you receive your spouse's benefits if you do not have a child in your care?

If you are a spouse age 62 to full retirement age (as defined in §723) entitled to spouse's benefits because you have a child in care, you are not paid any benefits for the months that the child is not in your care. You may be paid a reduced benefit, however, if you file a "certificate of election" to receive the reduced benefit for those months in which the child is not in your care. (See §729 and §1829.)

Note: The benefit of a divorced spouse between ages 62 and full retirement age is not subject to deductions for failure to have a child under age 16 or disabled in care. (See §320.)

(The conditions regarding nonpayment or partial payment of benefits are explained in Chapter 18.)

322. WHEN DO SPOUSE'S AND DIVORCED SPOUSE'S INSURANCE BENEFITS END?

Spouse's or divorced spouse's insurance benefits end when any of the conditions below are met:

A. The spouse dies;

B. The worker dies (in this case the spouse may be entitled to widow(er)'s, mother's, or father's benefits);

C. The worker's entitlement to disability insurance benefits ends and he or she is not entitled to retirement insurance benefits (unless the divorce spouse meets the requirements for an independently entitled divorced spouse, as explained in §311);

D. The spouse is under age 62 and there no longer is a child of the worker under age 16 or disabled who is entitled to child's insurance benefits;

E. The spouse becomes entitled to retirement or disability insurance benefits and his or her primary insurance amount is at least one-half of the worker's primary insurance amount;

F. The spouse and the worker are divorced, unless:
   1. The spouse had already turned 62 when the divorce became final; and
   2. The spouse and the worker had been married for at least 10 years before the date the divorce became final;

G. The spouse qualified for benefits only under the conditions explained in §306, and one of the following events occurs:
   1. The spouse enters into a valid marriage with someone other than the worker;
   2. Prior to January 1991, monthly benefits are awarded on the same earnings record to another person who qualifies as the legal spouse of the worker under the conditions in §306; or
   3. Prior to January 1991, the spouse obtains a divorce from the worker;

H. The spouse qualified for benefits only under the conditions explained in §306 and later learns that the marriage is invalid;

I. The divorced spouse marries someone of the opposite gender, other than the worker. However, the divorced spouse's benefit will not be ended by marrying an individual entitled to divorced spouse's, widow(er)'s, mother's, father's, or parent's monthly benefits, or to an

individual age 18 or over who is entitled to childhood disability benefits; or
J. For an independently entitled divorced spouse, the worker is no longer fully insured or he or she marries the worker.

A spouse is not entitled to spouse's insurance benefits for the month in which any one of the above events occurs.

323. WHO IS ENTITLED TO CHILD'S INSURANCE BENEFITS?

A child is entitled to child's insurance benefits on the Social Security record of a parent if the following conditions are met:
A. An application for child's insurance benefits is filed;
B. The child is (or was) dependent upon the parent (see §§333-337);
C. The child is not married;
D. The child meets any of the following conditions:
   1. Is under age 18;
   2. Is age 18-19 and a full-time elementary or secondary school student; or
   3. Is age 18 or older and under a disability (which must have begun before age 22) (see §517); and
E. The parent meets any of the following conditions:
   1. Is entitled to disability insurance benefits;
   2. Is entitled to retirement insurance benefits;
   3. Died and was either fully or currently insured at the time of death.

324. WHO IS A "CHILD" FOR SOCIAL SECURITY PURPOSES?

The term "child" includes the worker's:
A. Natural (i.e., biological) legitimate child, or any other child who would have the right under applicable State law to inherit intestate personal property from the worker as a child (see §326);

Note: Applicable State law is the law applied by the courts of the State where the worker was domiciled at the time of death. If the worker was not domiciled in any State, applicable State law is the law the courts of the District of Columbia would apply;

B. Stepchild, under certain circumstances (see §331);
C. Legally adopted child (see §329);
D. Child of invalid ceremonial marriage entered into under the conditions explained in §328;

E. Natural child, if the worker:
   1. Has acknowledged in writing that the child is his or her son or daughter;
   2. Has been decreed by a court to be the father or mother of the child;
   3. Has been ordered by a court to contribute to the support of the child because the child is his or her son or daughter; or
   4. Has been shown to be the child's father or mother by other acceptable evidence and was living with the child or contributing to the child's support when the child's application is filed (in life cases) or when the worker died (in survivor cases); or

   Note: The court action referred to in E.2. and 3. above must be made before the death of the worker.

F. Grandchild or step-grandchild, under certain circumstances (see §325).

325. WHEN CAN A DEPENDENT GRANDCHILD OR STEP-GRANDCHILD BE CONSIDERED THE GRANDPARENT'S "CHILD"?

A dependent grandchild or step-grandchild of the worker or spouse may qualify for benefits as a "child" if:

A. The grandchild's natural or adoptive parents are deceased or disabled:
   1. At the time the worker became entitled to retirement or disability insurance benefits or died; or
   2. At the beginning of the worker's period of disability which continued until the worker became entitled to disability or retirement insurance benefits or died; or

B. The grandchild was legally adopted by the worker's surviving spouse in an adoption decreed by a court of competent jurisdiction within the U.S. The grandchild's natural or adopting parent or stepparent must not have been living in the same household and making regular contributions to the child's support at the time the insured worker died.

Besides meeting the requirement in (A) or (B), the grandchild or step-grandchild must be dependent on the insured as described in §336.

326. LEGITIMACY OF A CHILD

326.1 Why is legitimacy of a child important for Social Security purposes?

A natural legitimate child (i.e., a child born of a valid marriage) has inheritance rights in the parents' intestate personal property under the laws of all States. Under the laws of most States, a child born out of wedlock has the status of "child" for the purposes of sharing the intestate personal property of the natural mother. The child does not have the status of child with regard to the estate of the natural father, unless certain conditions are met.

326.2 How does a State determine a child's legitimacy?

To determine the child's legitimacy, the courts of a State usually look to the law of the State where the parent was living when the child was born. The courts also look to the law of any other State under which the child's status may have been changed. Therefore, even if the State where the parent was living does not recognize the child as legitimate, the child may still be considered legitimate if born in some other State.

326.3 Is a child born during a valid marriage always considered legitimate?

A child conceived or born during a valid marriage is considered legitimate in all States. This presumption may be overcome, however, under certain conditions. In a controversy over a child's legal status, certain States follow the "Lord Mansfield Rule". Under this rule, neither the testimony of the child's mother, nor the testimony of the man who was her husband at the time the child was conceived or born, can disprove the child's legitimacy.

326.4 Are children of void marriages legitimate?

The legitimacy of children of void marriages differs by State. In some States, void marriage statutes provide that children of void marriages are legitimate. In other States, it may be necessary for a court of competent jurisdiction to declare the child legitimate.

327. LEGITIMATED CHILDREN

327.1 How does a child born out of wedlock acquire inheritance rights?

A child born out of wedlock may inherit the intestate personal property of the natural father if the child is "legitimated" (given the status of a legitimate child) under State law by performance of specific acts, e.g., the natural father's marriage to the child's natural mother.

In some States, a child may acquire inheritance rights without being legitimated only if certain acts prescribed by State law are performed; for example, acknowledgment of paternity of the child.

327.2 What is the effective date of legitimation?

The effective date of legitimation of a child may be important in determining when a child becomes entitled to Social Security benefits. In most States, a child legitimated after birth is considered legitimate from birth. In other States, such a child is legitimate only from the date of the legitimating act.

328. CAN A CHILD NOT MEETING THE STATE LAW TEST IN SECTION 326 OR 327 BE CONSIDERED THE CHILD OF THE WORKER?

A child is deemed to be your "child" even though the State Law Test is not met as described in §326 or §327 if the child is your son or daughter and:

A. You and the mother or father went through a marriage ceremony that would have resulted in a valid marriage except for an impediment arising:
   1. From the lack of dissolution of a previous marriage or otherwise arising out of such a previous marriage or its dissolution; or
   2. From a defect in the procedure followed in connection with the supposed marriage; or
B. One of the conditions set forth in §324 (E) is met.

329. LEGALLY ADOPTED CHILDREN

329.1 What is the definition of legally adopted child?

A "legally adopted child" of the worker means a child who was legally adopted under the adoption laws of the State or foreign country where the adoption took place.

A child who is legally adopted by the worker's surviving spouse after the worker's death is considered the worker's legally adopted child as of the date of the worker's death if:

A. The child was either living with or receiving one-half support from the worker at the time of the worker's death; and
B. One of the following is met:
   1. The worker started proceedings to adopt the child before his or her death; or
   2. The child was adopted by the worker's surviving spouse within two years after the worker's death.

329.2 What is the effective date of an adoption decree?

The effective date of an adoption decree is important in deciding when an adopted child becomes entitled to benefits. In some States, both an interlocutory and final decree of adoption may be issued. In other States, only one decree or order is issued. The effective date of an adoption is determined by the law of the State where the adoption took place.

330. INHERITANCE RIGHTS OF 'EQUITABLY ADOPTED' CHILDREN

330.1 If an adoption has not been completed, can the child still be considered a child of the worker?

In some cases, a worker may not complete a contemplated adoption. Most States give the child inheritance rights in the worker's intestate personal property if certain conditions are met. If so, the child may qualify for benefits as the worker's "equitably adopted child."

330.2 What are the conditions for qualifying as an 'equitably adopted' child?

Generally, the following conditions must be met:

A. An expressed or, in some States, implied contract for the worker to adopt the child;
B. A legal consideration for the worker's promise to adopt;
C. In some States, a promise to give the child inheritance rights in the worker's personal property;
D. Surrender of the child to the worker;
E. Performance by the child under the contract; and
F. Sufficient lapse of time so that the child could have been legally adopted under applicable State law.

330.3 What documentation must be provided?

All pertinent documents, together with complete and detailed statements of the parties and other persons having knowledge of the facts, setting forth full information about the factors listed above must be submitted. Each case must be handled on an individual basis.

Note: An equitably adopted child must have been living with or receiving contributions from the worker at the applicable time (see §337).

331. STEPCHILD-STEPPARENT RELATIONSHIP

331.1 When does a stepchild-stepparent relationship arise?

In general, a stepchild-stepparent relationship arises when you:
A. Marry the child's natural parent (in general, this must be after the child's birth); or
B. Marry the child's adopting parent after the adoption.

331.2 What is the effect of your death as a stepparent?

If you die, your stepchild's entitlement to benefits does not end.

331.3 What is the effect of divorce on a stepchild's benefits?

Once a stepchild is entitled, a divorce ending the parent's marriage (including an invalid ceremonial marriage-see §332) to the stepparent ends the child's benefits if the divorce becomes final in or after July 1996.

331.4 How long does the steprelationship have to exist?

A. If the parent is living, a stepchild must have been a stepchild of the insured worker for at least one year before filing an application; and
B. To qualify for survivors benefits, a stepchild must have been the stepchild of the insured worker for at least nine months before the day that the worker died, unless:
  1. The worker and the child's natural or adopting parent were previously married, divorced, and then remarried at the time of the worker's death, and
  2. The nine-month duration-of-relationship requirement was met at the time of the divorce.

Note: If the death of the worker was accidental or occurred in the line of duty while a member of a uniformed service serving on active duty, the nine-month requirement may be considered satisfied; unless the worker could not have been expected to live for nine months at the time of marriage. (See §404 for an explanation of the exception to the nine-month duration-of-marriage requirement.)

(The evidence required to establish the relationships described above is set forth in §§1707-1717.)

332. CAN A CHILD QUALIFY AS THE STEPCHILD OF AN INVALID MARRIAGE?

A child is considered the stepchild of the worker if the parent, or adopting parent, went through a marriage ceremony with the worker (who is not the child's parent or adopting parent). The marriage ceremony must have resulted in a marriage that would have been valid except for an impediment arising:

A. From the lack of dissolution of a previous marriage or otherwise arising out of such a previous marriage or its dissolution; or
B. From a defect in the procedure followed in connection with the purported marriage.

333. DOES A CHILD HAVE TO BE DEPENDENT ON THE WORKER TO QUALIFY FOR BENEFITS?

A child must be dependent upon the worker to qualify for benefits on the worker's Social Security record. The factors that determine whether a child is dependent upon a worker vary, depending upon whether the worker is the natural parent, the legally adopting parent, the stepparent, or the grandparent. The various dependency "tests" are set out in §§334-337.

334. WHEN IS A CHILD PRESUMED "DEPENDENT"?

A child is presumed "dependent" upon the worker if:

A. The child has not been legally adopted by someone other than the worker during the worker's lifetime; and
B. The child is one of the following:
   1. The legitimate child of the worker;
   2. A child born out of wedlock who would have the right under applicable State law to inherit intestate property from the worker as a child;
   3. The child of a void or voidable marriage;
   4. The child of an invalid ceremonial marriage;
   5. A deemed child under section 216(h)(3) of the Social Security Act, under certain circumstances (see §324 (E)); or

6. The legally adopted child of the worker adopted before the worker's entitlement to benefits.

Note: A natural or legally adopted child who was legally adopted by someone other than the worker during the worker's lifetime must have been living with or receiving contributions from the worker at the applicable time.

335. WHEN IS A CHILD DEPENDENT UPON A STEPPARENT?

A child is dependent upon a stepparent if the stepparent was contributing at least one-half the child's support at the applicable time (see §337). A stepchild entitled before July 1996 could meet an alternate requirement that he or she must have been "living with" the worker.

336. WHEN IS A CHILD DEPENDENT UPON A GRANDPARENT OR STEP-GRANDPARENT?

To be dependent on the worker, a grandchild (or step-grandchild) must have:

A. Begun living with the worker before the grandchild became 18 years old; and
B. Lived with the worker in the U.S. and received at least one-half support from the worker:
  1. For the year before the month the worker became entitled to retirement or disability insurance benefits or died; or
  2. If the worker had a period of disability that lasted until he or she became entitled to benefits or died, for the year immediately before the month in which the period of disability began.

If the grandchild was born during the one-year period, the worker must have lived with and provided at least one-half of the grandchild's support for substantially all of the period from the date of the grandchild's birth to the month indicated in (B) above.

337. WHEN A CHILD MUST BE DEPENDENT UPON INSURED PARENT

337.1 When must a child be dependent in order to obtain benefits?

In order to receive benefits, the child must have the status of a "child" (see §324) and must also be dependent or deemed dependent at one of the times set out in (A), (B), (C), or (D) below:

A. If the worker is entitled to disability insurance benefits the child must be dependent at one of the following points:

1. The beginning of the worker's period of disability;
2. The time the worker last became entitled to disability insurance benefits; or
3. The time the application for child's insurance benefits is filed;

B. If the worker is entitled to retirement insurance benefits and had a period of disability that did not end before that entitlement, the child must be dependent at one of the following points:
   1. The beginning of the worker's period of disability;
   2. The time the worker became entitled to disability insurance benefits;
   3. The time the worker became entitled to retirement insurance benefits; or
   4. The time the application for child's insurance benefits is filed;

C. If the worker is entitled to retirement insurance benefits not immediately preceded by a period of disability, the child must be dependent at the time the application for child's insurance benefits is filed; or

D. If the worker is deceased, the dependency requirement can be met at the time of the worker's death. If the deceased worker had a period of disability continuing until the month of death or until entitlement to retirement insurance benefits, the requirement can also be met:
   1. At the beginning of the worker's period of disability;
   2. At the time the worker became entitled to disability insurance benefits; or
   3. At the time the worker became entitled to retirement insurance benefits. If the parent was alive and entitled to disability or retirement insurance benefits within the retroactive life of the child's application, dependency can be met within the retroactive period.

Note: If the child is a dependent grandchild or step-grandchild, the use of the points in (A) through (D) of this section is subject to the limitations in §336 (B).

337.2 What are the dependency requirements for a child adopted by the worker after the worker's entitlement?

If the worker adopts a child after becoming entitled to either retirement or disability insurance benefits, the dependency requirement is met only if:

A. The child is the natural child or the stepchild of the worker; or

B. The child was legally adopted by the worker in an adoption decreed by a U.S. court; and
   1. The child was under age 18 when adoption proceedings began; or
   2. The child was living with or receiving at least one-half support from the worker for the year immediately before the month that the adoption is decreed.

338. AMOUNT OF CHILD'S INSURANCE BENEFIT

338.1 How is the child's monthly benefit amount determined?
A child's monthly benefit rate is:
A. One-half the insured parent's primary insurance amount if the parent is entitled to disability or retirement insurance benefits (see §302); or
B. Three-fourths of the parent's primary insurance amount if the parent is dead.

338.2 When is the child's benefit amount less?
The benefit paid to a child may be less if:
A. The "family maximum" applies and the benefit rate must be reduced (see §§731-732); or
B. A disabled "child" is entitled to disability or retirement insurance benefits on his or her own Social Security record. In this case, only the amount by which the child's monthly benefit rate exceeds the retirement or disability insurance benefit is paid as the child's insurance benefit.

(See §§733-737 for the effect of simultaneous entitlement to other Social Security benefits on the child's insurance benefit.)

339. WHEN ARE CHILD'S INSURANCE BENEFITS NOT PAYABLE (OR ONLY PARTLY PAYABLE)?

A child's insurance benefits may not be payable or may be payable only in part if any of the conditions below are met:
A. Some or all of the parent's retirement insurance benefits are not payable because the parent is under age 70, works, and earns more than the exempt amount (see §1803); or works outside the U.S. for more than 45 hours in a month (see §1823);
B. The child works and earns over the exempt amount (see §1803) or works outside the U.S. for more than 45 hours in a month (see §1823);

C. The parent has been deported or removed from the U.S. and the child is an alien who is outside the U.S.(see §1842). For information on payments while outside the U.S., see https://www.ssa.gov/international/payments.html;
D. The child is neither a citizen nor an alien lawfully present in the U.S. For information on payments while outside the U.S., see https://www.ssa.gov/international/payments.html;
E. The child is an alien who is outside the U.S. for more than six full calendar months in a row and the child does not meet an exception to the alien non-payment provisions or does not meet the additional U.S. residency requirements for dependents and survivors (see 1843-1846). For information on payments while outside the U.S., see "Your Payments While You Are Outside the United States" at https://www.ssa.gov/pubs/EN-05-10137.pdf and the *Payments Abroad Screening Tool* at www.ssa.gov/international/payments_outsideUS.html;
F. The child is in a U.S. Treasury restricted country where we cannot send U.S. Government payments (see 1847-1849). For information on payments while outside the U.S., see "Your Payments While You Are Outside the United States" at https://www.ssa.gov/pubs/EN-05-10137.pdf;
G. The child is in an SSA restricted country and does not meet an exception (see 1847-1849). For information on payments while outside the U.S., see "Your Payments While You Are Outside the United States" at https://www.ssa.gov/pubs/EN-05-10137.pdf;
H. The parent or child was granted a tax exemption as a member of a religious group opposed to insurance (see §§1128-1129);
I. The parent is receiving disability insurance benefits which are subject to offset because of workers' compensation payments; or
J. The child is entitled to childhood disability benefits and is married to a retirement insurance beneficiary whose benefit is not payable because he or she is working;
K. The child is confined within the U.S. to a correctional institution for more than 30 continuous days, as a result of a conviction of a criminal offense or a court of competent jurisdiction issues a verdict, finding or a ruling that declares the child is:
   • guilty but insane with respect to a criminal offense;
   • not guilty of such a criminal offense by reason of insanity;

- incompetent to stand trial under an allegation of a criminal offense;
- determined to have a similar verdict or finding with respect to a criminal offense based on similar factors (such as mental disease, mental defect or mental incompetence) *and*
- the child is confined to an institution at public expense for more than 30 continuous days;

or

- Immediately upon completion of confinement in a correctional institution (confinement in the correctional institution was based on a crime; an element of which was sexual activity), the child is confined by court order to an institution for more than 30 continuous days at public expense because he/she was determined to be a sexually dangerous person or a sexual predator or similar finding.

L. A court imposed an additional penalty upon conviction of the child of subversive activities. (See §1837).

M. The child has an outstanding warrant for a crime or attempted crime that carries a penalty of death or imprisonment for more than one year, or an outstanding warrant for a Federal or State probation or parole violation.

N. The parent requested voluntary suspension of his or her retirement benefits on or after April 30, 2016.

O. The disabled child who is full retirement age requests voluntary suspension of his or her own retirement benefits

(The provisions regarding nonpayment of benefits are explained in Chapter 18.)

340. TERMINATION OF CHILD'S INSURANCE BENEFITS

340.1 When do child's insurance benefit payments end?

A child's insurance benefit payments end when:

A. The child dies; or

B. The child reaches age 18 and is neither disabled nor a full-time student (For a situation where a student may continue to be entitled to child's benefits, even though he or she has reached age 19, see §342); or

C. The child marries (however, if the child is a childhood disability beneficiary and the marriage is to another Social Security beneficiary, see §1852. If the marriage is either void or subsequently annulled, see §1853); or

D. The child's parent is no longer entitled to disability insurance benefits, unless the entitlement ended because the insured parent became entitled to retirement insurance benefits or died.

The beneficiary is not entitled to child's insurance benefits for the month in which any of the above events occur. However, in the case of a disabled child, the child's benefits end with the second month following the month in which he or she is no longer disabled.

340.2 Do benefits of an adopted child end if the adoption is annulled?

If a child is entitled to a child's benefit based on a legal adoption, the benefit ends if the adoption is annulled. The effective date of the terminations of benefits is the month in which the annulment becomes effective.

340.3 Do benefits of a stepchild end in the case of a divorce?

A stepchild's benefits end if the marriage between the worker and the stepchild's parent ends in a divorce. The effective date of the termination of benefits is the month after the divorce becomes final.

341. CAN A CHILD BE RE-ENTITLED TO BENEFITS?

A child whose entitlement ended at age 18 or later may be re-entitled upon filing an application if:

A. He or she became and remains under a disability which began before age 22; or

B. He or she is age 18-19 and a full-time elementary or secondary school student; or

C. He or she was entitled to childhood disability benefits and becomes disabled again within seven years after the prior entitlement to those benefits ended. Effective for benefits payable for months beginning October 2004, a child may be reentitled to childhood benefits at any time if the child's previous entitlement had ended because disability ceased due to the performance of substantial gainful activity. The seven-year restriction continues to apply if childhood disability benefits ended because of medical improvement.

In addition to the above requirements, the child must not have married since last entitled to benefits, unless the marriage was void or annulled. Re-entitlement is not possible after a marriage that ended by death or divorce.

342. WHEN DO BENEFITS END FOR A CHILD WHO IS ATTENDING ELEMENTARY OR SECONDARY SCHOOL?

If a child is attending elementary or secondary school full time when he or she turns 19 and has not completed the requirements for a secondary school diploma or equivalent certificate, the child's benefits continue through whichever of the following occurs first:

A. The month he or she completes the course;
B. The second month after the month the child reaches age 19 (if the school operates on a yearly basis, which is the usual case); or
C. The last month of the quarter or semester that is in progress when he or she reaches age 19 (if the school operates on a quarterly or semester basis and requires students to reenroll for each new quarter or semester).

343. WHAT IS AN "EDUCATIONAL INSTITUTION"?

A school is considered an "educational institution" if it provides elementary or secondary education as determined under the law of the State or other jurisdiction in which it is located.

344. WHAT DOES "FULL-TIME" MEAN?

A student is attending an educational institution "full-time" if he or she is carrying a subject load that is considered full-time for day students under the standards and practices of the educational institution. An individual also may be considered a student regularly attending school when he/she is instructed at home in accordance with the home school law of the State or other jurisdiction in which he/she resides. However, a student will not be considered in full-time attendance if:

A. The student is enrolled in a course of study of less than 13 school weeks' duration;
B. The student's scheduled attendance is less than 20 hours a week (unless an exception applies);
C. The student is being paid while attending the educational institution by his or her employer who has requested or required that the student attend the educational institution; or
D. The student meets the requirements for suspension of benefits as required by prisoner or fugitive felon provisions (see §1850).

345. WHEN ARE BENEFITS PAID TO A CHILD WHO IS NOT ATTENDING SCHOOL?

Child's insurance benefits may be paid to a child as a full-time student for a period of four calendar months or less in which the child does not attend school if:

A. The child was in full-time attendance immediately before the four-month period;
B. The child has established an intent to continue full-time or actually does attend full-time after the end of the four-month period; and
C. The period of nonattendance is not due to the child's expulsion or suspension from school.

346. SPECIAL MONTHLY PAYMENT AT 72

346.1 Who can receive a special monthly cash payment?

You may be entitled to a special monthly cash payment if you meet the conditions below:

A. You turned 72 before 1972 (if you turned 72 between 1968 and 1971, you must have earned a specified number of credits (see §211));
B. You are a resident of one of the 50 States, the Northern Mariana Islands, or the District of Columbia;
C. You are either:
   1. A U.S. citizen; or
   2. An alien lawfully admitted to the U.S. and have lived in the U.S. continuously for the five-year period immediately before the month you filed the application;
D. You have properly filed an application for the special monthly cash payment (see §347); and
E. You do not qualify for a regular Social Security benefit under the fully insured provision discussed in §202. The special monthly payment ends with the month before the month you die.

346.2 What is the amount of the benefit?

The $276.40 amount was first payable for December 2008. These amounts may be increased when a cost-of-living increase in benefits is established. In 2024, the cost of living adjustment was 3.2% (See §719.)

Your special monthly payment amount is reduced by the amount of any periodic benefit under a governmental pension system for which you are eligible. (See §348.)

347. CAN SPECIAL MONTHLY PAYMENTS BE MADE FOR THE MONTHS BEFORE THE APPLICATION WAS FILED?

No, you are not entitled to the special monthly payment earlier than the month you filed the application. However, if you filed an application in one of the three months before the month you meet the requirements in §346, you can be paid under this special condition. Aside from these exceptions, the regular rules on applications in Chapter 15 apply to applications for the special monthly payment at age 72.

348. SPECIAL PAYMENTS AND GOVERNMENT PENSIONS

348.1 Are your payments reduced if you are under a governmental pension system?

Yes, your special monthly payment is reduced by the amount of any periodic benefit under a governmental pension system for which you are eligible for that month.

If you are married, your special monthly payment may be reduced if your spouse is eligible for a benefit under a governmental pension system. It does not matter whether you or your spouse is retired and receiving the governmental pension. Eligibility is the controlling factor.

348.2 What payments are considered periodic benefits?

A periodic benefit under a governmental pension system means any pension, annuity, or similar payment established by the U.S., a State, any political subdivision of a State, or any wholly owned instrumentality of one or more of these governmental entities. This includes monthly Social Security benefits and railroad retirement annuities and pensions. Lump-sums paid in place of a periodic benefit are also included. However, workers' compensation payments and payments by the Department of Veterans Affairs because of a service-connected disability or a service-connected death are not included.

348.3 What adjustments are made to your benefit payments if you are eligible for a governmental pension?

If you are eligible for a governmental pension, the amount of your pension is subtracted from your special monthly cash payment.

If your spouse is eligible for a governmental pension, but is not entitled to the special payment, your special payment is reduced. The reduction amount, after any reduction for your own governmental pension, is the total amount of any periodic pension for which your spouse is eligible.

If both you and your spouse are entitled to the special payment, each payment is first reduced by the amount of his or her own governmental pension (if any). The payment amount is further reduced by each monthly benefit amount that is more than any periodic pension for which the other spouse is eligible.

Chapter 4
Survivors Benefits

TABLE OF CONTENTS

GENERAL
400. Benefits Payable To Survivors of Deceased Insured Worker

WIDOWER'S INSURANCE BENEFITS
401. When is a widow(er) entitled to widow(er)'s insurance benefits?
402. Widow(er) Defined
403. Entitlement of a Surviving Divorced Wife or Husband
404. Exception to the Nine-Month Duration of Marriage Requirement
405. When an Application for Widow(er)'s Insurance Benefits is Not Required
406. Effect of Remarriage-Widow(er)'s Benefits
407. Amount of Widow(er)'s Insurance Benefit
408. When will you NOT receive widow(er)'s insurance benefits?
409. Termination of Widow(er)'s Insurance Benefits

SURVIVING CHILD'S INSURANCE BENEFITS
410. When is a surviving child entitled to child's insurance benefits?
411. What is the definition of "child" for Social Security purposes?

412. Amount of Surviving Child's Insurance Benefit
413. When are child's insurance benefit NOT payable?
414. When do child's insurance benefits end?

FATHER'S AND MOTHER'S INSURANCE BENEFITS

415. When is a widow(er) entitled to father's or mother's insurance benefits?
416. When is a surviving divorced parent entitled to father's or mother's insurance benefits?
417. Effect of Remarriage-Father's or Mother's Insurance Benefits
418. Amount of Father's or Mother's Insurance Benefit
419. When are father's or mother's insurance benefits NOT payable?
420. When do father's or mother's insurance benefits end?

PARENT'S INSURANCE BENEFITS

421. When is a parent of a deceased person entitled to parent's benefits?
422. Parent Defined
423. When must the support requirement be met?
424. When must you file evidence of support?
425. Amount of Parent's Insurance Benefit
426. When are parent's insurance benefits NOT payable?
427. When do parent's insurance benefits end?

LUMP-SUM DEATH PAYMENT

428. When is a lump-sum death payment paid?
429. When will you NOT receive a lump-sum death payment?
430. When is a lump-sum paid to the surviving widow(er)?
431. When No Spouse Living in Household
432. Lump-Sum Payable To Children
433. When Application Must Be Filed

400. BENEFITS PAYABLE TO SURVIVORS OF DECEASED INSURED WORKER

400.1 What cash benefits are paid to you as a survivor of an insured worker?

When the insured worker dies, your cash benefits as an eligible survivor may be paid as follows:

A. Monthly widow(er)'s insurance benefits (see §§401-409);
B. Monthly surviving child's insurance benefits (see §§410-414);
C. Monthly mother's or father's insurance benefits (see §§415-420);
D. Monthly parent's insurance benefits (see §§421-427); and/or
E. Lump-sum death payment (see §§428-433).

Your benefits rates are figured as a percentage of the deceased worker's primary insurance amount. (See §700.)

400.2 What conditions affect survivor benefits?

The following conditions may affect your benefits as a survivor of an insured worker:

A. If the deceased worker was insured under the Railroad Retirement Act, your benefits may be payable under that Act rather than under the Social Security Act. (See Chapter 23.);
B. If you or the insured worker was granted a tax exemption as a member of a religious group, whose members oppose insurance plans such as Social Security, you may not be eligible for survivor benefits. If you are eligible, your benefits may be smaller (See §1128.);
C. If you were convicted of the felonious and intentional homicide of the worker, you cannot become entitled to monthly benefits or the lump-sum death payment payable on the deceased's Social Security earnings record. (See §1722.); and
D. If you are a minor convicted of intentionally causing your parent's death, you may be denied survivor benefits on the earnings record of your parent.

(See §1837 and §1847 on how conviction by a court for an offense involving subversive activities and residence in a restricted country affect the payment of benefits.)

401. WHEN IS A WIDOW(ER) ENTITLED TO WIDOW(ER)'S INSURANCE BENEFITS?

You are entitled to widow(er)'s insurance benefits on a worker's Social Security record if the following conditions are met:

A. You are either (1) age 60 or over; or (2) at least age 50 but not age 60 and disabled (as defined in §515) and you meet the disability-related requirements in §513;

Note: A widow(er) age 60-64 and under a disability is entitled to disabled widow(er)'s benefits for Medicare purposes.

B. The worker died fully insured (see §203.1);
C. You are not entitled to a retirement insurance benefit that is equal to or larger than the worker's primary insurance amount;
D. You have filed an application for widow(er)'s insurance benefits (see §405 for exceptions and see §1511 for completing application forms);
E. You are not married or your marriage can be disregarded (see §406 for exceptions); and
F. *One* of the following conditions is met:
    1. You were married to the deceased worker for at least the nine months just before the worker died (see §404 for exceptions);
    2. You are the mother or father of the worker's son or daughter (this requirement is met if a live child was born to you and the worker, even if the child did not survive) (see §411);
    3. You legally adopted the worker's son or daughter during your marriage and before the child reached age 18 (see §329);
    4. You were married to the worker when you both legally adopted a child under age 18;
    5. The worker legally adopted (as defined in §329) your son or daughter during your marriage and before the child reached age 18; or
    6. In the month before the month you married the deceased worker, you were entitled or potentially entitled to either (1) spouse's, widow(er)'s, father's (based on the record of a fully insured worker), mother's (based on the record of a fully insured worker), parent's, or childhood disability benefits on the record of a fully insured individual under the Social Security Act; or (2)

widow(er)'s, child's (age 18 or over), or parent's insurance annuity under the Railroad Retirement Act.

Note: You are "potentially entitled" if you meet all requirements for entitlement, other than the filing of an application and attainment of the required age.

See §402.1 for definition of widow(er) for social security purposes.

402. WIDOW(ER) DEFINED

402.1 What is the definition of a widow(er) for Social Security purposes?

You are considered a widow(er) of the insured worker for Social Security purposes if:

A. Under applicable law, if at the time the insured worker died:
   1. You and the insured worker were validly married; or
   2. You would have the status of widow(er) with respect to the distribution of intestate personal property;
B. You entered into a ceremonial marriage with the insured worker that was invalid under the law, provided that:
   1. You married the insured worker in good faith, not knowing of any impediment to the marriage;
   2. You were living with the insured worker in the same household at the time of his or her death;

Note: This statement does not apply if you are divorced or if you were receiving spouse's benefits at the time of the insured worker's death.

   3. For periods prior to January 1991, there is no other person who is or was entitled to monthly insurance benefits on the insured worker's earnings record and still has the status as a legal widow(er); and
   4. The invalid marriage resulted from either (1) a prior marriage or its dissolution; or (2) a defect in the procedure followed in connection with your marriage.

402.2 What does under applicable law mean?

Applicable law is either:

A. The law applied by the courts of the State where the insured worker lived at the time he or she died; or

B. The law applied by the District of Columbia if the insured worker was not living in any State at the time of his or her death. See §402.1 A. footnote.[1]

403. ENTITLEMENT OF A SURVIVING DIVORCED WIFE OR HUSBAND

403.1 When is a surviving divorced wife or husband entitled to benefits on the worker's Social Security record?

You are entitled to surviving divorced wife's or husband's insurance benefits on the deceased worker's Social Security record if:

A. You are either (1) age 60 or over; or (2) at least age 50 but not age 60 and disabled (as defined in §515) and you meet the disability-related requirements in §513;
B. The worker died fully insured (see §203.1);
C. You are not married (see §406 for exceptions); and
D. You meet the requirements in §401 (C) and (D).

403.2 Who is a surviving divorced wife or husband?

You are a surviving divorced wife or husband if you were married to the worker for at least 10 years just before the date the divorce became final. You meet this definition even if you were divorced within the 10-year period, provided you remarried the worker no later than the calendar year after the year of the divorce.

404. EXCEPTION TO THE NINE-MONTH DURATION OF MARRIAGE REQUIREMENT

404.1 What are the exceptions to the nine-month duration of marriage requirement?

The nine-month duration of marriage requirement in §401(F)(1) is waived if the widow(er) was married to the insured worker at the time of his or her death and either:

A. The insured worker's death was accidental (see §404.2 in this section); or

---

1. On June 26, 2013, the Supreme Court ruled Section 3 of the Defense of Marriage Act (DOMA) unconstitutional. Therefore, Social Security no longer is prevented from recognizing same-sex marriages to determine entitlement or payment amount.

B. The insured worker's death occurred in the line of duty while he or she was a member of a uniformed service serving on active duty; or
C. The widow(er) was previously married and divorced from the insured worker and the previous marriage had lasted at least nine months; or
D. Effective for applications filed in or after March 2004,
- The insured worker had been married prior to his or her marriage to the widow(er); and
- The prior spouse was institutionalized during the insured worker's marriage to him or her due to mental incompetence or similar incapacity; and
- During the period of the prior spouse's institutionalization, the insured worker would have divorced the prior spouse and married the surviving spouse, but did not do so because the divorce would have been unlawful, by reason of the institutionalization, under the laws of the State of the insured worker's domicile at the time (this determination is based on evidence satisfactory to SSA); and
- The prior spouse remained institutionalized up to the time of his or her death; and
- The insured worker married the widow(er) within 60 days after the prior spouse's death.

Note: The exceptions to the nine-month duration of marriage requirement in A., B., and C. above do not apply if, at the time of the marriage, the insured worker could not reasonably have been expected to live for nine months.

404.2 When is a death considered accidental?

The insured worker's death is defined as accidental only if:
A. He or she received bodily injuries through violent, external, and accidental means;
B. The insured worker died within three months after the day that the injuries were received; and
C. The worker's death was a direct result of the bodily injuries, independent of all other causes.

405. WHEN AN APPLICATION FOR WIDOW(ER)'S INSURANCE BENEFITS IS NOT REQUIRED

405.1 When are you NOT required to file an application for widow(er)'s benefits?

You do not need to file an application for widow(er)'s benefits if:

A. You have reached retirement age (as defined in §723.5) and you were entitled to spouse's benefits for the month immediately before the month that your spouse died;

B. You were entitled to father's or mother's benefits for the month immediately before the month you reached retirement age; or

C. You were: (1) between ages 62 and retirement age at the time your spouse died and (2) entitled to spouse's benefits, but not to disability or retirement benefits. The spouse's benefits are automatically converted to widow(er)'s insurance benefits.

405.2 When must you file a certificate of election?

You must file a certificate of election to become entitled to widow(er)'s benefits if:

A. You are receiving reduced spouse's (or divorced spouse's) benefits and retirement or disability benefits in the month before the month of the worker's death; and

B. You are between age 62 and retirement age in the month of the worker's death.

406. EFFECT OF REMARRIAGE-WIDOW(ER)'S BENEFITS

406.1 Does the remarriage of a widow(er) or surviving divorced wife or husband affect widow(er)'s benefits?

Your remarriage *after age 60* does not prevent you from becoming entitled to benefits on your prior deceased spouse's Social Security earnings record.

406.2 Does the remarriage of a disabled widow(er) or surviving divorced wife or husband affect widow(er)'s benefits?

Your remarriage does not prevent you from becoming entitled to benefits on your prior deceased spouse's Social Security earnings records as long as:

A. Your remarriage occurs after you turn 50; and

B. Your remarriage occurs after you become disabled.

Note: If you remarry *before you turn 50*, you will not be entitled to survivor's benefits, unless the marriage ends.

406.3 How does remarriage of a widow(er) or a surviving divorced wife or husband before age 60 affect widow(er)'s benefits?

If you remarry before age 60, you will not be entitled to survivor's benefits, unless:

A. Your subsequent marriage ends, whether by death, divorce, or annulment; or

B. Your marriage occurred after age 50 and you were entitled to benefits as a disabled widow(er) or disabled surviving divorced spouse.

406.4 How does the termination of a remarriage of a widow(er) or surviving divorced wife or husband before age 60 affect widow(er)'s benefits?

If you remarry before you turn 60 and that marriage ends, you may become entitled or re-entitled to benefits on your prior deceased spouse's earnings record. Your benefits begin the first month in which the subsequent marriage ended if all entitlement requirements are met. If the remarriage was absolutely void or was annulled from the beginning, see §1853.

407. AMOUNT OF WIDOW(ER)'S INSURANCE BENEFIT

407.1 How is the widow(er)'s benefit rate computed?

The widow(er)'s insurance benefit rate equals 100 percent of the deceased worker's primary insurance amount *plus* any additional amount the deceased worker was entitled to because of delayed retirement credits. (See §720.)

407.2 When is the benefit rate less?

Your widow(er)'s insurance benefit payable may be less than what was computed above if any of the conditions below apply:

A. A reduction is necessary because the "family maximum" applies (this reduction is discussed in §§731-732);

B. You are also entitled to a smaller retirement insurance or disability insurance benefit (only the difference between the larger widow(er)'s insurance benefit and the other benefit is payable as the widow(er)'s insurance benefit; however, this amount is payable in addition to the other benefit);

C. You are entitled for months before the month you reach retirement age. See §§723-725 for an explanation of how the reduced rate is computed;
D. You choose to receive and are paid a reduced widow(er)'s benefit for months before you reach retirement age. A reduced benefit rate is payable for as long as you are entitled to widow(er)'s benefits. For a possible adjustment at age 62 and retirement age, see §728;

Note: Entitlement to this reduced rate may result in a reduction in any disability or retirement insurance benefit to which you may later become entitled.

E. You are caring for your deceased spouse's child and:
  1. The child is under age 16 or disabled;
  2. The child is entitled to child's insurance benefits; and
  3. You have not reached retirement age. In this case, your widow(er)'s benefits are not reduced for those months below 75 percent of the deceased spouse's primary insurance amount; or
F. The deceased worker was entitled to a reduced retirement benefit for the month before the month he or she died.

408. WHEN WILL YOU NOT RECEIVE WIDOW(ER)'S INSURANCE BENEFITS?

Widow(er)'s insurance benefits may not be payable for some months if any of the conditions below apply:

A. You are under full retirement age (as defined in 723.5), working, and earning more than the annual exempt amount (see §1803);
B. You are under full retirement age and working outside the United States (U.S.) for more than 45 hours in a month (see §1823);
C. You are an alien who is outside the U.S. for more than six full calendar months in a row and you do not meet an exception to the alien nonpayment provisions or do not meet the additional U.S. residency requirements for dependents and survivors. (see §1843-1846). For information on payments while you are outside the U.S., see "Your Payments While You Are Outside the United States" at https://www.ssa.gov/pubs/EN-05-10137.pdf and the *Payment Abroad Screening Tool* at www.ssa.gov/international/payments_outsideUS.html;
D. You are in a U.S. Treasury restricted country where we cannot send U.S. Government payments (see §1847-1849). For information on payments while you are outside the U.S., see "Your Payments While

You Are Outside the United States" at https://www.ssa.gov/pubs/EN-05-10137.pdf;
E. You are in an SSA restricted country and do not meet an exception (see §1847-1849). For information on payments while you are outside the U.S., see "Your Payments While You Are Outside the United States" at www.socialsecurity.gov/pubs/10137.html;
F. You are an alien who is outside the U.S., and you were deported;
G. You are entitled to a government pension (Federal, State, or a political subdivision of a State not covered by Social Security) based of your own employment and:
   1. The entitlement requires offset against the Social Security payment; and
   2. The exceptions in §1836 do not apply;
H. You are confined within the U.S. to a correctional institution for more than 30 continuous days, as a result of a conviction of a criminal offense or a court of competent jurisdiction issues a verdict, finding or a ruling that declares you are:
   - guilty, but insane with respect to a criminal offense;
   - not guilty of such a criminal offense by reason of insanity;
   - incompetent to stand trial under an allegation of a criminal offense;
   - determined to have a similar verdict or finding with respect to a criminal offense based on similar factors (such as mental disease, mental defect or mental incompetence) *and*
   - you are confined to an institution at public expense for more than 30 continuous days;
   or
   - Immediately upon completion of confinement in a correctional institution (confinement in the correctional institution was based on a crime; an element of which was sexual activity), you are confined by court order to an institution for more than 30 continuous days, at public expense because you were determined to be a sexually dangerous person or a sexual predator or similar finding (see §1850.1-1850.3).

You have an unsatisfied Federal, State or international law enforcement warrant for more than 30 continuous days for a crime, or attempted crime, of flight to avoid prosecution or confinement, escape from custody and flight-escape. In most jurisdictions these crimes are felonies or, in jurisdictions that do not classify crimes as felonies, a crime that is punishable by death or imprisonment for more than one year (regardless of the actual sentence imposed.

I. You do not have a Social Security Number, and you refuse to apply for one; or

J. You are in the U.S., and you are neither a U.S. citizen nor an alien lawfully present.

K. You requested voluntary suspension of your retirement benefits on or after April 30, 2016.

The conditions regarding nonpayment of benefits are explained in more detail in Chapter 18.

409. TERMINATION OF WIDOW(ER)'S INSURANCE BENEFITS

409.1 When do your widow(er)'s benefits end?

Your widow(er)'s insurance benefits end when:

A. You die;

B. You become entitled to a retirement insurance benefit that is equal to or larger than the worker's primary insurance amount;

C. For benefits payable prior to January 1991, you qualified only under the conditions explained in §402 (B) and monthly benefits were awarded on the same earnings record to another individual who either:
  1. Validly married the deceased worker; or
  2. Has the same status under State law with respect to the taking of intestate personal property as you would as the widow(er); or

D. Your disability ends. In this case, your last month of entitlement is the second month after the month in which your disability ended. However, your entitlement continues if you reach retirement age on or before the last day of the third month after your disability ends.

You are not entitled to widow(er)'s benefits for the month in which any one of the above events occurs, except as explained in (D).

409.2 Do benefits end or are they reduced upon remarriage?

Your benefits will not terminate or be reduced upon remarriage if:

A. You are a widow(er) or surviving divorced wife or husband age 60 or over; or

B. You are a *disabled* widow(er) or a *disabled* surviving divorced wife or husband age 50 or over.

See §406 for the effects of remarriage on benefits.

410. WHEN IS A SURVIVING CHILD ENTITLED TO CHILD'S INSURANCE BENEFITS?

A surviving child is entitled to child's insurance benefits if the conditions below are met:

A. The worker-parent died either fully or currently insured;
B. The child is the child of the deceased;
C. The child is:
   1. Under age 18;
   2. Under age 19 and a full-time elementary or secondary school student; or
   3. Age 18 or over and under a disability as defined in §507.1 (which began before age 22); and
D. The child was dependent upon the deceased parent (see §§334-337 for the dependency "tests");
E. The child is not married; and
F. An application for child's insurance benefits is filed. (See §511 for completing application forms.)

Note: An application is not required if the child was entitled to child's insurance benefits on the deceased parent's earnings record for the month before the month in which the parent died.

411. WHAT IS THE DEFINITION OF "CHILD" FOR SOCIAL SECURITY PURPOSES?

The term "child" includes the insured worker's:

A. Natural (e.g., biological) legitimate child, or any other child who would have the right under applicable State law to inherit intestate personal property from the insured worker as his or her child;

Note: Applicable State law is the law applied by the courts of the State where the insured worker was domiciled at the time of death. If the worker was not domiciled in any State, applicable State law is the law of the courts of the District of Columbia.

B. Stepchild, under certain circumstances (see §331);
C. Legally adopted child (see §329);
D. Child of an invalid ceremonial marriage entered into under the conditions explained in §328;
E. Natural child, provided the insured worker:
   1. Has acknowledged in writing that the child is his or her son or daughter;

2. Has been decreed by a court to be the parent of the child;
3. Has been ordered by a court to contribute to the support of the child because the child is his or her son or daughter; or
4. Has been shown to be the child's father or mother by other reasonable evidence. The worker must have lived with the child or contributed to the child's support or when the insured worker died; or
F. Dependent grandchild or step-grandchild (see §325).

Note: The court action in (E) above must be made before the worker's death.

412. AMOUNT OF SURVIVING CHILD'S INSURANCE BENEFIT

412.1 How is the surviving child's benefit rate computed?

The surviving child's insurance benefit rate is three-fourths (.75) of the deceased parent's primary insurance amount.

412.2 When is the benefit rate less?

The child's insurance benefit may be less than above if the "family maximum" applies and all the benefits on that earnings record have to be reduced.

(See §§730-732 for a discussion of the family maximum. See §§733-737 for the effect of simultaneous entitlement to more than one Social Security benefit.)

413. WHEN ARE CHILD'S INSURANCE BENEFIT NOT PAYABLE?

The child's insurance benefit may not be payable for some months if any of the conditions below are met:
A. The child works and earns more than the yearly exempt amount (see §1803);
B. The child works outside the U.S. for more than 45 hours in a month (see §1823);
C. The child is an alien who is outside the U.S. for more than six full calendar months in a row and does not meet an exception to the alien non-payment provision or does not meet the additional U.S. residency requirements for dependents and survivors (see 1843-1846). For information on payments while outside the U.S., see "Your Payments While You Are Outside the United States" at https://www.ssa.gov/pubs/EN-05-10137.pdf and the Payments Abroad Screening Tool at www.ssa.gov/international/payments_outsideUS.html

D. The child is in a U.S. Treasury restricted country where we cannot send U.S. government payments (see 1847-1849). For information on payments while outside the U.S., see "Your Payments While You Are Outside the United States" at https://www.ssa.gov/pubs/EN-05-10137.pdf;
E. The child is in an SSA restricted country and does not meet an exception (see 1847-1849). For more information on payments while outside the U.S., see "Your Payments While You Are Outside the United States" at https://www.ssa.gov/pubs/EN-05-10137.pdf;
F. The insured parent had been deported, and the child is an alien who is outside the U.S. For information on payments while outside the U.S., see https://www.ssa.gov/pubs/EN-05-10137.pdf;
G. The disabled child, age 18 or over, refuses to accept vocational rehabilitation services without good cause;

Note: The child's insurance benefit may be payable for all months while the disabled child is still under age 19, if a full-time student, as defined in §344.

H. The disabled child, age 18 or over, is married to a retirement insurance beneficiary whose benefit is not payable because of work activity;
I. The disabled child, age 18 or over, is married to a disability insurance beneficiary whose benefit is not payable because of refusal to accept vocational rehabilitation services without good cause;
J. The child is confined within the U.S. in a jail, prison, or other penal institution or correctional facility for conviction of a felony;

Note: The benefit may still be payable if the child is participating in a rehabilitation program that has been specifically approved for the child by a court of law. It must be expected that the child will be able to engage in substantial work upon release within a reasonable time.

K. The child does not have a Social Security Number, and the child or his or her parent, guardian, or person acting on the child's behalf refuses to apply for one; or
L. The child is in the United States and is neither a U.S. citizen nor an alien lawfully present.
M. The parent requested voluntary suspension of his or her own retirement benefits on or after April 30, 2016.
N. The disabled child who is full retirement age requests voluntary suspension of his or her own retirement benefits.

The conditions regarding nonpayment of benefits are discussed in more detail in Chapter 18.

414. WHEN DO CHILD'S INSURANCE BENEFITS END?

Surviving child's insurance benefits end when any of the conditions below are met:

A. The child dies;

B. The child reaches age 18 and is neither under a disability nor a full-time elementary or secondary school student;

Note: Entitlement to childhood disability benefits ends when the child age 18 or older is no longer under a disability that began before age 22. However, benefits may continue if the child is still under age 19 and a full-time elementary or secondary school student. (For a situation where a student may continue to be entitled to child's benefits even though he or she has reached age 19, see §342.)

C. The child marries;

Note: For exceptions: see §1852 if a disabled child age 18 or over marries another Social Security beneficiary; see §1853 if the marriage is absolutely void or has been annulled *from the beginning.*

D. The child's entitlement is based on a legal adoption and the adoption is annulled; or

E. The child is a stepchild of the worker, and the marriage between the worker and the stepchild's parent ends in divorce.

The effective date of the termination of benefits is the month in which any of the above events occurs. However, a *disabled* child's benefits terminate effective with the second month following the month in which he or she is no longer under a disability. Also, a stepchild's benefits terminate effective with the month after the divorce becomes final.

(See §341 for reentitlement conditions.)

415. WHEN IS A WIDOW(ER) ENTITLED TO FATHER'S OR MOTHER'S INSURANCE BENEFITS?

As a widow(er), you are entitled to father's or mother's insurance benefits if all of the conditions below are met:

A. The insured worker died either fully or currently insured (see §§203 and 206);

B. You have filed an application for father's or mother's insurance benefits;

Note: See §1511 for completing application forms. No application is required if you were entitled to spouse's insurance benefits for the month before the month in which the insured worker died.

C. You are not entitled to a retirement insurance benefit that is equal to or larger than the amount of the unadjusted father's or mother's insurance benefit;
D. You have in care a child of the deceased worker under age 16 or disabled who is entitled to child's insurance benefits (see §§312-315 for definition of "in care");
E. You are not married (see §417);
F. You are not entitled to widow(er)'s insurance benefits (see §402); and
G. You meet one of the conditions in §401 (F).

416. WHEN IS A SURVIVING DIVORCED PARENT ENTITLED TO FATHER'S OR MOTHER'S INSURANCE BENEFITS?

You are entitled to father's or mother's insurance benefits, as a surviving divorced father or mother of a worker who died fully or currently insured (as defined in §§203 and 206), if you meet the following conditions:

A. You and the worker were validly married under State law (see §402.1 A), or you were deemed to be validly married (see §402.1 B) but the marriage ended in a final divorce. After January 1, 1991, a marriage based on the requirements in §402 (B) also qualifies;
B. You filed an application for father's or mother's insurance benefits;

Note: No application is required if you were entitled to spouse's benefits for the month before the month the worker died.

C. You are not married;
D. You are not entitled to widow(er)'s insurance benefits (as defined in §402), or to a retirement insurance benefit that is equal to or larger than the father's or mother's full benefit;
E. You have in your care the worker's child (as defined in §411) who is entitled to child's insurance benefits and (see §§312-315 for definition of "in care"):
  1. The child is your natural or legally adopted child;
  2. The child is entitled to child's insurance benefits on the worker's earnings record; and
  3. The child is under age 16 or disabled; and
F. You meet one of the requirements in §401 (F).

417. EFFECT OF REMARRIAGE-FATHER'S OR MOTHER'S INSURANCE BENEFITS

417.1 How does remarriage affect father's or mother's insurance benefits?

If you receive father's or mother's benefits, your remarriage will generally end your entitlement. It also prevents any future entitlement to father's or mother's benefits on the prior deceased spouse's Social Security record.

417.2 Can you be entitled if the remarriage ends?

You can be entitled or re-entitled to father's or mother's or surviving divorced father's or mother's benefits if your subsequent marriage ends by death, divorce, or annulment. Entitlement or re-entitlement to father's or mother's benefits begins with the month your subsequent marriage ends.

Note: If your remarriage was absolutely void or was annulled *from the beginning*, see §1853.

418. AMOUNT OF FATHER'S OR MOTHER'S INSURANCE BENEFIT

418.1 How is the father's or mother's insurance benefit rate computed?

The father's or mother's insurance benefit rate is equal to three-fourths (.75) of the deceased worker's primary insurance amount.

418.2 When is the benefit rate less?

You father's or mother's insurance benefit amount may be less if either of the conditions below are met:

A. A reduction is necessary because the family maximum applies (see §§730-732); or

B. You are also entitled to a smaller retirement or disability insurance benefit. In this case, an amount equal to the difference between the father's or mother's benefit rate and the other benefit rate is payable as the father's or mother's benefit. This is paid in addition to the other benefit.

(For the effect of simultaneous entitlement to other Social Security benefits, see §§733-737.)

419. WHEN ARE FATHER'S OR MOTHER'S INSURANCE BENEFITS NOT PAYABLE?

Father's or mother's insurance benefits may not be payable for some months if any of the conditions below are met:

A. You work and earn more than the yearly exempt amount (see §1803);
B. You work outside the United States (U.S.) for more than 45 hours in a month (see §1823);
C. You are an alien who is outside the U.S. for more than six calendar months in a row. For information on payments while you are outside the U.S., see Publication "Your Payments While You Are Outside the United States" https://www.ssa.gov/pubs/EN-05-10137.pdf;
D. The deceased worker had been deported and you are an alien who is outside the U.S. For information on payments while you are outside the U.S., see Publication "Your Payments While You Are Outside the United States" https://www.ssa.gov/pubs/EN-05-10137.pdf;
E. You do not have in care a child of the deceased worker under age 16 or disabled who is entitled to benefits on any Social Security record; or, if you are a surviving divorced father or mother, you do not have in care a child of the deceased worker who is:
   1. Your natural or legally adopted child (as defined in §324);
   2. Under age 16 or disabled; and
   3. Entitled to benefits on the deceased worker's record; (see §§312-315 for definition of "in care")
F. You are married to an individual entitled to retirement insurance benefits and those benefits are not payable because of that individual's work activity;
G. You are married to an individual entitled to disability insurance benefits and those benefits are not payable because the individual is subject to workers' compensation offset;
H. You are entitled to a government pension (Federal, State, or a political subdivision of a State not covered by Social Security) based on your own employment and:
   1. The entitlement requires offset against the Social Security payment; and
   2. The exceptions in §1836 do not apply;
I. You do not have a Social Security Number and you refuse to apply for one; or you are in the U.S. for a full calendar month, and you are not a U.S. citizen, U.S. national, or alien lawfully present in the U.S.

J. You are confined within the U.S. to a correctional institution for more than 30 continuous days, as a result of a conviction of a criminal offense or a court of competent jurisdiction issues a verdict, finding or a ruling that declares you are:
- guilty, but insane with respect to a criminal offense;
- not guilty of such a criminal offense by reason of insanity;
- incompetent to stand trial under an allegation of a criminal offense;
- determined to have a similar verdict or finding with respect to a criminal offense based on similar factors (such as mental disease, mental defect or mental incompetence) *and*
- you are confined to an institution at public expense for more than 30 continuous days.

or;

- Immediately upon completion of confinement in a correctional institution, (confinement in the correctional institution was based on a crime an element of which was sexual activity), you were confined by court order to an institution for more than 30 continuous days at public expense because you were determined to be a sexually dangerous person or a sexual predator or similar finding.

K. You have an unsatisfied Federal, State or international law enforcement warrant for more than 30 continuous days for:
- A crime, or attempted crime, that is a felony or, in jurisdictions that do not classify crimes as felonies, a crime that is punishable by death or imprisonment for more than one year (regardless of the actual sentence imposed); or
- Violation of a condition of probation/parole imposed under Federal or State law (see §1854). The conditions regarding nonpayment of benefits are discussed in more detail in Chapter 18.

L. You requested voluntary suspension of your retirement benefits on or after April 30, 2016. The conditions regarding nonpayment of benefits are explained in more detail in Chapter 18.

420. WHEN DO FATHER'S OR MOTHER'S INSURANCE BENEFITS END?

Your father's or mother's insurance benefits end if any of the conditions below are met:

A. There are no children of the deceased worker under age 16 or disabled (as defined in §324) who are entitled to a child's insurance benefit;

B. If you are a surviving divorced father or mother, you have no natural or legally adopted child under age 16 or disabled who is entitled to a child's insurance benefit on the deceased worker's earnings record;
C. You become entitled to a widow(er)'s insurance benefit (see §§401-402);
D. You die;
E. You become entitled to retirement insurance benefits in an amount equal to or greater than three-fourths (.75) of the spouse's primary insurance amount;
F. You marry; or

Note: If you marry a person entitled to retirement, disability, divorced spouse's, widow(er)'s, father's, mother's, parent's, or childhood disability benefits, see §1852. If the subsequent marriage ends, you may be re-entitled (see §417).

G. For benefits payable before January 1991:
  1. You were qualified for benefits only under the conditions explained in §402 (B); and
  2. Your monthly benefits are awarded on the same earnings record to another individual who either:
     1. Is validly married to the worker; or
     2. Has the same status under State law with respect to the taking of intestate personal property as would a widow(er).

You are not entitled to father's or mother's insurance benefits for the month in which any of the terminating events above occur.

421. WHEN IS A PARENT OF A DECEASED PERSON ENTITLED TO PARENT'S BENEFITS?

You are entitled to parent's benefits as a parent of a deceased insured worker if the conditions below are met:

A. The insured worker was fully insured (as defined in §203) at the time of death;
B. You file an application for parent's benefits (see §1511 for completing application forms);
C. You have reached age 62;
D. You are not entitled to a retirement insurance benefit that is equal to or larger than the amount of the unadjusted parent's insurance benefit after any increase to the minimum benefit;

E. You were receiving at least one-half support from the insured worker at the applicable time (see §423);
F. You filed evidence that the support requirement was met with the Social Security Administration within the required time limit (see §424);
G. You have not remarried since the insured worker's death; and
H. One of the following conditions is met:
   1. You are the parent and would be eligible under the laws of the State where the worker had a permanent home when he or she died to share in the intestate personal property of the worker as the worker's parent (see §422);
   2. You legally adopted the insured worker before he or she turned 16; or
   3. You became the deceased's stepparent by a marriage entered into before the deceased turned 16.

422. PARENT DEFINED

422.1 Who is considered a parent for Social Security purposes?

You are considered the parent of the insured worker if, under applicable State law, it is found that you have the status of parent with respect to the taking of intestate personal property at the time of the insured worker's death.

422.2 What does under applicable State law mean?

Applicable State law is either:
A. The law applied by the courts of the State where the insured worker was domiciled at the time he or she died; or
B. The law applied by the District of Columbia if the insured worker was not domiciled in any State at the time of his or her death.

423. WHEN MUST THE SUPPORT REQUIREMENT BE MET?

The support requirement must be met:
A. At the time that the insured worker died; or
B. At the beginning of a period of disability that was established for the deceased if it continued up until the month that he or she died.

424. WHEN MUST YOU FILE EVIDENCE OF SUPPORT?

A parent as defined in §422 must file evidence of support within the two-year period:

A. After the date of the death of the insured worker, if that point is being used; or
B. After the month in which the insured worker had filed an application to establish a period of disability if that point is being used.

You must file evidence of support within the appropriate period, even if you may not be eligible for benefits at that time (e.g., you have not reached retirement age). (See §723.) The time limit may be extended for good cause. (See §1519.1 and §1520.)

425. AMOUNT OF PARENT'S INSURANCE BENEFIT

425.1 How is the parent's insurance benefit rate computed?

The parent's insurance benefit rate, if *only one parent is entitled* to benefits, equals to 82 1/2 percent (.825) of the deceased worker's primary insurance amount.

The parent's insurance benefit rate, if *two parents are entitled* to benefits on the same earnings record, equals 75 percent (.75) of the deceased worker's primary insurance amount. Each parent receives this amount.

425.2 When is the benefit rate less?

There is no actuarial reduction of benefits payable for months before you turn 65. However, your benefit payable may be less if any of the conditions below are met:

A. The "family maximum" is involved (see §§730-732). In this case, all benefits payable on the earnings record may be reduced;
B. You are entitled to a retirement or disability insurance benefit that is less than the parent's insurance benefit. In this case, only the difference between the amount of the parent's insurance benefit and the other benefit is payable as your insurance benefit.

(For the effect of simultaneous entitlement to other Social Security benefits, see §§733-737.)

426. WHEN ARE PARENT'S INSURANCE BENEFITS NOT PAYABLE?

Your parent's insurance benefits may not be payable for some months if:
A. You are under full retirement age (FRA) (as defined in §723), working, and earning more than the exempt amount (see §1803);
B. You work outside the United States (U.S.) for more than 45 hours in a month (see §1823);
C. You are an alien who is outside the U.S. for more than six full calendar months in a row and you do not meet an exception to the alien

nonpayment provisions or do not meet the additional U.S. residency requirements for dependents or survivors (see §1843-1846). For information on payments while you are outside the U.S. see "Your Payments While You Are Outside the United States" at https://www.ssa.gov/pubs/EN-05-10137.pdf and the *Payments Abroad Screening Tool* at www.ssa.gov/international/payments_outsideUS.html;

D. You are in a U.S. Treasury restricted country where we cannot send U.S. Government payments (see 1847-1849). For information on payments while you are outside the U.S. see "Your Payments While You Are Outside the United States" at https://www.ssa.gov/pubs/EN-05-10137.pdf;

E. You are in an SSA restricted country and do not meet an exception (see 1847-1849). For information on payments while you are outside the U.S. see "Your Payments While You Are Outside the United States" at https://www.ssa.gov/pubs/EN-05-10137.pdf;

F. The worker had been deported, and you are an alien who is outside the U.S. For information on payments while you are outside the U.S. see Publication "Your Payments While You Are Outside the United States" https://www.ssa.gov/pubs/EN-05-10137.pdf;

G. You are confined within the U.S. to a correctional institution for more than 30 continuous days as a result of a conviction of a criminal offense or a court of competent jurisdiction issues a verdict, finding or a ruling that declares you are:

- guilty, but insane with respect to a criminal offense;
- not guilty of such a criminal offense by reason of insanity;
- incompetent to stand trial under an allegation of a criminal offense;
- determined to have a similar verdict or finding with respect to a criminal offense based on similar factors (such as mental disease, mental defect or mental incompetence) *and*
- you are confined to an institution at public expense for more than 30 continuous days;

or

- Immediately upon completion of confinement in a correctional institution, (confinement in the correctional institution was based on a crime an element of which was sexual activity), you are confined by court order to an institution for more than 30 continuous days at public expense because you were determined to be a sexu-

ally dangerous person or a sexual predator or similar finding (see §1850.1-1850.3).
H. You have an unsatisfied Federal, State or international law enforcement warrant for more than 30 continuous days for:
- A crime, or attempted crime, that is a felony, or, in jurisdictions that do not classify crimes as felonies, a crime that is punishable by death or imprisonment for more than one year (regardless of the actual sentence imposed); or
- Violation of a condition of probation/parole imposed under Federal or State law (see §1854).
I. You do not have a Social Security Number and you refuse to apply for one.
J. You are in the U.S. for a full calendar month, and you are not a U.S. citizen, U.S. national, or alien lawfully present in the U.S.
K. You requested voluntary suspension of your retirement benefits on or after April 30, 2016.

The conditions regarding nonpayment of benefits are explained in more detail in Chapter 18.

427. WHEN DO PARENT'S INSURANCE BENEFITS END?

Your parent's insurance benefits end if any of the conditions below are met:
A. You die;
B. You become entitled to a retirement insurance benefit that is equal to or larger than the amount of the unadjusted parent's insurance benefit; or
C. You marry.

Note: If the marriage is to a person entitled to monthly Social Security benefits as a divorced spouse, widow(er), mother, father, parent, or a disabled child age 18 or over, see §1852.

If the remarriage was absolutely void or was annulled *from the beginning*, see §1853.

You are not entitled to parent's insurance benefits for the month in which any of the above events occurs.

428. WHEN IS A LUMP-SUM DEATH PAYMENT PAID?

A lump-sum death payment may be made on the Social Security record of a worker who dies either fully or currently insured. The lump-sum is a one-time payment of $255 (see §700 for an exception). It is paid in addition to any monthly survivors insurance benefits that are due.

429. WHEN WILL YOU NOT RECEIVE A LUMP-SUM DEATH PAYMENT?

You cannot be paid a lump-sum death payment on the Social Security record of a deceased worker, regardless of his or her insured status, if any of the following conditions are met:

A. The worker was deported after September 1, 1954, and, at the time of death, was not lawfully readmitted to the U.S. (see §1842 for a discussion of this condition);

B. The worker could not have been paid a monthly benefit for the month before the month in which he or she died.

At that time, the worker was an alien who was outside the U.S. for more than six calendar months in a row (see §1843 for a discussion of this condition);

C. You were convicted of the felonious homicide of the worker;

D. The worker was granted a tax exemption as a member of a religious group, which has not ended; or

E. The Railroad Retirement Board has jurisdiction in the survivor's claim; or has already paid a lump-sum death payment.

430. WHEN IS A LUMP-SUM PAID TO THE SURVIVING WIDOW(ER)?

You are eligible for the lump-sum death payment based on your relationship with the worker as husband and wife if both of the following conditions are met:

A. You were living in the same household as the worker when the worker died. This rule also applies when there is an absence; and

B. You filed an application for the lump-sum within the required time limit (see §§1517-1519). (See §402 for the definition of a "widow(er).")

431. WHEN NO SPOUSE LIVING IN HOUSEHOLD

431.1 Who receives the lump-sum death payment if there is no spouse living in the household?

Providing he or she is entitled to or eligible for benefits as a widow(er), mother, or father for the month the worker dies, the lump-sum is payable to a surviving spouse not living with the deceased worker at time of death if:

A. There is no spouse living in the same household with the worker when he or she died; or
B. The surviving spouse dies before the lump-sum is paid.

431.2 Who is considered an eligible person?

An "eligible" person is one who would have been entitled to benefits had a timely application been filed.

431.3 Can the lump-sum be paid to a divorced spouse?

No, the lump-sum is not payable to a divorced spouse.

431.4 Who receives the lump-sum if there are two surviving spouses?

In rare situations, there may be two surviving spouses (e.g., one meets the requirement in §402 (A)(1) and the other meets the requirement in §402 (A)(2)). Both spouses may be eligible for the lump-sum, even though neither was living in the same household as the worker when he or she died. In this situation, the lump-sum is equally divided between the spouses.

432. LUMP-SUM PAYABLE TO CHILDREN

432.1 Can the lump-sum be paid to children?

If there is no spouse to receive the lump-sum death payment, the lump-sum is payable to a child or the children of the deceased worker. The child or children must have been entitled to or eligible for benefits on the deceased's earnings record for the month the worker died.

432.2 How is the lump-sum paid of there is more than one child?

In the case of several children, each child is eligible for an equal share of the lump-sum.

432.3 What happens if one or more eligible children do not apply for the lump-sum?

If one or more of the children choose not to apply, those children who do apply are paid *only their equal share* of the lump-sum. The unpaid balance remains unpaid, unless those children who originally chose not to apply later decide to do so.

433. WHEN APPLICATION MUST BE FILED

433.1 When must you file the application for the lump-sum?
You must file the application for the lump-sum death payment within the two-year period ending with the second anniversary of the insured worker's death. The filing period may be extended under certain conditions as explained in §§1517-1519.

433.2 Who must file an application for the lump-sum payment?
You must file an application for the lump-sum death payment if:
A. You are *not* entitled to wife's or husband's benefits on the deceased person's Social Security record for the month just before the month in which the insured worker died; or
B. You are a child.
Note: If more than one child is entitled to the lump-sum, *each child* must apply to receive his or her share of the payment.

433.3 When do you NOT need to file an application for the lump-sum?
You do not need to file an application for the lump-sum as a widow(er) if you were entitled to wife's or husband's benefits on the deceased person's Social Security record for the month just before the month in which the insured worker died.

Chapter 5
Cash Disability Benefits and Related Disability Protection

TABLE OF CONTENTS

INTRODUCTION
500. What are the types of disability protection under Social Security?

ENTITLEMENT TO DISABILITY INSURANCE BENEFITS
501. Entitlement to Disabled Worker's Benefits
502. Waiting Period
503. Amount of Disabled Worker's Benefit
504. Reduction to Offset Workers' Compensation or Public Disability Benefits
505. When are your disabled worker's benefits NOT paid?
506. When do cash benefits for disabled workers' benefits end?
507. Definition of Disability for Disabled Worker's Benefits

PERIOD OF DISABILITY
508. What is a "period of disability?"
509. When may you establish a period of disability?
510. When does your period of disability begin?
511. When does your period of disability end?
512. How is "disability" defined for establishing a period of disability?

513. When can you receive widow(er)'s benefits based on disability?
514. When do disabled widow(er)'s benefits begin?
515. How is "disability" defined for determining entitlement for disabled widow(er)'s and surviving divorced spouse's benefits?

CHILDHOOD DISABILITY BENEFIT
516. What benefits may a child receive based on disability?
517. What is the definition of disability for Supplemental Security Income (SSI) children's disability benefits?
518. When is a child entitled to Social Security Disability Insurance (SSDI) benefits based on disability?

TICKET TO WORK AND VOCATIONAL REHABILITATION, EMPLOYMENT, OR OTHER SUPPORT SERVICES FOR PEOPLE WITH DISABILITIES
519. The Ticket to Work and Self-Sufficiency Program

TRIAL WORK PERIOD
520. Trial Work Period
521. When are you NOT eligible for a trial work period?
522. Beginning and Ending of Trial Work Period

BENEFICIARY'S OBLIGATION
523. What events must you report to the Social Security Administration?

THE APPEALS PROCESS
525. When and how can an appeal be filed?
526. How many appeal levels are there?
527. How to Read and Understand the Initial Determination
528. What to Do if You Are Found "Disabled"
529. What to do if You Are Found "Not Disabled"
530. Copying the Contents of the File
531. Filing a "Request for Reconsideration"
532. Submitting a "Request for Reconsideration"

Cash Disability Benefits and Related Disability Protection

533. What information should be in the Reconsideration Disability Report?
534. Filing the Reconsideration Request on Time
535. How to Submit a Late "Request for Reconsideration"
536. Communicating with DDS after Filing a "Request for Reconsideration"
537. How to Read, Understand, and Follow Up on the Reconsideration Determination
538. Filing the "Request for Hearing by Administrative Law Judge"

500. WHAT ARE THE TYPES OF DISABILITY PROTECTION UNDER SOCIAL SECURITY?

There are eight types of disability protection included under Social Security:

A. *Monthly cash benefits for a disabled worker* (see §§501-506) and family. Benefits for the disabled worker are often referred to as "disability insurance benefits." However, in this Chapter they are called "disabled worker's benefits." This is to distinguish them from other benefits for disabled persons.

B. *Monthly cash benefits for the needy, blind, or disabled individuals.* This also includes blind or disabled children (see §2110 for the definition of a child) under the Supplemental Security Income (SSI) program. The evaluation of disability is discussed in Chapter 6. Other conditions for eligibility are discussed in Chapter 21.

C. *The establishment of a period of disability for a disabled worker.* This protects against the loss of, or the reduction in, the disability amount or retirement insurance benefits for the worker or the worker's survivors. The establishment of a period of disability excludes the time that the worker is disabled when determining either insured status or the amount of benefits. This protects the worker since it is likely that the worker does not have substantial earnings when disabled. (See §§508-512.)

The requirements for disabled worker's benefits and for establishing a period of disability are nearly the same. A worker entitled to either one is usually entitled to both.

D. *Monthly cash benefits for a disabled widow(er) or disabled surviving divorced spouse.* These benefits apply to disabled widow(er)'s (or disabled surviving divorced spouses) age 50-59 who meet the other requirements for entitlement to widow(er)'s insurance benefits. (See §§401-403: the disability-related requirements are explained in §§513-515.) Statements in this Chapter that apply equally to disabled widow(er)'s and disabled surviving divorced spouses refer to them simply as *"disabled widow(er)'s."*

E. *Monthly cash benefits for a disabled child* of a worker entitled to disabled worker's or retirement benefits or of an insured worker who died. These benefits are payable as early as age 18 and there is no upper age limit. They are referred to as *childhood disability benefits* (see

§517) because the child must have become disabled before reaching age 22. (See Chapter 3 for an explanation of other requirements for entitlement to child's insurance benefits that must be met by a worker's child.)

F. *Vocational rehabilitation services, employment services, or other support services* for a Social Security disability beneficiary or an SSI disabled or blind recipient. These services help beneficiaries obtain the services and assistance they need to go to work. A State vocational rehabilitation agency or an employment network provides these services. (See §518.)

G. *Hospital and supplementary medical insurance protection for:*
1. A person under age 65 who has been entitled to disability benefits as a disabled worker, widow(er), or adult child for at least 24 months.

Note: The person must be entitled to benefits on the basis of insured status established under the Social Security Act. This does not include credits earned under the program of any other country.

2. A person who:
   1. Has chronic kidney failure requiring a regular course of dialysis or a kidney transplant; or
   2. Is disabled due to Amyotrophic Lateral Sclerosis and is entitled to disabled worker benefits; and
   3. Is fully insured, currently insured, or entitled to monthly insurance payments because of work covered by the Social Security Act or the Railroad Retirement Act. This includes the spouse or dependent child of a person who is insured or entitled to monthly benefits payable under these Acts; or
   4. Is disabled due to Amyotrophic Lateral Sclerosis and is entitled to disabled widow(er)'s or disabled adult child benefits.
3. A person whose disability did not end prior to December 1, 1980. The beneficiary may have his or her medical coverage continued for a maximum of 24 months after entitlement ends based on disability, provided medical recovery has not occurred.

Note: After this period, a person may elect to purchase premium Medicare coverage. This is provided if he or she continues to have a disabling impairment, files during an enrollment period, and his or her premium-free Medicare coverage ended because of substantial gainful activity (see §603).

H. *Prescription drug benefit to* a person entitled to hospital insurance or enrolled in supplementary medical insurance.

501. ENTITLEMENT TO DISABLED WORKER'S BENEFITS

501.1 When are you entitled to disabled worker's benefits?

If you are a disabled worker, you are entitled to monthly cash benefits if you meet the following conditions:

A. Are under a disability as defined in §507;
B. Have filed an application for disabled worker's benefits (see §1502 and §1513 for the period during which an application is effective);
C. Have disability insured status (see §207);
D. Have completed a five-month waiting period, unless you are exempt from this requirement (see §502); and
E. Have not reached full retirement age.

Your benefits begin with the first month that you meet all of the conditions above.

501.2 What are auxiliary benefits?

"Auxiliary benefits" are additional monthly benefits (see Chapter 3). These benefits may be payable to other family members on your earnings record if you are entitled to disabled worker's benefits. They are payable to your family members even when you are not receiving benefits because of imprisonment. (See §505(E).)

502. WAITING PERIOD

502.1 What is the waiting period?

The waiting period consists of five (5) full calendar months in a row. It begins with the earliest full calendar month (but not more than 17 months before the month you filed the application) that you:

A. Are disabled; and
B. Meet the disability insured status requirements for benefit purposes. (See §207.) You are not entitled to benefits for any month in the waiting period.

502.2 When is the waiting period NOT required?

No waiting period is required if any of the following conditions are met:

A. You were previously entitled to a period of disability and became disabled again within five years following the month your previous disability ended; or

B. You are entitled to Childhood Disability Benefits; or
C. You only filed for SSI benefits.

503. AMOUNT OF DISABLED WORKER'S BENEFIT

503.1 How is the amount of your disabled worker's benefit computed?

Your disabled worker's benefit rate is generally equal to the Primary Insurance Amount (PIA). For a definition of the PIA, and an explanation of how to figure the disabled worker's benefit amount and regular, reduced, and total family benefits, see Chapter 7.

503.2 When is your disabled worker's benefit rate less than the Primary Insurance Amount (PIA)?

Your actual disabled worker's benefit rate may be less than the Primary Insurance Amount if any of the conditions below are met:

A. A reduction becomes necessary because you receive workers' compensation and/or a public disability benefit based on your work relationship paid under a Federal, State, or local public law or plan (see §504); or
B. You become entitled to disabled worker's benefits after a reduced widow(er)'s or retirement insurance benefit (see §724).

504. REDUCTION TO OFFSET WORKERS' COMPENSATION OR PUBLIC DISABILITY BENEFITS

504.1 Why are disabled workers' benefits sometimes reduced?

Your Social Security (SS) disability insurance benefits, (and family benefits based on your earnings record) may be reduced to fully or partially offset your worker's compensation benefit.

SS disability insurance benefits may also be reduced if you receive public disability benefits, which are disability benefits paid under a Federal, State, or local public law or plan.

504.2 When is the reduction in the benefit made?

A reduction in your disabled worker's benefit (and family benefits based on your earnings record) may be made for any month before the month you turn 62 or 65 (See §504.5.B.). The reduction is made only if the total benefits payable to you and your dependents under the Social Security

Act *plus* your workers' compensation plus your public disability benefits (if applicable) exceed the higher of:
A. 80 percent of your "average current earnings" (see 504.3) before your disability began; or
B. Your family's total Social Security benefit (before the reduction).

The offset of benefits continues until you turn either age 62 or 65 depending on your onset of disability and month of entitlement to benefits.

504.3 What is average current earnings?

"Average current earnings" is the highest of:
A. Your average monthly wage upon which your un-indexed disability primary insurance amount is based (see Chapter 7);
B. Your average monthly earnings from covered employment and self-employment during the highest five years in a row after 1950; or
C. Your average monthly earnings based on the single calendar year of highest earnings from covered employment.

This single calendar year can be the year that your disability began or any of the five years immediately proceeding the year your disability began.

"Covered" employment (also known as covered wages, or covered service) is employment on which Federal Insurance Contribution Act (FICA) taxes are paid.

504.4 When is your disabled worker's benefit NOT reduced?

Some workers' compensation laws or plans reduce *their* benefit payments based on the amount of SS disability insurance benefits a disabled worker (and family) receives. If these particular workers' compensation laws or plans are in effect February 18, 1981 or earlier, SS disability benefits are not offset (not reduced).

504.5 What factors determine the offset and its amount?

Different factors are used to determine whether benefits are offset (reduced) and the amount of the offset. The factors depend on when you became disabled *and* the date you became entitled to benefits:
A. *Your workers' compensation benefits or public disability benefits* received under a Federal, State, or local public program are considered in determining the offset amount if:
   1. You became disabled after February 1981; and
   2. You became entitled to SS disability benefits after August 1981.

B. *Only benefits paid as workers' compensation* are considered in determining the amount of the offset if:
   1. You became disabled before March 1981; or
   2. You became entitled to SS disabled worker's benefits before September 1981.

   Note: The offset of benefits ends when you turn 62 (rather than 65).

504.6 What factors are NOT considered in determining the offset and its amount?

The following are not considered in determining the offset and its amount:

A. All Department of Veterans Affairs benefits;
B. Needs-based benefits;
C. Federal, State, or local disability benefits based on State or local employment, all or almost all of which were covered for Social Security purposes;
D. Private pension or private insurance benefits;
E. Black Lung Part B benefits;
F. Railroad Unemployment Insurance Act (RUIA) sickness benefits;
G. Railroad injury settlement payments under the Federal Employer's Liability Act (FELA);
H. Unemployment benefits;
I. Sick pay paid by an employer;
J. Proceeds from third party settlements;
K. Interest or other income generated by workers' compensation investments;
L. Jones Act payments;
M. Payments from tort (negligence) lawsuits;
N. Workers' compensation/public disability benefits paid under a law or plan enacted by an American Indian Tribal Government; and
O. Workers' compensation payments made to the employer.

504.7 How is the reduction amount computed?

The reduction is determined the first month you receive both SS disability benefits *and* workers' compensation benefits/public disability benefits. The reduction amount is computed using the higher of the following two amounts (the higher amount is known as the "*applicable limit*"):

A. Eighty percent of your "average current earnings" before your disability began (the "average current earnings" is derived by using your highest year(s) of earnings (see 504.3)); or
B. The total amount of Social Security disability insurance benefits you and your family receive (known as the "total family benefit") in the first month you also receive workers' compensation or public disability benefits.

SS disability benefits are reduced when the total of your monthly workers' compensation benefit plus any public disability benefit you receive exceeds the "applicable limit".

504.8 Can cost of living increases plus changes in the amount of workers' compensation benefits or public disability benefits change your Social Security benefits payable?

The amount of Social Security benefits payable to you and your family can go up or down based on increases or decreases in your workers' compensation or public disability benefits.

In addition, the amount of the reduction can be adjusted to take into account increases in the cost of living. In no event does a cost of living adjustment decrease the total amount of benefits payable on your earnings record.

504.9 How are lump-sum payments considered when computing the amount of offset?

Sometimes a State workers' compensation law, or a Federal, State, or local public disability benefit law or plan permits a lump-sum settlement. The lump-sum settlement can be in the form of a commutation or compromise agreement and releases the insurance company or the employer from liability. Such a settlement is a substitute for periodic payments and is subject to the offset. In this situation, the lump-sum is prorated to reflect the monthly rate that would have been paid had the lump-sum award not been made. Medical and legal expenses incurred by the worker in connection with the workers' compensation or public disability benefit claim may be excluded from computing the offset. (A check representing past due periodic payments which simply brings payments up to date is not considered a lump-sum settlement when we calculate offset.).

For additional information about Workers' Compensation go to: www.workerscompensationinsurance.com/index.htm.

505. WHEN ARE YOUR DISABLED WORKER'S BENEFITS NOT PAID?

You do not receive disabled worker's benefits for months during which you meet any of the following conditions:

A. You are deported or removed from the U.S. under certain provisions of law (see §1841). For information on payments while you are outside the U.S., see https://ssa.gov/pubs/EN-05-10137.pdf;

B. You are an alien who is outside the U.S. for more than six full calendar months in a row and you do not meet an exception to the alien nonpayment provisions (see §1843-1846). For information on payments while you are outside the U.S., see "Your Payments While You Are Outside the United States" at https://ssa.gov/pubs/EN-05-10137.pdf and the *Payments Abroad Screening Tool* at www.ssa.gov/international/payments_outsideUS.html;

C. You are in a U.S. Treasury restricted country where we cannot send U.S. Government payments (see §1847-1849). For information on payments while you are outside the U.S., see "Your Payments While You Are Outside the United States" at https://ssa.gov/pubs/EN-05-10137.pdf;

D. You are in an SSA restricted country and do not meet an exception (see §1847-1849). For information on payments while you are outside the U.S., see "Your Payments While You Are Outside the United States" at https://ssa.gov/pubs/EN-05-10137.pdf;

E. You are entitled to disabled worker's benefits only because you turned 55 and are blind (see §507.4), and you are engaging in substantial gainful activity;

F. You are imprisoned in the United States for conviction of a felony committed at any time;

Note: You may still be eligible for benefits if you are participating in a rehabilitation program that has been specifically approved for you by a court of law. It must be expected that you will be able to engage in substantial gainful activity upon your release within a reasonable time. (See §1850.)

G. You are engaging in substantial gainful activity following your completion of a trial work period (see §506 and §519), even though you may still have a disability; or

H. You are living in the United States and you are neither a U.S. citizen nor an alien lawfully present.

506. WHEN DO CASH BENEFITS FOR DISABLED WORKERS' BENEFITS END?

506.1 When do cash benefits for disabled workers end?

Your last month of entitlement to disabled worker's benefits is generally whichever of the following months occurs first:

A. The second month after the month your disability ends. However, there are certain conditions under which your benefits may continue; or re-entitlement to benefits may be established after your disability ends:

Continuation of Benefit Payments to certain individuals participating in a program of vocational rehabilitation, employment, training, or other support services, including the Ticket to Work Program. Your benefits as a blind or disabled worker (or a blind or disabled Supplemental Security Income recipient) may be continued after your impairment is no longer disabling if:

- You are participating in an approved program of vocational rehabilitation, employment, training or other support services, including the Ticket to Work Program;
- You began participating in the program before your disability ended; and
- We have determined that your completion of the program, or your continuation of the program for a specified period of time, will increase the likelihood that you will not have to return to the disability or blindness benefit rolls. Your benefits may continue until:
  - You complete the program; or
  - You stop participating in the program for any reason; or
  - We determine that your continued participation in the program will no longer increase the likelihood that you will not have to return to the disability or blindness benefit rolls.

Extended period of eligibility for reentitlement to benefits following trial work period. The extended period of eligibility (EPE) starts the month after the trial work period ends (whether you are working or not) and can continue forever depending on your work activity. The first 36 months after the trial work period is the reentitlement period. During the reentitlement period, benefits can be reinstated without having to file for a new period of disability. The earliest we can start your benefits again is the month after the end of the grace period.

(You are paid for the first month your benefits ceased due to substantial gainful activity, and the following 2 months.) After the grace period, benefits are paid for months your earnings/work activities are below the substantial gainful activity (SGA) limit. Benefits are not paid for months your earnings/work activities are above SGA. The latest we can start your benefits again is the 37th consecutive month after the end of the trial work period.

Note: The extended period of eligibility condition does not apply if you are entitled to supplemental security income disability payments.

B. The month before the month you reach full retirement age or when you reach full retirement age. When you reach full retirement age, your benefits are automatically converted to retirement insurance benefits; or

C. The month before the month you die.

506.2 Can you still qualify for Medicare coverage, even if you no longer receive disabled worker's benefits?

If you work you may still receive hospital and medical benefits under Medicare after you have stopped receiving disabled workers' benefits. Most people with disabilities who work will continue to receive at least 93 consecutive months of hospital and medical insurance under Medicare. You pay no premium for hospital insurance. Although cash benefits may cease due to work, you have the assurance of continued health insurance. The 93 months start the month after the last month of your trial work period. You may work and perform SGA, but must not be medically improved. You must satisfy your Medicare waiting period. Once that is complete, your continued Medicare coverage can start and continue for at least the remainder of the 93 consecutive months.

506.3 Can you still qualify for the prescription drug benefit even if you no longer receive disabled worker's benefits?

As long as you have hospital insurance or medical insurance under Medicare, you continue to qualify for prescription drug coverage.

506.4 Can you get benefits again if your benefits ended because of work?

If your benefits ended because you worked and had earnings, you can request to have your benefits started again without having to complete a new application, within 5 years from the month your benefits ended. We call this process "expedited reinstatement" or EXR. It was effective January 1, 2001.

You can be reinstated via EXR if:
- Your previous benefits ended due to work or earnings;
- You are not performing SGA in the month you request EXR;
- You are unable to perform SGA due to your medical condition;
- Your current disabling impairment(s) is the same as or related to the impairment(s) that was the basis for the previous disability entitlement;
- You request EXR within 60 months of when your previous benefits terminated, or you have good cause for filing your request late; and
- We determine that you are under a disability.

While we determine whether you can get benefits again, we can give you provisional (temporary) benefits for up to 6 months. These benefits include a cash payment and Medicare coverage. If we deny your request, we usually will not ask you to repay the provisional benefits. If we approve your EXR request, your eligible spouse and dependent children may also get benefits. We can pay you for up to 12 months before your request, if your condition kept you from working during that period. During the first 24 months you are eligible for benefits, we will not pay you for any month(s) you perform SGA, but your Medicare coverage will continue. Once you have received 24 months of benefits, which do not have to be in a row, you get a new trial work period and extended period of eligibility.

507. DEFINITION OF DISABILITY FOR DISABLED WORKER'S BENEFITS

507.1 When are you considered disabled?

You are considered "disabled" and entitled to disabled worker's benefits if you meet the following conditions:

A. You are unable to engage in any substantial gainful activity (see §603) because of a physical or mental impairment (see §601). You must not only be unable to do your previous work, but also any other type of work considering your age, education, and work experience (see §609);

Note: It does not matter whether such work exists in your immediate area, whether a specific job vacancy exists, or whether you would be hired if you applied for work.

B. Your impairment(s) must be established by objective medical evidence (see §§614-616);
C. It is expected that your impairment(s) will either result in death or last for at least 12 months in a row (see §602.1); and
D. You must meet the non-medical criteria needed to be insured by the program.

Note: The definition of disability also applies to persons applying for child's insurance benefits based on disability before age 22, for disability benefits payable after December 1990 as a widow, widower, or surviving divorced spouse and for adults (persons age 18 or over) for determining eligibility on the basis of disability under the SSI program.

507.2 Is blindness considered a disability?

Yes. For Social Security purposes, the statutory definition of "blindness" is either of the following:

A. Central visual acuity of 20/200 or less in the better eye with the use of a correcting lens; or
B. A limitation in the field of vision such that the widest diameter of the visual field in the better eye subtends an angle of 20 degrees or less.

Note: The same definition of blindness applies to all applicants for purposes of determining eligibility on the basis of blindness under the SSI program.

507.3 How is disability determined for blind persons who are age 55 or older?

Under title II, there is a special blindness rule if you are a blind worker who is at least 55. You are considered disabled if, by reason of such blindness, you cannot engage in substantial gainful activity requiring skills or abilities comparable to those of any substantial gainful activity that you previously engaged in with some regularity and over a substantial period of time.

No benefits are payable for any month that you engage in substantial gainful activity. (See §505(C).)

507.4 Are impairments relating to your commission of a felony considered in determining whether you are disabled and eligible for disability cash benefits?

Under title II, if you committed a felony after October 19, 1980, you are not eligible for disability *cash benefit*s if:

A. Your impairments (or the aggravation of preexisting impairments) are related to your commission of the felony; or
B. Your impairments (or the aggravation of preexisting impairments) are related to your confinement in a correctional facility for the conviction of the felony.

507.5 Can a period of disability be established for impairments relating to your commission of a felony?
Although you may not be eligible for cash benefits, your confinement-related impairments and impairments aggravated by your confinement may be used to *establish a period of disability*. You can apply to have your Social Security records show how long you are disabled. If a period of disability is established, the months in that period of time are not counted in computing your average earnings for any future benefits.

507.6 Are impairments relating to drug or alcohol abuse covered by disability benefits?
For both title II and title XVI, you cannot be considered disabled if drug or alcohol abuse is a contributing factor of disability. This is true regardless of age.

(See §512, §515, and §517, respectively, for definitions of disability relating to establishing a period of disability, establishing entitlement to disabled widow(er)'s or surviving divorced spouse's benefits, and benefits for a disabled son or daughter age 18 or over.)

(For a further explanation of how disability is evaluated, see Chapter 6.)

508. WHAT IS A "PERIOD OF DISABILITY?"
For title II, a "period of disability" is a continuous period of time when you are disabled. This period of disability is not counted when determining your insured status (§§206-209) and the monthly benefit amount payable to you and your family (see Chapter 7). The period of disability can also preserve your family's rights to benefits in another way: the beginning date of the period of disability is a point for determining dependency of a child (§333) and a parent (§421).

509. WHEN MAY YOU ESTABLISH A PERIOD OF DISABILITY?
For title II, you may establish a period of disability if you meet the conditions below:

A. You file an application either while you are disabled or no later than 12 months after the month in which your period of disability ends; (See §511.)

Note: A valid application on behalf of a deceased worker may be filed within three months following the month of the worker's death. It is filed by a person who would be qualified for unpaid monthly benefits (see §1902).

B. You have disability insured status (see §207);
C. You were disabled before a final decision was made on your application; and
D. You were disabled for a period of at least five months in a row before you reached full retirement age (or you are exempt from serving a waiting period (see §502)).

510. WHEN DOES YOUR PERIOD OF DISABILITY BEGIN?

For title II, your period of disability begins:

A. On the date your disability began, if you meet the requirements for disability insured status (see §207) as of that day; or
B. On the first day of the first calendar quarter after your disability began and you attain disability insured status.

511. WHEN DOES YOUR PERIOD OF DISABILITY END?

For title II, your period of disability generally ends with the last day of the month that the earliest of these events occurs:

A. The second month after the month your disability ends;
B. The month before the month you reach full retirement age; or
C. The month before the month you die.

Note: For the circumstances under which your period of disability may continue after your disability ends, see §506(A). This section also provides the circumstances under which your period of disability may continue if you have completed a trial work period and are doing substantial gainful activity.

512. HOW IS "DISABILITY" DEFINED FOR ESTABLISHING A PERIOD OF DISABILITY?

There are two definitions of disability for the purpose of establishing a period of disability:

A. The basic definition used for disabled worker's benefits (see §507.1); or

B. "Blindness", as defined in §507.5.
(See Chapter 6 for a further explanation of how disability is evaluated.)

513. WHEN CAN YOU RECEIVE WIDOW(ER)'S BENEFITS BASED ON DISABILITY?

You can receive disabled widow(er)'s benefits as a disabled widow(er) or surviving divorced spouse age 50-59 if, effective for benefits payable January 1991 or later, you meet the conditions below:

A. You meet the definition of disability for disabled workers in §507.1.;
B. You became disabled no later than seven years after the *latest* of the following months:
 1. The month the disabled worker died;
 2. The last month you were previously entitled to mother's or father's insurance benefits based on disability on the disabled worker's earnings record; or
 3. The month your entitlement to widow(er)'s insurance benefits ended because your disability ended;
C. You have been disabled throughout a waiting period of five full calendar months in a row; and

 Note: No waiting period is required if you were previously entitled to disabled widow(er)'s benefits.

D. You meet the non-disability requirements for a surviving spouse or a surviving divorced spouse (see Chapter 4).

 Note: A widow(er) age 60-64 and under a disability is entitled to Medicare benefits only. (See §407 concerning the amount of benefits.)

514. WHEN DO DISABLED WIDOW(ER)'S BENEFITS BEGIN?

The first month of your entitlement to disabled widow(er)'s benefits is the latest of the following months:

A. *If a waiting period is required*, the sixth consecutive full calendar month of disability; or
B. *If a waiting period is not required*, the first full calendar month of disability;
C. The month your insured spouse died;
D. The twelfth month before the month you applied for benefits (see §1513 for retroactivity of application); or
E. The month you turn 50.
 (See §409 for when disabled widow(er)'s benefits end.)

515. HOW IS "DISABILITY" DEFINED FOR DETERMINING ENTITLEMENT FOR DISABLED WIDOW(ER)'S AND SURVIVING DIVORCED SPOUSE'S BENEFITS?

For title II, the definition of "disability" for determining your entitlement to disabled widow(er)'s or surviving divorced spouse's benefits is the same as for disabled workers in §507.1. This definition applies to disabled widow(er)'s and surviving divorced spouse's benefits payable January 1991, or later.

(For a further explanation of how disability is evaluated, see Chapter 6).

Note: The following may *not* be used to establish disabled widow(er)'s or disabled surviving divorced spouse's benefits:

A. Impairments or the aggravation of preexisting impairments related to the commission of a felony after October 19, 1980, for which you are convicted; or

B. Impairments or the aggravation of preexisting impairments related to your confinement for committing such a crime.

516. WHAT BENEFITS MAY A CHILD RECEIVE BASED ON DISABILITY?

There are two Social Security disability programs that include disabled children.

Under the Supplemental Security Income (SSI) program, a child from birth to age 18 may receive monthly payments based on disability or blindness if:

- He or she has an impairment or combination of impairments that meets the definition of disability for children and
- the income and resources of the parents and the child are within the allowed limits.

Under the Social Security Disability Insurance (SSDI) program, an adult child (a person age 18 or older) may receive monthly benefits based on disability or blindness if:

- He or she has an impairment or combination of impairments that meets the definition of disability for adults; and
- the disability began before age 22; and
- the adult child's parent worked long enough to be insured under Social Security and is receiving retirement or disability benefits or is deceased.

Under both of these programs, the child must not be doing any "substantial" work, and must have a medical condition that has lasted or is expected either to last for at least 12 months or to result in death.

517. WHAT IS THE DEFINITION OF DISABILITY FOR SUPPLEMENTAL SECURITY INCOME (SSI) CHILDREN'S DISABILITY BENEFITS?

A child under age 18 is eligible to receive SSI based on disability if he or she:

A. Has very little income and resources (including the income and resources of family members in the same household) (see Chapter 21);
B. Is not engaging in substantial gainful work activity (see §603);
C. Has a physical or mental condition(s) that very seriously limits his or her activities (see §601): and
D. The condition(s) has lasted, or is expected to last, at least 1 year, or is expected to result in death.

Note: The SSI definition of disability for children is different from the definition of disability for adults under SSI and Social Security disability (see §507). A child's condition(s) must result in "marked and severe functional limitations," which is a level of severity that meets, medically equals, or functionally equals the listings. See Social Security regulations sections 416.924 through 416.926a for the rules about children's disability in the SSI program.

518. WHEN IS A CHILD ENTITLED TO SOCIAL SECURITY DISABILITY INSURANCE (SSDI) BENEFITS BASED ON DISABILITY?

518.1 When may a child receive Childhood Disability Benefits (CDB)?

An adult son or daughter, age 18 or over, is eligible to receive CDB if he or she:

A. Meets the definition of disability in §507.1;
B. Became disabled before age 22;
C. Meets the other requirements for child's insurance benefits (see §323); and
D. Is not imprisoned within the U.S. for conviction of a felony (see §1850). (See §340 for events that end these benefits.)

Note: There is no upper age limit for childhood disability benefits. Disabled adult sons and daughters can qualify on the record of a stepparent or grandparent in some cases.

518.2 When may a disabled adult child become re-entitled to benefits?

A disabled adult (age 18 or older) child may be re-entitled to CDB if he or she becomes disabled again. The recurrence of the disability must occur within seven years (84 months) of the month in which benefits were terminated because the earlier disability ended. These benefits are payable without a waiting period.

Effective 10/01/2004, P.L. 108-203 allows re-entitlement to childhood disability benefits after the 7-year period if the beneficiary's previous entitlement to disability terminated because of the performance of SGA.

519. THE TICKET TO WORK AND SELF-SUFFICIENCY PROGRAM

519.1 What is the Ticket to Work and Self-Sufficiency Program?

The Ticket to Work and Self-Sufficiency Program (Ticket to Work Program) is designed to give Social Security Disability Insurance (SSDI) or Supplemental Security Income (SSI) disability or blindness beneficiaries more choices to obtain vocational rehabilitation (VR) and employment support services to begin working or to increase their earnings. Beneficiaries ages 18-65 are eligible for the Ticket to Work Program. Organizations called Employment Networks (ENs), consisting of private, nonprofit, and public organizations, including many State VR agencies, have agreements with SSA to provide services to assist beneficiaries in meeting their individual work goals. When state VR agencies serve beneficiaries, they may choose to be paid under a ticket payment system or under SSA's long-standing authority to reimburse state VR agencies who assist beneficiaries age 16 and older to achieve substantial work.

519.2 How Does the Ticket to Work Program Work?

The Ticket gives eligible beneficiaries access to a network of ENs who can provide job training, career preparation, job placement and retention, and other employment support services at no cost to the beneficiary. SSA pays ENs for assisting individual beneficiaries in reaching certain monthly work-related milestones or outcomes that eventually eliminate financial dependence on SSDI and SSI benefits.

A beneficiary who wants to use his or her Ticket to return to work or increase earnings may contact an EN directly. ENs may also initiate contact with beneficiaries. When an EN and a beneficiary decide to work together, they must develop an individualized work plan outlining services and supports needed to achieve the beneficiary's vocational goal. The beneficiary's ticket is assigned when there is a signed work plan between the beneficiary and the EN and the beneficiary meets all Ticket regulation requirements. SSA will not conduct a continuing medical disability review while the beneficiary is using a Ticket with an EN or State VR agency as long as the beneficiary is making the expected progress.

VR agencies and ENs can both receive payment sequentially - VR under reimbursement and EN under the Ticket after VR closure. This is called Partnership Plus, and allows flexibility for increased collaboration among VR agencies and ENs.

519.3 For More Information about Ticket to Work

There are a variety of resources available on SSA's Work Site: https://www.ssa.gov/work for those who wish to learn more about the Ticket to Work Program. Beneficiaries may contact the Ticket Call Center by calling toll-free: 1-866-968-7842 (TTY 1-866-833-2967) for additional information. For a list of ENs in your geographic area, please visit the EN Directory on the web at https://www.yourtickettowork.ssa.gov.

519.4 Work Incentives Planning and Assistance and Protection and ADVOCACY

SSA has established cooperative agreements with community-based organizations called Work Incentives Planning and Assistance (WIPA) organizations to provide benefits planning and other assistance to SSA beneficiaries with disabilities. The goal of the WIPA program is to provide Social Security and SSI beneficiaries with disability-related support to achieve a work goal. WIPA projects assist beneficiaries to understand, and effectively use, work incentives. WIPA staff members, called Community Work Incentives Coordinators (CWICs), also assist beneficiaries to connect to vocational and financial supports. These supports include not only the SSA work incentives, but also services provided by ENs or State VR agencies, and a host of Federal, State, and local programs including Medicaid, housing, Food Stamps, etc. CWICs analyze a beneficiary's current benefit status, assist them to connect to needed supports, and follow the individual long-term as the beneficiary works towards economic self-sufficiency, or if that is not possible, improvement of the person's economic situation through earnings.

The Protection and Advocacy for Beneficiaries of Social Security (PABSS) program was also authorized by the Ticket to Work legislation.

In every State and U.S. territory, there is a designated Protection and Advocacy agency that receives Federal funding to provide advocacy services to individuals with disabilities. SSA provides grant funds to these agencies to administer the PABSS program. These agencies provide information and advice about vocational rehabilitation and employment services provided by ENs and State VR agencies. PABSS also provide systemic advocacy to improve available services or individual advocacy to assist beneficiaries to secure other related services that beneficiaries with disabilities need to secure or regain gainful employment. Both PABSS and WIPA services are free to individuals receiving SSDI or SSI benefits based on disability or blindness.

520. TRIAL WORK PERIOD

520.1 What is the purpose of the trial work period?

A trial work period provides an incentive for personal rehabilitation efforts for you as a disabled worker, disabled widow(er), or childhood disability beneficiary (who is still disabled) to return to work. It allows you to test your ability to work for up to nine months within a 60-consecutive-month period without your earnings for those months affecting your benefits.

520.2 Does the trial work period affect benefit rights?

If your disability does not improve and you continue to report your work activity, your rights to trial work period benefits are not affected.

520.3 Does the work you do during the trial work period determine the end of your disability?

Any work and earnings during the nine-month trial work period is disregarded in determining whether your disability ended *during* the trial work period.

520.4 Can your benefits end before the trial work period ends?

The trial work period does not prevent the consideration of any medical evidence that demonstrates your recovery before the ninth-month period. If your condition has improved, it is possible for your benefits to end before you complete your ninth month of trial work.

520.5 How many trial work periods are allowed?

Only one trial work period is allowed in any one period of disability.

(See §506 for conditions under which an extended period of eligibility occurs after the trial work period.)

520.6 When is your work during the trial work period not counted as a month of service?

For calendar year 2024, use the following guidelines to determine if your work during a trial work period does not count as a "month of service" for trial work period purposes:

A. Your earnings from employment are $1,110 or less in a month; or

B. Your earnings from self-employment activity are $1,110 or less in a month and you spend 80 hours or less in self-employment activity.

The dollar amount is adjusted each year based on the national average wage.

520.7 When are benefits in the trial work period not payable?

If you are convicted by a Federal Court of fraudulently concealing work activity that occurred during the TWP, you are not eligible to receive payment for any TWP months that occur in or after March 2004 and before the date of the conviction. If payments for those TWP months have already been paid to you, you will be liable for repayment.

521. WHEN ARE YOU NOT ELIGIBLE FOR A TRIAL WORK PERIOD?

A trial work period is not possible if you meet any of the following conditions:

A. Are entitled to benefits as a disabled widow(er) and your disability ended before December 1, 1980. After November 30, 1980, widow(er)s are entitled to a trial work period (see §521.);

B. Are a blind disabled worker (under certain circumstances) entitled only under the alternative definition of disability in §507.3);

C. Are entitled to a period of disability, but not to disability insurance cash benefits (see §500(C)); or

D. Are entitled only to supplemental security income disability payments.

522. BEGINNING AND ENDING OF TRIAL WORK PERIOD

522.1 When does the trial work period begin?

Your trial work period begins with the later of the month that you file your application or the month that you become entitled to disability benefits. If you have been reentitled under the expedited reinstatement provisions, your trial work period begins with the completion of your initial reinstatement period.

522.2 When does the trial work period end?

The trial work period ends with the month below that occurs first:

A. The ninth month (not necessarily consecutive) in which you perform services; or

B. The month in which it is determined that your impairment improves so that you no longer have a disabling condition.

(See §506 for conditions under which an extended period of eligibility occurs after the trial work period.)

523. WHAT EVENTS MUST YOU REPORT TO THE SOCIAL SECURITY ADMINISTRATION?

If you receive Social Security benefits based on a disability (or if you have a period of disability), you must notify the Social Security Administration of any of the following events:

A. Your disabling condition improves;

B. Your work status changes, such as:
   1. You begin working (employment or self-employment);
   2. You stop working (employment or self-employment);
   3. You increase your work activity;
   4. Your income increases; or
   5. Your disability-related work expenses change or stop.

When you report changes in your work activity to us, we will give you a receipt to verify that you have properly fulfilled your obligation to report. Keep this receipt with all of your other important papers from Social Security.

C. You apply for payments under a workers' compensation program or, where applicable, a public disability program;

D. You receive an increase or decrease in the amount of payment under a workers' compensation program or, where applicable, a public disability program;

E. You receive a lump-sum settlement under a workers' compensation program or a public disability program;
F. Your workers' compensation or public disability payments stop (see §504); or
G. You are confined within the U.S. for the conviction of a felony.

525. WHEN AND HOW CAN AN APPEAL BE FILED?

If you wish to appeal, you must make your request in writing within 60 days from the date you receive our letter informing you that your claim was disallowed or was only partially favorable. SSA assumes you receive the letter five days after the date on it, unless you can show us you received it later. Call the Social Security office (1-800-772-1213) if you need help with your appeal.

For more information on the administrative review process, see Chapter 20.

526. HOW MANY APPEAL LEVELS ARE THERE?

For information on the appeal levels, see §2000.

527. HOW TO READ AND UNDERSTAND THE INITIAL DETERMINATION

After the Disability Determination Services (DDS) completes its initial review of your application, a letter, which SSA calls a "notice," is mailed to you or your representative, if you appointed one, to explain the determination in your case and your right to appeal.

Initial determinations will include information about whether or not you have been found disabled. The following are three possible outcomes for medical determinations:

- *Fully favorable*—means that SSA has found that you are disabled as of the date you allege your disability began. If you are filing for Supplemental Security Income (SSI), a finding that your disability began as of the month of your application is a fully favorable determination because SSI payments cannot begin earlier than the month after the month of your application.
- *Partially favorable*—means one of two things. Either SSA has found that you are currently disabled, but SSA has determined that your disability started sometime after the date you said you became disabled, or SSA has determined that you were disabled for a specific period in the past but are no longer disabled.

- *Unfavorable*—means that SSA has found that you do not meet the requirements for disability benefits.
- The second part of the initial determination is a form letter which tells you how to appeal this determination. If a determination is fully favorable, there is never any reason to appeal the medical determination. If a determination is partially favorable, you must carefully review the reason behind this determination before deciding whether you should appeal. The benefit of filing an appeal is that you could be found to be disabled as early as the date you say your disability began. This could possibly provide you with retroactive payments and medical benefits.

However, you should be aware that by filing an appeal on a partially favorable determination, you must appeal the entire determination. This means that, on appeal, you could be found "not disabled". It also means that you will not receive any benefits while you are waiting for further appeals of your determination, whereas if you do not appeal the partially favorable determination, you will receive benefits shortly after receiving the determination. If a determination is unfavorable and you are not engaging in substantial gainful activity (SGA) (see §603 for the definition of SGA), and you disagree with SSA's determination, you or your representative should consider an appeal.

528. WHAT TO DO IF YOU ARE FOUND "DISABLED"

If you receive a fully favorable decision or a partially favorable decision that you decide not to appeal, go to Chapter 6, Chapter 7, or Chapter 8 of this *Handbook* for instructions explaining what to do after you have been approved. These chapters explain other aspects of the Social Security and Supplemental Security Income programs.

529. WHAT TO DO IF YOU ARE FOUND "NOT DISABLED"

If you choose to appeal an unfavorable or partially favorable determination, in most states, you or your representative's first appeal request is called a "Request for Reconsideration." The "Request for Reconsideration" (form SSA-561) and the Disability Report - Appeal form (SSA-3441) are available from the local Social Security office, SSA's toll-free service (1-800-772-1213), or on the SSA website, at https://www.ssa.gov/forms. This site is under the section of the page called "Other forms."

You or your representative can submit forms SSA-561 and SSA-3441 electronically by using iAppeals. SSA's website that allows you to file a medical reconsideration online is https://secure.ssa.gov/iApplsRe/start.

You can also file an appeal by sending a letter including your name, social security number, and a statement that you wish to appeal the determination. The statement does not have to be detailed, but an explanation as to why you or your representative do not agree with SSA's determination may be helpful. You must return all appeal forms to SSA before the appeal period ends, which is normally 60 days.

You will also need to complete a "Disability Report - Appeal" (form SSA-3441) and sign an "Authorization for Source to Release Information" (form SSA-827) to the Social Security Administration for any additional medical sources listed on the "Disability Report - Appeal". These are also available at the SSA website. In order for the reconsideration request to be accepted, you or your representative must send a SSA-561 or letter, the SSA-827s, and the SSA-3441 to the SSA office.

530. COPYING THE CONTENTS OF THE FILE

When a claim is denied, the SSA field office stores the file for at least 65 days in case you appeal the decision. Your representative can call the local SSA office to arrange to copy the file. The location and phone of where your file will be is listed on the denial notice. The information in your file may give your representative a clearer idea of how the decision was derived on your claim. Once you file the request for reconsideration, the claim file is returned to the Disability Determination Service. Your representative should arrange to copy your file before filing the reconsideration appeal request.

531. FILING A "REQUEST FOR RECONSIDERATION"

The "Request for Reconsideration" form (SSA-561) is one page long and asks for your name and claim number (usually your Social Security Number), the type of claim being appealed, the reason for filing an appeal, and the addresses for you and your representative.[1] The claim number and type of claim is listed on your notice of decision. Either you or your representative may sign the "Request for Reconsideration"; however, a signature is not required to process the reconsideration. If your whereabouts are not known at the time that the form must be filed, a representative can turn in a "Request for Reconsideration" for you. When entering the reason for filing an appeal, you and your representative should state the specific reasons why you feel that the determination made on the claim is incorrect. If you need additional space, use a separate sheet and make copies to attach to each copy of the appeal form.

532. SUBMITTING A "REQUEST FOR RECONSIDERATION"

You or your representative should request a date-stamped copy from the local SSA field office. You should keep this copy with all of your other case-related records. This gives you proof of the date that you filed your appeal. You may mail your appeal forms to the SSA office certified with a return receipt request to ensure that the date stamped copy of the certification reply will be sent to you or your representative.

533. WHAT INFORMATION SHOULD BE IN THE RECONSIDERATION DISABILITY REPORT?

The "Reconsideration Disability Report" asks you for new information about your claim. It asks whether there has been any change in the severity of your medical condition, if you have any new limitations due to your medical condition, or if there are any new restrictions that your doctor(s) has given you since you filed your claim. You will also be asked for information about new doctors you have seen or new hospitalizations since you filed your claim, and new agencies (such as VA or vocational rehabilitation) you have seen. The form also asks for information about any changes in your daily activities, and a description of how your impairments affect your ability to care for your personal needs.

---

1. The "Request for Reconsideration" form also states that for nondisability issues, the SSI applicants can choose whether their appeals will be handled through a "case review," an "informal conference", or a "formal conference". In SSI cases, this does not apply to cases where the issue is whether or not a person is disabled. Instead, it only applies to certain types of cases, such as cases where the question has to do with non-disability issues like income and resources.

534. FILING THE RECONSIDERATION REQUEST ON TIME

To be timely, the "Request for Reconsideration" must be filed, at an SSA office, within 60 days of the date on which you receive notice of the initial determination. SSA assumes unless an applicant can provide proof, or at least evidence to the contrary, that the determination is received five days after the date printed on it.

The question of timeliness is an important one. If an appeal is not accepted because it is filed too late, the claimant may have to file a new application, and begin the process all over again. When filing for reconsideration, representatives should help applicants submit the "Request for Reconsideration" as quickly as possible. Do not delay submitting the request if new medical evidence is forthcoming; instead, the representative should send the request indicating that the new medical evidence will be mailed at a specified future date.

See Section 2015 for information about filing a request for an extension of time for filing for a reconsideration.

535. HOW TO SUBMIT A LATE "REQUEST FOR RECONSIDERATION"

A "Request for Reconsideration" may be filed at an SSA office after 60 days from the date of the initial determination, but the applicant must provide a written statement explaining "good cause" for missing the 60 day deadline. A statement of "good cause" must contain one or more good reasons why the claimant did not request reconsideration within 60 days of the date on which he or she received the notice of the initial determination. Federal regulations state that SSA must consider the following in making their determination as to whether "good cause" exists: 1) all the circumstances which prevented a claimant from making the request on time; and 2) whether a claimant had any physical, mental, educational, or linguistic limitations (including problems speaking or reading in English) which prevented the claimant from filing the "Request for Reconsideration" within the 60 day period described above. If SSA finds that "good cause" exists for failure to file a timely request for reconsideration, the appeal will be accepted and forwarded to the DDS for a second medical determination. See Sections 2015.5 and 2015.6 for information on "good cause."

An example for possibly granting "good cause" for late filing is a severe disability, particularly mental illness, which prevented the claimant from contacting SSA. Other examples are the loss of important records due to fire or theft, incarceration, illiteracy, and the inability to understand or read English.

The most common reason for requesting good cause is non-receipt of a decision due to homelessness. If a claimant was unaware that a determination had been made in their case, then there is a solid argument to be made that they were unaware of when an appeal needed to be filed. If homeless people are hospitalized, they usually do not have any family that can communicate with SSA on their behalf. In addition, determinations or other important documents are sometimes lost or misplaced.

Many homeless persons may not see a case manager or representative right after receiving a notice saying that they were found "not disabled." Or, in the event that the homeless person loses the denial notice, a case manager might not find out about the determination or the ability to appeal until after the 60 days have passed. In these situations, the case manager must contact the SSA toll free number or the local field office number on behalf of the claimant to explain the situation and request appeal. Preferably, it would be advisable for the case manager keep the phone number of the SSA field office employee on file.

A case manager should work with a claimant to submit a written statement of "good cause" for missing the 60 day deadline.

536. COMMUNICATING WITH DDS AFTER FILING A "REQUEST FOR RECONSIDERATION"

When the DDS receives the "Request for Reconsideration", the applicant's claim file is given to a new disability examiner, who is responsible for making the reconsideration determination. The new disability examiner will be someone who played no role in making the initial determination.

Representatives or case managers should communicate with the new disability examiner in the same way that they did with the examiner who made the initial determination. To find out who the new disability examiner is, one should call the DDS - just as described in Chapter 3.

When speaking with the disability examiner handling the reconsideration, the representative or case manager should focus on providing both updated information (about impairments already disclosed in the initial application) and new information (about new impairments and/or new information that have arisen since the initial application was filed). For example, an individual may file for disability based on depression. Based on all the information previously submitted, the case may be denied. When a reconsideration is filed, it is important to provide the DDS with any new medical records about the individual's depression. But it is equally critical to provide any records relating to any newly developed medical conditions - for example, the applicant may have developed a physical impairment such as heart disease.

Representatives or case managers should work with the claimant's physician, psychiatrist, or psychologist to obtain a new medical statement explaining why the clinician believes that the claimant is disabled under SSA rules. Once all of the relevant information is submitted to the DDS, representatives or case managers should wait for the reconsideration determination. If additional new information is received at any time before a determination is issued, they should notify the DDS immediately and forward the relevant medical records/information to the disability examiner. It is appropriate for representatives or case managers to contact DDS or SSA to check the status of a determination. However, it is recommended that this not be overdone. In some states, advocates can check the status by calling the DDS "master files" number. A clerical employee is available to look up the case status in the computer and state whether the case is still pending or it is closed. SSA also has a toll free number that may be called for the status of a claim: 1-800-772-1213.

537. HOW TO READ, UNDERSTAND, AND FOLLOW UP ON THE RECONSIDERATION DETERMINATION

The reconsideration determination will look similar to the initial determination. It states whether or not the claimant is disabled, and will briefly list the evidence considered in making the determination. If the claimant is found "disabled," go on to Chapter 6 through Chapter 7, for an explanation of how to work with SSA to get the claimant's benefits processed. If the claimant is found "not disabled," advocates should work with them to file a second appeal. This appeal is called a "Request for Hearing by Administrative Law Judge (ALJ)."

538. FILING THE "REQUEST FOR HEARING BY ADMINISTRATIVE LAW JUDGE"

For information on hearing by administrative law judge, see Section 2007.

Chapter 6
Factors in Evaluating Disability

TABLE OF CONTENTS

DISABILITY DETERMINATIONS
600. Who qualifies for disability determinations?
601. What is a "medically determinable" impairment?
602. Impairment Lasting or Expected to Last at Least 12 Months
603. Definition of Substantial Gainful Activity
604. Independent Determinations Under the Social Security Act
605. Does SSA make disability determinations on a disability-rating schedule?

MEDICAL EVIDENCE
606. Medical and Other Evidence as Basis for Decision of "Not Disabled"
607. Medical Evidence as Basis for Decision of "Disabled"—Listing of Impairments

DISABILITY EVALUATION
608. What if your condition does not meet or medically equal a listing?
609. Evaluation Considering Age, Education, and Work Experience
610. What does "work that exists in the national economy" mean?

611. Does your employment condition affect a disability determination?

EVIDENCE OF DISABILITY
613. Are you considered disabled if you are receiving treatment for an impairment?
614. Evidence of Disability
615. Medical and Other Evidence
616. Consultative Examinations

SUBSTANTIAL GAINFUL ACTIVITY
617. Importance of Substantial Gainful Activity
618. How does work at the substantial gainful activity level affect disability?
619. Definition of "Make Work"
620. Significance of Earnings
621. How are your earnings as a self-employed person considered in determining substantial gainful activity?

DISABILITY STATUS CEASES
622. When are continuing disability reviews conducted?
623. When does disability end?

600. WHO QUALIFIES FOR DISABILITY DETERMINATIONS?

We make disability determinations for:

A. Insured individuals who apply for disability benefits or for a period of disability (as described in Chapter 5);

B. Widow(er)s and children who qualify because of relationship to an insured worker;

C. Adults who qualify and apply for Supplemental Security Income (SSI) disability payments;

D. Children under age 18 who qualify and apply for SSI disability payments (see §517).

This Chapter explains generally how the terms and requirements in Chapter 5 pertain to evaluating disability. It also covers what evidence is needed to make a disability determination.

601. WHAT IS A "MEDICALLY DETERMINABLE" IMPAIRMENT?

A "medically determinable" physical or mental impairment (see §507) is an impairment that results from anatomical, physiological, or psychological abnormalities, which can be shown by medically acceptable clinical and laboratory diagnostic techniques. A physical or mental impairment must be established by objective medical evidence from an acceptable medical source. Objective medical evidence includes signs, laboratory findings, or both.

602. IMPAIRMENT LASTING OR EXPECTED TO LAST AT LEAST 12 MONTHS

602.1 When does your impairment meet the 12-month duration requirement?

To meet the duration requirement, you must have a medically determinable physical or mental impairment which can be expected to result in death, or which has lasted or can be expected to last for at least 12 months in a row. Although your condition may not have lasted for 12 months at the time we decided you are disabled, the duration requirement may be met even though recovery is expected to occur after the 12-month period (see §507.1). This is provided your impairment keeps you from engaging in substantial gainful activity (see §603.1) for at least 12 months in a row.

(See §509, which describes the application requirements for entitlement to a period of disability.)

(Also see §§520-522 and §506.1, which describe the trial work period and extended period of eligibility (EPE), once you have been found to be "disabled" under the Social Security Act.)

602.2 Can you combine impairments to meet the 12-month duration requirement?

No. We cannot combine two or more unrelated severe impairments to meet the 12-month duration test. If you have a severe impairment(s) and then develop another unrelated severe impairment(s) but neither one is expected to last for 12 months, we cannot find you disabled, even though the two impairment in combination last for 12 months.

If you have two or more concurrent impairments that, when considered in combination, are severe, we must determine whether the combined effect of your impairments can be expected to continue to be severe for 12 months. If one or more of your impairments improves or is expected to improve within 12 months, so that the combined effect of your remaining impairments is no longer severe, we will find that you do not meet the 12-month duration test.

602.3 Does the 12-month duration requirement apply to SSI payments?

Yes. The 12-month duration-of-disability requirement also applies in establishing disability for SSI applicants. A medically determinable physical or mental impairment or combination of impairments must keep an adult from engaging in substantial gainful activity for at least 12 months in a row. A child who applies for SSI must have a medically determinable physical or mental impairment or combination of impairments that causes marked and severe functional limitations, and that can be expected to result in death or that has lasted or can be expected to last for a continuous period of not less than 12 months.

Note: There is no duration requirement for SSI payments based upon statutory blindness.

603. DEFINITION OF SUBSTANTIAL GAINFUL ACTIVITY

603.1 What does substantial gainful activity mean?

The term "substantial gainful activity" is used to describe a level of work activity and earnings.

Work is "substantial" if it involves doing significant physical or mental activities, or a combination of both. "Gainful" work activity is either of the following:

A. Work *performed* for pay or profit;
B. Work of a nature *generally performed* for pay or profit; or
C. Work *intended* for profit, whether or not a profit is realized.

603.2 Does work need to be performed on a full-time basis to be considered substantial gainful activity?

No. For work activity to be substantial, it does not need to be performed on a full-time basis. Work activity performed on a part-time basis may also be substantial gainful activity. (See §§618-621.)

603.3 Is there a different definition of substantial gainful activity for blind people?

Yes. A special definition of "substantial gainful activity" applies to individuals disabled by blindness. These individuals are considered to be performing substantial gainful activity if their earnings are higher than $2,590 a month for 2024. (see §617.2)

Note: If you are statutorily blind you do not need to show the inability to engage in substantial gainful activity to establish a period of disability (see §617).

604. INDEPENDENT DETERMINATIONS UNDER THE SOCIAL SECURITY ACT

604.1 How are disability determinations made?

We make independent disability determinations. Our determination is based on all of the facts in your individual case.

604.2 Do disability decisions by other agencies affect SSA's determination of disability?

A decision by any other governmental agency or a nongovernmental entity about whether you are disabled, blind, employable, or entitled to any benefits is based on their own rules. The decision is not binding on us and is not our decision about whether you are disabled or blind under our rules. In a claim filed on or after March 27, 2017, we will not provide any analysis in our determination or decision about a decision made by any other governmental agency or a nongovernmental entity about whether you are disabled, blind, employable, or entitled to any benefits.

However, we will consider all of the supporting evidence underlying the other governmental agency or nongovernmental entity's decision that we receive as evidence in your claim.

604.3 Do medical opinions from a medical source who regularly treats you affect SSA's determination of disability?

As part of our consideration of all evidence in a claim, we consider all medical opinions when we make our determinations and decisions. We consider several factors, which are listed in our regulations, to determine how we evaluate medical opinions. Some of these factors include: supportability, consistency, the medical source's relationship with the claimant, and the medical source's specialty. The medical source's relationship with the claimant including the length of the treatment relationship, frequency of examinations, purpose of the treatment relationship, extent of the treatment relationship, and examining relationship are factors we will consider when we consider the persuasiveness of that source's medical opinion(s). However, the most important factors in considering the persuasiveness of a medical source opinion(s) is supportability and consistency. Although not as important, we will also consider the medical source's specialization as well as other factors.

604.4 Do you consider evidence from nonmedical sources?

Yes. We consider all evidence we receive from all sources, including nonmedical sources. However, we are not required to articulate how we considered evidence from nonmedical sources using the requirements noted in §604.3.

605. DOES SSA MAKE DISABILITY DETERMINATIONS ON A DISABILITY-RATING SCHEDULE?

We do not make disability determinations on a rating schedule, for either adults or children. If the evidence of your impairment does not meet the threshold for a finding of disability under the Social Security Act, we will determine that you are not disabled, even if you have some work-related functional limitation(s). We do not evaluate a "percentage of disability" caused by a claimant's impairment(s).

606. MEDICAL AND OTHER EVIDENCE AS BASIS FOR DECISION OF "NOT DISABLED"

606.1 When does medical and other evidence alone establish that you are not disabled?

We will find that you are not disabled if the medical and other evidence in your case establishes that your impairment or combination of impairments is not severe. Your impairment(s) is not severe if it does not significantly limit your physical or mental ability to do basic work activities, such as: sitting, standing, walking, lifting, carrying, handling, reaching, pushing, pulling, climbing, stooping, crouching, seeing, hearing, speaking; understanding, carrying out, and remembering simple instructions; using judgment; responding appropriately to supervision, co-workers, and usual work situations; and dealing with changes in a routine work setting.

However, if we decide that your impairment is severe, we will continue to evaluate your claim to determine if you are disabled (see §§607 and §§608).

606.2 When does medical and other evidence establish that a child is not disabled under the SSI rules?

We will find that a child is not disabled under the SSI rules if the medical and other evidence in the child's case establishes that his or her impairment(s) is not severe. The child's impairment(s) is not severe if it is only a slight abnormality or a combination of slight abnormalities that causes no more than minimal functional limitations.

If we decide that your impairment(s) is severe, we will continue to evaluate your claim to determine whether you are disabled (see §§607 and 608)

607. MEDICAL EVIDENCE AS BASIS FOR DECISION OF "DISABLED" — LISTING OF IMPAIRMENTS

607.1 When is medical evidence enough to establish your disability?

Medical evidence may establish that you are disabled if:

A. You are an adult and the evidence shows that you have an impairment as described in Part A of the Listing of Impairments; or you are a child under age 18 applying for SSI and the evidence shows that you have an impairment(s) as described in Part B of the Listing (see §607.2); this is called "meeting" a listing; *or*

B. All the evidence in your case record shows you have an impairment or combination of impairments that is medically as severe as a listed impairment; this is called "medically equaling" a listing.

You must not be engaging in any substantial gainful activity.

607.2 How do we use the Listing of Impairments to establish disability?

The Listing of Impairments (the listings) is set out in our regulations. For each major body system, the listings describe examples of common impairments that we consider severe enough to keep an adult from doing any gainful activity.

We consider the listings that apply to a child under age 18 applying for SSI disability payments to be severe enough to cause marked and severe functional limitations. See appendix 1 of subpart P of part 404 of Social Security's regulations for the Listing of Impairments.

The listings are in two parts. There are listings for adults (part A) and for children (part B). If you are age 18 or over, we use part A when we assess your claim and we never use the listings in part B. If you are under age 18, we first use the listings in part B. If the listings in part B do not apply, and your specific disease process(es) has a similar effect on adults and children, we then use the listings in part A.

607.3 Is the diagnosis of an impairment in the Listings enough to establish your disability?

No. A diagnosis alone does not meet the guidelines of any listing simply because it is the same diagnosis as a listed impairment. To be considered as "meeting" a listing, an adult's or a child's impairment must have the symptoms, clinical signs, and laboratory findings specified in the Listing.

608. WHAT IF YOUR CONDITION DOES NOT MEET OR MEDICALLY EQUAL A LISTING?

608.1 What happens in adult claims?

If you apply for disabled worker's benefits, widow(er)'s benefits based on disability, childhood disability benefits ("disabled adult child"), a "period of disability," or adult SSI disability payments and have a severe impairment (see §606), we will decide if your condition meets or medically equals an impairment in Part A of the Listing of Impairments. (See §§607 and §§608.) However, if we decide that your condition is not a listed impairment and is not medically equal to a listed impairment, we may still decide that you are disabled under the definition in §507.1.

We will do this by assessing your residual functional capacity for work. That means we will look at how your condition affects your ability to do work-related activities and determine what you can still do despite your impairment(s). We will also consider your vocational background, including your age, education, and work experience.

A. First, we determine if your impairment prevents you from doing your past relevant work. Usually we consider past relevant work to be any substantial gainful work you did in the past 15 years that lasted long enough for you to have learned to do the work.

B. If you have no past relevant work or cannot do your past relevant work, we then look for other work you can do considering your impairment, age, education, and work experience. By "other work," we mean jobs that exist in significant numbers in the national economy.

608.2 What happens in children's SSI claims?

If you apply for SSI based on disability, and we decide that you have a severe impairment(s), we will decide if your condition meets or medically equals an impairment in Part B of the Listing of Impairments. If the listings in part B do not apply, and your specific disease process(es) has a similar effect on adults and children, we use the listings in part A to decide if your condition meets or medically equals a listed impairment. (See §607.) However, if we decide that your condition is not a listed impairment and is not medically equal to a listed impairment, we may still decide that you are disabled under the definition in §517.

We will do this by considering whether your condition(s) "functionally equals the listings"; that is, we will consider what you cannot do, have difficulty doing, need help doing, or are restricted from doing because of your condition. We will consider how your condition(s) affects you in your daily activities at home, at school, and in your neighborhood. Your activities are the things you do when you are acquiring and using information; attending and completing tasks; interacting and relating with others; moving about and manipulating objects; and caring for yourself. We will also consider your health and physical well-being.

To decide whether your condition(s) functionally equals the listings, we will compare your daily activities to the daily activities of other children your age who do not have impairments, and we will compare how you do your activities to how those children do theirs.

When we evaluate your claim, these are some of the things we will think about:

A. How well you can initiate, sustain, and complete your activities (for example, the range and pace of your activities; how much prompting you need to begin, carry through, and finish them).
B. How independently you are able to function compared to children your age who do not have impairments (for example, how much extra help or supervision you need in your activities).
C. Whether you spend some or all of your time in a structured or supportive setting, beyond what a child who does not have an impairment typically needs.
D. Whether symptoms such as pain, fatigue, decreased energy, or anxiety, as well as the effects of medication limit your functioning.

609. EVALUATION CONSIDERING AGE, EDUCATION, AND WORK EXPERIENCE

609.1 How do we consider your age, education, and work experience when making a disability determination?

If your impairment(s) prevents you from doing your past relevant work, we consider the combined effect of your impairment, age, education, and work experience on your ability to work. If these four factors meet any one of three special medical-vocational profiles, we will usually find that you are disabled without further evaluation.

We will generally find you are disabled if you meet all of the conditions of A, B or C.

A. 1. You are not working.
   2. You have long-time work experience (at least 35 years) limited to arduous, unskilled, physical labor; and
   3. You have a sixth grade or less education; and
   4. You have a more than "not severe" impairment that prevents you from performing your previous kind of work.
B. 1. You have no past relevant work; and
   2. You are at least 55 years old; and
   3. You have less than a high school education; and
   4. You have an impairment that is more than "not severe" (see §606).
C. 1. You have a lifetime commitment to a field of work you can no longer do because of a severe impairment; and
   2. You are age 60 or older; and

3. You have less than a high school education; and
4. Your work background is unskilled, semiskilled, or skilled work but you have no skills to do other work within your physical and mental capacities

609.2 Does your age affect disability determinations?
We only consider your age if we have not been able to make a disability determination based on work activity, medical evidence and ability to do past work. Advancing age can be an increasingly limiting factor in a person's ability to adjust to other work. This may be especially true when advancing age is combined with lower levels of education and an unskilled or no work background. We consider your age as well as your education and work background when we determine whether you can adjust to other work in spite of your severe impairment.

609.3 Is unemployment due to advancing age enough to show you are unable to do substantial gainful activity?
Your advanced age may affect your capacity to compete for jobs. However, to be found disabled, your severe medical impairment(s) must be the primary reason you are unable to work. Unemployment due mainly to advancing age does not show that you are unable to do substantial gainful activity.

609.4 Is lack of an education enough to show you are unable to do substantial gainful activity?
Formal education and work experience that provides skills can enhance your ability to work and to adapt to a new kind of job if you have an impairment that prevents you from doing your past work. However, a lack of formal schooling (or limited formal education) does not necessarily show you are unable to adjust to other work. For example, you may have developed skills in your past work that you can use in other work that is within your remaining capacities. If you do not have skills from past work, you may still be able to do unskilled work that is within your abilities even though you have little or no formal education.

610. WHAT DOES "WORK THAT EXISTS IN THE NATIONAL ECONOMY" MEAN?
"Work that exists in the national economy" is work in the U.S. economy. We will find that you are not disabled even if you cannot do any of your

past relevant work, if you can adjust to other work consisting of jobs that exist in significant numbers. The jobs must exist in the national economy, either in the region where you live or in several regions of the country.

611. DOES YOUR EMPLOYMENT CONDITION AFFECT A DISABILITY DETERMINATION?

Your impairment must be the main reason you cannot work. You will not be found disabled as defined in §507.1 if you are physically and mentally able to do any of your past relevant work or any other kind of work that exists in significant numbers in the national economy.

We *do not* consider any of the following reasons for unemployment when we make a disability determination:

A. Lack of work in local area;
B. Lack of job openings for particular work;
C. Your preferences for particular types of work;
D. Hiring practices of employers;
E. Cyclical economic conditions; or
F. Your efforts to obtain employment.

613. ARE YOU CONSIDERED DISABLED IF YOU ARE RECEIVING TREATMENT FOR AN IMPAIRMENT?

If you are following prescribed treatment for your impairment, we will use our regular rules to determine whether you are disabled. Also, if no treatment has been prescribed for your impairment, we will use our regular rules to determine whether you are disabled. However, if you are not following treatment prescribed for your impairment, we will use both: 1) our regular rules to determine whether you are disabled, and 2) additional rules to analyze the prescribed treatment. You must follow treatment prescribed by your medical source(s) if this treatment is expected to restore your ability to work (or, in a child's claims, to no longer results in marked and severe functional limitations), unless you have good cause.

614. EVIDENCE OF DISABILITY

614.1 Who is responsible for providing evidence of disability?

You are required to prove that you are disabled by providing medical and other evidence of disability. However, we are responsible for making every reasonable effort to help you get medical reports from medical sources. All evidence in your case record will be considered in making a determination.

614.2 What evidence must you submit with the application?

We will ask you or an individual filing the application on your behalf to provide the following:

A. Names and addresses of doctors and medical treatment facilities;
B. Dates of treatment and any other information that may relate to your disability;
C. Any sources of medical evidence supporting your disability;
D. Information relating to education, work experience, and daily activities both before and after the onset of disability; and
E. Any other pertinent facts showing the effects of the impairment on the ability to perform work-related functions.

614.3 What responsibility does SSA have in gathering evidence for disability determinations?

We will make every reasonable effort to help you get medical reports from your medical sources. We pay the reasonable cost for existing medical evidence from any non-Federal hospital, clinic, laboratory, or other provider of medical services, if we request it. If the information we need is not readily available from the records of your medical treatment source, or we are unable to obtain necessary clarification of information from your medical source, we will ask you to attend one or more consultative examinations at our expense. This includes necessary transportation costs. Generally, we will not request a consultative examination until we have made every reasonable effort to obtain evidence from your own medical sources.

614.4 What types of evidence must you submit if you are filing for SSI for a child?

A parent, guardian, or other individual applying for SSI disabled child payments on behalf of a child under age 18 is ordinarily required to furnish information about the child. We will ask the individual filing the application to provide the following:
- All of the medical evidence listed in §614.2;
- School records;
- Information from people who can tell us about the child's functioning on a day-to-day basis, such as parents, other caregivers, early intervention programs, preschool and school teachers; and
- Any information you can give us about the sources of information described in the following that will help us evaluate the child's case.

- Names, phone numbers, and addresses of doctors and medical treatment facilities, as well as day-care providers, schools, or other facilities that would have information about the child;
- Information about the child's developmental milestones;
- Information about the child's ability to do age-appropriate activities in self-care, play, recreation, school, relationships, and family life; and
- Any other facts about the effect of the child's condition(s) on his or her growth, development, and maturation.

615. CATEGORIES OF EVIDENCE

615.1 What types of evidence are from medical sources?
Evidence from medical sources include objective medical evidence, medical opinions, and other medical evidence.

A. Objective medical evidence is medical signs, laboratory findings, or both. We need objective medical evidence from an acceptable medical source to establish whether you have a medically determinable impairment. Acceptable medical sources are:
- Licensed physicians (medical or osteopathic doctor);
- Licensed psychologists, which include:
  - A licensed or certified psychologist at the independent practice level; or
  - A licensed or certified school psychologist, or other licensed or certified individual with another title who performs the same function as a school psychologist in a school setting, for impairments of intellectual disability, learning disabilities, and borderline intellectual functioning only;
- Licensed optometrists, for purposes of establishing visual disorders, or measurement of visual acuity and visual fields only, depending on the scope of practice in the State in which the optometrist practices;
- Licensed podiatrists, for impairment(s) of the foot, or foot and ankle only, depending on whether the State in which the podiatrist practices permits the practice of podiatry on the foot only, or the foot and ankle;
- Qualified speech-language pathologists, for purposes of establishing speech or language impairments only;

- Licensed audiologists for impairments of hearing loss, auditory processing disorders, and balance disorders within the licensed scope of practice only (on or after March 27, 2017);
- Licensed Advanced Practice Registered Nurses, or other licensed advanced practice nurses with another title, for impairments within his or her licensed scope of practice (on or after March 27, 2017); and
- Licensed Physician Assistants for impairments within his or her licensed scope of practice (on or after March 27, 2017).

B. Medical opinions

The definition we use for medical opinion depends on whether the claim is for an adult or a child and the filing date of the claim.

1. Medical opinion – adult claim – filing date on or after March 27, 2017
   - The ability to perform physical demands of work activities, such as sitting, standing, walking, lifting, carrying, pushing, pulling, or other physical functions (including manipulative or postural functions, such as reaching, handling, stooping, or crouching)
   - The ability to perform mental demands of work activities, such as understanding; remembering; maintaining concentration, persistence, and pace; carrying out instructions; and responding appropriately to supervision, co-workers, and work pressures in a work setting;
   - The ability to perform other demands of work, such as seeing, hearing, and using other senses
   - The ability to adapt to environmental conditions, such as temperature extremes and fumes

2. Medical opinion – child claim – filing date on or after March 27, 2017

   A medical opinion is a statement from a medical source about what you can still do despite your impairments and whether you have one or more impairment-related limitations or restrictions in the six domains of functioning:
   - Acquiring and using information
   - Attending and completing tasks
   - Interacting and relating with others
   - Moving about and manipulating objects

- Caring for yourself
- Health and physical well-being

3. Medical opinion – adult or child claim - filing date before March 27, 2017

    A medical opinion is a statement from an acceptable medical source (AMS) that reflects judgments about the nature and severity of your impairments, including symptoms, diagnosis and prognosis, what you can still do despite impairments, and your physical or mental restrictions.

C. Other medical evidence

   Other medical evidence is all other evidence from a medical source that is not objective medical evidence or medical opinion.

   1. Claims with a filing date on or after March 27, 2017

      Other medical evidence includes judgments about the nature and severity of your impairments, medical history, clinical findings, diagnosis, treatment prescribed with response, or prognosis.

   2. Claims with a filing date before March 27, 2017

      Other medical evidence includes medical history, clinical findings, prescribed treatment and response.

615.2 Evidence from nonmedical sources

In addition to medical evidence from medical sources (§615.1), we use evidence from nonmedical sources to show the severity of your impairment and how it affects your ability to work; or, if you are a child, your ability to perform age-appropriate activities compared to that of other children the same age who do not have impairments. Evidence from a nonmedical source means any information or statements from a nonmedical source about any issue in a claim. Nonmedical sources include but are not limited to: you; educational personnel (e.g., school teachers, counselors, early intervention team members, developmental center workers, and daycare center workers); public and private social welfare agency personnel; and family members, caregivers, friends, neighbors, employers, and clergy.

615.3 Prior administrative medical findings

A prior administrative medical finding is a finding of fact about a medical issue made by a medical consultant (MC) or psychological consultant (PC) at a prior administrative level in the current claim, such as:

- The existence and severity of an impairments
- The existence and severity of a symptoms
- A statement about whether an impairment(s) meets or medically equals any listing in the Listing of Impairments (Listings)
- If you are a child, a statement about whether the impairment(s) functionally equals the Listings
- If you are an adult, the residual functional capacity (RFC)
- Whether the impairment(s) meets the duration requirement
- How failure to follow prescribed treatment relates to the claim
- How drug addiction and alcoholism relates to the claim

We will include a written analysis or rationale about how we consider prior administrative medical findings in the determination or decision. We use the same standard for consideration as applied to medical opinion evidence

616. CONSULTATIVE EXAMINATIONS

616.1 When do you need a consultative examination?

We may require a consultative examination in situations including, but not limited to, the following:

A. To gather more evidence because the evidence obtained is not enough to make a disability determination;
B. To obtain more detailed medical findings about your impairment(s);
C. To obtain technical or specialized medical information;
D. To resolve conflicts or differences in medical findings in the evidence already in file; or
E. To resolve the issue of your ability to do substantial gainful activity, if you are an adult; or, if you are a child under age 18, your ability to function like other children your age who do not have impairments. We pay for necessary consultative examinations.

616.2 Who administers the consultative examination?

Your medical source will be the preferred source to perform the consultative examination. However, we may use a medical source other than your medical source in certain situations. In some situations, we pay travel expenses relating to a medical examination required in connection with a disability determination.

616.3 What happens if you refuse a consultative examination?

If you refuse a consultative examination without good cause, we make a decision based only on the evidence in your file.

617. IMPORTANCE OF SUBSTANTIAL GAINFUL ACTIVITY

617.1 Does the ability to do substantial gainful activity mean that you are not considered disabled?

If you are doing substantial gainful activity, you are not considered disabled. This is true even if your impairment is as severe as, or even more severe than, those in the Listing of Impairments. (See §607.)

617.2 Does the inability to do substantial gainful activity apply to all types of disability benefits?

You do not receive disability benefits if you can engage in substantial gainful activity, unless you meet one of two exceptions:

A. *A statutorily blind worker age 55 or over*-Evidence of your ability to do substantial gainful activity that does not require skills or abilities comparable to any gainful activity that you did in the past does not prevent a finding of disability for either entitlement to benefits or establishment of a period of disability. However, disabled worker's benefits are not payable for months you actually do substantial gainful activity. (See §505.)

B. *A statutorily blind applicant for SSI benefits*-Evidence of your ability to do substantial gainful activity does not prevent a finding of blindness. However, earnings are considered under the income and resources provisions. (See §§2128-2166.) This provision also applies to children under age 18.

618. HOW DOES WORK AT THE SUBSTANTIAL GAINFUL ACTIVITY LEVEL AFFECT DISABILITY?

Generally, we cannot find you disabled if you file an application for Social Security disability benefits or SSI disability payments while you are working and performing substantial gainful activity.

If you start performing substantial gainful activity after you begin to receive either Social Security disability benefits or SSI disability payments, we will determine whether you continue to qualify for disability.

619. DEFINITION OF ACTIVITY

The term "activity" in substantial gainful activity (SGA) means the performance of significant physical and/or mental activities in work. Significant activities are useful in the accomplishment of a job or the operation of a business, and have economic value. Activities involving self-care, household tasks, unpaid training, hobbies, therapy, school attendance, clubs, social programs, etc. are not generally considered to be SGA.

620. SIGNIFICANCE OF EARNINGS

620.1 Does the Amount of your earnings affect whether or not you can do substantial gainful activity?

Your earnings amount during a period of alleged disability may establish that you are able to engage in substantial gainful activity. Substantial earnings generally do so. However, low or no earnings during a period of work activity do not establish your inability to engage in substantial gainful activity. The circumstances under which work is performed are considered.

620.2 What if you must stop working because of the impairment?

If you must stop working after a short time (less than 6 months) because your impairment gets worse or prevents you from working, your earnings will not necessarily demonstrate your ability to engage in substantial gainful activity.

620.3 Does your work in a sheltered establishment affect whether or not you can do substantial gainful activity?

If you work under special conditions (e.g., in a sheltered workshop), only the earnings relating to your own efforts are considered. Subsidies based on financial need or other non-work factors are not considered. The fact that a "sheltered" establishment operates at a deficit or receives charitable or governmental aid is not material.

620.4 Can the costs of impairment-related items and services be deducted from your earnings?

The cost of certain impairment-related items and services (e.g., certain attendant care services, medical devices and equipment, prostheses, and similar items and services that are necessary to control your disabling condition) that you pay for and need in order to work are deductible from earnings.

620.5 Are there any earnings criteria that indicate whether or not you are doing substantial gainful activity?

Certain earnings criteria have been established as reasonable indications of whether you are doing substantial gainful activity. In 2024, the monthly SGA amount for statutorily blind individuals is $2,590, and $1,550 for non-blind individuals. The monthly substantial gainful activity amount can be adjusted each year based on the national average wage.

(For the definition of substantial gainful activity applicable to disabled blind individuals, see §603.3).

621. HOW ARE YOUR EARNINGS AS A SELF-EMPLOYED PERSON CONSIDERED IN DETERMINING SUBSTANTIAL GAINFUL ACTIVITY?

Your actual earnings as a non-blind self-employed worker may be given less weight in determining your ability to do substantial gainful activity than the extent of your activities in the business. This is so because earnings or losses from your business may be due to factors other than work activities. For example, your business may have only a small profit or may operate at a loss, even if your work is enough to be considered substantial and gainful.

(See §603.3 for the special definition of substantial gainful activity applicable to disabled blind individuals.)

622. WHEN ARE CONTINUING DISABILITY REVIEWS CONDUCTED?

We may conduct a continuing disability review from time to time to determine if your disability continues. Some examples of situations that may generate a continuing disability review are:

A. Occurrence of the date of a scheduled medical reexamination in cases in which your impairment is expected to improve or in which improvement is possible;

B. Voluntary reports received from individuals indicating medical improvement or return to work;

C. Substantial earnings posted to your employment record;

D. A report of medical improvement received from a vocational rehabilitation agency; or

E. A report from a third party indicating you are no longer disabled, not following required treatment, or failing to follow provisions of the Social Security Act.

Note: If you are eligible for SSI based on disability in the month before the month you turn age 18, we must redetermine your eligibility when you turn 18, and we must use the adult disability rules to decide whether you are still disabled.

623. WHEN DOES DISABILITY END?

If you are an adult, your disability ends when:

A. There has been medical improvement in your impairment(s) relating to your ability to work; *and*
B. The impairment does not meet or equal a current listing in the Listing of Impairments; *and*
C. You are not currently disabled; *or*
D. One of the following conditions exists:
   1. One of certain exceptions to medical improvement applies *and* your impairment(s) considered together with your age, education, and work experience (see §609) does not prevent you from doing substantial gainful activity (see §603);
   2. Subject to the trial-work period provisions (see §§520-521), you demonstrate the ability to do substantial gainful activity by working (see §603) (See §617 for exceptions.);

   Note: In SSI cases, disability does not end on this basis.
   3. You do not cooperate with us (e.g., you refuse to give us needed medical or other evidence);
   4. We cannot locate you (e.g., a question of whether you are still disabled needs to be resolved); or
   5. You fail to follow prescribed treatment that could restore your ability to do substantial gainful activity.

If you are a child under age 18, the process for determining when your disability ends is similar to the process we use in adult cases, but there are some important differences. In general, we will find that you are no longer disabled if we determine that:

- there has been medical improvement in any impairment(s) you had at the time of our most recent medical determination; and
- no impairment(s) that you had at the time of our most recent medical determination currently results in marked and severe functional limitations; and

- there are no exceptions to the medical improvement rules that apply to your case; and
- you have no new impairments that alone or in combination with another impairment(s) result in marked and severe functional limitations.

Chapter 7
Figuring the Cash Benefit Rate

TABLE OF CONTENTS

PRIMARY INSURANCE AMOUNT (PIA) - GENERAL
700. Primary Insurance Amount (PIA) as Basic Figure

AME OR AIME
701. How are the Average Monthly Earnings (AME) or the Average Indexed Monthly Earnings (AIME) computed?
702. When is the usual computation formula used?

COMPUTATION YEARS
703. Computation Years Defined

ELAPSED YEARS
704. Elapsed Years Defined

BASE YEARS
705. What are base years?

BENEFIT RATE COMPUTATIONS
706. Determining the PIA

OLD-START FORMULAS
707. The Simplified Old-Start Formula
708. When can the simplified old-start formula be used?
709. Figuring the AME Under the Simplified Old-Start Formula
710. How is the Primary Insurance Benefit (PIB) computed under the simplified old-start formula?

PERIOD OF DISABILITY EXCLUSION
711. Are established periods of disability excluded when benefits are computed?
712. Figuring the PIA Under the 1990 Consolidated Methods
713. What is included as "total earnings" when computing the AME or AIME?

MAXIMUM EARNINGS
714. What are the maximum earnings that can be counted for any calendar year for computing AME or AIME?
715. Allocation of Self-Employment Income
716. Elimination of the Minimum Benefit
717. Special Minimum PIA
718. Windfall Elimination Provision (WEP) - Modified Benefit Formula to Determine the PIA for Workers with Pensions from Non-covered Employment
719. Cost-of-Living Increases
720. Delayed Retirement Credit
721. Recomputation of the PIA
722. The Automatic Recomputation

REDUCED BENEFIT RATE
723. Reduction of Benefit Rate
724. Basic Reduction Formulas
725. How does SSA compute the number of reduction months?
726. Disability Insurance Benefit Reduced for Age
727. How is the reduction amount computed?
728. Adjustment of Reduction Factor at FRA
729. Certificate of Election for Husband or Wife Between Ages 62 and FRA-Child "In Care"

BENEFIT PAYMENTS
730. Maximum Monthly Benefits Payable on One Earnings Record
731. Adjustment of Individual Benefit Rates Because of Family Maximum
732. How Adjustment for Family Maximum is Figured
733. Entitlement to More Than One Social Security Benefit at the Same Time
734. Entitlement to Retirement or Disability Insurance Benefits and Another Benefit
735. What happens if a child is entitled to benefits on more than one earnings record at the same time?
736. When is a child automatically entitled on a second earnings record?
737. Family Maximum When Child is Entitled on More Than One Earnings Record
738. Rounding of Benefit Rates
739. How to compute your benefits

700. PRIMARY INSURANCE AMOUNT (PIA) AS BASIC FIGURE

In this Chapter, "first eligibility" means the year when you reach age 62 or when you begin a period of disability. "Entitlement" means that you meet all of the requirements for receiving benefits. This includes the filing of an application.

700.1 How do you figure your cash benefits?

The Primary Insurance Amount (PIA) is the figure used to determine almost all of your cash benefit amounts. These benefit amounts include your monthly benefits as a worker and benefits for your dependents and survivors. The PIA is based on your taxable earnings (see §713) averaged over the number of years you worked. This produces a monthly benefit that partially replaces the loss of your income because of retirement, disability, or death. The lump-sum death payment (see §428) is $255; however, it may be less if your PIA was computed under a totalization agreement. (See §107.) The only cash benefit not based on the PIA is the special monthly payment made to uninsured persons age 72 or over discussed in §346.

700.2 How does SSA determine your average earnings?

There are generally two methods for determining average earnings. The method we use depends upon when you are first eligible (or when you die if death occurs before you are eligible):
A. First eligibility or death before 1979; or
B. First eligibility or death in 1979 or later.

700.3 What is the PIA under first eligibility or death prior to 1979?

We base your PIA on your Average Monthly Earnings (AME). We use the actual earnings reported by your employers or reported by you as a self-employed worker. This method may also apply in limited circumstances for individuals whose first eligibility is after 1978 as defined in §706.2.

700.4 What is the PIA under first eligibility or death in 1979 or later?

We base your PIA on the Average Indexed Monthly Earnings (AIME). We index your earnings from 1951, through the second year before the year of your first eligibility or death, whichever comes first. "Indexed" means that your earnings are adjusted to put them in proportion to the earnings level of all workers for those years. Your actual reported earnings are used to compute the AIME for the years beginning with the year before your first year of eligibility.

This example shows how to calculate the PIA for an individual retiring at age 65 in the year 2000. Assume Mr. Francis retires at age 65 in 2000. The significant year for setting the index factor is 1995, which is the second year before the year in which he reached age 62. Average wages of all workers in 1995 are compared to average wages of all workers in each year after 1950. If Mr. Francis' earnings were $3,000 in 1951 and the wages of all workers in 1995 were 8.8160978 times higher than the average wages of all workers in 1951, (the index 1951 factor is 8.8160978). Therefore, the 1951 indexed earnings for Mr. Francis are $26,536.72 ($3,000 x 8.8260978). Index factors apply for each year to be indexed, depending on the ratio of average wage levels for all workers in each year compared to 1995. It is equally true that a different year of attainment of age 62 would change the index factors. In Mr. Francis' situation, earnings in years beginning with 1996 will not be indexed but will be the actual amounts reported.

700.5 What if an insured worker dies before reaching age 62 in 1979 or later?

If an insured worker dies before age 62, his or her earnings are indexed differently to compute the PIA on which widow(er)'s benefits are based, if this results in a higher benefit. In this case, the worker's earnings are indexed up to and including the earlier of the following:

A. The year in which the widow(er) reaches age 60; or

B. The second year before the widow(er) becomes eligible, but never earlier than the second year before the worker died.

700.6 Why are adjusted earnings used instead of actual earnings in computing the PIA?

Adjusted earnings are used instead of actual earnings to reduce the difference between a younger worker's average income and an older individual's average earnings. If not, the younger worker's benefit amounts would be based on fewer, more recent years of earnings while the older worker's average earnings would include lower amounts that were earned and taxable in earlier years of Social Security coverage.

700.7 Are there exceptions for individuals who have worked several years at low earnings?

A special minimum PIA is possible for workers who have worked under Social Security for many years at low earnings. (See §717.) At least 11 years of working at low earnings are required. Additional years are usually needed to bring the amount of the special minimum PIA to more than the PIA computed under the methods explained in subsections 700.3 - 700.5 above.

701. HOW ARE THE AVERAGE MONTHLY EARNINGS (AME) OR THE AVERAGE INDEXED MONTHLY EARNINGS (AIME) COMPUTED?

To compute your AME or AIME, divide your total earnings in the "computation years" (see §703) by the number of months in those years. The exception is explained in §709. If the result is not an exact multiple of $1, round down to the next lower multiple of $1.

702. WHEN IS THE USUAL COMPUTATION FORMULA USED?

The usual computation formula is used if:

A. You become entitled to retirement or disability insurance benefits;
B. You die without being entitled to retirement or disability insurance benefits; or
C. We need to compute your PIA again. (See §722.)

703. COMPUTATION YEARS DEFINED

703.1 What are computation years?

Your computation years are those years, selected from the "base years", that you earned the most income. Your total earnings in the computation years are then added together and divided by the number of months in those years to get the AME or the AIME.

703.2 How does SSA determine the number of years, selected as the computation years?

The *number* of years, which are selected as the "computation years" in a particular case, is determined in the following steps:

A. Determine the "elapsed years" using the rules in §704 or §707;
B. Select your type of claim from those shown below and follow the instructions shown:
  1. *Retirement or survivors' insurance benefits:* subtract five from the result attained in (A) above. Go to step (C).

2. *Disability insurance benefits where you were first entitled after June 1980:* divide the result attained in (A) above by five. Disregard any fraction (do not round up or down). Subtract the result (cannot exceed five) from the number of elapsed years. Go to step (C).
3. *Disability insurance benefits for months after June 1981:* divide the result attained in (A) above by five.

Disregard any fraction (do not round up or down). Subtract the result (cannot exceed five) from the number of elapsed years. You may further reduce the elapsed years by the number of years that a child, either yours or your spouse's, under age three was living primarily with you ("childcare years"), provided that: (1) you did not have earnings each childcare year; and (2) the combined total number of childcare years and regular years subtracted from the elapsed years (attained in step (A) above) does not exceed three. Go to step (C).

C. The number remaining is the number of "computation years." This number cannot be less than two. The computation years are selected from the base years, as defined in §705 or §709. The years selected are those of highest earnings. For the computation indexed method (see §700), the selection is made after the earnings are indexed.

D. To compute the AME or AIME, add together your total earnings in the computation years. Divide this result by the number of months in those years.

704. ELAPSED YEARS DEFINED

704.1 What are elapsed years?

Under the usual formula, "elapsed years" begin with those calendar years after 1950, or after you turn 21, if this is later and end with the year before first eligibility (or death if earlier).

704.2 How does SSA determine elapsed years for retirement insurance benefits?

For retirement insurance benefit purposes, elapsed years are those calendar years after 1950 up to the year you turn 62.

Example: An insured worker turned 62 on December 2, 1994, and filed his application for retirement insurance benefits on January 3, 1995. There are 40 elapsed years, counting the years from age 22 through 1993. The number of "computation years" is 35 (40 minus 5).

704.3 How does SSA determine elapsed years for survivors' insurance benefits?

For survivors' insurance benefit purposes, elapsed years are those calendar years after 1950 up to either: (1) the year of death; or (2) the year of attainment of age 62, whichever is earlier.

Determining elapsed years for survivors' insurance benefits (year of death). An insured worker died on November 3, 1994, at the age of 59. The widow filed a claim for mother's benefits on November 10, 1994. There are 37 elapsed years beginning with 1957 (age 22) through 1993. There are 32 computation years (37 minus 5).

Determining elapsed years for survivors' insurance benefits (attainment of age 62). An insured worker turned 62 in October 1993 and died on September 4, 1995. His widow filed for widow's insurance benefits on October 1, 1995. The elapsed years end the year before the year in which the worker attained age 62. There are 40 elapsed years beginning with 1953 through 1992. There are 35 computation years (40 minus 5).

704.4 How does SSA determine elapsed years for disability insurance benefits?

For disability insurance benefit purposes, elapsed years are those calendar years after 1950 up to either:

A. The year your waiting period for disability insurance benefits begins (see §502); or

B. If there is no waiting period, up to the year of your first month of entitlement.

The year you reach age 62 and later years are not counted as elapsed years. Also, whole or partial years within a period of disability are not normally counted as elapsed years. However, we can count them if your PIA would be higher if they were counted or if your insured status is affected by not counting them.

Example: An insured woman turned 50 in January 1995 and is found entitled to disability insurance benefits. It is determined that her waiting period began on March 1, 1995. The elapsed years run from 1967 (age 22) through 1994 and total 28. The number of computation years is 23 (28/5 = 5 and 28-5 =23).

705. WHAT ARE BASE YEARS?

Your base years are the years after 1950 up to the year of the first month you become entitled to retirement or disability insurance benefits. For a survivor's claim, the base years include the year of the worker's death. A year wholly contained in a period of disability is not included in the base years. Years partially within a period of disability are included.

Example: Mr. Clifford applied for retirement insurance benefits in October 1995. He is found entitled to a reduced benefit beginning October 1995, the month in which he is age 62 throughout the month. His base years for purposes of the initial computation of his benefit rate are the years 1951 through 1994, the year before the year in which he became entitled to benefits (1995). Since the elapsed years are 40 (1955 through 1994, the year before he attains age 62), the computation years are 35 (40 minus 5). To find the PIA, the earnings are averaged over the 35 highest of the base years 1951 through 1994 after the earnings are indexed. Mr. Clifford's PIA may be recomputed to take into account any earnings he had in 1995. This increase, if any, in his retirement insurance benefit will be effective January 1996. (See §722.)

706. DETERMINING THE PIA

706.1 How does SSA determine your PIA for first eligibility or death before 1979?

Your PIA is determined from the table that was in the Social Security Act as of December 31, 1978 if you:

A. Become eligible for retirement insurance benefits at age 62;
B. Have a period of disability established; or
C. Become eligible for survivors' insurance benefits on the basis of death before 1979.

This PIA is increased in December of each year in which there is a cost-of-living increase in benefit rates. (Before 1983, the increase was effective in June.) The table and the increases are not included in this *Handbook* because it is not possible to keep them current.

706.2 How does SSA determine your PIA for first eligibility or death after 1978?

Your PIA is determined by applying a mathematical formula to the AIME if you either:

A. Become eligible for retirement insurance benefits at age 62;
B. Have a period of disability established; or

C. Become eligible for survivors' insurance benefits on the basis of death in 1979 or later. The PIA, with first eligibility in 2024, equals the sum of the following:
   A. 90 percent of the first $1,174 of the AIME, *plus*
   B. 32 percent of the amount above $1,174 up through $7,078, *plus*
   C. 15 percent of any amount in excess of $7,078.

The dollar amounts at which these percentages change are called bend points. The bend points change for each year of eligibility based on the changes in your average total wages from the previous indexing year. The new bend points apply if you first become eligible or die in that year. They will remain applicable to PIA determinations in later recomputations.

Cost-of-living increases (see §719) are applied to compute your PIA beginning with the first year of eligibility, regardless of when you become entitled to benefits. Cost-of-living increases are not considered before the year of first eligibility, since your earnings in most of these years are "indexed" in computing the AIME.

706.3 How does SSA determine your PIA for first eligibility in years between 1979 and 1984?

You are guaranteed a PIA that is at least the amount computed under the pre-1979 method if you meet the following conditions:
A. You have at least one year of covered earnings before 1979;
B. You were not eligible for retirement or disability insurance benefits before 1979; and
C. You first became eligible for retirement insurance benefits between 1979 and 1984.

Your AME and PIA in effect on December 31, 1978, apply. Again, cost-of-living increases are effective beginning with the year of your first eligibility. This also applies to the survivors of a worker who was eligible but did not apply for benefits under this provision.

706.4 How is your PIA determined for entitlement at any time where the old-start formula yields a higher payment?

If the old-start formula (§§707-710) produces a higher payment, your PIA is based on the AME. This is determined from the December 31, 1978, table with cost-of-living increases beginning with the year of your first eligibility.

706.5 How does SSA determine the PIA if you had a prior period of disability?

If you had a prior entitlement to disability insurance benefits and you: (1) become eligible for a retirement insurance benefit; (2) become re-eligible for a disability insurance benefit; or (3) die, your PIA is the higher of the one computed as if you were first eligible after 1978, or the former PIA. (See (706.2) above.) This applies if more than 12 months have passed since your last entitlement to disability insurance benefits.

If fewer than 12 months have passed since your last disability entitlement after 1978, your current PIA is the higher of the former PIA (a continuation of the former PIA), or a new PIA computed under current methods.

707. THE SIMPLIFIED OLD-START FORMULA

707.1 What is the simplified old-start formula?

The simplified old-start formula is used to figure the AME and the Primary Insurance Benefit (PIB). It is used if an individual meets the requirements for its use and if it produces a higher PIA than the AME or AIME formula.

707.2 How is the simplified old-start formula used?

Under the simplified old-start formula, your earnings for 1937 through 1950 are considered a single total amount. This total amount is allocated equally to each of those years (1937-1950). These years are used along with years after 1950 to determine your average earnings.

This formula considers computation and elapsed years in the usual way (§§703-704) except that years are counted from after 1936 instead of after 1950. Base years, however, are determined differently as explained in §705.

708. WHEN CAN THE SIMPLIFIED OLD-START FORMULA BE USED?

Use of the simplified old-start formula requires that you meet the following conditions:

A. You have at least one quarter of coverage before 1951;

B. You have reached age 62, died, or become disabled after December 1977;

C. You have reached age 22 after 1937 and before 1951; or you have reached age 22 after 1950 and have less than six quarters of coverage after 1950; and

D. You did not have a period of disability that began before 1951, unless the period of disability is entirely ignored (because a higher PIA results by including the period of disability).

709. FIGURING THE AME UNDER THE SIMPLIFIED OLD-START FORMULA

709.1 How does SSA compute the AME under the simplified old-start formula for earnings after 1950?

Under the simplified old-start formula, your AME is figured by determining your base year earnings. Base years are determined the same way as under the AME formula (see §705). Earnings are used and credited up to the annual maximums. When eligibility is after 1978, earnings in and after the year of eligibility cannot be included.

709.2 How does SSA compute AME under the simplified old-start formula for earnings before 1951?

To compute your AME under the simplified old-start formula for earnings before 1951, we perform the steps below:

A. Add up your total pre-1951 earnings. This includes earnings posted to your earnings record plus any military wage credits, earnings under railroad retirement transferred to Social Security, and wages if you were an intern in the U.S. during World War II;

B. Divide this total by either: (a) *the number of years passed* since you turned 20 and prior to 1951; or (b) *one*, if you turned 21 after 1949. The result is your earnings in each year used in the divisor.
   1. We may not credit more than $3,000 to each of these years. We credit any remainder under $3,000 either: (a) to the year in which you turned 20 (if you turned 20 before 1951); or (b) to 1949, if you turned 21 after 1949. If there is anything left over more than $3,000, we credit this amount, in $3,000 increments, to the year in (a) and each consecutive preceding year.
   2. We may not credit more than $42,000 ($3,000 a year) to the period 1937 through 1950.

C. Divide your highest computation years by the number of months in the computation years to determine your AME.

710. HOW IS THE PRIMARY INSURANCE BENEFIT (PIB) COMPUTED UNDER THE SIMPLIFIED OLD-START FORMULA?

The PIB is computed from the AME under the simplified old-start formula as follows:

A. Take 40 percent of the first $50 of the AME;
B. Add 10 percent of the next $200 of the AME;
C. Increase the sum by one percent for each increment year; and
   Note: The number of increment years is the number, not more than 14 or less than four, that is equal to your total pre-1951 earnings divided by $1,650. Ignore any fraction.
D. Round the total to the nearest cent. The result is the PIB. You can convert the PIB to the PIA by using the benefit table that was in the Social Security Act as of December 31, 1978. Be sure to add any cost-of-living increases beginning with the year of eligibility or death. (See §706.)

711. ARE ESTABLISHED PERIODS OF DISABILITY EXCLUDED WHEN BENEFITS ARE COMPUTED?

Yes. We must exclude an established period of disability in figuring your benefit unless the exclusion of the period results in fewer benefits or a loss of insured status. This exclusion applies to all computation formulas. (See Chapter 5 for the requirements for establishing a period of disability and for the beginning and ending dates of this period.)

712. FIGURING THE PIA UNDER THE 1990 CONSOLIDATED METHODS

712.1 What computation methods are used for individuals eligible for benefits before the AME method?

Computation methods for individuals who were eligible for benefits before the AME method were consolidated into the two formulas for benefits payable June 1992, or later. The old computation methods continue to apply when:

A. An individual is entitled on the record in the month before the new entitlement; and
B. The PIA is based on a pre-1990 computation formula.

Because these old methods are rare, they are not discussed in this *Handbook*.

712.2 How are you eligible for either method of computing benefits?

To be eligible for either method of computing benefits, you must:

A. Become entitled to benefits on the record effective June 1992 or later. There is to be no other person on the record with benefits based on an old computation method in the month before the month you become entitled; and

B. Not qualify for any other new start method (methods enacted in 1965 or later which apply to earnings after 1950) or simplified old-start methods.

712.3 How does SSA compute elapsed years under the 1990 AME formula?

Under the 1990 AME formula, elapsed years for *retirement insurance benefits* are the later of either:

A. The years after 1950 up to 1961;

B. The year you turn 62; or

C. The year you turned 65 if you are a male born before January 2, 1913.

For survivors' benefits, the elapsed years are years after 1950 up to the year of death. However, if the worker attained retirement age and died prior to 1961, elapsed years go up to 1961.

Years before age 22 and years wholly or partially within a period of disability (if a higher primary insurance amount results) are excluded from the elapsed years.

712.4 How does SSA compute base years, computation years, and the divisor month under the 1990 AME formula?

For determining the base years, computation years, and the divisor month, see §§705-706.

712.5 How is the PIA determined for the AME under the 1990 AME formula?

The PIA for the AME is determined by a table. The table and the increases are not included in this *Handbook* because it is not possible to keep them current.

712.6 What is the difference between the 1990 old-start formula and the simplified old-start method?

The 1990 old-start formula is similar to the simplified old-start method (see §§707-708) but there are several basic differences:

A. Elapsed years are computed based on the retirement age of 65 for males born before January 2, 1911. For individuals born January 2, 1911, through January 1, 1913, retirement age occurs in 1975; and
B. Earnings in years prior to 1951 are allocated as follows:

The first year of the allocation period is:
1. 1937-if the worker was born before January 2, 1917;
2. 1950-if the worker was born January 2, 1929, or later;
3. The year the worker reaches age 21; or
4. 1950-if the worker died before 1951 and before age 22.

The last year of the allocation period is:
5. 1950-if the individual was alive on January 1, 1951; or
6. The year prior to the year of death if the individual died before January 1, 1951.

After the period is determined, the years are counted and the earnings are divided by the number of years.

Note: Recomputations of benefits for 1992 and later years of earnings are computed under one of the 1990 old-start methods whenever the eligibility year is prior to 1978. This is true regardless of the computation methods used to include earnings in previous years.

Example: Mr. Hile, was born in 1924 and died in 1950. His earnings for 1937 to 1950 equal $12,950. His earnings allocation period is 1945 (the year he reached age 21) through 1949 (the year prior to his death). There are five years in the allocation period. His earnings of $12,950 are divided by five (the number of years in the allocation period). $2,590 is allocated to each year (1945 - 1949). If Mr. Hile had a period of disability, it would have been excluded from the allocation period.

713. WHAT IS INCLUDED AS "TOTAL EARNINGS" WHEN COMPUTING THE AME OR AIME?

In computing your AME or AIME, we include the following as total earnings (subject to the yearly limits in §714):
A. Wages covered by Social Security and paid during the computation period;
B. Self-employment income covered by Social Security and allocated to this period;
C. Military service wage credits;
D. Railroad compensation creditable for Social Security purposes; and
E. Deemed wages if you were interned in the U.S. during World War II.

We may not count earnings from employment or self-employment not covered by Social Security in computing your AME.

714. WHAT ARE THE MAXIMUM EARNINGS THAT CAN BE COUNTED FOR ANY CALENDAR YEAR FOR COMPUTING AME OR AIME?

The table below shows the maximum earnings for each year that we can use when computing your AME or AIME.

Year	Maximum Earnings	Year	Maximum Earnings
2024	$168,600	1993	$57,600
2023	$160,200	1992	$55,500
2022	$147,000	1991	$53,400
2021	$142,800	1990	$51,300
2020	$137,700	1989	$48,000
2019	$132,900	1988	$45,000
2018	$128,400	1987	$43,800
2017	$127,200	1986	$42,000
2015–2016	$118,500	1985	$39,600
2014	$117,000	1984	$37,800
2013	$113,700	1983	$35,700
2012	$110,100	1982	$32,400
2011	$106,800	1981	$29,700
2010	$106,800	1980	$25,900
2009	$106,800	1979	$22,900
2008	$102,000	1978	$17,700
2007	$97,500	1977	$16,500
2006	$94,200	1976	$15,300
2005	$90,000	1975	$14,100
2004	$87,900	1974	$13,200
2003	$87,000	1973	$10,800
2002	$84,900	1972	$9,000
2001	$80,400	1968-1971	$7,800
2000	$76,200	1967	$6,600
1999	$72,600	1966	$6,600
1998	$68,400	1959-1965	$4,800
1997	$65,400	1955-1958	$4,200
1996	$62,700	1951-1954	$3,600
1995	$61,200	1940-1950	$3,000
1994	$60,600	1937-1939	$3,000 per employer

715. ALLOCATION OF SELF-EMPLOYMENT INCOME

715.1 How is self-employment income allocated for the years 1978 and later?

Self-employment income in taxable years (other than calendar years) is allocated proportionately to the two calendar years in which it was derived. The allocation is based on the number of months in each calendar year. Your self-employment income may be allocated for more than four calendar quarters if the taxable year includes parts of two calendar years. (See §214.) Only your self-employment income allocated to the calendar quarters in computation years is considered in figuring your AIME.

Example: A self-employed person has a fiscal taxable year beginning May 15, 1983, and ending May 14, 1984. His $6,000 self-employment income is allocated $3,500 (7/12) to calendar year 1983 and $2,500 (5/12) to 1984.

715.2 How is self-employment income allocated prior to 1978?

For taxable years beginning before 1978, your self-employment income is allocated equally to the calendar quarters, wholly or partly, in the taxable year in which it was derived. This allocation begins with the quarter in which the taxable year ended and continues to the preceding three calendar quarters.

715.3 What if you are self-employed and your taxable year has not ended when your PIA is computed?

If your self-employed taxable year has not ended at the time the PIA is computed, your net earnings from self-employment earned in the incomplete taxable year cannot be considered in computing the PIA. This is true even if the income may have been partially derived in the closed calendar year. The self-employment income is recorded and the PIA recomputed after you file your tax return.

716. ELIMINATION OF THE MINIMUM BENEFIT

716.1 Is there a minimum social security benefit?

The minimum social security benefit was eliminated in January 1982 for workers who initially become eligible for retirement or disability insurance benefits after December 1981. The PIA for these persons is either:

A. The actual amount computed by a mathematical formula; or

B. The amount determined from an extended version of the PIA table that was in the Social Security Act as of December 1978. That table has been extended downward from the original minimum of $121.80 to the lowest possible PIA ($1.70).

If you have covered employment for many years at low earnings, the special minimum PIA (see §717) may apply instead.

716.2 Is the elimination of the minimum social security benefit effective for members of religious orders?

If you are a member of a religious order, the elimination of the minimum social security benefit is effective January 1992 under the following conditions:

A. You are required to take a vow of poverty (see §932);

B. You become eligible for benefits or die in or after January 1992; and

C. Your religious order elected Social Security coverage before December 29, 1981.

717. SPECIAL MINIMUM PIA

717.1 What is a special minimum PIA?

A "special minimum PIA" is payable to some persons who have had covered employment or self-employment for many years at low earnings. It only applies if the resulting payment is higher than the benefit computed by any other method.

717.2 How is the special minimum PIA computed?

For 1979 and later, subtract ten from the number of years of coverage and multiply by $11.50. Between March 1974 and December 1978, subtract ten from the number of years of coverage and multiply by $9. Between January 1973 and February 1974, subract ten from the number of years of coverage and multiply by $8.50.

717.3 What is the Primary Insurance Amount (PIA) and Maximum family benefit?

The primary insurance amount (PIA) is the benefit (before rounding down to next lower whole dollar) a person would receive if they elect to begin receiving retirement benefits at their normal retirement age.

The PIA is the sum of three separate percentages of portions of average indexed monthly earnings. The portions depend on the *year* in which a worker attains age 62, becomes disabled before age 62, or dies before attaining age 62.

For 2024 these portions are the first $1,174, the amount between $1,174 and $7,078, and the amount over $7,078. These dollar amounts are the "bend points" of the 2024 PIA formula.

The dollar amounts in the maximum family benefit formula are $1,500 for the first bend point, $2,166 for the second bend point, and $2,825 for the third bend point.

717.4 How does SSA determine your number of years of covered work?

For 1951–1978, the amount of Social Security covered earnings needed for a year of coverage is 25 percent of the contribution and benefit base. For years after 1978, the amounts are 25 percent of what the contribution and benefit base would have been if the 1977 Social Security Amendments had not been enacted (hence the name "old-law" base). For special-minimum benefit purposes only, the applicable percentage is 15 percent for years after 1990. Please see the following table:

Year	"Old-Law" Contribution and Benefit Base	Year	"Old-Law" Contribution and Benefit Base
1979	$18,900	2002	$63,000
1980	$20,400	2003	$64,500
1981	$22,200	2004	$65,100
1982	$24,300	2005	$66,900
1983	$26,700	2006	$69,900
1984	$28,200	2007	$72,600
1985	$29,700	2008	$75,900
1986	$31,500	2009	$79,200
1987	$32,700	2010	$79,200
1988	$33,600	2011	$79,200
1989	$35,700	2012	$81,900
1990	$38,100	2013	$84,300
1991	$39,600	2014	$87,000
1992	$41,400	2015	$88,200
1993	$42,900	2016	$88,200
1994	$45,000	2017	$94,500
1995	$45,300	2018	$95,400
1996	$46,500	2019	$98,700
1997	$48,600	2020	$102,300
1998	$50,700	2021	$106,200
1999	$53,700	2022	$109,200
2000	$56,700	2023	$118,800
2001	$59,700	2024	$125,100

718. WINDFALL ELIMINATION PROVISION (WEP) - MODIFIED BENEFIT FORMULA TO DETERMINE THE PIA FOR WORKERS WITH PENSIONS FROM NON-COVERED EMPLOYMENT

718.1 What is the WEP PIA formula that is used for workers who are eligible for a pension from noncovered employment based on their own work?

The WEP benefit formula is used to determine the PIA for workers who are eligible for a pension from noncovered employment based on their own work and a Social Security retirement or disability benefit.

718.2 How does the WEP PIA formula affect workers who are eligible for a pension from noncovered employment?

The Social Security benefit formula provides a higher percentage of pre-retirement income for lifetime low-wage workers. The WEP benefit formula eliminates the "windfall" in Social Security benefits received by workers who have only minimal Social Security coverage and who receive a pension based on years of work in noncovered employment. A worker's PIA will never be reduced by more than one-half of the pension amount from noncovered employment. (See §706)

718.3 How is the revised formula used?

The revised formula substitutes 40 percent for the 90 percent factor in the first band of the Social Security benefit formula. The reduction is phased in as follows:

If you are initially eligible for retirement or disability benefits in...	Then the first percentage factor used in the Social Security benefit formula is...
1986	80 percent
1987	70
1988	60
1989	50
1990 or after	40

A worker may get a full or partial exemption based on earning "years of coverage." The worker receives the percentage that yields the higher benefit amount.

If your total years of coverage equal...	Then the first percentage factor in the formula is...
29	85
28	80
27	75
26	70
25	65
24	60

If your total years of coverage equal…	Then the first percentage factor in the formula is…
23	55
22	50
21	45
20 or fewer	40

A "year of coverage" is calculated as is the special minimum PIA. (See §717). For years 1991 and later, the amount needed for a year of coverage is 25% of the maximum earnings base.

718.4 Are any other methods considered?

In addition to the modified formula, we also consider the simplified old-start formula (see §707) and the special minimum PIA (see §717). We use the computation yielding the highest PIA to determine the amount of benefits payable.

718.5 When does the WEP benefit formula not apply?

The WEP provision does not apply under the following situations:
A. When the worker has 30 years of coverage;
B. When the noncovered pension benefits are paid under the Railroad Retirement Act;
C. To Federal employees who are mandatorily covered for Social Security purposes beginning January 1, 1984;
D. To most employees of nonprofit organizations who were exempt from coverage before 1984; and
E. When the worker receives noncovered pension benefits as a survivor.
F. To benefits paid to survivors entitled on the record.

719. COST-OF-LIVING INCREASES

719.1 How do cost-of-living increases affect benefits?

Benefits may be automatically increased to keep pace with increases in the cost-of-living if laws for general benefit increases are not passed. Benefit increases depend upon the condition of the Federal Old-Age, Survivors and Disability Trust Funds. The increases are based on the smaller of either: (1) *the Consumer Price Index* as published by the Department of

Labor; or (2) the average wage index, that is based on nationwide wages. Where the index for a current base quarter shows an increase over the same index for the last base quarter, the following happens: each PIA (the unreduced amount that would be paid at full retirement age), each related maximum family benefit, each transitionally insured benefit and each special age 72 payment is raised to reflect the same percentage of increase (rounded to the nearest one-tenth of one percent). The base quarter is either: (1) the third calendar quarter of each year after 1982, or (2) a later calendar quarter within which a general benefit increase became effective. After the cost-of-living is added, reductions and deductions are applied to the new amount.

For the most current Cost-of-Living Adjustment (COLA), see: https://www.ssa.gov/cola/.

719.2 When does the cost-of-living benefit increase become effective?

This cost-of-living benefit increase becomes effective beginning with December of the year that contains the base quarter for the index increase. The cost-of-living increase is published in the *Federal Register* on or about November 14 of the year preceding the year the benefits are payable.

719.3 How are Social Security program amounts determined under automatic adjustment provisions?

For current Social Security program amounts determined under automatic adjustment provisions, see: https://www.ssa.gov/OACT/COLA/autoAdj.html.

720. DELAYED RETIREMENT CREDIT

720.1 How does the delayed retirement credit affect benefits?

The delayed retirement credit increases your benefit amount if you did not receive benefits for months after you became full retirement age. Delayed retirement credit increases apply for benefits beginning January of the year following the year you reach full retirement age. However, it does not apply to the special minimum PIA, which is explained in §717.

720.2 What is an increment month?

Each month in which you are at least full retirement age, but not yet age 70 (age 72 if you turned age 70 before 1984), is an increment month. An increment month is also any month you are eligible, but did not receive a benefit.

720.3 How do increment months affect the delayed retirement credit?

The delayed retirement credit is based on increment months. They may increase your benefit amount:

A. If you are a retirement insurance beneficiary and you reach age 65 before 1982, then you receive an increase equal to 1/12 of one percent of the benefit for each increment month;
B. If you are a retirement insurance beneficiary and you reached age 65 after 1981 and before 1990, then you receive an increase equal to 1/4 of one percent of the benefit for each increment month; or
C. If you are a retirement insurance beneficiary who reached full retirement age after 1989, then your benefit amount is increased for each increment month at 1/4 of one percent, plus 1/24 of one percent for each even-numbered year from 1990 through 2008 in which you are full retirement age or older. The rates of credit are as shown in the table below.

If you reached full retirement age...	Then your monthly percentage is...and	Your yearly percentage is...
Prior to 1982	1/12 of 1%	1%
1982-1989	1/4 of 1%	3%
1990-1991	7/24 of 1%	3.5%
1992-1993	1/3 of 1%	4%
1994-1995	3/8 of 1%	4.5%
1996-1997	5/12 of 1%	5%
1998-1999	11/24 of 1%	5.5%
2000-2001	1/2 of 1%	6%
2002-2003	13/24 of 1%	6.5%
2004-2005	7/12 of 1%	7%
2006-2008	5/8 of 1%	7.5%
2009 or later	2/3 of 1%	8%

D. *If you are a widow(er) of a worker who had received or was eligible for delayed retirement credits*, then you are entitled to the same increase that had been applied to the benefit of your deceased spouse or for which the deceased was eligible as of the time of death. A surviving (including divorced) spouse receiving widow(er)'s benefits is also entitled to this increase.

721. RECOMPUTATION OF THE PIA

721.1 May we recompute the PIA?

We may recompute (and increase) your PIA one or more times after the first computation. We make the first computation at the time you become entitled to retirement or disability insurance benefits. You do not need to request or take any special action to have the benefit recomputed. There are two types of recomputations: automatic and railroad.

721.2 What is an automatic recomputation?

The automatic recomputation (see §722) gives you credit for any substantial additional covered earnings in the year you first became entitled to benefits or in a later year. A recomputation to include a particular year's earnings is effective in January following the year in which the earnings were paid. For example, a benefit increase resulting from an automatic recomputation to include 1992 earnings will first be paid for January 1993.

721.3 What is a railroad recomputation?

The railroad recomputation increases survivor benefits by including railroad earnings not permitted for use in figuring the Social Security benefit(s) when the worker was alive.

722. THE AUTOMATIC RECOMPUTATION

722.1 When is the automatic recomputation used?

The automatic recomputation is used to recompute the PIA. It is used if a person has wages or self-employment income for any year for any part of which he or she is entitled to retirement or disability insurance benefits.

722.2 How is the automatic recomputation determined?

The usual computation formula or the special minimum PIA formula (see §717) is used. If you qualify for either the simplified old-start or the

1990 consolidated methods, and each yields a higher PIA, the appropriate formula (see §707) is used. In effect, any year for which retirement or disability insurance benefits are paid can be a base year in the automatic recomputation of that year's retirement or disability insurance benefits.

722.3 What if a retirement or disability insurance beneficiary dies?

The automatic recomputation credits any earnings in the year that a retirement or disability insurance beneficiary dies. It is the same as above, except that it is effective with the month of death. Therefore, any resulting increase in the PIA is reflected in the amount of all monthly survivors' benefits, beginning with the first month of entitlement to survivors' benefits.

722.4 Can an automatic recomputation decrease your PIA or benefits?

No. A recomputation never decreases your PIA or benefits. However, an automatic recomputation can increase your PIA or benefits if your earnings in the additional base year considered are higher than earnings in the lowest computation year used in your last computation or recomputation.

723. REDUCTION OF BENEFIT RATE

723.1 When are benefit rates reduced?

Your benefit rate is reduced if you become entitled to the following benefits at the ages shown:

A. Retirement insurance benefits at age 62 through the month before you reach Full Retirement Age (FRA);

B. Husband's or wife's insurance benefits at age 62 through the month before you reach FRA, provided that you do not have in care a child of the worker either under age 16 or disabled and entitled to benefits;

C. Widow(er)'s insurance benefits beginning at any time from age 50 through the month before you reach FRA;

D. Widow(er)'s insurance benefits after the deceased worker has received a retirement insurance benefit reduced for age;

E. Disability insurance benefits received after a reduced retirement insurance benefit; or

F. Retirement or disability insurance benefits received after a reduced widow(er)'s insurance benefit. This applies only to workers born before 1928.

723.2 How is a reduction in benefits made?

The reduction is made by first determining your full benefit. This benefit rate is then reduced by a specified percentage for each month you are entitled before your FRA. The reduced rate is payable as of the first month of your entitlement to benefits. For retirement and spouse's benefits, you must be at least age 62 throughout the month before entitlement to reduced benefits begins.

These reduced benefits continue at a reduced rate even after FRA. The reduced disability insurance benefit is converted at FRA to a reduced retirement insurance benefit.

723.3 When is the reduced benefit rate recomputed?

The reduced benefit rate may be recomputed to include additional earnings. An increase in your benefits, either resulting from additional earnings or from a cost-of-living increase, is reduced in proportion to the reduction in effect in the first month your benefits were elected. A benefit rate may also be increased to give you credit for certain months before FRA in which the reduced benefit was not paid. (See §728.)

723.4 How will an increase in the retirement age affect reduced benefits?

Beginning with the year 2000 (workers and spouses born 1938 or later, widow(er)s born 1940 or later), the retirement age increases gradually from age 65 until it reaches age 67 in the year 2022. This increase affects the amount of the reduction for persons who begin receiving reduced benefits.

An additional reduction applies to primary insurance benefits and spouse's benefits based on the additional reduction period. The modification for widow(er)'s benefits is slightly different. The reduction amount at age 60 remains at 28 1/2 percent of the full benefit even as retirement age increases.

723.5 What is the full retirement age for workers and spouses born after 1937?

The following chart contains the full retirement age for workers and spouses born after 1937:

If your birth date is…	Then your full retirement age is…
1/2/38-1/1/39	65 years and 2 months
1/2/39-1/1/40	65 years and 4 months
1/2/40-1/1/41	65 years and 6 months
1/2/41-1/1/42	65 years and 8 months
1/2/42-1/1/43	65 years and 10 months
1/2/43-1/1/55	66 years
1/2/55-1/1/56	66 years and 2 months
1/2/56-1/1/57	66 years and 4 months
1/2/57-1/1/58	66 years and 6 months
1/2/58-1/1/59	66 years and 8 months
1/2/59-1/1/60	66 years and 10 months
1/2/60 and later	67 years

723.6 What is the full retirement age for widow(er)s born after 1939?

The following chart contains the full retirement age for widow(er)s born after 1939:

If your birth date is…	Then your full retirement age is…
1/2/40-1/1/41	65 years and 2 months
1/2/41-1/1/42	65 years and 4 months
1/2/42-1/1/43	65 years and 6 months
1/2/43-1/1/44	65 years and 8 months
1/2/44-1/1/45	65 years and 10 months
1/2/45-1/1/57	66 years
1/2/57-1/1/58	66 years and 2 months
1/2/58-1/1/59	66 years and 4 months
1/2/59-1/1/60	66 years and 6 months
1/2/60-1/1/61	66 years and 8 months
1/2/61-1/1/62	66 years and 10 months
1/2/62 and later	67 years

724. BASIC REDUCTION FORMULAS

724.1 What are the basic reduction formulas?

There are four basic reduction formulas:

A. A retirement insurance benefit is reduced by 5/9 of one percent (or 0.0056) for each month of entitlement before FRA;

B. Wife's and husband's insurance benefits are reduced by 25/36 of one percent (or 0.0069) for each month of entitlement before FRA;

C. Widow(er)'s insurance benefits are reduced for each month of entitlement between ages 60 and FRA. The amount of the reduction for each month is derived from dividing 28.5 percent by the number of possible months of early retirement. A person whose FRA is age 65 could be entitled up to 60 months before FRA. Each month is therefore 28.5 percent divided by 60 (or 0.00475). A person whose FRA is age 66 could be entitled up to 72 months before FRA. Each month is therefore 28.5 percent divided by 72 (or 0.00396). Widow(er)'s insurance benefits payable before age 60 based on disability are not further reduced for months before age 60; and

D. Retirement insurance benefits and spouse's benefits are reduced by 5/12 of one percent (or 0.0042) for each month of reduction in excess of 36 months. This applies to individuals whose full retirement age is after age 65. (See §723.)

724.2 How does the reduction formula affect retirement insurance benefits?

No matter what your full retirement age is, you may start receiving benefits as early as age 62. However, if you start your benefits early, they are reduced a fraction of a percent for each month before your full retirement age. This reduction is permanent.

724.3 How does the reduction formula affect widow(er)'s insurance benefits?

You can start receiving aged reduced widow(er)'s benefits at age 60. The most your widow(er)'s benefits can be reduced is 28.5 percent of the wage earner's PIA. Also, if you start receiving your widow(er)'s benefits at full retirement age and your deceased spouse received reduced benefits, your widow(er)'s benefits will always be reduced.

724.4 How does the reduction formula affect wife's or husband's insurance benefits?

A spouse can choose to retire as early as age 62, but doing so may result in a benefit as little as 32.5 percent of the worker's primary insurance amount. A spousal benefit is reduced 25/36 of one percent for each month before normal retirement age, up to 36 months. If the number of months exceeds 36, then the benefit is further reduced 5/12 of one percent per month. There is no reduction for the prior entitlement as a wife or husband.

725. HOW DOES SSA COMPUTE THE NUMBER OF REDUCTION MONTHS?

To compute the number of reduction months, we count all months, beginning with the first month of your entitlement to reduced benefits, up to the month in which you reach full retirement age.

For widow(er)'s insurance benefits that begin before age 60, the reduction formula in §724.3 requires using only months between age 60 and full retirement age.

726. DISABILITY INSURANCE BENEFIT REDUCED FOR AGE

726.1 When is a disability insurance benefit reduced for age payable?

A disability insurance benefit reduced for age may be payable if you are already entitled to either retirement insurance benefits or reduced widow(er)'s insurance benefits. This is true whether or not your benefit is based on disability.

726.2 What if a disability insurance benefit becomes payable to a beneficiary entitled to a reduced retirement insurance benefit?

If a disability insurance benefit becomes payable to you after becoming entitled to retirement insurance benefit, your disability benefit is reduced by the amount your retirement benefit is reduced for the months prior to the month of entitlement to the disability benefit in which you received retirement benefits.

727. HOW IS THE REDUCTION AMOUNT COMPUTED?

How your reduction amount is computed depends upon whether you are entitled only to: (1) a retirement insurance benefit, (2) a wife's or husband's insurance benefit, (3) a widow(er)'s insurance benefit, or (4) a disability insurance benefit. If you are entitled to a combination of benefits, the time at which you become entitled to each benefit can affect the method of figuring the reduction amount.

728. ADJUSTMENT OF REDUCTION FACTOR AT FRA

728.1 Why is an adjustment of the reduction factor made at FRA?
An adjustment of the reduction factor is made at FRA to determine your benefit payable for the month you reach full retirement age and later months. In addition, an adjustment may be made at age 62 for a widow(er)'s insurance benefit for the month of attainment of age 62 and later months.

728.2 Under what conditions are adjustments of the reduction factor made?
Adjustments are made under the following circumstances:
A. Your entitlement to retirement insurance benefits began between age 62 and full retirement age, and
   1. A work deduction (including a partial deduction) was imposed for any month before FRA; or
   2. You were also entitled to disability insurance benefits for any month of your entitlement to retirement insurance benefits.
B. Your entitlement to wife's or husband's insurance benefits began between age 62 and full retirement age, and one of the following conditions applies:
   1. A work deduction (including a partial deduction), based on your work and/or your spouse's work, was imposed for any month before full retirement age;
   2. A deduction was imposed because you refused vocational rehabilitation;
   3. A benefit was not payable for a month before full retirement age because you were entitled to other benefits which terminated the benefit; or
   4. A benefit was not payable for a month before full retirement age due to the worker's voluntary suspension request made on or after April 30, 2016.
   5. A full benefit was payable for some months because you had in care your spouse's child (under age 16 or disabled) who was also entitled to benefits.

C. Your entitlement to a widow(er)'s insurance benefit began between age 50 and full retirement age and one of the following conditions applies:
1. A work deduction (including a partial deduction) was imposed for any month;
2. A full benefit was payable for any month because you had a child in care as defined in §312; or
3. A benefit was not payable because of a terminating event.

728.3 How is the benefit amount recomputed?

An application is not required for this adjustment. The benefit amount is recomputed by using the reduction formula that was used to compute the original reduced benefit. The appropriate month(s) in (A) through (C) above are then excluded from the benefit reduction factor.

729. CERTIFICATE OF ELECTION FOR HUSBAND OR WIFE BETWEEN AGES 62 AND FRA-CHILD "IN CARE"

729.1 When is a certificate of election filed to reduce husband's or wife's insurance benefits?

You may file a certificate of election to receive reduced spouse's insurance benefits if you were receiving unreduced (full) insurance benefits that are suspended because a child under age 16 or disabled is no longer in your care.

729.2 When does the certificate of election become effective?

The certificate of election is effective for any month in which you are:
A. Between age 62 and full retirement age;
B. Entitled to husband's or wife's insurance benefits; and
C. Do not have in care a child (under age 16 or disabled) of the worker entitled to a child's insurance benefit.

729.3 Is the certification of election retroactive?

The certificate of election may be retroactive for as many as 12 months before the month you file it.

729.4 How long will the reduced spouse's benefit be payable?

Once you receive reduced spouse's insurance benefits, your insurance benefit rate will continue to be payable even after you reach full retirement age. The reduced benefits will continue as long as there is no entitled child in your care.

730. MAXIMUM MONTHLY BENEFITS PAYABLE ON ONE EARNINGS RECORD

730.1 Is there a maximum family benefit on a Social Security record?

Yes. A maximum family benefit is payable on a Social Security record. Generally, no more than the established maximum can be paid to a family, regardless of the number of beneficiaries entitled on that Social Security record. The family maximum is determined by the method of computing the PIA and the kind of benefits payable to the worker.

730.2 How is the maximum family benefit computed under first eligibility or death before 1979?

If you turn 62 or become disabled or die before 1979, your PIA is based on your average monthly earnings. It is determined from the table that was in the Social Security Act as of December 31, 1978, and increased by cost-of-living increases. A table of family maximums that is associated with special minimum PIA's is published in the Federal Register after each increase.

730.3 How is the maximum family benefit computed in 2024?

For the family of a worker who becomes age 62 or dies in 2024 before attaining age 62, the total amount of benefits payable will be computed so that it does not exceed:

A. 150 percent of the first $1,550 of the worker's PIA, plus
B. 272 percent of the worker's PIA over $1,550 through $2,166, plus
C. 134 percent of the worker's PIA over $2,166 through $2,825, plus
D. 175 percent of the worker's PIA over $2,825.

We then round this total amount to the next lower multiple of $.10 if it is not already a multiple of $.10.

730.4 How is the maximum family benefit computed under first entitlement to disability insurance benefits after June 1980, first eligibility after 1978?

The family maximum is 85 percent of the AIME (see §701). However, it cannot be less than the PIA nor more than 150 percent of the PIA.

731. ADJUSTMENT OF INDIVIDUAL BENEFIT RATES BECAUSE OF FAMILY MAXIMUM

731.1 When is an adjustment of individual benefit rates because of the family maximum required?

An adjustment is required whenever the total monthly benefits of all the beneficiaries entitled on one Social Security earnings record exceed the family maximum that can be paid on that record for the month. All benefit rates (except retirement or disability insurance benefits and benefits payable to a divorced spouse or surviving divorced spouse) must be reduced to bring the total monthly benefits payable within the family maximum.

731.2 What if a beneficiary's benefit rate is a percentage of the insured person's PIA?

Even if a beneficiary's benefit rate is originally set by law as a percentage of the insured person's PIA, the actual benefit paid to the beneficiary may be less if the family maximum is exceeded.

731.3 Can the family maximum ever be exceeded?

The family maximum may be exceeded only by the effect of "saving clauses" and certain entitlement exceptions.

731.4 What are savings clauses?

When the law was changed to add new categories of beneficiaries or to increase benefits, "savings clauses" were included. The purpose of the savings clauses was to prevent the reduction of the benefits of persons already on the rolls or to make sure they get the full increase intended.

For example, under the 1972 amendments, the amount of widow(er)'s insurance benefits was increased and exceptions were made with respect to the entitlement of divorced spouses and disabled children. Savings clauses were provided so that other beneficiaries who were already entitled would not be disadvantaged by these exceptions. Therefore, the total benefits paid on an earnings record may add up to more than the normal family maximum.

731.5 How do spousal benefits affect other beneficiaries under the savings clauses?

The entitlement of a divorced spouse to a spouse's insurance benefit does not result in reducing the benefits of other categories of beneficiaries.

Likewise, the entitlement of a legal spouse where a deemed or putative spouse is also entitled does not affect the benefit of other beneficiaries entitled in the month. The other dependents or survivors insurance benefits are reduced for the maximum. The existence of the divorced spouse, surviving divorced spouse, or the legal spouse is not taken into account. His or her benefits are not reduced because of the family maximum.

The examples above are the major exceptions to the family maximum currently in effect, although they are not exhaustive. They must be kept in mind in reading §732. To avoid repetition, the examples are not restated each time they might be pertinent.

732. HOW ADJUSTMENT FOR FAMILY MAXIMUM IS FIGURED

732.1 How is the adjustment for the family maximum calculated?

The adjustment for the family maximum is made by proportionately reducing all the monthly benefits subject to the family maximum on the Social Security earnings record (except for retired worker's or disabled worker's benefits). All benefits subject to the family maximum are reduced in order to bring the total monthly benefits payable within the limit for the particular case. (See §731 for other exceptions.)

732.2 How is the individual reduced benefit computed if the insured person is alive?

To compute the reduced benefit for an insured living person, we:
A. Subtract his or her PIA subtracted from the applicable family maximum amount; and
B. Divide any remainder among the other persons entitled to benefits on his or her Social Security earnings record.

732.3 How is the individual reduced benefit computed if the insured person is deceased?

If the insured person is deceased, the formula used depends upon the percentage of PIA that monthly benefits are based on:
A. If all monthly benefits are based on the same percentage (e.g., all are based on 100 percent of the PIA, or all are based on 75 percent), then the family maximum is divided equally among all those who are entitled to benefits on the Social Security earnings record; or

B. *Some benefits may be based on 100 percent, some on 82 and 1/2 percent, and/or others on 75 percent.* In cases where benefits are not based on the same percentage of PIA, each beneficiary is paid a proportionate share of the family maximum based on that beneficiary's original benefit rate.

732.4 When is the adjustment for the family maximum made?

This adjustment is made after any deductions that may be applicable. It occurs when reduction for the family maximum is required, and a benefit payable to someone other than the worker must be withheld. Redistributing for the maximum is made as if the beneficiary whose benefit must be withheld were not entitled to the amounts withheld.

Note: The total benefits payable to the family group are not necessarily reduced when monthly benefits are not payable to one member of the family group.

The following example illustrates the following: (1) the initial adjustment of benefit rates for the family maximum; (2) the readjustment of rates when benefits are not payable to one beneficiary; and (3) the readjustment of rates when benefits are not payable to two beneficiaries.

The PIA is $300.60 and maximum family benefits are $535.10. The insured person is entitled to retirement insurance benefits.

Beneficiary	Original Benefit	Adjusted for the Maximum	Adjustment When Benefits not Payable to One Child	Adjustment When Benefits not Payable to Two Children
Insured person	$300.60	$300.60	$300.60	$300.60
Spouse	150.30	58.60	78.10	117.20
First child	150.30	58.60	78.10	117.20
Second child	150.30	58.60	78.10	0.00
Third child	150.30	58.60	0.00	0.00
Total	$901.80	$535.00	$534.90	$535.00

733. ENTITLEMENT TO MORE THAN ONE SOCIAL SECURITY BENEFIT AT THE SAME TIME

733.1 Can you be entitled to more than one Social Security benefit at the same time?

Yes. You may be entitled to more than one benefit at the same time. For example, a person can be entitled to parent's insurance benefits on a deceased child's Social Security earnings record and to spouse's insurance benefits on another record.

733.2 If you are entitled to more than one benefit, which one is payable?

If you are entitled to more than one benefit, only the higher benefit is payable, unless one of the benefits is either: (1) a retirement or disability insurance benefit (see §734); or (2) both benefits are child's insurance benefits (see §735).

The lower benefit cannot be paid even if the higher benefit is not payable due to a suspension or deduction reason. However, if the higher benefit is terminated, the lower benefit will be automatically reinstated if you are still entitled to it.

Example: Mrs. Alicen is entitled to a spouse's insurance benefit of $102.10 and a parent's insurance benefit of $94.40. Her spouse's insurance benefit is suspended for several months because of her husband's work. Mrs. Alicen cannot be paid a parent's insurance benefit for these months. However, if she and her husband get divorced and she cannot meet the requirements for receiving benefits as a divorced spouse (see §311), her entitlement to spouse's insurance benefits is terminated. If she is still entitled to parent's insurance benefits, these will be paid to her, effective the month her spouse's insurance benefits terminate.

734. ENTITLEMENT TO RETIREMENT OR DISABILITY INSURANCE BENEFITS AND ANOTHER BENEFIT

734.1 Can you be entitled to retirement or disability insurance benefits and another higher benefit?

Yes. It is possible to be entitled to retirement or disability benefits as well as another higher benefit. In this case, you will receive the retirement or disability insurance benefit plus the difference between this benefit and the higher one. If the higher benefit is not payable, either in whole or in part for one or more months, the retirement or disability insurance benefit may be payable.

Example: Mrs. Martel is entitled to retirement insurance benefits of $128.10 and to spouse's insurance benefits of $159.10. The total benefit payable to her is $159.10, made up of a retirement insurance benefit of $128.10 and a spouse's insurance benefit of $31.00. If the spouse's insurance benefit is not payable for some months because of her husband's earnings, she will receive her own retirement insurance benefit of $128.10.

734.2 Could a larger benefit result if the smaller of the primary benefits were chosen?

Yes. In certain situations, e.g., the disability family maximum or the workers' compensation offset, a larger total family benefit would result if you chose the smaller of the two primary benefits.

735. WHAT HAPPENS IF A CHILD IS ENTITLED TO BENEFITS ON MORE THAN ONE EARNINGS RECORD AT THE SAME TIME?

In some cases, a child may be entitled to child's insurance benefits on more than one earnings record. In this case, the child receives benefits on only one earnings record. Usually benefits are received on the earnings record with the higher PIA. However, the child may be paid on the earnings record with the lower PIA, provided the following conditions are met:

A. The benefit on that earnings record, before reduction for the family maximum (see §731), is higher; and

B. No other beneficiaries, who are entitled on any earnings record involved, would receive a lower benefit than he or she would otherwise be paid.

736. WHEN IS A CHILD AUTOMATICALLY ENTITLED ON A SECOND EARNINGS RECORD?

A child entitled to benefits on one earnings record is automatically entitled on a second earnings record if:

A. The child is eligible for benefits on the second earnings record; and

B. The child eligible for benefits on both earnings records applies for benefits on the second earnings record.

737. FAMILY MAXIMUM WHEN CHILD IS ENTITLED ON MORE THAN ONE EARNINGS RECORD

737.1 What happens to the family maximum on the earnings record(s) on which the child is paid?

The monthly family maximum payable on the earnings record on which the child is being paid is the total of the family maximums on each of the earnings records involved. This total is subject to a combined maximum limit.

737.2 What happens to the family maximum on the earnings record(s) on which the child is entitled, but not paid?

The family maximum on the other earnings record(s) on which the child is entitled (but not paid) is based solely on that PIA.

Note: The benefits payable to the persons entitled only on the other earnings record(s) are computed as though the child were not entitled on that earnings record.

Example: Mr. and Mrs. Jones had eight children in the family group, five of whom were their natural children. The other three were Mr. Jones' stepchildren by a former marriage. Mr. Jones died and all the children and the widow became entitled on his earnings record. Mrs. Jones died shortly thereafter and her five natural children became entitled on her earnings record since it yielded the larger benefit for each (and had the higher PIA). The benefits are determined as follows:

	Original	Adjusted
Ann Day	$151.00	$100.60
Bob Day	151.00	100.60
Sid Day	151.00	100.60
Total		$301.80

	Original	Adjusted
Mary Jones	$160.50	$124.60
Peter Jones	160.50	124.60
Charles Jones	160.50	124.60
Marvel Jones	160.50	124.60
Ruth Jones	160.50	124.60
Total		$623.00

738. ROUNDING OF BENEFIT RATES

738.1 Are benefit rates rounded?

Yes. Benefit rates must be rounded.

738.2 How are benefit rates rounded?

Calculations that are not a multiple of 10 cents are rounded to the next lower multiple of 10 cents. For example, $100.18 is rounded down to $100.10.

The monthly amount payable is rounded to the next lower multiple of $1 if it is not already a multiple of $1. For example, $100.70 is rounded down to $100.

If you are entitled to Medicare, the Part B premium is deducted before rounding the monthly benefit payable to the lower multiple of $1.

739. HOW TO COMPUTE YOUR BENEFITS

For information on how to compute your benefits, see: https://www.ssa.gov/OACT/quickcalc/index.html

CHAPTER 8

Who Are Employees?

TABLE OF CONTENTS

INTRODUCTION
800. The Extent of Social Security Coverage
801. Who is an employer?

THE COMMON-LAW TEST
802. The Common-Law Test
803. Factors Which Show Control
804. Are you required to follow instructions at work?
805. Are you trained on how to do your job?
806. Are your services integrated in the business?
807. Do you personally perform your job functions?
808. Who hires, supervises, and pays assistants?
809. Is your work relationship continuing?
810. Do you have set hours at work?
811. Do you devote full time to the business?
812. Do you work on premises?
813. Do you perform your job duties in the order or sequence set by your employer?
814. Do you submit oral or written reports to your employer?
815. Are you paid at specified intervals?
816. Does your employer pay your business and traveling expenses?

817. Are you provided with tools, materials, etc., to do your job?
818. Do you invest in the facilities you use to do your job?
819. Do you have the opportunity for profit or loss?
820. Do you work for more than one person or firm at the same time?
821. Do you make your services available to the general public?
822. Can you be fired?
823. Do you have the right to end your relationship with your employer at any time?
824. Corporate Officers are Ordinarily Employees
825. What is a corporation?

EXCEPTIONS TO THE COMMON-LAW TEST
826. Certain Workers are Employees if the Common-Law Test is Not Met
827. Agent-Drivers or Commission-Drivers
828. Full Time Life Insurance Salespersons
829. Full Time Traveling or City Salespersons
830. Homeworkers
831. Are farm crew workers employees of the crew leader or the farm operator?

800. THE EXTENT OF SOCIAL SECURITY COVERAGE

800.1 Who are employees?
For Social Security purposes, you are considered an employee if:
A. You are an officer of a corporation (see §§824-825);
B. You meet the "common-law test" (see §§802-823);or
C. You are in one of the four specific occupations described in §§826-830.

800.2 Why is employment status important?
Employees and the self-employed are treated differently under the Social Security program. It is important for you to know if you are an employee or a self-employed person for Social Security purposes because your tax rate could be affected.

801. WHO IS AN EMPLOYER?
For Social Security purposes, you are an employer if you have the final authority or *right* to control workers in performing their services, including hiring, firing, and supervising. In cases of doubt, the common-law test must be applied (See §§802-823).

802. THE COMMON-LAW TEST

802.1 What is the common-law test?
Under the common-law test, the person you work for has the right to tell you what to do, how, when, and where to do your job. There are several factors, or elements, which indicate such control over the details of your work. These are discussed in §§804-823.

802.2 What if my relationship to my employer meets the common law test?
You are considered an employee if your relationship with your employer meets the common-law test. Even if your employer does not give you orders on what to do, how, when, and where to do your job, he or she only needs the *right* to do so for you to be considered an employee.

803. FACTORS WHICH SHOW CONTROL

803.1 How is evidence of control determined?
The factors, or elements, that show control over the details of work are discussed in §§804-823. These factors are weighed against and with factors that point to an employer-employee relationship or an independent

contractor status. It is important to note that *any single fact or small group of facts taken together is not necessarily evidence of control.* Determining evidence of control is based on a careful evaluation of all facts collectively.

803.2 How much weight is given to the factors of control?

The weight or amount of importance given to each factor is not always constant. Some factors are more important than others in determining evidence of control; also, the degree of importance changes by occupation. For example, some factors of control do not apply to certain occupations.

804. ARE YOU REQUIRED TO FOLLOW INSTRUCTIONS AT WORK?

If you follow instructions about when, where, and how to work, then you are ordinarily considered an employee. Instructions on how to do your job can be provided verbally or in written format (e.g., manuals and written procedures). Even if your employer does not give you specific instructions because you are a good worker and can be trusted, he or she only needs the *right* to instruct you.

805. ARE YOU TRAINED ON HOW TO DO YOUR JOB?

If you are trained by an experienced employee, then a factor of control exists. Your training shows that your employer wants you to do your job in a particular way. This is especially true if your training is provided periodically or frequently. On the other hand, independent contractors usually do their jobs using their own approach. They also are not trained by purchasers of their services.

806. ARE YOUR SERVICES INTEGRATED IN THE BUSINESS?

If your services are integrated into the business operations, a factor of control generally exists. Integration occurs when the services you perform merge with the scope and function of the business. If the job you do is critical to the success of the business you work for, you are subject to a certain amount of control by the business owner.

807. DO YOU PERSONALLY PERFORM YOUR JOB FUNCTIONS?

If you personally do your job without the use of a substitute, a factor of control exists. This shows that your employer is interested in who does the job, how the job gets done, and the results. On the other hand, if you have the right to hire a substitute without your employer's knowledge, a lack of control may exist.

808. WHO HIRES, SUPERVISES, AND PAYS ASSISTANTS?

If your employer hires, supervises, and pays assistants, control over all workers on the job generally exists. Sometimes, another worker may hire, supervise, and pay other workers at the direction of the employer. As long as the worker is acting as an employee in the capacity of a supervisor or a representative of the employer, control over workers on the job still exists. On the other hand, sometimes a worker hires, supervises, and pays other workers resulting from a contract under which materials and labor are provided for the attainment of a result. In this case, the worker is considered an independent contractor.

809. IS YOUR WORK RELATIONSHIP CONTINUING?

809.1 Does your working relationship continue with the person for whom you work?

If the working relationship continues between you and the person you work for, a factor of control generally exists. This relationship tends to indicate an employer-employee relationship.

809.2 How is an on-going working relationship determined?

If you are asked to work frequently on call or when work is made available, a continuing working relationship exists. This is true even under the following conditions:

A. Services are requested at irregular intervals;
B. Services are performed on a part-time basis;
C. Services are obtained on a seasonal basis; or
D. You only work a short time.

810. DO YOU HAVE SET HOURS AT WORK?

If your employer has established a fixed work schedule for you, a factor of control exists. In this instance, you are not able to set your own hours, which is a right of an independent contractor. In some cases, fixed hours may not be practical because of the nature of your job. As long as you are required to work at certain times, an element of control still exists.

811. DO YOU DEVOTE FULL TIME TO THE BUSINESS?

811.1 Do you work full time for the business of your employer?

If you work full time for your employer, a factor of control exists. Since your employer has control over the amount of time you spend working, you are restricted from doing other gainful work. On the other hand, an independent contractor can choose for whom to work and when to work.

811.2 What does full time work mean?

Full time does not necessarily mean an eight-hour work day or a five-day work week. The meaning of "full time" may vary by the nature of your job, the customs where you live, and your intentions as well as those of your employer.

811.3 What if there is no verbal or written agreement specifying full time employment?

Although you may not have a formal agreement, full-time services may be required of you. For example, some workers are not contractually permitted to work for anyone else. Another example is a worker who has to meet a production minimum. This production minimum may require that the worker devote all working hours to the business. In the previous examples, the workers are considered full time employees.

812. DO YOU WORK ON PREMISES?

812.1 Do you work on your employer's premises?

If you work at your employer's place of business, it is implied that your employer has control. This is especially true if the type of work you do could be done elsewhere. Working at the employer's place of business places you under your employer's direction and supervision.

812.2 Do you work off your employer's premises?

Even if you do not work on your employer's premises, it does not necessarily mean that you are not an employee. Some occupations require services to be performed off premises. For example, employees of construction contractors must work off premises to perform their job duties.

813. DO YOU PERFORM YOUR JOB DUTIES IN THE ORDER OR SEQUENCE SET BY YOUR EMPLOYER?

If you carry out your job duties in the order set by your employer, a factor of control exists. In this circumstance, you are not free to follow your own pattern of work. Instead, you must follow the established routines and schedules of your employer. Even if your employer does not set the order of your job tasks, he or she only needs the *right* to do so for control to exist.

814. DO YOU SUBMIT ORAL OR WRITTEN REPORTS TO YOUR EMPLOYER?

If you submit oral or written reports, a factor of control exists. The submission of reports shows that you are required to account for your actions.

815. ARE YOU PAID AT SPECIFIED INTERVALS?

815.1 Are you paid by the hour, week, or month?

If you are paid at regular intervals, a factor of control exists. In addition, if you are guaranteed a minimum salary, or if you are compensated through a drawing account (provided that you are not required to repay earnings in excess of your approved draw), an employer-employee relationship tends to exist.

815.2 Are you paid by the job?

If you are paid by commission or on a job basis, you are likely an independent contractor. Payment by the job includes a lump sum. This lump sum is normally computed by the number of hours worked against a fixed rate per hour. The lump sum payment may be broken out into weekly or monthly installments if this method of payment is convenient for a particular job.

816. DOES YOUR EMPLOYER PAY YOUR BUSINESS AND TRAVELING EXPENSES?

If your employer pays your business and traveling expenses, a factor of control exists. On the other hand, a lack of control may exist if you are paid on a job basis and you are responsible for business and traveling expenses.

817. ARE YOU PROVIDED WITH TOOLS, MATERIALS, ETC., TO DO YOUR JOB?

If your employer furnishes the various materials needed to do your job, a factor of control exists. On the other hand, furnishing your own tools, materials, and equipment may indicate a lack of control, unless it is common for employees in your field to use their own hand tools.

818. DO YOU INVEST IN THE FACILITIES YOU USE TO DO YOUR JOB?

Facilities generally include the equipment or premises necessary for work. If your employer provides all necessary facilities, you are generally considered an employee. On the other hand, if you invest in the equipment and premises necessary for work, you tend to be an independent contractor. Note that the tools, instruments, clothing, etc. that you may provide as a common practice in your particular field is not considered an investment in facilities.

819. DO YOU HAVE THE OPPORTUNITY FOR PROFIT OR LOSS?

819.1 Are you in a position to realize a profit or suffer a loss resulting from your services?
If you have an opportunity for profit or loss resulting from your services, we generally consider you an independent contractor. If you are not in such a position, you are likely to be an employee.

819.2 How do you establish the opportunity for profit or loss?
You may establish the opportunity for profit or loss by various circumstances. Examples of such circumstances are when someone:
A. Hires, directs, and pays assistants;
B. Has his or her own office, equipment, materials, or facilities to do the work;
C. Has continuing and recurring liabilities or obligations;
D. Succeeds or fails depending on the relation of receipts to expenses;
E. Agrees to perform specific jobs for prices agreed upon in advance;
F. Pays expenses incurred in connection with work performed; and
G. Performs services, or pays assistants to perform services, which establish or affect his or her business reputation, but not the reputation of those who purchase the services.

820. DO YOU WORK FOR MORE THAN ONE PERSON OR FIRM AT THE SAME TIME?
Independent contractors usually work for a number of people or firms at the same time. As an independent contractor, you are free from control by the people and firms for which you work. However, a person who works for several people or firms may still be an employee of one or all of them if he or she works under the control of each firm.

821. DO YOU MAKE YOUR SERVICES AVAILABLE TO THE GENERAL PUBLIC?
If the services you perform are made available to the general public, you are usually considered an independent contractor. Services are made

available to the general public by independent contractors in a variety of ways:

A. They may have their own office and assistants;
B. They may hang out a "shingle" in front of their home or office;
C. They may hold business licenses;
D. They may be listed in business directories;
E. They may maintain business listings in telephone directories; or
F. They may advertise in newspapers, trade journals, magazines, etc.

822. CAN YOU BE FIRED?

822.1 Does your employer have the right to fire you?

If your employer has the right to fire you, a factor of control exists, indicating an employer-employee relationship. On the other hand, independent contractors cannot be fired provided that they meet their contractual requirements.

822.2 Do labor union restrictions on firing affect the employer-employee relationship?

Sometimes an employer's right to fire is restricted because of a contract with a labor union. This restriction does not affect the existence of an employment relationship.

823. DO YOU HAVE THE RIGHT TO END YOUR RELATIONSHIP WITH YOUR EMPLOYER AT ANY TIME?

If you can end the relationship with your employer at any time without liability, you are generally considered an employee. An independent contractor usually agrees to complete a specific job before ending the work relationship. An independent contractor is also personally and legally responsible for satisfactory completion of the job.

824. CORPORATE OFFICERS ARE ORDINARILY EMPLOYEES

824.1 Are corporate officers employees of the corporation?

Yes. If you are a corporate officer, you are normally considered an employee of the corporation.

824.2 Are directors employees of the corporation?

If you are the director of a corporation, you are *self-employed* for any service you perform as director.

824.3 What if a director performs non-directorial services?

If you perform services outside the scope of your role as director, then you are considered an employee of the corporation for those services.

825. WHAT IS A CORPORATION?

825.1 How do we define a corporation?

A corporation is a business entity. Corporations are formed under state corporation laws and are subject to corporate income tax at the federal and state level. Other corporations may be formed as limited liability companies under state law, but elect to be treated as corporations for federal tax purposes. When the ownership of a corporation rests in a few persons, a few families, or within a family, the corporation is generally designated as a close or family corporation.

825.2 Forming a Corporation

The rules you must use to determine whether a business is a corporation changed for businesses formed after 1996. A business formed before 1997 and treated as a corporation under the old rules will generally continue to be treated as a corporation. The IRS and SSA treat the following businesses formed after 1996 as corporations:

- A business formed under a federal or state law that refers to it as a corporation, body corporate, or body politic;
- A business formed under a state law that refers to it as a joint-stock company or joint-stock association;
- An insurance company;
- Certain banks;
- A business wholly owned by a state or local government;
- A business specifically required to be taxed as a corporation by the Internal Revenue Code (for example, certain publicly traded partnerships);
- Certain foreign businesses; and
- Any other business that elects to be taxed as a corporation (for example, an LLC which elects corporate treatment).

See IRS Publication 542, Corporations for more information.

826. CERTAIN WORKERS ARE EMPLOYEES IF THE COMMON-LAW TEST IS NOT MET

826.1 Are you considered an employee even if you do not meet the common law test?

If you work in one of the four occupational groups set out in §§827-830, you are an employee for Social Security purposes even if you do not meet the common-law test as long as:

A. Your work contract expects that you will do mostly all of the work;
B. You have no substantial investment in the facilities used to do your work (except for tools, equipment, transportation, or clothing employees usually provide); and
C. You have an on-going work relationship with the person for whom you work.

826.2 Does it matter if the work contract is oral versus written?

No. The contract of service may be oral or written. The important issue in the contract is that you have no authority to delegate a substantial amount of your work to another person. However, there are cases where you might occasionally hire a substitute or assistant and still be an employee under this test. What is important is that it is intended that you perform the essential services of your job.

826.3 What does it mean to have a substantial investment in facilities?

A substantial investment in facilities would be the investment of items such as office furniture, fixtures, premises, and machinery. A salesperson who maintains a home office may not have substantial investment; however, a salesperson with an office elsewhere would be considered to have a substantial investment in facilities.

826.4 Are items workers have or use to do their jobs considered an investment in facilities?

Your investment in your education, training, tools, instruments, clothes, or vehicle (used to go to and from work) are not considered a substantial investment in facilities.

826.5 What is meant by an on-going work relationship?

You have an on-going work relationship if you work regularly and frequently for your employer. Regular part-time work and regular seasonal work are considered on-going. On the other hand, a single job transaction, even if it covers a considerable period of time, is usually not part of an on-going relationship.

827. AGENT-DRIVERS OR COMMISSION-DRIVERS

827.1 Are agent-drivers or commission-drivers employees?

If you meet the requirements in §826 and distribute any of the following items, you are considered an employee:

A. Meat or meat products;
B. Vegetables or vegetable products;
C. Fruit or fruit products;
D. Bakery products;
E. Beverages (other than milk); or
F. Laundry or dry cleaned clothing.

827.2 When are agent-drivers or commission-drivers NOT employees?

You must perform the services for the person engaging them to be considered an employee. If you buy merchandise on your own behalf and sell it to the public as part of your own independent business, you are not considered an employee. In addition, if you distribute items that are not incidental to handling items (A) - (F) above, you are not considered an employee.

827.3 Does how the driver operates affect employee status?

Several factors do not affect your employee status as an agent-driver or commission-driver:

A. You may sell at wholesale or retail;
B. You may operate from your own truck or from a company truck;
C. You may serve customers designated by the company or solicit your own;
D. You may distribute other products provided that the handling of these products is incidental to the handling of items A - F above; and
E. You may be compensated in any manner. How you are compensated is immaterial.

828. FULL TIME LIFE INSURANCE SALESPERSONS

828.1 Are full time life insurance salespersons employees?
You are considered an employee if you:
A. Meet the requirements in §826;
B. Solicit life insurance or annuity contracts as your entire or principal business activity; and
C. Work primarily for one life insurance company.

You should be provided with office space, stenographic help, telephone facilities, form, rate books, and advertising materials by the company or general agent.

828.2 Is the employment contract important?
Generally, the employment contract reflects the intention of you and the company regarding "full-time" work. How much time you spend working is not important. What is important is the contractual intent of full-time work. You may work regularly only a few hours a day yet still qualify as a full-time life insurance salesperson if your contract intends that you engage in full-time activity.

828.3 What does it mean to be a principal business activity?
A "principal business activity" takes the major part of a salesperson's working time and attention. This means that your efforts must be devoted primarily to the solicitation of life insurance or annuity contracts. Occasional or incidental sales of other types of insurance (e.g., surplus-line insurance) do not affect this requirement. On the other hand, if you are required to work substantially on selling applications for insurance contracts other than life insurance (e.g., health, accident, fire, etc.), you do not meet the requirement.

829. FULL TIME TRAVELING OR CITY SALESPERSONS

829.1 Are full time traveling or city salespersons employees?
You are considered an employee if you:
A. Meet the requirements in §826;
B. Solicit orders for merchandise on behalf of another person or firm as your principal activity;
C. Obtain your orders from businesses whose primary function is the furnishing of food and/or lodging (e.g., wholesalers, retailers, contractors, hotel and restaurant operators); and

D. Sell merchandise that is bought for resale or use as supplies in your customer's business operations.

"Full-time" means that you work primarily for one person or business. It does not matter how much time you spend on the job.

829.2 What types of salespersons are NOT considered employees?

Manufacturers representatives and multiple-line salespersons that work for a number of firms are usually not considered employees.

830. HOMEWORKERS

830.1 Are homeworkers employees?

You are considered an employee if you:
A. Meet the requirements in §826;
B. Work away from the employer's place of business;
C. Work according to your employer's guidelines;
D. Work on material or goods provided by your employer; and
E. Return the finished product to your employer or to someone whom your employer designates.

830.2 What type of worker is considered a homeworker?

Homeworkers include people who make quilts, buttons, globes, bedspreads, clothing, needlecraft products, etc. Homeworkers usually work in their own homes or in a workshop away from their employer's business. The type of work homeworkers do is usually simple and consists of following patterns or samples provided by the employer.

830.3 How is compensation computed for Social Security purposes?

If you receive wages less than $100 in a calendar year (the cash-pay test) from your employer, your pay is not counted for Social Security purposes. However, all of your pay is counted in applying the earnings test to a beneficiary, even if you do not meet the cash-pay test. If you do meet the cash-pay test, all of your pay is counted for benefits and the earnings test. (See §1303.)

831. ARE FARM CREW WORKERS EMPLOYEES OF THE CREW LEADER OR THE FARM OPERATOR?

Farm crew workers are employees of the crew leader if the crew leader:
A. Arranges with the farm operator to provide workers;
B. Pays the workers either on his or her own behalf or on behalf of the farm operator; and

C. Is not the farm operator's employee in a written agreement with the farm operator.

If items (A) - (C) above are met, the crew leader is self-employed. He or she is responsible for the payment of employment taxes and for reporting the farm crew workers for Social Security purposes.

If an agreement has been entered into in writing that the crew leader is an employee of the farm operator, all crew members are also *employees of the farm operator*. If the crew leader does not pay the workers and has not entered into a written agreement, the common-law test (see §§802-823) is applied. The common-law test determines the identity of the employer of the workers and the status of the crew leader.

Chapter 9
Special Coverage Provisions

TABLE OF CONTENTS

900. Does Social Security cover most types of work?
901. Is agricultural labor covered by Social Security?
902. How is the cash-pay test applied?
903. What is a farm?
904. What types of farm work are considered agricultural labor?
905. What are "agricultural and horticultural commodities"?
906. What types of work include cultivating, raising, and harvesting?
907. What types of work are not considered "raising"?
908. What types of work are considered "harvesting"?
909. What types of work are considered "agricultural labor"?
910. Is work performed in crude gum production covered by Social Security?
911. Is work performed in connection with cotton ginning covered by Social Security?
912. Work In Connection With Waterways, Ditches, Etc.
913. Processing or Packaging of Agricultural Commodities
914. Are services performed by foreign agricultural workers in the U.S. covered by Social Security?
915. Domestic Service in Private Home of Employer
916. Domestic Service Defined
917. Private Home Defined

918. Special Provision for Reporting Wages Paid to Domestics
919. Is domestic service performed by a student for a college club, fraternity, or sorority covered by Social Security?
920. Local College Club Defined
921. Service Performed by a Student For a School, College, or University
922. Is work performed by a student nurse covered by Social Security?
923. Is work performed as an intern for a hospital covered by Social Security?
924. Employment Not In The Course Of The Employer's Trade Or Business
925. Work Not in the Course of the Employer's Trade or Business — Defined
926. What types of family employment are not covered by Social Security?
927. Is domestic work performed by a parent for a son or daughter covered by Social Security?
928. What are the types of family employment covered by Social Security?
929. Delivering or Distributing Newspapers
930. Are services performed by vendors of newspapers and magazines covered by Social Security?
931. Work for Nonprofit Religious, Charitable, Educational, etc. Institutions
932. Ministers and Members of Religious Orders
933. How is work that is not in the exercise of the ministry treated for Social Security purposes?
934. What is an "ordained", "commissioned", or "licensed" minister?
935. What does "exercise of the ministry" mean?
936. Are services performed by crews on fishing boats covered by Social Security?
937. Employment for a Foreign Government, International Organization, or Instrumentality of a Foreign Government

938. Is work performed by U.S. citizens working in the U.S. as employees of foreign governments covered by Social Security?
939. Foreign Students, Exchange Visitors and International Cultural Exchange Visitors
940. Employment as Civilian for the U.S. Government
941. Are services performed by employees for the District of Columbia covered by Social Security?
942. Are services performed under Federally sponsored economic and human development programs covered by Social Security?
943. Is work as a volunteer or volunteer leader in the Peace Corps covered by Social Security?
944. Are services performed by Job Corps enrollees covered by Social Security?
945. Is work performed for community service programs for older Americans covered by Social Security?
946. Are services performed by students enrolled in a work-study program covered by Social Security?
947. Volunteers in Service to America (VISTA) Program
948. Member of the U.S. Uniformed Service
949. Definition of Member of a Uniformed Service
950. What does "active duty" mean?
951. What does "active duty for training" mean?
952. How are the amount of wages and the period of military service determined?
953. Deemed Wage Credits After 1956
954. Noncontributory Wage Credits Based on Military Service Before 1957
955. Definition of Military or Naval Service of the U.S.
956. Effect of Discharge Under Dishonorable Conditions
957. Are noncontributory wage credits granted for military service with a foreign country?
958. Are officers of the National Oceanic and Atmospheric Administration or the Public Health Service considered members of the Armed Forces?

959. Under what circumstances are veterans NOT eligible for non-contributory wage credits?
960. When is a deceased World War II veteran fully insured for Social Security Purposes?
961. Employment Outside The U.S.
962. Who can be considered an American employer?
963. Is work by a U.S. citizen for foreign affiliates outside the U.S. covered by Social Security?
964. What is a "foreign affiliate"?
965. Agreement to Cover Foreign Affiliates
966. Is work performed for private employers of Guam and American Samoa covered by Social Security?
967. Is work covered by the Railroad Retirement Act covered by Social Security?
968. The Included-Excluded Rule
969. When does the included-excluded rule NOT apply?
970. How do international Social Security agreements affect coverage?
971. Are services performed by employees of The Commonwealth of the North Mariana Islands (CNMI) covered by Social Security?

900. DOES SOCIAL SECURITY COVER MOST TYPES OF WORK?

Most types of employment in the U.S. are covered by Social Security. Some work, however, is specifically excluded by the law. Other types of work are covered only under certain conditions. This Chapter explains what employment is not covered by Social Security and what conditions must be met before certain types of employment otherwise excluded can be covered. The special coverage provisions for employment for State and local governments are explained in Chapter 10.

901. IS AGRICULTURAL LABOR COVERED BY SOCIAL SECURITY?

Most types of agricultural labor are covered by Social Security. However, only cash pay (as defined in §1303) for your farm work is counted as wages for Social Security purposes, and only if either:

A. The cash pay was paid to you by your employer whose expenditures for agricultural labor are $2,500 or more; or

B. The cash pay paid to you in a calendar year for agricultural labor by one employer amounts to $150 or more (the cash-pay test) if your employer spends less than $2,500 in the year for agricultural labor.

See SSA's electronic fact sheet "If You Are a Farm Worker," Publication No. 05-10074 at: https://www.ssa.gov/pubs/EN-05-10074.pdf.

902. HOW IS THE CASH-PAY TEST APPLIED?

In applying the cash-pay test, payments are credited as wages for Social Security purposes at the time your wages were *paid*. Therefore, if you were paid $150 in 1980 for agricultural labor, the entire $150 is counted as wages for 1980, even though part or all of the work may have been done in 1979.

903. WHAT IS A FARM?

A "farm" includes:
- dairy
- fruit
- fur-bearing animal farms
- lands
- nurseries
- orchards
- plantations
- poultry

- ranches
- ranges
- truck farms
- stock

The term also includes greenhouses (except those used primarily for display or storage purposes or for making wreaths or bouquets) and other similar structures that are used primarily for the raising of agricultural or horticultural commodities.

904. WHAT TYPES OF FARM WORK ARE CONSIDERED AGRICULTURAL LABOR?

If you do agricultural labor on a farm, your services are covered by Social Security if your work is performed in connection with:

A. Cultivating the soil; or

B. Raising or harvesting any agricultural or horticultural commodity (this includes the raising, shearing, feeding, caring for, training and/or management of livestock, bees, poultry, and fur-bearing animals and wildlife).

905. WHAT ARE "AGRICULTURAL AND HORTICULTURAL COMMODITIES"?

Agricultural or horticultural commodities raised for sale or for home use include:

A. Food crops (such as nuts, fruits, mushrooms, vegetables, and grain);

B. Flowers, cut flowers, trees, and shrubbery;

C. Animal feed or bedding, grass, vegetable, and cereal seed; and

D. Other crops (such as flax, cotton, tobacco, tung nuts, and medicinal herbs raised for sale or for home use.)

906. WHAT TYPES OF WORK INCLUDE CULTIVATING, RAISING, AND HARVESTING?

Cultivating, raising, and harvesting may include the following:

A. The actual cultivation of the soil;

B. The raising or harvesting of a commodity; or

C. An activity, such as irrigating crops, cutting of top soil, spraying or dusting, that is done in connection with such operations.

907. WHAT TYPES OF WORK ARE NOT CONSIDERED "RAISING"?

The term "raising" does not include service in potting, watering, heeling, or otherwise caring for trees, shrubbery, plants, etc., that are purchased in salable condition for the purpose of quick resale. However, if you keep these commodities long enough for them to grow and appreciate, the work in caring for them is agricultural labor.

908. WHAT TYPES OF WORK ARE CONSIDERED "HARVESTING"?

The term "harvesting" includes work usually performed as part of harvesting, such as: baling hay, shredding fodder, shucking and shelling corn, baling flax straw, hulling almonds, coarse grinding of alfalfa, and threshing small grains before storage. Horticultural commodities such as flowers, trees, shrubbery, and plants are harvested when they are taken up for sale or storage.

909. WHAT TYPES OF WORK ARE CONSIDERED "AGRICULTURAL LABOR"?

"Agricultural labor" is work performed with the operation, management, conservation, improvement, or maintenance of a farm and its tools and equipment. Salvaging timber or clearing land of brush and other debris left by a hurricane is also agricultural labor. The following conditions are required for work to be considered agricultural labor:

A. You must work in the employ of the owner, tenant, or other operator of the farm; and

B. The major part of your work is done on the farm.

Note: Work done in the wholesaling or retailing of raw or unmanufactured farm products (including displaying, actual selling, collecting, and depositing of sales receipts and the clerical and other work in connection with the selling of the products) is agricultural labor if the farm operator raised over one-half of the products sold, and the major part of the work is done on a farm.

910. IS WORK PERFORMED IN CRUDE GUM PRODUCTION COVERED BY SOCIAL SECURITY?

Crude gum production involves producing and harvesting crude gum from a tree, and processing crude gum into gum spirits of turpentine and gum rosin by the original producer of the crude gum. If you perform this type of work, you are covered by Social Security.

911. IS WORK PERFORMED IN CONNECTION WITH COTTON GINNING COVERED BY SOCIAL SECURITY?

Work done in connection with cotton ginning is agricultural labor. Therefore, it is covered by Social Security.

912. WORK IN CONNECTION WITH WATERWAYS, DITCHES, ETC.

912.1 Is work performed in connection with the normal upkeep of an existing water system covered by Social Security?

Work you do in connection with the ordinary upkeep, repair, and replacement of an *existing water system* is agricultural labor. Therefore, it is covered by Social Security provided that the waterways, ditches, canals, etc.:

A. Are not owned or operated for profit; and

B. Are used exclusively for supplying or storing water for farm purposes.

912.2 What if work is done in connection with a new water system. Is it covered by Social Security also?

Work you do in connection with the construction of a *new system or the extension of an existing system* is not agricultural labor. These services are not covered by Social Security.

913. PROCESSING OR PACKAGING OF AGRICULTURAL COMMODITIES

913.1 Is processing or packaging of an agricultural commodity covered by Social Security?

Work in connection with the processing or packaging of any agricultural commodity in its raw or unmanufactured state is covered by Social Security as agricultural labor if:

A. The work is not performed in connection with the commercial canning or freezing of the commodity;

B. The work is not performed after the delivery of the commodity to a terminal market for distribution for consumption; and

C. The work is performed in the employ of:
   1. A farm operator who produced more than one-half of the agricultural commodity being processed or packaged in a pay period; or
   2. An unincorporated group of farm operators who:
      1. Do not number more than 20 at any time during the calendar quarter, before 1978, in which the work was performed, or, after 1977, during the calendar year in which the work is performed;
      2. Are not a farmers' cooperative; and
      3. Produce the entire agricultural commodity being processed or packaged in a pay period.

913.2 Is the work involved in getting commodities to market covered by Social Security?

Activities performed to get commodities to market include: handling, planting, drying, packing, packaging, processing, freezing, grading, storing, or delivering to storage or to market or to a carrier for transportation to market. If you perform such activities in connection with an agricultural or horticultural commodity, the work you do is considered agricultural labor if the conditions in (A)-(C) above apply.

913.3 What if work changes a commodity from its raw or natural state?

If you process commodities in such a way that the work you perform changes them from their raw or natural state, the work you do is not agricultural labor. Likewise, any work you perform on a commodity after it has been changed from its raw or natural state is not agricultural labor.

914. ARE SERVICES PERFORMED BY FOREIGN AGRICULTURAL WORKERS IN THE U.S. COVERED BY SOCIAL SECURITY?

Your services are not covered by Social Security if you are a foreign worker lawfully admitted to the U.S. on a temporary basis to perform agricultural work.

915. DOMESTIC SERVICE IN PRIVATE HOME OF EMPLOYER

915.1 Is domestic service covered by Social Security?

Domestic service in the private home of the employer is covered by Social Security beginning January 1, 1951. However, cash (as defined in §1303) and non-cash remuneration is excluded from wages unless a regularity-of-employment and cash-pay test are met. Prior to 1994, only the cash pay paid to the domestic worker in the calendar quarter by the employer amounting to $50 or more counts for Social Security purposes.

915.2 What is the minimum amount that must be earned for domestic work to be covered by Social Security?

Beginning in 1994, rules for coverage of domestic services performed in the private home changed. The table below shows the minimum amount you must earn for Social Security purposes.

Calendar Year	Minimum Cash Pay
1998-1999	$1,100
2000	$1,200
2001-2002	$1,300
2003-2005	$1,400
2006-2007	$1,500
2008	$1,600
2009-2011	$1,700
2012-2013	$1,800
2014	$1,900
2015	$1,900
2016–2017	$2,000
2018–2019	$2,100
2020	$2,200
2021	$2,300
2022	$2,400
2023	$2,600
2024	$2,700

For calendar years after 1998, the earnings threshold will adjust in multiples of $100 in a given year, as average wages adjust. See SSA's electronic fact sheet on household workers, Publication No. 05-10021 for the current earnings threshold.

915.3 What if the domestic worker is under age 18?

Beginning in 1995, your services are excluded from Social Security coverage for any portion of a year that you work in a private home while you are under 18 years old. However, your services may be covered by Social Security if the service is your principle occupation.

915.4 How does the cash-pay test apply if the domestic worker has more than one employer?

If you perform domestic services for more than one employer, the cash-pay test applies separately to the cash pay paid by each employer. You cannot combine cash payments for a calendar quarter or a calendar year from various employers.

915.5 How is domestic service on a farm considered for Social Security purposes?

Your domestic service on a farm operated for profit is considered "agricultural labor" *for services rendered prior to 1995.* The agricultural labor cash-pay test, described in §900, must be met before cash wages paid for your employment can be considered covered for Social Security purposes.

Beginning in 1995, domestic work on a farm operated for profit is no longer treated as agricultural employment. You are subject to a new domestic threshold.

916. DOMESTIC SERVICE DEFINED

916.1 What does domestic service mean?

"Domestic service" means work normally performed as an essential part of household duties. Domestic service contributes to the maintenance of the employer's residence or administers to the personal wants and comforts of the employer, other members of the household, and guests.

916.2 What kind of work is included under domestic service?

In general, domestic service includes work performed by:
- baby sitters
- butlers
- caretakers
- chauffeurs of family automobiles
- companions
- cooks
- footmen
- furnace men
- gardeners
- governesses
- grooms
- handymen
- housekeepers
- housemen
- janitors
- laundresses
- maids
- nursemaids
- seamstresses
- valets
- waiters
- waitresses
- watchmen

917. PRIVATE HOME DEFINED

917.1 What is a private home?

A "private home" is the fixed place of residence of one or more people. Any shelter used as a dwelling may, depending on the circumstances, be considered as a private home. For example, a tent, boat, trailer, or a room or suite in a hospital, hotel, sanatorium or nursing home may all be considered private homes. A cooperative boarding and lodging facility may be a private home. Company-operated facilities are *not* private homes.

917.2 Is an apartment house considered a private home?

In an apartment house, each apartment together with its private stairways, halls, and porches, etc. is a private home. Parts of the premises devoted to common use, such as the office, furnace-room, lawns, public stairways, halls, and porches are not a part of the private home.

917.3 Is a house used for room and board considered a private home?

If a house is used mainly as a commercial rooming or boarding house, only that part of the house that is used as the operator's living quarters is considered to be a private home.

917.4 Do domestic workers who work in a property being rented as a private home work in the private home of the employer?

If you are a domestic worker employed by landlords or rental agencies to do work in or about property being rented as a private home, you are not performing work in the private home of the employer.

918. SPECIAL PROVISION FOR REPORTING WAGES PAID TO DOMESTICS

918.1 Are there special provisions for domestic employees for reporting wages?

For Social Security tax reporting purposes only, your cash wages paid for domestic service in the private home of your employer may be rounded to the nearest dollar. This simplifies computation of the Social Security tax. For example, you are paid daily and your cash pay is $22.50, your payment is considered $23 for reporting purposes. Similarly, a payment amounting to $22.49 is reduced to $22. Also rounding to the nearest dollar is permitted if you are paid on a weekly, semimonthly, or monthly basis.

918.2 Does the rounding method need to be applied consistently?

Yes. If you use the rounding method of reporting for any pay period in a calendar quarter, you must use it consistently throughout the calendar quarter.

919. IS DOMESTIC SERVICE PERFORMED BY A STUDENT FOR A COLLEGE CLUB, FRATERNITY, OR SORORITY COVERED BY SOCIAL SECURITY?

If you are a student performing domestic service for a local college club, fraternity, or sorority, your services are not covered by Social Security if:

A. You perform the domestic service in or about the club rooms or house; and

B. You are enrolled in a school, college, or university and you regularly attend classes there.

920. LOCAL COLLEGE CLUB DEFINED

920.1 What is a local college club?

A "local college club" is made up of members who are mainly students enrolled in the college, or people directly connected with the college. The membership of a local chapter of a college fraternity or sorority must be composed mostly of students enrolled in the college. However, the fact that a local college club or local chapter of a college fraternity or sorority has some alumni or faculty members is immaterial.

920.2 Is an alumni club or alumni chapter considered a college club?

No. An alumni club or alumni chapter of a fraternity or sorority is not considered a college club or chapter.

921. SERVICE PERFORMED BY A STUDENT FOR A SCHOOL, COLLEGE, OR UNIVERSITY

921.1 Is work done by a student for a school, college, or university covered by Social Security?

If you are a student working for a school, college, or university, you are not covered by Social Security provided that:

A. You are enrolled at the school, college, or university where you are working; and

B. You are regularly attending classes. (See §1002)

For application of this rule to students enrolled in Work-Study Programs, see §946.)

921.2 Is work done by a student after 1972 for a private, nonprofit auxiliary organization of a school, college, or university covered by Social Security?

If you are a student working for a private, nonprofit auxiliary organization of your school, college, or university after 1972, your services are not covered by Social Security provided you meet the conditions of (A) and (B) above. Also, the auxiliary organization must be:

A. Organized and operated for the benefit of, to perform the functions of, or to carry out the purposes of the school, college, or university;

B. Operated, supervised, or controlled by or in connection with the school, college, or university; and

C. Operated by a State or local government, unless the terms of the agreement between the State and the Social Security Administration cover the services performed by its student employees.

922. IS WORK PERFORMED BY A STUDENT NURSE COVERED BY SOCIAL SECURITY?

Beginning January 1, 1940, your work as a student nurse for hospital or nurses' training school is not covered by Social Security, provided that:

A. You are enrolled at the hospital or nurses' training school;

B. You are regularly attending classes; and

C. The hospital or nurses' training school is chartered or approved under State law.

Your work is excluded from coverage although the work of other employees of the hospital or nurses' training school is covered by Social Security. (See §1002)

923. IS WORK PERFORMED AS AN INTERN FOR A HOSPITAL COVERED BY SOCIAL SECURITY?

If you work as an intern for a hospital, your services may or may not be covered by Social Security depending upon the type of hospital for which you work:

A. If you work for a *privately owned and operated hospital*, then your services are covered by Social Security (see §931);

B. If you work for a *Federal hospital*, then your services are covered on the same basis as the work of other Federal employees; or

C. If you work for a *State or local government hospital*, your coverage depends on whether your position is in a group covered by the Federal-State Section 218 agreement. If your position is covered by the

Federal-State Section 218 agreement, your services are covered. If your position is not covered by a Section 218 agreement, you are subject to the rules of coverage under Section 210 of the Social Security Act. (See §1000 for information on a Section 218 agreement).

924. EMPLOYMENT NOT IN THE COURSE OF THE EMPLOYER'S TRADE OR BUSINESS

924.1 Is non-business work covered by Social Security?

Work done that is not in the course of your employer's trade or business (non-business work) may be covered by Social Security. Only cash pay (as defined in §1303) for this type of work may be counted for Social Security purposes. Also, you must be paid at least $100 in a calendar year to be considered for coverage.

924.2 How is the cash-pay test applied if work is done for more than one employer?

If you do non-business work for more than one employer, then apply the cash-pay test individually to the cash pay from each of your employers.

924.3 Is non-business work on a farm covered by Social Security?

Non-business work on a farm operated for profit is considered agricultural labor. You must meet the agricultural labor cash-pay test set out in §901 before your cash wages can be counted for Social Security purposes.

925. WORK NOT IN THE COURSE OF THE EMPLOYER'S TRADE OR BUSINESS — DEFINED

925.1 What is non-business work?

Non-business work is "work not in the course of the employer's trade or business." Any type of work that does not promote or advance the business of your employer is non-business work. For example, work relating to your employer's hobby or recreational activities, or work repairing your employer's private home would be considered non-business work.

925.2 Can work for a corporation be considered non-business work?

No. Any work you do for a corporation can never be considered non-business work or, "work not in the course of the employer's trade or business."

926. WHAT TYPES OF FAMILY EMPLOYMENT ARE NOT COVERED BY SOCIAL SECURITY?

Some types of family employment are not covered by Social Security. Your services are not covered by Social Security if you meet any of the following conditions. You are:

A. A child under age 18 working for your parent(s) (beginning January 1, 1988);

Note: Prior to January 1, 1988, a child, under age 21, in the employ of a parent.

B. A child age 18 to 21 working for your parent(s), but not performing work in the course of your parent's trade or business (beginning January 1, 1988);

C. A husband working for your wife, but not performing work in the course of your wife's trade or business (beginning January 1, 1988);

D. A wife working for your husband, but not performing services in the course of your husband's trade or business (beginning January 1, 1988); or

E. A parent working for your son or daughter performing:
   1. Domestic service in or about the private home of your son or daughter (see §927 for exception); or
   2. Work not in the course of your son's or daughter's trade or business.

927. IS DOMESTIC WORK PERFORMED BY A PARENT FOR A SON OR DAUGHTER COVERED BY SOCIAL SECURITY?

Beginning January 1, 1968, your services are covered by Social Security if you are a parent performing domestic service for your son or daughter in or about his or her private home, and:

A. There is a genuine employment relationship between you and your son or daughter;

B. Your son or daughter has a child living in his or her private home who is either: (1) under age 18; or (2) if older than 18, has a mental or physical condition requiring personal care and supervision by an adult. Adult care and supervision must be needed for at least four continuous weeks in the calendar quarter in which you perform domestic service; and

C. Your son or daughter is either:
   1. A widow or widower;
   2. Divorced and has not remarried; or
   3. Has a spouse living in the home that has a physical or mental condition that renders him or her incapable of taking care of the child. Adult care and supervision must be needed for at least four continuous weeks in the calendar quarter in which you perform domestic service.

Note: The term "child" includes a natural child, an adopted child, a stepchild, or a foster child.

928. WHAT ARE THE TYPES OF FAMILY EMPLOYMENT COVERED BY SOCIAL SECURITY?

The family employment exclusion does not apply to work you perform for either:

A. A corporation or an association classifiable as a corporation. This is true even though the relationship set out in §926(A), (B), (C), or (D) exists between you and the person or persons controlling the corporation; or

B. A partnership, unless the relationship in §926(A) exists between you and each of the partners.

929. DELIVERING OR DISTRIBUTING NEWSPAPERS

929.1 What are newspapers and shopping news?

"Newspapers or shopping news" includes news publications, shopping guides, handbills, and other types of advertising material.

929.2 What does delivery or distribution mean?

"Delivery or distribution" means retail sale, house-to-house delivery, or the passing out of handbills on the street.

929.3 Are services performed by newspaper deliverers covered by Social Security?

Effective January 1, 1996, your services are not covered by Social Security if you deliver or distribute newspapers or shopping news. You are considered a direct seller and your payment constitutes earnings from self-employment. See §1135.2 for further information on the treatment of these earnings as self-employment income. This exclusion does not apply to the delivery or distribution of magazines.

929.4 When were newspaper delivery services excluded from Social Security coverage prior to 1996?

Prior to January 1, 1996, newspaper delivery services were excluded from Social Security coverage if:

A. The work was performed as an employee and the person was under age 18; and

B. The material was delivered or distributed to the ultimate consumer and not to a point from which later distribution or delivery was made.

This exclusion does not apply to the delivery or distribution of magazines.

930. ARE SERVICES PERFORMED BY VENDORS OF NEWSPAPERS AND MAGAZINES COVERED BY SOCIAL SECURITY?

If you sell newspapers or magazines, your services are not covered by Social Security if:

A. The magazines or newspapers are sold:
  1. To the ultimate consumer; and
  2. At an arranged fixed price; and

B. Your pay is the difference between the fixed selling price of the newspapers or magazines and the amount at which they are charged to you whether or not:
  1. You are guaranteed a minimum wage for your services; or
  2. You are entitled credit for any unsold newspapers or magazines which are turned back.

If you are age 18 or over, your work is covered by Social Security as "self-employment" under a special provision of the law.

If you are under age 18 and you work in an independent capacity and not as an employee, the work may be covered by Social Security as self-employment.

931. WORK FOR NONPROFIT RELIGIOUS, CHARITABLE, EDUCATIONAL, ETC. INSTITUTIONS

931.1 Is work performed before January 1, 1984, for a nonprofit religious, charitable or educational organization covered by Social Security?

Work you performed prior to January 1, 1984, for a nonprofit religious, charitable, educational, or other organization exempt from income tax (under section 501(c)(3) of the Internal Revenue Code) is not covered by Social Security.

Note: If the organization waived its exemption from Social Security taxes by filing a waiver certificate and a list of concurring employees, then you may be covered by Social Security. The organization can terminate Social Security coverage by giving two years' advance notice, if coverage had been in effect for eight years or more.

See SSA's electronic fact sheet "If You Work For A Nonprofit Organization," Publication No. 05-10027 at: https://www.socialsecurity.gov/pubs/10027.html for more information.

931.2 Is work performed on January 1, 1984 or later for a nonprofit religious, charitable or educational organization covered by Social Security?

Beginning on January 1, 1984, work you perform for a nonprofit religious, charitable, educational or other organization is covered by Social Security. Your services are covered for work done on or after January 1, 1984, even if you previously terminated coverage.

Note: Since 1984, nonprofit organizations may not terminate coverage of employees.

931.3 Can nonprofit religious, charitable or educational organizations elect to be excluded from Social Security coverage?

A church or qualified church-controlled organization, opposed for religious reasons to payment of Social Security taxes, may elect to have services performed by their employees (beginning January 1, 1984) excluded from the definition of employment for Social Security purposes. Organizations in existence when the legislation was passed had to elect before October 31, 1984. Other organizations must elect before the date that the first quarterly tax return is due.

931.4 How are services of employees of a church or organization that elected to be excluded from Social Security coverage considered?

If you work for a church or organization that is excluded from the definition of employment for Social Security purposes, your work is treated as services performed in a trade or business. Your work is covered as self-employment (see §1136), provided payment for your work in a calendar year is $100 or more as required prior to 1984.

Note: Employees of a nonprofit organization required by law to be subject to the Civil Service Retirement System (such as the Legal Services Corporation) are treated like Federal civilian employees for Social Security coverage purposes.

932. MINISTERS AND MEMBERS OF RELIGIOUS ORDERS

932.1 Are services of ministers and members of religious orders covered by Social Security?

Your services as a minister or member of a religious order are covered by Social Security as *self-employment* if you:

A. Performed the services after 1967;
B. Are or were a duly ordained, commissioned, or licensed minister of a church in the exercise of your ministry or by a member of a religious order not under a vow of poverty;
C. Did not elect to be exempt from Social Security taxation and coverage (see §§1131-1132).

932.2 Can work performed by a minister or member of a religious order, under a vow of poverty, be covered by Social Security?

Your services may be covered by Social Security if the religious order has elected to have services performed by its members covered by Social Security.

932.3 How does a religious order elect to have the work of its members covered by Social Security?

To elect coverage, the order or subdivision of the religious order must file Form SS-16 *(Certificate of Election of Coverage)* with the Internal Revenue Service for members of religious orders under vows of poverty.

932.4 If services performed by a religious order are covered by Social Security, what do the members' covered wages include?

If are a member of a religious order that is covered by Social Security, your covered wages are the fair market value of any food, lodging, clothing, or other perquisites furnished by the order. Your wages must not be less than $100 a month in order to be covered by Social Security.

933. HOW IS WORK THAT IS NOT IN THE EXERCISE OF THE MINISTRY TREATED FOR SOCIAL SECURITY PURPOSES?

Work you perform that is not in the "exercise of the ministry or duties required by a religious order" is treated the same as the work of any other employee. Your services are covered or excluded from Social Security on the same basis as any other employee for the religious order.

934. WHAT IS AN "ORDAINED", "COMMISSIONED", OR "LICENSED" MINISTER?

You are an "ordained", "commissioned", or "licensed" minister if you have been vested with ministerial status according to the procedure followed by your particular church's denomination. You do not have to be connected with a congregation. Your ministerial authority continues until it is revoked by your church.

Some churches have formal ordination procedures. For Social Security purposes, your commissioning or licensing as a minister must be recognized by your church as an ordination if your church follows such procedures.

935. WHAT DOES "EXERCISE OF THE MINISTRY" MEAN?

The term "exercise of the ministry" includes the following activities:

A. The conduct of religious worship and the ministration of sacerdotal functions;

B. Service performed in the control, conduct, and maintenance of:
  1. A religious organization under the authority of a religious body constituting a church or church denomination; or
  2. An organization operated as an integral agency of a religious organization, church, or church denomination.

Note: Control, conduct, and maintenance of an organization do not include work such as operating an elevator or being a janitor. It refers to work in directing, managing, or promoting the activities of the organization.

C. Service performed for any organization under an assignment or designation by a church; or

Note: This does not include cases in which a church merely helps by recommending a minister for a position involving non-ministerial services for an organization not connected with the church.

D. Missionary service or administrative work for a missionary organization.

936. ARE SERVICES PERFORMED BY CREWS ON FISHING BOATS COVERED BY SOCIAL SECURITY?

If you are a member of a fishing boat crew or work on boats engaged in catching fish or other forms of aquatic life (such as shrimps or lobsters), you are considered self-employed. (See §1134 for special conditions.)

937. EMPLOYMENT FOR A FOREIGN GOVERNMENT, INTERNATIONAL ORGANIZATION, OR INSTRUMENTALITY OF A FOREIGN GOVERNMENT

937.1 Are services performed by employees of foreign governments, international organizations or instrumentalities of a foreign government covered by Social Security?

If you are a U.S. citizen, your work as an employee of a foreign government or of certain U.S.-designated international organizations is not covered by Social Security as employment. The same rule applies to work for a wholly owned instrumentality of a foreign government that exempts similar work if performed in that country by U.S. employees. (See §938 for treatment of work by U.S. citizens in the U.S. for foreign governments, international organizations, etc.)

If you are not a U.S. citizen, your work for a foreign government is not covered by Social Security.

If you are not a U.S. citizen, your work for a wholly owned instrumentality of a foreign government is not covered by Social Security if that foreign government exempts similar work if performed in that country by U.S. employees.

937.2 Are services performed by employees who participate in FERS or FSPS excluded from Social Security coverage?

Beginning in 1995, the services you perform for an international organization as a Federal employee participating in the Federal Employees' Retirement System (FERS) or Foreign Service Pension System (FSPS) are not excluded from employment. Your services are covered as employment by the Federal agency that transfers you. This includes employment outside and inside the United States.

938. IS WORK PERFORMED BY U.S. CITIZENS WORKING IN THE U.S. AS EMPLOYEES OF FOREIGN GOVERNMENTS COVERED BY SOCIAL SECURITY?

Your work is covered as self-employment if you are a U.S. citizen working in the U.S. as:

A. An employee of a foreign government;
B. An employee of a foreign government's wholly-owned instrumentality, if the foreign government exempts similar work if performed in that country by U.S. employees; or
C. An employee of certain U.S.-designated international organizations.

This provision and §937 do not change for Federal employees not under FERS or FSPS.

939. FOREIGN STUDENTS, EXCHANGE VISITORS AND INTERNATIONAL CULTURAL EXCHANGE VISITORS

939.1 Is work performed by foreign students, exchange visitors or international cultural exchange visitors covered by Social Security?

Work performed by foreign nonimmigrants temporarily admitted to the United States (U.S.) under sections 101(a)(15)(F), (J), (M), and (Q) of the Immigration and Nationality Act, as amended, is not covered by Social Security if:

A. The work is performed to carry out the purpose(s) for which the foreign nonimmigrants were admitted to the United States (U.S.); or

Note: Work by a student or exchange visitor other than that performed to carry out the purpose for which he or she was admitted is not excluded from Social Security coverage. However, if the foreign nonimmigrant has received special permission to work, then his or her services may be excluded from coverage.

B. Special permission to work has been granted by the Department of Homeland Security (in the case of a student) or by the sponsor of an exchange visitor.

939.2 What categories of visa holders does the Social Security exclusion apply?

The exclusion from coverage applies to authorized work performed by nonimmigrants with the following visa classifications:

- *F-1* - Foreign academic students admitted to pursue a course of study at an established school or other recognized place of study approved by DHS;
- *J-1* - Exchange visitors temporarily admitted to the United States (U.S.) to participate in a program designated by the Department of State, Bureau of Educational and Cultural Affairs for the purpose

of teaching, consulting, demonstrating special skills, or receiving training. The *J-1* exchange visitor classification includes: alien physician, au pair, camp counselor, government visitor, international visitor, professor, research scholar, short-term scholar, specialist, summer work travel, teacher, trainee and high school, college and university students;
- *M-1* - Foreign vocational students at an established vocational or other recognized nonacademic institution in the United States (U.S.). The course of study must be designated by the alien and approved by the U.S. Attorney General after consultation with the Secretary of Education; and
- *Q-1 or Q-2* - Beginning October 1, 1994, foreign exchange visitors admitted to participate in an international cultural exchange program for the purpose of providing practical training and sharing culture, history, and traditions of the visitor's country. This program is approved by the Secretary of State.

See SSA's electronic fact sheet "International Students and Social Security Numbers," Publication No. 05-10181 at: https://www.ssa.gov/pubs/EN-05-10181.pdf for more information.

939.3 Is work performed by a spouse or minor child of a foreign student or exchange visitor covered by Social Security?

Yes. Work performed by the spouse or minor child of an exchange visitor is covered by Social Security unless excluded by some other provision of law.

940. EMPLOYMENT AS CIVILIAN FOR THE U.S. GOVERNMENT

940.1 Are services performed by newly hired civilians for the U.S. Government covered by Social Security?

If you were hired as a civilian employee for the U.S. Government on or after January 1, 1984, then your services are covered by Social Security. Certain services performed by Federal officials are also covered.

Prior to 1984, most Federal civilian employment was exempt from regular Social Security coverage, but subject to the Hospital Insurance tax portion of the Federal Insurance Contributions Act beginning January 1, 1983.

940.2 Which services are covered by Social Security for civilian workers?

The following civilian positions are covered by Social Security:

A. Federal employees who on or after January 1, 1984:
   1. Are hired for the first time;
   2. Are hired after a separation exceeding 365 days from previous Federal employment (see §940.3 for exceptions);
   3. Return to Federal employment after a separation of less than 366 days *and* the prior employment was subject to full Social Security coverage and taxation under the prior law; or
   4. Were working for the Federal Government in a position subject to full Social Security coverage and taxation under the prior law (e.g., in the uniformed services or a temporary employee);

Note: Generally, work performed by re-employed Civil Service and other Federal annuitants, except retired members of the uniformed services, are specifically excluded from Social Security coverage other than Health Insurance coverage. Retired members of the Foreign Service who return to work for the Federal Government under temporary appointment (one year or less) as General Schedule employees, are subject to full Social Security coverage.

B. Legislative branch employees who were not participating in the Civil Service Retirement System (CSRS) or another Federal civilian retirement system as of December 31, 1983;

C. Legislative branch employees who were participating in the CSRS or another Federal retirement system (other than one for members of the uniformed services) on December 31, 1983, and
   1. Received lump-sum payments from the Federal retirement system after December 31, 1983; or
   2. Ceased to be subject to CSRS after December 31, 1983.

Note: Services performed by legislative branch employees covered by Social Security as a result of this provision who: (1) received or filed an application for a lump-sum payment before June 15, 1984, from a Federal retirement system; or (2) ceased to be subject to the CSRS after December 31, 1983, could be excluded from Social Security coverage if they joined the CSRS before August 18, 1984.

Services performed by legislative branch employees who: (1) were hired after July 18, 1984, after a break in Federal service of less than 366 days; and (2) otherwise meet these requirements, could be excluded from Social Security coverage if the employee joined CSRS within 30 days after they were hired.

D. Members of Congress, including Delegates and Resident Commissioners of or to the Congress;

E. The President, the Vice President, and most executive-level political appointees. Generally, this includes positions as Cabinet heads, sub-cabinet members, independent agency top staff, commission members, and political appointees designated by the President with the advice and consent of the Senate; and

F. Federal judges, magistrates, bankruptcy judges, and referees in bankruptcy. This does not apply to payment to retired senior status Federal justices and judges while actively performing judicial duties.

940.3 What are the exceptions to Social Security coverage for employees hired after a separation exceeding 365 days from previous Federal employment?

If you previously held a position not covered by Social Security and you meet any of the following conditions, your services are not covered by Social Security:

A. You return to non-covered Federal service after being detailed or transferred to service with certain international organizations;

B. You return to non-covered Federal service after separation to perform service with the American Institute in Taiwan; or

C. You exercise restoration or reemployment rights after service as a member of a uniformed service (including service in the National Guard and temporary service in the Coast Guard Reserve).

D. You return to non-covered Federal service after employment with an Indian tribal government.

940.4 How is employment for all Federal agencies and instrumentalities considered for Social Security purposes?

Employment for all Federal agencies and instrumentalities, including service as a member of the uniformed services, is considered as employment for the same employer.

940.5 What does the legislative branch consist of?

The legislative branch consists of the Congress, the Architect of the Capitol, the U.S. Botanical Gardens, the General Accounting Office, the Government Printing Office, the Library of Congress, the Office of Technology Assessment, the Congressional Budget Office, and the Copyright Royalty Tribunal.

940.6 What type of work performed for the U.S. government is usually NOT covered by Social Security?

Services that remain excluded from Social Security coverage includes work performed from the following:

A. Inmate of a Federal penal institution;
B. Interns, student nurses, and other student employees of a Federal hospital;
C. Emergency employees serving on a temporary basis during certain emergencies;
D. Many retired Federal judges (age 70 and above) who continue to remain on call to serve on the bench after retirement. These services would ordinarily be covered for Social Security purposes but have been excluded by law for all services performed after December 31, 1983; and
E. Certain students performing services for U.S. Army Corps of Engineers research and development laboratories.

These services are excluded from Federal employment by section 2360 of the Armed Forces Act. Since they are excluded from employment, their payment for services is not covered services for Social Security tax purposes; nor are they covered as independent contractors (self-employed individuals) since they are not in a trade or business.

941. ARE SERVICES PERFORMED BY EMPLOYEES FOR THE DISTRICT OF COLUMBIA COVERED BY SOCIAL SECURITY?

If you work for the District of Columbia and its wholly owned instrumentalities, including work as a substitute teacher in the District school system, your services are covered by Social Security beginning October 1, 1965, unless:

A. Your work is covered by a retirement system established by a law of the U.S.; or
B. Your services are specifically excluded by some provision of the law; or
C. You are performing services as any of the following:
   1. A patient or inmate of a District of Columbia hospital or penal institution;

2. A student employee of a District of Columbia hospital (including a student nurse, dietitian, and physical or occupational therapist but, not a medical or dental intern or resident in training);
3. An employee serving on a temporary basis in case of fire, storm, snow, earthquake, flood, or other similar emergencies; or
4. A member of a board, committee or council of the District of Columbia paid on a per diem, meeting, or other fee basis.

942. ARE SERVICES PERFORMED UNDER FEDERALLY SPONSORED ECONOMIC AND HUMAN DEVELOPMENT PROGRAMS COVERED BY SOCIAL SECURITY?

Some services performed under federally sponsored economic and human development programs are covered by Social Security and others are not. In some instances, these services are designated by public law to be performed in the employ of the U.S. In other instances, these services may be covered as State and local government employment. They may also be considered employment by private nonprofit organizations.

Whether or not the services are covered by Social Security depends on the particular program and the identity of the employer for whom the services are performed. A discussion of some of the major programs under which Social Security coverage may exist is contained in §§943-947.

943. IS WORK AS A VOLUNTEER OR VOLUNTEER LEADER IN THE PEACE CORPS COVERED BY SOCIAL SECURITY?

Your work as a volunteer or volunteer leader in the Peace Corps is covered by Social Security if:
A. You are a citizen or national of the U.S.; and
B. You enrolled in the Corps on or after September 22, 1961; or you had been engaged on that date by contract with the Peace Corps Agency established by Executive Order No. 10924 dated March 1, 1961.

944. ARE SERVICES PERFORMED BY JOB CORPS ENROLLEES COVERED BY SOCIAL SECURITY?

The Job Corps program is funded by the Federal Government and is administered by the Department of Labor. If you are enrolled in the Job Corps, you are considered an employee of the Federal Government for Social Security purposes. The Secretary of Labor (or your designated agent) decides what pay constitutes wages and the periods that you are paid wages.

945. IS WORK PERFORMED FOR COMMUNITY SERVICE PROGRAMS FOR OLDER AMERICANS COVERED BY SOCIAL SECURITY?

Community service programs for older Americans are generally assisted by State and local governments to provide services to older Americans. The Older Americans Act makes no provision regarding Social Security coverage. Social Security coverage questions are dependent on:

A. The identity of your employer (whether or not the State or local entity has coverage provided under a Federal-State Section 218 agreement); and

B. The application of the common-law test (see §§802-823). This will determine if an employment relationship exists between you and the agency for which you work.

946. ARE SERVICES PERFORMED BY STUDENTS ENROLLED IN A WORK-STUDY PROGRAM COVERED BY SOCIAL SECURITY?

Students enrolled in the Work-Study Program funded under the Higher Education Act may be employed by private, State, or local colleges and universities, or for public or private nonprofit organizations. Your Social Security coverage depends on the identity of your employer.

If your work is performed for a State or local government agency, your services may be covered under the agreement with the State if that State does not expressly exclude work performed by a student. (See §1002)

947. VOLUNTEERS IN SERVICE TO AMERICA (VISTA) PROGRAM

947.1 Are services performed by Volunteers in Service to America (VISTA) covered by Social Security?

Services performed by Volunteers in Service to America (VISTA) recruited to perform duties under the Domestic Volunteer Service Act may be covered as employees for Social Security purposes. If you are enrolled in a VISTA program for a period of service of at least one year, you are considered an employee of the U.S. Government. Your services (including training) are covered by Social Security.

947.2 How are decisions made concerning periods covered by wage payments?

Decisions concerning periods covered by wage payments are made by ACTION, an independent Federal agency.

948. MEMBER OF THE U.S. UNIFORMED SERVICE

948.1 Are services performed by members of the U.S. uniformed service covered by Social Security?

Your work as a member of the uniformed service of the U.S. is covered by Social Security beginning January 1, 1957, if performed while on active duty or active duty for training. This work is not covered by Social Security during any period when you are on leave without pay, or if the work is creditable under the Railroad Retirement Act. (See Chapter 23)

948.2 Are services performed by members of the Armed Forces Reserve covered by Social Security?

Your work as a member of the Armed Forces Reserve, while on inactive duty training (such as weekend drills), is covered beginning January 1, 1988. This work is not covered by Social Security during any period when you are on leave without pay, or if the work is creditable under the Railroad Retirement Act. (See Chapter 23)

948.3 Before 1957, how is Armed Forces service credited for Social Security purposes?

Before 1957, the service of a member of the Armed Forces of the U.S. was not covered by Social Security. However, you may be given military service "wage credits" for Social Security purposes based on this service. (See §§954-960.)

949. DEFINITION OF MEMBER OF A UNIFORMED SERVICE

949.1 Who is considered a member of a uniformed service?

You are considered a member of a uniformed service if you are any of the following:

A. An appointed, enlisted, inducted, or retired member of:
   1. One of the armed services without a specified component; or
   2. A component of the Army, Navy, Air Force, Marine Corps, or Coast Guard, including any of the following Reserve components: the Army, Navy, Marine Corps, Air Force, or Coast Guard Reserve, the Reserve Corps of the Public Health Service, the U.S. National Guard, the Air National Guard of the U.S., and, under limited circumstances, the National Guard or Air National Guard of the States or the District of Columbia;

B. A commissioned officer (including a retired commissioned officer) of the National Oceanic and Atmospheric Administration or the Regular or Reserve Corps of the Public Health Service;
C. A member of the Fleet Reserve or Fleet Marine Corps Reserve;
D. A midshipman at the U.S. Naval Academy, and a cadet at the U.S. Military, Coast Guard, or Air Force Academy;
E. A member of the Reserve Officers' Training Corps and the Naval or Air Force Reserve Officers' Training Corps, when ordered to annual training duty for 14 days or more, and while performing authorized travel to and from that duty; or
F. In route to or from a place of final acceptance for entry upon active military or naval service, provided that you:
  1. Were ordered or directed to proceed to such place; and
  2. Have been provisionally accepted for duty, or have been selected for active military, or naval service under the Universal Military Training and Service Act.

949.2 Is a temporary member of the Coast Guard Reserve considered a member of a uniformed service?

No. A temporary member of the Coast Guard Reserve is not considered a member of a uniformed service.

950. WHAT DOES "ACTIVE DUTY" MEAN?

The term "active duty" means:
- full-time duty (other than active duty for training) performed by a member of the uniformed services;
- full-time duty (other than for training purposes) as a commissioned officer of the National Oceanic and Atmospheric Administration or its predecessor organization the Coast and Geodetic Survey, or in the Regular or Reserve Corps of the Public Health Service;
- service as a cadet at the United States Military, Air Force, or Coast Guard Academy, or as a midshipman at the United States Naval Academy; and
- authorized travel to or from the duties described above.

951. WHAT DOES "ACTIVE DUTY FOR TRAINING" MEAN?

"Active duty for training" means:

A. Full-time duty performed by a member of a Reserve component of a uniformed service in the active military or naval service of the U.S. for training purposes;
B. Full-time duty as a commissioned officer of the Reserve Corps of the Public Health Service for training purposes;
C. Full-time duty as a member of the Army National Guard or Air National Guard of any State;
D. Annual training duty performed for a period of 14 days or more as a member of the Reserve Officers' Training Corps, the Naval Reserve Officers' Training Corps, or the Air Force Reserve Officers' Training Corps; and
E. Authorized travel to and from any duty or service described in (A) - (D) above.

952. HOW ARE THE AMOUNT OF WAGES AND THE PERIOD OF MILITARY SERVICE DETERMINED?

The head of your respective service department determines the following:

A. Whether and when you have performed work creditable for Social Security purposes;
B. The amount of your wages; and
C. The periods that your wages are paid.

953. DEEMED WAGE CREDITS AFTER 1956

953.1 What are deemed wage credits?

A member of a uniformed service may have wage credits in addition to basic pay received for active duty or active duty for training. These credits are subject to the maximum earnings limitation on income taxable for Social Security purposes. These "deemed wage credits" are granted in recognition of the fact that covered basic pay is increased by various allowances that are part of the actual reimbursement for services.

953.2 How are deemed wage credits granted?

You are granted deemed wage credits as follows:

A. *For years 1957 through 1977,* you are granted $300 for each calendar quarter that you receive any basic pay.

B. *For years 1978 through 2001*, you are granted credits in increments of $100 up to a maximum of $1,200 per calendar year. The $100 increments are granted for each full $300 of basic pay. No credit is granted if your annual wages are less than $300 and no further credit may be granted when the annual wages exceed $3,600.
C. Effective 01/01/02, deemed wage credits are *eliminated* for all years after calendar year 2001. Deemed wage credits will continue to be given for military wages for periods prior to calendar year 2002.

953.3 When are deemed wage credits NOT granted?

After September 7, 1980, wage credits may not be granted to service members discharged or released from active duty before completing the minimum active duty requirements. Therefore, wage credits will not be granted:

A. *After September 7, 1980*, if you were initially enlisted in a regular component of the Armed Forces and:
   1. You did not complete at least 24 months of your enlistment; or
   2. The full period of active duty you were called upon to serve was less than 24 months, unless you were discharged due to:
      1. Hardship as specified in section 1173 of Title 10 of the U.S. Code;
      2. The application of section 1171 of Title 10 of the U.S. Code (commonly referred to as "for the convenience of the government");
      3. Disability under certain circumstances; or
      4. Death during the period of enlistment;
B. Your entry on active duty occurred *after October 13, 1982*, in a regular component of the Armed Forces and:
   1. You did not previously complete a continuous period of active duty of at least 24 months; or
   2. You were discharged or released from active duty before completing the lesser of 24 months or the full period of the tour of active duty being served unless the individual was discharged or released from active duty due to:
      1. hardship as specified in section 1173 of Title 10 of the U.S. Code;

2. the application of section 1171 of Title 10 of the U.S. Code (commonly referred to as "for the convenience of the government");
3. disability under certain circumstances; or
4. death during the period of enlistment.

954. NONCONTRIBUTORY WAGE CREDITS BASED ON MILITARY SERVICE BEFORE 1957

954.1 How are noncontributory wage credits granted to veterans for service before 1957?

Veterans with active military or naval service with the Armed Forces of the U.S. during the World War II period (September 16, 1940-July 24, 1947) or the post-World War II period (July 25, 1947-December 31, 1956) are granted noncontributory wage credits of $160 for each month that the veteran:

A. Was discharged or released from active service under conditions other than dishonorable, either:
   1. After active service of 90 days or more; or
   2. After less than 90 days' service by reason of a disability or injury incurred or aggravated in service in the line of duty; or
B. Is still in active service; or
C. Died while in the active military or naval service (unless death was inflicted as lawful punishment for a military or naval offense by other than an enemy of the U.S.).

954.2 Will the noncontributory wage credits be part of the veteran's Social Security record?

The $160 a month noncontributory wage credits for military service are not actually posted on the veteran's Social Security record. However, when benefits are claimed on the veteran's Social Security record, the wage credits are then considered.

954.3 How are conditional discharges treated for Social Security purposes?

If an enlisted person received a "conditional discharge" to accept a commission with no break in service, the service is considered as performed in one period.

955. DEFINITION OF MILITARY OR NAVAL SERVICE OF THE U.S.

955.1 What does military or naval service of the U.S. mean?

"Military or naval service of the U.S." includes the following:

A. Service as a member of a Regular or Reserve component of the U.S. Army, Air Force, Navy, Coast Guard, or Marine Corps;

B. Service as a commissioned officer of the Public Health Service or the National Oceanic and Atmospheric Administration; or

C. Service by a midshipman at the U.S. Naval Academy or a cadet at the U.S. Military, Air Force, or Coast Guard Academies.

955.2 Which auxiliary military organizations are not eligible for noncontributory wage credits?

Noncontributory wage credits are not granted for service with certain auxiliary organizations such as: the Coast Guard Auxiliary; the temporary Coast Guard Reserve (unless service was full-time duty with military pay and allowances); Civilian Auxiliary to the Military Police; and the Civil Air Patrol.

956. EFFECT OF DISCHARGE UNDER DISHONORABLE CONDITIONS

956.1 What effect does a discharge under dishonorable conditions have on noncontributory military service wage credits?

A discharge under dishonorable conditions prohibits the granting of noncontributory military service wage credits for any period of active service to which the discharge applies.

956.2 What types of separations are considered to be under dishonorable conditions?

The following types of separations are issued under dishonorable conditions:

A. A dishonorable discharge;

B. A bad conduct discharge issued as a result of a sentence by a general court martial;

C. A discharge for desertion;

D. In the case of an officer, a resignation accepted "for the good of the service";

E. A discharge on the grounds that the person was a conscientious objector who refused to do military duty, to wear the uniform, or otherwise to comply with lawful orders of competent military authority; or

F. A discharge by reason of conviction by a civil court for treason, sabotage, espionage, murder, rape, arson, burglary, robbery, kidnapping, assault with intent to kill, assault with a dangerous weapon, or an attempt to commit any of these crimes.

956.3 How are wage credits considered if a veteran has more than one discharge involving separate periods of active service?

A veteran may have more than one discharge involving separate periods of active service. The period of active service that a discharge under dishonorable conditions applies cannot be used for determining military service wage credits. However, wage credits may be granted for any other period of active service that a veteran was released under conditions other than dishonorable.

957. ARE NONCONTRIBUTORY WAGE CREDITS GRANTED FOR MILITARY SERVICE WITH A FOREIGN COUNTRY?

Noncontributory wage credits may be granted for military service with a foreign country that was at war with the U.S. on September 16, 1940, during World War II if the service member:

A. Entered the active military or naval service of the foreign country before December 9, 1941;

B. Was a citizen of the U.S. throughout the period of service (or if the citizenship was lost, it was only because of the entrance into the naval or military service);

C. Had resided in the U.S. for at least four years out of the five-year period ending with the day the service member entered into this military or naval service;

D. Was living in the U.S. on the day of entrance into this military or naval service; and

E. The member meets one of the following conditions:
   1. Died while in service; or
   2. Was discharged or released from this military or naval service under conditions other than dishonorable:
      1. After at least 90 days' service; or
      2. Because of a disability or injury incurred or aggravated in service in the line of duty.

958. ARE OFFICERS OF THE NATIONAL OCEANIC AND ATMOSPHERIC ADMINISTRATION OR THE PUBLIC HEALTH SERVICE CONSIDERED MEMBERS OF THE ARMED FORCES?

Commissioned Officers of the National Oceanic and Atmospheric Administration (prior to 1965, the Coast and Geodetic Survey) or the Public Health Service are considered to be in the active service of the Armed Forces for the purpose of military service wage credits and the special insured status provisions only under the following conditions:

A. Commissioned officers of the National Oceanic and Atmospheric Administration may be granted wage credits for time spent:
   1. On active duty with an armed service department; or
   2. On active duty on military projects determined by the Secretary of Defense to be areas of immediate military hazard; or
   3. In service in the Philippines if the individual was serving there on December 7, 1941; or
   4. On active commissioned service with the National Oceanic and Atmospheric Administration after July 28, 1945, and before 1957.

B. Commissioned officers of the Public Health Service may be granted wage credits for time spent:
   1. On active commissioned service from July 29, 1945-July 3, 1952; or
   2. On active commissioned service, while on detail to a component of the uniformed forces, during the periods September 16, 1940-July 28, 1945, and July 4, 1952-December 31, 1956, inclusive; or
   3. On active commissioned service from July 4, 1952-December 31, 1956, even if not performed while on detail to a component of the uniformed services.

959. UNDER WHAT CIRCUMSTANCES ARE VETERANS NOT ELIGIBLE FOR NONCONTRIBUTORY WAGE CREDITS?

You are not eligible for noncontributory wage credits as a veteran for military service if you meet any of the following conditions:

A. Your Social Security benefit payable is larger without considering the wage credits; or
B. You have been convicted of certain offenses against the Federal Government such as treason, sedition, etc.; or

C. You refuse upon the ground of self-incrimination to appear, testify, produce books, etc. about your Government employment before a Federal grand jury, U.S. court, or U.S. congressional committee concerning matters of national security or your relationship with a foreign government; or
D. You are receiving a monthly benefit payable by another Federal agency (other than the Department of Veterans Affairs), based on military service prior to 1957. However, if you were on active duty or active duty for training after 1956, you may be granted Social Security wage credits for active service during the six-year period, 1951-1956. Therefore, even if a service organization uses any or all of your military service prior to 1957 in determining your rights to, or the amount of, a retirement benefit payable by that organization, you may be granted wage credits; or
E. The wage credits plus your covered earnings exceed the maximum earnings that may be credited for Social Security purposes for that year (see §714). In these cases, only wage credits that do not exceed the maximum earnings allowed will be credited.

960. WHEN IS A DECEASED WORLD WAR II VETERAN FULLY INSURED FOR SOCIAL SECURITY PURPOSES?

A deceased World War II Veteran is fully insured with an average monthly wage of $160 if:

A. The veteran died before July 27, 1954; or
B. The veteran died within three years after separation (death no later that July 26, 1954) from active military or naval service; and
C. The veteran's service was in the World War II period (September 16, 1940 - July 24, 1947).

Note: If a Veterans Affairs pension or a compensation benefit was ever paid, even if terminated, based on the veteran's death, deemed insured status benefits are prohibited.

See SSA's electronic fact sheet "Military Service and Social Security," Publication No. 05-10017 at: https://www.ssa.gov/pubs/EN-05-10017.pdf for more information.

961. EMPLOYMENT OUTSIDE THE U.S.

961.1 Is employment outside of the U.S. covered by Social Security?

Your work outside the U.S. is covered by Social Security if it is performed:

A. As a U.S. citizen, a U.S. resident for an American employer (see §962), or for an American employer's foreign affiliate for which coverage has been arranged as described in §§963-965; or

Note: Prior to the 1983 Amendments, enacted on April 20, 1983, coverage was available only to U.S. citizens (not U.S. residents). Also, the American employer and the American employer's foreign affiliate both had to be corporations.

B. On or in connection with an American vessel or aircraft, if the contract of employment was entered into within the U.S; or

C. On or in connection with an American vessel or aircraft, if the vessel or aircraft touches at a port or airport in the U.S. while you are working on it.

961.2 What does within the U.S. mean?

"Within the U.S." means on, in or over any of the 50 States, the District of Columbia, the Virgin Islands, Puerto Rico, Guam, American Samoa, the Northern Mariana Islands or the territorial waters of any of these places.

961.3 What does American vessel mean?

The term "American vessel" means:

A. Any vessel documented or numbered under the laws of the U.S.; or

B. Any vessel which is neither documented nor numbered under the laws of the U.S., nor documented under the laws of any foreign country if its crew is employed solely by:
   1. One or more citizens or residents of the U.S.; or
   2. Corporations organized under laws of the U.S. or any State.

961.4 What does American aircraft mean?

American aircraft means an aircraft registered under the laws of the United States.

962. WHO CAN BE CONSIDERED AN AMERICAN EMPLOYER?

An American employer includes:

A. The U.S. or any of its instrumentalities;
B. A State (including the District of Columbia, Puerto Rico, the Virgin Islands, Guam, the Northern Mariana Islands, and American Samoa) or any political subdivision of such State; or an instrumentality of the State or political subdivision;
C. A person who is a resident of the U.S.;
D. A partnership in which at least two-thirds of the partners are residents of the U.S.;
E. A trust, if all of the trustees are U.S. residents; or
F. A corporation organized under the laws of the U.S. or any State, including the District of Columbia, Puerto Rico, the Virgin Islands, Guam, the Northern Mariana Islands, and American Samoa.

963. IS WORK BY A U.S. CITIZEN FOR FOREIGN AFFILIATES OUTSIDE THE U.S. COVERED BY SOCIAL SECURITY?

Your work as a U.S. citizen or a U.S. resident outside the U.S. for a foreign affiliate (See §964) of an American employer is covered by Social Security if:

A. Your American employer arranges for coverage by entering into an agreement with the Internal Revenue Service by filing IRS Form 2032, *Contract Coverage Under Title II of the Social Security Act*; and
B. The agreement applies to all U.S. citizens and all U.S. residents employed outside the U.S. by the foreign affiliate. The agreement also applies to all citizens and residents subsequently employed by the affiliate if their work would be covered if performed in the U.S.

964. WHAT IS A "FOREIGN AFFILIATE"?

A "foreign affiliate" of an American employer is a foreign entity that:

A. The American employer has not less than a 10 percent direct interest or indirect interest in; and
B. Is defined in section 3121(l)(8) of the Internal Revenue Code.

965. AGREEMENT TO COVER FOREIGN AFFILIATES

965.1 When is the agreement to cover foreign affiliates effective?

The agreement to cover foreign affiliates is effective on the first day of the calendar quarter in which the agreement is approved by the Internal

Revenue Service; or the first day of the following calendar quarter. The American employer chooses the effective date of coverage.

965.2 Can the agreement be amended?

The agreement may be amended to include any other foreign affiliate of the American employer. However, coverage of the new group is effective only as of the first day of the calendar quarter in which the agreement is amended.

965.3 Can the agreement be terminated?

Effective June 15, 1989, an agreement to cover foreign affiliates may no longer be terminated by the employer.

Prior to June 15, 1989, a coverage agreement could be terminated by the American employer, but only after giving two years' notice of intention to terminate. Further, notice of intention to terminate could be given only after the agreement had been in existence for eight years. Thus, at least 10 years of Social Security coverage was assured. (However, the Secretary of the Treasury could terminate the agreement sooner.)

If, prior to June 15, 1989, an agreement was terminated in whole, the American employer may not again obtain coverage for any of its foreign affiliates. An agreement terminated with respect to one affiliate may not be reinstated with respect to that particular affiliate.

966. IS WORK PERFORMED FOR PRIVATE EMPLOYERS OF GUAM AND AMERICAN SAMOA COVERED BY SOCIAL SECURITY?

Work for private employers of Guam and American Samoa is covered by Social Security on the same basis as work of employees in the U.S. However, work in Guam by a resident of the Philippines under contract to work on a temporary basis as a nonimmigrant alien is not covered.

Work as an officer or employee of the government of American Samoa or any political subdivision or instrumentality thereof (except by a person covered under a retirement system established by law of the U.S.) has been covered since January 1, 1961. Beginning January 1, 1973, work as a temporary or intermittent employee of the government (or wholly-owned instrumentality) of Guam is covered by Social Security unless it is:

A. Covered by a retirement system established by a law of Guam or the U.S.;

B. Performed by an elected official;

C. Performed by a member of the legislature; or
D. Performed in a hospital or penal institution by a patient or inmate thereof.

967. IS WORK COVERED BY THE RAILROAD RETIREMENT ACT COVERED BY SOCIAL SECURITY?

Work covered by the Railroad Retirement Act is not covered by Social Security. However, earnings from railroad employment are counted for Social Security purposes at the death or retirement of a worker if he or she does not qualify under the railroad retirement program. For example, when a railroad worker retires with less than 120 months of railroad service and with less than 60 railroad service months accrued after December 31, 1995, no railroad retirement annuity is payable. However, we then consider his or her railroad earnings after 1936 in determining his or her rights to Social Security disability or retirement benefits.

In the event of disability, if you file with the Railroad Board, they will either advise you if you also need to contact Social Security or forward your claim to us for processing. Please go to https://www.benefits.gov to find additional information on the Railroad Retirement Act.

968. THE INCLUDED-EXCLUDED RULE

968.1 What happens if part of an employee's work is covered by Social Security and part is not covered by Social Security?

When part of your work during a pay period is covered by and part excluded from Social Security and all of the work is being performed for one employer, the following rules apply:
A. All of your work in that pay period is covered if 50 percent or more of your time during the pay period is spent in covered work; and
B. All of your work in that pay period is excluded if more than 50 percent of your time during the pay period is spent in excluded work.

968.2 What does pay period mean?

The term pay period means the period of not more than 31 consecutive calendar days for which the employer ordinarily pays the employee. Where there are seasonal fluctuations, there may be one customary seasonal pay period and another customary non-seasonal pay period.

969. WHEN DOES THE INCLUDED-EXCLUDED RULE NOT APPLY?

The included-excluded rule does not apply if:

A. Part of your work is covered by Social Security and part by the Railroad Retirement Act;

B. Part of your work is performed within the U.S. for a foreign employer, and part is performed outside the U.S.; or

C. There is no pay period, or the pay period covers more than 31 consecutive days, or there are separate pay periods for the covered and excluded work.

In all of the above instances, the wages paid for the work covered by Social Security are counted for Social Security purposes.

970. HOW DO INTERNATIONAL SOCIAL SECURITY AGREEMENTS AFFECT COVERAGE?

International Social Security agreements, often called "Totalization agreements" (see §107), provide certain exceptions to the normal coverage rules described above. For example, if a person performs work that is covered by both U.S. Social Security and the social security program of a foreign country, an agreement ordinarily assigns coverage of exempt that work to the program of only one of the two countries. Thus, an agreement can supersede the normal coverage rules in order to eliminate dual Social Security coverage and taxation.

See SSA's electronic fact sheet "How International Agreements Can Help You," Publication No. 05-10180 at https://www.ssa.gov/pubs/EN-05-10180.pdf for more information.

971. ARE SERVICES PERFORMED BY EMPLOYEES OF THE COMMONWEALTH OF THE NORTH MARIANA ISLANDS (CNMI) COVERED BY SOCIAL SECURITY?

Work as an officer or employee of the government of the CNMI or any political subdivision or wholly owned instrumentality is covered as employment beginning in October 1, 2012.

Service by a temporary or intermittent employee who is not covered by a CNMI retirement system is covered if performed on or after January 1, 1987.

However, work in the CNMI performed as a resident of the Republic of the Philippines under contract to work on a temporary basis as a nonresident alien is not covered.

Chapter 10
State and Local Employment

TABLE OF CONTENTS

1000. Social Security Coverage for State and Local Government Employees
1001. What type of work is excluded from mandatory Social Security and Medicare coverage?
1002. Terms Defined for Section 218 Agreement Purposes
1003. Social Security and Medicare Coverage Under a Section 218 Agreement
1004. Absolute Coverage Groups
1005. Retirement System Defined
1006. Retirement System Coverage Groups
1007. Social Security Coverage for Police Officers and Firefighters Under a Retirement System
1008. Divided Retirement Systems
1009. What are the procedures for conducting a referendum?
1010. Effective Date of Section 218 Agreement
1011. Can former employees be considered for retroactive coverage?
1012. What types of work are not covered by Section 218 Agreements?
1013. Public Transportation Systems
1014. Does the State have the option of including or excluding certain types of services under a Section 218 Agreement?

1015. Positions Compensated Solely by Fees
1016. Police Officers and Firefighters Not Covered by a Retirement System
1017. Rehired Annuitants
1018. Role of the State Social Security Administrator
1019. Wages Paid Before January 1, 1987
1020. Termination of Section 218 Agreements

1000. SOCIAL SECURITY COVERAGE FOR STATE AND LOCAL GOVERNMENT EMPLOYEES

1000.1 How are State and local government employees covered by Social Security and Medicare?

State and local government employees are covered for Social Security and Medicare in one of two ways. Their coverage is either: (1) mandated by law; or (2) under a Section 218 agreement between the State and SSA.

1000.2 What is a Section 218 Agreement?

A Section 218 agreement is a voluntary agreement between a State and SSA to provide Social Security and/or Medicare only coverage for State and local government employees. Section 218 agreements are authorized under section 218 of the Social Security Act. Under the 218 agreement, the State decides (within the limits of Federal and State law) whether to cover retirement system groups, non-retirement system groups, or both.

1000.3 What types of protections are provided under a Section 218 agreement?

A Section 218 agreement provides Old-Age, Survivors, Disability and Hospital Insurance (OASDHI) protection. Employees covered under a Section 218 agreement have the same Social Security and Medicare Hospital Insurance (HI) coverage and benefit rights as employees in the private sector who are mandatorily covered for Social Security and Medicare.

1000.4 Who is covered under Medicare Hospital Insurance?

If you are a State or local government employee hired or rehired *after March 31, 1986*, you are covered for Medicare Hospital Insurance (HI), unless the law excludes your services from coverage (see §1001).

If you were hired *before April 1, 1986*, you are exempt from mandatory Medicare HI if you meet the following conditions:
- You have been working continuously for the same State or local government employer since March 31, 1986; and
- You are a member of a public retirement system.

Public employers may obtain Medicare HI coverage for employees hired before April 1, 1986 through a Section 218 agreement (see §1000.2), by contacting the State Social Security Administrator.

1000.5 Is Social Security and Medicare Hospital Insurance coverage mandatory?

Beginning July 2, 1991, Social Security and Medicare HI coverage is mandatory for State and local government employees who meet the following conditions:

A. They are not members of a public retirement system; and
B. They are not covered under a Section 218 agreement, unless excluded by law (see §1001).

1001. WHAT TYPE OF WORK IS EXCLUDED FROM MANDATORY SOCIAL SECURITY AND MEDICARE COVERAGE?

You are excluded from mandatory Social Security and Medicare coverage if:

A. You were hired to be relieved from unemployment;
B. You perform services on a temporary basis in emergencies such as a fire, storm, snow, earthquake, flood or other similar emergencies;
C. You perform services as an election official or election worker and are paid less than the threshold amount mandated by Federal law (the limit will be automatically indexed each year thereafter for inflation):
   1. Less than $50 in a calendar quarter for years 1968 through 1977;
   2. Less than $100 for calendar years 1978 through 1994;
   3. Less than $1,000 for calendar years 1995 through 1999;
   4. Less than $1,100 for calendar years 2000 and 2001;
   5. Less than $1,200 for calendar years 2002 through 2005;
   6. Less than $1,300 for calendar years 2006 through 2007;
   7. Less than $1,400 for calendar year 2008; and
   8. Less than $1,500 for calendar years 2009 through 2012;
   9. Less than $1,600 for calendar years 2013 through 2015.
   10. Less than $1,700 for calendar year 2016.
   11. Less than $1,800 for calendar year 2017 through 2019.
   12. Less than $1,900 for calendar year 2020 forward.
   13. Less than $2,000 for calendar year 2021 and 2022 forward.
   14. Less than $2,200 for 2023 and 2024.

Note: In some States, election worker services are covered under a Section 218 agreement. Therefore, a lower dollar amount may apply, unless the State executes a modification to the State's 218 agreement to increase the threshold amount.

D. You perform services in a position compensated solely on a fee basis;
E. You perform services as a student at the school where you are enrolled and regularly attending classes; or

Note: In some States, student services are covered under a Section 218 agreement.

F. You perform services as a nonresident alien and meet the following conditions:
 1. You are temporarily residing in the U.S.;
 2. You are holding an F1, J1, M1 or Q1 visa; and
 3. The work you are doing carries out the purpose for which you were admitted to the U.S.

1002. TERMS DEFINED FOR SECTION 218 AGREEMENT PURPOSES

1002.1 What is a State?

A "State," for purposes of a Section 218 agreement, includes the 50 States, Puerto Rico, the Virgin Islands and interstate instrumentalities. It does not include the District of Columbia, Guam, American Samoa and the Commonwealth of the Northern Mariana Islands. All states have a Section 218 agreement with the Social Security Administration.

1002.2 What is a political subdivision?

A political subdivision is a separate legal entity of a State that has governmental powers and functions. Political subdivisions ordinarily include counties, cities, townships, villages, school districts, utility districts and other similar governmental entities.

1002.3 What is an interstate instrumentality?

An "interstate instrumentality" is an independent legal entity, organized by two or more states, to carry out some function of government (e.g., regional transportation systems). For purposes of a Section 218 agreement, an interstate instrumentality has the status of a State under the Social Security Act.

1002.4 What is an employee?

An employee, for purposes of a Section 218 agreement, must meet the definition of employee as defined in Section 210 of the Social Security Act (see Chapter 8). It includes an elected or appointed officer of a State or political subdivision.

1003. SOCIAL SECURITY AND MEDICARE COVERAGE UNDER A SECTION 218 AGREEMENT

1003.1 What is a coverage group?

State and local government employees are brought under a Section 218 agreement (see §1000.2) in groups known as "coverage groups." The

State decides, within the limits of Federal and State law, which groups of employees to cover under its agreement. The State also decides when Social Security coverage for the group begins.

1003.2 What types of coverage groups are there?
There are two types of coverage groups:
- Absolute coverage groups
- Retirement system coverage groups

1004. ABSOLUTE COVERAGE GROUPS

1004.1 What is an absolute coverage group?
An absolute coverage group is composed of employees in positions not covered by a State or local retirement system. Coverage is provided for all current and future employees in the group unless one of the exclusions in §1012 applies.

1004.2 What is an ineligible?
An "ineligible" is an employee who is in a position under a retirement system, but is not eligible for membership in the retirement system. Ineligibility for membership may be because of age, length of service, date of hiring, etc.

1004.3 Can a State cover ineligibles with an absolute coverage group?
Yes. A State can cover ineligibles as a part of or in addition to the absolute coverage group. However, the State must decide whether coverage of the ineligibles will continue or terminate if the ineligible later becomes eligible for membership in a retirement system (see §1006).

1005. RETIREMENT SYSTEM DEFINED

1005.1 What is a retirement system?
A retirement system is any pension, annuity, retirement or similar fund or system maintained by a State or local government or instrumentality. The purpose of the system is to provide retirement benefits to participating employees. The Internal Revenue Service has the responsibility for determining whether a retirement system not covered by a Section 218 Agreement (see §1000.2) qualifies to be exempt from mandatory Social Security and Medicare coverage. (See §1000.5.)

1005.2 Who determines if a worker is a member of a retirement system?

The State determines if you are a member of a retirement system under State law. Generally, you are considered a member of a retirement system if you can qualify for benefits under that system based on your present job.

1006. RETIREMENT SYSTEM COVERAGE GROUPS

1006.1 Can employees covered by a State or local retirement system also be covered for Social Security under a Section 218 agreement?

Yes. Employees covered by a State or local retirement system can be covered for Social Security under a Section 218 agreement (see §1000.2) after a referendum is held. The referendum is held under the State's authorization. (See §1018).

1006.2 What employees are eligible to vote in a referendum?

To be eligible to vote in a referendum, you must be:

A. A member of the retirement system at the time the referendum is held; and

B. In a position under the retirement system when:
  1. The notice of referendum is given; and
  2. The referendum is held.

1006.3 What does a retirement system coverage group consist of?

The state has the option to include any of the following in a retirement system coverage group:

A. All employees in positions under the retirement system;
B. Only employees of the State in positions under the system;
C. Employees of one or more political subdivisions in positions under the system;
D. Any combination of the groups referred to in (B) and (C);
E. Employees of a hospital that is an integral part of a political subdivision;
F. Employees of two or more hospitals. Each hospital must be an integral part of the same political subdivision; or
G. Employees in each institution of "higher learning," (e.g., colleges, junior colleges, and teacher's colleges). Generally, a retirement system

coverage group includes: (1) all current members of the retirement system; (2) employees who are ineligible for membership; and (3) employees who can choose to become members of the retirement system.

Some States may divide a retirement system and cover only members who want coverage and new members as in §1008.

1007. SOCIAL SECURITY COVERAGE FOR POLICE OFFICERS AND FIREFIGHTERS UNDER A RETIREMENT SYSTEM

1007.1 Can police officers and firefighters, covered by a retirement system, be covered for Social Security under a Section 218 agreement?

Yes. Police officers and firefighters covered by a retirement system can be covered under a Section 218 agreement (see §1000.2). However, the State must first conduct a majority vote referendum, or, if allowed, a divided vote referendum. Prior to August 15,1994, only the following 23 States (including interstate instrumentalities) were authorized to provide coverage for police officer and firefighter positions under a retirement system:

Alabama	Kansas	North Carolina	Tennessee
California	Maine	North Dakota	Texas
Florida	Maryland	Oregon	Vermont
Georgia	Mississippi	Puerto Rico	Virginia
Hawaii	Montana	South Carolina	Washington
Idaho	New York	South Dakota	

1007.2 Who is included in the retirement system coverage group for a majority vote referendum?

If a majority vote referendum is favorable, the retirement system coverage group consists of all current, future and ineligible employees in positions under the retirement system in which the referendum was held.

1007.3 Who is included in the retirement system coverage group for a divided vote referendum?

If a divided vote referendum is held, the retirement system coverage group consists of members who choose coverage as well as future members (see §1008). The State may elect to extend coverage to ineligibles of the retirement system.

1007.4 What if police officers and firefighters are under the same retirement system?

If police officers and firefighters are under the same retirement system, their positions may either be:

A. Considered separate retirement systems for referendum and coverage purposes;
B. Combined with each other, and other positions; or both.

In addition, a separate referendum can be held: (1) among the police officers; (2) among the firefighters; or (3) among the police officers *and* firefighters as one group.

1008. DIVIDED RETIREMENT SYSTEMS

1008.1 Can states divide retirement systems?

Under Federal law, 23 states are authorized to divide a retirement system. This division is based on whether the employees in positions under that retirement system want Social Security coverage. These states are:

Alaska	New Jersey	California
New Mexico	Connecticut	New York
Florida	North Dakota	Georgia
Pennsylvania	Hawaii	Rhode Island
Illinois	Tennessee	Kentucky
Texas	Louisiana	Vermont
Massachusetts	Washington	Minnesota
Wisconsin	Nevada	

1008.2 Can members have a second chance to obtain Social Security coverage?

If you previously voted "no" in a referendum for Social Security coverage, State law may permit your State to provide members with a second chance to obtain Social Security coverage. If you then want coverage, you must file a written request for coverage with the State. This coverage must be made a part of a State's agreement within two years after the date of execution of the agreement extending coverage to the retirement system. The State may, at any time, hold a majority vote referendum among all members who did not choose coverage. The outcome of the referendum may provide coverage for all positions under the system not already covered under the system.

1008.3 Can ineligibles obtain Social Security coverage?

If you are an employee in a position under the retirement system and you are ineligible for membership in the system, you will automatically be covered if the State conducts a favorable majority vote referendum. However, if the State conducts a divided vote referendum (see §1007.3), you will be covered at the option of the State. As an ineligible, you have no right of individual choice.

1009. WHAT ARE THE PROCEDURES FOR CONDUCTING A REFERENDUM?

The referendum is a State matter. However, Federal law does require the Governor of the State to certify that the following conditions have been met:

A. All eligible employees were given at least 90 days notice of the referendum; an extension of an additional 60 days for the entire eligible retirement system membership will be permitted if any retirement system members are called to military duty prior to the delegated State official issuing the advance 90-day notice of referendum;

B. An opportunity to vote was given and limited to eligible employees;

C. The referendum was held by secret written ballot for a majority vote referendum; or by written ballot for a divided vote referendum; and

D. A majority of all of the retirement system's eligible employees voted for coverage. (In a divided vote referendum, only those employees who voted "yes" for coverage and all future employees will be covered.)

The referendum procedures are conducted under the direction of the State Social Security Administrator (see §1018).

1010. EFFECTIVE DATE OF SECTION 218 AGREEMENT

1010.1 When does coverage under a Section 218 agreement begin?

The State decides when coverage will begin. Coverage under a Section 218 agreement (see §1000.2) may begin as early as five years before the year the State modifies its agreement to include the coverage group. Some State laws do not permit the agreement to be retroactive for as much as five years.

1010.2 How many effective dates can apply for each coverage group?

Generally, there can be only one effective date for each coverage group. If a retirement system includes: (1) employees of the State; and/or (2) employees of one or more political subdivisions of the State covered as one group, then the State may provide different effective dates for the employees of each participating entity.

1010.3 How is the effective date determined under a divided retirement system?

Under a divided retirement system (see §1008), members who did not originally vote for coverage, but later choose coverage, are included on the same date originally provided for the retirement system coverage group.

1011. CAN FORMER EMPLOYEES BE CONSIDERED FOR RETROACTIVE COVERAGE?

Ordinarily, only individuals in an employment relationship on a specific date, set out in the agreement, can obtain retroactive coverage for services. However, under certain conditions, a State may consider former employees, whose earnings were incorrectly reported to the Social Security Administration and to the Internal Revenue Service, to be in the coverage group for the period of retroactive coverage.

1012. WHAT TYPES OF WORK ARE NOT COVERED BY SECTION 218 AGREEMENTS?

Certain types of work are not covered by Section 218 agreements (see §1000.2) because Federal law excludes them. You are not covered under Section 218 agreements if:

A. You were hired to be relieved from unemployment;
B. You work as a patient or inmate in a hospital, home, or other institution thereof;
C. You work as a transportation system employee, which is compulsorily covered for Social Security (see §1013);
D. You work for a private employer and that work is not defined as employment under Section 210(a) of the Social Security Act; and
E. You are hired to work on a temporary basis in case of a fire, storm, snow, earthquake, flood or other similar emergency.

1013. PUBLIC TRANSPORTATION SYSTEMS

1013.1 Are public transportation system employees covered under Section 218 agreements?

Work you do for a public transportation system that is operated by a State or political subdivision of a State may be covered under a Section 218 agreement (see §1000.2).

1013.2 Are public transportation system employees covered under Social Security?

Generally, public transportation work is compulsorily covered under Social Security where the following conditions exist:

A. The transportation system was acquired from private ownership after 1950; and
B. No general retirement system became applicable to the employees at the time it was acquired.

1014. DOES THE STATE HAVE THE OPTION OF INCLUDING OR EXCLUDING CERTAIN TYPES OF SERVICES UNDER A SECTION 218 AGREEMENT?

Yes. Section 218 agreements (see §1000.2), at the option of the State, may include or exclude the following services:

A. Services in elective positions;
B. Services in part-time positions;
C. Services in positions compensated solely by fees (See §1015);
D. Agricultural labor (See §§901-914.);
E. Student services; and
F. Services performed by election officials and election workers paid less than the threshold amount mandated by Federal law.

Generally, if one of the types of work listed above was covered under the State's agreement, it cannot later be removed from coverage, except for the services in (F) above.

1015. POSITIONS COMPENSATED SOLELY BY FEES

1015.1 How are services compensated solely on a fee basis treated for Social Security coverage purposes?

If you perform work in a position compensated solely by fees received directly from the public, you are considered self-employed and covered under the SECA tax (See §1125). This does not apply to positions compensated by both salary and fees.

1015.2 What is a fee-based official?
A fee-based public official is one who receives and retains remuneration directly from the public, e.g., justice of the peace, local registrar of vital statistics. If you receive payment for services from government funds in the form of a wage or salary, you are not a fee-based public official even if the compensation is called a fee.

The fee-based public official provisions do not apply to notary publics. A notary public is not a public official even though he/she performs a public function and receives a fee for services performed. The services of a notary public are not covered for Social Security purposes.

1015.3 What if both salary and fees are used as compensation?
If you receive compensation in the form of both a salary and fees, your position is considered fee-based, if the fees are the primary source of compensation. However, State law may determine that any position, for which any salary is paid, is not a fee-based position. In this case, your position may not be considered fee-based.

1016. POLICE OFFICERS AND FIREFIGHTERS NOT COVERED BY A RETIREMENT SYSTEM

1016.1 What if police officer and firefighter positions are not covered by a retirement system?
These positions are generally covered as part of the political entity's absolute coverage group (see §1004) when the political entity is covered under the State's 218 agreement (see §1000.2). The absolute coverage group includes other city or town employees whose positions are not covered by a public retirement system.

If police or firefighter positions are covered as part of an absolute coverage group and later become covered under a retirement system, Section 218 coverage continues.

1016.2 Can ineligibles in police officer or firefighter positions be covered with an absolute coverage or retirement system coverage group?
Ineligibles in police officer or firefighter positions cannot be covered as part of an absolute coverage group or a retirement system coverage group (see §1006).

1017. REHIRED ANNUITANTS

1017.1 What is a rehired annuitant?

A "rehired annuitant" is a retiree who is rehired by his or her former employer or another employer that participates in the same retirement system as the former employer. A rehired annuitant is either drawing a retirement benefit from that retirement system, or has reached normal retirement age under the retirement system.

1017.2 Are rehired annuitants covered under Social Security?

Under Federal regulations, rehired annuitants are excluded from mandatory Social Security coverage. However, if you are rehired to perform services in a State or local government position that is covered for Social Security under a Section 218 agreement (see §1000.2), your services in that position are covered for Social Security. In addition, all retirees hired after March 31, 1986, are covered for Medicare HI by law.

1018. ROLE OF THE STATE SOCIAL SECURITY ADMINISTRATOR

1018.1 What is a State Social Security Administrator?

Each State has a designated official who is responsible for administering and maintaining the State's Section 218 agreement (see §1000.2). This official is the State Social Security Administrator.

1018.2 What does the State Social Security Administrator do?

The main roles of the State Social Security Administrator are listed below:

A. Administers and maintains the State's Section 218 Agreement that governs Social Security and Medicare coverage for State and local government employees;

B. Conducts referenda for Social Security and Medicare coverage, and prepares and executes modifications to the State's 218 agreement to include additional coverage groups; and

C. Provides information and advice to State and local employers and employees about Social Security and Medicare coverage, taxation, and reporting issues related to the State's Section 218 Agreement.

1019. WAGES PAID BEFORE JANUARY 1, 1987

1019.1 Who is responsible for the payment of contributions for wages paid before January 1, 1987?

The State is liable for the payment of contributions on all wages paid before January 1, 1987, for services covered under the State agreement. The amount due is equal to the sum of the employer and employee taxes imposed under the Federal Insurance Contributions Act (FICA) on private employers. Wages for covered services are subject to the wage limitations in §1301.

1019.2 How are contributions paid if an employee worked for more than one political entity?

If an employee worked for more than one political entity, contributions are due on all wages paid by each entity up to the maximum (see §1407).

1019.3 Is there a statue of limitations for State liability of contributions for wages?

A statute of limitations determines a time limit beyond which: (1) a State is not liable for amounts due on wages paid to employees whose services are covered under its agreement; and (2) SSA is not liable for refunding or crediting overpayments made by a State under its agreement.

In some situations, the earnings record of an individual may be corrected after the time limit for revising such records has expired. (See §§1424-1425.)

1019.4 What types of reviews may be requested of the Commissioner of Social Security?

Any State may request the Commissioner of Social Security to review:

A. An assessment of an amount due from the State under its agreement;
B. A disallowance of the State's claim for credit or refund of an overpayment of its contributions; or
C. An allowance to the State of a credit or refund of an overpayment of its contributions.

1019.5 When are requests for review by the Commissioner of Social Security filed?

The State must file its request for review within 90 days after the date of the notice to the State of the assessment, disallowance or allowance. The time for filing the request for review may be extended for good cause. The request for extension of time must be made before expiration of the 90-day period.

1019.6 What information is included with the request for review?

The request must show the specific issue on which review is being asked. Any additional evidence or information that the State wishes to submit is also included. SSA may allow a State an additional 90 days from the filing of the request for review to furnish evidence or information. If the State needs more time, an extension may be granted for good cause.

1019.7 What happens after the review?

SSA reviews whether or not the State has paid the amount assessed or has taken the credit allowed. If the State is not satisfied with the decision, it may file civil suit in the appropriate Federal district court for a redetermination. The appeal must be filed within two years of notification of SSA's decision. SSA may extend the time for filing a civil action for good cause. The State must request an extension of time before expiration of the two-year period.

Note: For wages paid after December 31, 1986, States are no longer liable for their political subdivisions' Social Security deposits. States and political subdivisions are required to follow FICA procedures, and the IRS is responsible for the administration and collection of the FICA taxes.

1020. TERMINATION OF SECTION 218 AGREEMENTS

1020.1 Can a Section 218 agreement be terminated?

No. A State may not terminate a Section 218 agreement (see §1000.2) either in its entirety or with respect to any coverage group, on or after April 20, 1983. The prohibition against terminating Section 218 agreements applies to any agreement in effect on April 20, 1983, regardless of whether a notice of termination was in effect on that date.

Prior to 1983, States could terminate a Section 218 agreement, in part or entirely, under certain specified conditions. The prohibition against terminating Section 218 agreements also applies to involuntary terminations for failure to comply with the agreement. This includes partial terminations in cases where an entity has been legally dissolved.

Note: States and interstate instrumentalities may modify their agreements to cover groups previously terminated.

1020.2 What should be done if an entity no longer exists?

There are instances where an entity is legally dissolved or is no longer in existence. When an entity is dissolved, the State must notify SSA and submit evidence of the dissolution. SSA notifies the State in writing whether the evidence is acceptable documentation that the entity no longer exists.

CHAPTER 11
Are You Self-Employed?

TABLE OF CONTENTS

1100. Social Security Coverage for the Self-Employed
1101. Trade or Business Defined
1102. Personal Services
1103. Does length of time engaged in an activity determine a trade or business?
1104. Can an illegal activity be a trade or business?
1105. Can more than one trade or business be operated?
1106. Is a hobby a trade or business?
1107. Partnership Defined
1108. What factors indicate a partnership or joint venture?
1109. Families and Partnerships
1110. What factors indicate a valid partnership?
1111. Does transfer of capital interest to a family member make the member a partner?
1112. Is an association taxable as a corporation or a partnership?
1113. Writers Receiving Royalties
1114. Nonprofessional Fiduciaries
1115. Is a beneficiary of a trust operating a trade or business engaged in the trade or business?
1116. Business Carried on by Executors or Administrators of Deceased's Estate
1117. What categories of mail carriers are self-employed?

1118. Owner of Land on Which Business is Operated
1119. Definition of Sharefarmer
1120. "Undertakes to Produce a Crop" Defined for Sharefarming Arrangements
1121. Partnership or Joint Ventures Between Farm Owner and Operator
1122. Exclusions from Trade or Business
1123. Are newspaper vendors self-employed?
1124. Are employees of foreign governments self-employed?
1125. State and Local Government Employees
1126. Public Office Holders
1127. Federal Court Reporters
1128. When may members of certain religious groups receive an exemption from the Social Security tax?
1129. Claiming the Tax Exemption
1130. Ministers, Members of Religious Orders, and Christian Science Practitioners
1131. Exemptions from Self-Employment Coverage
1132. Time Limit to File for Exemption
1133. Are services by chaplains self-employment?
1134. Crews on Fishing Boats
1135. Real Estate Agents and Direct Sellers
1136. Certain Church Employees Treated as Self-Employed

1100. SOCIAL SECURITY COVERAGE FOR THE SELF-EMPLOYED

1100.1 When did Social Security coverage begin for self-employed people?

Most self-employed people became covered by Social Security in 1951.

1100.2 What are the exceptions?

A. Farmers, ministers, and some other individuals (including certain professionals) were not covered until 1955;

B. Additional groups of professionals were covered for taxable years ending after 1955; and

C. Self-employed doctors of medicine were covered for taxable years ending on or after December 31, 1965.

Note: See §1122 for a detailed list of activities excluded from self-employment coverage.

1100.3 How is self-employment income calculated?

"Self-employment income" that is creditable for Social Security is based on "net earnings from self-employment" derived from a "trade or business" covered by the law.

Payment from self-employment that is not covered under Social Security is included when figuring income for earnings test purposes. (See Chapter 18)

1101. TRADE OR BUSINESS DEFINED

1101.1 How is trade or business defined?

For Social Security purposes, the term "trade or business" has the same meaning as when used in section 162 of the Internal Revenue Code relating to income taxes. However, certain occupations and the self-employed activities of members of certain religious groups who have been granted exemptions from the self-employment tax are not included in the term "trade or business" for Social Security purposes. They are included only if certain conditions are met.

1101.2 What are the guidelines for determining trade or business activity?

"Trade or business" is not specifically defined in section 162 of the Internal Revenue Code. However, certain guidelines for deciding whether a trade or business exists have been set forth in court decisions and Internal Revenue Service rulings. Briefly stated, these guidelines are:

A. You started and carried on the activity in good faith with the intention of making a profit or producing income;
B. You carried on the activity regularly, with a continuity of operation, a continual repetition of transactions, or a regularity of activities;
C. The activity is your regular occupation or calling that you carry on to make a living or a profit; and
D. You present yourself to the public as being engaged in the selling of goods and/or services.

Any one of these factors standing alone is not enough to show that a trade or business exists, but not all the factors need be present.

1102. PERSONAL SERVICES

1102.1 Are personal services required for income to count toward Social Security?

Personal services are not required. You may carry on a business through employees. Thus, absentee owners or silent partners can derive income from a trade or business.

1102.2 Are limited partners covered by Social Security?

For taxable years beginning after 1977, limited partners are excluded from Social Security coverage. Previously, limited partners could be covered on the same basis as other partners.

1103. DOES LENGTH OF TIME ENGAGED IN AN ACTIVITY DETERMINE A TRADE OR BUSINESS?

The length of time you engage in an activity usually is a factor in determining if it is a trade or business. If the activity is seasonal or of short duration, however, the period of time is not important.

For example, selling ice cream during the summer months or owning a grocery store for a short time before selling it. The short time period would not prevent the activity from being covered by Social Security.

1104. CAN AN ILLEGAL ACTIVITY BE A TRADE OR BUSINESS?

The illegality of an activity does not prevent it from being a trade or business. For example, professional gamblers, bookies, etc. may be engaged in a trade or business. If you are in this category, you are considered self-employed and are required to report your income and pay self-employment taxes.

1105. CAN MORE THAN ONE TRADE OR BUSINESS BE OPERATED?

You may own more than one trade or business. For example, you may operate both a wholesale grocery and a restaurant.

1106. IS A HOBBY A TRADE OR BUSINESS?

A hobby is not generally a trade or business. If you buy and sell stamps, pigeons, or coins to further the hobby rather than to make a profit, the activity is not a trade or business. If you conduct these activities to provide part or all of your livelihood, they may be a trade or business.

Consideration of the guidelines in §1101, in combination with the facts in each case, determine whether the activity is a trade or a business.

1107. PARTNERSHIP DEFINED

1107.1 Are business partners self-employed?

Yes, business partners are self-employed. A partnership is generally said to be created when two or more persons join together to carry on a trade or business. Each partner contributes in one or more ways with money, property, labor, or skill and shares in the profits and risks of loss in accordance with the partnership agreement or understanding.

1107.2 How does intention relate to partnership?

The intention of the parties that join together to carry on a trade or business is important in determining whether a partnership exists. Intention of the parties is determined not merely from their statements, but to a large degree, from how they carry on the business with each other and with third parties. The abilities and contributions of each partner and the control that each has over the operation of the business are also important factors.

1107.3 Is a partnership the same for Social Security as for income tax?

A partnership is the same for Social Security purposes as for income tax purposes except that Social Security excludes coverage of a limited partner in a limited partnership. Besides the ordinary partnership, the term "partnership" for Federal income tax purposes includes a syndicate, group, pool, joint venture, or any other unincorporated organization that carries on a business. The term does not include corporations, trusts, estates, or associations taxable as corporations. (See §825 for an explanation of these associations.)

1107.4 Must a partnership have a formal agreement?

No. Two or more persons, including husbands and wives, may be self-employed as partners for income tax and Social Security purposes. This may apply even if they do not operate under a formal partnership agreement, and even if they are not considered partners under State law because they have not complied with local statutory requirements.

1107.5 Is a partnership the same as a joint venture?

For Federal income tax purposes and for Social Security purposes, a partnership and a joint venture are essentially the same. The main distinction is that a partnership involves a continuing enterprise while a joint venture is usually for the accomplishment of a single project or transaction.

1108. WHAT FACTORS INDICATE A PARTNERSHIP OR JOINT VENTURE?

The following factors indicate a partnership or joint venture:

A. An intent on the part of two or more people to join together in good faith to carry on a trade or business;

B. Contribution of capital or services to the business by each party;

C. A sharing of the right to participate in management decisions and other responsibilities;

D. A sharing in the profits and risk of loss in accordance with the parties' agreement; and

E. Neither person is an employee of the other.

All of these basic factors must be present for an arrangement to be considered a partnership.

1109. FAMILIES AND PARTNERSHIPS

1109.1 May families form partnerships?

Yes. You may form valid partnerships with members of your family. For instance, a husband and wife or parents and children may conduct a business enterprise as a partnership.

1109.2 How is the validity of family partnerships determined?

The determination regarding partnerships with family members in a business depends on how you operate the business. You may have joint funds or mutual management with your spouse, but the legal incidents of the husband and wife relationship complicate the determination as to whether the business is jointly operated more than if the parties were unrelated. Merely "helping out" in the business or doing chores does not establish a partnership.

In cases involving closely related parties, the factors that usually indicate a partnership, such as the use of property, must be carefully evaluated to determine whether they indicate the existence of a partnership or a sole proprietorship.

1110. WHAT FACTORS INDICATE A VALID PARTNERSHIP?

The following factors help establish whether your business is conducted as a partnership:

A. Copies of any written agreements entered into by the parties or statements of the parties as to the terms of the arrangement;

B. Copies of partnership income tax returns on which the business income was reported;

C. Corroboration from the other partner(s); and

D. Statements from disinterested third parties, such as suppliers, wholesalers, customers, local business people, etc., who are familiar with the manner in which your business was conducted.

1111. DOES TRANSFER OF CAPITAL INTEREST TO A FAMILY MEMBER MAKE THE MEMBER A PARTNER?

Transfer of capital interest to a family member in a family partnership to a member of the same family (including only his or her spouse, ancestors and lineal descendants) generally makes the member a partner if:

A. A bona fide transfer by gift or purchase of a capital interest in the partnership has occurred;

B. The member actually owns the partnership interest and is vested with dominion and control over it;

C. The partnership is one in which capital is a material income-producing factor; and

D. A valid partnership was in existence before the transfer or was created at the time of the transfer.

1112. IS AN ASSOCIATION TAXABLE AS A CORPORATION OR A PARTNERSHIP?

An association taxable as a corporation (see §825) is not a partnership for self-employment tax purposes because it is not considered a partnership for income tax purposes.

1113. WRITERS RECEIVING ROYALTIES

1113.1 Are writers engaged in a trade or business?

Writers who receive royalties may be engaged in a trade or business. Each case must be decided from the facts. A one-time venture of short duration is usually not a trade or business, but a repetition of such ventures would constitute a trade or business. Thus, if you write only one book as a sideline and never revise it, the writing activities would probably not be a trade or business. However, if you prepare new editions from time to time or write several books, the writing and editing activities would be a trade or business.

1113.2 Is writing in combination with other activities considered a trade or business?

You may engage in other related activities which, when considered together with the writing activities, may be a trade or business. For example, if you are a college professor who writes a book on business administration and gives lectures and advice to business groups on the same subject, you would probably be in a trade or business.

Note: For the effect of the receipt of royalties on the payment of benefits, see §1812 (W).

1114. NONPROFESSIONAL FIDUCIARIES

1114.1 Are nonprofessional fiduciaries in a trade or business?

Nonprofessional fiduciaries serve as executors or administrators in isolated instances, and then only as personal representatives for the estate of deceased friends or relatives. Generally, they are not engaged in a trade or business, unless all of the following conditions are met:

A. There is a trade or business among the assets of the estate;
B. The fiduciary actively participates in the operation of this trade or business; and
C. The fees of the fiduciary are related to the operation of the trade or business.

1114.2 Can nonprofessional fiduciary activities be considered a trade or business if they are extensive?

Activities of a nonprofessional fiduciary of a single estate may be a trade or business if they are of sufficient scope and duration. This may occur when the executor manages an unusually large estate that requires extensive management activities over a long period.

1115. IS A BENEFICIARY OF A TRUST OPERATING A TRADE OR BUSINESS ENGAGED IN THE TRADE OR BUSINESS?

A beneficiary of a trust that operates a trade or business is not engaged in the trade or business. This is because the trust rather than the beneficiary is engaged in the activity. However, a trade or business that is carried on by a conservator, committee, or guardian on behalf of an incompetent is considered as carried on by the incompetent. This is true even if the person has been legally adjudged as incompetent.

1116. BUSINESS CARRIED ON BY EXECUTORS OR ADMINISTRATORS OF DECEASED'S ESTATE

1116.1 When income is generated by a business that is part of an estate, who receives the income?

When a business is part of an estate that is being administered, the income from the business is income of the estate and not of the heirs. This is true even if one or more of the heirs does the actual work and keeps the proceeds, and even if the heir is the administrator of the estate. However, this work may be a separate trade or business.

1116.2 When pay is received for running a business that is part of an estate, how is it classified?

If you receive pay designated specifically from running the business (as distinguished from an amount received as a distribution of estate assets to an heir), it counts as earnings from self-employment. (See also §1114 for rules where the administrator runs the business.)

1117. WHAT CATEGORIES OF MAIL CARRIERS ARE SELF-EMPLOYED?

Star route mail carriers, contract mail messengers, contract postal station operators, and contract postal branch operators work on a contract basis and are self-employed, unless determined by the U.S. Postal Service to be employees of that Service.

1118. OWNER OF LAND ON WHICH BUSINESS IS OPERATED

1118.1 When is an owner also a landlord?

Some facts that indicate an owner is a landlord are:

A. The owner's right of entry on the land is limited to the right to protect and maintain the property; and

B. The person occupying the land has:
1. Right to possession of the land;
2. Right to use of the land for his or her own purposes;
3. Right to use and possession for a definite period of time;
4. Obligation to pay rent;
5. Right to sublease; and
6. Control over the running of the business.

An owner of land can enter on it to prevent waste, make repairs, etc. In the case of a farm, an owner may take part in formulating the farm plan and may require the practice of good husbandry. An owner may also furnish supplies and equipment and share in the cost of seed, fertilizer, and other expenses for maintaining the fertility of the land or increasing its yield.

1118.2 Do these activities affect self-employment of the tenant or owner?

Neither the exercise of these rights nor the furnishing of these goods is inconsistent with a landlord-tenant relationship. In this case, the tenant is a self-employed farm operator and the farm owner is a landlord. The landlord's rental income counts for Social Security only if he or she materially participates in the crop production, as explained in §§1221-1232.

1119. DEFINITION OF SHAREFARMER

1119.1 When does a sharefarming arrangement exist?

A sharefarmer is a self-employed person. A sharefarming arrangement exists if the arrangement provides for all of the following:

A. The sharefarmer undertakes to produce a crop or livestock on the landowner's farm;
B. The sharefarmer receives a share of the crop or livestock, or a share of the proceeds from their sale; and
C. The amount of the sharefarmer's share depends upon the amount of the crop or the number of livestock produced.

If any one of these elements is not present, a "sharefarming" relationship does not exist.

1119.2 What are the other possible relationships?

There may, however, be a landlord-tenant relationship, or the person may be an employee of the landowner, or a partnership, or joint venture may exist between them.

1120. "UNDERTAKES TO PRODUCE A CROP" DEFINED FOR SHARE-FARMING ARRANGEMENTS

1120.1 What is a sharefarming arrangement?

A "sharefarming arrangement" is one in which the sharefarmer performs the labor for production of the crop. It is not one in which the landowner agrees to participate in the day-to-day physical labor in the production of the crop or livestock.

1120.2 What does undertakes to produce a crop mean?

The phrase "undertakes to produce a crop or livestock" means performing or assuming the responsibility for performing substantially all the physical labor involved in producing of the farm product.

1120.3 What activities are included under this definition?

Generally, this means that the tenant has the responsibility for caring for the crop from the beginning up to and including harvesting. In some circumstances, it may not include planting of the crop. For example, in fruit raising operations, the planting of fruit trees, bushes, or plants may have been done by the landowner in a prior year. This would not alter the relationship of the parties to a sharefarming arrangement with regard to the fruit crop.

1120.4 If the landowner harvests or sells the crop, does the sharefarming arrangement remain?

The landowner may sometimes harvest or sell the crop produced. If the person who produced a crop has the responsibility for planting, raising, and caring for the crop or livestock during substantially all of the growing period, the element of a sharefarming arrangement is still met.

1120.5 What activities are excluded from producing a crop or livestock?

Producing a crop or livestock does not include such specialized activities as custom sheep shearing, custom harvesting, dusting, or custom cultivating.

1121. PARTNERSHIP OR JOINT VENTURES BETWEEN FARM OWNER AND OPERATOR

1121.1 When are a farm owner and operator in a partnership?

If both the farm owner and the person working the land are involved in the management and control of the farm operations or in the day-to-day operations of the farm, they may be partners. (Some guidelines as to the existence of a partnership are set out in §§1107-1112.)

1121.2 If the operator alone produces the crop or livestock, is the arrangement a partnership?

No. In a partnership, the operator alone does not undertake to produce the crop or livestock, even though the agreement may name one partner to do the physical work and the other to contribute his capital, credit, management services, etc. In this case both parties are farm operators and self-employed.

1122. EXCLUSIONS FROM TRADE OR BUSINESS

1122.1 What exclusions apply to trade and businesses for Social Security purposes?

The term "trade or business" does not include the following for Social Security purposes:

A. Work as an employee, except newspaper vendors who are age 18 or older;

B. Work by U.S. citizens performing services in the U.S. as employees of a foreign government and, in some circumstances, as employees of an instrumentality wholly owned by a foreign government, or an international organization;

C. Employees of a State or political subdivision thereof who are paid solely on a fee basis and whose services are not otherwise covered as employment under a Federal-State coverage agreement (see §1125);

D. Work as an employee or employee representative covered by the Railroad Retirement system;

E. Work as a public official (except public officials of a State or political subdivision who are paid solely on a fee basis and whose services are not covered under a Federal-State coverage agreement) (see §1126);

F. Self-employment by members of certain religious sects exempt from self-employment taxes;

G. Services performed by ordained, commissioned or licensed ministers if they elected to be exempted from coverage under the Internal Revenue Code, and by members of religious orders who have not taken a vow of poverty;

H. Services performed by Christian Science practitioners, if they have elected to be exempted from coverage under the Internal Revenue Code; or

I. Deemed self-employment income of employees of church or church-controlled organizations that have elected to be exempt from payment of Social Security taxes for its employees.

1122.2 What trade or business rules apply to religious orders?
The term "trade or business" does not include services by a member of a religious order who has taken a vow of poverty when these services are performed in the exercise of the duties required by the order. However, effective October 30, 1972, these services may be covered as employment for the order if the order irrevocably elects coverage for its entire active membership and its lay employees. (For rules that apply see §932.)

1123. ARE NEWSPAPER VENDORS SELF-EMPLOYED?
Newspaper vendors who are age 18 or older are covered as self-employed persons if they are excluded from coverage as employees under the rules stated in §§929-930. Newspaper vendors under age 18 are considered as self-employed only if they are independent business people.

1124. ARE EMPLOYEES OF FOREIGN GOVERNMENTS SELF-EMPLOYED?
Services are considered self-employment (and excluded from employment) if they were performed in the U.S. by U.S. citizens who are employees of:
A. A foreign government;
B. An instrumentality wholly owned by a foreign government; or
C. An international organization.

1125. STATE AND LOCAL GOVERNMENT EMPLOYEES

1125.1 If Federal-State coverage for a government employee is not provided, are earnings covered as self-employment?
If you performed services after 1967 that were:
A. Compensated solely on a fee basis performed as an employee of a State or political subdivision of a State; and
B. Not covered under a Federal-State coverage agreement, then your earnings must be counted as self-employment earnings.

1125.2 Are exceptions applicable?
If you were an employee who in 1968 performed services as described above, you could have made an irrevocable election not to have such fees constitute net earnings from self-employment for 1968 and later.

1125.3 How is this exception obtained?

The exclusion of fees from net earnings would have been obtained by filing the certification of election with the Internal Revenue Service on or before the due date of your tax return for 1968. If you did not file this certification, you must count the earnings as self-employment earnings.

1125.4 If the services are covered by an agreement with the Secretary of HHS and the State, how are earnings counted?

If the services are covered under an agreement between the Secretary of Health and Human Services and the State for which the services are rendered, as described in Chapter 10, the services are covered as employment.

1126. PUBLIC OFFICE HOLDERS

1126.1 Are public office functions a trade or business?

The performance of functions of a public office is excluded by the Social Security law from the term "trade or business." A "public office" includes any elective or appointive office of the Federal Government, of a State or its political subdivisions, or of a wholly-owned instrumentality.

1126.2 What public offices are covered by this exclusion?

Public offices not considered a trade or business include, among many others, the President, the Vice President, members of the President's Cabinet, governors, mayors, members of Congress, State representatives, county commissioners, judges, county or city attorneys, marshals, sheriffs, registrars of deeds, and notaries public.

1126.3 Are earnings from other activities covered as Social Security earnings?

If a public official engages in an activity that is not part of the function of the public office, the income from that activity may be covered.

1126.4 When is a public official covered as an employee of a State or local government?

A public official may be covered as an employee of a State or local government under the conditions set out in Chapter 10.

1126.5 What public officials are covered as employees of the Federal government?
The President, the Vice President, members of the President's Cabinet, and members of Congress, among others, are covered as employees of the Federal Government effective January 1, 1984. (See §940.)

1127. FEDERAL COURT REPORTERS

1127.1 How are Federal court reporters paid?
Federal court reporters receive a salary from the Federal Government. They are also paid fees by the litigants for furnishing copies of transcripts.

1127.2 Is the employee's salary covered by Social Security?
The salary paid to the employee is not covered by Social Security, unless work for the Federal Government began after 1983, because it is covered by the Civil Service Retirement System. (See §940.)

1127.3 Are fees counted as income by Social Security?
The fees are counted as income from a trade or business and are covered by Social Security. They are not considered pay for work as a public employee or a public official.

1127.4 How is coverage determined?
The coverage of fees received by State court reporters depends upon the wording of the State law creating these positions. Work that the State law requires to be done is performed by the reporter as an employee. It may be covered by Social Security only if the job is included in a Federal-State coverage agreement as explained in Chapter 10. Fees for work not required by State law are normally earnings from self-employment covered by Social Security.

1128. WHEN MAY MEMBERS OF CERTAIN RELIGIOUS GROUPS RECEIVE AN EXEMPTION FROM THE SOCIAL SECURITY TAX?

As a member of certain religious groups, you may qualify for an exemption from the Social Security tax. You must waive your rights to all benefits under the Social Security Act, including hospital insurance benefits. You may be either an employee or self-employed. The following requirements must also be met:

A. You must be a member of a recognized religious sect that has established tenets and teachings by which you are conscientiously opposed to accepting benefits under a private or public insurance plan. This includes benefits such as payments in the event of death, disability or retirement, or payments towards the cost of medical care (including the benefits of any insurance system established by SSA);

B. Beginning after December 31, 1988, your wages are not subject to Social Security tax when you are paid by your employer if you and your employer are members of such a religious group. Both you and your employer must have approved applications for exemptions as provided in §1129. The employer for the purpose of this exemption is:
1. A self-employed individual;
2. A partnership provided all the partners have approved exemptions;
3. Effective with remuneration paid after December 31, 1988, a church or a church-controlled organization if the organization has in effect an exemption from payment of Social Security taxes (IRS Form 8274, *Certification by Churches and Qualified Church-Controlled Organizations Electing Exemption from Employers Social Security Taxes*) on its employees;

C. You have never received or been entitled to any benefits payable under Title II (Federal Old-Age, Survivors, and Disability Insurance) or Title XVIII (Health Insurance for the Aged and Disabled) of the Social Security Act;

D. The religious group of which you are a member has been in existence continuously since December 31, 1950; and

E. The religious group makes reasonable provision for its dependent members and has done so since December 31, 1950.

1129. CLAIMING THE TAX EXEMPTION

1129.1 How can the Social Security self-employment tax exemption be claimed?

To claim the exemption, you must file IRS Form 4029 (*Application for Exemption From Social Security Taxes and Waiver of Benefits*) with the IRS. The application for exemption must be filed on or before the due date for the tax return for the first taxable year in which you have self-employment income or are a member of an approved organization.

1129.2 How long does the exemption remain in effect?

Once granted, the exemption remains in effect until you or the religious group of which you are a member ceases to meet the requirements stated in §1128. If the exemption and waiver cease to be effective, any future Social Security benefits are payable only based on your earnings beginning with the first taxable year that the exemption is not in effect.

1130. MINISTERS, MEMBERS OF RELIGIOUS ORDERS, AND CHRISTIAN SCIENCE PRACTITIONERS

1130.1 Are ministers self-employed?

Ministers, members of religious orders who have not taken a vow of poverty, and Christian Science practitioners are covered as self-employed for Social Security purposes beginning in 1968, for their services as a minister, member, or practitioner.

1130.2 How are earnings reported?

You should report your income from these services as net earnings from self-employment, even if you perform your services as an employee.

1130.3 Is an exemption available?

Ministers, members, or practitioners who are conscientiously opposed to, or because of religious principles are opposed to, the acceptance of benefits based on their earnings from these services may elect to be exempt from coverage by applying to IRS for an irrevocable exemption. (See §§1131-1132.)

1130.4 Can the exemption ever be revoked?

Under a special provision of the 1977 amendments to the Social Security Act, individuals who had filed for exemption were given an opportunity to revoke the exemption. The revocation had to be filed before the due date of the income tax return for the individual's first taxable year beginning in 1978. Under the Tax Reform Act of 1986, enacted on October 22, 1986, individuals who had filed for exemption were again given an opportunity to revoke the exemption. The revocation had to be filed before the individual became entitled to Social Security benefits and no later than the due date (including any extension) of the Federal income tax return for the individual's first taxable year beginning after the date of enactment. The Ticket to Work and Work Incentives Improvement Act of 1999 allows members of the clergy who previously opted not to be covered under Social Security a two-year window in which to elect to be covered. The provisions of this law apply to services performed in taxable years beginning January 1, 2000. The application for revocation of the exemption must be filed with the IRS no later than the due date of the Federal Income Tax Return (including extensions) for the applicant's *second* taxable year beginning after December 31, 1999.

Therefore, the application for revocation must be filed by April 15, 2002 or October 15, 2002 (including all available extensions) respectively.

1130.5 What were the rules before 1968?

Before 1968, a minister, member or practitioner was exempt from coverage as self-employed, unless the person chose to be covered by filing a Form 2031 (*Waiver Certificate To Elect Social Security Coverage for Use by Ministers, Certain Members of Religious Orders, and Christian Science Practitioners*) with the IRS within a specified period. If you chose to be covered, you may not elect to be exempt from coverage for services performed as a minister, member, or practitioner for taxable years ending after 1967.

1130.6 Who is classified as a minister or practitioner?

A minister must be duly ordained, commissioned, or licensed by a church or church denomination. (See §934.)

A Christian Science practitioner is one who is a member in good standing of the Mother Church, the First Church of Christ, Scientist, in Boston, Massachusetts, and who practices healing in accordance with the teachings of Christian Science. Christian Science practitioners are specifically exempted from licensing by State laws. Some Christian Science practitioners also do work as Christian Science teachers and lecturers.

1130.7 Is income from teaching or lecturing treated differently from that received for work as a practitioner?

Income received by practitioners as teachers and lecturers is treated the same as income from their work as practitioners. Christian Science readers have the status of ordained, commissioned, or licensed ministers, and are covered in the same way as ministers.

1130.8 Are members who have taken vows of poverty covered by Social Security?

A member of a religious order who has taken a vow of poverty is not covered as a self-employed individual, but may be covered as an employee of the order if the order elects Social Security coverage for its members. (See §932.)

1131. EXEMPTIONS FROM SELF-EMPLOYMENT COVERAGE

1131.1 Who can obtain exemptions from self-employment coverage?

An exemption from self-employment coverage under Social Security can be obtained by:

A. Any duly ordained, commissioned, or licensed minister of a church, member of a religious order who has not taken a vow of poverty; or

B. Any Christian Science practitioner who is conscientiously opposed, or because of religious principles is opposed, to the acceptance of Social Security benefits (or other public insurance providing similar benefits) based on services as a minister, member or practitioner.

1131.2 How is an exemption obtained?

An exemption is obtained by the timely filing with IRS of a Form 4361 (*Application for Exemption From Self-Employment Tax for Use by Ministers, Members of Religious Orders, and Christian Science Practitioners*).

Applications filed after 1986 must also contain a statement that you have informed the ordaining, commissioning or licensing body of the church, or order of your opposition to the acceptance of Social Security benefits.

1131.3 Can the exemption be revoked?

Generally, this exemption is irrevocable. See §1130.4 for exemptions.

1131.4 What income is covered by the exemption?

The exemption applies only to net earnings from the exercise of the ministry, in the exercise of the duties required by the religious order, or from the practice as a Christian Science practitioner. Once having filed a valid application for exemption, a minister, member, or practitioner cannot later acquire Social Security credit for earnings from these services. However, Social Security taxes will continue to be paid by any minister, member, or practitioner filing such a certificate on any other self-employment income or covered wages.

1132. TIME LIMIT TO FILE FOR EXEMPTION

1132.1 What is the time limit to file for an exemption?

The time limit to file for an exemption with the IRS is the due date of the tax return (including extensions) for the second taxable year (whether or not consecutive) in which you had net earnings from self-employment of $400 or more. Any part of your self-employment earnings of $400 or more derived from services as a minister, member of a religious order, or Christian Science practitioner applies.

1132.2 When does the application become effective?

A valid application for exemption is effective for the first taxable year ending after 1967 for which you had net earnings of $400 or more, some part of which is derived from services as a minister, member, or practitioner.

1133. ARE SERVICES BY CHAPLAINS SELF-EMPLOYMENT?

No, service by a chaplain who is an ordained, commissioned, or licensed minister as an employee of the U.S., a State or political subdivision, or a foreign government is not self-employment. However, a chaplain may be covered as an employee of a State or local government (see Chapter 10) or as a member of the uniformed services of the U.S. (See §§948-960.)

1134. CREWS ON FISHING BOATS

1134.1 What fishing activities are considered a trade or business?

Services performed after December 31, 1954, by a person on a boat engaged in catching fish or other forms of aquatic life constitute a trade or business if the following conditions are met:

A. An arrangement exists between the person and the owner or operator of the boat whereby the person does not receive any remuneration other than a share of the catch or a share of the proceeds of the sale of the catch;

B. The amount of the share depends on the amount of the catch; and

C. The operating crew of the boat is normally made up of fewer than 10 persons. If all of the conditions are met, with one exception, the person is self-employed.

1134.2 What exception applies?

The exception applies if:

A. You received a share of a boat's catch of fish or other aquatic animal life (or a share of the proceeds therefrom) after December 31, 1954, and before October 4, 1976, for services performed on the boat after December 31, 1954; and

B. The boat's owner or operator reported such share as wages under the Federal Insurance Contributions Act (FICA).

If one or more of the three conditions in 1134.1 is not met or the exception applies, the person's status must be determined under common-law rules. (See §§802-823.)

1134.3 What rules apply after 1994?

Services after 1994 constitute a trade or business if you continue to meet all the requirements above and receive certain cash remuneration that:
A. Does not exceed $100 per trip;
B. Is contingent on a minimum catch; *and*
C. Is paid solely for additional duties (such as mate, engineer, or cook) for which additional cash remuneration is traditional in the industry.

1134.4 How is the size of the crew calculated?

The operating crew of a boat is treated as made up of fewer than 10 individuals if the average size of the operating crew on trips made during the preceding four calendar quarters consisted of fewer than ten individuals.

1134.5 When is the provision effective?

The new provision provided above is effective for payments after December 31, 1994. In addition, the provision applies to a payment made after December 31, 1984, and all years before January 1, 1995, unless the payer subjected the payment to FICA tax.

1134.6 If the conditions are not met, what rules apply?

If all of the conditions with respect to services performed after 1994 are not met, apply common-law rules.

1135. REAL ESTATE AGENTS AND DIRECT SELLERS

1135.1 Are real estate agents self-employed?

Effective January 1, 1983, certain qualified real estate agents are treated as self-employed persons. To be considered self-employed, you must:
A. Be a licensed real estate salesperson;
B. Derive substantially all payment received for services performed as a real estate salesperson directly from sales or other output, such as appraisal activities, rather than from the number of hours worked; and
C. Perform the services under a written contract or agreement which stipulates that you will not be treated as an employee with respect to the services for Federal tax purposes.

1135.2 What direct sellers are self-employed?

Effective January 1, 1996, The Small Business Job Protection Act of 1996, H.R. 3448, Section 1118 expanded the definition of "Direct Sellers" to include persons engaged in the delivering or distribution of newspapers or shopping news for Federal income tax purposes. To be considered self-employed, you must:

A. Be engaged in the trade or business of selling (or soliciting the sale of) consumer products:
   1. To any buyer on a buy-sell basis, a deposit-commission basis, or any similar basis, for resale (by the buyer or any other person) in the home or in other than a permanent retail establishment;
   2. In the home or in other than a permanent retail establishment; or
   3. Be engaged in the trade or business of the delivering or distribution of newspapers or shopping news (including any services directly related to such trade or business);
B. Derive substantially all payment for services performed as a direct seller directly from the sales of the product or the performance of services such as motivation, training, and recruitment activities, rather than from the number of hours worked; and
C. Perform the services under a written contract or agreement that stipulates you will not be treated as an employee with respect to the services for Federal tax purposes.

1135.3 What are the rules if these conditions are not met?

If all conditions are not met, your status as a real estate agent or direct seller must be determined under the common-law rules. (See §§802-823.)

1136. CERTAIN CHURCH EMPLOYEES TREATED AS SELF-EMPLOYED

1136.1 Can churches exclude income from employees from Social Security taxes?

Any church or church-controlled organization in existence on September 30, 1984, opposed for religious reasons to the payment of Social Security taxes, could make an election by October 31, 1984, to exclude from employment the services performed by its employees.

Any organization created after September 30, 1984, must file prior to the first date on which a quarterly employment tax return would otherwise be due if it wishes this exclusion.

1136.2 How is the exemption filed?

An election is made by filing with the IRS Form 8274 (*Certification by Churches and Qualified Church-Controlled Organizations Electing Exemption from Employers Social Security Taxes*). This election applies to services performed after 1983.

1136.3 What is the impact of excluding services from Social Security?

Where the exclusion is applicable, the services of those employees affected will be treated as services in a trade or business and covered as self-employment.

All present and future employees of churches and qualified church-controlled organizations that elect to exclude their employees' services from employment for Social Security purposes will be liable for self-employment taxes with respect to income from such services performed on or after January 1, 1984. Beginning with 1986, these persons must compute their "church employee income" separately from other earnings they may have from any other trade or business.

1136.4 How is church employee income defined?

For this purpose, "church employee income" is the gross income for service as an employee of the church. No deductions are made. The income is subject to $100 rather than $400 floor taxation and coverage (see §1201.1). The limitations of $100 unreduced by expenses also applied to income in 1984 and 1985.

1136.5 Does the exemption apply to church employee income?

As of 1986, the exemption from self-employment tax on grounds of religious belief (see §1128) does not apply to "church employee income."

1136.6 Is the exemption revokable?

The Tax Reform Act of 1986 permits a church or church-controlled organization that has elected not to pay Social Security employer taxes to revoke its election. This provision is effective as of October 22, 1986, the date of the Tax Reform Act of 1986.

Chapter 12
Net Earnings From Self-Employment

TABLE OF CONTENTS

NET EARNINGS FROM SELF-EMPLOYEMENT - GENERAL

1200. Net Earnings from Self-Employment
1201. Self-Employment Income
1202. What are gross business receipts?
1203. Are retirement payments received from partnerships included in net earnings?
1204. How is income credited when a partner dies?
1205. Deduction of Business Expenses
1206. Dividends on Stock and Interest on Bonds
1207. Is interest received by dealers counted as earnings?
1208. Is interest received by traders counted as earnings?
1209. Is interest received by a dealer/stockbroker counted as earnings?
1210. How is dividend and interest income calculated for partnerships?
1211. Are all gains and losses included in calculating earnings?
1212. What rental allowances must ministers include in net earnings?
1213. What rental income must be included in calculating earnings?
1214. Rent Received by Real Estate Dealers
1215. What items are counted as earnings for real estate brokers?

RENTAL INCOME - GENERAL
1216. Is rental income counted as earnings?
1217. Services Normally Provided by Landlords
1218. Services Provided for Convenience of the Occupant
1219. Are payments for parking lots, warehouses, and storage garages counted as earnings?
1220. Rental Income from Two or More Property Operations

RENTAL INCOME - FARM
1221. Does farm rental income count as net earnings?
1222. How is material participation established in a farm rental arrangement?
1223. How is material participation in farm production determined?
1224. What are the criteria for Test I: Financial Contribution, Periodic Inspection, and Consultation?
1225. What combination of activities is required to demonstrate material participation in farm rental agreements?
1226. What constitutes a "significant part" of production costs or equipment?
1227. Costs of Production
1228. Periodic Inspection of Production Activities
1229. Advice and Consultation
1230. What are the criteria for Test II: Decisions Affecting Success of Enterprise?
1231. Test III: 100 Hours of Work Over 5-Week Period
1232. If Tests I - III are not met, is material participation still possible?

OTHER METHODS OF COMPUTING EARNINGS
1233. Are other methods of computing net earnings for self-employment available?
1234. What is gross income for the optional method of reporting?
1235. Optional Method of Figuring Net Farm Earnings
1236. May grazing income be included in gross farm income?
1237. Is income from the sale of farm products grown in prior years included in gross farm income?

1238. Are federal agricultural program payments included in gross farm income?
1239. Is the landlord's share of a crop included in gross farm self-employment income?
1240. Income from the Sale of Timber
1241. Summary Table for Optional Methods of Computing Farm Self-Employment Income
1242. Optional Method of Computing Non-Farm Net Earnings
1243. Summary Table for Optional Methods of Computing Non-Farm Self-Employment Income
1244. Combining Farm and Non-Farm Net Earnings

OTHER INCOME
1245. Income of U.S. Citizen or Resident in Business Outside the U.S.
1246. Are exclusions in Section 911 of the Internal Revenue Code applicable to ministers outside the U.S.?

1200. NET EARNINGS FROM SELF-EMPLOYMENT

1200.1 How are net earnings from self-employment calculated?

To calculate the net earnings from self-employment, follow the steps below:

A. Add up your total gross income as calculated under the income tax law. Include income from all your trades and businesses.

B. Subtract all the deductions, including the allowances for depreciation that you are allowed when you calculate your income tax from the result in (A). This gives you your net earnings.

C. Effective with taxable years beginning after 12/31/89 multiply the result obtained in B. by .9235 (i.e., 100% - 7.65% = 92.35% or 0.9235) to derive your net earnings.

Note: If you have more than one business, calculate net earnings by adding up the net profits or losses from all the businesses. Net earnings also include any ordinary income or loss from partnerships. If any part of your income is included in gross earnings from self-employment, expenses connected with this income cannot be deducted.

1200.2 Are there other ways of calculating net earnings from self-employment?

Under certain circumstances, optional methods of computing net earnings from self-employment are available. For a discussion of these methods, see §§1233-1235 and §§1241-1244.

1200.3 What resources are available to help with calculations?

Definitions of terms used in calculating income for income tax purposes also apply to calculating net earnings from self-employment. For further information on these calculations, see the tax guides available from any Internal Revenue Service office, especially: *Farmer's Tax Guide*, Internal Revenue Service Publication No. 225, and *Tax Guide for Small Business*, Internal Revenue Service Publication No. 334.

1201. SELF-EMPLOYMENT INCOME

1201.1 What is self-employment income?

Self-employment income means your net earnings from self-employment for a taxable year. The following qualifications must be met:

A. Your net earnings for the taxable year must be at least $400;

Note: Certain church employees who are treated as self-employed must report earnings of $100 or more (see §1136). See §§1233-1235 and §§1241-1244 about the optional methods of computing net earnings.

B. Your trade or business must be covered by Social Security; and

C. If you are a nonresident alien, your earnings are not considered self-employment income except as provided by an international agreement (see §107).

1201.2 What are the limits on self-employed income?

Self-employment income cannot exceed the amounts listed in the table below. Any wages covered by Social Security that you earned during the taxable year must be subtracted from the limits shown below.

If the taxable year is...	Then your self-employment income limit is...
1968-1971	$7,800
1972	$9,000
1973	$10,00
1974	$13,200
1975	$14,100
1976	$15,300
1977	$16,500
1978	$17,700
1979	$22,900
1980	$25,900
1981	$29,700
1982	$32,400
1983	$35,700
1984	$37,800
1985	$39,600
1986	$42,000
1987	$43,800

(Continued)

If the taxable year is...	Then your self-employment income limit is...
1989	$48,000
1990	$51,300
1991	$53,400
1992	$55,500
1993	$57,600
1994	$60,600
1995	$61,200
1996	$62,700
1997	$65,400
1998	$68,400
1999	$72,600
2000	$76,200
2001	$80,400
2002	$84,900
2003	$87,000
2004	$87,900
2005	$90,000
2006	$94,200
2007	$97,500
2008	$102,000
2009	$106,800
2010	$106,800
2011	$106,800
2012	$110,100
2013	$113,700
2014	$117,000
2015–2016	$118,500
2017	$127,200
2018	$128,400
2019	$132,900
2020	$137,700
2021	$142,800
2022	$147,000
2023	$160,200
2024	$168,600

1201.3 What are the limits beginning in 1998?

Amounts for taxable years beginning in 1998 are subject to automatic increases in multiples of $300, if average total wages rise enough to cause a cost-of-living increase in benefits.

1201.4 Where is the amount for the current year published?

The amount for a taxable year is published in the *Federal Register* on or before November 1, of the year immediately preceding that taxable year.

1201.5 Are net earnings from self-employment and self-employment income the same?

Net earnings from self-employment and self-employment income are not the same. Only that part of net earnings that is included in the term "self-employment income" is subject to Social Security self-employment taxes and counted for Social Security benefit purposes. (However, even if net earnings do not count for these purposes, they are included in figuring the amount of benefits that must be withheld under the earnings test. See Chapter 18.)

1202. WHAT ARE GROSS BUSINESS RECEIPTS?

Gross business receipts for Social Security purposes include, among other things:

A. Professional fees received;
B. Compensation for services (other than as an employee);
C. Pay for work done on contract; and
D. Income from the sale, exchange, or conversion of goods held for sale in the ordinary course of business.

Gross business receipts do not include:

A. Income from the sale, exchange, or conversion of business assets that are not part of business inventory, such as delivery trucks and office equipment;
B. Dividends, interest, and rental income from real property; or
C. Gains and losses from the sale or exchange of capital assets, except those realized in the course of business by an options or commodities dealer.

Note: In computing gross income, the cost of goods that a person takes from the business for personal and family use must be excluded from the total amount of merchandise bought for sale.

1203. ARE RETIREMENT PAYMENTS RECEIVED FROM PARTNERSHIPS INCLUDED IN NET EARNINGS?

If you are a retired partner receiving retirement payments from a partnership of which you are a member or a former member, the payments are excluded from net earnings from self-employment (effective with taxable years ending on or after December 31, 1967) if:

A. The payments are made under a written plan of the partnership that meets the requirements prescribed by the Secretary of the Treasury. The written plan must also provide for periodic payments because of retirement, to partners generally or to a class or classes of partners, to continue at least until such partner's death; and

B. You provided no services in any business conducted by the partnership (or its successors) during the taxable year of the partnership ending within or with the taxable year in which you received payments; and

C. At the end of the partnership's taxable year referred to in (B) above, the other partners have no obligation to you other than for the retirement payments under the plan; and

D. Your share in the capital of the partnership has been paid in full by the end of the partnership's taxable year referred to in (B) above.

1204. HOW IS INCOME CREDITED WHEN A PARTNER DIES?

To calculate a partner's share of the profit or loss, follow the steps below:

A. Calculate the total profit or loss for the partnership.

B. Deduct any guaranteed payments from the total profits or losses.

C. Assume that the profits or losses occurred at a uniform rate throughout the year.

D. Multiply the monthly profit or loss from (A) by the number of months the partner was living, counting the month of death as a full month, and by the partner's proportional share in the partnership.

E. Add a proportion of the guaranteed payments equivalent to the number of months the partner was living during the taxable year.

Calculating partners' share of partnership when a partner dies.
A. John, Mary, and David were partners sharing in profits and losses in the proportions of 2/9, 3/9, and 4/9 respectively.
B. During the partnership taxable year which ended June 30, 1987, the partnership profit amounted to $15,000.
C. John died October 15, 1986.
D. John had a guaranteed payment of $2,400 a year because of an investment in the business.
E. Deducting John's share because of the capital interest (guaranteed payment) leaves $12,600 or $1,050 per month.
F. John is entitled to 2/9 of $1,050 for 4 months or $933.33.
G. John is also entitled to 4/12 of the $2,400 guaranteed payment because of the interest in the business.
H. Adding $800 to $933.33 gives $1,733.33 as John's distributive share of partnership earnings that is creditable for Social Security purposes for the year of John's death.

1205. DEDUCTION OF BUSINESS EXPENSES

1205.1 What expenses must be deducted?

All allowable business expenses, except those incurred by certain church employees who are treated as self-employed (see §1136), must be deducted in computing net earnings from self-employment.

1205.2 Who is responsible for taking the deduction?

If you are an operator of a business who becomes liable for a business expense, you must take the deduction even if the expense is paid by someone else.

If you rent the property where you conduct your business and your son pays the rent, you must deduct the rent because you became liable for it. If your son owns the property where the business is conducted, you cannot deduct expenses such as taxes, insurance, and repairs, paid by your son in connection with the property because you did not become liable for them.

1205.3 Must deductions be taken for non-cash expenses?

Yes, you must take a deduction for an expense even though it is paid with something other than cash. Expenses paid in property are deductible, usually in the amount of the cost or "adjusted basis" (generally it cost less than the amount it has depreciated) of the property transferred.

1206. DIVIDENDS ON STOCK AND INTEREST ON BONDS

1206.1 Are dividends on stock and interest on bonds included as earnings?

Dividends on stock and interest on bonds do not count for Social Security purposes, unless you receive them in the course of business as a dealer in stocks or securities.

Note: The term "bond" includes debentures, notes, certificates and other evidence of indebtedness issued with interest coupons or in registered form by a corporation. Bonds also include Government bonds.

1206.2 Is other interest included as earnings?

Other interest you receive in the course of business does count for Social Security purposes. For example, if you are a pawnbroker and receive interest on loans or a merchant and receive interest on accounts or notes receivable, you must include this interest in computing net earnings from self-employment.

1207. IS INTEREST RECEIVED BY DEALERS COUNTED AS EARNINGS?

If you are a dealer in stocks and securities, the dividends and interest that you receive from stocks and bonds while they are in your inventory are earnings from self-employment. Securities bought by a dealer but not held for resale are not part of the trade or business. They are considered a personal investment. The interest and dividends received do not count as earnings from self-employment.

Note: You are a dealer in stocks and securities if:

A. You are a merchant with an established place of business;
B. You regularly engage in buying stocks and bonds in your own name;
C. You sell stocks and bonds to customers for a profit.

Dealers do not buy for the purpose of obtaining dividends or interest, but for "stock in trade"; as another merchant buys hardware or dresses or groceries.

1208. IS INTEREST RECEIVED BY TRADERS COUNTED AS EARNINGS?

If you are a trader in stocks or securities, your interest and dividends are not counted as earnings for Social Security purposes.

Note: You are a trader if you buy and sell stocks and bonds for your own account only.

1209. IS INTEREST RECEIVED BY A DEALER/STOCKBROKER COUNTED AS EARNINGS?

Frequently, a dealer in securities will also be a stockbroker. If you fit both categories, profits earned as a broker and those earned as a dealer in securities are both included in net earnings. Dividends and interest paid on securities while they are part of your stock in trade are also counted.

Note: You are a stockbroker if you buy and sell stocks and bonds as an agent of the actual owner. As a stockbroker, you do not buy or sell in your own name. Your earnings come from commissions rather than from selling the stock or bond at a profit.

1210. HOW IS DIVIDEND AND INTEREST INCOME CALCULATED FOR PARTNERSHIPS?

Partnerships are treated as individuals when it comes to the dividend and interest exclusion. Dividends and interest on securities held for investment are excluded from net earnings of the partners. However, if a partnership is in business as a securities dealer, income on the securities held for resale by the partnership is included as net earnings of the partners.

1211. ARE ALL GAINS AND LOSSES INCLUDED IN CALCULATING EARNINGS?

When calculating earnings for Social Security purposes, you can exclude gains or losses from the disposition of certain properties if you do any of the following:

A. Sell or exchange a capital asset, except in the course of business of an options or commodities dealer;

B. Cut timber or dispose of timber, coal or iron ore, even though held primarily for sale to customers, if section 631 of the Internal Revenue Code applies; or
C. Sell, exchange, involuntarily convert or make other disposition of property that is not:
  1. Stock in trade or other property of a kind that would be included in inventory if it was on hand at the close of the taxable year; or
  2. Property held primarily for sale to customers in the ordinary course of business.

1212. WHAT RENTAL ALLOWANCES MUST MINISTERS INCLUDE IN NET EARNINGS?

If you are a minister, you must include the following in net earnings from self-employment (unless you are granted an exemption from coverage under Social Security (see §1131):

A. The rental value of a home furnished as part of your compensation;
B. A rental allowance paid as part of your compensation; and
C. The value of any meals or lodging furnished in connection with services performed in the exercise of your ministry.
D. Salary
E. Fees and honoraria for officiating at weddings, christenings, funerals and other services in the exercise of the ministry.
F. Value of meals when furnished as part of your compensation; and
G. Travel and automobile allowances, although these same items will be deducted as business expenses if incurred in the performance of your duties.

A minister excludes from gross income:
- Pensions and retirement pay
- Parsonage or housing allowances when included in retirement pay after the minister retires or any other retirement benefit received after retirement pursuant to a church plan as defined in Section 414(e) of the Internal Revenue Code must be excluded when computing net earnings from self-employment.

1213. WHAT RENTAL INCOME MUST BE INCLUDED IN CALCULATING EARNINGS?

Rental income you receive from real estate does not count for Social Security purposes unless:

A. You receive rental income in the course of your trade or business as a real estate dealer (see §§1214-1215);

B. Services are rendered primarily for the convenience of the occupant of the premises (see §1218); or

C. In the case of farm rental income, you materially participate in the production or in the management of the production of farm commodities on land rented to someone else. (See §§1221-1232.)

1214. RENT RECEIVED BY REAL ESTATE DEALERS

1214.1 Is rent received by real estate dealers counted as earnings?

Rentals from real estate being held for sale in the ordinary course of a trade or business are earnings from self-employment. The profit a dealer gets from selling the real estate is also earnings from self-employment.

Note: You are a real estate dealer if you are engaged in the business of selling real estate for a profit. Real estate is a dealer's stock in trade. As a real estate dealer, you are available to buy and sell property and are regularly engaged in negotiating sales of property that you own.

1214.2 Is all rental income received by real estate dealers counted as earnings?

Property held by real estate dealers for personal use or as investment is not held for sale. Rentals received from such property are not considered earnings from self-employment because they are not received in the regular course of a trade or business. Such property is not "stock in trade."

1215. WHAT ITEMS ARE COUNTED AS EARNINGS FOR REAL ESTATE BROKERS?

If you are a real estate broker, the following items are counted as earnings:

A. Fees you receive for buying, selling, and renting properties owned by someone else; and

B. Income you receive from the sale or rental of properties for which you have taken title in your own name until you can find a buyer.

Note: You are a real estate broker if you buy, sell or rent properties owned by someone else.

1216. IS RENTAL INCOME COUNTED AS EARNINGS?

Income you receive from renting rooms or apartments does not count for Social Security purposes unless you provide personal services for the convenience of the occupant.

Income you receive from renting property for business or commercial use, such as a store, factory, office space, etc. is usually excluded from earnings from self-employment. However, if you provide services primarily for the convenience of the tenant beyond those usually provided with rental of apartments or other space for occupancy only, rental income may be counted as earnings.

1217. SERVICES NORMALLY PROVIDED BY LANDLORDS

1217.1 What services are normally provided by landlords?

Services normally provided by landlords include furnishing heat, light, water, elevators, painting, repairing and redecorating, maintaining and replacing items furnished, collecting trash and garbage, cleaning hallways, common bathrooms, and entrances and cleaning the premises after the tenant leaves. These types of services are not considered personal services for the convenience of the occupant; rather, they are ordinary services performed by landlords.

1217.2 If these services are provided, is rental income counted as earnings?

When you provide these services to your tenants, the rental income is not counted as earnings.

1218. SERVICES PROVIDED FOR CONVENIENCE OF THE OCCUPANT

1218.1 What services are provided primarily for the convenience of the occupant?

These services may consist of room service, making beds, furnishing linens and towels, providing laundry service, preparing and serving meals, sweeping and mopping floors, dusting and cleaning, washing dishes, cleaning bathroom fixtures, emptying wastebaskets and picking up and replacing scattered or misplaced articles.

1218.2 If these services are provided, is rental income counted as earnings?

If you provide services rendered for convenience of occupant, services primarily for the convenience of the occupant of the dwelling space, the rental income is counted as earnings.

Note: No particular service or combination of these services will necessarily cause the income to be counted for Social Security purposes. Each case must be considered individually.

1219. ARE PAYMENTS FOR PARKING LOTS, WAREHOUSES, AND STORAGE GARAGES COUNTED AS EARNINGS?

Payments for the use or occupancy of space in parking lots, warehouses or storage garages are included in determining net earnings from self-employment.

1220. RENTAL INCOME FROM TWO OR MORE PROPERTY OPERATIONS

1220.1 How is rental income calculated for more than one property?

Rental income from two or more property operations is treated separately in figuring net earnings from self-employment. Your rental income does not count for Social Security purposes even if you have income from another property, such as a boardinghouse, which is included in earnings from self-employment.

1220.2 If part of the property is rented with services and part is rented without services, how is income calculated?

If you rent part of your property and provide significant services and part without such services, consider each separately. Income from the property rented with services is counted while the income from the other property is not counted. You should charge the expenses attributable to each type of operation accordingly.

1221. DOES FARM RENTAL INCOME COUNT AS NET EARNINGS?

Farm rental income counts as net earnings from self-employment if the landlord, as part of the rental arrangement, materially participates in the production of the crop or livestock. If the landlord does not materially participate, farm rental income does not count for Social Security purposes.

Note: "Landlord" means anyone who has rented to another individual, whether the land is owned or rented by the individual from a third party.

1222. HOW IS MATERIAL PARTICIPATION ESTABLISHED IN A FARM RENTAL ARRANGEMENT?

The farm rental arrangement must state that you will materially participate in the production of the farm commodities. The arrangement may be in writing or it may be oral, but should reflect the mutual understanding between you and your tenant. If the agreement is oral, you must be able to prove that it provides for your material participation. The written agreement or lease may not cover all the details of the understanding between you and the tenant. If the written agreement is supplemented by an oral agreement, material participation may be established if you actually participated in line with the oral agreement.

1223. HOW IS MATERIAL PARTICIPATION IN FARM PRODUCTION DETERMINED?

Four tests are used in determining whether your are materially participating in the production of farm commodities.

1224. WHAT ARE THE CRITERIA FOR TEST I: FINANCIAL CONTRIBUTION, PERIODIC INSPECTION, AND CONSULTATION?

You meet the conditions for Test I if you have an arrangement for participation and do any three of the following:

A. Advance, pay, or stand good for a significant part of the cost of production;
B. Furnish a significant part of the tools, equipment, and livestock used in producing the commodities;
C. Make periodic inspections of the production activities; or
D. Advise and consult with the tenant periodically.

1225. WHAT COMBINATION OF ACTIVITIES IS REQUIRED TO DEMONSTRATE MATERIAL PARTICIPATION IN FARM RENTAL AGREEMENTS?

A combination of factors showing material participation is required. Advancing, paying or standing for a significant part of production costs or furnishing a significant part of the equipment, tools and livestock helps to show that you may be materially participating. However, these two factors alone are not enough. Even paying all the expenses and furnishing all the equipment, tools and livestock are not enough to establish material participation. However, if you also participate in some other way to a significant degree, such as periodically inspecting the crop or advising and consulting with the tenant, you are participating to the required degree.

1226. WHAT CONSTITUTES A "SIGNIFICANT PART" OF PRODUCTION COSTS OR EQUIPMENT?

No precise amount can be defined as a significant part of the cost of production or of the tools, equipment and livestock. One-third or more of the total value of the tools, equipment and livestock used in producing the commodity or one-third or more of the total cost of producing the commodity would usually be considered a significant part. Whether less than one-third is a significant part depends on individual circumstances.

1227. COSTS OF PRODUCTION

1227.1 What expenses are included in costs of production?

Costs of production include expenses that relate directly to the production of the commodity, such as feed, seed, plants, fertilizer, fuel, machinery repair, pesticides and other supplies.

1227.2 What expenses are not included in costs of production?

Living expenses paid by the landlord for the tenants; overhead expenses such as taxes, depreciation, etc.; and the value of the labor furnished by the tenant cannot be counted in figuring the costs of production.

1228. PERIODIC INSPECTION OF PRODUCTION ACTIVITIES

1228.1 What is included in periodic inspection?

Periodic inspection of production activities counts toward material participation if it is conducted to promote production. To be counted, inspection of production activities must be for the purpose of seeing whether:

A. The farm work is being done properly;
B. Whether anything else needs to be done; or
C. When the work should be done.

Mere inspection to determine the condition of the buildings, fences or other improvements does not count.

1228.2 When are periodic inspections conducted?

The nature and size of the farming activities determine how often inspections need to be done. Making inspections during the soil preparation, planting, cultivating, and harvesting seasons count even if there is no inspection activity during some of the growing season. By itself, inspecting the farming activities, regardless of how often it is done, is not enough. However, regular and frequent inspections of the production activities, combined with other things showing participation, may be enough.

1229. ADVICE AND CONSULTATION

1229.1 What is considered advice and consultation?

To be counted toward material participation, your advice and consultation must be in connection with what, where, when, or how things are to be done in producing the commodities. It need not be connected directly with the actual planting, cultivating and harvesting work, but may be connected with:

A. Deciding what crops are to be planted;
B. The type of seed to be used;
C. How much fertilizer or spray should be used; or
D. When and at what price the crops should be sold.

Note: Advice and consultation does not count toward material participation unless the arrangement provides for it.

1229.2 Can advice and consultation alone considered material participation?

No, advice and consultation alone, regardless of how frequent, is not material participation. If you do other things, such as making periodic inspections and doing some of the work, this may be enough, together with advice and consultation, to be material participation.

1230. WHAT ARE THE CRITERIA FOR TEST II: DECISIONS AFFECTING SUCCESS OF ENTERPRISE?

Under Test II, you may be materially participating if you are regularly and frequently making decisions that significantly affect the success of the enterprise. Making final decisions contributing to or affecting the success of the enterprise count toward material participation. These decisions include:

A. What, when, and where to plant, cultivate, dust or spray;
B. When to harvest the crop;
C. What goods to buy, sell or rent;
D. What standards to follow; and
E. What records to keep, reports to make and bills to pay, etc., counts toward material participation.

1231. TEST III: 100 HOURS OF WORK OVER 5-WEEK PERIOD

1231.1 What are the criteria for Test III?

The criteria for Test III are:

A. If you work at least 100 hours spread over five or more weeks (not necessarily consecutive) on activities connected with the production of the crop, you are materially participating;

B. If you work less than 100 hours or conduct the 100 hours of work in fewer than five different weeks, you may still be materially participating if the work done adds up to a significant contribution to the production of the crop; or

C. If the work alone is not enough to establish material participation, it is considered along with the other things that are done that help establish material participation.

1231.2 Must the work involve physical activity in farming?

No, you do not have to help with the actual plowing, hoeing, etc. The work may be making purchases, keeping the records, caring for the livestock or repairing buildings, fences and farm equipment used in connection with the production of the crop.

1231.3 Does working for the tenant count toward material participation?

No. If you work as the employee of the tenant and if you are paid separately, your work does not count toward material participation.

Note: If you are in doubt, consult your nearest Social Security office or any Internal Revenue Service office.

1232. IF TESTS I - III ARE NOT MET, IS MATERIAL PARTICIPATION STILL POSSIBLE?

Even if Tests I-III (§§1224-1231) are not met, your total activities still may count as material participation. Those tests are for the more common types of arrangements. There may be different types of situations or combinations of factors that, based on the total picture, establish material participation.

Note: If you are in doubt, consult your nearest Social Security office or any Internal Revenue Service office.

1233. ARE OTHER METHODS OF COMPUTING NET EARNINGS FOR SELF-EMPLOYMENT AVAILABLE?

If certain requirements are met, optional methods of computing net earnings from self-employment are available to individuals engaged in the following activities:

A. Farm self-employment (see §1235, farm option);
B. Non-farm self-employment (see §1242, non-farm option); or
C. Both farm and non-farm self-employment (see §1244).

The purpose of the optional methods of computation is to enable a self-employed individual to maintain Social Security coverage during years of very low net earnings or a net loss.

1234. WHAT IS GROSS INCOME FOR THE OPTIONAL METHOD OF REPORTING?

Gross income for optional method of reporting is the gross receipts of the activity minus the cost of items purchased and sold in carrying on that activity. Gross income for this purpose is determined as follows:

A. If you are a single proprietor, use the gross profits as computed on *Schedule F* (farm) or *Schedule C* (non-farm), Form 1040, for Federal income tax purposes.
B. If you are a partner, first compute the gross income of the partnership as for a single proprietorship. Then allocate the gross income is allocated to each partner on the agreed profit-sharing basis.
C. If partners received guaranteed payments for services or use of capital, determine each partner's gross income as follows:
   1. Determine the partnership's gross income as for a single proprietorship;
   2. Deduct the total of all guaranteed payments made to all partners for services or use of capital from the partnership's gross income;
   3. Allocate the balance of the partnership's gross income to each partner on the agreed profit-sharing basis (this represents each partner's distributive share of the partnership's gross income); and

4. Add the guaranteed payment to the distributive share of the partnership's gross income. The total represents each partner's gross income from the partnership.

1235. OPTIONAL METHOD OF FIGURING NET FARM EARNINGS

1235.1 When is the optional method of computing net earnings from farm self-employment available?

The optional method of computing net earnings from farm self-employment is available for any taxable year for which you qualify.

1235.2 How is the optional method of calculating net earnings used?

Please see Publication 225 at https://www.irs.gov for more information.

1235.3 Is the optional method always available?

No. You can use this method if your gross farm income is $9,840 or less or your net farm profits are less than $7,103.

1235.4 If the optional method is used for one year, must it be used in years afterward?

No. If the optional method is used for one year, it does not have to be used for the next. However, if it is used, it must be applied to all farm earnings from self-employment for that year. It may be used to increase or decrease reported net farm earnings, and it may be used even if the farming operation resulted in a loss.

1236. MAY GRAZING INCOME BE INCLUDED IN GROSS FARM INCOME?

Grazing income may be included in gross farm income under certain conditions. The income is included if you perform services beyond those which landlords usually perform for the protection, maintenance, or improvement of your own land. These extra services may include:

A. Regular counting of the livestock;
B. Looking for strays;

C. Veterinary services;
D. Providing food, salt and water;
E. Protecting the livestock from exposure to disease from other animals in the same pasture; or
F. Other services showing that you have responsibility for the care of the livestock.

1237. IS INCOME FROM THE SALE OF FARM PRODUCTS GROWN IN PRIOR YEARS INCLUDED IN GROSS FARM INCOME?

Income from the sale of farm products grown or raised in prior years is included in gross farm income, even if you stopped farming before the year in which you received the income.

If you sell grain in 2009 that was raised in 2008, the gross farm income is for 2009 even if you stopped farming in 2008.

1238. ARE FEDERAL AGRICULTURAL PROGRAM PAYMENTS INCLUDED IN GROSS FARM INCOME?

Federal agricultural program payments to farm operators in cash, materials or services are generally included in gross farm income. If you are a landlord, payments made to you are included only if you meet the "material participation" requirements described in §§1221-1232.

1239. IS THE LANDLORD'S SHARE OF A CROP INCLUDED IN GROSS FARM SELF-EMPLOYMENT INCOME?

The landlord's share of a crop is not included in the gross farm income of a self-employed sharefarmer:
A. If you are a self-employed sharefarmer and turn over the landlord's share of the crop directly to the landlord, you must exclude the value of that share from your gross farm income; or
B. If you sell the landlord's share as well as your own, the amount turned over to the landlord must be excluded from your gross farm income. In these situations, the sharefarmer acts as an agent for the landlord.

1240. INCOME FROM THE SALE OF TIMBER

1240.1 Is income from the sale of timber included in gross farm income?

Income from the sale of timber is included in gross farm income if:

A. The timber was grown on the farm;
B. The income from the timber sales is not treated as a capital gain; and
C. The timber operation is incidental to or tied in with the operation of the farm so that farming and timber activities constitute one business.

1240.2 When is income from the sale of timber excluded from gross farm income?

If you are a farmer who receives substantial income from timber sales and if you have employees who are assigned to work only in timber operations, you generally would be considered to have two businesses: a farm business and a timber business. Income from the timber operations is not considered as farm income but rather is treated as non-farm income for use of the options.

1241. SUMMARY FOR OPTIONAL METHODS OF COMPUTING FARM SELF-EMPLOYMENT INCOME

For more information and examples see Publication 225 and IRS Form 1040 at www.irs.gov.

1242. OPTIONAL METHOD OF COMPUTING NON-FARM NET EARNINGS

1242.1 What is the optional method of computing non-farm net earnings?

The optional method of computing net earnings from non-farm self-employment is similar to the farm option, but is more limited in its operation. It may be used for no more than five taxable years, which need not be consecutive. It is available for a taxable year only if:

NET EARNINGS FROM SELF-EMPLOYMENT 341

A. Your actual net earnings were $400 or more (including your distributive share of the net income or loss from any partnership of which you are a member) in at least two of the three consecutive years immediately preceding the taxable year for which you elect to use the non-farm option; and

B. Your net nonfarm profits were:
   a) Less than $7,103 and
   b) Less than 72.189% of your gross nonfarm income.
   c) You have previously used this method less than five years. There is a five year lifetime limit.

1242.2 If the optional method is used for one year, must it be used in years afterward?

No. If the optional method is used for one year, it does not have to be used for the next year. However, if it is used, it must be applied to all farm earnings from self-employment for that year. It may be used only to increase reported net non-farm earnings and may be used even if the non-farm operation resulted in a loss.

1243. SUMMARY FOR OPTIONAL METHODS OF COMPUTING NON-FARM SELF-EMPLOYMENT INCOME

For more information and examples see Publication 225 and IRS Form 1040 at www.irs.gov.

1244. COMBINING FARM AND NON-FARM NET EARNINGS

1244.1 What options are available if both farm and non-farm self-employment are involved?

If both farm and non-farm self-employment is involved, both options (farm and non-farm) may be available. If you choose to use both options, the farm option (see §1235) is computed without regard to non-farm self-employment. However, the non-farm option (see §1242) requires consideration of farm self-employment to establish eligibility for its use.

1244.2 How are the options applied to determine net earnings?

The options are applied separately to the gross income from each activity to determine the reportable net earnings from each activity. However, if you are engaged in both activities during a taxable year beginning after

1972, you must combine net earnings or loss (either actual net earnings or earnings as computed under the farm and/or the non-farm optional methods) from both activities. Reporting the total net amount permits the use of several alternatives:

A. Report the actual net earnings from either activity with the optional net earnings from the other activity;
B. Report the actual net earnings from both activities; or
C. If otherwise eligible, use the option in computing net earnings from both activities.

1244.3 What is the maximum allowable total for combined net earnings?

If you elect to use both the farm option and the non-farm option in any one taxable year, the maximum combined total amount of your net earnings from self-employment cannot exceed $6,560.

1245. INCOME OF U.S. CITIZEN OR RESIDENT IN BUSINESS OUTSIDE THE U.S.

1245.1 Is income earned from a trade or business operated outside the U.S. counted as net earnings?

If you are a U.S. citizen or resident alien, income earned from a trade or business operated outside the U.S. is counted as net earnings from self-employment.

Note: International agreements may provide that the earnings will be covered under the social security program of another country, see §107.

1245.2 How have IRS rules changed regarding income earned outside the U.S.?

For many years, the Internal Revenue Code has provided special deductions or exclusions from foreign earned income of U.S. citizens and residents working outside the U.S. Effective with taxable years beginning after December 31, 1983, however, U.S. citizens or residents engaged in a trade or business outside the U.S. must compute net earnings from self-employment. This is true regardless of any foreign earned income exclusions for which they might be eligible for income tax purposes.

1246. ARE EXCLUSIONS IN SECTION 911 OF THE INTERNAL REVENUE CODE APPLICABLE TO MINISTERS OUTSIDE THE U.S.?

No. If you are a U.S. citizen or resident performing services outside the U.S. related to your ministry or duties required by your order, you must compute net earnings from self-employment, regardless of the exclusions in section 911 of the Internal Revenue Code. Section 911 of the Code relates to earned income from services performed outside the U.S.

CHAPTER 13
Wages

TABLE OF CONTENTS

1300. Wages for Social Security Purposes
1301. Maximum Earnings Creditable in any One Year
1302. Actual or Constructive Payment of Wages
1303. Cash-Pay Tests
1304. Pay for Work for Nonprofit Organization
1305. Does pay for military service after 1956 count as wages?
1306. Can you receive additional wage credits for military service after 1967?
1307. Can you receive wage credits for military service before 1957?
1308. Pay for Railroad Work
1309. Do commissions count as wages?
1310. Renewal Commissions of Life Insurance Salespersons
1311. Do payments from a plan or system for sickness, retirement, etc. count as wages?
1312. Does sick pay count as wages?
1313. Do payments to a profit-sharing or stock bonus plan count as wages?
1314. Do payments from or to a tax-exempt trust fund count as wages?
1315. Do payments to a Federal Thrift Savings Plan count as wages?
1316. Do payments from or to a tax-exempt annuity plan count as wages?

1317. Pension and Retirement Payments
1318. Do amounts deferred under a nonqualified deferred compensation plan count as wages?
1319. Do supplemental retirement plan payments count as wages?
1320. Do advance payments count as wages?
1321. Do loans count as wages?
1322. Do bonuses and wage dividends count as wages?
1323. Back Pay
1324. Do dismissal payments count as wages?
1325. Do strike benefits count as wages?
1326. Does idle time pay count as wages?
1327. Does vacation pay count as wages?
1328. Does veterans training pay count as wages?
1329. Tips
1330. Do prizes and awards from persons other than your employer count as wages?
1331. Do taxes withheld from pay count as wages?
1332. Do traveling and business expense payments count as wages?
1333. Do moving expense payments count as wages?
1334. Do wages paid after the worker's death count as wages?
1335. Do payments made to a disabled former employee count as wages?
1336. Are interns in the U.S. during World War II granted wage credits?
1337. Does group-term life insurance count as wages?
1338. Do payments from Individual Retirement Accounts (IRA's) and Keogh plans count as wages?
1339. Do payments provided by an employer for dependent care assistance count as wages?
1340. Do payments under or to a tax-sheltered annuity plan count as wages?
1341. Payments Under a Cafeteria Plan
1342. Do fringe benefits count as wages?
1343. Do meals and lodging count as wages?
1344. Do payments that are not intended as remuneration for employment count as wages?

1300. WAGES FOR SOCIAL SECURITY PURPOSES

1300.1 What are wages?

"Wages" means all payment for services you perform for your employer. Wages do not have to take the form of cash. The cash value of all compensation paid to you in any form other than cash is also considered wages (unless the form of payment is specifically not covered under the Social Security Act).

1300.2 What types of income are considered wages?

Wages include bonuses, commissions, fees, vacation pay, cash tips of $20 or more a month, and severance pay.

1300.3 What types of income are NOT considered wages?

Types of income that are not wages include capital gains, gifts, inheritances, investment income, and jury duty pay.

1301. MAXIMUM EARNINGS CREDITABLE IN ANY ONE YEAR

1301.1 What is the maximum amount of wages that can be credited to your record?

The following table lists the maximum amount of wages that can be credited to your Social Security record.

Year	Maximum Earnings	Year	Maximum Earnings
2024	$168,600	1993	$57,600
2023	$160,200	1992	$55,500
2022	$147,000	1991	$54,400
2021	$142,800	1990	$51,300
2020	$137,700	1989	$48,000
2019	$132,900	1988	$45,000
2018	$128,400	1987	$43,800
2017	$127,200	1986	$42,000
2015-2016	$118,500	1985	$39,600
2014	$117,000	1984	$37,800
2013	$113,700	1983	$35,700
2012	$110,100	1982	$32,400
2011	$106,800	1981	$29,700
2010	$106,800	1980	$25,900
2009	$106,800	1979	$22,900
2008	$102,000	1978	$17,700
2007	$97,500	1977	$16,500
2006	$94,200	1976	$15,300
2005	$90,000	1975	$14,100
2004	$87,900	1974	$13,200
2003	$87,000	1973	$10,800
2002	$84,900	1972	$9,000
2001	$80,400	1968-1971	$7,800/year
2000	$76,200	1967	$6,600
1999	$72,600	1966	$6,600
1998	$68,400	1959-1965	$4,800/year
1997	$65,400	1955-1958	$4,200/year
1996	$62,700	1951-1954	$3,600/year
1995	$61,200	1940-1950	$3,000/year
1994	$60,600		

1301.2 How is the maximum wage amount increased each year?

For the years after 1981, the maximum wage amount is usually increased by Congress. If Congress does not increase the maximum amount, it is automatically increased in multiples of $300 if there is a cost-of-living increase in Social Security benefits. The increased amount is officially published in the *Federal Register* on or before November 1 of the year before it goes into effect.

1302. ACTUAL OR CONSTRUCTIVE PAYMENT OF WAGES

1302.1 When are wages considered paid?
Your wages are generally considered paid when they are "actually" or "constructively" paid.

1302.2 What does actually paid mean?
Actual payment occurs when you are actually paid in the form of cash, check, bank deposit, or similar form other than cash.

1302.3 What does constructively paid mean?
Your wages are constructively paid when:
A. They have been credited or set aside for you, and you can get them at any time. It does not matter when or how you receive payment, just that you have access to your wages when you want them; or
B. Your employer intends to pay, set apart, or credit the wages and is able to pay you when due, but fails to do so because of a clerical error or mistake in the mechanics of payment.

1303. CASH-PAY TESTS

1303.1 When must you meet the cash-pay tests in figuring your wage amount?
In figuring your wage, you must meet the cash-pay tests if you perform any of the following types of work:
A. Agricultural labor (see §901);
B. Domestic service in a private home (see §915);
C. Non-business or casual labor (see §924);
D. Some services by homeworkers (see §830); or
E. Tips (see §1329).

1303.2 What cash counts as wages if you meet the cash-pay test?
If you meet the cash-pay test, you must count *all cash* as your wages. If you are a homeworker ((D) above), count both cash and payments-in-kind. Do not count payments-in-kind as wages if you are a worker described in (A), (B), (C), or (E) above, even you meet the cash-pay test.

1303.3 What cash counts as wages if you do NOT meet the cash-pay test?

If you do not meet the cash-pay test, do not count payment as wages for Social Security purposes, even if it is paid in cash. However, you must count all cash pay (except tips that total less than $20) to the earnings test. (See §1811.)

1303.4 What types of payment are considered cash?

Cash pay for cash-pay tests includes the following:

A. Cash;
B. Checks and other monetary forms of exchange;
C. The income you receive as an employee from the sale of a crop from the farm owner/operator; and
D. Cash given in place of such items as meals, lodging, car tokens, clothing, etc.

1303.5 What types of payment are NOT considered cash?

Cash pay for cash-pay tests does not include the following:

A. Payments-in-kind, such as meals and lodging;
B. A share of crops or animal increase;
C. Car tokens, clothing, transportation passes, or tickets; and
D. The furnishing of goods or limited credit made available at a store for the maintenance of you and your family.

1304. PAY FOR WORK FOR NONPROFIT ORGANIZATION

1304.1 What is the minimum pay test for work for a nonprofit organization?

If you work for a nonprofit organization that does not have to pay Federal income tax under section 501(a) of the Internal Revenue Code (IRC), your earnings are subject to a minimum pay test. Beginning in 1978, as an employee of such an organization, *you must be paid at least $100 in a calendar year* in order for the payments to count as wages. (Before 1978, such employment was covered only if wages of at least $50 were earned in a calendar quarter.)

Note: If you work for an organization described in section 401(a) or 521 of the IRC, the above may not apply.

WAGES   351

1304.2 How is your payment credited if you meet the minimum pay test?

If you meet the minimum pay test, your payment can be credited for Social Security purposes. If you are an employee of an exempt organization that is a religious, charitable, educational, etc. organization, your payment is covered beginning January 1, 1984. (See §931 for special rules for church or qualified church-controlled organizations.) Your pay may be either cash pay, payments-in-kind, or both.

Before 1984, payment could be credited only if the organization filed an appropriate waiver certificate for its covered employees. (See §931.)

1304.3 How is your payment credited if you do NOT meet the minimum pay test?

If your pay is less than the minimum pay in cash or payments-in-kind during the calendar year, your payment is not counted for Social Security purposes. However, it is still counted for the earnings test. (See Chapter 18.)

1305. DOES PAY FOR MILITARY SERVICE AFTER 1956 COUNT AS WAGES?

Military service you performed after 1956 is covered by Social Security. Basic pay is considered wages for active duty or active duty for training. Inactive duty for training (including weekend drills) is wages after 1987. (See §§948-952.)

1306. CAN YOU RECEIVE ADDITIONAL WAGE CREDITS FOR MILITARY SERVICE AFTER 1967?

If you are/were a member of the uniformed services, you may receive additional wage credits (also known as deemed wages). These credits are in addition to your basic pay. (See §953.)

1307. CAN YOU RECEIVE WAGE CREDITS FOR MILITARY SERVICE BEFORE 1957?

If you performed military service before 1957, you may receive "gratuitous military wage credits" (also known as non-contributory wage credits). You may be eligible for wage credits of $160 for each month of active duty if you are a veteran who was on active duty in the uniformed services after September 15, 1940, and before January 1, 1957 (see §954). Under certain circumstances, service with allied forces during World War II also qualifies you for gratuitous military wage credits. (See §957.)

1308. PAY FOR RAILROAD WORK

1308.1 Does payment for railroad work generally count as wages for Social Security purposes?

Your pay for railroad work generally does not count as wages for Social Security purposes. Railroad employees have a separate retirement system administered by the Railroad Retirement Board (see Chapter 23 to find information on other benefit programs). However, if your railroad work does not qualify you for a railroad retirement benefit, your railroad work may count as Social Security wages.

1308.2 Are there any special cases where railroad work does count for Social Security purposes?

Your railroad credits count for Social Security purposes if you have less than 10 years of railroad service and less than 5 years of railroad service after December 31, 1995. In some survivor cases, regardless of the number of railroad service months you have, your railroad credits count for Social Security purposes. If you are insured based on the combined earnings, Social Security benefits are payable.

1309. DO COMMISSIONS COUNT AS WAGES?

Your commissions paid on sales are considered wages. The commissions are credited to your earnings record in the calendar year that they are paid. If you receive an advance against commissions you will earn in the future, the advance is considered wages when you receive the advance.

1310. RENEWAL COMMISSIONS OF LIFE INSURANCE SALESPERSONS

1310.1 Do life insurance renewal commissions count as wages?

Your renewal commission as a life insurance salesperson is wages when paid if, at the time the policy was written, you are:

A. An employee under the common-law test (see §802); or
B. A full-time life insurance salesperson. (See §828.)

1310.2 Does employment status matter?

It does not matter whether you are an employee or self-employed at the time of payment. It also does not matter if you are required to perform any services in connection with the sale of the policy. Your status at the time the original sale was made determines if renewal commissions are wages, even if you are retired or have ended the employment relationship. Generally, renewal commissions are considered earned at the same time the original commission was earned if you were an employee at the time the policy was written.

1311. DO PAYMENTS FROM A PLAN OR SYSTEM FOR SICKNESS, RETIREMENT, ETC. COUNT AS WAGES?

Payments you receive from a plan or system established by your employer for insurance or annuities are not wages. The plan must generally provide for all employees and/or their dependents or for a class(es) of employees and their dependents. The terms and conditions of the plan must be communicated to all employees or the class(es) affected. In addition, the plan must provide payment eligibility standards that include:
A. Length of service, salary, classification, or occupation;
B. The minimum period payments are made; and
C. A formula for computing the minimum benefit for each eligible employee.

1312. DOES SICK PAY COUNT AS WAGES?

Payments you receive for sickness and accident disability count as wages for the first six calendar months after the last month you worked. (For payments made by an employer to a disabled former employee, see §1335.)

1313. DO PAYMENTS TO A PROFIT-SHARING OR STOCK BONUS PLAN COUNT AS WAGES?

Effective January 1, 1984, payments your employer makes to a profit-sharing or stock bonus plan are wages if:
A. You have the choice of receiving cash instead;
B. The payments and the amounts are not included in your gross income because of section 402(a)(8) of the IRC; and
C. One of the following conditions exists:
   1. The payments are made under a qualified cash or deferred arrangement; or
   2. The payments are made under section 401(k)(2) of the IRC.

The payments are counted as wages at the time the distributions are paid to the trust.

1314. DO PAYMENTS FROM OR TO A TAX-EXEMPT TRUST FUND COUNT AS WAGES?

Payments made from or to a tax-exempt trust fund on behalf of you or your beneficiary are not wages, if the payments made are "from or to a trust" that does not pay income tax under sections 401 and 501(a) of the Internal Revenue Code (IRC).

1315. DO PAYMENTS TO A FEDERAL THRIFT SAVINGS PLAN COUNT AS WAGES?

A Federal Thrift savings fund is treated as a trust in section 401(a) of the IRC. Therefore, *employer* contributions to your Thrift savings fund are not wages. However, your elective contributions to the fund are wages.

1316. DO PAYMENTS FROM OR TO A TAX-EXEMPT ANNUITY PLAN COUNT AS WAGES?

Payments made from or to an annuity or bond purchase plan on behalf of you or your beneficiary *do not* count as wages if at the time of payment the:

A. Annuity plan is qualified under section 403(a) of the Internal Revenue Code (IRC); or

B. Bond purchase plan is qualified under section 405(a) of the IRC.

1317. PENSION AND RETIREMENT PAYMENTS

1317.1 Do pension and retirement payments count as wages?

Effective January 1, 1984, your pension and retirement payments generally count as wages. However, they do not count as wages if the payments are made from tax-exempt trusts or qualified deferred compensation plans.

1317.2 Do retirement payments based on a disability count as wages?

If you receive retirement payments because of a disability, the payments are not wages if they are made under the following conditions:

A. They are made under your employer's plan;

B. They are made when or after your employment ends; and

C. Your retirement due to your disability was a condition or plan for the payment.

1318. DO AMOUNTS DEFERRED UNDER A NONQUALIFIED DEFERRED COMPENSATION PLAN COUNT AS WAGES?

Effective January 1, 1984, delayed payments under your Nonqualified Deferred Compensation Plan are wages:

A. When you perform services; or
B. When you meet the conditions required for payment.

Note: If an agreement was in existence on March 24, 1983, between you and a nonqualified deferred compensation plan for services you performed before 1984, the payments are excluded from wages if the payment would have been excluded from wages under Social Security before 1983.

1319. DO SUPPLEMENTAL RETIREMENT PLAN PAYMENTS COUNT AS WAGES?

Effective January 1, 1984, your supplemental retirement plan payments do not count as wages if the payments are made under a plan that:

A. Provides cost-of-living adjustments to pension benefits; and
B. Is treated as a welfare plan under section 3(2)(B)(ii) of the Employee Retirement Income Security Act of 1984.

1320. DO ADVANCE PAYMENTS COUNT AS WAGES?

Advance payments by your employer for work done in the future count as wages if:

A. You do the work (or part of it); and
B. Your employer considers the work as satisfaction for the advance payments.

1321. DO LOANS COUNT AS WAGES?

Loans from your employer to you do not count as wages, unless you pay the debt by work.

1322. DO BONUSES AND WAGE DIVIDENDS COUNT AS WAGES?

Bonuses and wage dividends count as wages if they are payment for services you perform for your employer.

1323. BACK PAY

1323.1 What is back pay?

"Back pay" is pay you receive in one period for actual employment in an earlier period. Back pay under statute is payment that is required by law, such as the National Labor Relations Act, the Fair Labor Standards Act, and other Federal and State laws. The purpose of back pay is to create an employment relationship or to protect employees' rights to wages.

1323.2 Does back pay count as wages?

Back pay, except penalties, interest, or legal expenses paid under a statute, is wages if it is paid for covered employment. For Social Security purposes, back pay may be assigned to the periods in which it should have been paid.

Back pay not under a statute is wages if it is extra pay for past employment. Back pay not under a statute is not assigned to any period other than the period in which it is paid.

1324. DO DISMISSAL PAYMENTS COUNT AS WAGES?

Dismissal payments from your employer to you when your services end count as wages.

1325. DO STRIKE BENEFITS COUNT AS WAGES?

If you are on strike, strike benefits paid by your union generally do not count as wages. It does not matter whether or not you are on picket duty during the strike or are subject to call.

Note: If payments other than strike benefits are made to you and you actually perform picket or other strike duties, the payments count for Social Security if they amount to $100 or more in any calendar year.

1326. DOES IDLE TIME PAY COUNT AS WAGES?

Idle time pay counts as wages if:
A. You are a non-striking employee; and
B. Your employer pays you for the time you are idle because of a strike.

1327. DOES VACATION PAY COUNT AS WAGES?

Vacation pay and pay you receive instead of taking a vacation count as wages. It does not matter whether you are paid for a period that you did not work. It also does not matter if the payment is for additional compensation for vacation time you did not use.

1328. DOES VETERANS TRAINING PAY COUNT AS WAGES?

Veterans training pay from the Department of Veterans Affairs does not count as wages. Subsistence or dependency allowances paid by the

Department of Veterans Affairs to you as a veteran while you are attending school or participating in on-the-job training do not count as wages. Such payments are not for employment.

Any additional payments made by your employer do count as wages if they are paid for employment covered by Social Security.

1329. TIPS

1329.1 Do cash tips count as wages?

Cash tips you receive in the course of employment by any one employer are wages if the tips total $20 or more in a calendar month. This includes tips you receive:

A. Directly from customers;
B. From charge customers that are paid by your employer to you; and
C. Under a tip-splitting arrangement.

1329.2 Do non-cash tips count as wages?

Non-cash tips, such as passes, tickets, or services, do not count as wages.

Note: A club, hotel, or restaurant may require customers who use its dining or banquet rooms to pay a service charge that is given to the employees. The employee's share of this service charge is not a tip. It is part of wages paid to the employee by the employer.

(For special rules concerning employee tip reporting to employers and payment of FICA tax on tips, see §1408.)

1330. DO PRIZES AND AWARDS FROM PERSONS OTHER THAN YOUR EMPLOYER COUNT AS WAGES?

Prizes and awards you receive from persons other than your employer generally do not count as wages. An example would be a prize or award given by a manufacturer to a salesperson that handles the manufacturer's product, but works for an employer.

1331. DO TAXES WITHHELD FROM PAY COUNT AS WAGES?

Taxes paid from your employer's funds or withheld from your pay count as wages.

Any Social Security taxes your employer pays from his/her own funds on wages for agricultural labor or domestic service you perform in his/her private home do not count as wages.

1332. DO TRAVELING AND BUSINESS EXPENSE PAYMENTS COUNT AS WAGES?

Travel and business expense payments you receive as reimbursement for business expenses you incur as part of furthering your employer's business count as wages if:

A. Your employer does not require you to verify the expenses; or

B. You can keep any amount in excess of the verifiable expenses. Expenditures for your personal use are not business expenses.

1333. DO MOVING EXPENSE PAYMENTS COUNT AS WAGES?

Payments you receive as reimbursement or allowance for moving expenses do not count as wages. It must be reasonable to believe that you could deduct the amount paid for income tax purposes under section 217 of the IRC.

1334. DO WAGES PAID AFTER THE WORKER'S DEATH COUNT AS WAGES?

Wages earned before death and paid to a survivor or the employee's estate after death count as wages if they are paid *in the calendar year* the worker died.

If the wages are paid *after the calendar year* that the worker died, they do not count as wages. In addition, they are not subject to FICA contributions.

1335. DO PAYMENTS MADE TO A DISABLED FORMER EMPLOYEE COUNT AS WAGES?

If you are a disability beneficiary, payments you receive from your employer after 1972 are not wages if:

A. You became entitled to disability insurance benefits before the year in which the payment is made; and

B. You did not work for your employer during the pay period in which the payment is made.

1336. ARE INTERNS IN THE U.S. DURING WORLD WAR II GRANTED WAGE CREDITS?

You are granted wage credits if you were interned at a camp in the U.S. during World War II, if you are of Japanese ancestry. Wage credits are granted for each week that you were 18 or older. The credit for each of these weeks is the greater of:

A. The highest hourly rate of pay for which you previously worked in any employment multiplied by 40; or
B. The Federal minimum hourly rate in effect during that time. The minimum wage rate during 1941-1944 was 30 cents per hour, and during 1945-1946, 40 cents per hour. If you were not employed or were self-employed before internment, the amount of wages credited are based on the Federal minimum hourly rate in effect for that period.

Note: You will not receive these credits if a larger benefit would be payable without them; or if you are receiving a monthly benefit from another Federal agency based on the same internment.

1337. DOES GROUP-TERM LIFE INSURANCE COUNT AS WAGES?

The employer's cost (premiums) for group-term life insurance that exceeds the cost of $50,000 is considered wages for Social Security purposes beginning January 1, 1988.

1338. DO PAYMENTS FROM INDIVIDUAL RETIREMENT ACCOUNTS (IRA'S) AND KEOGH PLANS COUNT AS WAGES?

Payments from your Individual Retirement Account (IRA) are not considered "earnings." Likewise, if you are self-employed, payments from your Keogh Plan are not considered earnings. These payments are counted when they are deferred, not when they are distributed.

1339. DO PAYMENTS PROVIDED BY AN EMPLOYER FOR DEPENDENT CARE ASSISTANCE COUNT AS WAGES?

Payments provided by your employer for dependent care assistance under a written program are not wages (provided the program qualifies under section 129 of the IRC).

1340. DO PAYMENTS UNDER OR TO A TAX-SHELTERED ANNUITY PLAN COUNT AS WAGES?

Tax-sheltered annuity payments do not count as wages if:
A. The payments are made under a plan that meets the requirements of section 403(b) of the IRC for income tax deferral; and
B. You do not make the payments under a salary reduction agreement.

1341. PAYMENTS UNDER A CAFETERIA PLAN

1341.1 What is a cafeteria plan?

A "cafeteria plan", under IRC section 125, is a written plan under which all participants are employees. The participants may choose among two or more employer-provided benefits consisting of cash and qualified benefits.

1341.2 Do cafeteria plan payments count as wages?

Whenever you select cash instead of a qualified benefit, these payments count as wages.

1342. DO FRINGE BENEFITS COUNT AS WAGES?

Any fringe benefit that is not specifically exempt from Social Security taxes counts as wages. The amount of wages is the difference between the discount price you pay for the benefit and its fair market value.

Effective January 1, 1985, the following five categories of fringe benefits do not count as wages:

A. The minimum fringe (a property or service furnished by your employer that is so small in value that counting it would be impractical);

B. Gyms and other athletic facilities (the value of an employer-provided on-premises athletic facility);

C. No additional cost service (any service provided to you by your employer for your use);

D. Qualified employee discount (employee discount with respect to property or services); and

E. Working condition fringe (any service or property provided by your employer, such as a parking space).

1343. DO MEALS AND LODGING COUNT AS WAGES?

Meals and lodging do not count as wages when they are provided to you at work for your employer's convenience (to the extent it is excluded under IRC section 119).

1344. DO PAYMENTS THAT ARE NOT INTENDED AS REMUNERATION FOR EMPLOYMENT COUNT AS WAGES?

Payments you receive that are not meant to be payment for employment do not count as wages. Such payments include damages, attorney's fees, interest, or penalties paid under court judgment or by compromise settlement with your employer based on a wage claim.

CHAPTER 14

Earnings Records and Tax Reports

TABLE OF CONTENTS

1400. Earnings as Basis for Benefits
1401. Social Security Numbers
1402. What precautions should be taken when using SSNs and SSN cards?
1403. Earnings Record
1404. Earnings Reports Filed by Employers
1405. Social Security and Medicare Tax Rates
1406. Employee Tax Deducted from Pay
1407. Employees Working for More Than One Employer
1408. Special Rules for Cash Tips After 1965
1409. What tax return forms do employers use?
1410. What are the due dates for filing returns and paying taxes?
1411. Statements of Earnings for Employees
1412. Records Employers Must Keep
1413. What Internal Revenue Service publications provide information on employer tax payments?
1414. Self-Employment Tax
1415. Social Security Taxes on Self-Employment Income
1416. What are the reporting requirements for self-employed people?
1417. What forms are filed for partnerships?

1418. What IRS publications provide information on self-employment tax payments?
1419. Earnings Information Available from Social Security Records
1420. Procedure for Correcting Earnings Record
1421. Evidence Needed to Change Earnings Record
1422. How are wage disputes between employer and employee resolved?
1423. Time Limit for Correcting Earnings Records
1424. When can earnings records be revised after the time limit?
1425. Time Limit Extended if an Investigation is in Progress
1426. Time Limit Suspended During Military Service
1427. Is notice given of changes in an earnings record?

1400. EARNINGS AS BASIS FOR BENEFITS

1400.1 What is the basis for Social Security benefit amounts?
Social Security benefits are based upon your earnings as reported to the Social Security Administration (SSA). For this reason, it is important that you report these earnings to us promptly and accurately. (See §§1402-1404.)

1400.2 What types of benefits are determined by earnings?
Your earnings are used to find out whether you are entitled to retirement, survivors, disability, and health insurance benefits (see Chapter 2). Also, they are used to calculate cash benefit rates (see Chapter 7).

1401. SOCIAL SECURITY NUMBERS

1401.1 When is a Social Security Number assigned?
A Social Security Number (SSN) is assigned after we receive and process your completed application (Form SS-5, *Application for a Social Security Card*).

1401.2 What information do you submit with the application?
You must submit documents that prove your age, identity, and U.S. citizenship or immigration and work authorization status before we can process your application. If you are age 12 or older, you must apply in person for a social security card. Your identity document must show your legal name.

1401.3 How long does it take to process the application?
Usually, it takes about two weeks, but may take longer depending on how long it takes to verify your documents. For example, if you were born in the United States and are requesting an original Social Security number, we must verify your birth record, which can add up to 12 weeks to the time it takes to issue a card. U.S.-born includes birth in the 50 States, the District of Columbia, American Samoa, Guam, the Northern Mariana Islands, Puerto Rico, and the U.S. Virgin Islands.

1401.4 What is the SSN used for?
The SSN is used for the following purposes:
A. SSA uses the SSN to record earnings covered by Social Security and/or Medicare. These earnings determine your eligibility and the amount of Social Security benefits when you retire, or become disabled; or survivor benefits if you die;

B. The Internal Revenue Service (IRS) uses the numbers assigned to you and your dependents as your taxpayer identification numbers (TIN) for processing tax returns;
C. You need a SSN to file for Social Security or Supplemental Security Income benefits, and Medicare; and
D. If you have a SSN, State-run programs, such as State tax programs, driver's license, motor vehicle registration, and public assistance, may require that you provide your SSN.

1401.5 How does the SSN provide accurate identification?

Although the SSN card is not considered an identity document (because it does not display identifying information about you), SSA uses your SSN to differentiate you from other SSN card holders. Many people have the same name, but each person has his or her own SSN. Your SSN allows your earnings to be credited to you.

1401.6 Can a person use someone else's SSN?

No one else may lawfully use your SSN.

1401.7 Can a person have more than one SSN?

Most persons have only one SSN. In certain limited situations, SSA can assign you a new number. If you receive a new SSN, you *should* use the new number. However, your old and new number will remain linked in our records to ensure that your earnings are credited properly. This could affect your benefits.

1402. WHAT PRECAUTIONS SHOULD BE TAKEN WHEN USING SSNS AND SSN CARDS?

A. Keep your Social Security card in a safe place with your other important papers. Do not carry it with you unless you need to show it to an employer or governmental agency.
B. Be careful when providing SSNs to employers, to ensure that the employer has the correct name and SSN, as it appears on the Social Security card, under which to file reports of earnings.
C. Self-employed persons should accurately report their names and SSNs as they appear on their Social Security cards, on their Federal tax reports and returns.
D. Be very careful about sharing your number and card with third parties, to protect against misuse of your number.

Giving your number is voluntary even when you are asked for the number directly, particularly by private agencies and businesses. If requested, you should ask:
- why your number is needed;
- how your number will be used;
- what happens if you refuse; and
- what law, if any, requires you to give your number.

The answer to these questions can help you decide if you want to give your SSN. The decision is yours.

1403. EARNINGS RECORD

1403.1 What does the earnings record show?
Your earnings record shows the amount of earnings reported by your employer or by you, if you are self-employed. Also, it shows the periods for which your earnings were reported.

1403.2 What happens to the Social Security taxes?
During working years, employees, their employers, and the self-employed pay Social Security and/or Medicare taxes. The equivalent of these taxes is pooled in special trust funds under automatic appropriation by Congress. (See §140.)

1404. EARNINGS REPORTS FILED BY EMPLOYERS

1404.1 When must employers file reports of earnings?
Reports of earnings must be filed annually with SSA by every employer who:
A. Is required to withhold income tax from wages; and/or
B. Is liable for Federal Insurance Contributions Act (FICA) taxes, also called Social Security and Medicare taxes.

1404.2 How do employers file W-2 forms?
A. Employers are encouraged to file electronically; even if you are filing fewer than 250 W-2 Copy A forms. Social Security no longer accepts magnetic tapes, cartridges, or 3 1/2" diskettes. Effective 2007, all wages must be filed either electronically or on paper.

Note: If you expect to file 250 or more W-2 Copy A forms (*Wage and Tax Statement*), you must use electronic reporting to report this information to us.

More information on Employer Reporting Instructions can be found at: https://www.ssa.gov/employer/.

B. Employers who are filing less than 250 W-2 Copy A forms and choose to file on paper may use Copy A of the W-2 form to report the wage and tax information for their employees. SSA records the employee's Social Security wages on his/her earnings record and then forwards the data to IRS.

1404.3 What other forms must employers file?

Employers must also file the following forms with the Internal Revenue Service (IRS):

A. Employers who are required to withhold income tax, FICA tax, or both, must file IRS Form 941 (Employer's QUARTERLY Federal Tax Return) or, only if notified by IRS, file Form 944 (Employer's ANNUAL Federal Tax Return).

B. Employers of agricultural employees must file annual returns with the IRS on Form 943 (Employer's Annual Federal Tax Return for Agricultural Employees).

C. Employers of household employees must file Form 1040, Schedule H (Household Employment Taxes).

These reports must be sent with the appropriate tax payments to IRS. These reports contain only summary information. To get more detailed information on employer reports and payment of taxes, contact any IRS office or visit their website at: www.irs.gov.

1404.4 What records of identification numbers must employers keep?

Each employer must keep the following records:

A. The name and Social Security number of each employee as it is shown on the employee's Social Security card (this information is needed for the earnings report); and

B. An employer identification number (EIN) obtained from IRS by filing an *Application for Employer Identification Number* (Form SS-4). The application may be obtained from any IRS or Social Security office, or employers can apply for an EIN online at www.irs.gov. The employer identification number must be shown on the employer's tax returns and earnings reports.

1404.5 What should an employer do if an employee does not have a Social Security card?

If an employee does not have a Social Security card, the employer advises the employee to:

A. Obtain an application Form SS-5, complete it, and send or take it to the nearest Social Security office along with the evidence required (See §1401);
B. Apply in person if the employee is 12 years or older; and
C. Provide the employer with the name and SSN exactly as it appears on the Social Security card. The employer makes a record of the number as soon as it is received from the employee.

1404.6 What is an employer?

An employer is any person or organization for whom a person performs any service and receives payment as an employee.

1404.7 What payments are counted as wages?

Pay for covered employment counts as wages (unless excluded by the Social Security Act).

1404.8 If a worker receives payment after he or she stops working for the employer, is the payment counted as wages?

Yes. Even if the relationship of employer-employee no longer exists when the payment is made, the payment is still counted as wages.

1405. SOCIAL SECURITY AND MEDICARE TAX RATES

1405.1 What rates do employers and employees pay on Social Security and Medicare taxes?

Employers and employees pay Social Security and Medicare taxes at the same rate on wages up to the maximum amounts creditable for each program for the year. (See §1301.) Certain employers did not pay Social Security Tax for qualified new hires for most of 2010. For 2011 and 2012, employees paid Social Security tax at a lower rate than employers.

1405.2 Are tips included in determining wages?

Yes. Tips are included in determining the maximum wages on which the employer's tax is payable. (See §1329.) See §1408 for allocated tips.

1405.3 How is the tax rate calculated?

The Social Security tax rate is the sum of the retirement, survivors, and disability insurance tax rate and the hospital insurance tax rate on the wages. The following chart shows the rates that apply to both employers and employees:

Calendar year	Retirement, survivors, and disability insurance rate	Hospital insurance rate	Combined rate
1985	5.70%	1.35%	7.05%
1986-1987	5.70%	1.45%	7.15%
1988-1989	6.06%	1.45%	7.51%
1990-2010[1]	6.20%	1.45%	7.65%
2011	4.20% (employees) 6.20% (employers)	1.45%	5.65% (employees) 7.65% (employers)
2012	4.20% (employees) 6.20% (employers)	1.45%	5.65% (employees) 7.65% (employers)
2013-2024[2]	6.20%	1.45%	7.65%

1406. EMPLOYEE TAX DEDUCTED FROM PAY

1406.1 When are Social Security and Medicare taxes deducted from wages?

Social Security and Medicare taxes are deducted when wages are paid. (See §1408 for special rules on cash and charged tips).

1406.2 Are taxes deducted if you do not meet the minimum dollar test?

If an employer is not sure if an employee will meet the minimum dollar test for household employees (as explained in §915), for agricultural

---

1. The Hiring Incentives to Restore Employment (HIRE) Act exempted employers from the employer's share of the Social Security tax on wages paid to qualified employees from March 19, 2010 through December 31, 2010.
2. As of January 2013, individuals with earned income of more than $200,000 and joint filers with wages above $250,000 pay an additional 0.9 percent in Medicare taxes. The tax rates shown above do not include the 0.9 percent.

employees (as explained in §901), or for some homeworkers (as explained in §830), the employer may:

A. Deduct the tax when the payment is made; or
B. Wait until the test is met.

1406.3 How are taxes deducted for tips?

If the employee submits written reports of tips more than once a month (§1408), the employer may collect the Social Security tax on tips even if the cash-pay test in §1408 is not yet met.

1406.4 If the employee does not meet the cash-pay test, what should the employer do?

If the employer collects the taxes and later finds that the employee does not meet the test, the employer must repay the Social Security taxes deducted to the employee. If the employer cannot locate the employee, the taxes should be sent to IRS.

1407. EMPLOYEES WORKING FOR MORE THAN ONE EMPLOYER

1407.1 Why is too much tax sometimes withheld?

If you work for more than one employer, you may not have to pay all the taxes deducted by the employers. This is because the tax is deducted on wages paid by each employer up to the maximum wages creditable for Social Security. The total deducted may be more than you owe. (Beginning with tax year 1994, there is no limit on Medicare wages.)

1407.2 How is Social Security tax calculated if too much was withheld?

Claim the excess as a credit against your income tax when you file your Federal income tax return. Your credit is the total Social Security that was deducted from your wages that year minus the taxes actually due.

1408. SPECIAL RULES FOR CASH TIPS AFTER 1965

1408.1 When are tips counted as wages?

Tips that total more than $20 in one calendar month are considered wages.

1408.2 When are tips considered received?

Tips are considered received when you report them to your employer. If you fail to report the tips to your employer, the tips are treated as received when you actually receive them.

1408.3 How are tips reported?

For each month that you receive $20 or more in tips, you must give your employer a written statement of cash and charge tips by the 10th day of the month after the month that you received the tips. Use IRS Form 4070 (*Employee's Report of Tips to Employer*) to report tips.

1408.4 Are tips of less than $20 per month reported?

No. Tips totaling less than $20 during a single calendar month while working for any one employer are not wages for FICA tax purposes. You do not need to report them to your employer.

1408.5 Are taxes withheld on tips?

Your employer must withhold Social Security, Medicare, and income taxes due on the tips you report. Your employer withholds FICA taxes due on tips from the employee's wages and pays both employer and employee portions of the tax in the same manner as the tax on your regular wages.

1408.6 What tax information is available for employers?

Employers should obtain IRS Circular E (*Employer's Tax Guide*) for information regarding employer's tax responsibilities.

1408.7 When is tip income allocated in food and beverage establishments?

Tip allocation is only required when the amount of tips reported by employees of a large food or beverage establishment is less than 8 percent (or an approved lower rate) of the gross receipts (other than nonallocatable receipts) for the given period. For additional information on tip allocation, visit the IRS website at www.irs.gov.

1408.8 How much tip income is allocated?

The amount allocated is the difference between eight percent of total sales and the amount of tips reported.

1408.9 How is allocated tip income reported?

Allocated tip income is reported as follows:

A. Employers are required to report tips allocated to employees on IRS Form W-2 (*Wage and Tax Statement*);

B. The employer withholds no Social Security, Medicare, or income taxes on allocated tips from the employees;

EARNINGS RECORDS AND TAX REPORTS   371

C. The employer is not liable for its portion of the FICA taxes on unreported tips until the IRS notifies the employer and demands payment; and

D. As an employee, you pay the FICA tax due by completing IRS Form 4137 (*Social Security and Medicare Tax on Unreported Tip Income*) and filing it with IRS Form 1040 (*U.S. Individual Income Tax Return*).

1408.10 Do allocated tips count as wages?

For Social Security purposes, allocated tips do not count as wages or income unless you report the allocated tips as additional income on IRS Form 1040.

1408.11 Must employees report allocated tip income?

You must report the allocated tip income amount as additional income unless you have records to show that the allocated tip amount was not received.

1408.12 How does an employee pay FICA taxes on allocated tip income?

If you include allocated tip income on Form 1040, you pay your portion of the FICA taxes by completing IRS Form 4137. The IRS reports the additional income to us to credit your earnings record.

1408.13 Where can you find more information on income and employment taxes on tips?

For more information regarding income and employment taxes on tips, see IRS Publication 531 (*Reporting Income from Tips*). For additional information on tip reporting, visit the IRS website at https://www.irs.gov.

1409. WHAT TAX RETURN FORMS DO EMPLOYERS USE?

Tax return forms used by employers include:

A. Form W-2 (*Wage and Tax Statement*);
B. Form W-2c (*Corrected Wage and Tax Statement*);
C. Form 941 (*Employer's QUARTERLY Federal Tax Return*);
D. Form 941-X, (*Adjusted Employer's QUARTERLY Federal Tax Return or Claim for Refund*);
E. Form 1040, Schedule H (*Household Employment Taxes*);
F. Form 943 (*Employer's Annual Tax Return for Agricultural Employees*);
G. Form 943-X, (*Adjusted Employer's Annual Federal Tax Return for Agricultural Employees or Claim for Refund*)

H. Form 944 (*Employer's ANNUAL Federal Tax Return*);
I. Form 944-X, (*Adjusted Employer's ANNUAL Federal Tax Return or Claim for Refund*)
J. Form W-3 (*Transmittal of Wage and Tax Statement*);
K. Form W-3C (*Transmittal of Corrected Wage and Tax Statement*).

1410. WHAT ARE THE DUE DATES FOR FILING RETURNS AND PAYING TAXES?

Due dates for filing returns and paying the balance of taxes due depend upon the type and size of the employer. Refer to the IRS publications mentioned in the later sections for detailed filing instructions.

1411. STATEMENTS OF EARNINGS FOR EMPLOYEES

1411.1 What items are shown on a statement of earnings?

Every employer subject to Social Security taxes must provide written statements of earnings to employees. IRS Form W-2 (*Wage and Tax Statement*) is generally used for this purpose. The statement must show:

A. The name, address, and identification number of the employer;
B. The name, address, and Social Security number of the employee;
C. The total amount of wages (including tips reported to the employer by the employee) subject to Social Security and Medicare taxes which were paid to the employee during the calendar year;
D. The amount of the Social Security and Medicare taxes deducted from the employee's wages;
E. The total amount of tips reported to the employer which is subject to Social Security and Medicare taxes; and
F. The amount of the Social Security and Medicare taxes, if any, the employee still owes on tips reported to the employer.

1411.2 When are statements provided to employees?

These statements must be given to employees as follows:

A. No later than January 31 following the calendar year in which the wages were paid; or
B. An employee who stops working before the end of a year and does not expect to return to work that year may ask the employer for an earlier statement. The statement must be furnished by the latest of the following:

EARNINGS RECORDS AND TAX REPORTS   373

1. 30 days after the date of the employee's request;
2. 30 days after the last wages were paid; or
3. 30 days after the death of the worker, in which case the statement is sent to the next of kin as well as to IRS.

1412. RECORDS EMPLOYERS MUST KEEP

1412.1 What information about employees must the employer keep?

Employers must keep the following records:

A. Names, addresses, and occupations of employees receiving wages;
B. Employees' periods of employment;
C. Employees' Social Security numbers;
D. The employer's identification number;
E. Total amount and date of each wage payment (including tips reported to the employer by the employee);
F. Amount of each wage payment subject to Social Security and Medicare taxes and the amount of tax withheld; and
G. Farm operators who utilize services of "crew leaders" must keep a record showing the name, home address, and employer's identification number of the crew leader.

1412.2 What copies of these records are kept?

The employer (except a household employer) must keep duplicate copies of the quarterly and annual returns on which employees' wages are reported for Social Security purposes.

1412.3 How long must the records be kept?

These records must be kept for a period of at least four years after the date the tax is due or is paid whichever is later.

1413. WHAT INTERNAL REVENUE SERVICE PUBLICATIONS PROVIDE INFORMATION ON EMPLOYER TAX PAYMENTS?

For more detailed information concerning employer deduction and payment of Social Security and Medicare taxes, employers can obtain the following publications from any IRS office or visit their website at: www.irs.gov:

A. General employment:
   1. Publication 15, Circular E, *Employer's Tax Guide*;
   2. Publication 15-A, *Employer's Supplemental Tax Guide*;

3. Publication 15-B, *Employer's Tax Guide to Fringe Benefits*;
4. Publication 15-T, *New Wage Withholding and Advance Earned Income Credit Payment Tables*;
5. Publication 80, Circular SS, *Federal Tax Guide for Employers in the U.S. Virgin Islands, Guam, American Samoa, and the Commonwealth of the Northern Mariana Islands*;
6. Publication 179, Circular PR, *Guia Contributiva Federal; Para Patronos Puertorriquenos* (*Federal Tax Guide for Employers in Puerto Rico*);
7. Publication 334, *Tax Guide for Small Business*;
8. Publication 957, *Reporting Back Pay and Special Wage Payments to the Social Security Administration*;

B. Agricultural employment:
   1. Publication 51 (Circular A), *Agricultural Employer's Tax Guide*;
   2. Publication 225, *Farmer's Tax Guide*;

C. Household employment:
   1. Publication 926, *Household Employer's Tax Guide*

1414. SELF-EMPLOYMENT TAX

1414.1 When do self-employed people pay self-employment tax?

If you are self-employed, you must pay the self-employment tax quarterly to IRS. You must pay any balance due when you file your Federal income tax returns on or before the 15th day of the fourth month following the end of your taxable year. (If you have a calendar tax year, this means on or before April 15th.)

1414.2 How does SSA obtain a record of earnings?

IRS reports the earnings to us for posting to the earnings record.

1414.3 Where can you obtain additional information on net earnings from self-employment?

For details about figuring net earnings from self-employment, including the optional ways of figuring net earnings which self-employed persons can use, see Chapter 12.

1415. SOCIAL SECURITY TAXES ON SELF-EMPLOYMENT INCOME

1415.1 What are the tax rates on self-employment income?

Social Security taxes are paid on self-employment income up to the maximum amount creditable for the year. Medicare taxes are paid on all self-employment income, as there is no yearly maximum. (See §1201.) The Social Security and Medicare tax rates on self-employment income are shown in the following chart:

Taxable year	Retirement, survivors, and disability insurance rate	Hospital insurance rate	Combined rate
1985	11.40%	2.70%	14.10%
1986-1987	11.40%	2.90%	14.30%
1988-1989	12.12%	2.90%	15.02%
1990-2012	10.40%	2.90%	13.30%
2013-2024	12.40%	2.90%	15.30%

1415.2 What tax credits are allowed for self-employed persons?
If you were self-employed in 1984-1989, you were allowed credit against your Social Security and Medicare tax liability for those years in the following percentages:

Taxable Year	Percentage Rate
1984	2.7%
1985	2.3%
1986-1989	2.0%

After 1989, the credit was replaced with special deduction provisions designed to treat the self-employed like employees and employers are treated for Social Security and income tax purposes.

1416. WHAT ARE THE REPORTING REQUIREMENTS FOR SELF-EMPLOYED PEOPLE?

If you are self-employed and have net earnings of $400 or more in any taxable year, you must:

A. Complete Form 1040 (*U.S. Individual Income Tax Return*) including Schedule C (Farmers use Schedule F instead of Schedule C);
B. Complete Schedule SE (*Computation of Social Security Self-Employment Tax*); and
C. Send the return and schedules to IRS with the balance of any self-employment tax that is due.

1417. WHAT FORMS ARE FILED FOR PARTNERSHIPS?

A partnership is required to file Form 1065 *(Partnership Return of Income)* to show each partner's share of partnership's income or loss. If you are a partner in a business, you should include your share of the partnership net earnings (or loss) from self-employment on your individual tax return.

1418. WHAT IRS PUBLICATIONS PROVIDE INFORMATION ON SELF-EMPLOYMENT TAX PAYMENTS?

For more detailed information on self-employment tax payments, refer to the following publications:

A. General self-employment
   - Publication 17, *Your Federal Income Tax.*
   - Publication 334, *Tax Guide for Small Business.*
B. Farm self-employment
   - Publication 225, *Farmer's Tax Guide.*
C. Foreign self-employment
   - Publication 54, *Tax Guide for U.S. Citizens and Resident Aliens Abroad.*
D. Commercial fishermen
   - Publication 595, *Capital Construction Fund for Commercial Fisherman.*

You can obtain these publications from any IRS office or visit their website at: www.irs.gov.

1419. EARNINGS INFORMATION AVAILABLE FROM SOCIAL SECURITY RECORDS

1419.1 How can you obtain more detailed information on coverage?

You may complete Form SSA-7050-F3 *(Request for Social Security Earnings Information)* to obtain detailed earnings information.

1419.2 Is there a cost to obtain the information?

No, if you need the information in connection with Social Security. For example, you may need earnings information to verify an employer's earnings report or to compute your amount of Social Security taxes.

Yes, charges are made if more detailed earnings information than that shown on the SSA-7005 is required for other than Social Security purposes. Charges are also made if certification by the custodian of the record is needed. Examples would be for the requestor's use in planning private pensions or civil litigation.

1419.3 How are charges calculated?

Charges are determined according to the fee provisions of section 1106(c) of the Social Security Act.

1420. PROCEDURE FOR CORRECTING EARNINGS RECORD

1420.1 What is the process for correcting earnings records, and when should it be done?

To correct your Social Security Earnings record, get in touch with the nearest Social Security office or call SSA's toll free number 1-800-772-1213. Do this when your earnings statement shows that earnings have not been correctly reported or credited. It will be helpful when you contact SSA to have any information such as forms W-2, pay stubs, etc. available.

1420.2 How does the SSA assist employees with correcting their record?

We do several things to help correct your record. We will first ask if you have any evidence of your earnings such as forms W-2, pay stubs, etc. We check to see if any missing reports of earnings can be found. If we cannot find the records, and you do not have any evidence of your earnings we will write your employer to get a statement of your earnings.

1421. EVIDENCE NEEDED TO CHANGE EARNINGS RECORD

1421.1 Can your earnings record be corrected?

Your earnings record can be corrected (subject to the requirements in §§1424-1425 if the time limit has passed) if there is acceptable evidence of wages paid to you.

1421.2 What evidence is acceptable?

The evidence may be a statement signed by your employer, Form W-2 (*Wage and Tax Statement*), pay envelopes or pay slips, or personal records of your wages. (See §§1726-1733 for a discussion of how to establish wages.)

1421.3 How can self-employed people establish earnings?

If you are self-employed, you may establish earnings by submitting a copy of your tax return. Include the applicable schedules (see §1416) and evidence that your return was filed on time with IRS. Evidence of filing your return includes canceled checks, IRS receipts, or other evidence of payment of tax shown on your return.

1421.4 How can partnerships establish earnings?

If a partnership is involved, a copy of Form 1065 should also be furnished.

1422. HOW ARE WAGE DISPUTES BETWEEN EMPLOYER AND EMPLOYEE RESOLVED?

If you and your employer disagree about the amount of wages paid, when they were paid, or whether your work was covered by Social Security, we help you obtain evidence to settle the matter. We will then make a decision as to:

A. Whether your earnings can be credited;
B. The amount of your earnings; and
C. The period to which they should be credited.

You are notified by SSA of the decision and the correction, if any, made to your earnings record.

1423. TIME LIMIT FOR CORRECTING EARNINGS RECORDS

1423.1 What is the time limit for correcting earnings?

An earnings record can be corrected at any time up to three years, three months, and 15 days after the year in which the wages were paid or the self-employment income was derived. "Year" means "calendar year" for wages and "taxable year" for self-employment income. If the last day of that period falls on a Saturday, Sunday, legal holiday, or other non-work day for Federal employees set by statute or Executive Order, the period for correction is extended to the end of the next work day.

1423.2 How can earnings be corrected after the time limit is passed?

After the time limit has passed, the earnings record can be corrected only as explained below in §§1424-1425. The following chart illustrates how the time limit operates:

If you were paid wages or you derived self-employment income in...	Then the Period of correction is...	And the record of wages or self-employment income is final on...
Calendar year 2000	1/1/01 through 4/15/04	4/16/04
Taxable year ending 6/30/91	7/1/91 through 10/17/94 (October 15th falls on a Saturday)	10/18/94
Taxable year ending 9/30/92	10/1/92 through 1/16/95 (January 15th falls on a Sunday)	1/17/95

1424. WHEN CAN EARNINGS RECORDS BE REVISED AFTER THE TIME LIMIT?

After the time limit has passed, earnings records can only be revised under the conditions described below and in §1425:

A. To correct an entry established through fraud;
B. To correct a mechanical, clerical, or other obvious error;
C. To correct errors in crediting earnings to the wrong person or to the wrong period;
D. To transfer items to or from the Railroad Retirement Board (if reported to the wrong agency), or to add railroad earnings to Social Security earnings records when the law permits;
E. To add wages paid in a period by an employer who made no report of any wages paid to the worker in that period, or if the employer is increasing the originally reported amount for the period;
F. To add or remove wages in accordance with a wage report filed by the employer with IRS; or, if a State or local governmental employer, with SSA if the report is filed within the time limitation specified for assessment, refund, or credit under a State's coverage agreement;

G. To add self-employment income in a taxable year if an individual or the individual's survivor establishes that:
   1. A self-employment tax return for that year was filed before the time limit ran out; and
   2. Either no self-employment income for that year has been recorded in the individual's earnings record, or the recorded self-employment income for that year is less than the amount reported on the self-employment tax return; or
H. To add self-employment income for any taxable year up to the amount of earnings that were wrongly recorded as wages and later deleted. This can be done only if a tax return reporting such self-employment income is filed within three years, three months, and 15 days after the taxable year in which the earnings wrongly recorded as wages were deleted. The self-employment income must:
   1. Be for the same taxable year as the year in which the wages were removed; and
   2. Have already been included on the individual's Social Security record.
I. Prior to the expiration of the time limit the worker or the worker's survivor has:
   1. Applied for benefits and stated that the earnings for a year(s) were incorrect; or
   2. Requested a revision of his or her earnings record for a year(s).

1425. TIME LIMIT EXTENDED IF AN INVESTIGATION IS IN PROGRESS

1425.1 Can revisions be made after the time limit has run out?

The earnings record for a year may be revised even after the time limit for that year has run out if, before it ran out, the worker or the worker's survivor:

A. Applied for benefits; or
B. Requested a revision of his or her earnings record for that year.

1425.2 When can the earnings record be corrected?

That part of the earnings record open to correction at the time of filing the application may be corrected up until a final decision is made on the earnings issue.

1425.3 Can the earnings record be revised after a final decision?

No, after a final decision has been made on the earnings issue, you may not revise your earnings record for that year.

1425.4 What years can be corrected?

The only years open to correction are:
A. Those years for which revision has specifically been requested before the time limit ran out; and
B. Those years in which the time limits ran out before the date of the final decision.

1425.5 What is the definition of survivor?

"Survivor" in this section means the worker's widow (including a surviving divorced wife or surviving divorced mother), widower (including a surviving divorced husband or surviving divorced father), child, or parent.

1426. TIME LIMIT SUSPENDED DURING MILITARY SERVICE

1426.1 Can the time limit be suspended for service personnel?

The time limit for making corrections is suspended while you are in the active military service. The suspension period can begin no earlier than October 17, 1940, and ends with the earliest of the following:
A. The date of your discharge from active service;
B. The date of your death; or
C. The date the Soldiers' and Sailors' Civil Relief Act of 1940 is no longer in force.

1426.2 Does the suspension apply to military service of heirs?

The time limit is also suspended during the military service of an heir of the worker. Heirs include spouse, child, and parent. Thus, if a worker's spouse was in the military service when the worker died, the time limitation is extended by the time between the worker's death and the date of the widow(er)'s discharge from service.

1427. IS NOTICE GIVEN OF CHANGES IN AN EARNINGS RECORD?

No. Notice of changes in an earnings record are not given unless:

A. The worker or the worker's survivor was previously given a report of the worker's wages for periods in which a deletion or reduction of wages is made; or

B. Amounts recorded as self-employment income are being reduced.

Note: A survivor is given notice of a change only if the worker or the survivor was previously given a report of wages or self-employment income for the period involved.

CHAPTER 15
Filing a Claim

TABLE OF CONTENTS

1500. Filing an Application
1501. Who Signs Applications
1502. When to File Applications
1503. Individuals Nearing Retirement Age
1504. Result of Delay in Filing for Benefits
1505. Where Applications May Be Filed
1506. Application Filed with Department of Veterans Affairs or Railroad Retirement Board
1507. When Your Application is Considered Filed
1508. What are the requirements for an application to be considered valid?
1509. Written Statement Considered As Application
1510. Can you file one application for more than one type of benefit?
1511. Completing the Application Form
1512. How can Social Security help you complete your application?
1513. Retroactive Effect of Application
1514. Claimant May Restrict Retroactivity
1515. Right to Withdraw Application
1516. How do you make a request to withdraw a claim?
1517. Time Limit for Applying for Lump-Sum Death Payment
1518. Can you file an application for the lump-sum death payment after the two-year filing period?
1519. Good Cause Defined
1520. What is the time limit for filing evidence of one-half support?

1500. FILING AN APPLICATION

1500.1 Why do you need to file an application for benefits?

You must file an application to:

A. Become entitled to benefits, including Medicare;

B. Establish a period of disability under the retirement, survivors, and disability insurance programs; or

C. Become eligible for Supplemental Security Income (SSI) payments.

1500.2 How do you apply for benefits?

Fill out the application on a form issued by the Social Security Administration (SSA). (See §1511.) File the completed and signed application form via the internet at www.socialsecurity.gov, at a Social Security office, or with a person authorized by us to receive applications. If you need an interpreter to communicate with us, we will provide one upon request, free of charge. SSA has a nationwide contract for telephone interpreter services in more than 150 languages and dialects. Based on SSA's signature alternatives to the traditional pen-and-ink signature, for teleclaims and in-person Title II (Retirement and Disability), Title XVI (Supplemental Security Income), and Title XVIII (Medicare) claims, the application is signed once the SSA interviewer confirms and annotates the system electronically of the claimant's intent to file, his or her affirmation of the correctness of the information that is provided under penalty of perjury, and agreement to sign the application. (See §§1505-1506 and 1511-1512.) When the signature is recorded electronically, it is no longer necessary for SSA to retain the paper application. Also, some applications for Social Security benefits are available to you on our Internet website; therefore, you can apply for some Social Security benefits online. For claims that are filed on the Internet website the application is signed when you press the "Sign Now" button.

1500.3 Do you have to file an application for hospital and medical insurance if you are 65 or older?

If you are age 65 or older and entitled to monthly benefits under Social Security or railroad retirement, you are automatically entitled to hospital insurance and medical insurance. You do not need to file a separate application for these benefits. If you are eligible for monthly benefits and are age 65 or older, you may apply for hospital insurance (Medicare Part A) and medical insurance (Medicare Part B) without applying for monthly benefits.

If you are age 65 or older and not entitled to monthly benefits under Social Security or railroad retirement, you need to file an application for hospital and medical insurance. You must be willing to pay the monthly premiums involved. (See Chapter 24.)

1500.4 Where can you find additional information about hospital and medical insurance benefits, the prescription drug benefit and extra help with prescription drug costs?

Chapter 24 includes information concerning entitlement to hospital and medical insurance (Medicare) for persons entitled to disability benefits and persons with end-stage renal disease requiring renal dialysis or kidney transplant. It also includes information about the prescription drug benefit. Chapter 26 includes information about extra help with prescription drug costs.

1501. WHO SIGNS APPLICATIONS

1501.1 Who normally signs the application form for Social Security benefits?

We normally expect the claimant to sign the application (which includes the use of signature alternatives to the pen- and-ink signature) personally if he or she is:

A. At least age 18;
B. Mentally competent; and
C. Physically able to do so.

Where good cause is shown, i.e., dire circumstances exist that preclude the claimant from filing his or her own application and a loss of benefits may result from the delay in obtaining an application from a person authorized to file for the claimant, an application may be signed by someone else. (See §1501.2. below)

Note: There is no similar provision for medical insurance coverage. These applications can only be filed at specific times. (See Chapter 24.)

1501.2 Who signs the application if the claimant can not?

If the claimant does not meet the conditions above, the application ordinarily is signed by the legal guardian, committee, or other legal representative of the claimant. It may also be signed by the relative or other person who cares for the claimant. If the claimant is in the care of an institution, the manager or principal officer of the institution may sign the application for the claimant.

1502. WHEN TO FILE APPLICATIONS

1502.1 When should you file an application for benefits?

You may file your application for benefits up to four months before you expect benefits to begin. However, you should file for monthly survivor's benefits as soon as you meet all the eligibility requirements on the deceased individual's record. If you are applying for retirement or aged spouse's benefits, the earliest you may file is three months before age 62. You may also file your application for disability before the first month you are entitled to benefits.

1502.2 When should you file an application for the establishment of a period of disability?

If you are applying for the establishment of a period of disability, you may file your application before the first day this period begins. Your application becomes effective some time before we make a final decision on your application.

1503. INDIVIDUALS NEARING RETIREMENT AGE

1503.1 Why should you contact us before you turn 62?

If you are a worker who is considering early retirement, you should get in touch with a Social Security office several months before turning 62 because age 62 is the earliest month possible for benefits to begin. We will give you the information you need so you can decide whether or not to file an application for reduced retirement benefits at that time.

1503.2 When should you contact us if you do not file an application for reduced retirement benefits at 62?

If you do not file an application for reduced retirement benefits at age 62, you should contact us again:

A. Up to 4 months before you plan to retire;
B. As soon as you know that you will neither earn more than the monthly exempt amount (see §1807.5) in wages nor render substantial services in self-employment in one or more months of the year, *regardless of expected total annual earnings* (see Chapter 18 for the earnings test); or
C. Up to 4 months before you reach Full Retirement Age (FRA), even if you are still working.

1504. RESULT OF DELAY IN FILING FOR BENEFITS

1504.1 What are the advantages of filing an application on time?

It generally works to your advantage to file your application for benefits promptly, even if you are still working. Any delay in filing your application may result:

A. In fewer payments, since:
1. Monthly benefits cannot be paid retroactively in some instances; and
2. Benefits cannot be paid for more than 12 months (depending on the particulars of the situation) before the month you file the application. (See §1513.)

B. In loss of some months of coverage under the hospital and medical insurance programs.

1504.2 When is it beneficial to delay the filing of your application?

It may be to your advantage to delay filing an application for monthly benefits if:

A. You have not yet reached FRA and you wish to wait and receive an unreduced benefit at FRA; or
B. You would lose benefits payable under some other program.

1505. WHERE APPLICATIONS MAY BE FILED

1505.1 Where do you file your application for Social Security or Medicare benefits?

File your application for Social Security benefits:

A. At a Social Security office or with an authorized Social Security employee (Retirement, Spouse, Disability, and Medicare applications may be filed on the Internet at https://www.socialsecurity.gov);
B. At a U.S. Foreign Service post if you are not a resident of the U.S. or could lose benefits because of extended absence from the U.S. (in the Philippines, applications may be filed at the U.S. Veterans Affairs Regional Office in Manila);
C. In certain cases, with the Railroad Retirement Board or the Department of Veterans Affairs (see §1506); or
D. In certain cases, with a provider of hospital services that is participating in the Social Security hospital insurance program. This provision protects you if you are:

1. Age 65 or older;
2. Eligible for hospital insurance benefits; and
3. Admitted to a hospital for inpatient services without ever having filed an application with us.

Note: There is no similar provision for medical insurance. These applications can only be filed at specific times. (See Chapter 24.)

1505.2 Where do you file your application for SSI benefits?
You may file your application for SSI benefits:
A. At a Social Security office or with an authorized Social Security employee;
B. At another Federal or State office with someone designated by us to receive applications, or
C. With another person designated by us to receive applications.

1505.3 Where do you file your application for extra help with Medicare prescription drug costs?
See Chapter 26.

1506. APPLICATION FILED WITH DEPARTMENT OF VETERANS AFFAIRS OR RAILROAD RETIREMENT BOARD

1506.1 Are applications you file with the Department of Veterans Affairs or the Railroad Retirement Board considered applications for Social Security benefits?
An application you file for survivor benefits with the Department of Veterans Affairs for benefits payable under its program is also considered an application for Social Security benefits. An application filed with the Railroad Retirement Board for benefits under its programs, is also an application for Social Security benefits. In these situations the claim or notice of the claim is sent to SSA.

1506.2 What types of Social Security benefits are considered when you file an application with the Department of Veterans Affairs?
When you file an application with the Department of Veterans Affairs for survivor's dependency and indemnity compensation, your application may also be considered an application for the following Social Security benefits:
A. Child's benefits;
B. Surviving spouse's benefits; or
C. Parent's monthly Social Security benefits.

Your application listed in (A) through (C) above is not considered an application for the lump-sum death payment.

1506.3 What types of Social Security benefits are considered when you file an application with the Railroad Retirement Board?

When you file an application with the Railroad Retirement Board for an annuity, your application is also considered an application for Social Security benefits (unless you specify otherwise). In the case of disability, your application is used to establish a period of disability under both the Railroad Retirement Act and the Social Security Act (unless you specify otherwise).

1507. WHEN YOUR APPLICATION IS CONSIDERED FILED

1507.1 When is your application for benefits generally considered filed?

We consider your application for benefits filed as of the day your application is received by:

A. A Social Security office;
B. Any other office we authorize to accept applications;
C. A Social Security employee authorized to receive applications; or
D. Any person designated by us to receive applications.

1507.2 Can a filing date other than the date of receipt be considered?

If we can establish an earlier filing date based on (A) - (E) below, we use that date as the application filing date instead of the receipt date:

A. The U.S. postmark date on the envelope containing the protective writing or application, if that date is more favorable than the date of receipt by such office or employee. (Only a U.S. postmark is acceptable.);
B. The date a written request for Social Security benefits is received;
C. The date a systems record is made of a telephone contact requesting benefits, and use of this date results in eligibility for additional benefits;
D. The date a written or verbal request for SSI benefits is received;
E. For SSI benefits: The date an Interim Assistance Reimbursement (IAR) authorization form is signed at a State agency.

F. For Social Security Benefits
1. The date a U.S. Foreign Service post (or in the U.S. Veterans Affairs Regional Office, Manila) receives an application; or
2. The date a social security agency of a foreign country with which the U.S. has a Social Security agreement (see §107) receives a written request for benefits.

1508. WHAT ARE THE REQUIREMENTS FOR AN APPLICATION TO BE CONSIDERED VALID?

Your application for benefits, including SSI, must be:

A. Made on a prescribed form;
B. Signed by a proper person (see §1501);
C. Received by one of the offices (or persons) specified in §§1505 and 1506; and
D. Received while you (or the person eligible for benefits) are still living.

Note: This requirement does not apply to applications for Social Security Disability Insurance benefits where the deceased was disabled prior to death. An application for disability insurance benefits may be filed by a qualified individual (see §1902) within three months after the month of death of the disabled person.

(Where an individual dies after requesting benefits in writing, but before filing a prescribed form, see §1509.)

1509. WRITTEN STATEMENT CONSIDERED AS APPLICATION

1509.1 When is a written statement used as the application filing date?

The receipt date of any written statement requesting benefits is used as the application filing date if the following requirements are met:

A. The statement indicates an intention on the part of the writer to claim benefits, the lump-sum death payment, or to establish a period of disability. The expression of intent may be made orally;
B. The statement is signed by the claimant or someone on his/her behalf, the claimant's spouse, or some other person who is authorized to file the application (see §1501);
C. The application is completed on a prescribed application form (see §1510) and is filed by the claimant (or a person who is authorized to file an application for the claimant). The valid application must be filed within six months for Social Security benefits (or within 60 days

for SSI) after the date we notify the claimant that a formal application is necessary; and
D. For Social Security Benefits, either:
1. The claimant is alive when the valid application is filed; or
2. If the claimant died before filing the valid application, the form is filed by a person acting on behalf of the claimant's estate or by a survivor eligible for benefits on his or her earnings record. The valid application must be filed within six months after our notice that a formal application is necessary.
E. For SSI Benefits:
1. The claimant is alive when the valid application is filed; or
2. If the claimant died before filing the valid application, the form is filed by a surviving living-with spouse or, in the case of a child, the child's living-with parent. The valid application must be filed within 60 days after our notice that a formal application is necessary.

1509.2 How are benefit rights protected for military service members who are missing in action?

Form DD-1300 (*Report of Casualty*) is prepared by a military service department, indicating a service member is missing. It is a written intent to claim benefits on behalf of the service member and all other persons eligible for benefits under the service member's Social Security record. This procedure serves, if the need arises, to protect the benefit rights of service members (and their dependents) missing in action. If an application is filed, we use the date the Form DD-1300 is prepared as the application filing date or if the form indicates that the service member was placed in MIA status earlier than the date the form is prepared, we will use the date the service member was placed in MIA status as the application filing date.

1510. CAN YOU FILE ONE APPLICATION FOR MORE THAN ONE TYPE OF BENEFIT?

Each application form is clearly worded to show its scope as an application for one or more types of benefits. Unless you restrict the scope of your application, the application will generally cover all classes of benefits on all Social Security Numbers (SSN), for which you are eligible, regardless of the title of the application. You can expand or restrict the scope of your application as long as you add appropriate remarks, in writing, on the application before we make a decision on your claim.

This rule has some exceptions.

If you are age 65 or older, you must file for Medicare Part A if filing for any monthly benefit. Following the rules for deemed filing, if you are eligible for both retirement insurance benefits and spouse's insurance benefits you must apply for both and cannot restrict your application to only one benefit when you are born:

- January 2, 1954 or later and eligibility for both benefits exists in any month; or
- Before January 2, 1954, under your full retirement age, and eligibility for both benefits exisits in the first MOET to either benefit.

The Social Security office determines the proper application form to use when you file your claim.

1511. COMPLETING THE APPLICATION FORM

1511.1 Do you need to fill out all questions on the application form?

You should answer all questions on the application form. If you do not know the answer to a question, answer "unknown". If you do not answer a question needed to establish your right to benefits, we cannot award benefits.

1511.2 How do you sign the application if you cannot write?

If you cannot write, signature by mark on the signature line is acceptable. The signature by mark must be witnessed as indicated on the application form. See §1500.2 which explains SSA's signature alternative to the pen-and-ink signature or mark which has been implemented for teleclaims and in-person claims.

1512. HOW CAN SOCIAL SECURITY HELP YOU COMPLETE YOUR APPLICATION?

If you find that you need help completing your application, any Social Security office will provide assistance free of charge. If you cannot go to the Social Security office personally because of poor health, or if there is no Social Security office nearby, call the toll-free number at 1-800-772-1213, or write the nearest Social Security office to:

A. Get full information and application forms;
B. Make an appointment for a telephone interview; or
C. Request that someone from the Social Security office go to your home. (See §110.)

If you need an interpreter to communicate with us, we will provide one upon request, free of charge. SSA has a nationwide contract for telephone interpreter services in more than 150 languages and dialects.

1513. RETROACTIVE EFFECT OF APPLICATION

1513.1 Can you be entitled to benefits retroactively?

You may be entitled to monthly benefits retroactively for months before the month you filed an application for benefits. For example, full retirement age claims and survivor claims may be paid for up to six months retroactively. In certain cases, benefits involving disability up to 12 months may be paid retroactively. (This is not true of the special age 72 payments (see §§346-348), black lung benefits (see Chapter 22), medical insurance (see Chapter 24), or SSI (see Chapter 21).)

1513.2 How is the retroactive entitlement date determined?

You are entitled to benefits beginning the first month in the retroactive period that you meet all requirements (except for the filing of an application) for entitlement. For example, suppose you reach FRA in March 2008 and you are fully insured. You do not file an application for retirement insurance benefits until March 2009. In this case, you may be entitled retroactively beginning with the month of September 2008 (six months before you filed an application).

1513.3 Are retroactive benefits payable if it results in a permanent reduction of the monthly benefit amount?

Retroactive benefits for months prior to attainment of FRA are not payable to a retired worker, spouse, or widow(er) if this results in a permanent reduction of the monthly benefit amount. However, this limitation does not apply if you are a surviving spouse or surviving divorced spouse under a disability, and you are not yet age 61 in the month of filing. You may possibly be entitled to benefits as a disabled widow(er) in the retroactive period.

1513.4 Is a widow(er) or surviving divorced spouse entitled to benefits in the month of the worker's death?

If you are a widow(er) or surviving divorced spouse and you file an application in the month after the month of the worker's death, you may be entitled to benefits in the month of the worker's death. In order to be entitled in the month of the worker's death, you must be otherwise eligible in that month.

1513.5 Is a widow(er) or surviving divorced spouse entitled to retroactive hospital insurance benefits?

If you are a widow(er) or surviving divorced spouse applying for hospital insurance benefits because of a disability, you may be deemed entitled retroactively for up to 12 months prior to the month of filing, even if monthly benefits are not payable because entitlement does not exist before age 60. You must meet all other conditions of entitlement.

1513.6 Can you be paid retroactively even if you are no longer eligible for monthly benefits?

Even if you file an application and are no longer eligible for monthly benefits, you may be paid benefits for the period beginning six months (or 12 months in certain cases involving disability) before the month you file the application if you meet all eligibility factors in the retroactive period. Payment ends with the month before the month you are no longer eligible.

1513.7 Are benefits payable if a claimant dies before filing an application?

If a person requests benefits in a written statement (see §1509) but dies before filing the valid application, benefits may be payable for the months in the period before death. Benefits for the months before the claimant's death may also be paid to a survivor whose right to benefits depended upon the claimant's entitlement to benefits.

1514. CLAIMANT MAY RESTRICT RETROACTIVITY

1514.1 Can you restrict your right to retroactive benefits?

Yes. You may restrict any retroactive right to benefits. Make your request in writing at any time before we make a decision on your application.

1514.2 Why might you want to restrict your right to retroactive benefits?

We do not use "waived" months in computing the reduction factor. (See §723.) This may result in a higher benefit amount for later months. You may want to give up benefits for certain months in order to receive somewhat higher benefits later on.

1514.3 What benefits may you NOT exclude from your application?

If you are age 65 or older, you must file for Medicare Part A if filing for any monthly benefit. Following the rules for deemed filing, if you

are eligible for both retirement insurance benefits and spouse's insurance benefits you must apply for both and cannot restrict your application to only one benefit when you are born:
- January 2, 1954 or later and eligibility for both benefits exists in any month; or
- Before January 2, 1954, under your full retirement age, and eligibility for both benefits exisits in the first MOET to either benefit.

1514.4 Can you change your decision to restrict retroactivity?
In certain cases, you may change your decision to restrict retroactivity. For example, if you discover that earnings in the year were more or less than you expected, you can change the month of entitlement to any month within the retroactive period of the original application. However, any other beneficiary who would lose some or all of those benefits because of such a change must agree to it in writing. Also, any benefits that were paid based on entitlement cancelled by the change must be repaid.

1515. RIGHT TO WITHDRAW APPLICATION

1515.1 Can you withdraw your application?
Yes. You may withdraw your application if:
A. You (or a person acting on your behalf) files a written request for withdrawal before we make a decision on your application; and
B. You are alive at the time the request is filed.

If we approve your request to withdraw an application, the application will be considered as if it was never filed. If we deny your request for withdrawal, the application is treated as if the request for withdrawal was never filed.

Note: There is no right to reconsideration or appeal based on a withdrawn claim. You must file a new application if you later wish to claim benefits.

1515.2 Can you withdraw your application after SSA makes a decision on your claim?
You may withdraw your application after we make a decision on your claim if the conditions in the above section are met *and* if:
A. All individuals whose entitlement would be voided by the withdrawal agree, in writing, to the withdrawal; and

B. The person who requested withdrawal repays any benefits received based upon entitlement on the claim that is voided by the withdrawal.

Even if you withdraw a claim, we keep your application form and all related papers.

1515.3 Can an application be withdrawn after a claimant dies?

After the claimant's death, an application may be withdrawn, regardless of whether we have made a decision on it if:

A. The application was for retirement benefits that would be reduced because of the claimant's age;

B. The claimant died before we certified his or her benefit entitlement to the Treasury Department for payment;

C. A written request for withdrawal is filed by or for the person eligible for widow(er)'s benefits based on the claimant's earnings; and

D. The conditions in (A) and (B) of the above section are met.

1515.4 What is the effective date of withdrawal?

Ordinarily, the filing date of the withdrawal is the day we receive the request and the filing date is used to determine if withdrawal is requested before or after a determination is made on the application. The withdrawal, however, does not become effective until SSA approves the withdrawal request.

1515.5 Can you cancel a request to withdraw an application?

You may cancel a request to withdraw an application if you file a written request at a proper place (see §1505), and the claimant is alive at the time you file the request for cancellation. For a cancellation request received after we approved the withdrawal, you must file the request no later than 60 days after the date of the notice of approval.

(To withdraw from medical insurance after a period of entitlement, see Chapter 24.)

1516. HOW DO YOU MAKE A REQUEST TO WITHDRAW A CLAIM?

We accept any written request for withdrawal of a claim. However, we have a special form for this purpose. You (the claimant) or someone acting on your behalf must sign the withdrawal request. Be sure to include a statement showing that you realize the effects of this action.

1517. TIME LIMIT FOR APPLYING FOR LUMP-SUM DEATH PAYMENT

1517.1 What is the time limit for applying for the lump-sum death payment?

If you are eligible for the lump-sum death payment, you must file the application within a two-year period.

Note: If you are the widow(er) of the deceased worker and you were entitled to spouse's benefits for the month before the month that the worker died, you do not need to file an application for the lump-sum.

1517.2 When does the two-year filing period end?

Normally, the two-year filing period ends with the second anniversary of the insured person's death. However, under the conditions set out in the following sections, the filing period may be extended. Also, there are conditions for extending the filing period for members of the U.S. Armed Forces.

Note: If the last day of the filing period is a Saturday, Sunday, legal holiday, or other non-work day for Federal employees set by statute or Executive Order, the application may be filed on the next work day.

1518. CAN YOU FILE AN APPLICATION FOR THE LUMP-SUM DEATH PAYMENT AFTER THE TWO-YEAR FILING PERIOD?

We may accept an application filed after the two-year filing period following the worker's death, provided there is good cause (defined in §1519) for your failure to file the application within that period.

1519. GOOD CAUSE DEFINED

1519.1 What does good cause mean?

"Good cause" means that you did not file the lump-sum death payment application within the time limit because of:
A. Circumstances beyond your control, such as extended illness, communication difficulties, etc.;
B. Incorrect or incomplete information given to you by us;
C. Your efforts to get the evidence to support the claim, not realizing you could file the application within the time limit and submit the supporting evidence later; or
D. Unusual or unavoidable circumstances that show that you could not reasonably be expected to have been aware of the need to file the application within a specified period.

1519.2 When is good cause NOT established?

Good cause is not established if:

A. You were informed that an application for the lump-sum death payment had to be filed within the initial two-year period; and

B. You did not file the application because of neglect, or because you did not then want to claim the lump-sum death payment.

1520. WHAT IS THE TIME LIMIT FOR FILING EVIDENCE OF ONE-HALF SUPPORT?

In order to establish potential entitlement to benefits on the insured worker's Social Security record, parents must file evidence of one-half support within the two-year time limit. The two-year period within which the evidence of support must be filed depends upon the circumstances. (See §423.)

We may extend the time if good cause, as explained in §1519, is established for failure to file the evidence within the time limit.

CHAPTER 16
Representative Payees

TABLE OF CONTENTS

1600. Representative Payees
1601. When does a beneficiary need a representative payee?
1602. What about a beneficiary under age 18?
1603. What if the beneficiary is age 18 or over?
1604. What kind of evidence shows that a beneficiary needs a representative payee?
1605. What is legal evidence of incapability?
1606. What is medical evidence of incapability?
1607. What is lay evidence of incapability?
1608. What factors does SSA consider in selecting payees?
1609. What is the usual order of preference in selecting a payee for a beneficiary under age 18?
1610. What is the usual order of preference in selecting a payee for a beneficiary age 18 or over?
1611. What evidence is needed before a payee is selected?
1612. SSA's Advance Notice of a Payee Selection
1613. When does SSA select new representative payee?
1614. Will SSA make direct payment to a beneficiary after a reevaluation shows he or she is now capable?
1615. What if a beneficiary's ability to manage benefits has improved?

1616. What are the responsibilities of a representative payee?
1617. Use of Benefit Payments
1618. Current Needs of Beneficiary
1619. Past Debts of Beneficiaries
1620. A Beneficiary's Savings
1621. Blind or Disabled Children Receiving SSI
1622. What should I do with a beneficiary's conserved funds when I stop serving as a representative payee?
1623. Accounting for Use of Funds
1624. State Mental Institutions that Serve as Representative Payees

1600. REPRESENTATIVE PAYEES

1600.1 What is a representative payee?

A representative payee is a person or organization SSA selects to receive and manage benefits on behalf of an incapable or legally incompetent beneficiary.

1600.2 What is SSA's policy on appointment of representative payees?

Our policy is that a legally competent adult beneficiary has the right to manage their own funds and we must pay them directly. However, if the evidence shows a beneficiary is unable to manage or direct the management of payments in his or her best interest, we will pay benefits through a representative payee.

1600.3 What does this chapter cover?

This chapter explains:

A. How we determine a beneficiary is incapable of managing or directing the management of funds;

B. How we select a representative payee; and

C. How a representative payee may use the payments they receive.

1601. WHEN DOES A BENEFICIARY NEED A REPRESENTATIVE PAYEE?

1601.1 When does SSA select a representative payee?

When we determine a beneficiary is unable to manage or direct the management of his or her funds, we select either an individual or an organization to serve as a representative payee. If we determine a representative payee is necessary, we say these beneficiaries are *incapable* of managing their benefits.

1601.2 Must a beneficiary be declared legally incompetent before a representative payee is selected?

No. While it is true that a legally incompetent beneficiary must have a payee, we may determine that other beneficiaries need a payee as well.

We initially presume that all legally competent adult beneficiaries are capable of managing or directing the management of their funds. The facts of a case may convince us that a legally competent beneficiary is not capable and we will select a payee.

We also generally consider beneficiaries under the age of 18 incapable of managing their own funds and in need of a payee.

1601.3 What will cause SSA to select a representative payee?

We will not select a representative payee unless we have convincing evidence that an adult beneficiary is incapable of managing or directing the management of his or her funds. (See §§1604-1607 for a discussion of evidence.)

1602. WHAT ABOUT A BENEFICIARY UNDER AGE 18?

1602.1 If a beneficiary is under age 18, is a representative payee necessary?

Yes. We generally consider a beneficiary under age 18 incapable of managing his or her own funds, and in need of a representative payee.

1602.2 Will SSA ever make direct payment to beneficiaries under age 18?

We may make direct payments to a beneficiary under age 18 if:
A. The beneficiary is age 15 or over; and
B. It serves the beneficiary's best interests; and
C. The beneficiary does not have a legal guardian; and
D. The beneficiary is:
  1. Receiving disability insurance benefits on his or her own Social Security earnings record; or
  2. Serving in the military services; or
  3. Self-supporting and living alone; or
  4. A parent and files for his or her own or his or her child's benefits, and has experience in handling his or her own finances; or
  5. Capable of using the funds to provide for his or her own current needs and no qualified payee is available; or
  6. Within seven months of reaching age 18 and is initially filing an application for benefits.

Note: If a minor beneficiary has the status of an adult under State law, we may also make direct payment.

1603. WHAT IF THE BENEFICIARY IS AGE 18 OR OVER?

1603.1 Under what circumstances will SSA select a representative payee for a beneficiary over age 18?

We will always pay benefits directly to a beneficiary age 18 or older unless the beneficiary:

A. Is judged legally incompetent; or
B. Is mentally incapable of managing his or her payments; or
C. Is physically incapable of managing or directing the management of his or her payments.

1603.2 What is required for a decision of incapability?

We determine a beneficiary is incapable only when there is convincing evidence he or she is unable to manage or direct the management of benefits. See §§1604-1607 for a discussion of evidence.

1603.3 If SSA's capability decision is pending, will SSA make direct payments?

If we are in the process of investigating a beneficiary's ability to manage funds, and the decision is taking longer than anticipated, we may pay benefits directly until the investigation is complete.

In these cases, we will generally make direct payments to a beneficiary who is:

A. Age 18 or over; and
B. Legally competent.

When the capability determination is complete, we may either select a representative payee or allow the beneficiary to continue receiving benefits directly.

1604. WHAT KIND OF EVIDENCE SHOWS THAT A BENEFICIARY NEEDS A REPRESENTATIVE PAYEE?

There are several kinds of evidence we will consider when determining whether an adult beneficiary needs help managing their payments. These are:

A. Legal evidence (see §1605), or
B. Medical evidence (see §1606), and
C. Lay evidence (see §1607).

1605. WHAT IS LEGAL EVIDENCE OF INCAPABILITY?

A court judgment that a beneficiary is legally incompetent, is legal evidence. If there is such a judgment, we will:

- Obtain a certified copy of the court order;
- Presume the beneficiary cannot manage payments; and
- Select an appropriate representative payee.

However, the appointment of a legal guardian alone doesn't necessarily mean the beneficiary is legally incompetent. The court order must specifically address the beneficiary's competency or must contain a statement regarding the individual's ability to handle his/her financial affairs. If the court order is more than one year old, SSA will obtain a court certification that the order is still in effect. Similarly, if a court order has restored a beneficiary's competency, SSA will obtain a certified copy of the order.

Note: As used here, a "legal guardian" means a person appointed or authorized by a court, or by law, to assume control of and responsibility for the beneficiary.

1606. WHAT IS MEDICAL EVIDENCE OF INCAPABILITY?

Medical evidence of a beneficiary's inability to handle payments is a signed statement from a physician, psychologist or other qualified medical practitioner who is in a position to provide an opinion of a beneficiary's ability to manage his or her funds. The statement should be based on an examination within the last year and must contain the actual/original signature of the person who conducted the examination or their authorized representative.

1607. WHAT IS LAY EVIDENCE OF INCAPABILITY?

Lay evidence is any non-legal or non-medical information that helps us understand how a beneficiary functions in day-to-day life. For example, it may be evidence of how the beneficiary has been managing any available funds, prior to Social Security payments, to meet his or her daily needs.

Some typical examples of lay evidence are:

A. Our observations (during a face-to-face interview) of the beneficiary's behavior, reasoning ability, how he or she functions with others and how effectively he or she pursues the claim; or

B. Any signed statements from people (such as relatives, close friends, neighbors or landlords) who are in a position to know of the beneficiary's ability to manage his or her funds.

1608. WHAT FACTORS DOES SSA CONSIDER IN SELECTING PAYEES?

When deciding whether to select a person as payee, we consider the person's:

A. Relationship to the beneficiary;
B. Concern for the beneficiary's well-being;
C. Ability to fulfill the duties of being a payee; and
D. Ability to know of and provide for the needs of the beneficiary.

1609. WHAT IS THE USUAL ORDER OF PREFERENCE IN SELECTING A PAYEE FOR A BENEFICIARY UNDER AGE 18?

The usual order of preference in selecting a payee for a beneficiary under age 18 is:

A. A natural or adoptive parent who has custody of the beneficiary, or a court-appointed legal guardian;
B. A natural or adoptive parent who does not have custody of the beneficiary but who demonstrates strong concern for the beneficiary's well-being;
C. A relative or stepparent who has custody of the beneficiary;
D. Any one of the following:
   1. A friend with custody who provides for the beneficiary's needs; or
   2. A relative or close friend who does not have custody of the beneficiary but who demonstrates concern for the beneficiary's well-being; or
   3. An authorized social agency or custodial institution.

1610. WHAT IS THE USUAL ORDER OF PREFERENCE IN SELECTING A PAYEE FOR A BENEFICIARY AGE 18 OR OVER?

1610.1 What is the usual order of preference in selecting a payee for a beneficiary age 18 or over?

The usual order of preference in selecting a payee for a beneficiary age 18 or over is:

A. A spouse, parent or other relative with custody or who shows strong concern;

B. A legal guardian/conservator with custody or who shows strong concern;
C. A friend with custody;
D. A public or nonprofit agency or institution;
E. A Federal or State institution;
F. A statutory guardian (see GN 00502.139);
G. A voluntary conservator (see GN 00502.139);
H. A private, for-profit institution with custody and is licensed under State law;
I. A friend without custody, but who shows strong concern for the beneficiary's well-being, including persons with power of attorney;
J. Anyone not listed above who is qualified and able to act as payee, and who is willing to do so;
K. An organization that charges a fee for its service.

1610.2 What is the usual order of preference in selecting a payee for a beneficiary age 18 or over who has a substance abuse condition?

The usual order of preference in selecting a payee for a disabled beneficiary who has a substance abuse condition is:

A. A community-based nonprofit social service agency bonded and licensed (if required) by the State;
B. A Federal, State or local government agency whose mission is to carry out income maintenance, social service, or health care-related activities;
C. A State or local government agency with fiduciary responsibilities;
D. A designee of an agency (other than of a Federal agency) referred to above, if appropriate; or
E. A family member who demonstrates strong concern and is able and willing to exercise adequate supervision of the beneficiary's behavior.

1610.3 Who is selected if the preferred payees are not available for a beneficiary age 18 or over who has a substance abuse condition?

When none of the preferred payees are available, select the best payee from this list of alternate sources:

A. A legal guardian with custody or who shows strong concern for the beneficiary's well-being;

B. A relative or friend with custody who shows strong concern for the beneficiary's well-being;
C. A public or nonprofit agency or institution with custody;
D. A private, for-profit institution with custody and is licensed under State law; or
E. Anyone not listed above who is qualified and able to act as payee, and who is willing to do so.

1611. WHAT EVIDENCE IS NEEDED BEFORE A PAYEE IS SELECTED?

1611.1 What evidence is needed to become a payee?

A payee applicant must produce evidence of his or her:
- Identity;
- Relationship to the beneficiary;
- Concern and responsibility for the care of the beneficiary; and
- SSN or EIN.

1611.2 What if a court has appointed a guardian?

A guardian, trustee, committee, conservator, or other court-appointed fiduciary must submit a certified copy of the letters or court order of appointment. This evidence must show that the appointment is still in full force and effect.

1611.3 Will SSA request information after the selection?

At least once a year, we will request a written report from the payee showing how the funds received were spent or saved.

We may also, at any time after the selection of a representative payee, ask the payee to furnish information showing a continuing relationship to the beneficiary and a continuing responsibility for the care of the beneficiary.

1611.4 What happens if the payee does not submit the required information?

If we do not receive the information when requested, we may initiate an investigation to determine if the payee has misused the beneficiary's funds. We may also select a different representative payee.

1612. SSA'S ADVANCE NOTICE OF A PAYEE SELECTION

1612.1 How does SSA notify a beneficiary of a proposed payee selection?

When we decide to pay benefits through a representative payee, we send the beneficiary (or the individual acting on his or her behalf) an advance notice of our proposed actions. The notice explains why we are selecting a representative payee and who that payee will be.

1612.2 Can the beneficiary object to the proposed decisions?

Yes, the notice advises the beneficiary (or the individual acting on his or her behalf) that they have the right to protest either our decision to pay benefits through a representative payee, or who we select as payee.

1612.3 What happens if there is an objection?

If the beneficiary (or the individual acting on his or her behalf) objects to either proposed action, he or she may review the evidence and submit any additional evidence.

When there is an objection, we will review the proposed determination, consider any additional information we receive, and issue our determination.

If the beneficiary (or the individual acting on his or her behalf) objects to either decision, he or she may appeal the decision.

1612.4 What happens if there is no objection?

If the beneficiary (or the individual acting on his or her behalf) does not object to the proposed actions, we will begin making payment through a representative payee.

1612.5 Can a beneficiary object after the decision is made?

Yes. If the beneficiary (or the individual acting on his or her behalf) is dissatisfied, he or she has 60 days from the date of our decision to appeal the decision.

1613. WHEN DOES SSA SELECT NEW REPRESENTATIVE PAYEE?

SSA will select a new representative payee if the current payee:
- Dies;
- Has misused the beneficiary's benefits as determined by SSA or a court of competent jurisdiction;
- Is unable to manage the benefit payments;

- No longer wishes to serve as payee;
- Fails to use and account for the payments properly;
- Is no longer responsible for the care or welfare of the beneficiary; or
- Is otherwise no longer suitable to serve as payee.

1614. WILL SSA MAKE DIRECT PAYMENT TO A BENEFICIARY AFTER A REEVALUATION SHOWS HE OR SHE IS NOW CAPABLE?

Yes. If a reevaluation of capability shows that the beneficiary is capable of managing or directing the management of benefits, SSA will make direct payment to the beneficiary.

1615. WHAT IF A BENEFICIARY'S ABILITY TO MANAGE BENEFITS HAS IMPROVED?

1615.1 When should a beneficiary submit evidence of capability?

Whenever an adult beneficiary has been receiving payments through a payee and believes he/she is now able to manage benefit payments, he or she should contact SSA and submit evidence of capability.

1615.2 What evidence should the beneficiary submit?

The beneficiary should submit:
- A signed statement from a physician or from a medical officer of the institution where he or she is or was residing, which shows the beneficiary's present capability to manage benefits (see §1607); or
- Any other evidence that establishes the beneficiary's ability to manage or direct the management of benefits; or
- A certified copy of a court order restoring the beneficiary's rights in a case in which he or she was previously judged legally incompetent.

1616. WHAT ARE THE RESPONSIBILITIES OF A REPRESENTATIVE PAYEE?

The responsibilities of a representative payee are to:
- Determine the beneficiary's current and future needs and to use the funds in the best interests of the beneficiary, conforming to SSA regulations and policies;
- Apply the benefit payments only for the beneficiary's use and welfare (see §1617);
- Maintain a continuing awareness of the beneficiary's needs and condition. If the beneficiary does not live with the representative

payee, the representative payee should keep in contact with the beneficiary by visiting and consultating with custodians;
- Keep written records of all payments received from SSA and how the payments were spent and/or saved along with receipts for shelter expenses and major purchases to prove how funds were spent and/or saved on behalf of the beneficiary;
- Report to us any event that will affect the amount of payments the beneficiary receives or the right of the beneficiary to Social Security or SSI payments;
- Give us written reports accounting for the use of the funds, when requested to do so;
- Notify us of any change in circumstances that would indicate he or she is no longer suitable to serve as payee or would affect the payee's performance; and
- Return conserved funds to SSA when no longer serving as the beneficiary's representative payee (see §1622) and return any payments not due when a beneficiary has died.

1617. USE OF BENEFIT PAYMENTS

1617.1 What is the proper use of funds?
A representative payee must apply the payments for the use and benefit of the entitled individual. Social Security and/or SSI funds are properly used if they are:
A. Spent for the beneficiary's current and reasonably foreseeable needs (see §1618); or
B. Saved or invested for the beneficiary, after current needs have been met (see §1620).

1617.2 May payments be applied to the needs of other individuals?
Yes. If the current and reasonably foreseeable needs of a Social Security beneficiary are being met, part of the benefits may also be used to support a spouse, child, or parent who is the beneficiary's legal dependent.

1617.3 May funds be used for someone other than the beneficiary, if the beneficiary is institutionalized?
For institutionalized beneficiaries whose current needs are being met, part of the beneficiary's Social Security funds may be used for:

A. The support of the community spouse (the legal spouse of the beneficiary); and
B. Any dependent family member as specified in the Medicaid determination.

Note: SSI funds may not be used to support a beneficiary's dependents.

1617.4 What expenditures are given priority for beneficiaries in institutions or nursing homes?

If a beneficiary is in an institution or nursing home that is not receiving Medicaid funds on behalf of the beneficiary, the representative payee will give priority to using funds for the current maintenance of the beneficiary. Current maintenance includes:

A. Customary charges made by an institution/nursing home for the beneficiary's care;
B. Items that will aid in the beneficiary's recovery or release; and
C. Personal needs to improve the beneficiary's condition while in the institution.

1617.5 How much money should be set aside for personal needs of beneficiaries who are in institutions or nursing homes?

The representative payee is required to set aside at least $30 each month for a beneficiary living in an institution or nursing home, to be used for the beneficiary's personal needs or saved on his or her behalf.

1617.6 What is misuse of Social Security and/or SSI funds?

Misuse occurs when a representative payee converts Social Security and/or SSI payments for purposes other than the "use and benefit" of the beneficiary or for certain legal dependents of the beneficiary after the beneficiary's current and reasonably foreseeable needs are met as explained in 1617.2.

1617.7 Does a representative payee who misuses funds owe the beneficiary the money?

When SSA determines that a representative payee has misused a beneficiary's Social Security and/or SSI payments, the payee owes the beneficiary the full amount of funds misused. SSA will reissue the misused benefits to the beneficiary and recover the misused funds from the payee when the payee is:

A. An organization or an individual payee serving 15 or more beneficiaries; or
B. An individual representative payee serving 14 or fewer beneficiaries and SSA was negligent in following procedures to investigate or monitor the representative payee's actions.

SSA will seek restitution of the misused benefits from the representative payee by treating the misused amounts as an overpayment to the misuser payee.

1617.8 What are the penalties for misused Social Security or SSI funds?

When a representative payee misuses funds, we may refer the case for criminal prosecution. The penalty upon conviction for a payee's misuse of funds may be a fine of up to $250,000, imprisonment up to 10 years, or both.

When the case is not criminally prosecuted, SSA may impose a civil monetary penalty up to $5,000 for each payment or partial payment misused and an assessment of not more than twice the amount of the misused benefits.

1618. CURRENT NEEDS OF BENEFICIARY

1618.1 What are current needs?

"Current needs" are the immediate and reasonably foreseeable essentials for housing, food, clothing, utilities, medical care and insurance, dental care, personal hygiene, education, and the rehabilitation expenses of the disabled beneficiaries.

1618.2 How should the representative payee evaluate and respond to the beneficiary's needs?

The representative payee is responsible for knowing and providing for the needs of the beneficiary. Current needs should never be sacrificed to pay other expenses, to conserve or invest funds, or to accumulate funds for a future purpose.

1619. PAST DEBTS OF BENEFICIARIES

1619.1 Can creditors seize funds?

In order to assure an income for a beneficiary's current needs, Section 207 of the Social Security Act specifically exempts funds from seizure by creditors. However, some exceptions may apply.

1619.2 What are the exceptions?

Section 459 of the Social Security Act permits garnishment for the legal enforcement of providing child support and alimony, and the IRS may levy for taxes owed. In addition, SSA may seek refund of a Social Security or SSI overpayment.

1619.3 Should representative payees use funds to cover bills incurred before the payee began receiving the payments?

Provided the beneficiary's current and reasonably foreseeable needs are met, a representative payee may use funds to pay bills incurred by a beneficiary before the first month we began to pay benefits to the representative payee.

1619.4 What if the beneficiary owes a debt to the representative payee?

If a debt is owed to the representative payee, the payee must obtain approval from SSA prior to using funds for self-reimbursement.

1619.5 Where can a representative payee obtain further information on payment of past debts?

Refer questions concerning payment of past debts to the local Social Security office.

1620. A BENEFICIARY'S SAVINGS

1620.1 How should I handle funds not required for current needs?

You must conserve or invest any funds not required for the beneficiary's current or reasonably foreseeable needs, or for the support of legal dependents. You can set aside part of the funds for definite foreseeable needs such as the beneficiary's education or rehabilitation if disabled.

1620.2 How should I invest funds?

You should place accumulated funds of more than $500 in an interest-yielding account or investment on behalf of the beneficiary. Any interest and dividend payments that result from checking accounts, savings or an investment are the property of the beneficiary and not your property.

1620.3 What investments does SSA prefer?

Preferred investments include:

A. U.S. Savings Bonds; or
B. Deposits in an interest or dividend paying account in a bank, trust company, savings and loan association, or credit union that is insured under either Federal or State law.

Otherwise, you may invest funds according to State laws governing the investment of trust estates by trustees.

1620.4 Does the SSA have restrictions on investing funds?

Guidelines for managing the beneficiary's money are as follows:

A. You may not invest funds in any company, corporation, or association when such an investment will involve you in a conflict of interest;
B. You should not keep money at home or mingle it with your own money or with other funds; and
C. You must keep accurate records in order to account for the use of funds.

1620.5 How must I title an investment?

You must title conserved and invested funds in a form that shows you hold the property in trust for the beneficiary. The preferred forms of titling follow:

A. U.S. Savings Bonds bought for a beneficiary under age 18 - (*Name of Beneficiary*), (*Social Security Number*), a minor, for whom (*Name of Payee*) is representative payee for Social Security funds.
B. U.S. Savings Bonds bought for a beneficiary age 18 or older - (*Name of Beneficiary*), (*Social Security Number*), for whom (*Name of Payee*) is representative payee for Social Security funds.
C. Various forms of accounts recognized by banks, trust companies, savings and loan associations, or credit unions as establishing the trust relationship between the beneficiary and the representative payee are acceptable as long as they clearly establish that relationship under the applicable State law.
D. For a savings or checking account, an acceptable title is (*Name of Payee*), representative payee for (*Name of Beneficiary*). A statement such as (*Name of Payee*) in trust for (*Name of Beneficiary*) should not be used because some States treat the funds in this type of account as belonging to the representative payee.

Note: The examples listed above are not all-inclusive. You should always consult with the bank to verify that, under State law, the titling of an account:

A. Shows you only have a fiduciary interest;
B. Permits you ready access to the funds when needed for the beneficiary's current maintenance; and
C. Does not permit the beneficiary to have direct access to the funds.

1621. BLIND OR DISABLED CHILDREN RECEIVING SSI

1621.1 What funds must the SSA pay into a dedicated account?

The SSA must pay certain large, past-due SSI payments to blind or disabled children directly into a separate, "dedicated account" in a financial institution.

1621.2 Why does the SSA call it a dedicated account?

We call this separate account a "dedicated account" because you can use the funds in this account only for certain expenses, primarily those related to the child's disability.

1621.3 How should I maintain the dedicated account?

You should maintain the dedicated account as follows:

A. You must keep it separate from any other savings or checking account you set up for the beneficiary; and
B. Except for certain subsequent underpayments, you must not put other funds in the account.

1621.4 Does the SSA count money in the account as a resource?

No, the SSA does not count money in the dedicated account as a resource. Also, interest earned on the money in a dedicated account does not count as income or a resource.

1621.5 How can I use the money in a dedicated account?

You can use money in a dedicated account only for the following allowable expenses for the benefit of the child:

A. Medical treatment and education or job skills training;
B. If related to the child's disability, personal needs assistance, special equipment, housing modification, and therapy or rehabilitation; and
C. Any other item or service related to the child's disability that we determine to be appropriate.

If you have doubt whether an expense in this category is appropriate, you should first get our approval.

1621.6 What happens if I use the money incorrectly?

If you use money from the dedicated account for anything other than the expenses shown above, you must repay us from your own funds in an amount equal to what you spent.

1621.7 What records of the account must I keep?

You must keep a record of all money taken from this account and keep receipts for all items or services bought. You must maintain these records for a minimum of two years because periodically we may ask to review them.

1622. WHAT SHOULD I DO WITH A BENEFICIARY'S CONSERVED FUNDS WHEN I STOP SERVING AS A REPRESENTATIVE PAYEE?

When you stop serving as a payee, you must return savings or other investments and any interest earned on the funds to us. We will reissue the returned funds to either a new representative payee or to the beneficiary currently receiving direct payment.

In the event of the beneficiary's death, conserved funds become the property of the beneficiary's estate. Rather than returning them to us, you must give them to the legal representative of the deceased beneficiary's estate for disposition under State law. If no legal representative exists, you must contact the State probate court (or the State agency handling estate matters) for instructions on what to do with the remaining conserved funds.

1623. ACCOUNTING FOR USE OF FUNDS

1623.1 How do I account for the use of the beneficiary's funds?

We send you an annual report (Representative Payee Report) to explain how you used the funds for the prior 12-month report period. You should keep records throughout the year so that you can provide an accurate accounting. In addition to the annual report, you may have to submit a report at other times as well.

1623.2 Do State mental institutions receive this report form?

Some State mental institutions receive this report form for each beneficiary. However, most State mental institutions are subject to a different monitoring process (see §1624).

1623.3 How does SSA evaluate my performance?

We assess your performance by asking the following information on the report:

A. Did you determine how to spend or save the funds;
B. How did you use the funds;
C. How much of the funds did you save and how did you invest the savings;
D. Did you have a felony conviction during the report period; and
E. Did the beneficiary live alone, or with the same person, or in the same institution during the report period.

1623.4 Does SSA request additional information?

Based on your responses, we may interview you, the beneficiary, and the custodian. In addition, we may require a more detailed report (*Representative Payee Evaluation Report*) in order to determine if you continue to be the most suitable payee.

1623.5 Does SSA conduct any additional monitoring of payees?

We visit some organizational and individual payees and examine their beneficiary accounting records. In addition, we interview some of the beneficiaries' concerning their payee's performance. This site visit program gives us the opportunity to provide ongoing education to payees about their responsibilities. Furthermore, it helps to improve the lines of communication between the payees and us.

1624. STATE MENTAL INSTITUTIONS THAT SERVE AS REPRESENTATIVE PAYEES

1624.1 Must State mental institutions complete annual report forms?

We do not require State mental institutions that participate in our onsite review program to complete the annual report form.

1624.2 How does SSA monitor participating State mental institutions?

We monitor participating State mental institutions through a process we call onsite review.

1624.3 How often does SSA monitor State mental institutions?

We review each participating institution at least once every three years. However, if we find an institution is not performing its representative payee duties satisfactorily, we may review it more often.

Chapter 17
Evidence Required to Establish Right to Benefits

TABLE OF CONTENTS

1700. Evidence Requirements
1701. Can information submitted to SSA be disclosed anywhere else?
1702. Type of Evidence to be Submitted - General
1703. What factors do we consider when we evaluate evidence you submit?
1704. When do you need to provide proof of age?
1705. How do you prove your age?
1706. Other Evidence of Date of Birth
1707. How Natural Parent-Child Relationship is Proved
1708. What evidence is required for a child born out of wedlock to be considered yours?
1709. What constitutes as a written acknowledgment of a child?
1710. Does a court decree of paternity prove a child is yours?
1711. Does a court order for support prove a child is yours?
1712. What other evidence proves paternity?
1713. How do you prove a legal adoption?
1714. How Do You Prove a Step-Relationship
1715. School Attendance
1716. Evidence of Ceremonial Marriage
1717. Evidence of Common-Law Marriage
1718. When Evidence of Termination of Prior Marriage is Required

1719. Establishing Termination of Marriage
1720. Evidence of Death
1721. When is a missing person presumed dead?
1722. Felonious and Intentional Homicide
1723. How do you prove that a child is in your care?
1724. What constitutes evidence of support?
1725. Evidence of U.S. Citizenship
1726. Evidence of Wages
1727. What evidence can you submit if your employer's records are not available?
1728. How do we verify your unsigned employer's wage statements?
1729. Union Records
1730. Do certified copies of your State or Federal tax returns constitute evidence of wages?
1731. Do findings by State unemployment compensation agencies constitute evidence of wages?
1732. Statement by Person Knowing About Employment
1733. Personal Records of Worker
1734. Can wages be credited to your record even if you cannot obtain any evidence of wages?
1735. How does IRS help gather evidence?
1736. Are you a self-employed partner?

1700. EVIDENCE REQUIREMENTS

1700.1 Do you need to provide evidence to support your claim for benefits?

You must prove your identity and that you have met all the requirements necessary to be entitled to the benefit you are claiming. The Social Security office handling the claim will advise you as to what you must prove and what evidence you need to submit.

(This Chapter does not discuss evidence of disability; it is discussed in Chapter 5. Nor does it discuss entitlement to hospital insurance protection or medical insurance coverage. See Chapter 24 for a discussion of these programs.)

1700.2 What evidence do you need to submit for a claim for monthly benefits?

The following chart summarizes the evidence you usually need to submit to us to get monthly benefits. However, in some cases, additional evidence may be required.

Then the evidence the claimant needs to submit is....[1]

If the beneficiary is....	Age	Relationships: Marriage	Relationships: Divorced	Parent-Child	Dependency or Support	School Attendance	Child-in-Care	Death of Worker
Insured person[2]	X	–	–	–	–	–	–	–
Spouse (62 or over)	X	X	–	–	–	–	–	–
Spouse under 62 (child in care)	–	X	–	–	–	–	X	–
Divorced spouse (62 or over)	X	X	X	–	–	–	–	–
Child[2]	X	–	–	X	X[3]	X[4]	–	X[6]
Widow(er) (60 or over, 50 or over if disabled)[2]	X	X	–	–	–	–	–	X
Surviving divorced spouse[2]	X	X	X	–	–	–	–	X
Mother/Father or surviving divorced mother or father (child in care)	–	X	X[5]	X	–	–	X	X
Parent	X	–	–	X	X	–	–	X

[1] See Chapter 3, Chapter 4, or Chapter 5 for all the requirements for specific types of benefits.
[2] If disability is involved, see Chapter 5 for evidence required to establish disability.
[3] A legitimate or adopted child is ordinarily considered dependent on his or her parent; however, certain evidence may be needed in the case of other types of children.
[4] Proof of full-time school attendance required if child is 18-19 and is not disabled.
[5] Surviving divorced mother or father only.
[6] For survivor claims.

1700.3 What evidence do you need to submit for a claim for the lump-sum death payment?

The following chart summarizes the evidence you usually need to submit to us to get the lump-sum death payment. However, in some cases, additional evidence may be required.

Then the evidence the claimant needs to submit is...

If the beneficiary is....	Age	Relationships — Marriage	Relationships — Divorced	Relationships — Parent-Child	Dependency or Support	School Attendance	Child-in-Care	Death of Worker
Surviving spouse living in same household	–	X	–	–	–	–	–	X
Eligible surviving spouse, excluding divorced spouse	$X^{(3)}$	$X^{(3)}$	–	–	–	–	–	X
Eligible children	$X^{(3)}$	–	–	$X^{(3)}$	$X^{(1,3)}$	$X^{(2,3)}$	–	X

[1] A legitimate or adopted child is ordinarily considered dependent on his or her parent; however, certain evidence may be needed in the case of other types of children.

[2] Proof of full-time school attendance required if child is 18–19 and is not disabled.

[3] To qualify for the lump-sum, the claimant must present evidence that proves he or she does (or could) qualify for monthly benefits in the month the worker died.

1701. CAN INFORMATION SUBMITTED TO SSA BE DISCLOSED ANYWHERE ELSE?

Information you submit to us in connection with your claim cannot be disclosed to any other person, except for very limited purposes. (See §118.)

1702. TYPE OF EVIDENCE TO BE SUBMITTED - GENERAL

1702.1 What types of evidence can you submit to support your claim?

Descriptions of the various types of evidence you should submit with your claim are below:

A. *An original document or a certified copy of the original record.* If the document is not original, it should be certified by the custodian of the record. Documents in foreign languages are acceptable and can be translated by Government translators. If you submit a photocopy of a document as evidence, you must also submit the original document for comparison. Otherwise, we will return the photocopy, unless it is certified by the official custodian of the original document to be an exact copy of the original.

B. *A statement of the individual.* Where an individual's statement is submitted as evidence, it should be complete and detailed. Submit any supporting evidence if it is available. Statements must be signed but do not need to be notarized. If you sign your statement by mark, two persons who know you need to sign as witnesses.

1702.2 What happens if you give false information?

Make sure you have full knowledge of any statement you sign. Be aware that your statement is used for Social Security purposes. *Any false statement you make in an attempt to obtain benefits not due you or another person is punishable under the Social Security Act by fine, imprisonment, or both.* Other penalties may also apply under another part of the United States Code. (See §142.)

1703. WHAT FACTORS DO WE CONSIDER WHEN WE EVALUATE EVIDENCE YOU SUBMIT?

When we evaluate a particular document you submit as evidence, we consider factors such as:

A. The source of information from which the record was made. Was the person originally furnishing the information in a position to know the facts?
B. The purpose for which the record was made. Was there any reason to falsify or distort the facts?
C. The formality of the document. Was it made under oath? Is it a public record? Were there witnesses to its execution? Was a penalty provided for a false statement?
D. The age of the document. Was the record made at, or shortly after, the time the event occurred?
E. The custody of the document. Has it been in possession of someone who might have reason to change it?
F. Its appearance. Lack of erasures, etc. Does it appear altered from its original form?
G. The consistency of all the evidence relating to a particular matter; and
H. Whether the person furnishing the information has an interest in the claim for which the proof is needed.

1704. WHEN DO YOU NEED TO PROVIDE PROOF OF AGE?

You must submit proof of age when age is a factor in determining benefit rights. For example:

A. Age of child for child's insurance benefits (see Chapter 3 for age requirement);
B. Age 62 and over for retirement or dependent's insurance benefits;
C. Age of deceased worker when it affects the benefit computation or insured status; or
D. Age of disabled worker for disability insurance benefits.

1705. HOW DO YOU PROVE YOUR AGE?

The following types of evidence, established or recorded before your fifth birthday, are acceptable in proving your age:

A. A public record of your birth; or
B. A religious record of your age that shows your date of birth.

If such a document is unavailable, you must submit another document or documents that may serve as the basis for a determination of your date of birth. The evidence must be confirmed by other evidence or by information contained in our records.

1706. OTHER EVIDENCE OF DATE OF BIRTH

1706.1 Can you submit other evidence to prove your date of birth?

If a public or religious record of your birth established before your fifth birthday is not available, we accept other documentation.

1706.2 What other evidence can you submit to prove your of date of birth?

Some records you may submit are listed below. These records must show your date of birth or age. This list is not complete or listed in order of importance:

A. School record;
B. Census record;
C. Bible or other family record;
D. Religious record of confirmation or baptism in youth or early adult life;
E. Insurance policy;
F. Marriage record;
G. Employment record;
H. Labor union record;
I. Fraternal organization record;
J. Military record;
K. Voting record;
L. Vaccination record;
M. Delayed birth certificate;
N. Birth certificate of child showing age of parent;
O. Physician's or midwife's record of birth;
P. Passport;
Q. Immigration record; and
R. Naturalization record.

1706.3 What evidence do you need to submit if you are foreign-born?

If you were born in a foreign country, submit a record of your entry into the U.S. Also, submit your naturalization record, if applicable.

1707. HOW NATURAL PARENT-CHILD RELATIONSHIP IS PROVED

1707.1 How do you prove a natural parent-child relationship?

You can prove a natural legitimate parent-child relationship by the child's birth or religious certificate or hospital record, if it shows you as the child's parent. If evidence raises doubt about the record or if the record cannot be obtained, we will ask for other evidence of the relationship.

1707.2 Can a child born out of wedlock be considered your child for Social Security purposes?

If the child was born out of wedlock, he or she may be considered your child for Social Security purposes if he or she:

A. Is legitimated; or

B. Can inherit your intestate personal property under applicable State law.

The evidence required depends on the State law requirements for legitimization or inheritance rights.

1708. WHAT EVIDENCE IS REQUIRED FOR A CHILD BORN OUT OF WEDLOCK TO BE CONSIDERED YOURS?

If your child was born out of wedlock, he or she may be considered your child if he or she is the child of an invalid ceremonial marriage, or if the special test described in §324(E) is met. The evidence required to meet this special test may be:

A. A written acknowledgment by you stating the child is your son or daughter;

B. A court decree finding that you are the father or mother;

C. A court order directing you to support the child because the child is your son or daughter; or

D. Other satisfactory evidence that you were the father or mother of the child and were living with, or contributing to, the child's support.

1709. WHAT CONSTITUTES AS A WRITTEN ACKNOWLEDGMENT OF A CHILD?

A written acknowledgment can be any writing from you confirming that the child is your son or daughter. A variety of written statements are acceptable, for example:

A. An income tax return listing the child as yours;
B. A soldier's application for an allotment listing the child as yours;
C. A will referring to the child as yours;
D. An application for insurance naming the child as yours (e.g., as beneficiary); or
E. A letter indicating the child is yours.

1710. DOES A COURT DECREE OF PATERNITY PROVE A CHILD IS YOURS?

A court decree finding that you are the child's mother or father must:
A. Identify you and the child;
B. Include a specific finding that you are the child's biological parent; and
C. Must have been issued before your death and be certified by the proper official.

1711. DOES A COURT ORDER FOR SUPPORT PROVE A CHILD IS YOURS?

A court order for support must:
A. Identify the child;
B. Direct you to contribute to the child's support;
C. Either name you as the child's parent or have been issued under a child support statute; and
D. Have been issued before your death.

1712. WHAT OTHER EVIDENCE PROVES PATERNITY?

Several types of evidence may prove that you are a child's father, including:
A. Hospital, religious, or school records;
B. A court order or decree that does not meet the requirements for court orders set out above;
C. A statement from the attending physician, relative, or other person who knows the child's relationship to you, including the basis for that knowledge; and
D. Evidence that you and the child's mother were living together at the time of the child's conception.

1713. HOW DO YOU PROVE A LEGAL ADOPTION?

You can prove the legal adoption of a child by an amended birth certificate issued as the result of an adoption. If the date of a U.S. adoption is material, it may be proved by:

A. Records of the court that granted the adoption;
B. Official notice you received as the adopting parent(s);
C. Records of the State's Attorney or child welfare division; or
D. The adoption decree (if you have it and voluntarily submit it).

1714. HOW DO YOU PROVE A STEP-RELATIONSHIP

You can prove a step-relationship by:

A. Proving the relationship between the child and the natural (or adopting) parent (see §§1707-1713); and
B. Proving the marriage between the natural (or adopting) parent and the stepparent (see §1716 and §1717).

1715. SCHOOL ATTENDANCE

1715.1 When is evidence of school attendance needed?

We require evidence of full-time school attendance (see §344) if a child age 18-19 is not under a disability.

1715.2 How is evidence of school attendance obtained?

We obtain the necessary information from the child. This information is verified by the school or schools involved.

1716. EVIDENCE OF CEREMONIAL MARRIAGE

1716.1 How do you prove a ceremonial marriage?

You prove a ceremonial marriage by providing:

A. A certified copy of the public record of the marriage;
B. A certified copy of the religious record of the marriage; or
C. The original marriage certificate.

1716.2 Is any other evidence acceptable?

We prefer the types of evidence listed above. If none of this evidence is available, you may submit the following types of evidence:

A. A signed statement from a member of the clergy or public official who performed the marriage; or
B. Other evidence of investigative value, e.g., statements of witnesses, newspaper accounts, photos taken of the ceremony.

In some cases, evidence obtained for other purposes may also serve as evidence of marriage. You must provide statements concerning certain details of your marriage and document the fact that the preferred proofs are not available.

1717. EVIDENCE OF COMMON-LAW MARRIAGE

1717.1 How do you prove a common-law marriage?

Evidence to prove a common-law marriage in the States that recognize such marriages must include:

A. *If the husband and wife are living,* a statement from each and a statement from a blood relative of each;

B. *If either the husband or wife is dead,* a statement from the surviving widow or widower and statements from two blood relatives of the decedent; or

C. *If both a husband and wife are dead,* a statement from a blood relative of the husband and from a blood relative of the wife.

1717.2 How should the statements be made?

The statements of the husband, wife, and relatives must be made on special forms, Statement Regarding Marriage or Statement of Marital Relationship, available at any Social Security office or on the Social Security Administration's website. You must fully answer all items on the forms and in your own words. Also, submit evidence that confirms that you had a common-law marriage, such as mortgage/rent receipts, bank records, insurance policies, etc.

1717.3 What if you cannot get statements from your relatives?

If you adequately explain why you cannot obtain the required statements from relatives, you may submit statements from other persons who know the facts. Provide any other investigative evidence relating to your case.

1718. WHEN EVIDENCE OF TERMINATION OF PRIOR MARRIAGE IS REQUIRED

1718.1 When do you need to provide evidence that your prior marriage ended?

You may be required to provide evidence that your marriage ended if your right to benefits depends on:

A. The validity of a later marriage; or
B. The termination of a prior marriage.

If you are claiming benefits as a divorced spouse (see §311), you must establish that the marriage lasted for at least 10 years before the divorce became effective.

1718.2 How does a marriage end?

A valid ceremonial or common-law marriage ends only by death, divorce, or annulment.

1719. ESTABLISHING TERMINATION OF MARRIAGE

1719.1 How do you prove your marriage ended?

You prove that your marriage ended by providing:

A. A certified copy of the divorce decree;
B. A certified copy of the annulment decree; or
C. A certified copy of the death certificate (or other proof of death, see §1720).

1719.2 What other evidence is acceptable?

If none of the above is available, you can submit any other evidence of investigative value. You must explain why none of the items above is available.

1719.3 Do you live in a state that restricts remarriage?

If your prior marriage ended by a divorce in a State that imposes a restriction on remarriage, you must show that your remarriage does not violate the restriction.

1720. EVIDENCE OF DEATH

1720.1 How do you prove someone's death?

You can prove death by providing any of the following evidence:

A. A certified copy of a public record of death;
B. A statement of death by the funeral director;
C. A statement of death by the attending physician or the superintendent, physician, or intern of the institution where the person died;
D. A certified copy of the coroner's report of death or the verdict of the coroner's jury;

E. A certified copy of an official report of death or finding of death made by an agency or department of the United States (U.S.) that is authorized or required to make such a report; or
F. If death occurred outside the United States (U.S.), an official report of death by a U.S. Consul or other employee of the State Department; or a copy of the public record of death in the foreign country.

1720.2 What other evidence is acceptable?

If you cannot obtain any of the evidence above, you can submit statements from two or more persons (preferably not related to you) who saw the body. These statements must be complete and indicate the following:
A. Why none of the types of evidence in (A) through (F) above can be obtained;
B. The date and place of death;
C. The date and place of viewing the body;
D. The cause of death, if known;
E. The occupation, age, sex, and race of the deceased;
F. The relationship of the deceased, if any, to the person making the statements; and
G. The basis for identification of the body.

1720.3 Does a presumptive finding of death by an armed service department prove death?

A presumptive finding of death by an armed service department establishes the fact of death, but not the date of death. The date of death shown by the armed service department in these cases is a statutory date. It is usually a year and a day from the "missing" date, but may be later or earlier. If there is no evidence to establish a later date, the date the individual was "missing" is used as the date of death.

1720.4 How do you prove death in a disappearance case?

In a disappearance case where the body is not recovered, you must clearly prove the death of the missing person. Submit all available evidence, including:
A. Statements of persons having knowledge of the situation;
B. Letters or notes left by the missing person that have a bearing on the case;
C. The results of insurance or police investigations; and
D. The complete facts surrounding the person's disappearance.

1721. WHEN IS A MISSING PERSON PRESUMED DEAD?

We presume a person is dead if he or she has been missing from home and has not been heard from for seven years or more. This presumption applies regardless of the reason for the absence.

Once the presumption applies, it can only be disputed if we:

A. Prove the person is alive; or
B. Provide an explanation that explains the individual's absence and continued life.

1722. FELONIOUS AND INTENTIONAL HOMICIDE

1722.1 How does the felonious and intentional homicide of the worker affect benefits?

You cannot be entitled to benefits on the worker's earnings record if you were convicted of the felonious and intentional homicide of the worker. Further, you are considered as non-existent when we decide the rights of other persons entitled to benefits on the worker's record.

1722.2 What evidence do you submit if you were convicted or acquitted of the felonious homicide of the worker?

If you were either acquitted or convicted of the felonious homicide of the worker, submit either:

A. A certification of the final verdict or court record; or
B. A statement from the proper official advising of the nature of the case.

1723. HOW DO YOU PROVE THAT A CHILD IS IN YOUR CARE?

You can prove you have a child in your care by providing:

A. Statements from you;
B. If you and the child are living apart, a statement from one or both of the following:
   1. The person with whom the child is living; or
   2. An official of the school the child is attending; and
C. Statements from other people who know the facts. We furnish you with the forms you need.

1724. WHAT CONSTITUTES EVIDENCE OF SUPPORT?

Evidence of support includes your statement and whatever other evidence may be necessary to prove your statement concerning your support. Make sure your statement:

A. Is on the form we give you. The form is designed to bring out all the information about your total income from all sources during the appropriate period;
B. Includes the cost of your support during the same period; and
C. Shows the amount and frequency of your support payments.

1725. EVIDENCE OF U.S. CITIZENSHIP

1725.1 Why is evidence of U.S. citizenship or lawful alien status necessary?

Evidence of U.S. citizenship or lawful alien status is necessary because:
A. It is required to pay monthly benefits to an individual who is lawfully present and meets the residency requirements in the U.S;
B. It applies for Title II benefits on December 1, 1996, or later; and
C. It *may* be required in certain cases, for instance, to determine:
  1. The payment of monthly benefits in the U.S. under the lawful presence payment provision;
  2. The applicability of the alien nonpayment provision (see §1843);
  3. Eligibility to hospital or medical insurance protection of a person who is not entitled to cash benefits or
  4. Eligibility for special age 72 payments (see §§346-348).

1725.2 How do you prove that you are a U.S. citizen?

You may be a citizen of the U.S. by birth or by naturalization. Acceptable evidence is a birth certificate showing birth within the U.S. Other acceptable evidence of U.S. citizenship includes:
A. Form N-550 and N-570 (Certificate of Naturalization issued currently by U.S. Citizenship and Immigration Services (USCIS), part of the Department of Homeland Security (DHS) - formerly issued by the Immigration and Naturalization Service (INS));
B. A U.S. passport issued by the U.S. Department of State (DOS);
C. Form I-197 (*U.S. Citizen Identification Card* issued by the former INS); (*Note:* This card was issued only to naturalized citizens who lived along the U.S. - Mexican border. INS discontinued issuance of this card in 1983; however these cards are still valid as proof of U.S. citizenship.)
D. Form FS-240 (*Consular Report of Birth Abroad of a Citizen of the U.S.* issued by DOS);

E. Form FS-545 (*Certification of Birth Abroad of a Citizen of the U.S.* issued by a foreign service post);
F. Form N-560 and N-561 (*Certificate of Citizenship* issued by DHS); or
G. Form DS-1350 (*Certification of Report of Birth* issued by DOS).
H. U.S. Passport Card, issued after July 13, 2008.

1725.3 How do you prove that you are a lawful alien?
You may be determined to be lawfully present in the U.S. as defined by the Attorney General if you are an alien who is in possession of a valid immigration documents that shows status or admission as:
A. Lawfully admitted for permanent residence;
B. Admitted as a refugee under section 207 of the Immigration and Nationality Act (INA);
C. Granted asylum under section 208 of the INA;
D. Paroled under section 212(d)(5) of the INA for at least one year (except for aliens paroled for an exclusion hearing or prosecution in the U.S.);
E. Whose deportation has been withheld under section 243(h) of the INA as in effect prior to April 1, 1997, or whose removal has been withheld under section 241(b)(3) of the INA;
F. Granted conditional entry as a refugee under section 203(a)(7) of the INA as in effect prior to April 1, 1980;
G. Inspected and admitted as a non-immigrant to the U.S. and who has not violated the applicable terms of your status (*Note:* Generally non-immigrants, with a few exceptions, are not eligible for SSI benefits; this applies to all non- immigrant classes of admissions with the exception of "T" or "U" non-immigrant visas.);
H. With a pending application for political asylum under section 208(a) of the INA or a pending application for withholding of deportation under section 243(h) of the INA, and employment authorization; or
I. Belonging to any specific class of aliens permitted to remain in the U.S. under U.S. law or policy, for humanitarian, medical or other public interest policy reasons.

1726. EVIDENCE OF WAGES

1726.1 When is evidence of wages needed?

You need to provide evidence of the amount of wages paid to you and the period they were paid if:

A. The wages are not recorded in the earnings record maintained by us or the Railroad Retirement Board; or

B. There is reason to believe that the amounts recorded are not correct.

1726.2 What constitutes evidence of your wages?

Evidence must be based directly on your employer's records, if available, and may consist of:

A. Form W-2 (*Wage and Tax Statement*);

B. Notice from us to you showing wages credited to your earnings record, e.g., Form SSA-L987 (*Social Security Earnings Information*);

C. SSA-7011 (*Statement of Employer*) used in claims and earnings discrepancy cases as evidence of non-agricultural wages, if signed by employer or custodian of employer's records;

D. SSA-1002 (*Statement of Agricultural Employer*) used in claims and earnings discrepancy cases as evidence of agricultural wages, if signed by employer or custodian of employer's records;

E. Any other statement signed by an employer;

F. Statement signed by custodian of employer's records;

G. Certification by SSA of contents of employer's records;

H. Certification by SSA of contents of employer tax returns in possession of IRS;

I. Certification by SSA of report of IRS audit of employer's records; or

J. SSA-4500-U6 (*Federal Determination of Error in State's Wage Reports*) when signed by an authorized State or local official.

1727. WHAT EVIDENCE CAN YOU SUBMIT IF YOUR EMPLOYER'S RECORDS ARE NOT AVAILABLE?

When evidence based directly on employer records is not available, you can submit *two or more* of the following:

A. Pay envelopes, vouchers, and similar unsigned employer wage statements given to you, a State agency, or another Federal agency (see §1728);

B. Union records (see §1729);

C. Your income tax returns (see §1730);
D. Records of State unemployment compensation agencies based on evidence other than the employer's records (see §1731);
E. Statements of persons having knowledge of the facts (see §1732);
F. Your personal records (see §1733); or
G. Other acceptable evidence.

The types of evidence listed in this section must show clearly the amount of wages paid and when they were paid.

1728. HOW DO WE VERIFY YOUR UNSIGNED EMPLOYER'S WAGE STATEMENTS?

When you submit pay envelopes, vouchers, and similar unsigned employer wage statements, make sure they:

A. Show your name and your employer's name;
B. Show the amount of wages paid and dates of payment or employment;
C. Are accompanied by your signed statement showing:
   1. When your employer furnished the voucher or wage statements;
   2. Whether your employer made all the entries; and
   3. Whether this information correctly shows the wages paid and dates of employment.

1729. UNION RECORDS

1729.1 What information is needed on your union records?

When you submit union records as evidence of your wages, the information you submit must include:

A. Your name and your employer's name;
B. The beginning and ending dates of employment;
C. The amount of wages paid;
D. Breakdown by calendar quarters of amounts shown on union records;
E. The name and title of the union official giving the information and the name and local number of the union;
F. Whether the amounts shown in the records were reported by the employer, shop steward, or you, etc.; and
G. Intervals at which the reports are made.

1729.2 Are the amounts on your union records dues rather than wages paid?

If the amounts shown on your union records are dues rather than wages paid, the information should show whether:

A. The dues are fixed or based on wages actually paid to you; and
B. Any charges not related to wages are also included in the dues figure.

1729.3 Are the amounts on your union records total wages?

If the amounts shown on your union records are total wages, the evidence should show whether:

A. They are the actual wages paid; or
B. They were figured by using the prevailing union rate of pay.

1730. DO CERTIFIED COPIES OF YOUR STATE OR FEDERAL TAX RETURNS CONSTITUTE EVIDENCE OF WAGES?

You may use certified copies of your State or Federal Income Tax Returns as evidence of wages if they show the actual wages paid to you. You can obtain certified copies of your Federal income tax returns from IRS for a small fee. You may use *uncertified copies* of State or Federal income tax returns only if you cannot obtain a certified copy.

1731. DO FINDINGS BY STATE UNEMPLOYMENT COMPENSATION AGENCIES CONSTITUTE EVIDENCE OF WAGES?

Findings by State Unemployment Compensation Agencies based on evidence other than your employer's records may be used as evidence if they are based on evidence that is acceptable to us. You must submit a copy or certification of the State agency's findings showing:

A. Your employer's name;
B. Wages paid to you; and
C. A description of the evidence on which the finding was based.

1732. STATEMENT BY PERSON KNOWING ABOUT EMPLOYMENT

1732.1 How do you submit statements of persons who know about your employment and wages?

Persons who know about your employment and wages should make their statements on a Form SSA-795 (*Statement of Claimant or Other Person*), available at all Social Security offices. The statements must:

A. Set out the facts on which the person bases his or her conclusions about the wages paid to you; and
B. Show the periods for which the wages were paid.

1732.2 Who qualifies as a person who knows about your employment and wage?

Sources for statements include your:

A. Supervisors;
B. Fellow employees;
C. Banks, or others who regularly cashed your pay checks;
D. Employment agencies; and
E. Union officials.

1733. PERSONAL RECORDS OF WORKER

1733.1 Do your personal records constitute evidence of wages?

Your personal records showing wages paid to you are not of high investigative probative value. However, regular, complete, and genuine records may be used to support other types of evidence.

1733.2 What information do you submit with your personal records?

You must provide a statement along with your personal records showing:

A. Who made the entries;
B. When the entries were made;
C. The basis for the entries;
D. What happened to any wage statements that were given to you by your employer; and
E. An explanation of all discrepancies and inaccuracies in the records.

1734. CAN WAGES BE CREDITED TO YOUR RECORD EVEN IF YOU CANNOT OBTAIN ANY EVIDENCE OF WAGES?

If you cannot obtain evidence of wages, we may accept your statement as to the amount of wages and credit your earnings record if all of the following conditions are met:

A. The year in question is 1978 or later;
B. Only one year is involved in the allegation;
C. The year in question is not the current year or the year immediately preceding the current year, i.e., the "lag" year;
D. There are postings from the same employer in the year immediately before and/or after the year in question;
E. The amount of earnings alleged is consistent with the earnings posted both prior to and after the year in question;

F. All attempts to obtain any other evidence have been exhausted;
G. No contradictory evidence exists; and
H. In claims cases, the missing wage amount affects insured status or the benefit amount.

1735. HOW DOES IRS HELP GATHER EVIDENCE?

If you do not have a copy of the Form 1040, Schedule SE, Schedule C, or Schedule F and we need the form(s) to establish the amount of self-employment income, we may ask IRS to furnish the information in its files. Normally, we request the information from IRS. If IRS cannot find the return but you know one was filed, you may complete and sign a written request asking IRS to furnish a statement of the amount of self-employment income for the year in question. You must give IRS complete identifying information, place of filing, etc. so that they can find your tax return.

1736. ARE YOU A SELF-EMPLOYED PARTNER?

If you are self-employed and a partner in a business, you may need to submit Form 1065 *(Partnership Return)*. We may need to know whether your share of the partnership income contains any income that is not included in earnings from self-employment (such as capital gains, rent, etc.).

Chapter 18
Reduction or Nonpayment of Social Security Benefits

TABLE OF CONTENTS

1800. Are there conditions where your benefits are not payable?
1801. The Earnings Test
1802. Excess Earnings - Defined
1803. Annual Exempt Amounts
1804. How Excess Earnings are Charged Against Benefits
1805. When are you NOT charged for excess earnings?
1806. Payment of Partial Benefit
1807. Grace Year and Non-Service Month Defined
1808. Exempt Amounts for Short Taxable Years
1809. Total Earnings for Earnings Test Purposes
1810. When are wages and net earnings from self-employment counted?
1811. What types of income count under the earnings test?
1812. What types of income do NOT count under the earnings test?
1813. Does the recipient of income determine whether the earnings count under the earnings test?
1814. Annual Report of Earnings
1815. When is the annual report of earnings due?
1816. Extension of Time for Filing Annual Report of Earnings
1817. How do you request an extension of time for filing your annual report?
1818. The Annual Report Form

1819. Delay in Filing Annual Report
1820. Number of Additional Benefits Lost for Failure to Report on Time
1821. Are benefits of those entitled to benefits on your earnings record affected when you do not file your annual report on time?
1822. Report of Expected Earnings Also Required
1823. The Foreign Work Test
1824. What is considered work "outside of the U.S."?
1825. Non-Covered Work for Pay Defined
1826. Determining Number of Hours a Retirement Beneficiary Works Per Month
1827. Do you need to report your work activity performed outside the U.S.?
1828. What is the penalty for your failure to report foreign work?
1829. Child in Care Requirement
1831. Reporting Failure to Have a Child in Care
1832. Do we still impose a penalty if you have good cause for your failure to report to us?
1833. Good Cause Defined
1835. Does the receipt of periodic workers' compensation payments or public disability benefits affect your benefits?
1836. Receipt of a Governmental Pension
1837. Conviction for Subversive Activities
1838. What earnings are disregarded when a convicted person makes a claim for benefits?
1839. Penalty Applies to Convicted Person Only
1840. How does a pardon for a previous conviction affect your benefits?
1841. Deportation or Removal of Retirement or Disability Insurance Beneficiary
1842. Effect of Deportation or Removal on Auxiliary or Survivor Benefits
1843. Aliens Outside the U.S. for Six Months or More
1844. Absence from the U.S.
1845. Exceptions to Alien Nonpayment Provision

1846. Limitations on Use of Certain Exceptions
1847. Residence in a Restricted Country
1848. What are the restricted countries?
1849. When can you receive benefits you earned while you lived in a restricted country?
1850. Confinement in a Correctional Institution
1851. What events end benefits?
1852. How does the marriage of one beneficiary to another affect benefits?
1853. Reinstatement of Benefits When Marriage Terminates
1854. Certain Outstanding Warrants

1800. ARE THERE CONDITIONS WHERE YOUR BENEFITS ARE NOT PAYABLE?

There are certain conditions under which your retirement, auxiliary, survivors, and disability benefits are not payable or are payable only in part. This is true even if you meet all of the "entitlement" requirements. You may do things (or fail to do things) that require us to withhold all or some part of your benefits. For example, if you are entitled to retirement insurance benefits and you work, we may make deductions from your benefits and from others entitled to benefits on your record.

The chart in §1851 summarizes the events that may require withholding of part or all of the various types of benefits.

1801. THE EARNINGS TEST

1801.1 How is your amount of benefits generally determined?

Social Security benefits are meant to partly replace earnings you (or your family) lose because of retirement, disability, or death. Therefore, the amount of Social Security benefits you receive each year depends on whether you are fully or partially retired.

1801.2 What is the earnings test?

We use the "earnings test," also referred to as the retirement test, to:

A. Measure the extent of your retirement;
B. Determine the amount, if any, to be deducted from monthly benefits; and
C. Measure the work activity of other individuals entitled to benefits on your record and the amount of benefits payable to them.

1801.3 What beneficiaries are not subject to the earnings test?

The earnings test does not apply to you if you are:

A. Full retirement age (FRA) (see §723.5 for definition of Full Retirement Age);
B. Entitled to benefits because of a disability;
C. Living outside the U.S. and your work is not covered by Social Security. In this case, the "foreign work test" applies as described in §1823; or
D. A divorced spouse of NH whose MOET is prior to the month of divorce.

1802. EXCESS EARNINGS - DEFINED

1802.1 What are excess earnings?

"Excess earnings" are your earnings that exceed the annual exempt amount. (See §1803).

1802.2 How do excess earnings affect your benefit amount?

If you are younger than full retirement age (FRA) (see §723.5), your excess earnings are subject to a $1 deduction from benefits for each $2 you earn. In the year you reach FRA, you are subject to a different annual exempt amount, and your excess earnings are subject to a $1 deduction from benefits for each $3 you earn.

1803. ANNUAL EXEMPT AMOUNTS

1803.1 How is the annual exempt amount determined?

There is an annual exempt amount prior to year of FRA (see §723.5) attainment. In the year you reach FRA, you are subject to a different annual exempt amount. The exempt amounts may change from year to year to take into account the change in the national average wage index. The exempt amounts are computed each year according to the formula provided in the Social Security Act. This formula takes into account increases in national earnings levels.

1803.2 What are the annual exempt amounts?

The chart below shows the annual exempt amounts for the years 1985 through 2024:

Year	Age 65-69	Under Age 65
1987	$8,160	$6,000
1988	$8,400	$6,120
1989	$8,880	$6,480
1990	$9,360	$6,840
1991	$9,720	$7,080
1992	$10,200	$7,440
1993	$10,560	$7,680
1994	$11,160	$8,040
1995	$11,280	$8,160
1996	$12,500	$8,280
1997	$13,500	$8,640
1998	$14,500	$9,120

(Continued)

Year	Age 65-69	Under Age 65
1999	$15,500	$9,600
	Year of Full Retirement Age	Prior to Year of Full Retirement Age
2000	$17,000	$10,080
2001	$25,000	$10,680
2002	$30,000	$11,280
2003	$30,720	$11,520
2004	$31,080	$11,640
2005	$31,800	$12,000
2006	$33,240	$12,480
2007	$34,440	$12,960
2008	$36,120	$13,560
2009	$37,680	$14,160
2010	$37,680	$14,160
2011	$37,680	$14,160
2012	$38,880	$14,640
2013	$40,080	$15,120
2014	$41,400	$15,480
2015-2016	$41,880	$15,720
2017	$44,880	$16,920
2018	$45,360	$17,040
2019	$46,920	$17,640
2020	$48,600	$18,240
2021	$50,520	$18,960
2022	$51,960	$19,560
2023	$56,520	$21,240
2024	$59,520	$22,320

1803.3 How do you know which exempt amount applies?

The higher exempt amount applies if you reach full retirement age (65 and 2 months in 2003) (see §723.5) on or before the last day of the taxable year involved. The lower exempt amount applies if you do not turn full retirement age on or before the last day of the taxable year.

Dr. James, who reports his earnings on a calendar year basis, turns age 65 and 2 months on June 18, 2003. The lower exempt amount ($11,280) applies for calendar year 2002, and the higher exempt amount ($30,720) applies January through May for calendar year 2003. The FRA no longer applies from the month of FRA attainment and on.

(See §1808.2 for test used when a beneficiary dies in the year of turning FRA.)

1804. HOW EXCESS EARNINGS ARE CHARGED AGAINST BENEFITS

1804.1 When are excess earnings charged against your benefits?
When you have excess earnings, these earnings are charged against and deducted from your benefits. The deductions begin with the first chargeable month of the taxable year and continue each month until all excess earnings have been charged.

(See §1805 for months to which earnings cannot be charged.)

1804.2 How do excess earnings affect family insurance benefits?
If you receive retirement insurance benefits, your excess earnings are charged against the total monthly family benefit. This reduces the total family benefit. The family benefit includes all monthly benefits (other than disability insurance benefits) payable to you and anyone else (e.g., spouse or child) entitled to benefits on your earnings record. It also includes benefits payable to your spouse on any earnings record as a disabled child, a mother, or a father.

Note: Your excess earnings do not cause deductions from the benefits of an entitled divorced spouse if your month of entitlement is prior to the month of divorce or if you have been divorced from the entitled spouse for at least two years in a row.

Mr. Bond is entitled to a retirement insurance benefit of $378. His wife and child are each entitled to an auxiliary benefit of $160. Mr. Bond worked and had excess earnings of $2,094. These earnings are charged against the total monthly family benefit of $698 ($378 plus (2 x $160)). Therefore, no benefits are payable to the family for January through March (3 x $698 = $2,094).

1804.3 How do excess earnings of someone entitled to benefits on your record affect benefits?
If a survivor or other person entitled to benefits on your Social Security record has excess earnings, only his or her monthly benefit amount is charged and deducted.

Same facts as the example in (1804.2) above, except it was the wife who worked. Her excess earnings were $800, which are charged only against her own monthly benefit of $160. She therefore receives no payments for January through May (5 x $160 = $800).

1804.4 How are your benefits affected if you and someone entitled to benefits on your record have excess earnings?
If you and a person entitled to benefits on your earnings record (auxiliary) both have excess earnings:

A. First, your excess earnings are charged against the total monthly family benefit; and

B. Next, the auxiliary's excess earnings are charged against his or her own benefits. However, they are only charged to the extent that those benefits have not already been charged with your excess earnings.

Mrs. Malcolm is entitled to a retirement insurance benefit of $346, and her husband is entitled to a spouse's insurance benefit of $173. Mrs. Malcolm had excess earnings of $2,076. Her husband had excess earnings of $865.

Mrs. Malcolm's earnings are charged against the total monthly family benefit of $519 ($346 plus $173), so neither Mrs. Malcolm nor her husband receives payments for January through April (4 x $519 = $2,076). The husband's excess earnings are charged only against his own benefit of $173. Since his benefits for January through April were charged with the worker's excess earnings, the charging of his own earnings cannot begin until May; therefore, he receives no benefits for May through September (5 x $173 = 865).

1805. WHEN ARE YOU NOT CHARGED FOR EXCESS EARNINGS?
Your excess earnings are not charged against your benefits for any month in which you:

A. Were not entitled to benefits;

B. Were FRA (see §723.5) or over in any part of the month;

C. Met the following conditions:
 1. You were in a "grace year;" (§1807)
 2. You did not work for wages of more than the monthly exempt amount; and
 3. You did not perform substantial services in self-employment (see §1807.4);

D. Were entitled to a disability insurance or a childhood disability benefit;

E. Were entitled to a widow(er)'s or surviving divorced spouse's insurance benefit because of a disability;
F. Were entitled to a wife's, husband's, mother's, or father's insurance benefit, but were subject to a deduction because you did not have the spouse's (or former spouse's) child in care (see §1829);
G. Were subject to a deduction because of your own non-covered work for pay outside the U.S.;
H. Were subject to a deduction because the worker on whose earnings record you are entitled to benefits performed non-covered work for pay outside the U.S. (see §1823);
I. Were subject to a deduction because the worker on whose earnings record you are entitled to benefits refused to accept vocational rehabilitation services;
J. Did not receive payment because periodic workers' compensation benefits prevented such payment (see §1835); or

Note: Excess earnings of a retirement insurance beneficiary are not charged against the benefits of person entitled to benefits on the worker's earnings record (the auxiliary) for any month in which the auxiliary is subject to a deduction under (D), (E), or (F) above.

K. Were entitled to student benefits based on full-time attendance at a post-secondary school and did not receive benefits for the summer months.

1806. PAYMENT OF PARTIAL BENEFIT

1806.1 When do you receive a partial monthly benefit because of your excess earnings?

You may receive a partial monthly benefit when your excess earnings remaining to be charged for the year are less than the amount of your total benefit for the next month subject to charging.

1806.2 When is the partial monthly benefit paid?

The partial payment is paid only at the close of the taxable year when you file your annual report of earnings (see §1814), unless otherwise requested. Where the partial monthly benefit is not a multiple of $1, the monthly benefit amount is rounded to the next lower multiple of $1. (See the example in 1806.3 below.)

1806.3 What is the partial monthly benefit amount if there is only one beneficiary involved?

If you are the only beneficiary involved, the partial benefit paid is the difference between the monthly benefit amount and the excess earnings charged to the month.

Ms. Ridgely has a monthly benefit amount of $288.20. She had excess earnings of $700 that are charged against her benefits beginning with January. This results in the loss of her entire benefit for January and February plus $123.60 of the March payment ((2 x $288.20) plus $123.60 = $700). She receives a partial monthly benefit of $164.00 for March ($288.20 minus $123.60 = $164.60 rounded to the next lower multiple of $1).

1806.4 What is the partial monthly benefit amount if there is more than one beneficiary involved?

Where excess earnings are charged against the family benefits of a retirement insurance beneficiary and one or more persons entitled to benefits on the worker's earnings record, the partial benefit is allocated to each person entitled to benefits. The partial benefit is allocated in the proportion to the "original entitlement rate" of beneficiary on the worker's earnings record. However, a beneficiary's prorated share of the partial benefit may not be more than the benefit amount that would have been paid if there were no work deductions.

1806.5 What is the original entitlement rate?

The "original entitlement rate" means the respective benefit rate as figured without:

A. Adjustment for the family maximum;
B. Adjustment for entitlement before FRA; and
C. Any reduction because of an auxiliary's entitlement to a retirement or disability insurance benefit.

Mr. Star, his wife, and two children are entitled to benefits. After charging Mr. Star's excess earnings against the total monthly family benefit, a partial benefit of $100 is payable to the family. The chart below shows the amount each family member will receive.

Family Member	Original Benefit Amounts	Proportionate Part of Original Benefit	Actual Benefits Under Family Maximum	Prorated Share of Partial Benefit
Mr. Star	$194.00	(2/5)	$194.00	$ 40 (2/5 x 100)
Wife	97.00	(1/5)	32.40	20 (1/5 x 100)
Child	97.00	(1/5)	32.40	20 (1/5 x 100)
Child	97.00	(1/5)	32.40	20 (1/5 x 100)
Total	$485.00	-	$291.20	$100

1807. GRACE YEAR AND NON-SERVICE MONTH DEFINED

1807.1 What is a grace year?

A "grace year" is the first year you receive your full benefit amount for any month of entitlement in that year that has a non-service month before the month of FRA.

1807.2 What is a non-service month?

A "non-service month" is a month you do not:

A. Perform substantial services in self-employment; and

B. Do not have earnings from employment that are more than the monthly exempt amount.

1807.3 When are you entitled to a grace year?

You are entitled to a grace year under the following circumstances:

A. The first year you have at least one non-service month and the non-service month is before the month of FRA is a grace year;

B. If you are entitled to one type of benefit (e.g., mother's) and then have a break in entitlement of at least one month before becoming entitled to a different type of benefit (e.g., widow's): the first year you are entitled to the second benefit in which you have at least one non-service month is a grace year.

C. If you are entitled to benefits as a child, a young wife or husband with a child in care, a mother or a father: the year that your entitlement ends is an additional grace year, unless entitlement ends:
   1. Because of death; or
   2. Because you are entitled to another type of benefit with no break in entitlement.

1807.4 How is substantial services determined for a self-employed beneficiary?

We determine whether you, as a self-employed beneficiary, perform "substantial services" by the actual service you perform, not by the amount of profit or loss. In applying this test, we consider the following factors:

A. The amount of time you devote to the trade or business. Generally, services of 45 hours or less in a month are not considered substantial. However, as few as 15 hours of service a month could be substantial if, for example, the hours:
  1. Involved management of a sizeable business; or
  2. Were spent in a highly skilled occupation.

  Note: Services of less than 15 hours a month are never considered substantial.

B. The nature of the services;
C. The relationship of the activities performed before retirement to those performed after retirement; and
D. Other circumstances, such as:
  1. The amount of capital you invested in the business;
  2. The type of business establishment;
  3. The presence of a paid manager, partner, or family member who manages the business; and
  4. The seasonal nature of the business.

1807.5 What are the monthly exempt amounts?

The monthly exempt amounts that apply to earnings from employment for years 1985 through 2024 are listed in the chart below.

Year	Age 65-69	Under Age 65
1987	$680	$500
1988	$700	$510
1989	$740	$540
1990	$780	$570
1991	$810	$590
1992	$850	$620
1993	$880	$640
1994	$930	$670
1995	$940	$680
1996	$1,042	$690
1997	$1,125	$720
1998	$1,209	$760

Year	Age 65-69	Under Age 65
1999	$1,292	$800
	Year of Full Retirement Age	Prior to Year of Full Retirement Age
2000	$1,417	$840
2001	$2,084	$890
2002	$2,500	$940
2003	$2,560	$960
2004	$2,590	$970
2005	$2,650	$1,000
2006	$2,770	$1,040
2007	$2,870	$1,080
2008	$3,010	$1,130
2009	$3,140	$1,180
2010	$3,140	$1,180
2011	$3,140	$1,180
2012	$3,240	$1,220
2013	$3,340	$1,260
2014	$3,450	$1,290
2015-2016	$3,490	$1,310
2017	$3,740	$1,410
2018	$3,780	$1,420
2019	$3,910	$1,470
2020	$4,050	$1,520
2021	$4,210	$1,580
2022	$4,330	$1,630
2023	$4,710	$1,770
2024	$4,960	$1,860

1807.6 What is your benefit amount when the monthly earnings test applies?

When the monthly earnings test applies, regardless of the amount of annual earnings, you receive full benefits for any month that:

A. Your earnings do not exceed the monthly exempt amount; and

B. You do not perform substantial services in self-employment.

Note: Earnings for the entire year, i.e., January through December, are always used to determine the maximum amount we withhold from benefits if you are under FRA. However, the monthly test prevents us from withholding benefits for months that meet the above rules.

1808. EXEMPT AMOUNTS FOR SHORT TAXABLE YEARS

1808.1 When does a short taxable year occur?

A short taxable year is a taxable year of less than 12 months. It may occur when an individual:

A. Dies before November 11, 1988; or

B. Changes from one taxable year to another, usually from a calendar to a fiscal year or from one fiscal year to another.

Congress eliminated the short taxable year for deaths that occur on or after November 11, 1988. The number of months in such taxable year of death is 12.

1808.2 How is the exempt amount computed for a short taxable year?

The exempt amount for a short taxable year is figured by multiplying the monthly exempt amount by the number of months in the short taxable year. The monthly exempt amounts in §1807.5 are used to compute the exempt amounts for a short taxable year.

If a beneficiary dies in any month of the taxable year that he or she would have attained FRA, the year of FRA attainment exempt amount is used.

Miss Rose's date of birth is August 29, 1935. She is on a calendar taxable year and died on October 15, 2000. Her exempt amount is thus $17,000, the exempt amount for the year of FRA attainment for 2000. If 2000 is her initial grace year, the monthly exempt amount of $1,417 for the year of FRA attainment is used in determining non-service months.

Dr. Carey's date of birth is December 2, 1935. He is on a calendar taxable year and died on October 26, 2000. Although he had not turned FRA before his death, his exempt amount is $17,000, the exempt amount for the year of FRA attainment for 2000.

1809. TOTAL EARNINGS FOR EARNINGS TEST PURPOSES

1809.1 How do you compute your total earnings?

Under the earnings test, your earnings for a taxable year consist of:

A. The sum of your wages for services performed in the year; *plus*

B. All net earnings from self-employment for the year; *minus*

C. Any net loss from self-employment for the year.

1809.2 Are earnings counted even if you were not entitled to benefits for the entire year?

Yes, we count your earnings for the entire taxable year in applying the earnings test. This is true even if you may not have been entitled to benefits for the entire year.

1809.3 Are earnings counted when you reach FRA?

No, we do not count your earnings if they were earned in or after the month you reach FRA.

1810. WHEN ARE WAGES AND NET EARNINGS FROM SELF-EMPLOYMENT COUNTED?

For earnings test purposes, we count wages as earnings for the taxable year in which they are earned, regardless of when they are paid. We generally count net earnings from self-employment as earnings for the taxable year in which they are received. (However, note the exclusion in §1812(B).)

1811. WHAT TYPES OF INCOME COUNT UNDER THE EARNINGS TEST?

The following types of earnings count for earnings test purposes:

A. All wages for employment covered by Social Security (see Chapter 13);

B. All cash pay (even if not considered as "wages" under the cash-pay test explained in §901 and §1303) for:
   1. Agricultural work;
   2. Domestic work in a private home; or
   3. Service not in the course of the employer's trade or business;

C. All pay, cash and non-cash, for work as a homeworker or for a non-profit organization whether or not the $100 per year test is met (see §931);

D. Cash tips that equal or exceed $20 a month (see §1329);

E. All pay for work not covered by Social Security, if the work is done in the U.S., including pay for:
   1. Family employment;
   2. Work by students, student nurses, interns, newspaper and magazine vendors;
   3. Work for Federal or State or foreign governments or instrumentalities; or
   4. Work covered by the Railroad Retirement Act;

F. All net earnings from self-employment;
G. All pay for incentive, suggestion, and outstanding work awards;
H. All pay for occasional and regular bonuses;
I. All pay from a "cafeteria" plan if the payments meet the definition of wages and the plan is not a "qualified benefit";
J. All pay from a non-qualified deferred compensation plan/system;
K. All pay by an employer for educational assistance;
L. All pay from federally sponsored economic and human development programs only if payments are wages;
M. All pay for non-work periods including idle time, standby, and subject to call related payments;
N. All pay for prizes, awards and gratuities only if it is part of the salesperson's wage structure; and
O. All pay from television, radio and motion picture residuals if the performer was an employee at the time of the original performance.

1812. WHAT TYPES OF INCOME DO NOT COUNT UNDER THE EARNINGS TEST?

The following types of earnings income (or losses) do not count as earnings from employment or self-employment under the earnings test:

A. Any income from employment or self-employment earned in or after the month the individual turns FRA;
B. Any income from self-employment received in a taxable year after the year the individual becomes entitled to benefits. Such income must not be attributable to services performed after the first month of entitlement to benefits;

Note: This income is excluded from gross income only for purposes of the earnings test.

C. Damages, attorneys' fees, interest, or penalties paid under court judgment or by compromise settlement with the employer based on a wage claim;

Note: Any back pay recovered in a wage claim does count for the earnings test.

D. Payments to secure release of an unexpired contract of employment;
E. Certain payments made under a plan or system established for making payments because of the employee's sickness or accident disability, medical or hospitalization expenses, or death (see §1311);
F. Payments from certain trust funds that are exempt from income tax (see §1314);

G. Payments from certain annuity plans that are exempt from income tax (see §1316);
H. Pensions and retirement pay;
I. Sick pay if paid more than six months after the month the employee last worked;
J. Payments-in-kind for domestic service in the employer's private home for:
   1. Agricultural labor;
   2. Work not in the course of the employer's trade or business; or
   3. The value of meals and lodging furnished under certain conditions;
K. Rentals from real estate that cannot be counted in earnings from self-employment. For instance, the beneficiary did not materially participate in production work on the farm, the beneficiary was not a real estate dealer, etc.;
L. Interest and dividends from stocks and bonds (unless they are received by a dealer in securities in the course of business);
M. Gain or loss from the sale of capital assets, or sale, exchange, or conversion of other property that is not stock in trade nor considered inventory;
N. Net operating loss carry-over resulting from self-employment activities;
O. Loans received by employees unless the employees repay the loans by their work;
P. Workers' compensation and unemployment compensation benefits and strike benefits;
Q. Veterans' training pay or allowance;
R. Pay for jury duty;
S. Payments for achievement awards, length of service awards, hobbies or prize winnings from contests, unless the person enters contests as a trade or business;
T. Tips paid to an employee that are less than $20 a month or are not paid in cash (see §1329);
U. Payments by an employer that are reimbursement specifically for travel expenses of the employee and are so identified by the employer at the time of payment;
V. Payments to an employee as reimbursement or allowance for moving expenses, if they are not counted as wages for Social Security purposes (see §1333);

W. Royalties received in or after the year a person turns FRA. The royalties must flow from property created by the person's own personal efforts that he or she copyrighted or patented before the taxable year in which he or she turned FRA;

Note: These royalties are excluded from gross income from self-employment only for purposes of the earnings test.

X. Retirement payments received by a retired partner from a partnership provided certain conditions are met (see §1203);

Y. Certain payments or series of payments paid by an employer to an employee or an employee's dependents on or after the employment relationship has ended due to:
1. Death;
2. Retirement for disability; or
3. Retirement for age.

The payments are made under a plan established by the employer (see §1319); and

Z. Payments from Individual Retirement Accounts (IRA's) and Keogh Plans (see §1338).

1813. DOES THE RECIPIENT OF INCOME DETERMINE WHETHER THE EARNINGS COUNT UNDER THE EARNINGS TEST?

It does not matter who the final recipient of your income is when applying the earnings test. If the income is actual wages for services you perform or net earnings from self-employment, you must include the income when applying the earnings test. It also does not matter what you call your earnings: "dividends," "rent," "refund of loans," etc. We look closely at arrangements of this nature.

For example, Mr. Smith continues to perform services for a family, close corporation, trade, or business owned by him. Mr. Smith later transfers ownership to a relative. If Mr. Smith is receiving income, directly or indirectly, that is wages for the services or net earnings from self-employment, he must include that income in applying the earnings test.

1814. ANNUAL REPORT OF EARNINGS

1814.1 Who must file an annual report of earnings?

You must file an annual report of earnings if you are:

A. A Social Security beneficiary (unless you are entitled to benefits because you are disabled); or

B. Receiving benefits on a beneficiary's behalf, if the beneficiary:
1. Was entitled to Social Security benefits for the taxable year;
2. Had not reached FRA in or before the first month of entitlement in that year;
3. Had total earnings (wages and net earnings from self-employment) more than the yearly exempt amount; and
4. Did not have all benefits withheld in the year for all entitlement months in which he or she was under FRA.

1814.2 Who is NOT required to file an annual report of earnings?

You do not have to file an annual report for a taxable year that you (or the beneficiary on whose behalf you are receiving benefits) were not paid any benefits because of work and high earnings.

1814.3 What happens if you are required to file an annual report and you fail to do so?

If you do not file an annual report or other information showing that benefits are payable for that year, benefits that might otherwise have been payable may not be paid after three years, three months and 15 days after the close of the taxable year. Be sure to file your report within the time limit in §1815.

1814.4 What type of information qualifies as an annual report?

In 1997, we changed our rules so that, for reports due on or after April 15, 1997, we may accept the W-2 information reported by your employer. If you are self-employed, the self-employment tax information you file with the IRS is acceptable. We use the information in those reports along with other pertinent information on our records to adjust your benefits under the earnings test.

You may still report your earnings to us if you want to have your benefits adjusted sooner. Otherwise, we will adjust benefits based on the earnings posted to your record.

1814.5 Who is responsible for the accuracy of the amount of earnings posted to your record?

We notify you of the amount of earnings used to adjust your benefits. However, you have the primary responsibility to ensure that the adjustment to your benefits was based on the correct amount of earnings. Be sure to notify us promptly if the earnings used were not correct for deduction purposes.

1815. WHEN IS THE ANNUAL REPORT OF EARNINGS DUE?

The law requires that a report of earnings be filed with the Social Security Administration within 3 months and 15 days after the close of your taxable year. You may file a report by calling your local Social Security office or the 800 number, or you may visit any office in person to file. If you do not file a report, we will accept the report of your earnings filed by your employer, i.e., your W-2 form as the report of your earnings, or the amount reported on your self-employment tax return to the IRS if you are self-employed.

1816. EXTENSION OF TIME FOR FILING ANNUAL REPORT OF EARNINGS

1816.1 Can you get an extension for filing your annual report of earnings?

We may grant an extension of time for filing your annual report of earnings if there is a valid reason. You (or someone acting on your behalf) must make a written request for an extension before your annual report is due.

1816.2 What are examples of valid reasons for getting an extension?

A valid reason is a real need, problem, or situation that makes it impossible or difficult for you to file your annual report by the regular due date. A valid reason may be:

A. Illness or disability;

B. Absence or travel so far from home that you do not have and cannot readily obtain records needed to file your report;

C. Inability to get evidence you need from another source;

D. Inability of an accountant to compile the data needed for your report; or

E. Any similar situation that has a direct bearing on your obligation to file your annual report.

1816.3 What happens if you are granted an extension?

If we grant your request for an extension, we will set a new due date for your annual report. You will receive a written notice of the approved extended reporting date. If you need another extension, you must make your request before the due date of your new approved reporting date.

1816.4 What is the maximum amount of time you can receive for an extension?

More than one extension may be granted in a taxable year. However, the total amount of time of all extensions granted for any one taxable year cannot be more than four months. This is so you avoid a penalty (see §1820) for late reporting when you know your annual report will be unavoidably late.

1817. HOW DO YOU REQUEST AN EXTENSION OF TIME FOR FILING YOUR ANNUAL REPORT?

If you believe that you have a valid reason for an extension, file a request with a Social Security office before your annual report is due. The request must be in writing and must:

A. Clearly identify you (or the beneficiary, if you are filing on his or her behalf) by name and claim number;
B. Establish the year that your annual report is due;
C. State the reason you need the extension;
D. State the amount of additional time you need;
E. Show the date you are making the request;
F. Be signed by you (or the person requesting the extension on your behalf); and
G. If you are making the request on behalf of a beneficiary, show the beneficiary's authorization or include a statement by you giving the basis for your authority.

Note: For reports due on or after April 15, 1997, we consider all adjustments based on posted earnings to be based on a timely filed report. (See Section §1814.) However, beneficiaries requesting an extension of time for filing a self-employment tax return with IRS should also request an extension of time for filing the annual report with us.

1818. THE ANNUAL REPORT FORM

1818.1 How do you file an annual report?

SSA may consider the Wage and Tax Statement (W-2) information and self-employment tax return information to be the annual earnings report required under 203(h) of the Social Security Act. Beneficiaries will need to contact us to provide additional information only when the information on the W-2 and self-employment tax return, along with other information on our records will not allow us to correctly determine benefits payable.

Although we may accept W-2 information and special payment information from employers, the beneficiary still has primary responsibility for making sure that the earnings we use for deductions purposes is correct.

1818.2 What information do you need for your annual report?

The following summarizes the information you need for your annual report:

A. Your total amount of wages (before payroll deductions) earned during the taxable year for which the report is being made;

B. Your total net earnings or net loss from self-employment for the taxable year;

C. Months during a grace year (see §1807) in which you did not earn over the monthly exempt amount as an employee and did not perform substantial services in self-employment; and

D. An estimate of your expected total earnings (wages and net earnings from self-employment) for the next taxable year.

1819. DELAY IN FILING ANNUAL REPORT

1819.1 Under what conditions does the late filing of your annual report result in a reduction of benefits?

There may be a penalty deduction (see §1820) in your benefits if you fail to file your annual report of earnings in a timely manner, if all of the following factors exist:

A. You did not make an annual report of earnings within three months and 15 days after the close of the taxable year;

B. We cannot find good cause for your not reporting on time (see §1832);

C. A work deduction (part or all of one month's benefit) is required because of your earnings; and

D. You received and accepted a benefit check for one or more months during that taxable year.

1819.2 If you do not file your annual report on time, what benefit payments are withheld?

If you fail to file your annual report on time, you will not receive:

A. Any benefit payments withheld due to your failure to file an annual report on time; and

REDUCTION OR NONPAYMENT OF SOCIAL SECURITY BENEFITS   465

B. Any monthly benefit payments that must be withheld because of your excess earnings in the year the annual report was due.

Note: See sections §1814 and §1819 above. We accept the information on the W-2 forms and the SE tax return to be the annual report of earnings required by law. We assume that all adjustments to benefits were based on a report filed on time. No penalty is imposed unless you knowingly and intentionally attempted to hide your earnings from us in an effort to avoid the payment of taxes and/or to avoid deductions under the earnings test.

1820. NUMBER OF ADDITIONAL BENEFITS LOST FOR FAILURE TO REPORT ON TIME

1820.1 What is the penalty deduction amount for failing to file the annual report on time?

The penalty deduction that may be imposed due to your failure to file the annual report of earnings on time is as follows:

A. *For the first time you fail to file the report*, the amount of the penalty is equal to your monthly benefit rate for the last month you are entitled in the taxable year. However, if the work deduction is less than your full benefit for the month, the amount of the penalty equals the amount of the work deduction, but not less than $10;

B. *For the second time you fail to file the report*, the amount of the penalty is two times your monthly benefit rate; and

C. *For the third and any subsequent time you fail to file the report*, the amount of the penalty is three times your monthly benefit rate.

1820.2 Is there a maximum number of months that can be imposed for the penalty?

The number of months imposed for the penalty cannot be more than the number of months that work deductions are imposed for the year. The amount of the penalty is the same no matter how long you delay filing each report, whether for one month or one year after the due date.

A beneficiary with a monthly benefit rate of $136 has excess earnings of $190 for that year. This requires a loss of benefits in two months. Therefore, the maximum amount of the penalty is $272 (two times the monthly benefit rate) even if that year may have been the third year that the beneficiary failed to file the annual report on time.

1821. ARE BENEFITS OF THOSE ENTITLED TO BENEFITS ON YOUR EARNINGS RECORD AFFECTED WHEN YOU DO NOT FILE YOUR ANNUAL REPORT ON TIME?

Benefits of your spouse or child are not affected if a penalty is imposed on you for failing to submit your annual report of earnings on time. However, their benefits are affected for any month you lose part or all of your benefit because of excess earnings.

1822. REPORT OF EXPECTED EARNINGS ALSO REQUIRED

1822.1 When do you need to file a report of expected earnings?

If you go to work and expect that your total earnings will be more than the yearly exempt amount (see §1803), you should file a report of expected earnings. This report prevents payment of monthly benefits to you that may have to be returned at the end of the year if, under the earnings test, you were not due all the payments received.

When you file your expected earnings report, you are encouraged to make a high estimate of earnings for the year. Based on your report, we suspend benefits for the number of months required by your estimate.

1822.2 How is your earnings report validated at the end of the year?

At the end of the taxable year, we figure the amount of benefit payments due for that taxable year. If all payments that were due have not been made, you are paid whatever amount we find that is due to you. If, on the other hand, you have been paid too much, we either withhold the amounts from future benefits payable, or you must refund the amount. (See Chapter 19.)

1823. THE FOREIGN WORK TEST

1823.1 What is the foreign work test?

The "foreign work test" is a separate retirement test that applies to beneficiaries (other than those entitled because of disability) who work in employment or self-employment outside the U.S. that is not covered by the U.S. Social Security system. This test is based only on the amount of time during which the beneficiary is employed or self-employed. It is not based on the amount of the beneficiary's earnings or losses. The foreign work test was intended to make it unnecessary to convert earnings in a foreign currency into earnings in specific dollar amounts.

1823.2 When are benefits withheld under the foreign work test?

The foreign work test only applies to monthly benefits of those who work before attaining their full retirement age. Under the foreign work test, your monthly benefit is withheld for each calendar month that you (or a person entitled to benefits on your record) work:

A. Outside the U.S.;
B. In work for pay not covered by Social Security; and
C. For more than 45 hours.

1823.3 Are benefits withheld if you are over full retirement age and you work?

No. If you are at least full retirement age, we do not withhold benefits for any month you work.

1823.4 Are family benefits withheld if a retirement insurance beneficiary loses benefits?

If you are a retirement insurance beneficiary and you work and lose benefits for one or more months, family benefits are also withheld for the same months. (See the exception below.) Family benefits include:

A. Benefits payable to auxiliaries (spouse or child) on your earnings record; and
B. Benefits payable to your spouse on any earnings record as a disabled child, mother, or father.

Note: The benefits of a divorced spouse, who has been divorced at least two years, are not subject to withholding because of the retirement insurance beneficiary's work.

1823.5 How does work activity of someone entitled to benefits on your record affect benefits?

The work activity of your spouse, child, or survivor beneficiary affects only his or her own benefits.

1824. WHAT IS CONSIDERED WORK "OUTSIDE OF THE U.S."?

We consider your work "outside of the U.S." if your work takes place outside the territorial boundaries of the 50 States, the District of Columbia, Puerto Rico, the U.S. Virgin Islands, Guam, American Samoa, and the Commonwealth of the Northern Mariana Islands. However, the law specifically provides that self-employment by nonresident aliens in Puerto Rico, the U.S. Virgin Islands, Guam, American Samoa, or the

Commonwealth of the Northern Mariana Islands is considered to be outside the U.S. unless the alien is a resident of a State, the District of Columbia, Puerto Rico, the U.S. Virgin Islands, Guam, American Samoa, or the Commonwealth of the Northern Mariana Islands.

1825. NON-COVERED WORK FOR PAY DEFINED

1825.1 What is non-covered work for pay?

You are performing "non-covered work for pay" if:

A. You are employed outside the U.S. in a job not covered by U.S. Social Security (see Chapter 9); or

B. You are self-employed outside the U.S. in a trade or business and your income is not subject to the U.S. Social Security tax;

C. You are a self-employed owner or part-owner of a trade or business outside the U.S. not subject to the U.S. Social Security tax and hold yourself out to the public as available to work in excess of 45 hours a month, whether or not you actually work.

1825.2 Is income excluded from net earnings considered non-covered work for pay?

A trade or business that produces only income that would be excluded from net earnings if carried on in the U.S. (e.g., dividends, rentals from real estate, etc.) is not "non-covered work for pay." Neither the foreign work test nor the earnings test applies to such income.

1826. DETERMINING NUMBER OF HOURS A RETIREMENT BENEFICIARY WORKS PER MONTH

1826.1 How do you count the number of hours you work each month?

To determine the number of hours you work each month, count each hour you are engaged in employment or self-employment.

1826.2 How do you know if you are engaged in employment or self-employment?

You are engaged in employment or self-employment when you:

A. Actually perform services as an employee or self-employed person;

B. Have an employment agreement to work even though you may not perform actual services because of sickness, vacation, etc.;

C. Are the owner or part owner of a functioning trade or business; or
D. Hold yourself out to the public as carrying on a trade or business, whether or not you perform actual services.

1827. DO YOU NEED TO REPORT YOUR WORK ACTIVITY PERFORMED OUTSIDE THE U.S.?

If you are under full retirement age and receive retirement benefits or receive disability benefits as the worker, spouse, survivor or dependent of a worker, you must file a report with us if you become employed for 45 hours or more per month or become self-employed outside the U.S. You must file the report before the receipt and acceptance of a benefit for the second month following the month in which you worked. For example, if you work 45 hours or more in January, you must report your work activity before you receive and accept your benefits in March. Report employment or self employment to the nearest U.S. Embassy or Consulate if you are outside the United States.

1828. WHAT IS THE PENALTY FOR YOUR FAILURE TO REPORT FOREIGN WORK?

If you fail to report foreign work activity within the time limit, penalty deductions may be imposed as follows:

A. *For the first time you fail to file the report*, a penalty of one month's benefit is withheld, even if you may have worked several months before we discovered your failure to report;

B. *For the second time you fail to file the report*, a penalty of two months' benefits may be imposed; and

C. *For the third and subsequent times you fail to file the report*, three additional months' benefits may be withheld. The above penalties are imposed in addition to the monthly benefits you lose because of the application of the foreign work test. We cannot impose any more penalty deductions than the number of months for which foreign work deductions were required for that year.

1829. CHILD IN CARE REQUIREMENT

1829.1 What types of beneficiaries must have a child in care to receive benefits?

The following types of beneficiaries must have in care a child entitled to benefits in order to receive monthly benefits:

A. A spouse under age 62;
B. A mother or father; or
C. A surviving divorced mother or father.

The child in care must be under age 16 (or disabled, if age 16 or over). Benefits are not payable for any month in which the child is not in the parent's care, or the child is age 16 or over and not disabled. (For the definition of "child in care", see §312.)

1829.2 Are beneficiary benefits reduced if there is a child in care?

The amount of the benefit payable to a spouse or divorced spouse is not reduced for any month he or she has a child in care, unless the spouse/divorced spouse has excess earnings. Similarly, the amount of the benefit payable to a widow(er), surviving divorced spouse, or disabled widow(er) is not reduced below 75 percent of the primary insurance amount of the deceased worker in any month he or she has such a child in care (unless reduction for the family maximum or excess earnings is required). (For the definition of "in care," see §§312-319.)

1829.3 What must be the relationship of the child to the worker?

The child entitled to benefits must be the worker's child; e.g., the natural child, stepchild, or adopted child:

A. *Where a wife or husband* is concerned, the child must be entitled to benefits on the same worker's Social Security earnings record;
B. *Where a surviving divorced mother or father* is concerned:
  1. The child must be his or her child or legally adopted child; and
  2. The child's insurance benefit must be payable on the same worker's Social Security earnings record; or
C. *Where a divorced spouse, a widow(er), a surviving divorced spouse, a mother, or a father* is concerned, the child may be entitled to child's benefits on any Social Security record.

1831. REPORTING FAILURE TO HAVE A CHILD IN CARE

1831.1 Is it required to report to SSA if there is no longer a child in care?

If you have rights to benefits based on having a child in care, you must report to us if you no longer have a child in your care. The mother or father must report this fact before receiving and accepting benefits for the second month following the month in which they first did not have the child in care.

1831.2 What is the penalty for failure to report no longer having a child in care?

The mother of father must report when there is no longer a child in care within the time limit. Failure to do so may result in the following penalties:

A. *For the first time the mother or father fails to report*, a penalty equal to one month's benefit may be withheld;

B. *For the second time the mother or father fails to report*, a penalty equal to two months' benefits may be withheld; and

C. *For the third and each subsequent failure to report*, a penalty equal to three months' benefits may be withheld. The withholding of the penalty for failure to report is in addition to the withholding of benefits because the mother or father did not have a child in care.

We cannot impose any more penalty deductions than the number of months for which deductions for failure to have a child in care were required for that period.

1832. DO WE STILL IMPOSE A PENALTY IF YOU HAVE GOOD CAUSE FOR YOUR FAILURE TO REPORT TO US?

If you have good cause for failing to report an event that requires benefits to be withheld, there is no penalty deduction for the late report. (See §§1819, 1828, and 1831.)

1833. GOOD CAUSE DEFINED

1833.1 What is good cause for failing to report an event?

"Good cause" for your failure to make a required report on time may exist if the failure was the result of:

A. Unfavorable circumstances;

B. Your confusion as to the law resulting from amendments to the Social Security Act or other legislation; or

C. Misleading action on our part.

You must prove that your failure to report was for good cause and was not due to willful neglect. When we decide whether there is good cause, we consider the circumstances in each case.

1833.2 What are examples of good cause?

Below are examples good cause for failure to report. We consider evidence of failure to report due to:

A. Your serious illness, or death or serious illness in your immediate family;
B. In the case of an annual report, your inability to get earnings information from an employer within the time required to file the report because of:
   1. Death or serious illness of your employer or his or her immediate family;
   2. Unavoidable absence of the employer; or
   3. Destruction by fire or other damage of the employer's records;
C. Destruction by fire or other damage of your business records;
D. Your timely sending of the report to another governmental agency (that caused a delay in the report reaching us), if you did so in good faith;
E. Your lack of awareness that an annual report is required in the year you reach age 70 if earnings exceeded the yearly exempt amount;
F. Our failure to give you the reporting forms in enough time to complete and file the report, provided you made a timely request for the forms;
G. Your belief that an extension of time granted to you by the Internal Revenue Service for filing income tax returns also applied to the Social Security annual earnings report;
H. Your reliance on a report to us made by (or on behalf of) you before the close of the taxable year was adequate. You believed the report provided enough information about your work to require suspension of benefits, provided the report was not later found untrue or voided; or
I. You had a physical, mental, educational, or linguistic limitation (including any lack of familiarity with the English language) that kept you from understanding the reporting responsibilities. Therefore, you did not file a timely report.

1833.3 Is good cause established if you have the same reason for failing to file a report more than once?

Generally, good cause does not exist if you fail to file a report on time for a later period under similar circumstances under which you have been found to have good cause in the past.

1835. DOES THE RECEIPT OF PERIODIC WORKERS' COMPENSATION PAYMENTS OR PUBLIC DISABILITY BENEFITS AFFECT YOUR BENEFITS?

Your Social Security disability insurance benefit amount, and the benefits of others entitled on your record, may be reduced if you receive:

A. Workers' compensation payments; or
B. Certain disability benefits paid under a Federal, State or local public disability law or plan. (See §504.)

1836. RECEIPT OF A GOVERNMENTAL PENSION

1836.1 How does the receipt of a governmental pension affect benefits?

If you receive a government pension, certain circumstances cause an offset against your Social Security benefit. Benefits payable as a spouse, divorced spouse, surviving spouse, surviving divorced spouse, or a deemed spouse may be reduced if the person receives periodic payments based on his or her own employment in the Federal Government, State or political subdivision that was not covered under Social Security.

1836.2 What is a periodic payment?

A periodic payment is a:

A. Payment received on a monthly or other than monthly basis; or
B. Lump-sum payment that replaces a monthly payment.

1836.3 What is a State or political subdivision?

For government pension purposes, a State or political subdivision includes the 50 States, the District of Columbia, the Commonwealth of Puerto Rico, the Virgin Islands, Guam, American Samoa, and the Northern Mariana Islands.

1836.4 Are there any exceptions to the government pension offset?

The offset is effective if you apply for Social Security benefits in or after December 1977, unless you meet one of the following exceptions:

A. The offset does not apply for any month you:
   1. Were entitled to or eligible for the government pension for any month between December 1977 through November 1982; and
   2. Meet all the requirements for entitlement that were in effect and being administered in January 1977;

B. The offset does not apply to benefits payable December 1982 and later if you:
   1. Were entitled to or eligible for the government pension before July 1, 1983; and
   2. Were receiving one-half support from the retirement or disability insurance beneficiary at the time that beneficiary either became entitled to benefits, began a period of disability, or died;
C. You were a Federal, State or local government employee and you were eligible for and filed an application for Social Security spouse's benefits before April 1, 2004; and you were entitled based on that filing and your last day of government employment was under both social security and the pension plan (you may work your last day at anytime); or
D. You were a Federal, State or local government employee whose pension is based on work covered by both Social Security and the pension plan on your last day of employment and your last day at work was before July 1, 2004; or
E. You were a Federal, State or local government employee whose pension is based on a job where you were paying Social Security taxes during the last 60 months of employment and your last day of employment was July 1, 2004, or later; or
F. You were a Federal employee first hired after December 31, 1983, and you are covered under Social Security by law; or
G. You were a Federal employee who chose to switch from the Civil Service Retirement System (CSRS) to employment covered under Social Security on or before December 31, 1987, and you worked under Federal covered employment in the last 60 months of Federal service; or
H. You were a Federal employee who chose to switch from the CSRS to employment covered under Social Security after December 31, 1987, you worked under Federal covered employment in the last 60 months or more during the period beginning January 1988, and ending with the first month of entitlement to spouse's benefits. The 60 months need not be consecutive but must be worked prior to entitlement to spouse's benefits.

1836.5 How much is the Social Security benefit reduced?

If you do not meet one of the exceptions above and you receive a government pension, your Social Security benefit is reduced by one of the following amounts:

A. If you were eligible for a government pension *before July 1983*, your Social Security benefits are reduced by 100 percent of your government pension; or

B. If you are eligible for a government pension *after June 1983*, your Social Security benefits are reduced by two-thirds the amount of your government pension.

Effective with benefits payable for December 1984 and later, the two-thirds reduction rate applies to all situations where the offset applies. This is true regardless of when you were first eligible for a government pension.

1837. CONVICTION FOR SUBVERSIVE ACTIVITIES

1837.1 How does the conviction of subversive activities affect your benefits?

If you are convicted of subversive activities, you may lose the right to Social Security benefits if you are convicted of an offense:

A. Under title 18 of the United States Code, chapter 37 (relating to espionage and censorship), chapter 105 (relating to sabotage), or chapter 115 (relating to treason, sedition, and subversive activities); or

B. Under section 4 of the Internal Security Act of 1950, as amended (relating to subversive activities).

1837.2 Can additional penalties be imposed?

Upon conviction of one of these offenses, the judge may impose an additional penalty that affects your right to monthly Social Security benefits. It does not matter whether the benefit is payable on your own or on anyone else's Social Security earnings record.

1838. WHAT EARNINGS ARE DISREGARDED WHEN A CONVICTED PERSON MAKES A CLAIM FOR BENEFITS?

If the additional penalty is imposed and you make a claim for monthly Social Security benefits, the following earnings creditable to any Social Security record on which you have claimed benefits are ignored:

A. All wages paid:
   1. For convictions prior to 1978-All wages paid in or before the calendar quarter in which you were convicted; or

2. For convictions after 1977-All wages paid in or before the calendar year in which you were convicted; and

B. All net earnings from self-employment derived in or before the taxable year in which you were convicted.

1839. PENALTY APPLIES TO CONVICTED PERSON ONLY

1839.1 Does the penalty apply to others entitled to benefits on the convicted person's record?

The penalty applies only to you as the person convicted of subversive activities. It does not affect the rights of others who are entitled to benefits on your Social Security earnings record. Their benefit rights and benefit amounts are based on your earnings before and after the conviction.

1839.2 Is the right to the lump-sum death payment affected by a conviction?

Your right to the lump-sum death payment is not affected by your conviction for subversive activities. The payment may be paid to you if you are otherwise entitled to the payment. The lump-sum death payment may also be paid on the full earnings record of a worker convicted of subversive activities.

1840. HOW DOES A PARDON FOR A PREVIOUS CONVICTION AFFECT YOUR BENEFITS?

If you were previously convicted of subversive activities, a pardon removes the additional penalty affecting your Social Security benefit rights. The penalty is removed the month after the month the pardon is granted. Thereafter, your right to benefits and the benefit amount is determined as if there had been no conviction. However, the pardon has no effect on your benefit rights for the months before the pardon.

1841. DEPORTATION OR REMOVAL OF RETIREMENT OR DISABILITY INSURANCE BENEFICIARY

1841.1 How does deportation or removal affect your benefits?

If you are deported or removed from the U.S. after September 1, 1954, you cannot receive retirement or disability benefits beginning with the month after the month the Department of Homeland Security notifies us of your deportation or removal. (If notification occurs before your entitlement, nonpayment applies with the first month of your entitlement.) For this nonpayment provision to apply:

A. Deportation must have been ordered under section 241(a) of the Immigration and Nationality Act (INA), in effect before the Act was amended in April 1997; or
B. Removal must have been ordered under sections 212(a)(6)(A) or 237(a) of the INA as amended in April 1997. Nonpayment applies until the month you are lawfully admitted to the U.S. for permanent residence after the deportation or removal.

1841.2 Are there any exceptions to nonpayment under the deportation/removal provisions?

The following deportations or removals do not affect payment of your retirement or disability benefits:

A. Deportations ordered under paragraph (3), (8), (9), (13), or (1)(C) of INA section 241(a);
B. Removals ordered under paragraph (1)(C) of INA section 237(a); or
C. Deportations or removals ordered under paragraph (1)(E) of INA sections 241(a) or 237(a), but only if we received notice of the deportation or removal before March 3, 2004.

1842. EFFECT OF DEPORTATION OR REMOVAL ON AUXILIARY OR SURVIVOR BENEFITS

1842.1 How does your deportation or removal affect benefits of others entitled on your earnings record?

Generally, others who are receiving benefits on your earnings record can continue to receive those benefits if you are deported or removed. However, if they are aliens, they cannot receive benefits on your record for any month they are outside the U.S. for any part of the month, regardless of how short the stay. If a person entitled to benefits on your earnings records is deported or removed (but you are not), the benefit that person receives on your record continues.

1842.2 Is the lump-sum death payment affected by deportation or removal?

The lump-sum death payment cannot be paid on the earnings record of a worker who dies in or after the month we receive notice of deportation or removal. However, nonpayment does not apply if the worker was lawfully admitted to the U.S. for permanent residence after deportation or removal but before death.

1843. ALIENS OUTSIDE THE U.S. FOR SIX MONTHS OR MORE

1843.1 If an alien lives outside the U.S. for more than six consecutive calendar months, how are benefits affected?

If you are an alien and you live outside the U.S. (as defined in §1824) for six full calendar months in a row, you may not receive monthly benefits effective with the seventh month, unless you meet one of the exceptions listed in §1845. This rule applies if you are a retirement and disability insurance beneficiary. It also applies to those entitled to benefits on your earnings record. For information on payments while you are outside the U.S., see https://www.ssa.gov/pubs/EN-05-10137.pdf and the *Payments Abroad Screening Tool* at https://www.ssa.gov/international/payments_outsideUS.html.

1843.2 Are benefits of others entitled to benefits on your record affected if you live outside the U.S. for more than six months?

Each beneficiary is treated individually. The suspension of one beneficiary's payments does not cause suspension of payments to any other beneficiary.

1843.3 How is the lump-sum death payment affected?

No lump-sum death payment is paid on the record of a worker who dies outside the U.S. if a monthly benefit was not (or would not have been) payable for the month before the month of death because of the worker's absence from the U.S.

1843.4 Is an alien entitled to special age 72 benefits?

To be entitled to special age 72 payments, an alien must have:

A. Been legally admitted for permanent residence in the U.S.; and
B. Resided in the U.S. continuously for five years.

1844. ABSENCE FROM THE U.S.

1844.1 When does a period of absence from the U.S. begin if you are not a United States citizen or national?

If you are an alien, a period of absence from the U.S. begins with the first full (24-hour) day you are outside the U.S.

1844.2 Are benefits affected if you return within 30 days?

If you are an alien and return to the U.S. before 30 full days in a row have passed, we consider your period of absence as broken. Your benefits are not affected.

EXAMPLE: Ms. Kopper leaves the U.S. on March 31 and returns on April 30. Since she is outside the U.S. for only 29 full days (April 1-April 29), her period of absence is considered broken and her benefits are not affected.

1844.3 Are benefits affected if you remain outside the U.S. for 30 days?

If you are an alien and have been outside the U.S. for 30 consecutive days, the 6 month period of absence begins and is counted from the first day of the first full month of absence. A return to the U.S. of at least 30 consecutive days causes a break in the 6 month period of absence. When the 6 month period is broken, it does not start again until you again leave the U.S. for at least 30 consecutive days. The 30 consecutive days is defined as 24 hours of each and every day of the period.

EXAMPLE: Miss Kelly leaves the U.S. on May 15, returns on August 1, and leaves again on August 20. Because she is outside the U.S. for (at least) 30 consecutive days, her August visit of less than 30 days does not break her period of absence and her benefits are suspended effective December, the seventh month after her departure month of May. If Miss Kelly had delayed her second departure until September 1, she would have been in the U.S. for 30 full days (August 2-August 31). The period of absence that began on May 16 would have been broken and a new period of absence would have begun effective September 2.

1844.4 Can benefits start again after they have been suspended?

If you are an alien, once your benefits have been suspended because of your absence from the U.S. for six consecutive calendar months or more, they may not start again until you return to the U.S., lawfully present, and remain for one full calendar month. NOTE: It is not always necessary for a beneficiary in alien suspense to return to the United States in order to receive payments. A beneficiary may reside in one of the Totalization countries (a country with which the U.S. has an international social security agreement) or reside in the United States. Your benefits continue if you reside in a country with which the U.S. has an international social security agreement and the withholding of benefits would be against the terms of that agreement (see §107).

EXAMPLE: Mr. Michael's benefits are suspended in October because of his absence from the U.S. for six consecutive calendar months or more. He returns to the U.S. on January 31. Mr. Michael's benefits are resumed for February, the first full calendar month he spends in the U.S. (Note that the number of days in the calendar month is not a factor.) He again leaves the U.S. on March 1 to live in Spain. Since Spain has an international social security agreement with the U.S., his benefits are continued as long as he lives in Spain.

1845. EXCEPTIONS TO ALIEN NONPAYMENT PROVISION

1845.1 What are the exceptions to the alien nonpayment provision?
There are exceptions to the alien nonpayment provision that permit the payment of benefits, even if you are absent from the U.S. The alien nonpayment provision does not apply if:

A. The worker on whose earnings record benefits are being paid:
   1. Had at least 40 quarters of coverage (see §1846 for limitations);
   2. Resided in the U.S. for a period or periods totaling 10 years or more (see §1846 for limitations);
   3. Had earnings from railroad employment that were counted for Social Security because no railroad benefits were payable on the basis of these earnings (see §1846 for limitations);
   4. Died while in military service of the U.S.; or
   5. Died as the result of a disease or injury certified by the Department of Veterans Affairs to have been incurred or aggravated in line of duty during a period of military service, and the service member was discharged or released under conditions other than dishonorable; or

B. The alien beneficiary (whether the insured worker or a person entitled to benefits on the worker's record):
   1. Was entitled (or upon filing an application would have been entitled) to a monthly benefit of any kind on the same Social Security earnings record for December 1956;
   2. Is outside the U.S. because he or she is in the active military or naval service of the U.S. (see §1846 for limitations);

3. Resides in a country with which the U.S. has an international social security agreement and the withholding of benefits would be against the terms of that agreement (see §107);
4. Is a citizen of a country that has a treaty with the U.S. requiring payment[s] of U.S. Social Security benefits to citizens of the other country (i.e. Germany, Greece, Ireland, Israel, Italy, Japan, and the Netherlands (survivor benefits only)); or
5. Is a citizen of a foreign country that has a social insurance system that is of general application in that country and under which (see §1846 for limitations):
   1. Periodic benefits are payable because of old age, retirement, or death; and
   2. Benefits are payable at the full rate to eligible citizens of the U.S. who are not citizens of that foreign country, even while outside the foreign country, and these benefits are payable regardless of how long they remain outside that country.

1845.2 What countries have social insurance or pension systems of general application?

The following countries, not already listed in §1845.1.B.4., currently have social insurance or pension systems that meet the conditions described in §1845.1.B.5.:

Albania
Antigua and Barbuda
Argentina
Austria
Australia
Bahamas
Barbados
Belgium
Belize
Bolivia
Bosnia-Herzegovina
Brazil

Latvia
Liechtenstein
Lithuania
Luxembourg
Macedonia
Malta
Marshall Islands
Mexico
Micronesia, Fed. States of
Monaco
Montenegro
Nicaragua

Bulgaria
Burkina Faso
Canada
Chile
Colombia
Costa Rica
Cote D'Ivoire
Croatia
Cyprus
Czech Republic
Denmark
Dominica
Dominican Republic
Ecuador
El Salvador
Finland
France
Gabon
Grenada
Guatemala
Guyana
Hungary
Iceland
Jamaica
Jordan
Norway
Palau
Panama
Peru
Philippines
Poland
Portugal
Romania
St. Kitts and Nevis
St. Lucia
St. Vincent and the Grenadines
Samoa
San Marino
Serbia
Slovakia
Slovenia
South Korea
Spain
Sweden
Switzerland
Trinidad - Tobago
Turkey
United Kingdom
Uruguay
Venezuela

1846. LIMITATIONS ON USE OF CERTAIN EXCEPTIONS

1846.1 What limitations apply to the exceptions to the alien non-payment provision?
Limitations apply to the use of several of the exceptions listed in §1845 beginning July, 1968. The exceptions in §1845 (A.1) and (A.2) cannot be applied to any alien who is:
A. A citizen of a country that has a social insurance or pension system of general application paying periodic old age, retirement, or death benefits that does not provide for full payment to eligible U.S. citizens who are outside the country; or
B. A citizen of a country that has no social insurance or pension system of general application and is a country to which Treasury Department

regulations currently or within 5 years prior to January 1968 prohibit the delivery of checks. These countries are:
C. The limitations on the exceptions in §1845 (A.1.) and (A.2.) apply to citizens of the countries shown below.

Algeria
Andorra
Angola
Armenia
Azerbaijan
Bahrain
Belarus
Benin
Brunei
Bulgaria
Cambodia
Comoros
Congo, Democratic Republic of the
Cuba*
Djibouti
Egypt
Equatorial Guinea
Estonia
Georgia
Guinea
Guinea-Bissau
Iran
Iraq
Kazakhstan
Kiribati
Kuwait
Kyrgyzstan
Libya
Maldives
Moldova

Mongolia
Mozambique
Namibia
Nauru
New Zealand
Niger
North Korea*
Oman
Papua-New Guinea
Paraguay
Qatar
Romania
Russia
Rwanda
Sao Tome and Principe
Saudi Arabia
Seychelles
Suriname
Syria
Tajikistan
Turkmenistan
Tuvalu
Ukraine
United Arab Emirates
Uzbekistan
Vanuatu
Vietnam
Zambia
Zimbabwe

*Treasury restrictions apply. See also §§1847-1848.

Note: This limitation applies only to those beneficiaries who are citizens of the countries listed above. It does not affect payment to other beneficiaries on the same earnings record who are not citizens of those countries.

1846.2 What limitations to the exceptions apply to aliens entitled to benefits on another person's record?

The exceptions listed in §§1845 (A.1), (A.2), (A.3), (B.2), and (B.5) cannot be applied to an alien entitled to spouse or child (auxiliary) or survivor benefits unless certain residency requirements are met. The auxiliary or survivor must have:

A. Resided in the U.S. for a total period of at least five years; and
B. Had a relationship during the five-year period with the worker as a parent, a child, or one or more of the following:
   1. Spouse;
   2. Widow(er);
   3. Divorced spouse; or
   4. Surviving divorced spouse.

Note: The U.S. residency requirements do not apply to aliens who are citizens or residents of a country with which the U.S. has an international social security agreement (see §107) except for Australian citizens who do not reside in an agreement country and Danish citizens who do not reside in an agreement country.

1846.3 How does a child meet the residency requirement, other than on his or her own?

A child of the worker who cannot meet the residency requirement on his or her own may meet it if the worker and the child's other parent, if any, each resided in the U.S. for a total period of at least five years. In addition, if the child was adopted, the worker must have adopted the child in the U.S., lived with the child in the U.S. and meet a support requirement. During the period the child lived with the worker in the U.S., the worker must have provided at least one-half of the child's support for a period:

A. Beginning before the child turns age 18; and
B. Consisting of the year immediately before the month the worker:
   1. Began a period of disability;
   2. Became entitled to retirement or disability insurance benefits; or
   3. Died.

1847. RESIDENCE IN A RESTRICTED COUNTRY

1847.1 What is a restricted country?
A restricted country is one to which payments cannot be sent to you or to anyone on your behalf either because of U.S. Treasury Department regulations or SSA restrictions (see §1848).

1847.2 Can you receive benefits if you live in a restricted country?
If you live in a country where U.S. Treasury Department regulations prohibit payment, you cannot receive benefits, nor can we send your payments to anyone on your behalf or to a financial institution for you. No exceptions to the nonpayment policy can be made for U.S. Treasury Department restricted countries.

Generally, if you live in an SSA restricted country, you cannot receive payments while you are in one of these countries, nor can we send your payments to anyone on your behalf or to a financial institution for you. However, exceptions can be made for certain eligible beneficiaries in SSA restricted countries. For information on payments while you are outside the U.S., see https://www.ssa.gov/pubs/EN-05-10137.pdf.

1848. WHAT ARE THE RESTRICTED COUNTRIES?

The U.S. Treasury Department regulations prohibit sending payments to you or to anyone on your behalf if you are in the following countries:

Cuba
North Korea

Social Security restrictions prohibit sending payments to you or to anyone on your behalf if you are in the following countries unless you meet an exception for certain eligible beneficiaries:

Azerbaijan, Belarus, Kazakhstan, Kyrgyzstan, Tajikistan, Turkmenistan, or Uzbekistan

1849. WHEN CAN YOU RECEIVE BENEFITS YOU EARNED WHILE YOU LIVED IN A RESTRICTED COUNTRY?

If you are a citizen or national of the United States and are a resident in a U.S. Treasury restricted country (Cuba or North Korea), you can receive all of your payments that were withheld once you leave that country and go to another country where the U.S. Treasury can send payments. Generally, if you are not a citizen or national of the United States, you cannot receive any payments for months in which you are a resident of a U.S.

Treasury restricted country, even though you leave that country and satisfy all other requirements.

If you are a resident in an SSA restricted country (see §1848) and do not qualify for an exception (see §1847.2), once you leave that country and go to another country where we can send payments, you can receive all the benefits for which you were eligible but were withheld because of Social Security restrictions.

1850. CONFINEMENT IN A CORRECTIONAL INSTITUTION

1850.1 Do you receive benefits if you are in a correctional institution?

Your benefits are withheld for any month, or any part of a month, you are confined for more than 30 continuous days in a correctional institution in the U.S. based on a conviction.

1850.2 Are your benefits withheld even if you have a mental impairment?

Your benefits are also withheld if you are confined by court order for more than 30 continuous days to an institution in the U.S. at public expense in connection with a verdict or finding that you are:

A. Guilty but insane with respect to a criminal offense;
B. Not guilty of a criminal offense by reason of insanity;
C. Incompetent to stand trial under an allegation of a criminal offense; or
D. Found to be under similar conditions (such as mental disease, mental defect, or mental incompetence) with respect to a criminal offense.

1850.3 Are there any other situations when benefits are withheld because you are confined in an institution?

Your benefits are withheld if, after completing a sentence based on conviction of a crime, an element of which was sexual activity, you are confined by court order for more than 30 continuous days in a U.S. institution at public expense based on a finding that you are a sexually dangerous person, sexual predator, or a similar finding.

1851. WHAT EVENTS END BENEFITS?

In addition to the circumstances discussed in the preceding sections that can cause deductions from or suspension of benefit payments, there are events that can end your entitlement to benefits. They are provided in the chart below.

Ends Payment to These Beneficiaries:
(Benefits end with the month before the month the event occurs unless otherwise noted)

The occurrence of this event...	Retired Worker	Disabled Worker	Spouse	Divorced Spouse	Child Under 18	Child 18-19 full-time Student	Disabled Child 18 or Over	Widow-(er)	Disabled Widow-(er)	Surviving Divorced Spouse	Mother or Father	Surviving Divorced Mother or Father	Parent
Turning age 18 and not a full-time student or disabled.	–	–	–	–	X	–	–	–	–	–	–	–	–
Turning age 19.	–	–	–	–	–	X (9)	–	–	–	–	–	–	–
Turning age 65.	–	X (1)	–	–	–	–	–	–	–	–	–	–	–
Student not in full-time school attendance and not disabled.	–	–	–	–	–	X (12)	–	–	–	–	–	–	–
Disability of worker getting disability benefits ends.	X (2)	–	X (2)	X (2)	X	X	X	–	–	–	–	–	–
Disability of beneficiary ends.	–	–	–	–	–	–	X (3)	–	X (3)	X (11)	–	–	–
Death of worker.	X	–	X (4)	X (10)	–	–	–	–	–	–	–	–	–
Death of beneficiary other than worker.	–	X	X	X	X	X	X	X	X	X	X	X	X
Divorce or annulment (final decree).	–	–	X (5)	–	–	–	–	–	–	–	–	X	–

(Continued)

Ends Payment to These Beneficiaries:
(Benefits end with the month before the month the event occurs unless otherwise noted)

The occurrence of this event...	Retired Worker	Disabled Worker	Spouse	Divorced Spouse	Child Under 18	Child 18-19 full-time Student	Disabled Child 18 or Over	Widow-(er)	Disabled Widow-(er)	Surviving Divorced Spouse	Mother or Father	Surviving Divorced Mother or Father	Parent
Entitlement to retirement or disability insurance benefit based on primary insurance amount equal to or exceeding the worker's primary insurance amount.	–	–	X	X	–	–	–	–	–	–	–	–	–
Entitlement to retirement insurance benefit equal to or exceeding amount of survivor's benefit.	–	–	–	–	–	–	–	X	–	X	X	X	X
Entitlement to widow(er)'s insurance benefit.	–	–	–	–	–	–	–	–	–	–	X	X	–

(Continued)

Ends Payment to These Beneficiaries:

(Benefits end with the month before the month the event occurs unless otherwise noted)

The occurrence of this event...	Retired Worker	Disabled Worker	Spouse	Divorced Spouse	Child Under 18	Child 18-19 full-time Student	Disabled Child 18 or Over	Widow-(er)	Disabled Widow-(er)	Surviving Divorced Spouse	Mother or Father	Surviving Divorced Mother or Father	Parent
Certification of entitlement of another person as legal spouse.	–	–	X (6)	–	–	–	–	X (6)	X (6)	–	X (6)	–	–
Marriage or remarriage.	–	–	–(6)	X (7)	X	X	X (7)	–	–	–	X (7)	X (7)	X (7)
Valid marriage to someone other than worker.	–	–	X (6)	–	–	–	–	–	–	–	–	–	–
No child of worker under age 16 or age 16 or over and disabled.	–	–	X (8)	–	–	–	–	–	–	–	X	X	–
No natural or adopted child of beneficiary entitled on worker's earnings record.	–	–	–	–	–	–	–	–	–	–	–	X	–

(1) Retirement insurance benefit payable instead.
(2) The last month of entitlement is the second month after the month in which the disability ends, or the month before the month in which the individual turns age 65, whichever occurs first.

(Continued)

(3) The last month of entitlement is the second month after the month in which the disability ends or the beneficiary is under age 65.

(4) Widow's or widower's benefits usually payable.

(5) Except where spouse had attained age 62 at the same time of the divorce and her marriage to the worker had been in effect for 10 years immediately preceding the effective date of the final divorce.

(6) If beneficiary is entitled as "de facto" spouse, that is, if he or she is qualified for benefits only under the provisions explained in §§306.1.B, or 402.1.B.

(7) See Chapters Chapter 3 and Chapter 4 for information on when marriage to another beneficiary does not end benefits.

(8) Unless spouse is at least full retirement age (FRA), or is at least age 62 and has elected to receive reduced benefits.

(9) If the student has not completed the requirements for a secondary school diploma or equivalent certificate, benefits continue through the month the course is completed or for 2 months after attainment of age 19, whichever is less.

(10) Surviving divorced wife's benefits usually payable.

(11) Only if entitlement is as a disabled surviving divorced spouse.

(12) A student, otherwise in full-time attendance, is deemed not to be in full-time attendance if the student meets the requirements for suspension of benefits as required by prisoner or fugitive felon provisions (see §1850).

1852. HOW DOES THE MARRIAGE OF ONE BENEFICIARY TO ANOTHER AFFECT BENEFITS?

The effect of one beneficiary's marriage to another is summarized in the following chart:

If you are the following type of beneficiary…	Then marrying another Social Security beneficiary has the following effect…
Retired or disabled worker, widow(er), disabled widow(er), surviving divorced spouse or disabled surviving divorced spouse	No effect on entitlement.
Child under age 18 or student	Always terminates entitlement.
Parent or divorced spouse	No effect on entitlement unless marriage is to a retired or disabled worker, a child under age 18, or a student, in which case benefits of the parent or divorced spouse terminate.
Mother, father, surviving divorced mother/father or childhood disability beneficiary	No effect on entitlement unless marriage is to a child under age 18 or a student, in which case both benefits terminate.

1853. REINSTATEMENT OF BENEFITS WHEN MARRIAGE TERMINATES

1853.1 Can your benefits start again if your marriage ends?

Your benefits may start again under the following conditions:

A. If your marriage is voided, your benefits may begin again as of the month they ended because of the marriage, subject to the rules on administrative finality (see §2016); or

B. If your marriage has been annulled from the beginning in accordance with State law by a court having jurisdiction over the matter, your benefits can be reinstated as of the month the decree of annulment was issued. You must file a timely application.

1853.2 Who may have benefits on a prior spouse's earnings record in the event of remarriage?

If benefit rights ended because of remarriage, the following individuals may also have benefits on the prior spouse's Social Security earnings record:

A. Divorced spouse;
B. Mother or father;
C. Widow(er);
D. Surviving divorced spouse; or
E. Surviving divorced mother or father.

1854. CERTAIN OUTSTANDING WARRANTS

SSA will not pay a monthly benefit to any individual for any month when the individual has an unsatisfied arrest warrant for more than 30 continuous days for a crime, or attempted crime, of flight to avoid prosecution or confinement, escape from custody, and flight-escape. In most jurisdictions these crimes are felonies or, in jurisdictions that do not classify crimes as felonies, a crime that is punishable by death or imprisonment for more than one year (regardless of the actual sentence imposed).

SSA will find a good cause exception to this non-payment rule if a court finds the person not guilty, the charges are dismissed, a warrant for arrest is vacated, or there are similar exonerating circumstances identified by the court. SSA will also apply the good cause exception to the non-payment rule if the individual establishes to the satisfaction of SSA that he or she was the victim of identity fraud and the warrant was issued on this basis.

SSA also may apply the good cause exception to the non-payment rule if the arrest warrant was for a crime that was non-violent and not drug-related, and in the case of probation or parole violators, both the violation and the underlying offense were non-violent and not drug-related.

CHAPTER 19

Underpayments and Overpayments

TABLE OF CONTENTS

1900. What is an underpayment?
1901. Is a written request required for an unpaid benefit to be paid to a living person?
1902. Unpaid Amounts Owed to a Deceased Person
1903. Legal Representatives
1904. What is an overpayment?
1905. Written Notice of Overpayments
1906. Liability for Repayments
1907. How are overpayments recovered?
1908. Refunds of Overpayments
1909. Adjustment of Benefits to Recover Overpayments
1910. Rate of Withholding
1911. Compromise Settlement of an Overpayment
1912. Recovery by Civil Suit
1913. Recovery Efforts
1914. Relief from Making Repayment (Waiver)
1915. When is an individual "without fault" in receiving an overpayment?
1916. What factors does SSA consider in deciding whether a person is without fault?

1917. When is an individual "at fault" in receiving an overpayment?
1918. Defeat the Purpose as a Factor in Waiver
1919. What is the definition of "against equity and good conscience"?
1920. What is the definition of "impede effective or efficient administration" of the SSI program?
1921. Waiver of Recovery from Estate of Deceased Person
1922. If SSA changes its position on a prior decision, can recovery of overpayments be attempted?
1923. If the Department of Defense reports a service member's death on active duty but the report is later found to be incorrect, what is the effect on benefits paid?

1900. WHAT IS AN UNDERPAYMENT?

An underpayment is an amount that is owed to a person and that has not yet been paid. Underpayments usually result from unpaid benefits that have accumulated or checks that have not been cashed.

1901. IS A WRITTEN REQUEST REQUIRED FOR AN UNPAID BENEFIT TO BE PAID TO A LIVING PERSON?

No, a written request is not required. We generally pay an unpaid amount owed to a living person automatically. It may be paid in a single check or added to other benefits that are payable.

1902. UNPAID AMOUNTS OWED TO A DECEASED PERSON

Can we release an underpayment to a beneficiary or recipient who is not receiving benefits or payments because he or she is confined to a correctional facility or institution because of a court order, or has an unsatisfied arrest warrant for flight or escape?

No, we cannot release the underpayment. Once the beneficiary or recipient is no longer confined to a correctional facility or institution because of a court order, or no longer has an unsatisfied arrest warrant for flight or escape, we can release the underpayment to him or her.

See Section 1854 for additional information on warrants that qualify.

1902.1 Is a written request required to obtain payments owed to a deceased person?

We pay unpaid amounts owed to a deceased person automatically without a separate written request if our records contain sufficient information to determine the identity and current address of all people entitled to the underpayment.

1902.2 If complete information is not available on all those entitled to the underpayment, what should be done?

If complete information is not available, we need a separate written request from at least one person entitled to receive a portion of the underpayment.

1902.3 What is the order of payment for people entitled to the underpayment for retirement, survivors, and disability insurance (RSDI)?

Payments are made in the following order:

A. The widow(er) of the underpaid person if:
   1. Living in the same household with the underpaid person at the time of death; or
   2. Entitled to a monthly benefit on the same earnings record as the underpaid person for the month of death.
B. The child or children of the underpaid person entitled to monthly benefits on the same earnings record as the underpaid person for the month of death. If there is more than one entitled child, payment is made in equal parts to each child;
C. The parent or parents of the underpaid person entitled to monthly benefits on the same earnings record as the underpaid person for the month of death. If there is more than one entitled parent, payment is made in equal parts to each parent;
D. A widow(er) who does not meet the requirements of (A);
E. A child or children who do not meet the requirements of (B). If there is more than one child, payment is made in equal parts to each child;
F. A parent or parents who do not meet the requirements of (C). If there is more than one parent, payment is made in equal parts to each parent; and
G. The legal representative of the underpaid person's estate.

A surviving divorced spouse does not qualify as the "widow(er)" under this provision.

1902.4 How are Supplemental Security Income (SSI) payments made?

We pay Supplemental Security Income (SSI) underpayments to a surviving eligible spouse or surviving spouse who was living in the same household with the underpaid person at any time in the month of death or the preceding six months.

1902.5 How are payments made for a disabled or blind child?

If the underpaid person was a disabled or blind child, underpayments are payable to a surviving parent(s) who was living in the same household with the child at any time in the month of death or the preceding six months.

1902.6 Can we release an underpayment to a beneficiary or recipient who is not receiving payments because he or she is a prisoner, fugitive felon, or probation or parole violator?

No, we cannot release the underpayment. However, once the beneficiary or recipient can receive payments because he or she is no longer a prisoner, fugitive felon, or probation or parole violator, we can release the underpayment to him or her.

1903. LEGAL REPRESENTATIVES

1903.1 What is the definition of legal representative?

As used in this Chapter, "legal representative" means an administrator or executor or other person who qualifies under a State statute (or, where applicable, the law of a foreign country) to receive payment on behalf of the estate.

1903.2 What must a person do to become a legal representative?

In order to be a legal representative, a person acting on behalf of an unadministered estate must:

A. Prove to us that payment will relieve us of legal liability to any other person; and

B. Provide proof of appointment or other evidence showing authorization under a State statute (or, where applicable, the law of a foreign country).

Note: Under the SSI program, an underpayment cannot be paid to an estate.

1904. WHAT IS AN OVERPAYMENT?

An overpayment is an excess payment. It is the amount by which payments exceed the amount that should have been paid for that period.

1905. WRITTEN NOTICE OF OVERPAYMENTS

1905.1 How are individuals notified of overpayments?

When we decide an overpayment has been made, we send a written notice to the overpaid individual (and/or the representative payee, if any, and the legal representative, if any).

1905.2 What information is in the notice?

If you receive an overpayment notification, you will find the following information:

A. The amount overpaid, including correct and incorrect amounts for each month in the overpayment period;
B. How and when the overpayment occurred;
C. Your right to appeal (to request reconsideration of) the overpayment determination (see Chapter 20);
D. Action required by you:
   1. *For RSDI or black lung benefits*: a request for full, immediate refund, unless the overpayment can be withheld from the next month's benefit, and the proposed adjustment (see §1909) if adjustment is available. Adjustment action is effective with the second month following the date of the notice unless full refund or a request for reconsideration, waiver, or a different rate of adjustment is received within 30 days. (See §1910, §1914, and §2004.)
   2. *For SSI payments*: a request for full, immediate refund, and the proposed rate of adjustment if payment continues. Adjustment begins with the first month occurring 60 days after the date of the overpayment notice, unless a full refund or request for reconsideration, waiver, or a different rate of adjustment is received within 30 days;
E. Your right to request waiver of recovery of the overpayment (see §1914);
F. In the case of overpaid RSDI, the automatic scheduling of a personal conference if the waiver request cannot be approved;
G. The availability of:
   1. A different rate of adjustment when full withholding of RSDI benefits is proposed, or for SSI payments, a different rate of adjustment;
   2. Installment payment when adjustment is not currently available;
   3. Availability of cross program recovery when you are receiving benefits under more than one SSA program (e.g., retirement benefits, or SSI payments, or disability benefits).
H. Mandatory cross program recovery when you are no longer receiving SSI payments but are receiving benefits under another SSA program (e.g., retirement benefits or disability benefits);

I. The need to notify a Social Security office promptly if you want reconsideration, waiver, a lesser rate of adjustment, or to repay by installments or cross-program adjustment; and

J. The appropriate penalty notification, if applicable.

1906. LIABILITY FOR REPAYMENTS

1906.1 Who is liable for repayments?

A beneficiary and/or a representative payee receiving retirement, survivors or disability insurance, benefits on behalf of a beneficiary or SSI, may be equally liable for repayment of any overpayment received, as follows:

A. The beneficiary is liable if he or she received the benefit of the monies;

B. The representative payee is personally liable if he or she:
   1. Was at fault in creating the overpayment; or
   2. Did not apply the monies for the beneficiary's use and benefit.

1906.2 Can other individuals be liable for overpayments?

Liability for repayment may move from the overpaid beneficiary or payee to certain others in particular situations:

A. If the overpaid beneficiary or payee has died, the estate is liable for repayment. We may ask the legal representative to make a refund, or we may withhold benefits due the estate. We may also require the recipients of the estate to refund an overpaid amount to the extent of funds received from the estate; and

B. If an RSDI overpayment cannot be recovered from the overpaid beneficiary, the payee, or the estate, benefits may be withheld from other persons entitled to benefits on the same earnings record.

However, Effective 12/04/2008, a representative payee who receives payments on the beneficiary's behalf after the death of the beneficiary is solely responsible for repayment of the overpayment.

Since the representative payee is solely liable for these types of overpayments, we will not recover these types of overpayments from the representative payee's spouse, the estate of the spouse, or the auxiliaries of the overpaid representative payee, or the deceased beneficiary's estate.

1906.3 Who is liable for repayment of SSI benefits?

An individual and spouse who receive SSI payments as a married couple are equally liable if either is overpaid. If overpayment of SSI benefits was made to an alien, the alien and the person who sponsored the alien for admission to the U.S. are equally liable if the overpayment resulted from the sponsor's failure to provide correct information about income and resources. (See §2170.)

Note: When an alien sponsored under a legally enforceable agreement of support receives SSI payments, the individual sponsoring the alien SSI recipient is liable to repay the entire amount of the SSI payments made to the alien recipient.

1907. HOW ARE OVERPAYMENTS RECOVERED?

Overpayments are generally recovered by means of:

A. Refund;
B. Adjustment or withholding of benefits payable;
C. Compromise settlement;
D. Civil suit; or
E. Existing debt collection tools, including tax refund offset, administrative offset, administrative wage garnishment, Federal salary offset and credit bureau reporting.
F. Adjustment of SSA benefits to recover an SSI overpayment when the SSI recipient is no longer receiving SSI payments.

1908. REFUNDS OF OVERPAYMENTS

1908.1 When are refunds of overpayments requested?

We request refunds as soon as the overpayment is detected.

1908.2 How should refund payments be made?

If you were overpaid, make your refund payment by check or money order to "Social Security Administration, Claim No. __." For RSDI debts, and for SSI debts when the SSI *individual is not receiving monthly payments*, we accept credit card refund payments. We will provide a pre-addressed envelope for return of the check, money order, or credit card authorized form. Refund payments are sent to the Social Security Administration, Mid-Atlantic Program Service Center, P.O. Box 3430, Philadelphia, PA 19122-9985.

1908.3 What happens if SSA does not receive the full refund?

If we do not receive a full refund, we may withhold benefits as described in §1910 in an amount required to cover the overpayment. (See §134 for return of benefit checks.) If you do not send the full refund and the overpayment cannot be withheld from benefits as described in §1910, you may arrange an installment plan of repayment. If you have a SSI overpayment and if you receive SSA payments after your SSI payments end, we will adjust your SSA benefits to recover your SSI overpayment.

1908.4 What should be done with uncashed benefit checks?

If an overpayment has been made, return any benefit checks on hand.

1909. ADJUSTMENT OF BENEFITS TO RECOVER OVERPAYMENTS

1909.1 How are benefits adjusted to recover overpayments for RSDI programs?

We may adjust or withhold benefits to recover an overpayment for benefits payable under the RSDI programs as follows:

A. The amount of the overpayment may be withheld from any benefits to which the overpaid person is entitled as follows:
   1. From his or her own earnings record or on the earnings record of any other person; or
   2. From benefits payable to others on the earnings record on which the overpayment was made.

1909.2 If the overpaid person is deceased, how is the repayment made?

When the overpaid person is deceased, we may withhold the amount of the overpayment from the lump-sum death payment payable on deceased's earnings record. If a lump-sum death payment has already been made despite an overpayment, the individual who received the payment must refund it.

1909.3 Are overpayments recovered by adjustment against SSI payments?

We may recover overpayments under RSDI programs by adjustment against an SSI payment.

1909.4 How are overpayments under the SSI program recovered?

For benefits payable under the SSI program, we may adjust or withhold benefits to recover overpayments as follows:

A. Adjustment may be made against any payment due an overpaid individual or eligible spouse (as defined in §2110) or the estate of either or both if benefits have not been recovered prior to the death of either or both;

B. Overpayments are adjusted against any payments due an eligible individual and eligible spouse (as defined in §2110) before any further payment is made if the overpayment was created by the disposition of resources or is related to non-excluded resources; (See §§2148-2166.)
C. Overpayments are never adjusted against Medicare payments but will be adjusted against benefits payable under the RSDI programs if one of the following conditions applies:
  1. Effective 01/01 adjustment will be made against benefits payable under the RSDI program to recover SSI overpayments when it is not possible to adjust benefits payable under the SSI program; or
  2. The overpayment resulted from the deeming of income or resources to an alien from the person who sponsored him or her for admission to the U.S. (See §2170.)

1910. RATE OF WITHHOLDING

1910.1 What is the rate of withholding under the RSDI programs?
If you are under the RSDI program, we withhold all benefits until the overpayment is recovered, unless:
A. You request a lesser withholding; and
B. You demonstrate that full withholding will cause financial hardship.

1910.2 What is the rate of withholding under the SSI program?
If you are under the SSI program, your benefits are withheld at the lesser rate of:
A. Your entire monthly benefit; or
B. An amount equal to 10 percent of your total countable income (including SSI and State supplementary payments). (See Chapter 21.)

1911. COMPROMISE SETTLEMENT OF AN OVERPAYMENT

1911.1 What is a compromise settlement?
A compromise settlement occurs when we accept an amount less than the full overpayment because full recovery cannot be accomplished and forgive repayment of the rest of the debt.

1911.2 What law permits compromise settlements?
The Federal Claims Collection Act of 1966 permits Federal agencies to arrange compromise settlements of overpayment claims.

1911.3 Can compromise settlements be appealed?

No, compromise settlements cannot be appealed because the settlement is at our discretion.

1911.4 When are compromise settlements acceptable?

Generally, we accept a compromise when one of the following conditions exists:

A. The debtor is unable to pay the full amount within a reasonable time;
B. The Government is unable to enforce collection of the full amount within a reasonable time;
C. The Government is unable to obtain full recovery through court action because of the legal issues involved or there is a legitimate dispute as to the facts; or
D. The cost of collecting the claim is likely to exceed the amount to be recovered.

1912. RECOVERY BY CIVIL SUIT

1912.1 Can a civil suit be used to recover overpayments?

Yes, a civil suit can be used to recover an overpayment. A civil suit is a legal proceeding that can be filed in a Federal court of law.

1912.2 What Federal agency handles civil suits for overpayments?

Appropriate cases are referred to the Department of Justice for civil action.

1912.3 When must civil suits for overpayments be filed?

Generally, we must file a civil suit before the later of:

A. Six years after an overpayment has been made; or
B. One year after a final decision has been rendered in an administrative proceeding.

1912.4 Who can be sued for overpayments?

The representative payee and the beneficiary may both be sued in a civil suit if both are liable.

1913. RECOVERY EFFORTS

1913.1 When does SSA stop trying to recover overpayments?

The Federal Claims Collection Act of 1966 permits SSA to stop trying to recover an overpayment from you when the overpayment:

A. Does not exceed $100,000;
B. Was not received as a result of fraud; and
C. Any one of the following conditions also exists:
   1. Collection of a significant portion of the overpayment cannot be accomplished by compromise settlement or civil suit considering your current and future financial prospects;
   2. You cannot be located after diligent search; or
   3. The cost of further collection efforts is likely to exceed the amount recovered.

1913.2 What law permits recovery of delinquent Title II debts by withholding Federal income tax refunds?

The Omnibus Budget Reconciliation Act of 1990 permits SSA to have the Department of the Treasury (Treasury) withhold or reduce (called "offsetting") Federal income tax refunds to collect delinquent Title II debts.

1913.3 What law permits recovery of delinquent Title XVI debts by withholding Federal income tax refunds?

The Deficit Reduction Act of 1984 permits SSA to have the Treasury offset Federal income tax refunds to collect delinquent Title XVI debts. We use this debt collection technique to recover debts owed by former beneficiaries and recipients.

1913.4 What law permits recovery of delinquent Title II/Title XVI debts by Administrative Wage Garnishment (AWG)?

The Debt Collection Improvement Act of 1996 authorized Federal agencies to recover delinquent non-tax debts by AWG. SSA regulations implemented AWG under guidance provided by the Department of Treasury.

1913.5 How are delinquent debtors selected for AWG?

Delinquent debtors selected for AWG is based on the following criteria:
- You are not entitled to Title II or Title XVI benefits or Medicare based on disability, *and*
- You are not active in the Ticket to Work and Self-Sufficiency Program, *and*
- Your social security number is available, *and*
- Your debt is $200 or more, *and*
- Your debt is past-due, *and*

- The debt was established after you attained age 18, *and*
- You have regular wages, state and local government wages, non-profit or railroad wages from a domestic employer, *and*
- You were not involuntarily separated from employment, or if you were, you have been re-employed continuously for at least 12 months, *and*
- You do not have a pending waiver or appeal, *and*
- Cross Program Recovery is not available.

1913.6 How are debtors notified of SSA's intent to use AWG?

If we plan to use AWG, SSA will send a notice to inform you. The notice provides due process rights associated with AWG.

1913.7 How are delinquent debtors referred to the Treasury?

The selection and referral of delinquent debtors to the Treasury is a weekly automated operation, that results in offsets on a continual basis. We select debtors for this program based on many criteria, including the following:

A. You must be at least 18 years old;
B. The debt is greater than $25;
C. The debt has been delinquent for less than 10 years;
D. You are no longer receiving Social Security payments; and
E. You are alive.

1913.8 How are debtors notified of SSA's intent to refer a debt to Treasury for collection through income tax refunds?

If we refer your debt to the Treasury for offset, SSA will send a notice to inform you. The notice provides due process rights and gives you the chance to repay the debt.

1913.9 What is the definition of administrative offset?

"Administrative offset" is the withholding or reduction of Federal payments other than tax refunds.

1913.10 When can SSA use administrative offset and credit bureau reporting to collect unrecoverable Title II debts?

The Debt Collection Improvement Act of 1996 permits SSA to use administrative offset and credit bureau reporting to collect unrecoverable Title II debts. The Foster Care Independence Act of 1999 permits SSA to use these tools to collect unrecoverable Title XVI debts. Treasury performs this activity for us. Credit bureau reporting involves notifying credit bureaus that a former Title II beneficiary or Title XVI recipient owes SSA a debt that has been determined to be unrecoverable.

1913.11 How are debtors referred to the Treasury for administrative offset and to credit bureaus?

Selection and referral of debts to the Treasury for administrative offset is a weekly automated operation. For credit bureau reporting, selection and referral to credit bureaus is a monthly automated operation.

1913.12 How are debtors notified of SSA's intent to refer a debt to the Treasury for administrative offset and credit bureau reporting?

If you are selected for these collection techniques, SSA will send a notice to inform you. The notices provide due process rights and give you the chance to repay the debt to avoid the administrative offset and credit bureau reporting.

1914. RELIEF FROM MAKING REPAYMENT (WAIVER)

1914.1 What is the definition of waiver?

A "waiver" occurs when you are given relief from making repayment. Your debt does not have to be paid.

1914.2 When is waiver granted?

We may grant a waiver when:
A. You are without fault, and
B. Recovery or adjustment:
   1. Would defeat the purpose of the program involved; or
   2. Would be against equity and good conscience; or
   3. For the SSI program only, would impede efficient or effective administration of the program because of the small amount involved.

1914.3 When can waiver be requested?

You may request a waiver of recovery of an overpayment at any time.

1914.4 What happens when SSA receives a request for waiver?

When we receive a request for waiver, all recovery actions stop until your request is either approved or denied and you had the opportunity for a personal conference.

1914.5 What happens if the request is approved?

If your request is approved, you do not have to repay the overpayment. We may refund any monies we previously withheld to recover the overpayment.

1915. WHEN IS AN INDIVIDUAL "WITHOUT FAULT" IN RECEIVING AN OVERPAYMENT?

"Without fault" means that the overpayment did not result from your lack of care, such as:

A. Furnishing full and accurate information affecting basic rights to benefit payment;
B. Complying with annual earnings and other reporting requirements; and
C. Returning checks believed not due.

Even if we caused the overpayment, you must show that you are without fault.

1916. WHAT FACTORS DOES SSA CONSIDER IN DECIDING WHETHER A PERSON IS WITHOUT FAULT?

In deciding whether you are without fault in causing an overpayment, we consider your:

A. Understanding of the reporting requirements and of the obligation to return payments which are not due;
B. Knowledge of the occurrence of events which should have been reported;
C. Efforts and opportunities to comply with the reporting requirements; and
D. Ability to comply with the reporting requirements i.e., any physical, mental, educational, or linguistic limitations (including having difficulty with the English language).

1917. WHEN IS AN INDIVIDUAL "AT FAULT" IN RECEIVING AN OVERPAYMENT?

You are "at fault" if the overpayment results from:

A. A willful misstatement;
B. Hiding of facts or fraud which directly or indirectly caused the overpayment;
C. Your failure to furnish information that you knew or should have known was important; or
D. Acceptance of a payment that you knew or should have known was incorrect.

1918. DEFEAT THE PURPOSE AS A FACTOR IN WAIVER

1918.1 When does recovery of an overpayment in the RSDI programs defeat the purpose of the program?

Recovery of an overpayment of the RSDI programs defeats the purpose of the program if:

A. You need substantially all of your income (including Social Security benefits) to meet ordinary and necessary living expenses;

B. Refund or adjustment of benefits would reduce your total assets to:
 1. Below $3,000, if you have no dependents; or
 2. Below $5,000, you have one dependent. For each subsequent dependent, beginning with the second, an additional $600 is allowed; and

C. You receive any type of cash welfare payments (including SSI payments).

1918.2 When does recovery of an overpayment in the SSI program defeat the purpose of the program?

Recovery of an overpayment in the SSI program defeats the purpose of the program if refund or adjustment of benefits would deprive you of income or financial resources needed for ordinary and necessary living expenses.

1918.3 How is ordinary and necessary living expenses defined?

An individual currently receiving SSI payments is considered to have met the financial requirement if your total income:

A. Does not exceed the applicable Federal Benefit Rate (see §2113(A)); *plus*

B. Any State supplement (see §2106); *plus*

C. The applicable monthly income disregard (i.e., $20 for a non-working recipient or $20 plus $65 for a working recipient).

Note: Regardless of a person's financial situation, recovery cannot defeat the purpose of any program to the extent of incorrect or overpaid funds in the person's possession when he or she is notified of the overpayment. This means that if the $500 in a person's bank account is the $500 payment he should not have received, he is able to repay $500 of the overpayment. Because the person was not due the money that was deposited into the bank account, no harm is suffered by refunding the money to the Agency.

1919. WHAT IS THE DEFINITION OF "AGAINST EQUITY AND GOOD CONSCIENCE"?

"Against equity and good conscience" can be established regardless of your financial ability to repay or possession of any part of the overpayment when you:

A. Changed your position for the worse or neglected a valuable right because of your reliance upon a notice that a payment would be made or because of the overpayment itself (e.g., a beneficiary, relying on benefit payments, signed a lease on a more expensive apartment or retired from a job and cannot get it back);

B. Were living in a separate household from the overpaid person at the time of the overpayment and did not receive the overpayment (RSDI overpayments only); or

C. Were a member of an eligible couple legally separated or living apart and did not receive the overpayment (SSI overpayments only).

In these cases, waiver would be granted and you do not need to repay the overpayment debt.

1920. WHAT IS THE DEFINITION OF "IMPEDE EFFECTIVE OR EFFICIENT ADMINISTRATION" OF THE SSI PROGRAM?

"Impede effective or efficient administration" of the SSI program means that the average cost of recovering the overpayment equals or exceeds the amount of the overpayment.

1921. WAIVER OF RECOVERY FROM ESTATE OF DECEASED PERSON

1921.1 When can the estate of a deceased person be granted waiver?

The estate of a deceased person may be relieved from repayment if:

A. The overpaid person was without fault; and

B. Recovery during the lifetime of the overpaid person would have been against equity and good conscience.

1921.2 Can waiver of recovery from an estate be based on defeat the purpose?

No, waiver of recovery from an estate cannot be based on "defeat the purpose" even if waiver of recovery on that basis would have been proper during the overpaid person's lifetime. This is because an estate cannot be considered to require income for ordinary and necessary living expenses.

1922. IF SSA CHANGES ITS POSITION ON A PRIOR DECISION, CAN RECOVERY OF OVERPAYMENTS BE ATTEMPTED?

Yes, we can reopen a case and make a different decision under the rules given in §2016. Payments made on the basis of the first decision may then be incorrect and constitute overpayments. Such overpayments are subject to recovery unless waiver is granted.

1923. IF THE DEPARTMENT OF DEFENSE REPORTS A SERVICE MEMBER'S DEATH ON ACTIVE DUTY BUT THE REPORT IS LATER FOUND TO BE INCORRECT, WHAT IS THE EFFECT ON BENEFITS PAID?

If the Department of Defense makes an incorrect report of the death of a service member on active duty, payments made to survivors are considered correct for the months before we were informed that the service member was alive. Repayments do not need to be made.

CHAPTER 20
Determinations and the Administrative Review Process

TABLE OF CONTENTS

2000. Administrative Review Process
2001. Time Limits for Requesting Review
2002. Initial Determinations
2003. Administrative Actions that are not Initial Determinations
2004. Reconsideration
2005. The Reconsideration Process
2006. Disability Hearing
2007. Hearing by an Administrative Law Judge (ALJ)
2008. ALJ Actions
2009. Notice of Hearing
2010. Pre-Hearing or Post-Hearing Conferences
2011. Assistance from the Social Security Office
2012. ALJ's Decision
2013. Review by the Appeals Council
2014. Appeals Council Procedures
2015. Extension of Time for Filing
2016. Time Limit for Reopening Final Determinations and Decisions
2017. Representation of Claimant
2018. Representatives' Fees
2019. Direct Payment of Authorized Fee to a Representative

2000. ADMINISTRATIVE REVIEW PROCESS

2000.1 What does this chapter cover?

This chapter provides a general description of the administrative review process and explains the rules for reopening determinations and decisions after they become final. Exceptions to these rules apply under certain circumstances. Where the exceptions apply, individuals are made aware of them in the notice of the determination or decision.

Note: For information concerning the hospital and medical insurance review process, see Chapter 24. See Chapter 21 for information concerning the supplemental security income (SSI) review process.

2000.2 What is the administrative review process?

The administrative review process provides for an appeal if you are dissatisfied with our initial determination concerning your entitlement or continuing entitlement to benefits, or other matters. After we make an initial determination, we may request further information from you or another person who disagrees with our determination or shows in writing that his or her rights may be adversely affected by the initial determination.

2000.3 What are the steps in the administrative review process?

The administrative review process consists of several steps that must be requested in writing, usually within specified time periods (see §2001), and in the following order:

A. In most states, you may request that the initial determination be reconsidered. Reconsideration is a re-examination of the administrative record in your case and an opportunity to submit additional evidence that results in a reconsidered determination;

B. If you disagree with the reconsidered determination or initial determination in some states, you may request a hearing before an Administrative Law Judge (ALJ) of the Office of Disability Adjudication and Review;

C. If you disagree with the ALJ's decision or dismissal, you may request a review by the Appeals Council of the Office of Disability Adjudication and Review;

D. If you are dissatisfied with the Appeals Council's action, you may be able to file a civil action in a Federal district court.

The written request for further review at any step of the administrative appeals process may be on a special form, available at any Social

Security office, or it may be in a letter. This request may be filed at any Social Security Office, the Department of Veterans Affairs (VA) Regional Office in the Philippines, or an office of the Railroad Retirement Board, if the claimant has 10 or more years of service in the railroad industry. If you received a disability determination finding you do not meet our medical criteria and wish to file a request for reconsideration or a request for hearing, you now have the option of filing your appeal via the Internet (https://secure.ssa.gov/apps6z/iAppeals/ap001.jsp).

2000.4 What is the expedited appeals process?

In certain cases, at the reconsideration level or higher where the determination has not become final, you may use the expedited appeals process. This process permits you to go directly to a Federal district court if the only issue is the constitutionality of a provision of the Social Security Act that prevents the payment of benefits or receiving a favorable determination in a non-claim earnings discrepancy case. The Social Security office can advise you or your authorized representative of the exact requirements and procedure for requesting this process. (See also §2001 for time limit for requesting the expedited appeals process.)

2001. TIME LIMITS FOR REQUESTING REVIEW

2001.1 Are time limits imposed for requesting review?

Yes, there are time limits for requesting each review in the administrative review process. It is generally 60 days from receipt of the notice of the determination or decision. See §§2004.3, 2007.2, 2013.3, 2014.3, 2015.1.

2001.2 What happens if you do not request a review within the time limit?

If you or your representative do not appeal within the prescribed time limit (unless a longer period is allowed for good cause as explained in §2015), the determination or decision becomes final and binding on the parties affected, except as provided in §2016.

2001.3 Are time limits extended when they end on non-work days?

Yes. If the time limit for requesting review ends on a Saturday, Sunday, legal holiday, or Federal non-work day set by law or Executive Order, the time limit is extended to the next following work day.

2001.4 What are the time limits for each type of determination?

In the following situations, we presume you received notice no later than the fifth day following the date of the notice, unless you can show that the notice was received later or not at all.

A. An initial determination becomes final unless you or another person shows in writing that your rights may be adversely affected by the initial determination. Reconsideration must be requested in writing within 60 days after the date of receiving the notice of the initial determination (See §2004.);

B. A reconsidered determination becomes final unless you or another person shows in writing that your rights may be adversely affected by the reconsidered determination. A hearing before an ALJ must be requested in writing within 60 days after the date of receiving the notice of the reconsidered determination (See §2007.);

C. A decision of the ALJ becomes final unless:
   1. You or another party to the hearing decision request review by the Appeals Council in writing; or
   2. The Appeals Council reviews the decision on its own motion. (See §2013.)

   The review request must be filed within 60 days after the date of receiving the notice of the ALJ's decision. However, after a federal court remand, you must file a written statement with reasons why you disagree with the ALJ decision or request an extension of time from the Appeals Council within 30 days of the date you receive the decision.

D. An expedited appeals process (see §2000.4) may be requested:
   1. Within 60 days after the date you receive notice of the reconsidered determination;
   2. At any time after you have filed a timely request for a hearing but before you receive notice of the ALJ's decision;
   3. Within 60 days after the date you receive a notice of the ALJ's decision; or
   4. At any time after you have filed a timely request for Appeals Council review, but before you receive notice of the Appeals Council's action.

2001.5 How can you get a court review of hearing decisions?

You may obtain a court review after the Appeals Council has issued its action by filing a civil action within 60 days after the date of receiving the notice of the Appeals Council's action.

2001.6 What court has jurisdiction if the Appeals Council denies a request for review or makes a decision?

A Federal district court has jurisdiction after the Appeals Council has denied a request for review or made a decision. (See §2014.)

2001.7 What court has final say on the SSA's decision?

If a civil action is filed, a Federal district court decides whether to review our decision. The decision of the court, if not appealed, is final.

2001.8 What courts have jurisdiction if a decision is appealed?

If the court's decision is appealed, it is subject to further review and affirmation, modification, or reversal by a Court of Appeals or the Supreme Court. (See §2015 concerning granting an extension of time for filing appeals.)

2002. INITIAL DETERMINATIONS

2002.1 What is an initial determination?

An initial determination is a determination we make about your entitlement or continuing entitlement to benefits that is subject to administrative and judicial review.

2002.2 What topics can initial determinations cover?

Initial determinations include, but are not limited to, determinations about:

A. Entitlement or continuing entitlement to benefits;
B. Reentitlement to benefits;
C. The amount of benefits;
D. Recomputation of benefits;
E. Revisions of Social Security earnings records;
F. A deduction from benefits because of work;
G. Termination of benefits;
H. The establishment or termination of a period of disability;
I. Whether benefits should be paid to another person on behalf of the beneficiary (unless the beneficiary is under age 18 (see §1602 for exception) or legally incompetent);
J. Who will act as payee if we determined that representative payment will be made;
K. Any overpayment or underpayment of benefits;
L. How an underpayment of benefits due a deceased person will be paid;

M. An offset of benefits because of SSI previously received for the same period;
N. A deduction from disability benefits because of refusal to accept rehabilitation services;
O. Whether completion of or continuation for a specified period of time in an appropriate vocational rehabilitation program will significantly increase the likelihood that the person will not have to return to the disability benefit rolls and thus, whether benefits may be continued even though the person is not disabled;
P. Whether an overpayment of benefits must be repaid to us;
Q. Reduction in disability benefits because the person also receives benefits under a workers' compensation law;
R. Penalty deductions imposed because of failure to report certain events;
S. Nonpayment of benefits because of claimant's confinement for more than 30 continuous days in a jail, prison, or other correctional institution for conviction of a criminal offense;
T. Whether or not the person has a disabling impairment(s) as defined in §507. Nonpayment of benefits because of claimant's confinement for more than 30 continuous days in a mental health institution or other medical facility because a court found the individual was not guilty for reason of insanity; a court found that he/she was incompetent to stand trial or was unable to stand trial for some other similar mental defect; or, a court found that he/she was sexually dangerous; and
U. Nonpayment of benefits because the person has not furnished us satisfactory proof of their Social Security number, or, if a Social Security number has not been assigned, a proper application has not been filed.
V. Nonpayment of benefits, unless good cause is found, for any month in which a beneficiary has an unsatisfied warrant for more than 30 continuous days for:
  - A crime, or attempted crime, that is a felony or, in jurisdictions that do not classify crimes as felonies, a crime that is punishable by death or imprisonment for more than one year (regardless of the actual sentence imposed); or
  - Violation of a condition of Federal or State probation/parole.

2002.3 How does SSA notify you of decisions?
We will mail you a written notice of the initial determination, stating:
A. The reasons for the determination;
B. The effect of the determination; and
C. Information concerning the right to a reconsideration or to a hearing.

We will not mail a notice if the beneficiary's entitlement to benefits has ended because of his or her death.

2002.4 What can you do if you disagree with SSA's decision about your claim or benefits?
If you are dissatisfied with any action taken affecting your right to monthly benefits, a lump-sum death payment, or entitlement to hospital or medical insurance protection, you may appeal. We will explain your appeal rights. We will also assist you in your appeal, your request for a hearing by an administrative law judge, or your request for review by the Appeals Council. If you are dissatisfied with any action taken regarding your request for extra help with Medicare prescription drug costs, see Chapter 26. If you want to appeal a determination regarding your Medicare Part B Income-Related Monthly Adjustment Amount see Chapter 26.

2003. ADMINISTRATIVE ACTIONS THAT ARE NOT INITIAL DETERMINATIONS

2003.1 What is the review process for administrative actions that are not initial determinations?
We may review administrative actions that are not initial determinations. These actions are not subject to:
A. The administrative review process; and
B. Judicial review.

2003.2 What actions are included?
Administrative actions that are not initial determinations include, for example:
A. Withholding part of a monthly benefit to recover an overpayment;
B. Authorizing fees for representation; and
C. Denying a request to extend the time period to request review of a determination or decision.

Other administrative actions that are not determinations are listed in our regulations. See 20 CFR §404.903.

2004. RECONSIDERATION

2004.1 What is the first step in the administrative review process?

Generally, reconsideration is the first step in the administrative review process.

2004.2 How is a request for reconsideration made?

To make a request for reconsideration, you (or another party) must show in writing that you are dissatisfied with the initial determination or that your rights may be adversely affected by the initial determination.

2004.3 What is the deadline for requesting a reconsideration?

You must file a request for reconsideration in writing within 60 days after the date of receiving the notice of the initial determination (see §2001 and §2015).

2004.4 What is reconsideration in Title II cases?

In Title II cases, reconsideration is a case review or, in medical cessation cases, a disability hearing. (See §2006 for more information.)

2004.5 What is reconsideration in Title XVI cases?

In Title XVI cases, reconsideration is a case review, an informal conference, a formal conference, or in medical cessation cases, a disability hearing. See Sections 2005.5 and 2192 for more information.

2005. THE RECONSIDERATION PROCESS

2005.1 What is the reconsideration process?

The reconsideration process is a thorough and independent reexamination of all evidence on record related to your case. It is based on the evidence submitted for the initial determination, and any additional evidence and information that you or your representative submits in connection with the reconsideration.

2005.2 What issues can be raised in the reconsideration process?

The reconsideration is a completely new and independent review of all the evidence in your case. It is not limited to the issues that you raise.

2005.3 Is the person who makes the reconsidered determination the same one who made the initial one?

No. The person who makes the reconsidered determination must have had no prior involvement with the initial determination.

2005.4 How is the claimant notified of the determination?

You will receive a notice of the reconsidered determination detailing the basis for the determination in your case. (See §111.2.)

2005.5 What are the options for the reconsideration process in Title XVI cases?

In Title XVI cases, the reconsideration process may be a case review, or, under certain circumstances, an informal conference, a formal conference, or a disability hearing.

A. *Informal Conference.* A review in which you may participate. You may present witnesses and may present the case in person.

B. *Formal Conference.* In addition to participating in an informal conference, you may request that adverse witnesses be issued a subpoena and cross-examined by you or your representative. This type of reconsideration is available only if you are eligible for SSI payments and are notified that the payments will be reduced, suspended, or terminated.

C. *Disability Hearing.* A disability hearing is a face-to-face evidentiary meeting that enables you to review the evidence, to introduce new evidence, and to present your objections of a medical determination to a disability hearing officer (DHO). This type of disability hearing is available if you have already been receiving disability benefits, and we find that your impairment has ceased, did not exist, or is no longer disabling

2005.6 Is the reconsidered determination binding?

The reconsidered determination is binding unless:

A. You or any other party to the reconsideration requests a hearing before an ALJ within the stated time period and a decision is made;

B. The expedited appeals process (see §2000.3 and §2001) is used; or

C. The reconsidered determination is revised.

2006. DISABILITY HEARING

2006.1 When can a disability hearing be held?

A disability hearing can be held if:

A. You have been receiving benefits based on a medical impairment that causes you to be disabled (in Title XVI cases, blind or disabled);

B. We have made an initial or revised determination, based on medical factors, that you are no longer disabled (in Title XVI cases, blind or disabled) because the impairment:
1. Has ceased;
2. Did not exist; or
3. Is no longer disabling; and
C. You make a timely request for reconsideration of the initial or revised determination.

2006.2 What issues does the disability hearing address?

The disability hearing addresses only the initial or revised determination, based on medical factors, that you are not now disabled (in Title XVI cases, blind or disabled).

2006.3 Who conducts the disability hearing?

The hearing is conducted by a disability hearing officer who was not involved in making the decision you are appealing.

2006.4 How does the hearing officer announce the results of the hearing?

The disability hearing officer issues a written reconsidered determination.

2006.5 What other outcomes are possible?

In some cases, the disability hearing officer may ask for further development, SSA may make a determination based on work activity, or the disability hearing officer's decision may be reviewed.

2007. HEARING BY AN ADMINISTRATIVE LAW JUDGE (ALJ)

2007.1 When can a claimant request a hearing before an ALJ?

A hearing before an ALJ may be requested if:
A. You disagree with the reconsidered determination;
B. You show in writing that your rights may be adversely affected by the decision; or
C. We have made a reconsidered determination or another type of determination that provides the right to a hearing before an ALJ. These are listed in section 404.930 and 416.1430 of SSA's regulations.

2007.2 When must the request be made?

You must make a request for a hearing in writing within 60 days after you receive the notice of the determination. (See §2000, §2001, and §2015.)

2007.3 What are the procedures at the hearing?

At the hearing you may:

A. Appear in person with or without a designated representative or by video teleconference;
B. Testify under oath or affirmation;
C. Submit new evidence;
D. Examine the evidence used in making the determination under review; and
E. Present and question witnesses. (See §2011.)

2007.4 What happens if a claimant waives the right to an oral hearing?

If you waive the right to an oral hearing, the ALJ will ordinarily make a decision based on the evidence already submitted and any additional evidence that you or any other party presented.

2007.5 What is the basis for the ALJ's decision?

The ALJ makes a decision on the basis of:

A. The evidence already submitted;
B. Any additional evidence you present;
C. Evidence that is otherwise obtained; and
D. Any testimony given at the hearing.

2008. ALJ ACTIONS

2008.1 When may the ALJ dismiss the request for hearing?

The ALJ may dismiss the request for a hearing if:

A. You request a dismissal in writing or orally on the record at the hearing;
B. Neither you nor your representative appears at a scheduled hearing, you have not waived the right to appear, and good cause for not appearing cannot be established;
C. You did not file the request within the time limit and the ALJ does not find there was good cause for missing the time limit;
D. The person requesting the hearing has no right to a hearing;
E. A previous determination or decision was made for the same people, involving the same facts and issues, and that determination has become final;
F. You die and no substitute pursues the request for hearing; or
G. A fully favorable revised reconsideration determination has been made.

2008.2 What actions may an ALJ take on the request for a hearing?

The ALJ may:

A. Hold a hearing and issue a decision;
B. Hold a limited hearing to determine whether there is new and material evidence that would warrant reopening and revision of a prior determination or decision;
C. Send back a case involving a mental impairment for preparation of a standard form required in such cases and a new reconsidered determination under certain circumstances;
D. Send back a case to the appropriate component of SSA for a revised determination, if there is reason to believe that the revised determination would be fully favorable to you. If the ALJ holds a hearing, it will not be sent back to the DDS for a fully favorable decision; or
E. Make a fully favorable decision without holding a hearing

2009. NOTICE OF HEARING

2009.1 When are claimants sent hearing notices?

Notice of the time and place of the hearing is sent by the ALJ to the parties to the hearing at least 20 days before the date set for the hearing, to allow time to prepare for it.

2009.2 Where is the hearing held?

The hearing before the ALJ is usually held in the area where the person requesting the hearing resides, although the person may be required to travel up to 75 miles without travel expense reimbursement. The person may have to travel over 75 miles for a hearing but can request travel expense reimbursement in that situation. In setting the time and place of the hearing, the ALJ determines whether appearance at the hearing will be made in person or by video teleconferencing. The ALJ may direct that the hearing be conducted by video teleconference if video conferencing technology is available and there are no circumstances that prevent use of video teleconference. However, a claimant may object to having his or her hearing by video teleconference. If the claimant refuses to appear by video teleconference, an in-person hearing will be scheduled.

2009.3 Are travel expenses paid?

The Government will pay travel expenses to you and reasonably necessary witnesses only if travel over 75 miles is required. The Government may pay a representative for travel expenses to attend a hearing. The amount of reimbursement under this section for travel by your representative to attend a disability hearing or a hearing before an administrative law judge may not exceed the maximum amount allowable under this section for travel to the hearing site from any point within the designated geographic service area of the office having jurisdiction over the hearing. The Government specifies a maximum travel allowance.

2009.4 Can an ALJ issue subpoenas?

Yes, an ALJ has authority to issue subpoenas requiring the attendance and testimony of witnesses and the production of any evidence that relates to the issues involved in the hearing.

2009.5 Can hearings be held outside of the United States?

There is no provision for holding a hearing outside the U.S. The U.S. is defined as the 50 States, the District of Columbia, Puerto Rico, the U.S. Virgin Islands, Guam, American Samoa, and the Northern Mariana Islands.

2009.6 What should a person do who is outside the U.S. and wishes a hearing?

If you live outside the U.S. and inform the ALJ assigned to conduct the hearing, in writing that you do not wish to appear at a hearing, the ALJ may decide the case based on the record and any additional evidence submitted, with no one appearing in person. If you wish to have an in-person hearing, you may travel to the U.S. at your own expense or appoint a representative to appear on your behalf.

2010. PRE-HEARING OR POST-HEARING CONFERENCES

2010.1 When is a pre-hearing or post-hearing conference called?

A pre-hearing or post-hearing conference may be called by the ALJ on his or her own, or at the request of any party to the hearing. The purpose is to facilitate the hearing or the hearing decision.

2010.2 When are people notified of the conference?

The ALJ will notify the parties of the conference at least seven days before the conference date, unless the parties waive advance written notice of the conference.

2010.3 Are topics other than those in the notice considered?

Yes. At the conference, the ALJ may consider matters in addition to those stated in the notice, if the parties consent in writing.

2010.4 What procedures are followed at the conference?

A record of the conference will be made. The ALJ will issue an order stating all agreements and actions resulting from the conference. If the parties do not object, the agreements and actions become part of the hearing record and are binding on all parties.

2011. ASSISTANCE FROM THE SOCIAL SECURITY OFFICE

2011.1 How can the Social Security office help a claimant?

The Social Security office or hearing office can help you or other interested parties prepare for the hearing by:

A. Explaining the issues involved in the case;
B. Explaining how the hearing will be conducted;
C. Telling you how to arrange for the appearance of witnesses;
D. Advising you how to obtain any documents that may be needed for the presentation of the case; and
E. Telling you how to arrange for a representative.

2011.2 Can claimants review written materials about the hearing?

Yes, you or your representative may review the record and receive copies of the evidence.

2012. ALJ'S DECISION

2012.1 What actions may the ALJ take after the hearing?

After the hearing, the ALJ usually issues a written decision based on all the evidence obtained, including your testimony and that of witnesses. The ALJ may also:

A. Request additional evidence or information necessary to make a decision;
B. Send the case with a recommended decision to the Appeals Council for decision (though this happens very infrequently); or
C. Dismiss the request as described in §2008.

2012.2 What notification is provided about the results?

All parties to the hearing are notified of the ALJ's action and the reasons for it in a written decision.

2013. REVIEW BY THE APPEALS COUNCIL

2013.1 When is a review by the Appeals Council requested?

You or any other party to the hearing decision may file a request for review by the Appeals Council if you disagree with the hearing decision or with the dismissal of the hearing request.

2013.2 What does the Appeals Council do when it receives a request?

The Appeals Council may:

A. Deny or dismiss the request; or

B. Grant the request and either issue a decision or remand the case to an ALJ.

2013.3 How should a request for a review by the Appeals Council be filed?

Your request for a review by the Appeals Council must be in writing. It must be filed within 60 days after the date you or your representative receive notice of the ALJ's action. The request for review may be filed with any Social Security office, at a hearing office, or directly with the Appeals Council. The request can be made by letter or on a special form, HA-520 Request for Review of Hearing Decision/Order, which is available online at: https://www.ssa.gov/forms/ha-520.pdf or at any Social Security office. (See §2000, §2001, and §2015.)

2013.4 When may the Appeals Council decide to review a decision or dismissal without a party or party's representative filing a request for review?

Within 60 days after the date of the ALJ's decision or order of dismissal, the Appeals Council may on its own initiative (motion) decide to review the action that was taken.

2013.5 How is notice of the own motion review provided?

Notice of this review is mailed to all parties at the last known address.

2013.6 When does the Appeals Council review a case?

The Appeals Council will review a case if:

A. There appears to be an abuse of discretion by the ALJ;

B. There is an error of law;

C. The action, findings, or conclusions of the ALJ are not supported by substantial evidence;

D. There is a broad policy or procedural issue that may affect the general public interest; or
E. New and material evidence is submitted, the evidence submitted relates to the period on or before the date of the ALJ decision, and the Appeals Council finds that the ALJ's action, findings, or conclusion is/are contrary to the weight of the evidence currently of record.

2014. APPEALS COUNCIL PROCEDURES

2014.1 What are the steps in the appeals process?

The steps in the appeals process are as follows:
A. The Appeals Council notifies you whether it will review the case.
B. If the Council decides to review the case, you or your representative may request an appearance before the Council for the presentation of oral arguments.
C. If the Appeals Council determines that a significant question of law or policy is presented or that oral arguments would be beneficial in rendering a proper decision, the appearance will be granted.
D. You may also file written statements in support of your claim. The Appeals Council will notify you of its action in the case.

2014.2 What action may a claimant take if dissatisfied with the Appeals Council's action?

If you are dissatisfied with the decision of the Appeals Council or denial of the request for review of the ALJ's decision by the Appeals Council, you may bring suit in a Federal district court.

2014.3 When must a civil action be filed?

The civil action must be filed within 60 days after the date of receipt of the notice of the Appeals Council decision or denial of the request for review.

2014.4 What actions may the court take?

The court may enter a judgment affirming, modifying, or reversing our decision, with or without sending the case back to us. Under certain circumstances, the court may return the case to us so we can take additional evidence before the court enters a judgment.

There is no right to court review where the Appeals Council has dismissed a request for review or denied a request for review of an ALJ's dismissal.

2015. EXTENSION OF TIME FOR FILING

2015.1 Can an extension be granted for filing a request?
Yes, an extension of time may be granted for filing a request for reconsideration, hearing, Appeals Council review, the expedited appeals process, or to bring suit in a Federal district court.

2015.2 What is the procedure for requesting an extension?
You must request an extension of time in writing and/or establish good cause for failing to file the request within the specified time limit.

2015.3 Who makes the decision about granting an extension?
The decision about granting extension of time is made by the field office, the ALJ, or the Appeals Council, depending on who has jurisdiction.

2015.4 Who makes the decision about granting an extension for filing a civil action in a Federal district court?
The Appeals Council may grant an extension of time for filing a civil action in a Federal district court and decide whether good cause exists for failure to file within the appropriate time.

2015.5 What does SSA consider in deciding whether an individual had good cause for missing a deadline?
In determining whether you had good cause for missing a deadline to request review, we consider:

A. What circumstances kept you from making the request on time;
B. Whether our action misled you;
C. Whether you did not understand the requirements of the Social Security Act, resulting from amendments, other legislation, or court decisions; and
D. Whether you had any physical, mental, educational, or linguistic limitations (including any lack of facility with the English language) that prevented you from filing a timely request or from understanding or knowing about the need to file a timely request for review.

2015.6 What are examples of good cause?
Examples of circumstances where good cause may exist include, but are not limited to, the following situations:

A. You were seriously ill and were prevented from contacting us in person, by phone, in writing, or through a friend, relative, or other person;

B. There was a death or serious illness in your immediate family;
C. Important records were destroyed or damaged by fire or other accidental cause;
D. You were making serious efforts to find necessary information to support the claim but had not been able to obtain it within the stated time periods;
E. You requested additional information from us explaining this action within the time limit. Within 60 days of receiving the explanation you requested reconsideration or a hearing, or within 30 days of receiving the explanation requested Appeals Council review or filed a civil suit;
F. We gave you misleading, incorrect or incomplete information about when and how to request administrative review or to file a civil suit;
G. You did not receive notice of the determination or decision;
H. You sent the request to another Government agency in good faith within the time limit and the request did not reach us until after the time period had expired; or
I. Unusual or unavoidable circumstances exist, including the circumstances described in paragraph 2015.5 of this section, which show that you could not have known of the need to file timely, or which prevented you from filing timely.

2016. TIME LIMIT FOR REOPENING FINAL DETERMINATIONS AND DECISIONS

The following sections discuss the time limitations on the reopening of final determinations and final decisions, except those dealing with a Social Security earnings record. (Earnings records are corrected in accordance with the statute of limitations (see §1423)).

2016.1 Can a determination or decision be reopened and revised?

Even though a determination or decision has become final, it may be reopened and revised (by the SSA field office, DDS, reviewing office, ALJ, or Appeals Council) as described below.

2016.2 When may a determination or decision be reopened?

A determination or decision which has become final (see §2001) may be reopened and revised:
A. Within 12 months from the date of the notice of the initial determination for any reason;

B. Within four years (two years in the SSI program) from the date of the notice of the initial determination, if there is good cause for reopening it. "Good cause" can be found to exist if:
1. New and material evidence is submitted;
2. A clerical error was made; or
3. The evidence that was considered in making the determination or decision clearly shows that an error was made.

Note: "Good cause" does not exist where the only basis for reopening the determination or decision is a change of legal interpretation or administrative ruling on which the determination or decision was based. Action reopening the determination or decision under either (A) or (B) above must be started within the time limit specified.

C. At any time if the determination or decision was based on fraud or similar fault. For Title II cases only, several other provisions listed in our regulations permit reopening a determination at any time. In Title XVI cases, the "at any time" rule applies only if fraud or similar fault is involved.

We may decide to reopen a determination or decision on our own initiative or as the result of receiving a written request from you, an eligible spouse, or representative payee. The decision to not reopen is not an initial determination, as defined by our regulations, and is not subject to appeal. It is an administrative action that we will usually take if the above criteria are met.

2017. REPRESENTATION OF CLAIMANT

2017.1 Who can represent you?

A qualified attorney or a qualified non-attorney may represent you at any proceedings before us, such as at an initial determination, a reconsideration, a hearing, or an Appeals Council review.

2017.2 Are there restrictions on who may represent you?

The following restrictions apply:
A. No one who has been suspended or disqualified by us from representing Social Security claimants or another agency who is otherwise prohibited by law from acting as a representative may be appointed as your representative; and
B. You may appoint only individuals as your representative(s). You may appoint a qualified member in a firm, labor union, or other

organization as your representative, but we will not recognize the firm, labor union, or other entity as your representative.

2017.3 How do you appoint a representative?

To appoint a representative, whether an attorney or non-attorney, you must tell us in writing (preferably on a Form SSA-1696-U4, Appointment of Representative, available online at www.socialsecurity.gov/online/ssa-1696.pdf or at any Social Security office). You must sign, date, and file the written appointment with us. If the representative you are appointing is not an attorney, he or she must also sign the SSA-1696-U4 or submit a written acceptance to us. It is not necessary for an attorney to sign the appointment.

2017.4 What information is available to your representative?

Your representative may obtain the same information about the claim that would be available to you for as long as the individual is appointed and acting on your behalf.

2017.5 What actions may your representative take?

Your representative may submit evidence, make statements about facts and law, appear at an interview or hearing with or without you, and make any request or give any notice concerning the proceedings. He or she cannot sign an application for benefits or other rights on your behalf, or testify on your behalf in any administrative proceeding.

2017.6 How does SSA notify your representative?

We will send your representative a notice and a copy of any administrative action, determination, or decision, and requests for information or evidence. These notices or requests will have the same force and effect as if we had sent them to you.

2018. REPRESENTATIVES' FEES

2018.1 Who sets the fees for your representative's services?

Your representative cannot charge and collect a fee from you or another individual unless we first authorize the fee.

2018.2 When we do not need to authorize a representative's fee?

There is an exception to the requirement that we must authorize the amount of the fee your representative may charge. Sometimes a third-party entity such as a business, firm, or other association (including but not limited to partnerships, corporations, for-profit or nonprofit organizations, or a government agency) will provide you with representation and pay your representative's fee. If a third-party pays your representative's fee and expenses, then we do not have to authorize the fee if all of the following conditions are met:

A. You and any auxiliary beneficiaries are free of direct or indirect financial liability to pay a fee or expenses, either in whole or in part, to your representative or to someone else;
B. A third-party entity, or a government agency from its own funds, pays the fee and expenses incurred, if any, on behalf of you and any auxiliary beneficiaries; and
C. The representative submits a written statement to SSA waiving the right to charge and collect a fee and expenses from you and any auxiliary beneficiaries.

2018.3 How does SSA authorize fees?

We have two methods of authorizing representatives' fees: (1) fee agreement and (2) fee petition processes.

If you and your representative elect to use the fee agreement process, you must file a written agreement with us before the date that we make a favorable determination or decision on the claim. We usually approve the fee agreement if:

A. Both you and your representative have signed it; and
B. The fee specified in the agreement does not exceed 25 percent of the past-due benefits or $6,000 (or such higher amount as the Commissioner of Social Security may prescribe pursuant to section 206(a)(2)(A) of the Social Security Act), whichever is less; and
C. Our determination or decision in the claim is fully or partially favorable; and
D. The claim results in past-due benefits.

2018.4 When does SSA approve or disapprove the fee agreement?

We approve or disapprove the fee agreement at the time we make a favorable determination or decision on a claim. We then notify you and your representative of our determination on the fee agreement.

2018.5 If SSA disapproves the fee agreement, can the claimant request review?

Yes. If we disapprove the fee agreement, you and your representative have 15 days after the date of receiving notice of the disapproval to request review of the determination.

2018.6 If SSA approves the fee agreement, what actions take place?

If we approve the fee agreement, we notify you and your representative of:

A. The amount of the past-due benefits;
B. The amount of the past-due benefits payable to you;
C. The amount of the fee that the representative may charge and collect; and
D. An explanation that, within 15 days after the date of receiving the notice, you, an affected auxiliary beneficiary(ies), your representative, or the decision maker may ask us to review the amount of the fee.

2018.7 If the determination or decision on the claim is unfavorable or SSA does not approve the fee agreement, how can a representative charge a fee?

If the determination or decision on the claim is unfavorable or we do not approve the fee agreement, the representative must file a fee petition if he or she wishes to charge and collect a fee.

2018.8 When must the representative file the fee petition be filed?

If your representative uses the fee petition process, he or she must file a petition with us after completing his or her services on a claim. Your representative should submit the petition for a fee for services as soon as possible after his or her services end.

2018.9 Does the claimant receive a copy of the fee petition?

Yes, the representative must also send a copy of the fee petition to you.

2018.10 Where can the representative obatin a fee petition form?

Any Social Security office has a form available, listing all the required information to petition for a fee. Form SSA-1560, Petition to Obtain Approval of a Fee for Representing a Claimant, is also available online at https://www.ssa.gov/forms/ssa-1560.pdf.

2018.11 When does SSA set the fee?

When we receive the petition from the representative stating the amount of the fee requested and giving a detailed description of services that the representative provided to you, with the amount of time spent on each service, we will set the amount of the fee.

2018.12 What is the basis for the authorized fee?

We use several factors to determine the amount of the fee authorized under the fee petition process. These factors include:

A. The extent and type of services the representative performed;
B. The complexity of the case;
C. The level of skill and competence required of the representative in giving the services;
D. The amount of time the representative spent on the case.
E. The results the representative achieved;

2018.13 What information does SSA provide about the fee?

We notify both you and your representative of the fee authorized under the fee petition process, and give a complete explanation of how we determined the amount of the fee.

2018.14 Can the claimant request a review of the fee?

You, an affected auxiliary beneficiary(ies), or your representative may request a review of the fee determined under a fee petition within 30 days after receipt of the notice.

2019. DIRECT PAYMENT OF AUTHORIZED FEE TO A REPRESENTATIVE

2019.1 When does SSA make (or certify) direct fee payments to your representative?

Prior to February 28, 2005, if you were represented by an attorney and your claim was for old age, survivors, or disability insurance benefits (title II benefits), we could withhold up to 25 percent of past-due benefits. We could certify for direct payment to the attorney the lesser of the amount of the authorized fee or 25 percent of past-due benefits. Also for appointments prior to February 28, 2005, we assumed no responsibility for the payment of any fees, if the representative was not an attorney or the claim was for SSI (title XVI) benefits.

For representation agreements entered into on or after February 28, 2005, we continue to make payments to attorneys for title II benefits as before, but also can make direct payment to an attorney if your claim is for SSI benefits. In addition, we can make direct payment to a non-attorney representative whom we determine is eligible to receive direct payment, if your claim is for SSI or old age, survivors, or disability benefits.

After December 31, 2006 any eligible representative who wants his or her fee directly paid by SSA from withheld past-due benefits must register with SSA by completing Form SSA-1699. The representative is also required to submit Form SSA-1695 (Identifying Information for Possible Direct Payment of Authorized Fees) for each claimant that he represents before SSA. If your representative is not eligible for direct payment, he or she is not required to register.

We do not make direct payment to a representative if the representative waives the right to direct payment.

2019.2 Does SSA charge to pay your representative directly?

When SSA makes direct payment to a representative, the law requires us to deduct 6.3 percent from the representative's fee to cover administrative costs. This "user fee" cannot exceed $117.00 (effective December 2023, or a higher amount based on annual adjustments). The representative cannot charge or collect this expense from you.

2019.3 When does SSA pay the fee?

We will pay an authorized fee to a representative soon after we determine the fee amount, unless one of the parties (e.g., you or your representative) requests review before we issue the payment. If that occurs, we will not pay the representative until we have completed the review and notified the parties of the determination.

2019.4 How does a representative receive direct payment if there is no fee agreement?

If there is no fee agreement or we disapprove a fee agreement, the representative must file a fee petition or notice of intent to submit a fee petition with us in order to receive direct payment of a fee from past-due benefits. The representative must file the petition or notice of intent within 60 days of notification of a favorable determination, i.e., the Award Notice.

2019.5 If the claimant has deposited a fee into an escrow account, what must the representative who is eligible to receive direct payment do to receive payment?

When you and a representative have a trust or escrow agreement (to assure payment of an authorized fee), the representative must identify and disclose the amount of the trust or escrow account when he or she files a fee agreement or petitions us for a fee. The representative must also disclose any payment(s) toward this fee that may have come from a source other than you. We reduce direct payment to the representative by any amount you deposited into a trust or escrow account and any payments toward the fee from some other source.

2019.6 What must the representative do if the total amount of the authorized fee is unavailable from your withheld past-due benefits?

If we cannot certify the total amount of the authorized fee for direct payment out of past-due benefits, the representative must look to you and any auxiliary beneficiaries for the balance.

2019.7 If a Federal court rules in favor of a claimant, what fee may an attorney collect and how?

If a Federal court rules in your favor, the court may allow, as part of its judgment, a reasonable fee to an attorney who represented you in court. The court may award your representative court fees under the Social Security Act as well as fees under the Equal Access to Justice Act (EAJA). If your attorney receives court fees for the same work under both Acts, the attorney must refund the smaller fee to you.

Prior to February 28, 2005, the fee allowed by the court cannot exceed 25 percent of your and your family's title II past-due benefits resulting from the favorable judgment. Beginning February 28, 2005, the fee allowed by the court may also include 25 percent of your title XVI past-due benefits. We may certify the amount of the fee awarded by the court (if the PDBs amount we withheld is sufficient) to directly pay your attorney out of your past-due benefits. If it is not sufficient, your attorney will look to you for payment of the balance due.

In addition, if a Federal court rules in your favor, your attorney may request, under EAJA, reimbursement of the expenses he or she incurred in representing you in the course of the court action.

CHAPTER 21

Supplemental Security Income

TABLE OF CONTENTS

INTRODUCTION
2100. What is the Supplemental Security Income (SSI) program?
2101. Who administers the SSI program?
2102. Purpose and Basic Principles
2103. Where does the SSI program operate?
2104. When are SSI benefits paid?
2105. How are SSI benefits financed?
2106. State Supplementation of Basic SSI Benefits
2107. Medicaid
2108. Supplemental Nutrition Assistance Program (SNAP)
2109. Were you eligible for assistance under a Federal/State matching grant program for the aged, blind, or disabled in December 1973?
2110. SSI Definitions

ELIGIBILITY
2111. What are the general eligibility requirements for SSI?
2112. What are the categories of eligibility?
2113. Eligibility Criteria Based on Need
2114. What are other requirements for SSI eligibility?
2115. Citizenship/Alien Status
2116. Absence from the United States

2117. Filing for Other Benefits
2119. Are fugitive felons eligible for SSI?
2120. Are probation and parole violators eligible for SSI?
2121. Institutionalization
2122. Marriage
2123. Eligible Couples
2124. Eligibility Under More Than One Category
2125. Continuing Eligibility
2126. Recipient Reporting Requirements
2127. Fraud

INCOME
2128. How does income affect SSI benefits?
2129. How is income defined for SSI purposes?
2130. What is NOT income for SSI purposes?
2131. Countable Income
2132. How Income is Counted
2133. When Income is Counted
2134. What is earned income?
2135. What are the earned income exclusions?
2136. What is "unearned income"?
2137. What are the unearned income exclusions?
2138. Assistance Related to Disasters
2139. Can home energy or support and maintenance assistance be excluded from income?
2140. In-Kind Income
2141. What is "in-kind support and maintenance"?
2142. Valuation of In-kind Support and Maintenance
2143. One-Third Reduction Rule
2144. Presumed Maximum Value Rule
2145. Temporary Absences and In-kind Support and Maintenance
2146. Acting as an "Agent"
2147. Tables of Federal Benefit Rates, One-third Reduction Values, and Presumed Maximum Values

RESOURCES
2148. Role of Resources
2149. What is considered a resource for SSI purposes?
2150. Liquid and Non-liquid Resources
2151. What is NOT considered a resource?
2152. Ownership of Resources
2153. Countable Resources
2154. How Resources are Valued
2155. When are resources valued?
2156. What are the resource exclusions?
2157. Exclusion of an Automobile or Other Vehicle
2158. Is property needed for self-support excluded from resources?
2159. Life Insurance
2160. Do burial spaces count as resources?
2161. Burial Funds
2162. Resources Affected by a Disaster
2163. Real Property that Cannot be Sold
2164. Conditional Payments Despite Excess Resources
2165. Is your SSI eligibility affected if you dispose of a resource below its market value?
2166. What are the statutory resources limits?

DEEMING
2167. Deeming of Income and Resources
2168. Deeming from an Ineligible Spouse to an Eligible Individual
2169. Deeming from a Parent to a Child Under Age 18
2170. Deeming from a Sponsor to an Alien
2171. Deeming from an Essential Person to an Eligible Qualified Individual

SPECIAL PROVISIONS FOR CONVERTED RECIPIENTS
2172. Special Provisions for Converted Recipients

WORK INCENTIVES
2173. What is the purpose of work incentives for the blind and disabled?

2174. Continued Benefits for Participants in a Program of Vocational Rehabilitation, Employment, Training, or Other Support Service
2175. Impairment-Related Work Expenses
2176. Work Expenses of the Blind
2177. Plan to Achieve Self-Support (PASS)
2178. Special Cash Benefits to Disabled Individuals Who Engage in SGA
2179. Medicaid While Working

PAYMENTS
2180. What is the Federal SSI payment amount?
2181. State Supplementary Payments
2182. Computation of Payments
2183. Retrospective Monthly Accounting
2184. Proration of SSI Payments
2185. Windfall Offset
2186. Interim Assistance Reimbursement
2187. Direct Field Office Payments
2188. Presumptive Blindness or Presumptive Disability Payments

DETERMINATIONS, APPEALS AND REOPENINGS
2189. Initial Determinations
2190. What administrative actions are NOT initial determinations?
2191. How does the appeals process work?
2192. Reconsideration
2193. Hearing
2194. Appeals Council Review
2195. What is the time limit for filing for civil action in a Federal District Court?
2196. Can the time limit for filing an appeal or hearing be extended?
2197. Reopening Determinations/Decisions Under the Rules of Administrative Finality

2100. WHAT IS THE SUPPLEMENTAL SECURITY INCOME (SSI) PROGRAM?

Supplemental Security Income (SSI) is a cash assistance program funded and administered by the Federal Government. The program is authorized by Title XVI (Supplemental Security Income for the Aged, Blind, and Disabled) of the Social Security Act.

Beginning in January 1974, SSI replaced the Federal/State matching grant program of adult assistance to the aged, blind, and disabled. Under SSI, there is no minimum age limit for establishing eligibility based on blindness or disability.

2101. WHO ADMINISTERS THE SSI PROGRAM?

The Social Security Administration (SSA) administers the SSI Program. Local Social Security offices (see §1505 and §1507) handle applications.

2102. PURPOSE AND BASIC PRINCIPLES

2102.1 What is the purpose of SSI?

The basic purpose of SSI is to assure a minimum level of income to people who are aged, blind, or disabled and who have limited income and resources.

2102.2 What are the basic principles of SSI?

There are several basic principles under the SSI program:

A. Payments are to be made to aged, blind, and disabled people whose income and resources are below specified amounts. This provides objective, measurable standards for determining your eligibility and the amount of payment;

B. Title XVI determines:
   1. Your right to SSI benefits;
   2. Your benefit amount; and
   3. The conditions under which you are eligible.

If you disagree with our decision on your case, you can obtain an administrative review of the decision. If you are still not satisfied, you may take court action.

C. SSI benefits are paid under conditions that protect your dignity as much as possible. [*Note:* There is a restriction on expenditures of retroactive benefits paid to children under the age of 18 and placed into a dedicated account.]

D. The eligibility requirements and the Federal income floor are identical everywhere the program operates (see §2103). This provides assurance of a minimum income that States and the District of Columbia may choose to supplement.

E. Although some of your earned income is counted against the SSI income limit, benefit amounts are not reduced dollar-for-dollar as the result of income from work. Thus, you are encouraged to work if you can. (See §§2173-2179 for a discussion of work incentives.) Blind and disabled recipients, if they are capable, are referred to the appropriate State vocational rehabilitation agencies for services to help them enter the labor market. (See §2176 for more information on work incentives for the blind and disabled.)

2103. WHERE DOES THE SSI PROGRAM OPERATE?

The SSI program operates in the 50 States, the District of Columbia, and the Northern Mariana Islands. The program also covers blind or disabled children of military parents stationed abroad and certain students studying outside the U.S. for a period of less than one year.

2104. WHEN ARE SSI BENEFITS PAID?

SSI benefits are not paid in the month that you first apply. After the month of application or the month in which you first become eligible and meet SSA requirements, SSI benefits are normally paid on the first day of the month they are due. For example, benefits for August are paid August 1. (See §§2180-2188 for more information on payments.) It is important to project eligibility and to estimate future income and resources as accurately as possible. We identify and correct errors in payments due to inaccurate estimates when we review your eligibility.

2105. HOW ARE SSI BENEFITS FINANCED?

SSI benefits are financed from the general funds of the United States Treasury. They are not paid out of the Social Security or Medicare trust funds. States that supplement the Federal benefits make these payments from State funds.

2106. STATE SUPPLEMENTATION OF BASIC SSI BENEFITS

2106.1 Can states supplement basic SSI benefits?

States may supplement the basic SSI benefits as explained in §2181. In addition, any State may make an agreement with us to administer its supplementation program. We would pay the State supplementary amounts along with the basic SSI benefits. Each month, we charge the State an administration fee for every State supplementary payment issued during that month.

2106.2 What is the administration fee if a State asks SSA to administer its SSI supplementation program?

For fiscal year 2024, the fee is $14.78 per payment. The rate will increase by the rate of increase in the Consumer Price Index each year.

2107. MEDICAID

2107.1 Can SSA make eligibility decisions for the States?

Under Section 1634 of the Social Security Act, States can contract to have us make Medicaid eligibility decisions for SSI recipients. In these States, the SSI application serves as an application for Medicaid.

2107.2 What roles do the States play in administering Medicaid?

The States are responsible for sending Medicaid notices and issuing Medicaid cards or coupons. For SSI recipients in States contracting with us per 2107.1 above, Medicaid eligibility notices will be based on information given to them by the State data exchange (SDX) system.

2107.3 What if SSA does not make Medicaid decisions in a certain State?

If we do not make Medicaid eligibility decisions in a certain State, local Social Security offices advise applicants who have questions about Medicaid to visit their local Medicaid office.

2108. SUPPLEMENTAL NUTRITION ASSISTANCE PROGRAM (SNAP)

2108.1 What is SNAP?

The Food and Nutrition Act of 2008 changed the name of the Food Stamp Program to the Supplemental Nutrition Assistance Program (SNAP). SNAP safeguards the health and well-being of the nation's population by raising levels of nutrition among low-income households. SNAP benefits are paid by means of an electronic benefits transfer (EBT), or other means of providing assistance.

2108.2 How does an SSI applicant or recipient apply for SNAP benefits?

Social Security offices provide information about SNAP to all SSI applicants and recipients and offer the opportunity to apply or recertify for SNAP benefits while in the office or during an initial claim or redetermination interview if:

A. You live alone or in a household where all members are either receiving or applying for SSI;

B. You are not already receiving SNAP benefits; and

C. You do not have a pending SNAP application.

SNAP applications may be taken with initial SSI claims or upon redetermination. You have the choice of applying at a local Social Security office or at a State SNAP office.

2108.3 How is SNAP eligibility determined?

SNAP eligibility is based on your household circumstances, not on your individual circumstances. The State SNAP agency determines your eligibility for SNAP.

For SNAP purposes, an SSI household is a household in which all members are either receiving SSI or have an application pending for SSI. Social Security offices forward the SNAP application and any supporting documents to the local SNAP office within one day of taking the application.

2109. WERE YOU ELIGIBLE FOR ASSISTANCE UNDER A FEDERAL/STATE MATCHING GRANT PROGRAM FOR THE AGED, BLIND, OR DISABLED IN DECEMBER 1973?

The SSI program went into effect in January 1974. If you were eligible for assistance under one of the prior Federal/State matching grant programs for the aged, blind, or disabled in December 1973, you were "converted" to SSI. Congress wanted to be sure that you were not disadvantaged by your conversion to SSI. Therefore, it enacted certain special provisions applicable only to you as a converted recipient. These special provisions are called "grandfather" provisions and are discussed in §2172.

2110. SSI DEFINITIONS

2110.1 Who is an eligible individual?

An "eligible individual" is a person who files an application and meets all of the eligibility criteria in §§2111-2114.

2110.2 Who is an eligible spouse?

An "eligible spouse" is an eligible individual's husband or wife who meets all of the eligibility criteria in §§2111-2114 and is living in the same household with the person.

2110.3 Who is an eligible couple?

An "eligible couple" is an eligible individual and his or her eligible spouse.

2110.4 Who is an ineligible spouse?

An "ineligible spouse" is an eligible individual's husband or wife who does not meet all of the criteria for SSI eligibility.

2110.5 Who is an essential person?

An "essential person" is an *ineligible* person:

A. Who lives in the same household as the eligible individual or couple; and

B. Whose needs were taken into account in computing the amount payable to a recipient prior to conversion from one of the State adult assistance programs. (See §2172.)

2110.6 Who is a child?

For the purposes of evaluating income and resources, a "child" is a person who is:

A. Unmarried;
B. Not the head of a household;
C. Either:
   1. Under age 18; or
   2. Under age 22 and a student, regularly attending an educational or vocational training institution in a course of study designed to prepare him or her for a paying job.

2110.7 Who is a sponsor?

A "sponsor" is an individual who signs an affidavit of support or similar agreement on behalf of an alien.

2111. WHAT ARE THE GENERAL ELIGIBILITY REQUIREMENTS FOR SSI?

To be eligible for SSI, you must meet all of the eligibility criteria described in §§2111-2114.

No one (except for converted recipients described in §2109 and §2172) can become eligible for SSI benefits without filing an application.

2112. WHAT ARE THE CATEGORIES OF ELIGIBILITY?

In order to be eligible for SSI benefits, you must fit one of the following three categories:

A. *Aged* - An "aged" person is someone who is age 65 or older;
B. *Blind* - A "blind" person is someone whose vision, with use of a correcting lens, is 20/200 or less in the better eye or who has tunnel vision of 20 degrees or less. There is no minimum age limit (for converted blind recipients, see §2172); or
C. *Disabled*
   1. A "disabled" person *age 18 or older* is someone who meets the definition of disability for adults under Social Security law. He or she must be unable to engage in substantial gainful activity (SGA) due to a medically determinable physical or mental impairment which can be expected to result in death, or which has lasted or can be expected to last for a continuous period of not less than 12 months.
   2. A "disabled" person *under the age of 18* is someone who meets the definition of disability for children under Social Security law. He or she must have a medically determinable physical or mental impairment that results in marked and severe functional limitation(s), and which can be expected to result in death, or has lasted or can be expected to last for a continuous period of not less than 12 months.

2113. ELIGIBILITY CRITERIA BASED ON NEED

2113.1 Does your income amount determine whether you are eligible for SSI?

Yes. In order to receive SSI benefits, you cannot have monthly countable income more than the current Federal benefit rate (FBR). The FBR for an eligible couple is approximately one and one half as much as that for an individual. These amounts are set by law and are subject to annual increases based on cost-of-living adjustments. As of January 2024, the FBR for an individual is $943 and that for an eligible couple is $1,415.

(See §§2128-2147 for more information on how income affects both eligibility and payment amount.)

2113.2 Does the amount of real or personal property you own determine whether you are eligible for SSI?

Yes. In order to receive SSI benefits, you cannot own countable real or personal property (including cash) in excess of a specified amount at the beginning of each month. For an individual with an eligible or ineligible spouse, the applicable limit is one and one-half times as much as that for an individual without a spouse. These limits are set by law, and they are not subject to regular cost-of-living adjustments. But they are subject to change. The limits for 2024 are $2,000 for an individual and $3,000 for a couple.

Note: Resources do not affect payment amount. (See §§2148-2166 for more information on how resources affect eligibility.)

2114. WHAT ARE OTHER REQUIREMENTS FOR SSI ELIGIBILITY?

In addition to the categorical and need criteria described above, you must file an application and meet all of the following eligibility requirements:

A. Be a resident of one of the 50 States, the District of Columbia, or the Northern Mariana Islands, or be a child who is a U.S. citizen and lives outside the U.S. with a parent in the U.S. armed forces;

B. Be a citizen of the U.S., or an alien in an immigration category qualified to receive Federal benefits and meet certain additional requirements (see §2115);

C. Not be a resident of a public institution throughout a month (see §2121);

D. Not be absent from the U.S. for a calendar month unless:
   1. You are a child who is a U.S. citizen and lives outside the U.S. with a parent in the U.S. armed forces; or
   2. You are a student who is temporarily abroad for the purpose of conducting studies, (see §2116);

E. File for any other benefits for which you are potentially eligible (see §2117);

F. Not be a fugitive felon (see §2119);

G. Not be violating a condition of parole or probation (see §2120); and

H. Give SSA permission to contact any financial institution at any time and request any financial records that financial institution may have about you. Other people who are responsible for your support must also give SSA their permission to contact any financial institution at any time and request any financial records that financial institution may have about them (see §2167 for more information about the process we call "deeming").

2115. CITIZENSHIP/ALIEN STATUS

2115.1 How does an individual become a U.S. citizen?

You are a U.S. citizen either by birth or by naturalization (see §1725).

2115.2 How is an alien eligible for SSI benefits?

A qualified alien can be eligible for SSI benefits if he or she meets one of the categories listed in "A" through "H" below:

A. Who is lawfully admitted for permanent residence (LAPR), *and*:
   1. Has 40 qualifying quarters of creditable work; or
   2. Is a veteran, active duty member of the U.S. military or a spouse or dependant child of a veteran or member of the U.S. military; or
   3. Was lawfully residing in the United States on 8/22/96 and is blind or disabled; or
   4. Is lawfully residing in the United States and was receiving SSI on 8/22/96; or
   5. Was granted one of the alien classifications listed below within the last seven years:
      1. Refugee under section 207 of the INA;
      2. Asylee under section 208 of the INA;
      3. Alien whose deportation is being withheld under section 243(h) of the INA or whose removal has been withheld under section 241(b)(3) of the INA;
      4. Cuban/Haitian entrant under one of the categories in Section 501(e) of the Refugee Education and Assistance Act of 1980 or alien in a status that is to be treated as a Cuban/Haitian entrant for SSI purposes (see SI 00502.108B.); or
      5. Amerasian immigrants under section 584 of the Foreign Operations, Export Financing, and Related Programs Appropriations Act, 1988.

B. Refugee under section 207 of the INA *and*:
   1. Is a veteran, active duty member of the U.S. military, or a spouse or dependant child of a veteran or member of the U.S. military; or

2. Was lawfully residing in the United States on 8/22/96 and is blind or disabled; or
3. Is lawfully residing in the United States and was receiving SSI on 8/22/96; or
4. Was granted refugee status under section 207 0f the INA within the last seven years.

C. Granted asylum under section 208 of the INA *and*:
  1. Is a veteran, active duty member of the U.S. military or a spouse or dependant child of a veteran or member of the U.S. military; or
  2. Was lawfully residing in the United States on 8/22/96 and is blind or disabled; or
  3. Is lawfully residing in the United States and was receiving SSI on 8/22/96; or
  4. Was granted asylum within the last seven years.

D. Deportation withheld under section 243(h) of the INA or removal withheld under section 241(b)(3) of the INA *and*:
  1. Is a veteran, active duty member of the U.S. military or a spouse or dependant child of a veteran or member of the U.S. military; or:
  2. Was lawfully residing in the United States on 8/22/96 and is blind or disabled; or
  3. Is lawfully residing in the United States and was receiving SSI on 8/22/96; or
  4. Deportation or removal was withheld within the last seven years.

E. Conditional entrant under section 203(a)(7) of the INA *and*:
  1. Is a veteran, active duty member of the U.S. military or a spouse or dependant child of a veteran or member of the U.S. military; or
  2. Was lawfully residing in the United States on 8/22/96 and is blind or disabled; or
  3. Is lawfully residing in the United States and was receiving SSI on 8/22/96.

F. Paroled into the U.S. for one year or more under section 212(d)(5) of the INA *and*:
  1. Is a veteran, active duty member of the U.S. military or a spouse or dependant child of a veteran or member of the U. S. military; or

2. Was lawfully residing in the United States on 8/22/96 and is blind or disabled; or
3. Is lawfully residing in the United States and was receiving SSI on 8/22/96; or
4. Was granted Cuban/Haitian entrant status within the last 7 years or was granted a status that is to be treated as a Cuban/Haitian entrant for SSI purposes (see SI 00502.108B.) within the last 7 years.

G. Cuban/Haitian entrant under Section 501(e) of the Refugee Education and Assistance Act of 1980 *and*:
1. Is a veteran, active duty member of the U.S. military or a spouse or dependant child of a veteran or member of the U.S. military; or
2. Was lawfully residing in the United States on 8/22/96 and is blind or disabled; or
3. Is lawfully residing in the United States and was receiving SSI on 8/22/96; or
4. Was granted Cuban/Haitian entrant status within the last seven years or was granted a status that is to be treated as a Cuban/Haitian entrant for SSI purposes (see SI 00502.108B.) within the last 7 years.

H. Battered spouse or child who petitioned for status as a lawfully admitted permanent resident under section 204(a)(1)(A)(i)-(iv) or 204(a)(1)(B)(i)-(iii) of the INA, or suspension of deportation under section 244(a)(3) or 240A(b)(2) of the INA, *and*:
1. Is a veteran, active duty member of the U.S. military or a spouse or dependant child of a veteran or member of the U.S. military; or
2. Was lawfully residing in the United States on 8/22/96 and is blind or disabled; or
3. Is lawfully residing in the United States and was receiving SSI on 8/22/96. Certain other aliens who are not qualified aliens may also get SSI. They include:
   - Noncitizen Indians who are members of a Federally recognized Indian tribe.
   - American Indians born in Canada who are admitted to the United States under Section 289 of the INA.

- Aliens who are victims of a severe form of trafficking in persons who meet the requirements of the Trafficking Victims Protection Act of 2000.
- Certain Iraqi or Afghan nationals who provided valuable service as translators or interpreters for the U.S. Armed Forces in Iraq or Afghanistan, or worked for the U.S. Chief of Mission in Iraq, and were granted lawful permanent resident status as special immigrants pursuant to Section 101(a)(27) of the INA.

2116. ABSENCE FROM THE UNITED STATES

2116.1 Are you still eligible for SSI benefits if you leave the United States?

You are not eligible for SSI benefits for the month or months that you are:

A. Outside the United States for a full calendar month or more; and
B. Not a child living outside the United States with a parent in the military service or a student temporarily abroad for the purpose of studying.

2116.2 When are you considered back in the United States?

If you have been outside the United States for 30 days in a row, you are not considered "back" until you have spent 30 days in a row in the United States.

2116.3 When does your eligibility begin again after you have been outside of the United States?

After an absence of 30 days in a row, your SSI eligibility may resume effective with the day following the 30th day of your continuous presence in the United States. You must continue to meet all other eligibility criteria.

2116.4 Can a blind or disabled child still be eligible for SSI benefits while living outside the United States?

A blind or disabled child may be eligible for SSI benefits while outside the United States if the child:

A. Is a United States citizen; and
B. Lives with a parent who is a member of the U.S. armed forces assigned to permanent duty ashore outside the United States

2116.5 Can a student still be eligible for SSI benefits while living outside the United States?

A student of any age may be eligible for SSI benefits while temporarily outside the United States if:

A. The student is conducting studies that are not available in the United States;
B. The student is sponsored by an educational institution in the United States;
C. The studies abroad are designed to enhance the student's ability to get gainful employment; and
D. The student was eligible to receive a SSI benefit for the month before the first full month outside the United States.

2117. FILING FOR OTHER BENEFITS

2117.1 What other benefits do you need to apply for before you can be eligible for SSI?

SSI is a program of last resort. Therefore, you must file for any other benefits for which you may be eligible. This means benefits such as Social Security benefits, private pensions, etc., which share all of the following characteristics:

A. Require an application or similar action;
B. Have conditions for eligibility;
C. Provide either periodic or one-time payments; and
D. Are sources of income that reduce SSI benefits.

2117.2 How do you know of other benefits for which you could be eligible?

We must provide you with written notice of potential eligibility for other benefits and of your requirement to "take all appropriate steps" to pursue these benefits. You have 30 days from receipt of the notice to file for the benefits involved.

2117.3 What does it mean to take all appropriate steps to pursue benefits?

"Taking all appropriate steps" to pursue other benefits for which you could be eligible means:

A. Applying for the benefit;
B. Providing the other payment source with any information necessary to establish eligibility; and

C. Agreeing to receive the other benefits if you are found eligible.

Note: It is not necessary for an individual to pursue a claim for other benefits through an appeals process.

2119. ARE FUGITIVE FELONS ELIGIBLE FOR SSI?

No. A person cannot be eligible for SSI benefits for any month during which he or she has an unsatisfied arrest warrant for a crime, or attempted crime, of flight to avoid prosecution or confinement, escape from custody, and flight-escape. In most jurisdictions these crimes are felonies or, in jurisdictions that do not classify crimes as felonies, a crime punishable by death or imprisonment for more than one year (regardless of the actual sentence imposed).

SSA will find a good cause exception to this non-payment rule if a court finds the person not guilty, the charges are dismissed, a warrant for arrest is vacated, or there are similar exonerating circumstances identified by the court. SSA will also apply the good cause exception to the non-payment rule if the individual establishes to the satisfaction of SSA that he or she was the victim of identity fraud and the warrant was issued on that basis.

SSA also may apply the good cause exception to the non-payment rule if the arrest warrant was for a crime that was non-violent and not drug-related, and in the case of probation or parole violators, both the violation and the underlying offense were non-violent and not drug-related.

2120. ARE PROBATION AND PAROLE VIOLATORS ELIGIBLE FOR SSI?

No. Probation and parole violators are not eligible to receive SSI benefits. You may not receive SSI payments for any month during which you are violating a condition of probation or parole imposed under Federal or State law. However, effective March 18, 2011, we no longer suspend or deny payments based solely on an outstanding warrant for a violation of probation or parole.

2121. INSTITUTIONALIZATION

2121.1 Are you eligible for SSI if you are institutionalized?

Institutionalization affects your eligibility and your benefit rate. If you are a resident of a public institution (an institution administered by the

Federal government or by a State or local government) for a full calendar month, you *are not eligible for SSI unless one of the following exceptions applies*:

A. The public institution is a medical treatment facility and Medicaid pays more than 50 percent of the cost of care. In the case of a child under age 18, Medicaid and/or private health insurance pays more than 50 percent of the cost of care. If these conditions are met, you are eligible for a monthly payment of $30. However, you may be eligible to receive full SSI benefits for up to the first three full months of institutionalization if:
- A physician certifies that your stay in a medical facility is not likely to last more than three months; and
- You can demonstrate that you need to continue to maintain and provide for the expenses of your home to which you may return.

B. You are living in a publicly operated community residence that serves no more than 16 residents. Such a facility must be residential (i.e., not a correctional, educational, or medical facility) and be based in a community, not part of a large institution;

C. The public institution is a public emergency shelter for the homeless. Such a facility provides food, a place to sleep, and some services to homeless individuals on a temporary basis. Payments to a resident of a public emergency shelter for the homeless are limited to no more than six months in any nine-month period;

D. You are in a public institution primarily to receive educational or vocational training. To qualify, the training must be an approved program and must be designed to prepare you for gainful employment;

E. You were eligible for SSI under one of the special work incentive provisions described in §2178 and §2179 in the month before the first full month you lived in a medical or psychiatric institution and the institution agrees to permit you to retain benefit payments. Payments under the special work incentive provisions may be made for the first two full months of institutionalization. If your stay in the institution is expected to be temporary, you may be eligible for one additional month if you meet the conditions for a full benefit per (A) in this section.

2121.2 When is your payment limited to the $30 Federal Benefit Rate?

In general, payment is limited to a maximum of $30 per month (minus any countable income) when:

A. You are a resident throughout a month in a public or private medical treatment institution; and

B. Medicaid pays over 50 percent of the cost of care for that month. In the case of a child under age 18, Medicaid or private health insurance pays more than 50 percent of the cost of care.

As with other benefits, States can supplement the $30 payment.

2121.3 Are there exceptions to the maximum payment limit?

There are two exceptions to the maximum payment limit:

A. If you meet the requirements of 2121.1 (A), you may receive full payment for the first three full months of institutionalization; or

B. If you meet the requirements of 2121.1 (E), you may receive full payment for the first two full months of institutionalization or for three months if 2121.1 (A) also applies.

2121.4 What is the prerelease program?

The prerelease program helps aged or disabled institutionalized individuals return to community living. You may have nearly completed your sentence in a correctional facility or are ready to be released from a medical facility, but cannot financially support yourself. The prerelease program allows you to apply for SSI payments and food stamps several months before your anticipated release so your benefits can begin quickly after you leave the institution.

2121.5 How can you participate in the prerelease program?

A formal prerelease agreement can be developed between an institution and the local Social Security office. However, you can file an application for benefits under the prerelease procedures even if your institution does not have a formal agreement.

2122. MARRIAGE

2122.1 How does marriage affect SSI benefits?

Marriage helps determine whether:

A. There is an eligible couple (rather than two eligible individuals);

B. The rules for deeming income and resources apply if a spouse is *not* eligible (see §2167); or

C. An individual under age 22 is a child who qualifies for special income exclusions.

2122.2 When are two people considered married?

Two people are married for SSI purposes if:

A. They are living in the same household and are married under the laws of their State;
B. They are holding themselves out as a married couple to the community in which they live; or
C. One is entitled, as the spouse of the other, to Social Security benefits.

2122.3 When does SSA evaluate the existence of a marriage?

We generally evaluate the existence of a marriage as of the first day of a month. However, there are exceptions:

A. If both members of an eligible couple file an application in the same month, we evaluate couple status for that month on the first day of the month following the date the application is filed; and
B. If both members of a formerly eligible couple seek reinstatement as a couple in the same month, we evaluate couple status for that month as of the latest request for reinstatement.

2122.4 Who is considered the spouse if marriage status changes?

The spouse you were living with at the beginning of a month is your spouse for SSI purposes, regardless of changes later in the month. For example, a "holding-out" spouse with whom you are living takes precedence over a legally married spouse from whom you are separated.

2123. ELIGIBLE COUPLES

2123.1 What is the income and resources limit for an eligible couple?

The income and resources limits for an eligible couple are higher, but less than twice the individual's limit. The couple's eligibility is established by comparing their *combined* countable income and resources with the applicable couple's limits.

2123.2 How is a couple's benefit computed?

An eligible couple's federal benefit is the difference between:

A. The *combined* countable income of both members; and
B. The couple's FBR.

Whatever benefit is due an eligible couple is usually paid in two equal payments, one to each spouse.

2123.3 When does couple status end?

The members of an eligible couple continue to be treated as such until:

A. The marriage ends through death, divorce, or annulment; or

B. The members of the couple begin living apart.

2123.4 How does SSA recognize a couple who shares a room in an institution?

We consider the members of an eligible couple who share a room in an institution as separated. We treat them as two eligible individuals for purposes of determining eligibility and payment amount.

2124. ELIGIBILITY UNDER MORE THAN ONE CATEGORY

2124.1 Can you qualify for benefits under more than one of the eligibility categories?

It is possible for you to qualify for SSI under more than one of the three eligibility categories of aged, blind, or disabled. For example, you may be both blind and disabled, or you may be over age 65 and blind or disabled.

2124.2 How are Federal SSI benefits affected if you fit more than one of the eligibility categories?

The Federal SSI benefit rate is the same for all categories. However, because of differences in income/resources exclusions, a blind or disabled individual may receive a higher SSI benefit than an aged person. However, the individual age 65 or older must have an established onset of blindness or disability before the month he or she turned age 65 in order to qualify for the higher exclusions.

2124.3 How are Federally Administered State Supplementation benefits affected if you fit more than one of the eligibility categories?

States with Federally administered supplementation programs may vary their supplementation amounts by category. For example, if a person was blind before age 65 but was age 65 or older at the time of filing, he or she may choose to receive a higher State supplement based on blindness, if that option is provided. However, such an individual's Federal SSI payment is based on age 65 and not on blindness.

2125. CONTINUING ELIGIBILITY

2125.1 Why does SSA reevaluate eligibility for SSI?

We periodically reevaluate the eligibility of each SSI recipient to ensure that eligibility continues and that payments are in the proper amount.

2125.2 What is covered in the reevaluation?

Except for individuals turning age 18, reevaluation covers all factors of eligibility except age, citizenship, and continuing disability or blindness. Every individual eligible based on a disability in the month before the month of turning 18 is subject to a reevaluation of disability based on the initial adult standards.

2125.3 How often does SSA reevaluate eligibility?

The length of time between scheduled reevaluations varies depending on the likelihood that your situation may change in a way that affects your eligibility and/or payment amount.

2125.4 What is your role in a reevaluation?

We contact eligible individuals and couples for the reevaluation. It may be conducted by mail, telephone, or personal interview. You will be asked to provide the same kind of information that you gave when you applied. We may also ask you to provide evidence on factors subject to change, such as income, resources, living arrangements, etc.

2126. RECIPIENT REPORTING REQUIREMENTS

2126.1 Do you need to report events that affect your SSI benefits?

You must report events or changes in circumstances if they affect your eligibility or payment amount. You must make the report within 10 calendar days after the end of the month the event or change occurred.

2126.2 What happens if you do not report an event?

If you do not report an event that affects your SSI benefits, there may be a penalty deduction in later benefit payments as follows:

A. $25 penalty for the first time;
B. $50 penalty for the second time; and
C. $100 for each subsequent failure.

We do not impose a penalty if you were without fault or had good cause for not reporting an event.

2126.3 What types of events must be reported?

You must report such matters as:

A. Change in amount of earned and unearned income;

When you report to us about changes in your earnings or work activity, we will give you a receipt to verify that you have properly fulfilled your obligation to report. Keep this receipt with all of your other important papers from Social Security.

B. Change of residence;
C. Marriage, divorce, or separation;
D. Absence from the U.S;
E. If you receive benefits because you are disabled you must tell us if your medical condition improves so that you can go to work;
F. Certain deaths;
G. Changes in income or resources for you or individuals whose income and resources are considered as yours;
H. Eligibility for other benefits;
I. Change in school attendance;
J. Change in composition of the household;
K. Change in citizenship or alien status;
L. Becoming a fugitive felon; or
M. Violating a condition of probation or parole.
N. Admission to or discharge from a medical facility, public or private institution.

2127. FRAUD

2127.1 What are the penalties for fraud?

Penalties for fraud include possible fines and imprisonment.

2127.2 What actions are considered fraudulent?

Penalties are imposed if a person with intent to defraud:

A. Willfully and knowingly deceives, misleads, or threatens any claimant, prospective claimant, or beneficiary regarding benefits by word, circular, letter, or advertisement;
B. Knowingly charges or collects, whether directly or indirectly, any fee more than the maximum fee set by the Commissioner of Social Security;
C. Makes false statements or misrepresentations in applying for benefits;

D. Makes false statements or misrepresentations of material facts at any time if for use in determining benefit rights;
E. Conceals, or fails to reveal, information about events affecting initial or continued right to benefits or the amount of payment; or
F. Converts payments received on behalf of another to a use other than for the use and benefit of the eligible person.

2128. HOW DOES INCOME AFFECT SSI BENEFITS?

The amount of your income determines your eligibility for SSI and the amount of your benefit. Generally, the more income you receive the lower your SSI benefit. If you have too much income, you are not eligible for SSI benefits. However, not everything you get is considered income and not all income counts in determining your eligibility.

In certain situations, other people are expected to share financial responsibility for an individual. In these situations, the income (and resources) of others are considered in determining the individual's eligibility and payment amount (see §2167).

2129. HOW IS INCOME DEFINED FOR SSI PURPOSES?

Income is anything you receive during a calendar month that is used or could be used to meet your needs for food or shelter. It may be in cash or in-kind. In-kind income is not cash; it is food, shelter, or something you can use to get food or shelter.

2130. WHAT IS NOT INCOME FOR SSI PURPOSES?

Certain things you receive are not income, even if they have value. Among them are:

A. Medical care and services, provided by anyone, including room and board, provided by the medical treatment facility or paid directly to the facility by a government medical or social service program, while you are living in a medical treatment facility such as a hospital or nursing home;

Note: Cash provided by an individual, a non-governmental medical services program, or health insurance *is income* if it is not reimbursement for, or restricted to the future purchase of, program-approved services.

B. Social Services;

Any social service, related cash or in-kind item from a government social service program.

Note: Cash provided by an individual or a non-governmental social services program *is income* if it is not reimbursement for, or restricted to the future purchase of, program-approved services.

C. Receipts from the sale, exchange, or replacement of a resource. These receipts are simply resources that have changed their form. This includes any cash or in-kind item provided to replace or repair a resource that has been lost, damaged, or stolen (see §2138);
D. Income tax refunds;
E. Payments by credit life or credit disability insurance;
F. Proceeds of a loan. This includes money you borrow or receive as repayment of a loan;
G. Money paid by someone else directly to a supplier on your behalf. However, goods or services you receive as a result of the payments may be income even if the third-party payments themselves are not;
H. Replacement of income already received, e.g., replacement of a stolen paycheck;
I. Assistance you receive to protect your residence from bad weather, such as insulation or storm doors; and
J. Any item (other than an item of food or shelter) that would be an excluded non-liquid resource (see §2156) if you kept it.

2131. COUNTABLE INCOME

2131.1 What is countable income?

Countable income is the amount left over after:

A. Eliminating from consideration all items that are not income; and
B. Applying all appropriate exclusions to the items that are income.

Countable income is determined on a calendar month basis. It is the amount actually subtracted from the FBR to determine your eligibility and to compute your monthly benefit amount. (See §2132.)

2131.2 Why is it important to distinguish earned income from unearned income?

It is important to distinguish earned income from unearned income because not as much earned income is countable.

2132. HOW INCOME IS COUNTED

2132.1 How does SSA count income?

We count income by determining countable income for each calendar month of eligibility. This means looking at income you received (or deemed to have received, see §2167) in a given month. We then apply exclusions appropriate to that month's income.

2132.2 What happens if countable income is more than the FBR?

If your countable income is more than the FBR, you are not eligible for a Federal benefit. Since SSI payments are made on the first day of a month for that same month, we need to use an estimate of countable income to project your eligibility for that month.

2132.3 When does SSA review the estimates of countable income?

We review the estimates (and revise them, if necessary) whenever there is a report of change or a redetermination.

2132.4 What month is used to compute your benefit amount?

If you are eligible for a particular month, we usually compute your SSI benefit amount for the month using your countable income from two months before the current month. This is called retrospective monthly accounting (see §2183).

2133. WHEN INCOME IS COUNTED

2133.1 When does SSA count your income?

Generally, we count both earned and unearned income in the month of actual or "constructive" receipt, whichever is earlier.

2133.2 What does constructive receipt mean?

"Constructive" receipt means that income is credited to your account or set aside for your use, whether or not you actually receive it in hand. (See §1302.) For example, if an individual asks an employer to hold his or her regular July 15 paycheck pending return from vacation on August 3, the wages are income in July. Similarly, a month's income includes certain amounts withheld at the source. For example, amounts deducted from a payment to satisfy a garnishment or to make certain payments, such as insurance premiums, are considered income in the month the withholding occurs.

Note: There is an exception. Net earnings from self-employment are determined on an annual basis and allocated equally over all 12 months of the tax year.

2134. WHAT IS EARNED INCOME?
Earned income is:
A. Wages paid or constructively paid (as defined in §1302) for services you perform as an employee;
B. Military pay and allowances except for on-base and privatized military housing and combat-related pay (i.e., hostile fire and imminent danger pay);
C. Net earnings from self-employment estimated for a current year on the basis of volume of business, past experience, etc.;
D. Payments for participating in a sheltered workshop or work activities center program;
E. Sickness or temporary disability payments received within the first six months of stopping work; and
F. Royalties you earned in connection with any publication of your work and any honoraria received for your services.

Earned income may be paid in cash or in-kind. If it is in-kind, its full current market value is the amount used to determine your countable income.

2135. WHAT ARE THE EARNED INCOME EXCLUSIONS?
In figuring countable earned income, certain exclusions are authorized by other Federal laws and by Title XVI of the Social Security Act. Countable earned income can never be less than zero, nor can any earned income exclusion apply to unearned income.

We apply earned income exclusions in the following order:
A. Exclusions authorized by Federal laws other than Title XVI;
B. The full amount of any Federal earned income tax credit payments;
C. The first $30 per calendar quarter of earned income if received infrequently or irregularly. For example, if the income is received only once during a calendar quarter from a single source and the individual did not receive it in the month immediately preceding that month or in the month immediately following that month regardless of whether or not the payments occur in different calendar quarters, or if its receipt cannot reasonably be expected (effective 9/8/06);

D. Up to $2,290 in a month for 2024 (but no more than $9,230 per year) for a working student under age 22 and regularly attending school;
E. Any portion of the $20 per month general income exclusion that is not used against unearned income in the same month;
F. $65 of earned income;
G. Impairment-related work expenses of a disabled (not blind) individual who:
   1. Is under age 65; or
   2. Received SSI based on a disability for the month before turning age 65;
H. One-half of the month's remaining earned income;
I. Any expenses reasonably attributable to the earning of income for a blind (not disabled) individual who:
   1. Is under age 65; or
   2. Received SSI because of blindness for the month before turning age 65; and
J. Any earned income used to fulfill an approved Plan to Achieve Self-Support (PASS) in the case of a blind or disabled individual who:
   1. Is under age 65; or
   2. Received SSI based on blindness or disability for the month before turning age 65.

Note: An eligible couple gets the same income exclusions as an eligible individual. However, the benefit rate is higher for an eligible couple.

2136. WHAT IS "UNEARNED INCOME"?

"Unearned income" is all income that is not earned. Some common types of unearned income are:

A. In-kind support and maintenance (food or shelter) given to an individual or received by an individual because someone else paid for it (see §§2140-2142);
B. Private pensions and annuities;
C. Periodic public payments such as Social Security benefits, Railroad Retirement benefits, Department of Veterans Affairs pension and compensation payments, civil service annuities, workers' compensation, unemployment compensation, and payments based on need involving Federal funds;

D. Life insurance proceeds and other death benefits, to the extent that the total amount is more than the expenses of the deceased person's last illness and burial paid by the individual;
E. Gifts and inheritances;
F. Support and alimony payments in cash or in-kind;
G. Prizes and awards;
H. Dividends and interest;
I. Rents and royalties (except those royalties defined as earned income); and
J. Certain payments not considered wages for Social Security purposes:
   1. In-kind payments to certain agricultural workers;
   2. Tips under $20 per month;
   3. Jury fees;
   4. Money paid to individuals who are residents, but not employees, of institutions.

2137. WHAT ARE THE UNEARNED INCOME EXCLUSIONS?

As with earned income, certain unearned income exclusions are authorized by other Federal laws as well as by Title XVI. Countable unearned income can never be less than zero. However, there is one unearned income exclusion that can be applied to earned income (see (M) in this section). Unearned income exclusions are applied in the following order:
A. Payments or benefits excluded by provisions of a Federal statute other than Title XVI of the Social Security Act;
B. Any public agency's refund of taxes on real property or food;
C. Assistance based on need and funded wholly by a State or one of its political subdivisions (including Indian tribes). It does not matter whether these payments are made directly to an individual or are paid to someone else on his or her behalf. This exclusion includes all State payments used to supplement SSI;
D. Any portion of a grant, scholarship, fellowship, or gifts used for paying tuition, fees or other necessary educational expenses (effective 6/1/04). However, any amount set aside or actually used for food or shelter is not excluded;
E. Food raised by an individual or by his or her spouse if consumed by the household;
F. Assistance received under the Disaster Relief and Emergency Assistance Act and assistance provided under any Federal statute because

of a catastrophe declared by the President to be a major disaster (see §2138);

G. The first $60 per calendar quarter of unearned income if received infrequently or irregularly; for example, if the income is received only once during a calendar quarter from a single source and the individual did not receive it in the month immediately preceding that month or in the month immediately following that month regardless of whether or not the payments occur in different calendar quarters, or if its receipt cannot reasonably be expected;

H. Payments received by certain recipients under the Alaska Longevity Bonus program;

I. Payments to an individual for providing foster care to a child placed in the individual's home by a qualified agency;

J. Any interest earned on excluded burial funds and any appreciation in the value of an excluded burial arrangement left to accumulate and become part of the separately identifiable burial fund (see §2161);

K. Certain home energy and other needs-based support and maintenance assistance (see §2139);

L. One-third of support payments made by an absent parent to or for an eligible child;

M. The first $20 per month of an individual's total unearned income other than income based on need. Payments are based on need if the recipient's income is a factor in determining eligibility for the payments. (Any portion of this exclusion that cannot be used up against unearned income is applied against earned income received in the same month);

Note: A needs-based payment funded solely by any combination of a State and its political subdivisions (including Indian tribes) is called "assistance based on need" and is excluded totally (see (C) in this section). A needs-based payment funded wholly or partially by a non-governmental organization or by the Federal Government is called "income based on need." It does not qualify for this $20 general exclusion; (For an exclusion that may apply to assistance provided by nonprofit organizations, see §2139).

N. Any unearned income used to fulfill an approved plan for achieving self-support in the case of a blind or disabled individual who:
  1. Is under age 65; or
  2. Received SSI based on blindness or disability for the month he or she turned 65;

O. Federal housing assistance, whether provided directly by the Federal Government or through other entities such as local housing authorities, nonprofit organizations, etc.;
P. Any interest accrued on (or after April 1, 1990) and left to accumulate as part of the value of an excluded burial space purchase agreement;
Q. The value of any commercial transportation ticket received as a gift and not converted to cash. This applies to travel among the 50 states, District of Columbia, Puerto Rico, Virgin Islands, Guam, American Samoa, and the Northern Mariana Islands;
R. Hostile fire or imminent danger pay from the Uniformed Services received in or after October 1993;
S. Payments received from a State fund to aid victims of crime;
T. Relocation assistance provided under Title II of the Uniform Relocation Assistance and Real Property Acquisitions Policies Act of 1970;
U. Austrian Social Insurance payments that are based, in whole or in part, on wage credits received for certain losses suffered before and during World War II;
V. Payments made by the Dutch Government under the Netherlands Act on Benefits for Victims of Persecution 1940-1945 to individuals who were victims of persecution and suffering from illnesses or disabilities resulting from the persecution;
W. Dividend or interest income earned on countable resources or resources excluded under other Federal laws (effective 7/1/04);
X. Interest or earnings on a dedicated account which is excluded from resources;
Y. Certain gifts to children with life-threatening conditions;
Z. Any annuity paid by a State for certain veterans or the veteran's spouse (effective 9/1/08);
AA. Americorps State and National payments, and National Civilian Community Corps (NCCC) payments (effective 9/1/08).
AB. Filipino Veterans Equity Compensation Fund payments (effective 2/17/09);
AC. The one-time $250 economic recovery payment under the American Recovery and Reinvestment Act of 2009 (ARRA) (effective 2/17/09);
AD. Incentives provided to Medicaid beneficiaries from the Incentives for Prevention of Chronic Diseases in Medicaid program (IPCDM) under the Affordable Care Act (effective 3/23/10);

AE. The first $2000 per calendar year of compensation received for participating in certain clinical trials.

Note: An eligible couple gets the same income exclusions as an eligible individual, although there is a higher benefit rate for a couple.

2138. ASSISTANCE RELATED TO DISASTERS

2138.1 What is considered a major disaster?

A "major disaster" is one declared by the President. It is declared for purposes of the Robert T. Stafford Disaster Relief and Emergency Assistance Act (formerly the Disaster Relief Act of 1974).

2138.2 What exclusions apply when there is a major disaster?

When a major disaster occurs, the following exclusions apply:

A. Support and maintenance you begin receiving within 30 days of the disaster, if the disaster caused you to leave a household that you maintained as your own home. The support and maintenance may be provided in a residential facility or in a private household maintained by another person;

B. Any assistance provided under the Robert T. Stafford Disaster Relief and Emergency Assistance Act or under any other Federal statute because of the catastrophe (e.g., cash to repair or replace the home or other property); and

C. Any interest earned on assistance payments described under (B) above.

2138.3 What is considered a personal disaster?

A "personal disaster" occurs when your resource is lost, damaged, or stolen (e.g., destruction of a home by fire or flood).

2138.4 What exclusions apply when there is a personal disaster?

When a resource is lost, damaged, or stolen, the following rules apply:

A. You may receive cash to repair or replace the resource, or the resource may be repaired or replaced for you. Neither the cash nor the repair/replacement is income;

B. Temporary housing provided until your excluded home is repaired or replaced is not income; and

C. Up to nine months (which can be extended to 18 months for good cause) of interest earned on cash received to repair or replace a non-cash resource is not income.

2139. CAN HOME ENERGY OR SUPPORT AND MAINTENANCE ASSISTANCE BE EXCLUDED FROM INCOME?

Home energy or support and maintenance (i.e., food or shelter) assistance received by you (or by any person whose income or living arrangement affects your income) may be excluded if:

A. The appropriate State agency certifies that the assistance is based on need; and
B. The assistance is provided in one of the following ways:
   1. In cash or in-kind by a supplier of home heating fuel or a municipal utility providing home energy;
   2. In cash or in-kind by a rate-of-return entity that provides home energy; or
   3. In-kind by a private nonprofit organization.

Note: You receive "in-kind" assistance, not cash, when you receive a voucher or a third-party check; or when an organization pays cash directly to a provider (e.g., your landlord).

2140. IN-KIND INCOME

2140.1 What is in-kind income?

"In-kind income" is income that is not in the form of cash or negotiable instruments. Examples of in-kind income include real property, food, and occasionally, wages (e.g., room and board or clothing as compensation for employment).

2140.2 How is in-kind income valued?

In-kind income that is unearned and directly satisfies the need for food or shelter is called "in-kind support and maintenance." It has special rules for valuation. Any other in-kind income is valued at its current market value.

2141. WHAT IS "IN-KIND SUPPORT AND MAINTENANCE"?

"In-kind support and maintenance" means unearned income in the form of food or shelter that you receive and that is paid for by someone else. In-kind support and maintenance can be received from someone inside or outside the home.

Shelter includes room, rent, mortgage payments, real property taxes, heating fuel, gas, electricity, water, sewerage and garbage collection service. You are not receiving in-kind support and maintenance in the form of room or rent if you are paying the amount charged under a business arrangement.

2142. VALUATION OF IN-KIND SUPPORT AND MAINTENANCE

2142.1 How is in-kind support and maintenance valued?

There are two rules we use for placing a value on in-kind support and maintenance: the "one-third reduction rule (VTR)" and the "presumed maximum value rule (PMV)." These rules are explained in the subsections below.

2142.2 What is the one-third reduction rule?

Under the one-third reduction rule, an amount equal to one-third of the applicable FBR is considered the value of the in-kind support and maintenance.

Note: The $20 general income exclusion does not apply to the income counted under the one-third reduction rule.

2142.3 When does the one-third reduction rule apply?

The one-third reduction rule applies if you:

A. Live in another person's household throughout a calendar month, except for temporary absences (see §2145); and

B. Receive both food and shelter from within the household. (See §2143 and §2147 for additional information on the one-third reduction rule.)

2142.4 What is the presumed maximum value rule?

Under the presumed maximum value rule, we presume that the value of support and maintenance does not exceed a certain maximum amount (see §2144). However, if you can show that the actual value is lower than the presumed maximum value, we use the lower value to determine your countable income. (See §2147.)

2142.5 When does the presumed maximum value rule apply?

This rule applies in situations when you receive in-kind support and maintenance and the one-third reduction rule does not apply.

2143. ONE-THIRD REDUCTION RULE

2143.1 How much of the reduction amount applies under the one-third reduction rule?

The value of the one-third reduction (see §2142) applies in full or not at all. If the value of the one-third reduction applies, no other in-kind support and maintenance you receive is considered.

2143.2 What is a household under the one-third reduction rule?

A household is your personal place of residence. A commercial establishment, such as a hotel or boarding house, is not a household although one or more households can exist within these establishments. An institution is not a household, and a household cannot exist within an institution.

2143.3 What is another person's household under the one-third reduction rule?

You live in another person's household if the person who provides the support and maintenance lives in the same household and is not:

A. A minor child; or
B. An ineligible person whose income can be deemed to you (see §2167).

You are not living in another person's household when:

A. You or your living-with spouse (or any person whose income can be deemed to you) have an ownership or life estate interest in the home;
B. You or your living-with spouse (or any person whose income can be deemed to you) are liable to the landlord for payment of any part of the rental charges;
C. You have been placed in the household under a program of protective care such as foster care or adult care;
D. You pay at least a pro rata share (see 2143.5 below) of average household operating expenses;
E. All members of the household receive public income-maintenance payments; or
F. None of the food is provided by the household. You buy or eat all of your meals elsewhere.

2143.4 What are average household operating expenses under the one-third reduction rule?

Household operating expenses are the household's total monthly expenditures for food, rent, mortgage, property taxes, heating fuel, gas, electricity, water, sewerage, and garbage collection services. Generally, household operating expenses are averaged over a 12-month period.

2143.5 What is pro rata share under the one-third reduction rule?

A pro rata share of average household operating expenses is the average monthly operating expenses divided by the number of people in the household. The ages of the people in the household do not matter.

2144. PRESUMED MAXIMUM VALUE RULE

2144.1 How is in-kind support and maintenance valued under the presumed maximum value rule?

Instead of determining the actual value of in-kind support and maintenance, we presume that its value is not more than an amount equal to one-third of the applicable FBR plus $20. Unlike the value of the one-third reduction, the presumed maximum value amount can be contested.

2144.2 Can you show that the actual value of in-kind support and maintenance is less than the presumed value?

If you can show that the actual value of the food or shelter you receive is less than the presumed maximum value, we use the actual value in computing countable income.

2144.3 When does the presumed maximum value rule apply?

The presumed maximum value rule applies whenever you receive food or shelter and the one-third-reduction rule does not apply. (See §2142.4.) Presumed maximum value situations are:

A. Living throughout a month in another person's household but not receiving *both* food and shelter from that person;
B. Living in your own household, but someone outside your household pays for the rent, utilities or food; or
C. Living in a non-medical institution.

Note: Room and board provided by anyone during a medical confinement does not count as income at all.

2144.4 Are there any exceptions to applying the presumed maximum value rule?

The value of any in-kind support and maintenance provided to you while living in a private nonprofit retirement home or similar institution is excluded, provided:

A. The in-kind support and maintenance is furnished by the institution itself or a nonprofit tax-exempt organization; and
B. The institution or private nonprofit organization does not have an express obligation to provide you with in-kind support and maintenance.

2145. TEMPORARY ABSENCES AND IN-KIND SUPPORT AND MAINTENANCE

2145.1 How does your temporary absence affect the value of in-kind support and maintenance?

A temporary absence may be due to employment, hospitalization, vacations, or visits. When you are temporarily absent from a permanent living arrangement, in-kind support and maintenance continues to be valued based on your permanent living arrangement. We do not count in-kind support and maintenance you receive during your temporary absence.

If the value of the one-third reduction applies in your permanent living arrangement, the value of the one-third reduction continues to apply while you are temporarily absent. This is true even if you pay for food or shelter during your absence.

2145.2 When are you considered temporarily absent?

You are temporarily absent when you:

A. Were in a permanent living arrangement for at least one full calendar month; and

B. Intend to and do return to the permanent living arrangement in the same calendar month or the next month.

2145.3 Are there any other situations when you may be considered temporarily absent for the purpose of valuing in-kind support and maintenance?

There are other situations where you are considered temporarily absent. In the following situations, we value your in-kind support and maintenance based on your permanent living arrangement, regardless of the length of your stay in the facility.

A. When you are away because of a stay in a medical treatment facility under circumstances such that the $30 payment limit applies, but you intend to return to your permanent living arrangement.

Note: Room and board provided during a medical confinement is not income. No in-kind support and maintenance is considered during the absence.

B. A child under age 22 is generally temporarily absent while away at school, regardless of the length of the absence. As long as the child comes home on some weekends, or for lengthy holidays or vacations, the child is temporarily absent.

Note: If a child is under age 18 and his or her permanent living arrangement is with an ineligible parent, the deeming rules continue to apply during the temporary absence (see §2167). Any in-kind support and maintenance received at the school and not paid for by the parent is income.

2146. ACTING AS AN "AGENT"

2146.1 Can an SSI beneficiary have someone act as their agent?

It is not uncommon to find an individual (or an institution or other organization, such as a State welfare agency) acting as an "agent" on behalf of another individual.

2146.2 What does an agent do?

Acting as an agent is somewhat similar to being a representative payee (see Chapter 16) and may even include the representative payee function. Being an agent simply means that the agent is acting on behalf of another person.

2146.3 Do agents get paid?

An agent does not derive income or resources from that function unless:

A. The agent is paid a fee for services; or

B. The agent misuses the other person's funds.

A SSI recipient may give money to another recipient who will do some grocery shopping for the first recipient. The money belongs to the first recipient and any food purchased with it has been paid for by that first recipient, so the food is not considered in-kind support and maintenance. The second recipient, acting as an agent of the first, does not receive income when the first person's funds are used on behalf of that first person.

2147. TABLES OF FEDERAL BENEFIT RATES, ONE-THIRD REDUCTION VALUES, AND PRESUMED MAXIMUM VALUES

2147.1 What are the applicable Federal benefit rates?

Federal Benefit Rates	2012	2013	2014	2015-2016	2017	2018	2019	2020	2021	2022	2023	2024
Individual Full FBR	$698	$710	$721	$733	$735	$750	$771	$783	$794	$841	$914	$943
Eligible-couple Full FBR	$1,048	$1,066	$1,062	$1,100	$1,103	$1,125	$1,157	$1,175	$1,191	$1,261	$1,371	$1,415

2147.2 What are the applicable one-third reduction rule values (VTR)?

	2013	2014	2015-2016	2017	2018	2019	2020	2021	2022	2023	2024
Individual Full FBR	$236.67	$240.33	$244.33	$245.00	$250.00	$257.00	$261.00	$264.66	$280.33	$304.66	$314.33
Eligible-couple Full FBR	$355.33	$360.67	$366.67	$367.67	$375.00	$385.66	$391.66	$397.00	$420.33	$457.00	$471.67

2147.3 What are the applicable presumed maximum values (PMV)?

	2013	2014	2015-2016	2017	2018	2019	2020	2021	2022	2023	2024
Individual Full FBR	$256.67	$260.33	$264.33	$265.00	$270.00	$277.00	$281.00	$284.66	$300.33	$324.66	$334.33
Eligible-couple Full FBR	$375.33	$380.67	$386.67	$387.67	$395.00	$405.66	$411.66	$417.00	$440.33	$477.00	$491.61

2148. ROLE OF RESOURCES

2148.1 How do resources affect SSI benefits?

The amount of your resources determines whether you are eligible for any given month. If your countable resources are within the limit for eligibility, they have no effect on the amount of your SSI payment. If you have too many resources, you are not eligible for SSI benefits. However, not everything you own is a resource and not all resources count.

2148.2 Does somebody else share responsibility for you?

In certain situations, a person is expected to share financial responsibility for another individual. If someone else shares financial responsibility for you, like a spouse or a parent if you are a child, the resources (and income) of that person(s) are also considered in determining your eligibility. (See §2167.)

2149. WHAT IS CONSIDERED A RESOURCE FOR SSI PURPOSES?

For SSI purposes, a resource is any of the following owned by you (or your spouse, if any): cash, liquid assets, and real or personal property that can be converted to cash to obtain food and shelter. If you have the right, authority, or power to liquidate the property, it is considered a resource.

2150. LIQUID AND NON-LIQUID RESOURCES

2150.1 How are resources categorized?

Resources generally are categorized as either "liquid" or "non-liquid." The difference between the two types of resources is important when determining whether:

A. A resource can be excluded as non-business property essential to self-support (see §2158); or

B. You qualify for conditional payments (see §2164).

2150.2 What are liquid resources?

Liquid resources are those resources that are:

A. In the form of cash; or

B. Convertible to cash within 20 working days.

The most common types of liquid resources are savings and checking accounts, stocks, bonds, mutual funds, promissory notes, certain trusts, and certain types of life insurance.

2150.3 What are non-liquid resources?

Non-liquid resources are all resources that cannot be converted to cash within 20 working days. They include both real and personal property. Examples are automobiles, machinery, livestock, buildings and land.

2151. WHAT IS NOT CONSIDERED A RESOURCE?

The term "resource" does not apply to:

A. Any property right that has a legal restriction preventing its sale or liquidation;
B. Home energy or support and maintenance assistance (see §2139);
C. Restricted allotted land owned by an enrolled member of an Indian tribe if the individual cannot sell, transfer, or otherwise dispose of the land without the permission of others;
D. Except for cash reimbursement of medical or social services expenses already paid by the individual, cash received for medical or social services that is not income under §§2130(A) and (B);

Note: This exclusion applies *only* for the calendar month following the month of its receipt. Cash retained until the first moment of the second calendar month following its receipt is a resource at that time.

E. Retroactive in-home supportive services payments to ineligible spouse and parent, but only for the month following receipt.
F. Death benefits an individual will use to pay the deceased's last illness and burial expenses for the first month following the month of receipt. This only applies for one calendar month following receipt; and
G. Certain gifts of domestic travel tickets if excluded from income and not converted to cash.

2152. OWNERSHIP OF RESOURCES

2152.1 Can more than one person own a resource?

Resources may be owned outright by just one person or ownership may be shared by two or more people.

2152.2 How do you determine what is your resource if you share ownership with another person?

Only that portion of a property that is designated as belonging to you can be considered your resource (except for deeming as described in §2167). If there is more than one owner and the consent of the co-owner(s) is needed for you to liquidate your share, then your share is not a resource if the co-owner(s) do not agree to sell.

If you have a time deposit, checking, or savings account and you have unrestricted access to the funds, you are considered to own the entire amount, even if there is a co-owner on the account. However, if you own the account with another or others who receive or who have filed for SSI benefits, we assume the funds are owned in equal shares.

2152.3 How are your resources valued if you are married?

The total value of a countable property owned only by you and your (eligible or ineligible) spouse is compared with the resource limit for a couple. (See §2166.)

2153. COUNTABLE RESOURCES

2153.1 What resources are countable?

Not all of your resources count in determining your eligibility for SSI (See §2156.) Countable resources are those left after we:

A. Eliminate from consideration any asset that is not a resource; and
B. Apply all appropriate exclusions to the assets that are resources.

Countable resources are determined on a monthly basis. We compare them with the applicable statutory resources limit to determine whether you are eligible for that month.

2153.2 What are the applicable resource limits?

For 2024, the applicable limits are:

A. $2,000 for an individual without a spouse; and
B. $3,000 for an individual with an eligible spouse or a living-with ineligible spouse. See §2166 for a table of resource limits.

2154. HOW RESOURCES ARE VALUED

2154.1 How does SSA value resources?

We generally value both liquid and non-liquid resources at their equity value. Equity value is the price for which the item can reasonably be expected to sell for on the open market, in the particular geographic area, minus any encumbrances (e.g., a loan, a mortgage).

2154.2 Are there any exceptions to valuing cash?

Cash is always valued at its face value. The fact that you owe money does not mean that a specific amount of cash in hand or in a bank account is actually "encumbered."

2155. WHEN ARE RESOURCES VALUED?

Your countable resources are established for each month using their value as of the first moment of the month. We do not consider any change in the value of countable resources, or any conversion of a resource from an excluded to a non-excluded form (or vice versa), until the beginning of the following month. When you file a claim or seek reinstatement during a month, your resources are valued as of the first moment of that month to determine eligibility.

2156. WHAT ARE THE RESOURCE EXCLUSIONS?

In determining countable resources, certain exclusions are authorized by Title XVI of the Social Security Act, by other Federal laws, and by certain court cases. These exclusions are:

A. An individual's home, regardless of value. This exclusion applies to a home owned by the individual or the individual's spouse if it is the principal place of residence. A home includes any adjacent land and related buildings on it;
B. Restricted allotted Indian lands;
C. Household goods and personal effects regardless of value;
D. One vehicle, regardless of value, if you or a member or your household uses it for transportation (see §2157);
E. Property of a trade or business without limit;
F. Non-business property of a reasonable value that is needed for self-support;
G. Resources of a blind or disabled individual that are needed to carry out an approved plan for achieving self-support (see §2177);
H. Life insurance as described in §2159;
I. Burial spaces and certain burial funds up to $1,500 as explained in §2160 and §2161;
J. Disaster relief as described in §2162;
K. Payments or benefits excluded by provisions of a Federal statute other than Title XVI of the Social Security Act;
L. Title XVI or Title II retroactive payments as provided in 20 CFR §416.1233;
M. Housing assistance as provided in 20 CFR §416.1238;
N. Refunds of Federal income taxes and advances made by an employer relating to an earned tax credit as provided in 20 CFR §416.1235;
O. Shares of stock held by a native of Alaska in a regional or village corporation during the 20-year period in which, under the provisions

of the Alaska Native Claims Settlement Act, such stock cannot be transferred;

P. Payments received as compensation for expenses incurred or losses suffered as a result of a crime for nine months following the month of receipt;

Q. Relocation assistance from a State or local government for nine months; and

R. Dedicated financial institution accounts required to be established for the payment of past-due benefits to disabled children as provided in 20 CFR 416.1247;

S. Grants, scholarships, fellowships or gifts provided for tuition, fees or other necessary educational expenses for 9 months after the month of receipt (effective 6/1/04);

T. State annuities for certain veterans (effective 9/1/08);

U. Filipino Veterans Equity Compensation Fund payments (effective 2/17/09);

V. The one-time $250 economic recovery payment under the American Recovery and Reinvestment Act of 2009 (ARRA) for 9 months after the month of receipt (effective 2/17/09);

W. Incentives provided to Medicaid beneficiaries from the Incentives for Prevention of Chronic Diseases in Medicaid program (IPCDM) under the Affordable Care Act (effective 3/23/10);

X. The first $2000 per calendar year of compensation received for participating in certain clinical trials.

Note: An eligible couple gets the same resource exclusions as an eligible individual. However, the resource limit is higher for an eligible couple.

2157. EXCLUSION OF AN AUTOMOBILE OR OTHER VEHICLE

Are automobiles or other vehicles excluded from resources?

One automobile or other vehicle belonging to you (or spouse, if any) is excluded from resources if you or a member of your household uses it for transportation. The value of the automobile or vehicle does not matter.

2158. IS PROPERTY NEEDED FOR SELF-SUPPORT EXCLUDED FROM RESOURCES?

We exclude certain property from resources on the basis that it is necessary for your self-support. Such property, that may be business or non-business, can be excluded as follows:

A. Liquid or non-liquid property used in a trade or business and any non-liquid property you use as an employee can be excluded without limit.
B. Non-liquid non-business income producing property that:
   1. Has an equity value of no more than $6,000 (equity value above $6,000 is countable); and
   2. Produces a net annual return of at least six percent of its excluded equity value.
C. Non-liquid non-business property that:
   1. Has an equity value of no more than $6,000 (equity value above $6,000 is countable); and
   2. Is used to produce goods or services essential to your daily activities. (For example, land or tools used to produce food solely for consumption by you or your household.)

Note: You cannot exclude liquid non-business property.

2159. LIFE INSURANCE

2159.1 Is life insurance considered a resource?
Life insurance is a resource if:
A. You own it; and
B. It has a cash surrender value.

For example, burial insurance and most kinds of term insurance have no cash surrender value. These are not resources.

2159.2 Can life insurance with a cash surrender value be excluded from resources?
Life insurance that has a cash surrender value and is owned by you (or your spouse) is excluded from countable resources if the total face value of all policies you own on any one person is not more than $1,500. However, if the total face value of such insurance is more than $1,500, then the total cash surrender value of the insurance counts as a resource, unless it is designated as funds set aside for burial. (See §2161.)

2160. DO BURIAL SPACES COUNT AS RESOURCES?
The value of burial spaces for you, your spouse, or for any member of your immediate family does not count as resources. This includes grave sites, vaults, crypts, caskets, mausoleums, urns, and other repositories traditionally used for the remains of a deceased person. It also includes headstones and grave markers.

2161. BURIAL FUNDS

2161.1 Do burial funds count as resources?

Money you set aside for burial up to $1,500 each for you and your spouse are excluded from resources if:

A. The resource is designated as funds specifically set aside for burial; and

B. The funds set aside for burial are not combined with non-burial assets.

Note: This exclusion also applies to burial funds set aside for the burial of an eligible child's ineligible parent, parents, or stepparent when parent-to-child deeming applies (see §2169).

2161.2 What do burial funds include?

Burial funds include revocable burial contracts, burial trusts or other burial arrangements, cash, financial accounts, or other financial instruments with a definite cash value that is clearly designated for burial expenses.

2161.3 When does SSA reduce your exclusion?

We must reduce your $1,500 exclusion by:

A. The face value of insurance policies you own if the cash surrender value of the policies has been excluded as described in §2159; and

B. Amounts in an irrevocable burial trust or any other irrevocable arrangement that is available to meet your (or your spouse's) burial expenses, unless it is for excluded burial spaces.

2161.4 Does interest earned on your burial fund count as resources?

Interest earned on your excluded burial funds and appreciation in the value of the funds do not count as income and resources if you leave them as part of your burial fund.

2161.5 What if I use my burial fund for another purpose?

If you use any excluded burial funds, including excluded interest or appreciation for a purpose other than burial, we may withhold your SSI check in an amount up to the amount of burial funds you spend.

2162. RESOURCES AFFECTED BY A DISASTER

2162.1 What is considered a major disaster?

A "major disaster" is one declared by the President under the Robert T. Stafford Disaster Relief and Emergency Assistance Act (formerly the Disaster Relief Act of 1974).

2162.2 What resource exclusions apply when there is a disaster?

When a major disaster occurs, any assistance you receive from any of the following is excluded from resources:

A. The Robert T. Stafford Disaster Relief and Emergency Assistance Act;
B. Any other Federal statute because of the disaster;
C. Comparable assistance received from a State or local government or;
D. A disaster assistance organization.

Any interest earned on assistance described in (A)-(D) above is also excluded.

2162.3 What if something happens to an excluded resource?

If an *excluded* resource is lost, damaged, or stolen, cash or in-kind replacement from any source is excluded from resources for 9 months from the date of receipt, unless a permanent exclusion applies. Under this exclusion, "cash" includes any interest earned on the cash. Both cash and in-kind receipts can be excluded up to an additional 9 months for (good cause).

Note: For victims of disasters declared by the president, if good cause is shown, the exclusion may be extended for up to 12 additional months beyond the nine-month extension for good cause for a total of up to 30 months.

2163. REAL PROPERTY THAT CANNOT BE SOLD

2163.1 Does real property you cannot sell count as resources?

Real property that you cannot sell is excluded from your resources as long as it cannot be sold because:

A. You own the property jointly with another owner(s) and:
  1. It is the other owner(s) principal place of residence; and
  2. The sale would cause undue hardship (due to loss of housing) to the other owner(s); or
B. Your reasonable efforts to sell have been unsuccessful.

2163.2 How long is the property excluded from resources based on reasonable effort to sell?

Initially, we evaluate your reasonable but unsuccessful efforts to sell under a nine-month conditional benefits arrangement. After the nine months, the property is excluded as long as it cannot be sold and your efforts to sell continue.

2164. CONDITIONAL PAYMENTS DESPITE EXCESS RESOURCES

2164.1 Can you receive conditional payments even if you have excess resources?

If your countable resources are more than the applicable limit, you may be able to receive conditional payments. Conditional payments are made when your countable resources include some that are non-liquid. We recognize that it can take months to convert non-liquid resources to cash for support and maintenance.

2164.2 Are you still eligible for regular SSI benefits if you receive conditional payments?

If you receive conditional payments, you are not eligible for regular SSI benefits. You must refund the payments at the end of the conditional payment period.

2164.3 Under what circumstances can you receive conditional SSI payments?

You can receive conditional SSI payments only if:
A. Your total countable liquid resources do not exceed the statutory limit of $2,000 for an individual and $3,000 for a couple; and
B. You agree to dispose of the excess non-liquid resources within nine months if real property (three months for other property) and refund the SSI payments you receive during that period. The time limit for personal property may be extended an additional three months for good cause. If you do not sell the property, see §2163.

2165. IS YOUR SSI ELIGIBILITY AFFECTED IF YOU DISPOSE OF A RESOURCE BELOW ITS MARKET VALUE?

If you give away or sell a resource at less than fair market value on or after December 14, 1999, you may be ineligible for SSI for up to 36 months. We also must report such a transfer to the State Medicaid agency. A transfer of assets may result in a period of ineligibility for some Medicaid covered nursing home services.

2166. WHAT ARE THE STATUTORY RESOURCES LIMITS?

The following table shows the applicable statutory resources limits:

Effective Date	Single Individual	Individual and Spouse
1/1/87	$1,800	$2,700
1/1/88	$1,900	$2,850
1/1/89 and later	$2,000	$3,000

2167. DEEMING OF INCOME AND RESOURCES

2167.1 What is deeming?

When we determine the eligibility and amount of payment for an SSI recipient, we consider the income and resources of people responsible for the recipient's welfare. This concept is called "deeming." It is based on the idea that those who have a responsibility for one another share their income and resources. It does not matter if money is actually provided to an eligible individual for deeming to apply.

2167.2 In what situations are income and resources deemed?

There are four types of situations where income and resources are deemed:
A. From an ineligible spouse to an eligible individual (see §2168);
B. From a parent to a child under age 18 (see §2169);
C. From a sponsor to an alien (see §2170); and
D. From an essential person to an eligible qualified individual (see §2171).

2167.3 What items are not included in the deeming of income?

The following items are not included when deeming the income of an ineligible spouse or parent. Item A is not included when deeming the income of a sponsor or an essential person, but items B through AB are included.
A. Income excluded by Federal laws other than the Social Security Act;
B. Any public income-maintenance payments received by an ineligible spouse or parent, and any income counted or excluded in figuring the amount of those payments;

C. Any income of an ineligible spouse or parent used by a public income-maintenance program to determine the amount of that program's benefit to someone else;
D. Any portion of a grant, scholarship, fellowship, or gift used to pay tuition or fees (effective 6/1/04);
E. Money received for providing foster care to an ineligible child;
F. The value of food stamps and the value of Department of Agriculture donated foods;
G. Food raised by an ineligible spouse or parent and consumed by household members;
H. Tax refunds on income, real property, or food purchased by the family;
I. Income used to fulfill an approved plan for achieving self-support (for blind and disabled individuals);
J. Income used to comply with the terms of court-ordered support, or child support payments enforced under Title IV (Grants to States for Aid and Services to Needy Families with Children and for Child-Welfare Services, Part D-Child Support and Establishment of Paternity) of the Social Security Act;
K. The value of in-kind support and maintenance;
L. Payments received by certain recipients under the Alaska Longevity Bonus program;
M. Disaster assistance (see §2138);
N. Certain home energy and support and maintenance assistance (see §2139);
O. Income received infrequently or irregularly (see §2135(C) and §2137(G));
P. Work expenses if the ineligible spouse or parent is blind;
Q. Income of an ineligible spouse or parent paid under a Federal, State, or local governmental program to provide chore, attendant, or homemaker services;
R. Certain housing assistance;
S. The value of any commercial transportation ticket received as a gift. This applies to travel among the 50 States, District of Columbia, Puerto Rico, Virgin Islands, Guam, American Samoa and the Commonwealth of the Northern Mariana Islands. If a ticket is converted to cash, the cash is income in the month the spouse or parent receives the cash;

T. Refunds of Federal income taxes and advances made by an employer relating to an earned income tax credit;
U. Payments from a fund established by a State to aid victims of crimes;
V. Relocation assistance;
W. Hostile fire and imminent danger pay received from one of the uniformed services;
X. Impairment-related work expenses incurred and paid by an ineligible spouse or parent, if the ineligible spouse or parent receives Social Security disability benefits;
Y. Any interest earned on excluded burial funds and any appreciation in the value of an excluded burial arrangement left to accumulate and become part of the separately identifiable burial fund;
Z. Any additional increment in pay, other than any increase in basic pay, received while serving as a member of the uniformed services, if:
 1. The spouse or parent received the pay as a result of deployment to or while serving in a combat zone, *and*
 2. The spouse or parent was not receiving the additional pay immediately prior to deployment to or service in a combat zone;
AA. Dividend or interest income earned on countable resources or resources excluded under other Federal laws (effective 7/1/04);
AB. Earned income of a student under the age of 22 and regularly attending school.

2167.4 What is excluded from the deeming of resources?

Any resources excluded for an eligible individual are also excluded for an ineligible spouse or ineligible parent for purposes of deeming. In addition, the following two exclusions apply to deemed resources:
A. Pension funds owned by an ineligible spouse or by an ineligible parent or spouse of a parent are excluded from resources for deeming purposes. Pension funds are defined as funds held in Individual Retirement Accounts (IRA's) or in work-related pension plans.
B. For 9 months following the month of receipt by an ineligible spouse or ineligible parent, the unspent portion of any retroactive payment of:
 1. Hostile fire and imminent danger pay received from one of the uniformed services, *and*
 2. Family separation allowance received from one of the uniformed services as a result of deployment to or while serving in a combat zone.

2167.5 When does a change for an eligible individual into or out of a deeming situation become effective?

A change for an eligible individual into or out of a deeming situation is effective the month following the month of change. This rule also applies for changes within the deeming household that affect the computation of deemed income, such as the birth or death of an ineligible child, the marriage or separation of an ineligible parent, etc.

2168. DEEMING FROM AN INELIGIBLE SPOUSE TO AN ELIGIBLE INDIVIDUAL

2168.1 How are income and resources deemed from an ineligible spouse to an eligible individual?

When an eligible individual lives in the same household with an ineligible spouse, the income and resources of the ineligible spouse are deemed available to the eligible individual. If there are ineligible children under age 22 (who are students) in the household, an allocation for their living allowance is provided. A living allowance is also provided for the ineligible spouse.

2168.2 When does deeming NOT apply?

Deeming does not apply when the eligible individual is not in the same household as the ineligible spouse unless:

A. The absence is temporary; or
B. The ineligible spouse is absent from the household due only to a duty assignment as a member of the armed forces on active duty.

2168.3 What income is excluded?

Certain types of income are excluded when determining the income to be deemed from the ineligible spouse. They are listed in §2167.3. Also, there are additional exclusions provided based on whether the ineligible spouse receives earned or unearned income.

2168.4 Can deeming result in a higher payment?

Under spouse-to-spouse deeming, an individual can never receive a higher payment with deeming than would be received if deeming was not done. If deeming does apply, the ineligible spouse's income is combined with the income of the eligible individual and compared to the FBR for a couple (see §2147).

2168.5 What resources are excluded?

The same resource exclusions that apply to an eligible individual apply to an eligible individual with an ineligible spouse. The resources of the eligible individual and the ineligible spouse are counted together and compared to the resource limit for a couple (see §2166).

2169. DEEMING FROM A PARENT TO A CHILD UNDER AGE 18

2169.1 How are income and resources deemed from a parent to a child under age 18?

A child under age 18 is subject to deeming from a natural or adoptive parent or a stepparent living in the same household. However, if a child lives only with the stepparent due to the death or divorce of the natural parent, the stepparent is not considered a parent for deeming purposes.

2169.2 What income is excluded?

The same exclusions that apply to the income of an ineligible spouse, as listed in §2167.3, apply to the ineligible parent. There are also living allowances for the parent(s) and an allocation for each ineligible child under age 22 (and is a student) living in the household. Any income of an ineligible child reduces the amount of the allocation.

The type of calculation used to figure the amount of deemed income for the child depends on the type of income the parent has after allocations are made for ineligible children.

2169.3 When does deeming NOT apply?

Deeming does not apply if the eligible child does not live in the same household as the parent, unless the absence is temporary (e.g., the child is away at school).

2169.4 What resources are excluded?

Any resources excluded for an eligible individual are excluded for an ineligible parent(s). However, two additional exclusions explained in §2167.3 apply to an ineligible parent(s). Currently, the balance of countable resources more than $2,000 in the case of one parent, or $3,000 in the case of two parents (or one parent and the parent's spouse), is deemed to the child.

2169.5 Is there an exception to normal parent-to-child deeming?

There is a provision that allows a waiver of the normal parent-to-child deeming rules. This waiver applies in very few circumstances. Beginning July 1, 1990, parental income or resources are not deemed to any child under age 18 who:

A. Is disabled;
B. Received one or more months of SSI benefits limited to the $30 reduced benefit rate because of residence in a medical treatment facility;
C. Is eligible for Medicaid under a State home care plan; and
D. Would be ineligible for SSI benefits because of deemed parental income or resources.

2170. DEEMING FROM A SPONSOR TO AN ALIEN

2170.1 What is sponsor-to-alien deeming?

The income and resources of an individual who sponsors an alien's entry into the U.S. (by signing an affidavit of support) are considered in determining the alien's eligibility for SSI. The income and resources of the sponsor's spouse are also considered when the spouse is living with the sponsor. This process is called sponsor-to-alien deeming. Deeming applies whether or not the alien lives with the sponsor.

2170.2 What is an affidavit of support?

The sponsor of an alien must sign an affidavit of support, an agreement in which the sponsor promises to provide assistance to the alien. The U.S. Citizenship and Immigration Service (USCIS) (formerly called the Immigration and Naturalization Service (INS)) currently uses two different types of affidavits:

A. For aliens who applied for admission to the U.S. (or applied for a change in their immigrant status) prior to December 19, 1997, an unenforceable affidavit (INS Form I-134) was used; and
B. For aliens applying for admission or change of status on or after December 19, 1997, a new legally enforceable affidavit (INS Form I-864) is generally used. The new affidavits are used only in family situations, including employment-based immigration with family involvement.

Different deeming rules apply to aliens, depending on which type of affidavit their sponsor signed.

2170.3 When does sponsor-to-alien deeming apply?

Deeming applies to all aliens sponsored under the legally enforceable affidavit of support. When the enforceable affidavit is used, deeming continues until the alien becomes a U.S. citizen, or the alien's sponsor dies, or the alien is no longer lawfully admitted the United States for permanent residency (LAPR) and departs the U.S., or obtains 40 work credits. Deeming can be suspended in certain cases, if the alien is subjected to battery or cannot obtain food and shelter.

Deeming also applies to aliens sponsored under the unenforceable affidavit of support, unless:

A. The alien has been granted asylum by the Attorney General;
B. The alien is living in the U.S. under color of law and has not been admitted for permanent residence;
C. The alien filed for SSI prior to October 1, 1980;
D. The alien is sponsored by an organization; or
E. The alien becomes blind or disabled after admission for permanent residence. In this case, deeming applies up until the month disability or blindness begins.

2170.4 What income is excluded?

The exclusions that apply to the income of an ineligible spouse or parent listed in §2167.3 do not apply to a sponsor, except for certain types of income excluded by other Federal laws. Allocations are provided for the sponsor, the sponsor's spouse in the same household, and the sponsor's dependents as defined by the Internal Revenue Service.

These allocations are subtracted from the income of the sponsor and the living-with spouse to determine the amount of income to deem to the alien.

2170.5 What resources are excluded?

Resources excluded from the resources of an eligible individual are also excluded from the resources of a sponsor. Currently, the balance of countable resources above $2,000 (or $3,000 for a sponsor with a living-with spouse) are deemed to an alien.

2171. DEEMING FROM AN ESSENTIAL PERSON TO AN ELIGIBLE QUALIFIED INDIVIDUAL

2171.1 How are income and resources deemed from an essential person to an eligible qualified individual?

An eligible qualified individual with an essential person in the household receives an amount of SSI that is increased by an increment for the essential person. All of the essential person's income is deemed to the qualified individual.

2171.2 What income is excluded?

None of the exclusions from income that apply to an ineligible spouse or parent and are listed in §2167.3 apply to an essential person except those exclusions provided by Federal statutes other than the Social Security Act.

2171.3 What resources are excluded?

The resources of an essential person are deemed to the qualified individual. Restitution payments for Social Security and Supplemental Security Income benefits that were misused by certain representative payees are excluded from the essential person's resources for the 9 months after the restitution is received. If the amount of income or resources to be deemed would make the qualified individual ineligible, or if the qualified individual so chooses, the essential person and the increment are not considered in computing the SSI payment. Once either of these situations occurs, the essential person cannot be reinstated later.

2171.4 Does your temporary absence affect how income and resources are deemed to you from an essential person?

If you are absent from a permanent living arrangement that is with an essential person, the essential person deeming rules continue to apply during a temporary absence. The absence cannot exceed six months, even if for hospitalization.

2172. SPECIAL PROVISIONS FOR CONVERTED RECIPIENTS

2172.1 What is a converted recipient?

You are a "converted" recipient (see §2109) if you, for December 1973, were:

A. Eligible for assistance under one of the Federal/State adult assistance programs for the aged, blind, or disabled; and

B. Automatically transferred ("converted") to the SSI rolls for January 1974.

There are still in effect certain special "grandfather" provisions to ensure you are not disadvantaged by your conversion to SSI. These are explained in the subsections that follow.

2172.2 Are your countable resources more than the allowable limit?

Your countable resources as a converted recipient may be more than the allowable limit described in §2166. When that occurs, you are considered to be within the allowable limit for SSI eligibility if your resources are not more than the maximum amount of resources specified in the appropriate State plan as in effect in October 1972. This is known as the *"State Plan Resources Limits."*

You may have been converted in any category; i.e., as blind, as aged, or as disabled. You are entitled to the use of the State plan resource limits provided, since December 1973:

A. You have lived continuously in the same State as that under whose plan you were eligible for that month; and
B. You have not been ineligible for SSI benefits for a period of more than six months in a row.

2172.3 Were you converted because of blindness?

There are alternative rules for computing countable income if you were converted based on blindness. This provision is known as *"State Plan Income Disregards."* These rules do not apply to anyone converted as aged or as disabled.

Under this alternative, your countable income is computed using whichever of the following results in the lower amount:

A. The SSI income exclusions described in §2135 and §2137; or
B. The disregards that would have applied under the State plan for October 1972.

In order to qualify for the use of the State plan income disregards, you must have lived continuously in the same State as that under whose plan you were eligible for that month.

2172.4 Is your State's definition of disability different from ours?

Occasionally, a State plan for aid to the permanently and totally disabled had a less strict definition of disability than appears in Title XVI of the

Social Security Act. If so, the *"State Plan Disability Definition"* provision may apply. When that occurs, you are considered eligible for SSI on the basis of disability if you:

A. Met the disability criteria in the State's approved plan as in effect for October 1972;
B. Received aid under that State plan for the month of December 1973 and for at least one month before July 1973; and
C. Continue to be disabled as defined under that State plan.

This grandfather provision does not require continuous SSI eligibility or residence in the same State from which you were converted.

2172.5 Do you have an essential person living in your household?

Your FBR may be increased if you have an "essential person" living in your household. This is known as the *"Essential Person Increment."* You may receive this "essential person increment" to the FBR only if:

A. You were a recipient for December 1973 of aid or assistance under:
   1. A State plan approved under Title I (Grants to States for Old-Age Assistance for the Aged);
   2. Title X (Grants to States for Aid to the Blind);
   3. Title XIV (Grants to States for Aid to the Permanently and Totally Disabled); or
   4. Title XVI (Grants to States for Aid to the Aged, Blind, or Disabled) of the Social Security Act, and
B. You had the essential person's needs taken into account in determining your need for aid or assistance.

The essential person increment is $472 per month in 2024. It is added to the FBR, and the total is due you if you have no countable income. Like the FBR for an individual and the FBR for an eligible couple, the essential person increment is increased each January by the cost-of-living adjustment.

2173. WHAT IS THE PURPOSE OF WORK INCENTIVES FOR THE BLIND AND DISABLED?

SSI payments provide a basic level of support for blind or disabled individuals with low earnings ability due to their impairments. A number of work incentive provisions have been incorporated into the SSI program. The purposes of the work incentives are to:

A. Enable blind and disabled individuals to return to work;

B. Increase their levels of work activity without the loss of SSI disability status; and/or
C. Have their SSI benefits protected from reduction based on the increased earnings. In most States, they also permit continued Medicaid coverage after cash payments end.

2174. CONTINUED BENEFITS FOR PARTICIPANTS IN A PROGRAM OF VOCATIONAL REHABILITATION, EMPLOYMENT, TRAINING, OR OTHER SUPPORT SERVICE

2174.1 Are your benefits continued if you medically recover while participating in a program of vocational rehabilitation or similar program?

Your benefits as a blind or disabled Supplemental Security Income recipient may be continued after your impairment is no longer disabling if you are participating in an approved program of vocational rehabilitation, employment, training, or other support services, including the Ticket to Work Program; you began participating in the program before your disability ended; and we have determined that your participation in the program will increase the likelihood that you will not have to return to the disability or blindness benefit rolls. Your benefits may continue until:

- You complete the program; or
- You stop participating in the program for any reason; or
- We determine your continued participation in the program will no longer increase the likelihood that you will not return to the disability or blindness rolls.

2175. IMPAIRMENT-RELATED WORK EXPENSES

2175.1 Do work expenses related to your impairment count as income?

The cost of certain impairment-related services and items you as a disabled (but not blind) person need in order to work can be deducted from earnings in determinations of SGA. This is true even if you need these items and services for non-work activities. Your impairment-related work expenses (IRWE) are also excluded from earned income in determining monthly countable income (see §2135).

2175.2 How are impairment-related work expenses calculated?

In calculating an IRWE, an amount equal to the cost of certain attendant care services, medical devices, equipment, prostheses, and similar items and services is deducted from your earnings. The costs of routine drugs and routine medical services are not deductible unless these drugs and services are necessary to control your condition.

2176. WORK EXPENSES OF THE BLIND

2176.1 Do your work expenses count as income if you are blind?

Your work expenses do not count as income if you:
A. Are eligible to SSI based on blindness (not disability);
B. Received SSI benefits on the basis of blindness for the month before you turned 65; and
C. Receive earned income and the expenses relate to your earning the income.

A deductible expense does not need to be directly related to your blindness. It only needs to be an ordinary and necessary work expense.

2176.2 How much can you deduct?

There is no specific dollar limit on the amount you can deduct. However, the amount must be reasonable and not be more than your earned income in the month. Work expenses are deducted in the month you pay for them.

2176.3 What are some examples of work expenses?

Some frequently encountered work expenses include:
A. Transportation to and from work;
B. Meals consumed during work hours;
C. Job equipment;
D. Licenses;
E. Income or Federal Insurance Contributions Act (FICA) taxes; and
F. Costs of job training.

Expenses for life maintenance (such as life insurance or self-care) are not work-related and are not deductible.

2177. PLAN TO ACHIEVE SELF-SUPPORT (PASS)

2177.1 What is a Plan to Achieve Self-Support (PASS)?

A Plan to Achieve Self-Support (PASS) allows you, as a disabled or blind person, to set aside income and/or resources for a work goal such as education, vocational training, or starting a business. You can even set aside funds to purchase work-related equipment. A PASS does not affect an SGA decision. Income and resources that are set aside are excluded only under the SSI income and resources tests.

Any blind or disabled SSI individual can have a PASS. It is important to keep in mind that as earnings go up, the individual who does not need one now may need one next month to remain eligible or to increase his or her SSI payment amount.

2177.2 When does SSA recognize your PASS?
We recognize your PASS if you:
A. Have a feasible work goal;
B. Have a specific savings/spending plan;
C. Provide for a clearly identifiable accounting for the funds you set aside; and
D. Follow the plan and negotiate revisions as needed.

2177.3 Who can help you with your PASS?
Anyone may help you with your PASS: vocational counselors, social workers, or employers. Our responsibilities are to evaluate your PASS and determine its acceptability. It is also our job to help you put your plan in writing.

2178. SPECIAL CASH BENEFITS TO DISABLED INDIVIDUALS WHO ENGAGE IN SGA

2178.1 Do you engage in Substantial Gainful Activity (SGA)?
We provide special SSI cash benefits if your gross earned income is at the amount designated as the SGA level ($1,550 a month in 2024 for non-blind individuals). You must continue to be disabled and meet all other eligibility rules.

2178.2 How is the special cash benefit computed?
There are no special computations. The only difference between the regular rules and the special rules is that the special rules allow you to be eligible even if you are performing SGA. Your payment amount is still calculated in the usual way. States that pay SSI supplements have the option of supplementing special benefit cases.

2178.3 How do you get the first month of the special benefit?

To get the first month of special SSI cash benefits, you must have been eligible to receive a regular SSI cash payment in a previous month within the current period of eligibility. Then, special benefits may be paid for later months until you become eligible again under the regular rules or become ineligible.

2179. MEDICAID WHILE WORKING

2179.1 Are you eligible for Medicaid even if you work?

Many States provide Medicaid eligibility (see https://www.benefits.gov) based on SSI eligibility regardless of whether you meet the State's own definition of medical need. Even if you lose your cash benefits because countable income is more than the FBR plus the State supplement, if any, you may be eligible for continued Medicaid coverage. Medicaid coverage continues for most working disabled or blind people when earnings (alone or combined with other income) become high enough to cause SSI cash benefits to stop.

Note: Performance of SGA is not an issue. One dollar in countable earned income is enough to qualify if all other requirements are met.

2179.2 How do you qualify for Medicaid while working?

To qualify for Medicaid while working, you must:

A. Have a disabling condition;
B. Need Medicaid in order to work;
C. Not be able to afford equivalent medical coverage and publicly funded personal or attendant care that you would lose without assistance;
D. Meet all non-disability requirements for SSI payment (other than earnings); and
E. Have been eligible to receive a regular SSI cash payment in a previous month within your current period of eligibility.

Note: In some states, you must have qualified for Medicaid the month before these rules apply.

2179.3 Can you get SSI cash benefits again if your benefits ended because of your earned income?

If your benefits ended because you worked and had earnings, you can request to have your benefits started again without having to complete a new application, within 5 years from the month your benefits ended.

We call this process "expedited reinstatement" or EXR. It was effective January 1, 2001.

You can be reinstated via EXR if:
- Your previous SSI disability/blindness eligibility was terminated because of excess earned income or a combination of earned and unearned income;
- You are unable to perform substantial gainful activity because of your medical condition;
- You are not performing SGA in the month you request EXR;
- Your current disabling impairment(s) is the same as or related to the impairment(s) that was the bases for the
- previous disability entitlement;
- You request EXR within the consecutive 60-month period beginning with the month we terminated your eligibility for SSI payments or you have good cause for filing your request late;
- We determine that you are under a disability; and
- You meet all non-medical requirements for eligibility to SSI.

While we determine whether you can get benefits again, we can give you provisional (temporary) benefits for up to 6 months. These provisional benefits may include a cash payment and Medicaid coverage. If we deny your request, we usually will not ask you to repay the provisional benefits. If we approve your EXR request, your benefits will begin the month after your request. Your spouse may also be eligible for reinstatement of his/her SSI benefits.

2180. WHAT IS THE FEDERAL SSI PAYMENT AMOUNT?

Federal SSI benefits are paid at different rates depending on whether you have an eligible spouse and whether you have an "essential person" (see §2110):

A. *If you do not have an eligible spouse* – you are due the FBR of $943 per month in 2024, provided you have no countable income; or

B. *If you are an eligible couple* – You are due the FBR of $1,415 per month in 2024, provided you have no countable income.

Both of these rates are established in the Social Security Act, and are subject to annual cost-of-living adjustments (COLA's). The COLA increases the FBR effective in January based on the increase in the Consumer Price Index.

2181. STATE SUPPLEMENTARY PAYMENTS

2181.1 What are the types of State supplementary payments?

There are two types of State supplementary payments: mandatory and optional.

2181.2 When are State supplementary payments mandatory?

If you were converted to SSI from a State assistance program, your State must supplement the SSI amount. The amount of the supplement is what is necessary to provide you the same level of payment you had before you were converted to SSI.

Payments may be issued directly by the State or the State may elect Federal administration where the mandatory payment and the SSI payment are combined in one payment by the Federal Government.

2181.3 When are State supplementary payments optional?

Most States provide supplementary payments to SSI recipients. These payments vary from State to State and reflect differences in regional living costs. Supplementary payments may be made directly by the State or combined with the SSI payment (by mutual agreement of SSA and State agencies).

A Social Security office can let you know whether your State participates in this program. If so, you can file an application at a Social Security office or at a local welfare office.

2182. COMPUTATION OF PAYMENTS

2182.1 How are payment rates reduced?

Payment rates described in §2180 are reduced by your countable income. If the remainder is more than $0 but less than $1, you are paid $1 for the month. If the amount is less than $1, but being paid as a retroactive payment of more than $1, the actual amount will be paid. For example, you are due $.50 for 4 months. We will pay you $2.00 in one payment.

2182.2 What is the benefit paid to a couple?

The SSI benefit due a couple is:
A. The couple's FBR; *plus*
B. Any essential person increment (see §2172.5) and federally administered State supplementary payment (see §2181) due; *less*
C. The couple's countable income; plus

D. Federally administered State supplementary payment (see §2181); less
E. Any remaining countable income.

Generally, each member of an eligible couple is paid one-half of the couple benefit.

2182.3 Who receives payment if payment is higher due to an essential person?

If your payment computation includes an amount due because of an essential person, the increment is paid to you (and/or your eligible spouse), and not to the essential person.

2182.4 How are you paid if SSA administers the State supplementary payment?

When a Federal/State agreement allows us to administer your State supplementary payment, we add the supplementary payment to your monthly SSI payment. We pay you the total in one check.

2183. RETROSPECTIVE MONTHLY ACCOUNTING

2183.1 What is retrospective monthly accounting?

SSI payments are based on known circumstances for a past month. This is "retrospective monthly accounting" (RMA). Payments are computed for each month. RMA has two parts: an eligibility determination and a payment computation.

2183.2 How does the eligibility determination of RMA work?

If you are ineligible based on the current month's factors (including the current month's countable income), no payment is due and none is paid, except where your income is too high to be eligible for a Federal payment, but low enough to be eligible for a State payment.

2183.3 How does the payment computation of RMA work?

If you are eligible based on the current month's factors, your payment is computed. The payment for a month is generally based on your countable income from the second month before the current month. The basic formula is as follows:

A. Subtract the countable income from two months ago from the current month's FBR (plus any essential person increment); and

B. Compute any federally administered State supplementary payment by subtracting any remaining countable income.

It is possible for you to be eligible only for the State supplementary payment.

2183.4 Are there exceptions to the payment computation formula?

There are exceptions to the payment computation formula:

A. *An individual or couple first becomes eligible for Federal SSI or re-attains Federal eligibility after a period of ineligibility.* The SSI benefit for the first, second and third month is based on the countable income (see §2131) in the first month. Sometimes a type of income in the first month is not received in the second month. We call this "nonrecurring income." Beginning April 2005, where there is nonrecurring income, the SSI benefit for the second and third month is based on the countable income from the first month, minus the nonrecurring income.

These exceptions apply either when an individual or couple has been eligible for and paid only State supplementary payments and attains or re-attains eligibility for Federal SSI; or when an individual or couple first becomes eligible for Federal SSI or re-attains Federal eligibility after a period of ineligibility. After we apply these exceptions, we apply the regular RMA computation; i.e., the SSI benefit is based on the countable income from two months ago.

B. *"COLA coordination."* This exception applies only to SSI recipients who have Title II (Social Security) income and certain in-kind income. In COLA coordination, payment for January and February (the month of the COLA and the next month) is based on countable income from a prior month (as described above). The increase in Title II income, and certain in-kind income, in January and February is used immediately to compute the payments for January and February. There is no delay in using these increased income amounts.

C. *Assistance under certain programs.* Effective April 1, 1988, retrospective monthly accounting does not apply to income received as assistance under:

1. Title IV, Part A (Temporary Assistance for Needy Families) of the Social Security Act;
2. Title IV, Part E (Federal Payments for Foster Care and Adoption Assistance) of the Social Security Act;

3. Refugee cash assistance;
4. Cuban/Haitian entrant assistance; and
5. General and child welfare assistance provided by the Bureau of Indian Affairs.

These payments are used to determine the SSI benefit only for the month they are actually received. Effective February 4, 1994, people can receive Title IV, Part E and SSI at the same time.

2184. PRORATION OF SSI PAYMENTS

2184.1 What does proration of SSI payments mean?

"Proration" means that you receive a fraction of your SSI benefit (Federal benefit plus any federally administered State supplement) that would otherwise be due for the month.

2184.2 When does proration of benefits occur?

Proration happens only in the first month you re-attain eligibility after a period of ineligibility. The fraction is based on the date you first re-attain all factors of eligibility for SSI. Both Federal SSI and federally administered State supplementary payments are subject to proration.

2184.3 What causes proration of benefits?

Factors that can cause proration are:

A. No longer being a resident of a public institution;
B. Being present in the U.S. after an absence;
C. Regaining residency status in the U.S.;
D. Again meeting the definition of citizen, alien lawfully admitted to U.S., or alien permanently residing in the U.S. under color of law; and
E. Compliance to file for other benefits.

2184.4 What is the formula for proration?

The proration formula is as follows:

A. Take the benefit that you would otherwise be due for the month;
B. Multiply the amount in (A) by the number of days in the month from (and including) the date you meet all factors of eligibility through the end of the month; and
C. Divide the amount in (B) by the total number of days in the month.

2185. WINDFALL OFFSET

2185.1 What is the windfall offset?

The "windfall offset" is an important provision that affects individuals and couples eligible for SSI. It applies to people due both SSI and Social Security benefits. The windfall offset prevents a person from receiving more benefits retroactively than would have been received if all benefits were paid in the months they were due.

We use the general rules for computing SSI payment amounts, e.g., RMA, COLA coordination, and proration, to decide the windfall offset amount. Then, the windfall offset amount reduces either the Social Security or SSI retroactive payment, depending on which we pay first.

2185.2 How does the windfall offset work?

It is our policy to pay the SSI benefits first in order to protect possible Medicaid eligibility in the retroactive period. If you are due retroactive Social Security benefits, they are reduced by the amount of SSI you would not have been due had your Social Security benefits been paid in the months they were due. The amount of the reduction is transferred from the trust funds to the general funds of the U.S. Treasury and to the States (for any State supplementary amount you would not have been due). Your eligibility and payments under SSI are not affected for the retroactive period.

In rare situations, you may receive retroactive Social Security benefits first. In this case, your Social Security benefits count as income in the months they were due to compute SSI eligibility and payments. Your SSI benefits are reduced instead of your Social Security benefits. The amount of the reduction is transferred from the general funds to the trust funds. If no SSI benefits are payable, we will pay $1.00 as a monthly SSI payment to protect Medicaid eligibility in the retroactive period.

2186. INTERIM ASSISTANCE REIMBURSEMENT

2186.1 What is interim assistance?

"Interim assistance" is cash or vendor payments furnished by States or political subdivisions to you for meeting basic needs while your application for SSI or appeal of SSA's eligibility determination is pending.

2186.2 How does interim assistance affect your benefit payment?

We may withhold the retroactive SSI payments due you at the time the first payment is made when:

A. We receive a written authorization from you or the State; or
B. We receive notice from the State that it has such an authorization, if the automated authorization notification procedure applies.

When SSA decides you are eligible for SSI, SSA tells the State what months are available for reimbursement from your retroactive SSI payments. We then ask the State the amount of interim assistance paid to you. Once we pay the State what they are due, we will pay the remaining money (if any) to you based SSI payment rules.

2186.3 What is the scope of interim assistance?

Effective January 1, 1989, the definition of interim assistance was expanded to cover aid provided by States or political subdivisions to individuals:

A. Whose SSI benefits are suspended or terminated; and
B. Are later found eligible for payments.

2187. DIRECT FIELD OFFICE PAYMENTS

2187.1 Can Social Security offices make direct payments of SSI benefits?

Social Security offices are authorized to make direct field office payments. There are two types of direct payments: SSI emergency advance payments (EAP) and SSI or Social Security immediate payments.

2187.2 Under what conditions can a Social Security office make an emergency advance payment?

SSI emergency advance payments are available only at the time of initial application if you need assistance before the first payment arrives. You must present strong evidence of the following:

A. Qualifying for payment in the current or in the following month by meeting the qualifications for eligibility (age, disability, blindness, citizenship or alien status as applicable); and
B. A financial emergency exists where you have insufficient income or resources to meet an immediate need for food, clothing, shelter or medical care.

2187.3 How much is the payment under an emergency advance payment?

The maximum EAP is the smallest of these three amounts:

A. The Federal benefit rate (FBR) plus any federally administered State supplement;
B. The amount of that month's payment (computed according to §2182 - §2183); or
C. The amount requested for the emergency.

2187.4 How does SSA recover the emergency advance payment?

If you are due retroactive SSI benefits, the amount of the emergency advance payment is withheld from the retroactive benefits. If there are no retroactive SSI benefits, we recover the emergency advance payment in up to six monthly increments starting the first month you are eligible for benefits.

2187.5 Under what conditions can a Social Security office make an immediate payment?

SSI or Social Security immediate payments are available at the field office management's discretion. To be considered for immediate payment, the following criteria apply:

A. Your case involves delay in payment of benefits due;
B. All development to establish eligibility is complete; and
C. You have a financial emergency which the FO cannot otherwise resolve.

Issuance of an SSI EAP does not mean you cannot receive an immediate payment of SSI or Social Security benefits. An immediate payment is limited to the smaller of:

- $999 for an individual or each member of an eligible couple, or
- The total unpaid benefits due at the time the FO makes the immediate payment.

2188. PRESUMPTIVE BLINDNESS OR PRESUMPTIVE DISABILITY PAYMENTS

2188.1 Under what conditions does SSA make presumptive disability or presumptive blindness payments?

We can make a presumptive disability or presumptive blindness payment to you if:

A. You are applying for the first time for SSI based on disability or blindness;
B. Your medical condition is such that it presents a strong likelihood that you will be found disabled or blind under our rules; and
C. You meet all non-medical factors of eligibility.

Presumptive disability or blindness payments are computed like other SSI benefits (RMA, COLA coordination, proration).

2188.2 How long are the payments made?

These payments may be made for up to six months while you wait for the formal disability or blindness decision. They normally begin with the month after the month a disability/blindness finding is made (by the local Social Security office or State disability determination agency based on specific criteria). Payments end after six months even if a formal decision has not been made.

2188.3 What happens if SSA decides you are not disabled or blind?

If we make a formal decision that you are not disabled or blind, the decision does not cause you to be overpaid SSI benefits. Any overpayment would have to be based on a non-medical factor of eligibility.

2189. INITIAL DETERMINATIONS

2189.1 What is an initial determination?

An "initial determination" is the first decision made on an application, post-eligibility event, or a periodic redetermination of eligibility. An initial determination generally involves eligibility for, or the amount of, SSI payments (including federally administered State supplementary payments). See §2002.1.

2189.2 What should you do if you are not satisfied with SSA's initial determination?

We offer several independent reviews of your case if you are dissatisfied with our determination. Each review is a step in the administrative appeals process. You *must* request review within specified time limits. If you do not request the next step within the time limit, our decision becomes final and binding on the parties affected (except for determinations/decisions reopened under the rules of administrative finality (see §2197)). We may extend the time limit for good cause.

2189.3 What matters can you appeal?

Your legal right to appeal flows from findings that are initial determinations. You do not have the legal *right* to appeal matters that are not the subject of an initial determination. However, we may, at our discretion, review, reopen, and revise our initial (or appellate) determination.

2189.4 What are examples of initial determinations?

The following are examples of initial determinations:

A. Eligibility as an aged, blind, or disabled individual;
B. Eligibility for and the amount of an SSI payment;
C. Eligibility for and the amount of an SSA (or Federally) administered State supplementary payment;
D. Eligibility for and the amount of payment to an eligible recipient who has an essential person living in the home;
E. Residency, citizenship, or alien status;
F. Amount of income and what constitutes income and exclusions from income for a period. However, there are no appeal rights on findings based on income estimates for a *future period*. Any changes of income estimates are disposed of as redeterminations;
G. Amount of resources, what constitutes resources for a period, allocation of resources, tests of ownership, determination of value, exclusion from resources, and disposition of resources;
H. Marital relationship of an individual and spouse for SSI purposes;
I. Living arrangements for SSI purposes;
J. Failure to file for and/or pursue benefits under other programs;
K. Status as a child;
L. Status as a resident of a public institution;
M. Status as a drug addict or alcoholic and compliance with the terms, conditions, and requirements of treatment deemed appropriate for those conditions;
N. Status as a patient, through any month, in a medical treatment facility receiving payments under Title XIX (Grants to States for Medical Assistance Programs) of the Social Security Act;
O. Ineligibility for benefits because of refusal, without good cause, to accept available vocational rehabilitation services for the blind and disabled;
P. Imposition of a penalty deduction for failure, without good cause, to report, or to report timely, any change in circumstances or events that would affect eligibility and/or payment amount;
Q. Reduction, suspension, or termination of payments;

R. Reinstatement of payments, as well as denial of reinstatement, when the individual has requested reinstatement in writing;
S. Fact and amount of underpayment or overpayment;
T. Waiver of recovery of overpayment;
U. Need for a representative payee (except for a recipient under age 18, a person adjudged legally incompetent or a drug addict or alcoholic), the selection of a payee, that a designated payee will no longer serve, or suspension of payments for lack of a suitable payee. In cases of drug addiction and alcoholism, payment through a representative payee is mandatory and this is not an initial determination with administrative appeal rights. However, a legally competent drug addict or alcoholic may appeal the determination that a particular person should serve as representative payee. Only the recipient, the recipient's representative, or an essential person can appeal a decision on the selection of a representative payee;
V. Decisions of ineligibility for failure to submit evidence;
W. Denial of a request for withdrawal of an application, or the denial of a request for cancellation of a withdrawal request;
X. Deemed redeterminations (i.e., the redetermination of eligibility that is presumed to have taken place on the first day of any month for which eligibility and payment amount do not change, but only for the purposes of administrative finality); and
Y. Decision to recover an overpayment, including through a 10 percent check adjustment.

2190. WHAT ADMINISTRATIVE ACTIONS ARE NOT INITIAL DETERMINATIONS?

The following are examples of administrative actions, but they are not initial determinations:

A. Determination of misuse of payments by a representative payee;
B. Method of recovering an overpayment (e.g., by withholding part of a regular monthly payment, netting against an underpayment, etc.);
   Note: The amount to be withheld is an initial determination. (See §2189 (Y).)
C. Compromise settlement for an overpayment;
D. Representative's fees (i.e., a finding as to the amount an attorney or other representative may charge for representing a claimant before SSA);
E. Eligibility for and the amount of an emergency advance payment;

F. Eligibility for presumptive disability or presumptive blindness payments;
G. Timing and frequency of payment;
H. Termination of eligibility after 12 months in a row of suspension;
I. Finding that a prior determination may not be re-opened or revised under the rules of administrative finality;
J. Finding that the expedited appeals process does not apply;
K. Finding that good cause for extending the appeals period does not exist;
L. Findings based on income estimates for a future period (Any changes of income estimates are handled as redeterminations.);
M. Reduction, suspension, or termination of the federally administered State supplementary payment;
N. Denial of a request to be made a representative payee;
O. Disqualifying or suspending a person from acting as a representative in connection with a proceeding before SSA;
P. Determining whether (and the amount of) travel expenses incurred are reimbursable in connection with a proceeding before SSA;
Q. Denying a request to re-adjudicate a claim and apply an Acquiescence Ruling; and
R. Actions to pay, adjust or terminate provisional benefits related to an Expedited Reinstatement (EXR) request. See §2003.

2191. HOW DOES THE APPEALS PROCESS WORK?

An eligible individual or eligible spouse who is a recipient or applicant for SSI payments has a right to appeal our decision as to eligibility or amount of payment. Time limits apply to each step in the appeals process. Extensions are possible if good cause for the delay can be established. (See §2196.) For the purpose of determining the expiration of a time limit, a notice or decision is presumed to have been received within five days of its date, unless there is evidence to the contrary. See §2014. The appeals process consists of four levels described in §§2192-2195 and is to be pursued in the order shown.

2192. RECONSIDERATION

2192.1 What is the time limit for requesting a reconsideration?

You must request a reconsideration within 60 days after receiving notice of our determination. We presume that you receive the notice no later than five days following the date of the notice, unless you show the notice was received later or not at all. See §2004.

2192.2 What are your appeal options?
You have three options when requesting reconsideration:
A. *Case Review*-An independent review of the record with or without additional evidence. This is the only option available in cases involving the medical aspects of a disability denial of an initial application;
B. *Informal Conference*-A review as in (A) above in which you may participate. You may present witnesses and may present the case in person; or
C. *Formal Conference*-Same as (B) above and you may request that adverse witnesses be issued a subpoena and cross-examined by you or a representative. This type of reconsideration applies only in adverse post-eligibility situations (i.e., when your SSI payments are going to be reduced, suspended, or terminated).

2192.3 Who can request reconsideration?
Reconsideration of an initial determination may be requested by the claimant, the eligible spouse, a parent, or the representative payee. An initial determination may also be reexamined by SSA on its own motion. (See §2197.)

2192.4 How do you request a reconsideration?
You must request the reconsideration in writing within 60 days of receipt of the notice of the initial determination. If the initial determination involves an adverse post-eligibility issue (e.g., a hearing in a medical/blindness cessation case), you must request reconsideration within 10 days of receipt of the notice of initial determination. This will ensure payment continues until we make a reconsideration determination, pending an initial appeal determination. Make the request on a special form available at any Social Security office or by letter.

2192.5 How does the reconsideration process work?
The reconsideration process is a thorough and independent review of your case. It is based on the evidence you submitted for the initial determination plus any further evidence you submit in connection with the reconsideration.

A reconsideration is made by a member of the Social Security office staff who was not involved in the initial decision under appeal. This person has been trained in handling reconsiderations.

2193. HEARING

2193.1 What is a hearing?

A hearing is provided to individuals who disagree with the reconsideration determination or any other matter that provides the right to a hearing held before an administrative law judge (ALJ) of SSA's Office of Disability Adjudication and Review. See §2006.

The hearing is a thorough review of your record. You or your representative may appear in person. The ALJ makes a decision based on the evidence already submitted, any additional evidence you provide, evidence that is otherwise submitted, and any testimony given at the hearing. The ALJ has authority to issue subpoenas requiring the attendance and testimony of witnesses and the producing of any evidence that relates to the issues involved in the hearing.

2193.2 How do you request a hearing?

You must request a hearing within 60 days of receipt of the reconsidered determination. A hearing may be requested in writing by you, your eligible spouse, or a representative payee who disagrees with the reconsidered determination.

You may make the request for a hearing on a special form available at any Social Security office or by letter, and file the request with the Social Security office or an ALJ.

2193.3 What is done after you request a hearing?

Upon reviewing your request for a hearing, the ALJ may:
A. Dismiss the case if:
　1. You request it;
　2. You do not appear at a scheduled hearing;
　3. You did not file the request within the time limit;
　4. You were not a party to the reconsideration; or
　5. There has been a previous determination or decision as to your rights on the same facts and issues now present, which has become final; or
B. Hold a hearing on the case and issue a decision.

2193.4 How are you notified of a scheduled hearing?

The ALJ sends you and all other parties involved notice of the time and place of the hearing at least 75 days before the date set. This allows you time to prepare for it. The hearing before the ALJ is usually held in the area where you live, although you may be required to travel up to 75 miles, without travel expense reimbursement. If you have to travel more than 75 miles, you can request travel expense reimbursement. Hearings are held in the 50 States, the District of Columbia, and the Northern Mariana Islands.

2193.5 What help does SSA provide in preparing for the hearing?

The Social Security office is ready to help you prepare for the hearing by:
A. Explaining the issues involved in the case;
B. Explaining how the hearing will be conducted;
C. Explaining how to arrange for the appearance of witnesses; and
D. Advising how to obtain any documents that you may need for the presentation of the case.

2193.6 Do you need a representative?

You may represent yourself, be represented by an attorney, or by any other person you select to have represent you. However, you do not have to be represented by anyone.

2193.7 What happens after the hearing?

After the hearing, the ALJ issues a decision affirming, revising, or reversing the reconsidered determination. The ALJ may also certify the case with a recommended decision to the Appeals Council for decision (though this would happen very infrequently). All parties to the hearing are notified of the ALJ's decision and the reasons for it.

2194. APPEALS COUNCIL REVIEW

2194.1 Why would you request an Appeals Council review?

You may request a review by the Appeals Council if you are not satisfied with the action of the ALJ, whether a decision or dismissal. The Council will grant, deny, or dismiss your request for review as it decides is proper. See §2013.

2194.2 How do you request an Appeals Council review?

You must make a request for a review by the Appeals Council in writing. File your request within 60 days from the date you receive the notice of the ALJ's decision or dismissal. The request may be filed with any Social Security office, at a hearing office, or directly with the Appeals Council. You can make the request by letter or on a special form HA-520, Request for Review of Hearing Decision/Order, which is available at any Social Security office or online at: www.socialsecurity.gov/online.

2194.3 What does the Appeals Council do with the request for review?

The Appeals Council makes a thorough inspection of your claim:

A. The Appeals Council notifies you whether it will review your case.
B. If the Council decides to review your case, you or your representative may request an appearance before the Council for presentation of oral arguments.
C. If the Appeals Council determines that a significant question of law or policy is present or that oral arguments would be beneficial in rendering a proper decision, the appearance will be granted.
D. You may also file written statements in support of your claim. The Appeals Council will notify you of its action in the case.

2195. WHAT IS THE TIME LIMIT FOR FILING FOR CIVIL ACTION IN A FEDERAL DISTRICT COURT?

You must file for civil action in a Federal District Court within 60 days of:

A. Receipt of the Appeals Council's notice of denial of the request for review of the ALJ's decision; or
B. Receipt of the Appeals Council's revised decision.

The court's jurisdiction is limited to rendering a decision on the record. Also, the Commissioner's findings of fact are binding on the court, if supported by substantial evidence. See §2014.2.

2196. CAN THE TIME LIMIT FOR FILING AN APPEAL OR HEARING BE EXTENDED?

Your time limit for filing a request for reconsideration, hearing, or review by the Appeals Council, or a civil action in U.S. District Court may be extended if you show you had good cause for failing to file the request within the appropriate time limit. The decision as to whether or not to grant the extension is made by the office responsible for making the reconsideration, by the ALJ, or by the Appeals Council, depending upon who has jurisdiction over the case. See §2015.

2197. REOPENING DETERMINATIONS/DECISIONS UNDER THE RULES OF ADMINISTRATIVE FINALITY

2197.1 Can final decisions/determinations be reopened?

Even though a determination, revised determination, decision, or revised decision has become final, it may be reopened and revised by the Social Security field office, reviewing office, ALJ, or Appeals Council within certain time limitations and under certain conditions. See §2016.

We may decide to reopen a determination or decision on our own or as the result of receiving a written request from a claimant, eligible spouse, or representative payee. The decision to reopen or not to reopen is not an initial determination and is not subject to appeal.

2197.2 How are decisions reopened?

Determinations or decisions may be reopened as follows:

A. Within 12 months from the date of notice of the initial determination for any reason;

B. After such 12-month period but within two years (for Title XVI) from the date of notice of the initial determination if there is "good cause" for reopening it. After such 12-month period, but within four years (for Title II) from the date of notice of the initial determination if there is "good cause" for reopening it. "Good cause" may exist when:

   1. New and material evidence is submitted;
   2. A clerical error was made; or
   3. The evidence that was considered in making the determination clearly shows on its face that an error was made.

   Note: "Good cause" does not exist where the only basis for reopening the determination or decision is a change of legal interpretation or administrative ruling on which the determination or decision was based.

C. At any time if the determination or decision was based on fraud or similar fault. For Title II cases only, several other provisions listed in our regulations permit reopening a determination at any time. In Title XVI cases, the "at any time" rule applies only if fraud or similar fault is involved.

CHAPTER 22

Black Lung Benefits

TABLE OF CONTENTS

2200. How to Find Black Lung Benefit Information

2200. HOW TO FIND BLACK LUNG BENEFIT INFORMATION

Please go to https://www.dol.gov/owcp/dcmwc to find black lung benefit information.

On November 2, 2002, the President signed H.R. 5572 - the Black Lung Consolidation of Administrative Responsibilities Act - (Public Law 107-275). The Act is effective 90 days after the date of enactment and provides that the Commissioner of Social Security shall transfer to the Secretary of Labor all property and records that the Director of OMB determines relate to the Part B program. This transfer became effective 02/01/03.

Enactment of the legislation represents the culmination of activities that began in 1997 when SSA and DOL signed a Memorandum of Understanding under which the Office of Workers' Compensation Programs (OWCP) in DOL provided selected programmatic, administrative management and general support functions in assisting the SSA in the administration of the Black Lung Part B program.

CHAPTER 23
Other Benefit Programs

TABLE OF CONTENTS

INTRODUCTION
2300. How to Find Other Benefit Program Information

2300. HOW TO FIND OTHER BENEFIT PROGRAM INFORMATION

Please go to https://www.benefits.gov/ to find other Federal and State benefit program information.

CHAPTER 24
Health Insurance Protection (Medicare)

TABLE OF CONTENTS

MEDICARE
2400. How to Find Medicare Information

2400. HOW TO FIND MEDICARE INFORMATION

Please go to this page for information about Medicare: https://www.ssa.gov/benefits/medicare.

CHAPTER 25

Medicare Income-Related Monthly Adjustment Amount

TABLE OF CONTENTS

INTRODUCTION
2500. Description of Medicare Income-Related Monthly Adjustment Amounts (IRMAA)
2501. What is Modified Adjusted Gross Income (MAGI)?
2502. What are the Thresholds ?
2503. What are Sliding Scale Tables?
2504. Description of the Medicare Income-Related Monthly Adjustment Amount Determination Process
2505. How Does the Income-Related Monthly Adjustment Amount Affect the Total Medicare Premium?
2506. What is the New Initial Determination Process?
2507. What are Life Changing Events?
2508. Overview of the Appeal Process for Medicare Income-Related Monthly Adjustment Amount

2500. DESCRIPTION OF MEDICARE INCOME-RELATED MONTHLY ADJUSTMENT AMOUNTS (IRMAA)

Two Medicare laws changed how Medicare Part B and D premiums are calculated for some higher income beneficiaries.

Historically, the government has paid approximately 75 percent of the Part B premium and the beneficiary paid the remaining 25 percent.

As of January 2007, beneficiaries enrolled in Medicare Part B with modified adjusted gross incomes (MAGI) above a set threshold are required to pay a higher percentage of their total Part B premium costs. This is the Income-Related Monthly Adjustment Amount (IRMAA), also referred to as the Medicare subsidy reduction or IRMAA-B.

As of January 2011, beneficiaries enrolled in a Medicare prescription drug plan also known as Medicare Part D, with modified adjusted gross incomes (MAGI) above a set threshold are required to pay an Income-Related Monthly Adjustment Amount (IRMAA). The Income-Related Monthly Adjustment Amount for prescription drug coverage is also referred to as IRMAA-D.

2501. WHAT IS MODIFIED ADJUSTED GROSS INCOME (MAGI)?

Modified Adjusted Gross Income is the sum of:

- The beneficiary's adjusted gross income (AGI) (last line of page 1 of the IRS Form 1040 (U.S. Individual Income Tax Return)), plus
- Tax-exempt interest income (line 8b of IRS Form 1040)

2501.1 How is MAGI used?

MAGI is used to determine if an Income-Related Monthly Adjustment Amount (IRMAA) applies. It is provided by IRS and is generally information that is two years prior (but not more than 3 years prior) to the year for which the premium is being determined. We will use the appropriate sliding scale table (§2503) to determine the IRMAA.

2502. WHAT ARE THE THRESHOLDS?

The Modified Adjusted Gross Income (MAGI) thresholds used for Income-Related Monthly Adjustment Amount (IRMAA) determinations are tied to the consumer price index and are published annually by the Centers for Medicare & Medicaid Services. They vary for individuals with a tax filing status of married and for all other tax filing statuses.

2503. WHAT ARE SLIDING SCALE TABLES?

The IRMAA sliding scale tables are a set of tables containing modified adjusted gross income (MAGI) ranges and income-related monthly adjustment amounts (IRMAA). If your modified adjusted gross income amount is above a certain amount, you pay an IRMAA. Medicare uses the modified adjusted gross income reported on your IRS tax return from 2 years ago.

Your Part B premium based on your 2022 income:

File individual tax return	File joint tax return	File married and separate	You pay (in 2024)
$103,000 or less	$206,000 or less	$103,000 or less	$174.70
Above $103,000 up to $129,000	Above $206,000 up to $258,000	Not applicable	$244.60
Above $129,000 up to $161,000	Above $258,000 up to $322,000	Not applicable	$349.40
Above $161,000 up to $193,000	Above $322,000 up to $386,000	Not applicable	$454.20
Above $193,000 and less than $500,000	Above $386,000 and less than $750,000	Above $103,000 and less than $397,000	$559.00
$500,000 or above	$750,000 or above	$397,000 or above	$594.00

Your Part D premium based on your 2022 income:

File individual tax return	File joint tax return	File married and separate tax return	You pay (in 2024)
$103,000 or less	$206,000 or less	$103,000 or less	Your Plan Premium (YPP)
Above $103,000 up to $129,000	Above $206,000 up to $258,000	Not applicable	$12.90 + YPP
Above $129,000 up to $161,000	Above $258,000 up to $322,000	Not applicable	$33.30 + YPP
Above $161,000 to $193,000	Above $322,000 up to $386,000	Not applicable	$53.80 + YPP
Above $193,000 and less than $500,000	Above $386,000 and less than $750,000	Above $103,000 and less than $397,000	$74.20 + YPP
$500,000 or above	$750,000 or above	$397,000 or above	$81.00 + YPP

2504. DESCRIPTION OF THE MEDICARE INCOME-RELATED MONTHLY ADJUSTMENT AMOUNT DETERMINATION PROCESS

SSA uses Federal income tax return information from the Internal Revenue Service (IRS) about beneficiaries' modified adjusted gross income (MAGI) to make Income-Related Monthly Adjustment Amount (IRMAA) determinations.

SSA requests MAGI information from IRS for the tax year that is two years prior to the premium year, for certain Medicare beneficiaries. If IRS does not have data for that tax year, it will send us data for the tax year that is three years prior to the premium year if it is available and above the threshold. When SSA uses data from three years prior, we will make a correction when data from two years prior becomes available. If data from two years prior and three years prior is not available for an individual or MAGI is at or below the threshold, IRMAA will not be imposed.

Note: Data from two years prior will usually be the most recent income tax return the beneficiary has filed with the IRS. Example—for Medicare beneficiaries in 2007, Medicare Part B costs (including IRMAA) were set during 2006 for premium year 2007. The most recent completed tax return was for tax year 2005, which equals two years before the premium year (PY-2).

When SSA receives MAGI information from IRS, we will use the appropriate Sliding Scale table to determine the IRMAA. Beneficiaries will receive notification with information about SSA's determination and their appeal rights.

When SSA uses MAGI received from the beneficiary in conjunction with a request for a New Initial Determination (§2506), SSA will later verify the MAGI data with IRS. SSA will make any necessary adjustments to the beneficiary's IRMAA based on the MAGI information that IRS provides to SSA.

2505. HOW DOES THE INCOME-RELATED MONTHLY ADJUSTMENT AMOUNT AFFECT THE TOTAL MEDICARE PREMIUM?

The Income-Related Monthly Adjustment Amount (IRMAA) is only one part of the cost of a beneficiary's Medicare premium. The amount a beneficiary ordinarily pays for Part B each month consists of:

- The Standard premium, plus
- Surcharges that may be due for late enrollment or reenrollment (if applicable), plus
- IRMAA (if applicable), minus
- Medicare Advantage reduction in premium credited (if applicable), see §127.5.

The amount a beneficiary ordinarily pays for Part D each month consists of:

- The premium amount for the plan for which the beneficiary has enrolled, plus
- Surcharges that may be due for late enrollment or reenrollment (if applicable), plus
- IRMAA (if applicable)

2506. WHAT IS THE NEW INITIAL DETERMINATION PROCESS?

A new initial determination is a new decision made by SSA that does not require reopening or revising a prior initial determination during a specified period. New initial determinations are only used in the Income-Related Monthly Adjustment Amount (IRMAA) process.

In order for SSA to make a new initial determination of IRMAA:
- the beneficiary must have a qualifying circumstance, and
- the beneficiary must request, either verbally or in writing, that SSA use other tax information.

2506.1 When can a beneficiary request a new initial determination?

There are five qualifying circumstances when SSA may use modified adjusted gross income (MAGI) provided by the beneficiary rather than the information received from IRS to make a new initial determination about the income-related monthly adjustment amount.

The five circumstances are:
- Amended Tax Return
- Correction of IRS information
- Use of two-year old tax return when SSA used IRS information from three years prior to the premium year
- Report of a change in living arrangement when tax filing status is "Married filing separately"
- Life-changing event(s) from the list in §2507.

2507. WHAT ARE LIFE CHANGING EVENTS?

There will be cases when a beneficiary or the spouse of a beneficiary will have experienced one or more events causing a significant reduction in modified adjusted gross income (MAGI). A "significant" reduction in MAGI is a reduction that decreases or eliminates the Income-Related Monthly Adjustment Amount (IRMAA) for a specific year. A beneficiary who has experienced a life-changing event that caused a significant reduction in MAGI may request SSA to make a new initial determination using a more recent tax year than the tax year used previously.

A life changing event can be one or more of the following eight events:
- Death of Spouse
- Marriage
- Divorce or annulment
- Work reduction
- Work stoppage
- Loss of Income-Producing Property
- Loss or reduction of pension income
- Receipt of employer settlement payment.

2508. OVERVIEW OF THE APPEAL PROCESS FOR MEDICARE INCOME-RELATED MONTHLY ADJUSTMENT AMOUNT

Once an Income-Related Monthly Adjustment Amount (IRMAA) determination is made for Medicare Part B or D or both, SSA mails a notice to the beneficiary. The notice informs the beneficiary of the determination and appeal rights. The notice also provides information about what a beneficiary should do if they have other information about their income or if their circumstances have changed. The IRMAA determination will apply to both Medicare Part B and D where applicable. If an appeal is filed, the appeal determination will also apply to both Part B and D if applicable.

2508.1 When can an appeal be filed?

A beneficiary or his authorized representative can request an appeal within 60 days of receipt of an IRMAA determination notice.

2508.2 What are the levels of appeal?

There are four levels of appeal that apply to IRMAA determinations:

- A reconsideration processed by the Field Office or Processing Center
- A hearing before an Administrative Law Judge of the Department of Health and Human Services (HHS) Office of Medicare Hearings and Appeals
- A review by the HHS Medicare Appeals Council, and
- Federal Court action.

CHAPTER 26
Extra Help with Medicare Prescription Drug Costs

TABLE OF CONTENTS

INTRODUCTION
2600. Description of Extra Help Available for Medicare Prescription Drug Costs
2601. Eligibility for Extra Help with Prescription Drug Costs

ENTITLEMENT TO SVB
2602. What is income?
2603. What is not income?
2604. Whose income is counted?
2605. What is earned income?
2606. What is unearned income?
2607. How is unearned income counted?
2608. What are unearned income exclusions?
2609. What are resources?
2610. Whose resources are counted?
2611. How are resources counted?
2612. What are resource exclusions?
2613. Verification Process (General)
2614. Overview of the Appeals Process
2615. Redeterminations

2600. DESCRIPTION OF EXTRA HELP AVAILABLE FOR MEDICARE PRESCRIPTION DRUG COSTS

The Medicare Prescription Drug Program offers extra help with prescription drug costs. If you have limited income and resources, Social Security can help. The Extra Help will provide relief for some or all payments of premiums, annual deductible, and co-payments related to the Medicare Prescription Drug Program.

Note: Unless you tell us not to on your Extra Help application, SSA will transmit data used to determine Extra Help eligibility and the amount of Extra Help from the application process to your Medicaid State agency to initiate an application for the Medicare Savings Programs (MSP). The State may then contact you for any additional information needed.

2601. ELIGIBILITY FOR EXTRA HELP WITH PRESCRIPTION DRUG COSTS

2601.1 When are you entitled to Extra Help with Prescription Drug Costs?

You are entitled to Extra Help with prescription drug costs if you:
A. Are entitled to benefits under Medicare Part A (hospital insurance) or enrolled in Medicare Part B (medical insurance) or both, and
B. Reside in one of the 50 states or the District of Columbia, and
C. Your combined savings, investments, and real estate are not worth more than $33,950, if you are married and living with your spouse, or $17,010 if you are not currently married or not living with your spouse. **(Do NOT count your home, vehicles, personal possessions, life insurance, burial plots, irrevocable burial contracts or back payments from Social Security or SSI.)** If you have more than those amounts, you may not qualify for the extra help. However, you can still enroll in an approved Medicare prescription drug plan for coverage.

2601.2 How do I apply for this Extra Help?

You may apply online at: https://www.socialsecurity.gov, at a local Social Security office, or with your State Medicaid Agency. You can also call 1-800-772-1213 (TTY 1-800-325-0778). For more information, please visit https://www.ssa.gov/pubs/EN-05-10508.pdf.

2601.3 When Is It NOT Necessary to File an Application?

You do not need to file an application if you:
- receive Supplemental Security Income (SSI) payments and have Medicare, or
- you have full Medicaid and Medicare coverage.

If your State Medicaid program pays your Medicare Part B premiums because you belong to a Medicare Savings Program, contact your State whether you should file an application for Extra Help. You may be able to get this coverage automatically.

2602. WHAT IS INCOME?

Income is anything you receive in cash that can be used to meet your needs for food or shelter. Income can be earned or unearned.

2603. WHAT IS NOT INCOME?

An item received is not income if it is neither food nor shelter and it cannot be used to obtain food or shelter.

Note: We do not count in-kind support and maintenance (food or shelter) as income when determining eligibility for Medicare Part D Extra Help. That is, we do not count the help you receive from someone else to pay your household expenses, such as, food, mortgage, rent, heating fuel or gas, electricity, water, and property taxes.

2604. WHOSE INCOME IS COUNTED?

We count only your income if you are not married, or if you are married but not living with your spouse at the time that you apply for Extra Help.

If you are married and are living with your spouse in the same household in the month you apply for Extra Help, we count the income of both spouses.

If the amount of Extra Help you are eligible for is based on the income of both spouses, we stop counting your spouse's income in the month following the month that a report is received that you and your spouse stopped living together.

2604.1 Periods for which income is counted

For purposes of determining your eligibility for Extra Help and how much Extra Help you will receive, we consider all of the countable income you and your living-with spouse receive (or expect to receive) during the year for which your eligibility is being determined.

2605. WHAT IS EARNED INCOME?

Earned income consists of the following:
- Wages - Wages are what an individual receives (before any deductions) for working as someone else's employee. Wages include salaries, commissions, bonuses, severance pay, and any other special payments received because of employment. Wages may also include the value of food and shelter, or other items provided instead of cash. For example, shelter provided to an employee can be considered wages. This is considered in-kind earned income. However, for domestic or agricultural workers, in-kind pay is treated as unearned income.
- Net earnings from self employment
- Payments for services in a sheltered workshop, and
- Most royalties and honoraria.

2605.1 How is earned income counted?

We may count more earned income than the individual actually receives. We count more than the individual actually receives if amounts are withheld from earned income because of a garnishment, or to pay a debt or other legal obligation such as taxes, or to make any other payments such as for health insurance.

We count wages, services in a sheltered workshop, royalties, and honoraria at the earliest of the following points:
- when the individual receives them;
- when they are credited to the individual's account; or
- when they are set aside for the individual's use, i.e., the employer sets aside the wages for payment at a future date as requested by the employee (e.g., deferred wages).

We count the current market value of in-kind earned income. If the individual receives an item that is not fully paid for and is responsible for the unpaid balance, only the paid up value is counted as income.

We count net earnings from self-employment on a taxable year basis. If the individual has net losses from self-employment, we deduct them from the individual's other earned income. We do not deduct net losses from the spouse's earned income. If the individual with a net loss does not have other earned income, no deduction is applicable. We do not deduct the net losses from the individual's or spouse's unearned income.

2605.2 What are earned income exclusions?

While it is necessary to ascertain the sources and amounts of all of an individual's earned income, we do not count all of it to determine whether the individual is eligible for Extra Help with prescription drug costs. These are earned income exclusions.

We do not count as earned income the following:
- Any refund of Federal income taxes received under section 32 of the Internal Revenue Code (relating to the earned income tax credit), and any payment received from an employer under section 3507 of the Internal Revenue Code related to advance payments of the earned income tax credit;
- The first $30 per calendar quarter of earned income which is received infrequently or irregularly;
- Any portion of the $20 per month general income exclusion which has not been excluded from the unearned income of the individual (or of the combined unearned income of the individual and living-with spouse) received in that same month;
- $65 per month of the individual's earned income (or the combined earned income of the individual and living-with spouse) received in that same month;
- Earned income used to pay impairment-related work expenses if the individual receives Social Security disability benefits not based on blindness and is under age 65;
- One-half of the remaining earned income that the individual (or the individual and living-with spouse) receives in that same month; and
- Earned income used to meet any expenses that are reasonably attributable to the earning of the income if the individual receives Social Security disability benefits based on blindness and is under age 65.

2606. WHAT IS UNEARNED INCOME?

Unearned income is all income that is not earned income.
A. Private pensions and annuities;
B. Periodic public payments such as Social Security benefits, Railroad Retirement benefits, Department of Veterans Affairs pension and compensation payments, civil service annuities, workers'

compensation, unemployment compensation, and payments based on need involving Federal funds;

C. Life insurance proceeds and other death benefits, to the extent that the total amount is more than the expenses of the deceased person's last illness and burial paid by the individual;

D. Gifts and inheritances;

E. Support and alimony payments in cash or in-kind;

F. Prizes and awards;

G. Rents and royalties (except those royalties defined as earned income); and

H. Certain payments not considered wages for Social Security purposes:
   1. Tips under $20 per month;
   2. Jury fees;
   3. Money paid to individuals who are residents, but not employees, of institutions; and
   4. Military pay and allowances, except basic pay.

2607. HOW IS UNEARNED INCOME COUNTED?

Unearned income is counted at the earliest of the following points:
- when it is received;
- when it is credited to an individual's account; or
- when it is set aside for his or her use.

We may count more or less of income than the individual actually receives.

Overpayment Recovery

We count more income than the individual receives where a benefit payment (such as a Social Security benefit) has been reduced to recover an overpayment. In such a situation, the individual is repaying a legal obligation through the withholding of a portion of his or her benefit amount, and the amount of this withholding is part of the individual's unearned income.

Garnishment or Debts

We also include more than the individual receives if amounts are withheld from unearned income because of a garnishment, or to pay a debt or other legal obligation, or to make any other payment such as payment of the individual's Medicare Part B, C, or D premiums.

Expenses of Obtaining Income
We count less than the individual actually receives if part of the payment is for an expense incurred to obtain the payment. For example, if money is received from an accident settlement, we subtract from the amount of the payment any medical, legal, or other expenses connected with the accident. Similarly, if the individual receives a retroactive check from a benefit program such as workers compensation, we subtract legal fees connected with the claim. We do not subtract from any taxable unearned income the amount used to pay personal income taxes. The payment of taxes is not considered an expense of obtaining income.
Retroactive Benefits
We count retroactive monthly benefits such as Social Security benefits as unearned income in the month the individual receives the retroactive benefits.
One-Time Payment
We evaluate one-time payments following normal income counting rules. Since a one-time payment is not a recurring monthly payment, we count the payment like it was received in equal payments spread over 12 months. For example, if an individual receives a one-time payment of $3,600, we divide the payment amount by 12 months count the one-time payment as unearned income in the amount of $300 per month for 12 months.
Veterans Benefits
If the individual receives a veteran's benefit that includes an amount paid because of a dependent, we do not count as unearned income the amount paid because of the dependent. However, the portion of the payment to the veteran that is attributable to the dependent is counted as the unearned income of the dependent, if the dependent resides with the veteran or receives a separate payment from the Department of Veterans Affairs.
Rental Income
We count rental income as unearned income after expenses are deducted. We use the amount of net rental income reported on your last Federal tax return and divide the amount by 12 months to determine your average monthly net rental income.

"Patrimony" Funds Received by Members of Religious Orders Who Have Taken a Vow of Poverty
Patrimony traditionally refers to a family inheritance. Members of religious orders often relinquish control of the patrimony to the religious order when required by the terms in his or her vow of poverty. If the member can access the funds for his or her own use, we count funds placed into the patrimony as unearned income in the month the member receives funds (e.g., the inheritance). We count only funds that the member can withdraw from the patrimony as income. We do not count any interest and dividends earned by the patrimony as income for the member. Patrimony funds are not a resource if the member has no access to the funds to pay for his or her food and shelter expenses, even if he or she retains ownership of the patrimony.

2608. WHAT ARE UNEARNED INCOME EXCLUSIONS?

For purposes of determining countable income for Extra Help with Medicare prescription drug costs, the unearned income exclusions that apply to the SSI program also apply to Extra Help with Medicare prescription drug costs determinations (see §2137).

Note: We do not count in-kind support and maintenance as income when we determine your eligibility for Extra Help. That is, we do not count the help you receive from someone else to pay your household expenses, such as, food, mortgage, rent, heating fuel or gas, electricity, water, and property taxes.

2609. WHAT ARE RESOURCES?

Resources are cash or other assets that an individual owns and could convert to cash to be used for his or her support and maintenance.

For purposes of determining eligibility for Extra Help with Medicare prescription drug costs, the following are countable resources:

Liquid Resources
We count liquid resources. Liquid resources are cash or other property, which can be converted to cash within 20 workdays. Examples of resources that are ordinarily liquid are stocks, bonds, mutual fund shares, promissory notes, mortgages, financial institution accounts (including savings, checking, and time deposits, also known as certificates of deposit), retirement accounts such as individual retirement accounts (IRA), 401(k) accounts, trusts if they are revocable or the trust beneficiary can direct the use of the funds, and similar items.

Non-Home Real Property
The equity value of non-home real property is counted as a resource.
Note: The home that serves as the individual's principal place of residence is excluded from resource counting.

2610. WHOSE RESOURCES ARE COUNTED?

When we determine countable resources for the Extra Help, we need to determine if the individual filing for the Extra Help lives with his or her spouse.

1. Individual is not Married
If the individual is not married when the Extra Help application is filed or the month that eligibility is redetermined, we count only the resources owned by the individual. We do not count the resources of relatives or non-relatives (roommates) who live with the individual.

2. Married Couple Living Together
If the individual is married and living with his or her spouse when the Extra Help application is filed or the month that eligibility is redetermined, we count the resources of both the individual and his or her spouse. This is true whether one or both members of the married couple apply or are eligible for the Extra Help.

3. Individual Marries
If an individual's eligibility for the Extra Help has been determined as a single individual, we start counting the spouse's resources in the month after we receive a report the individual married and is living with his or her spouse.

4. Individual is Married but not Living with Spouse
If the individual is married but separated from his or her spouse at the time the individual applies for Extra Help or in the month we redetermine eligibility, we count only the individual's resources.

5. Marriage Ends
If eligibility for the Extra Help is based on the resources of both the individual and the spouse, we stop counting the spouse's resources the month after we receive a report the marriage ended due to death, divorce, or annulment.

6. Married but Separated
If the individual is married but separated from his or her spouse in the month that the Extra Help application is filed or the month that we redetermine eligibility, we count only the individual's resources.

If the individual's Extra Help is based on the resources of both spouses, we will stop counting the spouse's resources in the month after we receive a report that the individual and spouse stopped living together.

7. *Married Couple Resumes Living Together*

If an individual's eligibility for the Extra Help has been determined as a single individual, we start counting the spouse's resources in the month after we receive a report the individual is living with his or her spouse again.

8. *Temporary Absence*

If the individual's eligibility for the Extra Help is based on the resources of both the individual and his or her living-with spouse, we will continue counting the resources of both the individual and his or her living-with spouse if one member of the married couple is temporarily away from home and it was due to one of the following:

- Service in the U.S. Armed Forces;
- An absence of 6 months or less and neither the individual nor his or her living-with spouse was outside of the United States during this time, and the absence was due to business, employment, or confinement in a hospital, nursing home, other medical institution, or a penal institution.
- An absence based on other circumstances, and it is alleged by the spouses that they expect to live together in the near future.

2611. HOW ARE RESOURCES COUNTED?

An individual's countable resources are determined as of the first moment of the month that an application for the Extra Help is filed or the month that eligibility is redetermined. A resource determination is based on resources the individual (or the individual and living-with spouse) have as of the first moment of the month.

Resources, other than cash, are evaluated according to an individual's equity in the resources. For purposes of determining eligibility for the Extra Help, the equity value of an item is defined as the price that item can reasonably be expected to sell for on the open market in the particular geographic area involved, minus any encumbrances. If resources are jointly owned, the individual's equity value is determined following SSI rules for determining ownership and equity (see §2152).

Cash an individual receives during a month is evaluated under the rules for counting income during the month of receipt. If the individual retains the cash until the first moment of the following month, the cash is countable as a resource unless it is otherwise excludable.

2612. WHAT ARE RESOURCE EXCLUSIONS?

We do not count all of an individual's resources when we determine eligibility for the Extra Help.

For purposes of determining countable resources for the Extra Help with Medicare prescription drug costs, we apply the exclusions applicable to the SSI program unless a specific exception is noted. SSI resource exclusions applicable to Extra Help determinations include the following:

- Your primary residence
- Your personal possessions
- Your vehicle
- Resources you can't easily convert to cash, such as jewelry or home furnishings
- Property you need for self support, such as rental property or land you use to grow produce for home consumption
- Non-business property essential to your self-support
- Life insurance policies
- Burial expenses
- Interest earned on money you plan to use for burial expenses

Certain other money you are holding is not counted for 9 months, such as:

- Retroactive Social Security benefits or Supplemental Security Income (SSI) payments
- Housing assistance
- Tax advances and refunds related to earned income tax credits and child tax credits
- Compensation you receive as a crime victim
- Relocation assistance from a State or local government

Note: Unless identified as exceptions, other SSI exclusions not listed above are also considered exclusions for purposes of determining eligibility for the Extra Help.

2613. VERIFICATION PROCESS (GENERAL)

Determinations of eligibility for the Extra Help are based on a comparison of the income and resource information provided on the application with income and resource data that SSA obtains from its own records and through matching agreements with other agencies.

Verification may be needed for income, liquid resources, or real property or a combination of the three issues, depending on the comparison of the application data with the agency data. If the application data and the agency data are in relative agreement (within certain tolerances), the Extra Help determination is processed. If the application data and agency data are not within these tolerances, the case is sent through a verification process where the applicant is contacted to resolve the discrepancies.

The purpose of verification is to reconcile discrepancies between the application data and the agency data and determine the correct amount of income and resources for the individual.

2614. OVERVIEW OF THE APPEALS PROCESS

The appeal process for Extra Help determinations consists of one formal SSA administrative step. The individual can choose a hearing either by telephone or case review. Case review will be based on the information in the file and any additional information the individual or his or her personal representative provides. Both, the hearing by telephone and the hearing by case review are the same level of the administrative appeal process for Extra Help determinations. If an individual is dissatisfied with SSA's final decision, he or she may file an action in Federal district court.

2614.1 What can you do if you do not agree with Social Security's decision about your claim for Extra Help with Medicare prescription drug costs?

If you are not satisfied with the decision you may request an appeal by calling the national toll-free 800 number (1-800-772-1213, TTY 1-800-325-0778) or by calling, writing, or visiting any Social Security office to request an appeal. You can also obtain a copy of the SSA-1021 (Appeal of Determination for Extra Help with Medicare Prescription Drug Plan Costs) from our website at https://www.ssa.gov/forms/ssa-1021.pdf.

2615. REDETERMINATIONS

There are no mandatory reporting rules in the program for Extra Help with Medicare prescription drug costs. However, the law requires that SSA periodically redetermine a person's continuing eligibility for Extra Help with Medicare prescription drug costs and the amount of that help.

We will schedule a redetermination of a person's eligibility for the Extra Help about a year after eligibility began. Each year, we will select cases for redetermination in the period August through December, rather than throughout the year. The redeterminations will generally be conducted by mail rather than face-to-face. Also, if you experience one of the events in §2615.1, you may want to request a redetermination if the event reduces your income and/or resources.

Note: Beginning January 1, 2011 a special rule applies to widows and widowers. When one member of a married couple dies, a redetermination can be delayed until one year after the report of death if the death could decrease or eliminate the amount of Extra Help.

2615.1 What events can result in a redetermination of the amount of Extra Help you receive before the periodic redetermination?
A. You get married;
B. You and your spouse who lives with you divorce;
C. Your spouse who lives with you dies;
D. You and your spouse who lives with you separate;
E. You and your spouse who lives with you have your marriage annulled; or
F. You and your previously separated spouse begin living together again.

2615.2 What happens to your Extra Help with Medicare prescription drug costs after you notify SSA of an event?
Certain changes in your situation (above) may affect the amount of Extra Help that you can receive to pay for your prescription drug costs. Based on the event and circumstances reported, SSA may adjust the amount of help you receive.

Chapter 27
Special Veterans Benefits

TABLE OF CONTENTS

INTRODUCTION
2700. What are Special Veterans Benefits?
2701. What is the purpose of Special Veterans Benefits (SVB)?

ENTITLEMENT TO SVB
2702. How can you become entitled to SVB?
2703. When are you qualified for SVB?
2704. Who is a veteran of World War II?
2705. When are you eligible for SSI?
2706. When are you not eligible for SSI?
2707. What is other benefit income?
2708. When are you disqualified for SVB?
2709. Where can you file for SVB?
2710. What happens when you file an application for SVB?
2711. When are you residing outside the United States?

PAYMENTS
2712. How are SVB payments calculated?
2713. When are SVB payments made?
2714. Are State supplementary payments made as they are for SSI?
2715. What countries can we not send payments to?

REPRESENTATIVE PAYEE
2716. What happens if you become unable to manage your SVB?

VISIT OR MOVE TO THE UNITED STATES
2717. What happens if you return to the United States to visit?
2718. When can you be entitled to SVB payments for more than 1 month while you are in the United States?
2719. What if you return to the United States for a visit and decide to live here?
2720. What if you return to the United States to live?

DETERMINATIONS, APPEALS AND REOPENINGS
2721. Initial determinations
2722. Appeal Process
2723. Reconsideration
2724. Hearing
2725. Appeals Council Review
2726. U.S. District Court
2727. Extension of Time for Filing
2728. Reopening Final Determinations or Decisions Under the Rules of Administrative Finality

2700. WHAT ARE SPECIAL VETERANS BENEFITS?

Special Veterans Benefits (SVB) are benefits funded by the Federal Government and are administered by the Social Security Administration. Under the SVB program, special benefits are paid to certain veterans of World War II who reside outside the United States.

SVB is authorized by Title VIII (Special Benefits for Certain World War II Veterans) of the Social Security Act.

SVB is not the same as Supplemental Security Income (SSI). It is a separate benefit program and is financed from the general funds of the United States Treasury.

2701. WHAT IS THE PURPOSE OF SPECIAL VETERANS BENEFITS (SVB)?

SVB payments are intended to provide an income so that certain World War II veterans who were entitled to SSI can leave the United States and live with their families abroad.

2702. HOW CAN YOU BECOME ENTITLED TO SVB?

In order to become entitled to SVB, you must be qualified for SVB and living outside the United States.

2703. WHEN ARE YOU QUALIFIED FOR SVB?

You are qualified for SVB if you:
A. Were age 65 or older on December 14, 1999, the date the law was enacted;
B. Are a World War II veteran (as explained in section 2704);
C. Were eligible for SSI benefits for December 1999, the month the law was enacted (as explained in section 2705);
D. File an application for SVB;
E. Are eligible for SSI benefits for the month in which you file an application for SVB; and
F. Do not have other benefit income (as explained in section 2707) that is equal to, or more than, 75 percent of the SSI Federal benefit rate.

2704. WHO IS A VETERAN OF WORLD WAR II?

You are a World War II veteran if:
A. You served in the:
   1. Active military, naval or air service of the United States at any time during the period beginning on September 16, 1940 and ending on July 24, 1947; or

2. Organized military forces of the Government of the Commonwealth of the Philippines, while the forces were in the service of the U.S. Armed Forces pursuant to the military order of the President dated July 26, 1941. The term military forces includes organized guerrilla forces under commanders appointed, designated, or subsequently recognized by the Commander in Chief, Southwest Pacific Area, or other competent authority in the U.S. Army. This military service must have been rendered during the period beginning on July 26, 1941 and ending on December 30, 1946.

and

B. You were discharged or released from this military service under conditions other than dishonorable
  1. After service of 90 days or more, or
  2. Because of a disability or injury incurred or aggravated in the line of active duty.

2705. WHEN ARE YOU ELIGIBLE FOR SSI?

Generally, you are eligible for SSI and meet this requirement for qualification for SVB, if you were entitled to SSI for the applicable month and that entitlement has not been terminated.

2706. WHEN ARE YOU NOT ELIGIBLE FOR SSI?

You are not eligible for SSI for any month for which your SSI:

A. Claim was denied;

B. Entitlement was not timely terminated (for example, if you did not report your departure from the United States and your SSI entitlement should have been terminated); or

C. Benefits are subject to penalty deductions because you knowingly made false or misleading statements of a material fact in order to receive SSI benefits.

2707. WHAT IS OTHER BENEFIT INCOME?

Other benefit income is any recurring payment you receive as an annuity, pension, retirement or disability benefit. It includes such payments as:

A. Social Security old-age or survivors insurance benefits;

B. U.S. veterans compensation or pension payments;

C. Veterans benefits from another country (for example, PVAO in the Philippines);

D. Civil Service benefits (for example, GSIS in the Philippines);
E. Military pensions (for example, AFP in the Philippines);
F. Railroad annuities or pensions; and
G. Unemployment insurance benefits.

This income must have been received from the same source, or a related, source during the 12-month period before the month in which you file your application for SVB.

2708. WHEN ARE YOU DISQUALIFIED FOR SVB?

You cannot be qualified for SVB in any month:

A. That begins after the month in which the Attorney General notifies us that you have been removed (deported) from the United States under section 237(a) or 212(a)(6)(A) of the Immigration and Nationality Act and before the month in which you are subsequently lawfully admitted to the United States for permanent residence; or

B. During any part of which you are fleeing to avoid prosecution, custody or confinement after conviction for a crime that is a felony, under the laws of the United States or the jurisdiction in the United States from which you have fled or, in the jurisdictions that do not define crimes as felonies, is punishable by death or imprisonment for a term exceeding one year regardless of the actual sentence imposed; or

C. During any part of which you violate a condition of probation or parole imposed under Federal or State law; or

D. During which you are not a citizen or national of the United States and reside in a country to which payments to residents of that country are withheld by the Treasury Department under section 3329 of title 31, United States Code. Treasury Regulations prohibit payments to residents of Cuba and North Korea.

2709. WHERE CAN YOU FILE FOR SVB?

You can file for SVB at any of the following places:

A. An SSA office;
B. The SSA Division of the U.S. Veterans Affairs Regional Office in Manila, Philippines; or
C. A U.S. Embassy or consulate abroad.

2710. WHAT HAPPENS WHEN YOU FILE AN APPLICATION FOR SVB?

2710.1 What happens if you are outside the United States when you file?

We will determine whether you are entitled to SVB. If you are entitled to SVB, we will send you a notice of this and tell you what your benefit amount is and the month in which your entitlement began.

If you are not entitled to SVB, we will send you notice of this and tell you why you are not entitled to SVB.

Whether you are entitled to SVB or not entitled to SVB, we will also tell you what you can do if you are not satisfied with our determination (as explained in section 2721.3).

2710.2 What happens if you are in the United States when you file?

We will determine whether you are qualified for SVB. If you are not qualified for SVB, we will send you a notice of this and explain why you are not qualified. We will also tell you what you can do if you are not satisfied with our determination (as explained in section 2721.3).

If you are qualified for SVB, we will send you a notice of this and tell you that in order to receive monthly benefits you must establish residence outside the United States within 4-calendar months. For example, if the notice that you are qualified for SVB is dated May 15, we will tell you that you have to begin residing outside the United States no later than September 30 of that year. Your application for SVB will be denied if you do not begin residing outside the United States by that date.

If you establish that you began residing outside the United States within the specified time, we will advise you of your entitlement to SVB, your benefit amount and the month your benefits will begin. We will also tell you what you can do if you are not satisfied with our determination (as explained in section 2721.3).

2711. WHEN ARE YOU RESIDING OUTSIDE THE UNITED STATES?

You are considered to be residing outside the United States if you have established a home outside the United States and intend to continue living outside the United States.

You can receive SVB for any month in which you are residing outside the United States on the first day of the month.

Outside the United States means outside the 50 States, the District of Columbia and the Northern Mariana Islands.

SPECIAL VETERANS BENEFITS   651

2712. HOW ARE SVB PAYMENTS CALCULATED?

The current SSI Federal Benefit Rate in 2024 is $943. This means that your total other monthly benefit income must be less than $707.50 (75 percent of $943) in order for you to receive Special Veterans Benefits.

2713. WHEN ARE SVB PAYMENTS MADE?

SVB payments are normally paid on the first day of the month for which they are due. For example, the benefit for May is paid May 1.

2714. ARE STATE SUPPLEMENTARY PAYMENTS MADE AS THEY ARE FOR SSI?

Only the State of California provides a monthly supplement to SVB payments. The California Veterans Cash Benefit (CVCB) program provides a cash supplement to certain World War II veterans of the Philippines military forces and certain U.S. military forces who:

A. Were eligible, as California residents, for SSI California State Supplementary Payment benefits for December 1999; and

B. Have returned to the Philippines to live.

If you qualify for the CVCB supplement, you can only be paid for months in which you are also entitled to an SVB payment.

The CVCB supplement is administered by SSA. The supplement amount is combined with your monthly SVB payment in one payment issued by the Federal Government.

2715. WHAT COUNTRIES CAN WE NOT SEND PAYMENTS TO?

If you are a citizen or national of the United States and are a resident in a U.S. Treasury restricted country (Cuba or North Korea), you can receive all of your payments that were withheld once you leave that country and go to another country where the U.S. Treasury can send payments. Generally, if you are not a citizen or national of the United States, you cannot receive any payments for months in which you are a resident of a U.S. Treasury restricted country, even though you leave that country and satisfy all other requirements.

If you are a resident in a SSA restricted country (see §1848) and do not qualify for an exception (see §1847.2), once you leave that country and go to another country where we can send payments, you can receive all the benefits for which you were eligible but were withheld because of Social Security restrictions.

2716. WHAT HAPPENS IF YOU BECOME UNABLE TO MANAGE YOUR SVB?

We believe that you have a right to manage your own SVB. If, however, you become unable to manage or direct the management of your benefit payments, we will select a person or organization to receive these payments on your behalf and to use these benefits in your best interests. This person or organization is called a representative payee.

See Chapter 16 for information on how we determine if a representative payee is needed, how a representative payee is selected and what is the proper use of benefits by a representative payee.

2717. WHAT HAPPENS IF YOU RETURN TO THE UNITED STATES TO VISIT?

If you visit the United States and stay for more than one full calendar month, we will no longer consider you to be residing outside the United States for any month after the first full calendar month you are in the United States. You will not be entitled to any SVB payments until you leave the United States and re-establish residence outside the United States.

A calendar month means all of the first day of a month through all of the last day of that month. For example, if you enter the United States on May 25 and stay throughout the entire month of June and leave the United States on July 5, you will not be entitled to SVB for the month of July.

2718. WHEN CAN YOU BE ENTITLED TO SVB PAYMENTS FOR MORE THAN 1 MONTH WHILE YOU ARE IN THE UNITED STATES?

Under special circumstances, we will consider you to be residing outside the United States even though you are in the United States for more than 1 full calendar month. For example:

A. You came to the United States to visit and made an attempt to return to your home abroad, but had to remain in the United States for more than 1 full calendar month due to circumstances beyond your control. This could include such circumstances as sickness, a death in the family or a transportation strike.

or

B. You must remain in the United States for more than 1 full calendar month in order to attend a proceeding for the appeal of a Social Security Administration decision on a claim.

You may receive SVB payments for any month in which these special circumstances occur.

2719. WHAT IF YOU RETURN TO THE UNITED STATES FOR A VISIT AND DECIDE TO LIVE HERE?

If you return to the United States to visit and later decide to live here and not to return to your home abroad, you will no longer be considered to be residing outside the United States. You will not be entitled to SVB payments for the earlier of the following:

A. The month after the month in which you decided to live in the United States; or

B. The month after the first full calendar month you were in the United States.

2720. WHAT IF YOU RETURN TO THE UNITED STATES TO LIVE?

If you return to the United States to live, you will not be entitled to an SVB payment for any month after the month in which you leave your home outside the United States.

2721. INITIAL DETERMINATIONS

2721.1 What are initial determinations?

Initial determinations are the first decisions that we make in response to your application to qualify for and become entitled to SVB. They are also decisions that we make on whether you can continue to receive SVB based on events that occur after your entitlement. Initial determinations generally involve your qualification for and entitlement to SVB, the amount of your SVB benefit, and your residence outside the United States. See §2002.

2721.2 How do we notify you when we make an initial determination?

We notify you of our initial determination by mail. In our notice, we will tell you the reasons for, and the effects of, our determination. We will also advise you of your right to appeal if you do not agree with our determination.

2721.3 What should you do if you are not satisfied with our initial determination?

We offer several independent reviews of your case if you are not satisfied with our initial determination. Each review is a separate step in the administrative appeals process. You must request a review within specified time limits. However, we may extend the time limit if you establish that you had a good reason for not requesting a review timely (as explained in section 2727). If you do not request the next review step within the time limit, our decision becomes final and binding (except as explained in section 2728).

In determining if your request was made within the time limit, we generally presume that you received our notice no later than 5 days following the date of the notice. However, we will not make this assumption if you establish that you received the notice later or you did not receive it at all.

Your request can be filed at any of the offices listed in section 2709.

2721.4 What decision can you appeal?

You have a legal right to appeal our initial determinations (per 2721.1 in this section). You do not have a legal right to appeal other matters. However, we may, at our discretion, review, reopen and revise our initial (or appellate) determinations.

2722. APPEAL PROCESS

2722.1 How does the appeal process work?

The appeals process consists of four levels as described in sections 2723-2726. See also §2014.

2723. RECONSIDERATION

2723.1 What is reconsideration?

Reconsideration is the first step in the appeals process. It is a thorough and independent review of your case. It includes the evidence you submitted for the initial determination and any additional evidence you submit with your reconsideration request. The reconsideration determination is made by a Social Security employee who has been trained in this process and who was not involved in the initial determination you are appealing. See §2004.

2723.2 How do you request a reconsideration?

You, or your authorized representative, must request a reconsideration in writing within 60 days after the day you receive notice of our initial determination. (See section 2721.3 for information about when we presume you received our notice.)

If our initial determination indicates that we will reduce, suspend or end your entitlement to SVB, you must request reconsideration within 10 days after the day you receive the notice *to ensure that your payments continue* until we make a reconsideration determination.

2723.3 What are your options during the reconsideration process?
The reconsideration process may consist of a case review, or under certain circumstances, informal or formal conferences.

A. *Case review*: This is an independent review of your record, per 2723.1 in this section. It is the only option available when you request reconsideration of the initial determination(s) that we made on your SVB application.

B. *Informal conference*: This is a review per 2723.1 in this section, in which you may participate. You may bring witnesses and present your case in person. You can select this option only in situations where you are entitled to SVB and our initial determination indicates that we will reduce or suspend your SVB payments or terminate your SVB entitlement.

C. *Formal conference*: This includes the same steps as an informal conference. However, you may also request that adverse witnesses be issued a subpoena and cross-examined by you or your representative. The restrictions on selecting this option are the same as for the informal conference per 2723.2 in this section.

We hold informal and formal conferences only in the United States. We cannot pay your expenses to come to the United States and participate in one of these conferences.

2724. HEARING

2724.1 What is a hearing?
If you are not satisfied with the reconsideration determination, you may request a hearing. This is a thorough review of your record by an Administrative Law Judge (ALJ) in the SSA Office of Disability Adjudication and Review. You, or your representative, may appear in person at a hearing. You may review the evidence used in making the determination under review and submit additional evidence. You may also present and question witnesses. See §2007.

If you are outside the United States, we will not schedule an oral hearing unless you tell us you wish to appear. If you want to travel to the

United States to appear, the hearing will be held at a site nearest to your port of entry into the United States. We cannot pay your travel expenses.

If we do not hold an oral hearing, an ALJ will make a decision based on the evidence in file and any new evidence that you may submit.

2724.2 How do you request a hearing?

You, or your authorized representative, must request a hearing in writing within 60 days of the date you received the notice of the reconsideration determination or decision. (See section 2721.3 for information about when we presume you received our notice.)

2724.3 Where are hearings held?

SSA holds hearings in the 50 States, the District of Columbia and the Northern Mariana Islands.

2724.4 What happens after the hearing?

After the hearing, the ALJ issues a decision affirming, revising or reversing the reconsidered determination. The ALJ may also certify the case with a recommended decision to the Appeals Council (see section 2725). You will be notified of the ALJ's decision and the reasons for it.

2725. APPEALS COUNCIL REVIEW

2725.1 How do you request an Appeals Council review?

If you are not satisfied with the action of the ALJ, whether a decision or a dismissal of your case, you may request a review by the Appeals Council. You, or your appointed representative, must request an Appeals Council review in writing within 60 days after the date you received the notice of the ALJ's decision. (See section 2721.3 for information about when we presume you received our notice.)

2725.2 What happens when the Appeals Council receives your request?

The Appeals Council will thoroughly examine your claim and decide whether to deny, grant or dismiss your request for a review of the ALJ's action. It will notify you of its decision. See §2014.

If the Appeals Council decides to review your case:

A. You or your representative may request an appearance before the Appeals Council in Falls Church, Virginia.

B. If the Appeals Council determines that a significant question of law or policy is present or that oral arguments would be beneficial in rendering a proper decision, the appearance will be granted.
C. If the request for appearance is granted, you can present oral arguments as well as submit additional evidence or written statements in support of your case. We cannot pay your travel expenses to the United States for an appearance.
D. You may also file written statements in support of your claim.

The Appeals Council decision, or the ALJ decision if the Appeals Council denied the request for review, is binding unless you file an action in a U.S. District Court or we reopen and revise the decision under the rules in section 2728. A dismissal of the request for review by the Appeals Council is binding and not subject to further review.

2726. U.S. DISTRICT COURT

2726.1 When do you file for civil action in a U.S. District Court?

If you are not satisfied with the Appeals Council decision or its notice of denial of your request for review of the ALJ's decision, you may file for civil action in a U.S. District Court. You may file within 60 days after the date you received notice of the Appeals Council decision or denial. (See section 2721.3 for information about when we presume you received our notice.) You have no right to court review where the Appeals Council has dismissed your request for review or denied your request for review of the dismissal of an ALJ decision.

2726.2 What actions may the court take?

The court may enter a judgment affirming, modifying or reversing our decision, with or without sending the case back to us. Under certain circumstances, the court may return your case to us so that we can obtain additional evidence before the court enters a judgment.

2727. EXTENSION OF TIME FOR FILING

2727.1 When can we extend the time limit for filing an appeal?

We can extend the time limit for you to file your request for reconsideration, an ALJ hearing or an Appeals Council review, or a civil action in U.S. District Court if you show that you had good cause for not filing timely. The decision on whether or not to extend the time limit is made by the field office, the ALJ, or the Appeals Council, depending on who has jurisdiction. See §2015.

2727.2 What do we consider when we decide if you had good cause for not filing within a time limit?

In deciding whether you had good cause for not filing within a time limit, we consider:

A. What circumstances kept you from making the request on time;
B. Whether our action mislead you;
C. Whether you did not understand the requirements of the Social Security Act, resulting from amendments, other legislation or court decisions; and
D. Whether you had any physical, mental, educational or linguistic limitations (including any lack of facility with the English language) that prevented you from filing a timely request or knowing about the need to file a timely request for review.

2728. REOPENING FINAL DETERMINATIONS OR DECISIONS UNDER THE RULES OF ADMINISTRATIVE FINALITY

2728.1 When can we reopen a final determination or decision?

A final determination, revised determination, decision or revised decision may be reopened and revised by a Social Security office, an ALJ or the Appeals Council within certain time limits and under certain conditions. See §2016.

We may decide to reopen a final determination or decision on our own or as a result of receiving a written request from a claimant or beneficiary. A decision not to reopen a determination or decision is not an initial determination and is not subject to appeal.

2728.2 When can we reopen a determination or decision within 12 months?

We can reopen determinations or decisions within 12 months from the date of the notice of the initial determination for any reason.

2728.3 When can we reopen a determination or decision within 24 months?

We can reopen determinations or decisions within 24 months from the date of the notice of the initial determination if:

A. We receive new and material evidence;
B. We made a clerical error; or
C. The evidence that we used in making the determination or decision clearly shows on its face that the determination or decision was incorrect.

2728.4 When can we reopen a determination or decision at any time?

We can reopen a determination or decision at any time if:

A. It was fully or partially unfavorable to you, but only to correct:
 - a clerical error; or
 - an error that appears on the face of the evidence that we considered when we made the determination or decision.
B. It was obtained by fraud or similar fault by the SVB claimant or beneficiary, or some other person.

Index

Note: Index citations are to section numbers, not page numbers.

A
Absence from U.S., alien nonpayment provisions, §1843
Absence from U.S., SSI, §2116
Accidental death, exception to 9-month duration-of-marriage requirement, §404
Accounting by representative payee, discontinuance, §1622
Accrued benefits, unpaid, §1900
Acknowledgment of children, §1709
Active duty (military), §950
Active duty pay, coverage, §1305
Actual or constructive payments, §1302
Additional penalty conviction for subversive activities, §1837
Address, reporting change for mailing of check, §124
Adjustment against current and future benefits, overpayment, §1909
Adjustment for family maximum benefits, §731 adjustment of reduction factor at ages 62 and FRA, §728
Adjustment of reduction factor at FRA, §728
Administrative actions which are not initial determinations, SSI, §2190
Administrative actions, distinguished, §2003

Administrative appeals process: ALJ actions, §2008
ALJ's decision, §2012
- appeals process, §2007, §2008, §2009, §2010, §2011, §2012, §2013, §2014 appeals review, §2013
- claimant's representative, §2017, §2018
- extension of time for filing request for reconsideration, hearing or review, §2015
- hearing notices, §2009
- pre/post hearing conferences, §2010
- reconsideration, §2000, §2001, §2002, §2003, §2004, §2005
- reopening and revision of determination or decision, supplemental security income (SSI), §2197
- Social Security Office assistance, §2011
- time limit for reopening determinations, §2001, §2016
Administrative finality, §2001
Administrative policy with respect to appointment of representative payees, §1600
Administrative review process:
- defined, §2000
- prehearing or posthearing conference, §2010

661

- State's assessment, disallowance, credit or refund, §1019
Administrator, §1903
Administrator Law Judge, locations, §110
Administrator of estates, trade or business, §1114
Adopted child:
- deemed stepchild, §332 dependency, §334
- dependent upon insured parent, §334 effective date of adoption decree, §329 inheritance rights, §330
- legal, §329, §330, §331, §332, §333, §334, §335, §336, §337, §1713 legal adoption defined, §329
- past indebtedness, §1619 proof, §1713
- State law test, §328
- step-relationships, §331, §332 termination of benefits, §340

Adult beneficiary (representative payee):
- ability to manage benefits, §1613, §1614 advance notice of proposed actions, §1611 conservation of funds, §1619
- current needs and maintenance, §1617 evidence of capability of beneficiary, §1614
- evidence of incapability of beneficiary, §1604, §1606
- legal guardian appointed, beneficiary adjudged incompetent, §1605 past indebtedness, §1618
- payee preference guide, §1609
- payments made directly to beneficiary over age 18, §1603 proper use of benefits, §1616
- responsibilities of payee, §1616 transfer of funds, §1622

Advance filing of applications for benefits, §1502
Advance payment of wages, §1309
Advancing age, capacity to work, §609
Against equity and good conscience, recovery of overpayment, §1919
Age 62:
- quarters of coverage required, §204
- reduced benefits, §302, §723, §724, §725, §726, §727, §728, §729 reduction factors adjustment, widow(er), §728
- retirement insurance requirements, §301
- spouse's insurance benefits, §119, §305, §311, §322

Age 65:
- blind or disabled, SSI, §126
- hospital and medical insurance protection, §127, §1500 period of disability ends, §511
- prescription drug benefit, §128, §1500, §2400
- reduced spouse's benefits, §320 reduced widow(er)'s benefits, §407 reduction factor adjustment, §728
- SSI, §2102

Age 72, special monthly cash payment entitlement, §119
Age, education, and work experience, disability evaluation, §608
Age, proof required, §1704
Aged, blind or disabled, SSI, §2100
Agent-drivers or Commission-drivers, §827
Agents, SSI, §2146
Agreement for farm rental, §1222
Agreement to cover foreign affiliates, §965
Agricultural inspectors, State and local employment, §1005
Agricultural labor (coverage): cash-pay test, §901, §902 commodities listed, §905 cotton ginning, §911
- cultivating, raising or harvesting any agricultural or horticultural commodities, §904 cultivation of soil, raising or harvesting of commodities, §906
- domestic service in a private home for profit, §915 domestic service, defined, §916
- farm crew workers and leaders, §831 farm defined, §903
- foreign workers admitted to U.S. on temporary basis, §914 nonbusiness work on a farm operated for profit,

INDEX 663

§924 operating, managing, maintaining farm, §909
- processing or packaging commodities, §913 production and harvesting of crude gum, §910 quarters of coverage, cash-pay test, §214
- raising and harvesting, terms, §906, §907, §908 sharefarm arrangement, §1119, §1120, §1121 types, §909
- water system upkeep, §912

Alien nonpayment provisions:
- absence from U.S., §1844
- absence from U.S. for 30 full consecutive days, §1844 accrued benefits, restricted countries, §1849 beneficiary outside U.S. 6 months or more, §1843 countries restricted, §1847, §1848
- countries with social insurance or pension systems, §1845 exception limitations, §1846
- exceptions, §1843, §1845
- limitations on use of certain exceptions, §1846 lump-sum death payment, §429, §1843, §1847 outside the U.S., 6-months or more, §1843 period of absence, §1844
- retirement insurance benefits, §303

Aliens:
- child's benefits, §339, §413
- foreign students, exchange visitors, and international cultural exchange visitors, §939 mother's or father's benefits reduced, §419
- parent's benefits nonpayable for some months, §426 spouse's benefits, §321
- SSI, §2115
- widow(er)'s benefits, §408
- work performed under Immigration and Nationality Act, §939

ALJ's decision, §2012

Allied armed forces services:
- before 1957, gratuitous military wage credits, §1307 noncontributory military wage credits, §957

Alternative definitions of disability, §512
American employer defined, §962
American Samoa, coverage, §966
American vessel or aircraft defined, §961
Annual earnings test
   See Earnings test
   See Earnings test
Annual exempt amounts, §1803
Annual report of earnings:
- additional reports, when required, §1822 beginning or stopping employment, §522 deadline for filing, §1815
- exempt amounts, §1803
- extension of time for filing, §1816, §1817 failure to file timely, §1819, §1820, §1821 failure to file, good cause, §1832, §1833 filing requirements, §1814
- information required, §1818 payment of partial benefit, §1806
- request for extension of time for filing, §1817

Annuity plan payments, §1316
Apartment house, private home, §917
Apartments or rooms, rental income, §1216
Appeal levels, §526
Appeal levels, IRMAA, §2508
Appeals Council process, §2013
Appeals Council review, SSI, §2194
Appeals Council review, SVB, §2725
Appeals office, purpose, §110
Appeals process, IRMAA, §2508
Appeals process, SSI, §2191
Appeals process, SVB, §2722
Applicant outside U.S., application or enrollment for benefits, §103
Application for a Social Security Card, Form SS-5, §101
Application for Exemption from Self-Employment Tax for Use by Ministers, Members of Religious Orders, and Christian Science Practitioners, Form 4361, §1131
Application for Exemption from Social Security Taxes Income and Waiver of Benefits, IRS Form 4029, §1129

664　Social Security Handbook 2024

Applications:
- answering questions, §1511
- by guardian, committee or legal representative, §1501 child's, §323
- child's reentitlement to benefits, §341 completion, §1511, §1512
- date of effectiveness, §1502 delayed filing result, §1504
- disabled worker's, §509, §602, §1502 divorced spouse's, §311
- false statements, penal provisions, §142 filing, §1500
- food stamp program, SSI, §2108
- good cause for extension of time limit, §1518, §1519 help in completing, §1512
- individuals nearing retirement age, §1503
- lump-sum death payments, §433, §1517, §1518, §1519
- Medicaid, SSI, §2107
- medical evidence, §614, §615 medical insurance benefits, §103
- Medicare prescription drug benefit, §1500, §2400
- Medicare prescription drug costs, extra help with, §103, §1500, §2600
- missing in action, Form DD-1300 (Report of Casualty), used as intent to claim benefits, §1509 prerequisites, §1508, §1509
- processing, §105
- proof of support, time limit for filing, §1520 retirement insurance benefits, §301, §1502 retroactive entitlement, §301, §1513, §1514 right to withdraw, §1515, §1516
- scope of application, §1510
- signature, written or signed by mark and witnessed, §1511 special monthly cash payments, age 72, §347
- spouse's, §305
- survivors insurance benefits, §1502 when considered filed, §1507, §1509 where to file, §1505, §1506
- who must execute, §1501 widow(er)'s benefits, §401, §405 wife's, §305
- written statement requesting benefits acceptable, §1509

Appropriations for hospital benefits, §137
Assignment of benefits prohibited, §129
Assistance in completing applications for benefits, §1512
Association classifiable as corporation, §928
Association of several persons classifiable as corporation, §825
Association taxable as a corporation, §1112
Attachment of benefits, past indebtedness, §129
Attorney, representative of claimant, §2017
Automatic recomputation of primary insurance amount (PIA), §722
Automobile, exclusion from resource, SSI, §2157
Auxiliaries or survivors of deported worker, §1842
Auxiliary benefits, §300
Auxiliary insured person, excess earnings, §1804
Average current earnings, defined, §504
Average indexed monthly earnings, §700
Average monthly earnings, §700
Awards, exclusion from wages, §1330

B

Back pay as wages, §1323
Base years defined, §705
Beneficiary:
- current needs, defined, §1618
- days worked in a calendar year, §1826 evidence of incapability, §1605
- hours worked per month, §1826 overpayment liability, §1905 past debts, §1619
- regains competency, §1613, §1614 retired, determining work hours, §1826 trust, trade or business, §1115

Benefit forfeiture, conviction for subversive activities, §1837
Benefit Planning and Assistance Organizations (BPAO), §519
Benefits:
- adjustment at FRA, §728 adult son or daughter, §517
- annual report, failure to file, §1821 application requirements, §1500 assignment or transfer prohibited, §129 auxiliary, §300
- check payments, monthly, §121 checks, §120, §121, §122, §123, §124
- child entitled on more than one earnings record, §735, §736
- child's, §410, §411, §412, §413, §414 computation of payments, SSI, §2182 correctional institutions, §1850
- cost-of-living increase, §719
- criteria for absence from the U.S., §1844 direct deposit, §122
- disability exclusions, §711 disability protection, types, §500
- disabled worker's terminating events, §506 earnings as basis, §1400
- elapsed years, §704
- eligibility criteria, based on need, §2113
- eligibility under more than one category, SSI, §2124 estate of deceased, waiver provisions, §1921
- events that affect, §106 exceptions, §1843, §1845, §1846
- excess earnings, §1802, §1804, §1805, §1806 expedited payments, special requests, §130 false statements, penal provisions, §143 family maximum, §730, §731, §732
- father's/mother's, §415, §416, §417, §418, §419, §420
- Federal benefit rate (FBR), SSI, §2113 fringe, §1342
- funding sources, §136
- governmental pension offset, §1836 hospital intern coverage, §923 institutionalized effects, §1850 insured status requirements, §200 liability for repayments, §1906
- lump-sum death payment, §428, §429, §430, §431, §432, §433 marriage effects, §1852
- marriage, termination, §1853
- Medicare, health insurance, §127 minimum, §716
- mother's/father's, §415, §416, §417, §418, §419, §420 non-payment conditions, §1800
- non-transferable, §129
- not payable, or payable only in part, §1800
- overpayments, §1904, §1905, §1906, §1907, §1908, §1909, §1910, §1911, §1912, §1913, §1914, §1915, §1916, §1917, §1918, §1919, §1920, §1921, §1922, §1923
- overpayments, without fault situations, §1915, §1916 paid at different rates, SSI, §2180
- parent's, §421, §422, §423, §424, §425, §426, §427 partial payment, excess earnings, §1806
- payable to, §119
- payment to person other than beneficiary, §1600, §1601, §1602, §1603, §1604, §1605, §1606, §1607, §1608, §1609, §1610, §1611, §1612, §1613, §1614, §1615, §1616, §1617, §1618, §1619, §1620, §1621, §1622
- prescription drug benefits, §128 proration, SSI, §2184
- rate of withholding, §1910 recovery by civil suit, §1912 recovery efforts, §1913
- reduced, §723, §724, §725, §726, §727, §728, §729 remarriage effects, §417
- replace, in part, earnings, §1801
- reporting events affecting eligibility, §106, §114, §133 retirement, §300, §301, §302, §303, §304

- retroactivity, §301, §1513, §1514
- retrospective monthly accounting, SSI, §2183
- revised prior determination, overpayment recovery, §1922 rounding, §738
- separate checks to spouses, §131
- simultaneous entitlement, §733, §734, §735, §736, §737 sources of funds, §136
- spouse's, §305, §306, §307, §308, §309, §310, §311, §312, §313, §314, §315, §316, §317, §318, §319, §320, §321, §322
- SSI
  See Supplemental Security Income (SSI) SSI payment amounts, §2180
- terminating events, §1851 totalization coordination, §216 underpayment, §1900, §1901, §1902
- widow(er)'s, §401, §402, §403, §404, §405, §406, §407, §408, §409 withheld, §1909

Birth or baptismal certificate, parent-child relationship, §1707
Birthdate, proof of, §1705
Blind:
- disability defined, §507
- disabled worker's, trial work period, §520 special provisions, §208
- SSI, §2100, §2101, §2102 substantial gainful activity, §603 work expenses, §2176
- work incentives, SSI, §2173

Board of Trustees for the Social Security Trust Funds, §141
Bond purchase plan, §1316
Bonds, interest, §1206
Bonuses and wage dividends, §1322
Burial funds excluded from resources, SSI, §2161
Burial spaces, excluded resources, SSI, §2160
Business
  See Trade or business
Business expenses, computing net earnings from self-employment, §1205

C

Cafeteria plan, not included as wages, §1341
Calendar quarter defined, §212
Calendar quarters not counted as quarters of coverage, §213
Capital gains or losses, §1211
Cash or vendor payments, SSI, §2186
Cash-pay test:
- agricultural labor, §214, §901, §902, §924
- domestic service in private home or farm, §915, §916 employee does not meet test, §1406
- general, §1303 homeworkers, §830 nonbusiness work, §924 nonprofit organization, §1304 tips, §1329

Categories of payees, factors in selection, §1607
Ceremonial marriage, proof, §1716
Certificate of election, reduced husband's/wife's benefits, §321
Certification by Churches and Qualified Church-Controlled Organizations Electing Exemption from Employer's Social Security Taxes Form 8274, §1128
Change of address, reporting for mailing checks, §124
Change of name on Social Security records, §101
Chaplains, coverage, §1133
Checks:
- assignment or transfer prohibited, §129 change of address, §123
- child payments, §132 direct deposit, §122 disbursement for children, §132 endorsement, §124
- expedited payments, §130 husband/wife payments, §131 issuer, §120
- lost or stolen, §123 mailing, §123
- non-receipt, §123
- overpayment, refund of benefits, §135 received outside the U.S., §123 reporting address changes, §123
- return of, §134

INDEX   667

- separate payments, child, §132 signature by mark, §124, §1511 time limits for cashing, §124
Child, §323:
  See Also Adopted child
  See Also Child-in-care
  See Also Dependency of child
  See Also Grandchild or stepgrandchild
  See Also Illegitimate child
  See Also Legitimacy of child
  See Also Step-child
- court order of support, §1711 decree of paternity, §1710, §1712 deemed, §328
- deemed stepchild, §332 defined, §324, §411
- dependency, §333, §334, §335, §336, §337 dependent grandchild, §325
- employed by parent, §926 legally adopted, defined, §329 legitimacy, §326, §327, §411 legitimation or acknowledgment, §327
- separation from parent, child-in-care, §315, §316, §317, §318, §319 step-relationship, §331, §332, §333, §334, §335, §336, §337

Child's insurance benefits:
- amount, §412
- automatic entitlement, more than one earnings record, §736 benefit rate, §338, §412
- child-in-care, §312
- dependency requirements for child beneficiaries, §333, §334, §335, §336, §337 disabled child, §338
- educational institutional, defined, §343
- entitlement on more than one earnings record, §735, §736, §737 entitlement requirements, §323, §324, §325, §326, §327, §328, §410, §516 full-time student, §344
- grand-child, §325, §336, §411
- grand-parent/step grand-parent, §336
- listing of insured status requirements for Social Security benefits, §211 lump-sum benefits, §432

- nonpayment or partial payment situation, §339, §413
- parent-child relationship, §411, §1707, §1708, §1709, §1710, §1711, §1712, §1713, §1714 reentitlement, §341
- representative payee, beneficiary under age 18, §1602, §1608
- school attendance, proof, §1715
- SSDI entitlement, §518
- SSI disability entitlement, §517 stepchild/step-parent, §331, §332 student beneficiary, §342, §344
- terminating events, §340, §341, §342, §414

Child-in-care:
- child at school, §318 defined, §312
- disabled child age 18 or over, §1829
- employment of parent, reason for separation, §317 evidence to establish, §1723
- failure to report child no longer "in care", penalty deductions, §1831 father's or mother's benefits as a surviving divorced spouse, §416 illness or disability, reason for separation, §319
- parental responsibility, §313 personal services, §314 requirements not met, §315 spouse's benefits, §320, §321
- temporary separation, §315, §316, §317, §318, §319

Childhood disability benefits:
- beginning of trial work period, §521
- child-in-care, §314, §315, §316, §317, §318, §319 disability determination, §600
- entitlement requirements, §516, §517, §518
- identifying sources of medical evidence on application, §614 impairments, §607
- protection under worker, §500
- reentitlement, §341
- terminating events, §340, §414 trial work period, §519

Christian Science practitioners, self-employment, §1130

Church employee exclusions, §1136
Citizen outside U.S. performing services in exercise of ministry, §1246
Citizenship, evidence, §1725
City or traveling salespersons, full-time, §829
Civil action in a Federal District Court, SSI, §2195
Civil suit recovery, §1912
Civilian employee, U.S. Government, §940
Claimant residing abroad, §114
Claims:
- copying rights, §530 denied, §530
- evidence to support, §104 processing, §105
- reporting events, §106

Coast and Geodetic Survey, commissioned officers, §958
Collection of monthly premiums for medical benefits, §138
College club, domestic service by student, §919
College or university student employment, §921
College, educational institution, §343
Commercial or business properties, rental income, §1216
Commission-driver, status as employee, §827
Commissioned employees, §827
Commissioned officers, §949
Commissions, as wages, §1309
Common-law marriage, §307
Common-law test:
- agent-drivers or commission-drivers, §827 defined, §802
- factors of control, §803, §804, §805, §806, §807, §808, §809, §810, §811, §812, §813, §814, §815, §816, §817, §818, §819, §820, §821, §822, §823
- farm crew workers and leaders, §831 fishing boat crews, §936, §1134 homeworkers, §830
- identity of employer, §801

- life insurance salespersons, §828 requirements for special occupations, §826 traveling or city salespersons, full-time, §829
- weights and factors, §803, §804, §805, §806, §807, §808, §809, §810, §811, §812, §813, §814, §815, §816, §817, §818, §819, §820, §821, §822, §823

Community programs, referral to, §118
Community service programs for older Americans, §945
Compensation by fees, §1015
Compromise settlement of overpayment, §1911
Compulsory coverage rule, retirement system coverage group, §1005
Computation of benefits: automatic recomputation, §722 base years, §705
- computation years defined, §703 computing AME/AIME, §701, §712 consolidated methods, §712
- cost-of-living increases, §719 delayed retirement credit, §720 disability period excluded, §711
- elapsed years under usual formula, §704
- elimination of minimum PIA, §716 family maximum, §731, §732, §737 formula, §701, §702
- maximum earnings creditable in calendar year, §714
- maximum monthly benefits payable on one earnings record, §730, §731, §732 minimum benefit, elimination, §716
- payment rates, SSI, §2182
- Primary Insurance Amount (PIA), §700, §706, §710 primary insurance benefit converted to PIA, §710 recomputation of PIA, §721, §722
- reduction effect, §723, §724, §725, §726, §727, §728, §729 requirements for use of simplified old-start formula, §708 retrospective monthly accounting, SSI, §2183
- rounding rates, §738 savings clauses, §731

Index 669

- self-employment income, allocation in taxable year, §715 simplified old-start formula, §707, §708, §709, §710
- simultaneous entitlement, more than one benefit, §733, §734, §735, §736, §737 special minimum PIA, §717
- total earnings, §713
- windfall elimination provision (WEP), modified benefit formula, §718

Computation of farm income, optional methods, §1233
Computation years defined, §703
Concealment or failure to report event affecting benefits, criminal prosecutions and penalties, §143
Confidentiality of evidence, §1701
Confinement-related impairment, §507
Conservation of farm, agricultural labor, §909
Constructive payment, wages, §1302
Consultative examinations, disability, §616
Continuing disability reviews, §622
Control, conduct, and maintenance of an organization, §935
Conversion of recipients from prior State programs, SSI, §2109
Converting excess resources to liquid resources, SSI, §2164
Coordination of U.S. and foreign country social security systems, §216
Corporation: defined, §825 employment, §925
- family employment, §928
- foreign affiliates, §963, §964, §965, §966 officers and directors as employees, §824

Corrected Income and Tax Amounts, Form W-2c, §1409
Correctional institution, §344
Cost-of-Living Adjustment (COLA):
- affect on benefits, §719 automatic increases, table, §143 retrospective monthly accounting, §2183
- SSI coordination, §2183

Costs of production, material participation, §1225
Cotton ginning, §911
Countable income, exclusions, SSI, §2130
Countable income, SSI, §2131
Countable resources, SSI, §2153
Countries listed under alien nonpayment provisions, §1848
Court decree of paternity, parent-child relationship, §1710
Court order for support, parent-child relationship, §1711
Court reporters, Federal and State, §1127
Court review on Appeals Council action in a case, §2014
Court-allowed fee for representing claimant, §2018
Coverage and exceptions:
- agricultural labor, §901, §902, §903, §904, §905, §906, §907, §908, §909, §910, §911, §912, §913, §914
- American employee, defined, §962
- American Samoa, work coverage, §966 civilian Federal employee, §940
- community service programs for older Americans, §945
- District of Columbia employees, §941
- domestic services in private home of employer, §915, §916, §917, §918, §919 employee status, §800
- family employment, §926, §927, §928 fishing boat crews, §1134
- foreign affiliates, §964, §965
- foreign affiliates of domestic corporations, §963, §964, §965, §966 foreign government and international organization employees, §937
- foreign students, exchange visitors, and international cultural exchange visitors, §939
- Guam, work coverage, §966 included-excluded rule, §968, §969 interns, hospital, §923
- Japanese internees during WWII, §1336 limited partners, §1102

- local college club, defined, §920 military service after 1956, §1305
- military service, special wage credits, §210
- ministers and members of religious orders, §932, §933, §934, §935 newspaper deliverers, §929
- newspaper or magazine vendors, §930 non-business work, §924
- nonprofit religious, charitable, educational, etc. institutions, §931
- nonresident aliens temporarily admitted to U.S., §939 occupations not covered, §108
- Peace Corps volunteers, §943 personal services, §1102
- Railroad Retirement Act (RRA), §967
- self-employed persons and effective dates, §1100 student nurses, §922
- students, §919, §920
- U.S. citizens working within the U.S. as employees of foreign governments, §938
- uniformed service of the U.S., §948, §949, §950, §951, §952, §953, §954, §955, §956, §957, §958, §959, §960
- Visa holder, exclusion categories, §939
- Volunteers in Service to America (VISTA), §947
- work not in course of employer's trade or business, §924, §925 work outside the U.S., §961, §962, §963, §964, §965, §966 work performed under Immigration and Nationality Act, §939

Crew leaders (farm), §831
Criminal prosecutions for fraud, §143
Crude gum production, agricultural labor, §910
Cultivating, raising or harvesting any agricultural or horticultural commodity, §904
Cultivation of soil, raising or harvesting of commodities, §906
Currently insured status, §206

D

Data processing, Office of Central Records Operations, §110
Dealer in stocks or securities, net earnings from self-employment, §1207
Death:
- accidental, §404
- benefits on behalf of deceased worker, §509 evidence, §1720, §1721
- felonious homicide, claimant involved, §400, §1722 incorrect report of death by Department of Defense, §1923 missing person, §1721
- nine-month duration of marriage requirement, exceptions, §404 partnership, effect on taxable year, §1204
- survivor of deceased insured worker, §400

Decision on reconsideration determination and notice, §2012
Decree of paternity, parent-child relationship, §1710
Deductions from benefits:
- annual report of earnings, §1814, §1815, §1816, §1817, §1818, §1819, §1820, §1821, §1822 child-in-care requirement, §1829
- earnings test, §1801 excess earnings, §1802
- failure to have child-in-care, §1833
- foreign work test, §1823, §1824, §1825, §1826, §1827, §1828 good cause for failure to file required reports, §1832, §1833 months not charged, excess earnings, §1805
- non-covered work for pay, defined, §1825
- non-payment of disability benefits, §505
- penalty, failure to report annual earnings on time, §1820, §1821 penalty, failure to report foreign work, §1828
- receipt of periodic workers' compensation payment, §1835 worker and auxiliary have excess earnings, §1804

Deemed military wage credits, §953
Deeming of income and resources, SSI, §2167
Defeat the purpose of Social Security program, factor in waiving recovery of overpayment, §1918
Defeat the purpose of Social Security program, recovery of overpaid benefits, §1918
Delayed filing of benefit applications, §1504
Delayed retirement credits, §720
Dependency of child:
- child defined, Social Security purpose, §411 dependent upon insured parent, §337 grandchild, §325, §411
- natural or legally adopted, §334 requirements, §337 stepgrandchild, §325
- stepparent, §335 surviving child, §410

Dependent care assistance, payments provided by employer, §1339
Deported worker, nonpayment of benefits, §303
Determination or decision:
- administrative actions, distinguished, §2003 administrative review process, §2000 disability, §115, §600, §604, §605
- dismissal of case by administrative law judge (ALJ), §2008
- extension of time for filing request for reconsideration, hearing, or review, §2015 hearing by ALJ, §2007, §2008, §2009, §2010, §2011, §2012
- initial determination, §2002
- initial determinations, SSI, §2189 reconsideration process, §2004, §2005 request for reconsideration, §2004
- review of the decision by the Appeals Council, §2000 review of the final administrative decision, §2000
- Social Security office assistance, §2011 time limit for reopening, §2001, §2016

Direct deposit:
- outside the U.S., §122
- Social Security benefits, §122

Direct field office payments, SSI, §2187
Disability: cessation, §623 continuing reviews, §622 defined, §507
- determinations, §115, §600, §604, §605 hearing, §2006
- medical evidence, §606, §607, §615 medically determinable impairment, §601
- presumptive blindness and presumptive disability payments, SSI, §2188 processing claims, §105
- SSI, §2102
- Ticket-to-work Program, §519 trial work period, §520
- types, under Social Security, §500 work incentives, SSI, §2173

Disability Determination Services (DDS), §115
Disability evaluation:
- age, education and work experience, consideration, §608, §609 cessation, §623
- child impairments, §607
- complete clinical and laboratory findings consistent with other evidence, §604 condition does not meet medical impairment, §608
- consultative examination, §616 continuing reviews, §622 earnings, §620
- employment conditions, §611 evidence, §614
- impairment, 12-month duration, §602 independent of other decisions, §604 initial decision, §527
- listing of impairments, §607
- medical evidence, §606, §614, §615, §616 medically determinable impairments defined, §601 periodic review, required by law, §622 qualifications, §600
- rating schedule not used, §605 severe impairments, §613

- substantial gainful activity defined, §603
- substantial gainful activity, evidence, §617, §618, §619, §620, §621 terminating events, §623
- work availability, §610, §611

Disability insurance benefits: administration of program, §115 applications
See Applications
- base years, §705
- benefit computation, §507
- certification of election, husband/wife, §729 cessation, §623
- childhood, §516, §517, §518 dependent child, §337 deported worker, §1841
- disability insured status requirements, §207 disabled adult child, §518
- disabled widow(er)'s, §513, §514, §515 disabled worker defined, §505
- elapsed years, §704
- entitlement of underpayment due a deceased person, §1902 entitlement requirements, §501, §502, §503, §504, §505, §506, §507 entitlement to other benefits, §734
- felony affect, §507
- financing the program, §136
- listing of insured status requirements for Social Security benefits, §211 overpayment liability, §1905, §1906
- overpayment, adjustment, §1908, §1909, §1910
- period of disability, §209, §508, §509, §510, §511, §512 periodic workers' compensation payments, §1835 reduced, §723, §724, §725, §726, §727, §728, §729 reduction for age, §726
- terminating events, §623
- trial work period, §519, §520, §522 types of protection, §500 unfavorable decision, §529
- VR services, §518
- wages, disabled former employee, §1335 waiting period, §502
- without fault situations, overpayment, §1915, §1916

Disability insurance, Office of Disability Operations (ODO), §110
Disability insured status, exclusions, §209
Disability Operations, Office of, §110
Disability, period of
See Period of disability
Disabled son or daughter age 18 or over, §517
Disabled widow(er)'s benefits:
- benefit rate, §407
- date of entitlement, §514
- disability defined, entitlement purposes, §515 disability determinations, §600
- disability protection, types, §500 entitlement requirements, §513
- impairments related to the commission of a felony, §515 medical evidence, §607
- terminating events, §409
- trial work period not possible, §520

Disabled worker's benefits:
- amount, §503 appeals, §525 application, §1502 benefit rate, §503, §711
- dedicated account, defined, §1621 definition, §507
- disability determination, worker's impairment(s), §507
- entitlement requirements, §500, §501 events to report, §523
- felony affect, §507
- fully favorable decision, §528 impairments related to a felony, §515 last month of entitlement, §506
- lump-sum payments, §504 medical evidence, §607
- medicare coverage, qualifications, §506 nonpayment situations, §505
- offset determination, §504
- period of disability, §508, §509, §510, §511, §512 reduction to offset workers' compensation, §504
- substantial gainful activity, effect, §505, §617, §618, §619, §620, §621 terminating events, §506
- trial work period, §519, §520
- types of disability protection, §500 unreduced, §504

- waiting period, §502
- when trial work period begins and ends, §521 worker convicted of a felony, §505, §1850

Disaster, exclusions from resources, SSI, §2162

Disasters, major or personal, exclusions from income, SSI, §2138

Disclosure of official information:
- confidentiality of evidence, §1701
- Freedom of Information Act, §117
- Privacy Act, §117

Dishonorable discharge, effect of, §956

Dismissal of case by ALJ, §2008

Dismissal pay as wages, §1324

Disposal of resources, uncompensated value, SSI, §2165

Disposition of preferred investments, representative payee, §1619

Disposition of underpayment, §1901

Distributive shares of ordinary net income (or loss) from partnerships, §1200

District of Columbia employees, §941

Divided retirement system coverage group, §1015

Dividends or interest as earnings, §1206

Divorce decree, §308

Divorced spouse's insurance benefits:
- entitlement, §311, §403
- lump-sum death benefits, §431 termination, §322

Document or record as evidence, §1702

Document submitted as evidence, evaluation, §1703

Domestic service: cash-pay test, §915 duties defined, §916
- local college club, §919, §920
- parent performing for son or daughter, §926, §927, §928 private home or apartment, §917
- student, §919, §920, §921, §922 wages, tax reporting, §918

Due dates for filing returns and paying balance of taxes due, §1410

Duty of claimant to report certain events, §106

E

Earned income, SSI, §2133

Earning report
See Earnings record Earnings, §1300:
See Also Wages
- annual exempt amount, §1802, §1803
- annual report, §1814, §1815, §1816, §1817, §1818, §1819, §1820, §1821, §1822 clarification of report, §113
- countable, §2131, §2132, §2133 earnings test, types, §1811
- excess, §1802, §1803, §1804, §1805 excess earnings, defined, §1802 excluded under earnings test, §1812 foreign work test, §1823, §1824, §1825 grace years, defined, §1807
- in-kind, defined, §2140
- included under earnings test, §1811 maintenance of records, §112 maximum creditable in year, §714 monthly exempt amounts, §1807
- non-covered work for pay, defined, §1825 non-service months, defined, §1807 number of hours worked, §1826
- partial payments, §1806
- quarters of coverage, §212 recording process, §113 rental income, §1216
- reported or credited incorrectly, §1420 reports must be filed annually, §1404
- self-employed, §1414, §1810
- short taxable years, §1808
- Social Security credits, §212
- SSI effect on, §2128, §2129, §2130, §2131, §2132, §2133, §2134, §2135, §2136, §2137, §2138, §2139, §2140, §2141, §2142, §2143, §2144, §2145, §2146, §2147
- substantial gainful activity, §620, §621 substantial services, defined, §1807 total computable, §713
- total, for taxable year, §1809
- Wage and Tax Statement, Form W-2, §1409, §1726, §1727 wages, §1810
- work outside the U.S., §1824

Earnings record:
- basis for benefit rate and insured status, §1400
- benefits payable on more than one earnings record, §733, §734, §735, §736, §737 convicted persons, §1838
- correction procedure, §1420, §1421, §1423 correction, State and local employment, §1019 crediting, §113
- deportation or removal of beneficiary, §1841 disclosure of information, §117
- evidence of unrecorded wages, §1726, §1727, §1728, §1729, §1730, §1731, §1732, §1733 extension of time limit, §1425
- filing requirements by employers, §1404
- insured status, quarters of coverage, §200
- IRS publications, employer tax payments, §1413 maintenance, §112
- notice of changes, §1427 recording, §114
- records kept by employers, §1412 reports filed annually, §1404
- revisions after time limit expires, §1424
- Social Security and Medicare tax rates, §1405
- Social Security number precautions, §1402
- Social Security number, application and use, §1401, §1402
- Social Security taxes, §1403
- subversive activities, benefit affects, §1837 suspension of time limit, military service, §1426 tax deductions, §1406
- tax forms, §1409
- time limit for review and correction, §1421, §1423, §1424, §1425, §1426 tips, §1303, §1329, §1406, §1408
- wage disputes between employer/employee, §1422 wage statements conflict, §1422

- what is shown on earnings record, §1403

Earnings reports, employer filing procedures, §1404

Earnings test:
- annual exempt amounts, §1803
- annual exempt amounts for short taxable years, §1808 defined, §1801
- excluded income, §1812 homeworkers, §830
- included income, §1811, §1813
- total earnings, §1809
- wages and self-employment income counted, §1810 without fault provisions, overpayments, §1915, §1916

Economic and human development programs, coverage, §942

Education, age, and work experience, disability evaluation, §608

Educational institution defined, §343

Elapsed years defined, §704

Election to receive reduced spouse's benefits, §320

Emergency advance payments, SSI, §2187

Employee's Report of Tips to Employer, Form 4070, §1408

Employees:
- agent-drivers or commission-drivers, §827 awards, exclusions from gross income, §1330
- beneficiary working outside U.S., deductions, §1823, §1824, §1825, §1826, §1827, §1828 citizens working outside U.S., §961, §962, §963, §964, §965, §966
- civilian Federal employee, §940
- classes of workers defined by the Social Security Act, §800 common-law test not met, §826
- common-law test, control factor, §802, §803, §804, §805, §806, §807, §808, §809, §810, §811, §812, §813, §814, §815, §816, §817, §818, §819, §820, §821, §822, §823
- compensation, §815

- controlling factors or elements of common-law test, §803, §804, §805, §806, §807, §808, §809, §810, §811, §812, §813, §814, §815, §816, §817, §818, §819, §820, §821, §822, §823
- corporation officers and directors, §824 court reporters, §1127
- defined, §800
- differences in treatment of employees and self-employed persons, §800 domestic services, §915, §916, §917, §918, §919
- earnings conflict with employer, §1422
- earnings report, §1404 employer identification, §801 farm crew workers, §831
- foreign government, instrumentality, or international organization, §937, §1124 homeworkers, §830
- life insurance salespersons, full-time, §828 ministers and members of religious orders, §932 newspaper or magazine vendors, §930, §1123 nonprofit organizations, §931
- partnerships, §825
- requirements other than common-law test, §826
- Social Security card, issuance procedure, §101
- Social Security number, application and use, §1401, §1402, §1404
- State and local
  See State and local employment statement of earnings, §1417
- tax payments, deducted or paid by employer, §1406 tip income, §1303, §1329, §1408
- traveling or city salespersons, full-time, §829
- U.S. citizens working in U.S. for foreign governments, §938
- Wage and Tax Statement, Form W-2, §1409, §1411 wages
  See Wages
- work relationships, §809

- working for two or more employers, §1407

Employer: American, §962
- crew leader (farm), §831 defined, §801, §1404
- earnings conflict with employee, §1422
- earnings reports, §1404, §1405, §1406, §1407, §1408, §1409, §1410, §1411, §1412, §1413 group-term life insurance, wages, §1337
- household employment and employer tax return forms, §1409
- Internal Revenue Service tax guides, §1413
- payment of Federal Insurance Contributions Act (FICA) tax, §1406 record maintenance, §1412
- State
  See State and local employment tax return forms, §1409
- tip income reports, §1329, §1408

Employer's Annual Tax Return for Agricultural Employees, Form 943, §1409

Employer's Application for Identification, Form SS-4, §1404

Employer's Quarterly Federal Tax Return, Form 941, §1404

Employer's Quarterly Tax Return for Household Employees (For Social Security), Form 942, §1404

Employer-employee relationship:
- agent-drivers or commission-drivers, §827
- common-law control test, §802, §803, §804, §805, §806, §807, §808, §809, §810, §811, §812, §813, §814, §815, §816, §817, §818, §819, §820, §821, §822, §823
- earnings reports, §1404 facilities, §818
- family employment, §926, §927, §928 farm crew workers and leaders, §831 full-time employment, §811 homeworkers, §830

- identity of employer, §801 instructional requirement, §804 job functions, §807
- life insurance salespersons, §828
- place of employment, §812 report submissions, §814
- requirements other than common-law test, §826 retroactive coverage, former employees, §1011
- State and local
  See State and local employment training, §805
- traveling expenses, §815
- traveling or city salespersons, full-time, §829 wage disputes, §1422
- work schedules, §810

Employment (coverage):
- beneficiary working outside U.S., deductions, §1823, §1824, §1825, §1826, §1827, §1828 domestic services, §915, §916, §917, §918, §919, §926, §927
- family, §926, §927, §928
- farm or agricultural, §901, §902, §903, §904, §905, §906, §907, §908, §909, §910, §911, §912, §913, §914
- Federal employee, §940
- fee compensated services, §1122, §1125 fishing boat operators and crews, §1134
- foreign government, instrumentality, or international organization, §937, §938 general discussion, §900
- included-excluded rule, §968, §969 interns, hospital, §923
- nonprofit organizations, §931
- outside the U.S., §961, §962, §963, §964, §965, §966 railroad, §967
- special minimum PIA, §717
- State and local
  See State and local employment student, §919, §920, §921, §922
- work not in course of employer's trade or business, §924, §925 work performed under Immigration and Nationality Act, §939

Employment outside the U.S., §1827

End-stage renal disease
See Hospital insurance benefits
Endorsement of checks, §124
Entitlement:
- child's benefits, §323, §410
- disabled widow(er)'s benefits, §513, §514, §515
- disabled worker's benefits, §501, §502, §503, §504, §505, §506 divorced spouse's insurance benefits, §311
- earnings, insured status, §1400 health insurance protection, §127
- hospital and medical insurance protection, §127, §1500
- Medicare prescription drug benefit, §128
- Medicare prescription drug costs, Extra Help with, §2600, §2601, §2602, §2603, §2604, §2605, §2606, §2607, §2608, §2609, §2610, §2611, §2612, §2613, §2614, §2615
- mother's or father's benefits, §415, §416, §417, §418, §419, §420 parent's benefits, §421
- retirement insurance benefits, §301 retroactivity, §301, §1513, §1514 spouse's benefits, §120, §305 student's benefits, §345
- surviving divorced spouse, §403 widow(er)'s benefits, §407

Equity value, SSI, §2154
Estate:
- administrator or executor, §1114 legal representative defined, §1903 refund of overpayment, §1921
- trade or business, §1116
- waiver of overpayment recovery, §1921

Events affecting benefits, need to report, §106
Events or changes in circumstances affecting eligibility, SSI, §2126
Evidence or proof: adoption, legal, §1713 age, §1704, §1705, §1706
- appointment of representative payee, §1610 beneficiary able to manage own benefits, §1614

INDEX 677

- beneficiary incapable of managing own benefits, §1604, §1606 beneficiary legally incompetent, §1605
- ceremonial marriage, §1716
- chart of evidence requirements, §1700 child born out of wedlock, §1707, §1708 child-in-care, §1723
- citizenship, U.S., §1725 common-law marriage, §1717 date of birth, §1706
- death, §1720, §1721
- disclosure of information, §1701 documents, acceptability, §1702, §1703 earnings record corrections, §1421 employer wage statements, §1728 employment statement requests, §1732 evaluation of document, §1703
- false information, §1702
- felonious and intentional homicide, §1722 full-time school attendance, §1715
- identity of claimant, §1700
- IRS, §1735
- lump-sum death payments, §1700 marriage validity, §310
- medical, §614, §615, §616
- medical evidence, incapable adult beneficiary, §1604, §1606 missing person, §1721
- parent-child relationships, §1707, §1708, §1709, §1710, §1711, §1712, §1713, §1714 partnerships, §1110
- paternity decree, §1710, §1712 personal records, §1733
- representative payee, selection process, §1611 requirements, §1700
- school attendance, §1715
- self-employment income, §1734, §1735, §1736
- State/Federal tax returns, §1730
- Statement of Claimant or Other Person, SSA-795, §1732 step-relationship, §1714
- stepchildren, §331
- support of claimant, §1724

- support, 2-year filing period, §424, §1520 termination of marriage, §1718, §1719 types, acceptability, §1702
- unemployment compensation, §1731 union records, §1729
- unsigned wage statements, §1728
- wage evidence unobtainable, §1734
- wages, §1726, §1727, §1728, §1729, §1730, §1731, §1732, §1733, §1734, §1735, §1736 written acknowledgement, defined, §1709

Excess earnings:
- defined, §1802
- earnings charged against benefits, §1804 grace years and nonservice months, §1807 months not charged to benefits, §1805 payment of partial benefit, §1806

Excluded resources, SSI, §2156
Excluded services, Federal-State agreement, §1002
Exclusions from coverage, international social security agreements, §970
Exclusions from trade or business, §1122
Exclusions of employment, not covered by Social Security, §900
Exclusions, computing gross business income, §1202
Exclusions, employer payments from employer funds under or to a tax-sheltered annuity plan, §1340
Exclusions, real property, SSI, §2163
Executor, §1903
Executor of estate, trade or business, §1114
Exemption from Social Security taxes, members of religious orders, §1128
Exercise of ministry defined, §935
Expedited payment provisions, §130
Expenses allowable in computing net earnings from self-employment, §1205
Extended period of eligibility, §506
Extension of time for filing annual report of earnings, §1816
Extension of time for filing request for reconsideration, hearing, or review, §2015

Extra Help with Medicare Prescription Drug Costs:
- appeal process, §2614 application, §103, §2601
- earned income, §2605 eligibility, §2601
- income, defined, §2602, §2603, §2604, §2605, §2606, §2607, §2608 income, not considered, §2603, §2604
- prescription drug cost plan, §2600 program defined, §2600
- protective filing for Medicare Savings Programs, §2601 redeterminations, §2615
- resource exclusions, §2612
- resources, §2609, §2610, §2611, §2612 resources, countable, §2610, §2611 resources, defined, §2609
- unearned income, §2606, §2607 unearned income, exclusions, §2608 verification, §2613

F

Failure to file, or late filing of, annual report of earnings, penalty deductions, §1819

Failure to report child no longer in care, penalty deductions, §1831

Failure to report foreign work activity, penalty deductions, §1828

False statements, penal provisions, §143

Family employment, §927

Family maximum:
- adjustment of individual rates and exceptions, §731, §732 amount payable, §730
- benefit rate, adjustment, §731, §732
- child entitled on more than one earnings record, §737 child's benefit, effect on, §338, §412
- cost-of-living increase, §719 excess earnings, §1804
- individual reduced benefit rates, §732 parent's benefits reduced, §425
- payment of partial benefit, excess earnings, §1806 spouse's benefit, effect on, §320

Family partnerships, §1109

Farm:
- agricultural or horticultural commodities listed, §905 defined, §903
- domestic services, §915, §916
- domestic services on a farm operated for profit, §915 income from prior year products, §1237
- material participation
  See Material participation by landlord (farm)
- nonbusiness work, §924
- operating, managing, maintaining, etc., §909 partnerships and joint ventures, §1121
- rental arrangement, material participation, §1221, §1222, §1223, §1224, §1225, §1226, §1227, §1228, §1229, §1230, §1231, §1232
- types of work covered, §904, §906

Farm employee, quarters of coverage, §214

Farm income computation (self-employment):
- chart on optional methods, §1241
- combined farm and nonfarm earnings, §1244

Federal program payments, §1238 grazing land, income from, §1236
- gross income, optional reporting, §1234, §1235, §1236, §1237, §1238, §1239, §1240, §1241 nonfarm self-employment, net earnings optional method, §1242, §1243
- optional methods of computing net earnings from self-employment, §1233, §1234 sale of prior year products, §1237
- self-employment, net earnings, optional method, §1235 sharefarmer's and landlord's share of gross income, §1239 timber, sale of, §1240

Farmer's Tax Guide, Internal Revenue Service Publication No. 225, §1200

Father's insurance benefits, §416: *See Also* Parent's insurance benefits benefit rate, §418

INDEX **679**

- child-in-care, §312, §1829, §1831
- entitlement requirements, §415, §416, §417, §418, §419, §420, §421 non-payment situations, §419, §426
- reduction, family maximum applies, §418
- remarriage, effect, §417 terminating events, §420

Federal agencies, disclosure of information, §118
Federal agricultural program payments, §1238
Federal benefit rates, SSI, §2113
Federal benefit rates, table, SSI, §2147
Federal court reporters, §1127
Federal Determination of Error in State's Wage Reports, Form SSA-4500-U6, §1726
Federal Disability Insurance Trust Fund, §141
Federal Employee's Retirement System (FERS), §937
Federal employees and coverage, §940
Federal Hospital Insurance Trust Fund, §141
Federal Insurance Contributions Act (FICA), §1019
Federal Medical Insurance Trust Fund, §141
Federal Old-Age and Survivors Insurance Trust Fund, §141
Federal-State agreements
  See Disability insurance benefits See Medical insurance benefits See State and local employment
Federal-State matching grant programs, conversion to SSI, §2109
Federally administered State supplementation, SSI, §2124
Federally sponsored economic and human development programs, §942
Fee for representing claimant, §2018
Fee-based official, defined, §1015
Fee-compensated positions, State and local employment, §1009

Felonious homicide of worker, claimant involved, §400
Felony-related impairments, §507
Fiduciaries, trade or business, §1114
Filing date, application for benefits, §1507
Filing for other benefits, SSI, §2117
Final decision on application, §1502
Finality of determination or decision, §2001
Financial contributions (Test I), criteria, §1224
Firefighters' and police officers', positions under a retirement system, §1012
Firefighters' positions under a retirement system, §1012
Fishing boat operators and crews, §936
Food stamp program, SSI, §2108
Foreign (allied) military service, §957
Foreign affiliate of domestic corporation, §964
Foreign agricultural workers admitted to U.S. on a temporary basis, §914
Foreign claims, beneficiaries residing abroad, §103
Foreign countries, totalization agreements with U.S., §107
Foreign employment, included-excluded rule, §969
Foreign government, instrumentality, or international organization, §1124
Foreign government, instrumentality, or international organization employees, §937
Foreign language documents as evidence, §1702
Foreign Service Pension System (FSPS), §937
Foreign students, exchange visitors, and international cultural exchange visitors, §939
Foreign subsidiary of domestic corporation, §964
Foreign work test, §1823
Foreign-born applicant, evidence of age, §1706

Formal education and work experience, §609

Forms, IRS:
- 1040, U.S. Individual Tax Return, §1416, §1735
- 4029, Application for Exemption from Social Security Taxes and Waiver of Benefits, §1129
- 8274, Certification by Churches and Qualified Church-Controlled Organizations Electing Exemption from Employer's
- Social Security Taxes, §1128

Forms, SSA:
- 1065, Partnership Return of Income, §1417, §1421, §1736
- 1099, Social Security Benefit Statement, §125
- 2031, Waiver Certificate to Elect Social Security Coverage for Use by Ministers, Certain Members of Religious
- Orders, and Christian Science Practitioners, §1130
- 225, Farmer's Tax Guide, Internal Revenue Service Publication, §1200
- 334, Tax Guide for Small Business, Internal Revenue Service Publication, §1200
- 4070, Employee's Report of Tips to Employer, §1408
- 4137, Social Security and Medicare Tax on Unreported Tip Income, §1408
- 4361, Application for Exemption from Self-Employment Tax for Use by Ministers, Members of Religious Orders, and
- Christian Science Practitioners, §1131
- 941, Employer's Quarterly Federal Tax Return, §1409
- 941E, Employer's Quarterly Federal Tax Return for Employees of Governmental Organizations, §1404
- 942, Employer's Quarterly Tax Return for Household Employees (For Social Security), §1409
- 943, Employer's Annual Tax Return for Agricultural Employees, §1409
- DD-1300, Report of Casualty, used as intent to claim benefits, §1509
- I-197, United States Citizen Identification Card, §1725
- L987, Social Security Earnings Information, §1726
- Schedule C (Profit (or Loss) from Business or Profession), §1416
- Schedule SE (Computation of Social Security Self-Employment Tax), §1416
- SS-16, Election of Covered Wages for Members of Religious Order Under Vow of Poverty, §932
- SS-4, Employer's Application for Identification Number, §1404
- SS-5, Application for a Social Security Card, §101, §1401, §1404
- SSA-1002, Statement of Agricultural Employer, §1726
- SSA-4500-U6, Federal Determination of Error in State's Wage Reports, §1726
- SSA-7011, Statement of Employer, §1726
- SSA-795, Statement of Claimant or Other Person, §1732
- W-2, Wage and Tax Statement, §1404, §1408, §1409, §1411, §1726
- W-2c, Statement of Corrected Income and Tax Amounts, §1409
- W-3, Transmittal of Wage and Tax Statement, §1409
- W-3C, Transmittal of Corrected Wage and Tax Statement, §1409

Fraud:
- benefit claims and earnings records, §143 criminal prosecutions and penalties, §143, §2016
- criminal prosecutions and penalties, SSI, §2016, §2127, §2197

Freedom of Information Act (FOIA), §117

Fringe benefits, §1342

Fugitive Felons: SSI, §2119
- Title II, §1854

Full Retirement Age (FRA): adjustment of reduction, §728 certification of election, §729 reduction factors, §723
- workers/spouses born after 1937, §723

Full-time school attendance, evidence, §1715

Full-time student defined, §344

Fully insured status: deceased veteran, §960 deemed, §205
- defined, §203
- delayed retirement credits, §720 exceptions, §203
- quarters of coverage requirement, §203, §204
- totalization agreements between U.S. and foreign countries, §216

Fully insured worker, delayed retirement credits, §720

G

Gainful work activity defined, §603

Garnishment of benefits, §129

Good cause:
- deemed to exist, §2016 defined, §1519, §1833
- extension of time limit for filing application, §1518, §1519, §1520
- extension of time limit for filing request for reconsideration, hearing or review, SSI, §2196 extension of time limit for filing request for reconsideration, hearing, or review, §2015 failure to file required reports, §1832, §1833
- proof of, §1833
- refusal of consultative examinations, §616 refusal of VR services, §505
- signature on application, §1501

Governmental functions, State and local employment, §1003

Governmental pension offset, §348

Grace years, §1807

Grandchild or stepgrandchild, §325

Grandchild, dependent, §336

Grandfather provisions for converted recipients, SSI, §2172

Grazing land, income as net earnings, §1236

Gross business receipts, §1202

Gross income, farm option, §1234

Group-term life insurance, employer cost, §1337

Guam, coverage, §966

H

Harvesting agricultural commodities, §906

Health insurance, Medicare, §127

Hearing by Administrative Law Judge (ALJ):
- action on case before judge, §2008 authority of ALJ, §2009
- decision on determination and notice, §2012
- extension of time for filing request for hearing or review, §2015 hearing, defined, §2193, §2724
- notice of hearing, §2009
- prehearing or posthearing conferences, §2010 request for hearing or review, §2007
- review by Appeals Council, §2013, §2014
- SSI, §2193 subpoenas, §2009

Hearings, disability, §2006

Hearings, SVB, §2724

Hobbies as trade or business, §1106

Home energy or support and maintenance, SSI, §2139

Homeworkers, §830

Horticultural or agricultural commodities, §903

Hospital insurance benefits, §138: application requirements, §1500 appropriations from general revenues, §137 disability, under age 65, §500
- end-stage kidney disease, §127, §500 entitlement, §1500
- funding sources, §137

Hospital interns, coverage, §923

Household employment and employer tax return forms, §1409
Husband's insurance benefits
   See Spouse's insurance benefits

I
Identity of claimant, §1700
Identity of employer, §801
Idle time pay as wages, §1326
Illegal activities as trade or business, §1104
Illegitimate child:
- acknowledgment or recognition, §327 inheritance rights, §327
- parent-child relationship, §1708
- State laws, §326, §327
Immediate payments, SSI, §2187
Immigration and Nationality Act, §939
Impairment-related work expenses, SSI, §2175
Impairments (disability): confinement-related, §507 definition, §507, §601 felony-related, §507
- listing, §607 severe, §613
Impede effective or efficient administration, SSI, §1920
Imprest fund checks, SSI, §2187
Improvement or maintenance of farm, agricultural labor, §909
In care, child
   See Child-in-care
In-kind income, SSI, §2140
In-kind support and maintenance, SSI, §2141
Included-excluded rule, §968
Income and resource limits for eligible couples, SSI, §2123
Income counted for earnings test purposes, §1811
Income earned outside U.S. from a trade or business, net earnings from self-employment, §1245
Income for SSI purposes, §2129
Income from renting rooms or apartments, §1216
Income or losses not counted for earnings test, §1812

Income producing property, excluded resource, SSI, §2158
Income tax returns, evidence of earnings, §1730
Income tax returns, evidence of self-employment income, §1734
Income-Related Monthly Adjustment Amount, §2500
Incompetent person owns business, §1115
Individual Retirement Accounts (IRA's) and Keogh Plans, §1338
Ineligibles, retirement system coverage group, §1015
Information program in Social Security offices, §117
Informational facilities/records available for public inspection, §118
Inheritance rights of adopted children, §330
Initial determination, §2000
Initial determinations, SSI, §2189
Initial determinations, SVB, §2721
Inspection in Social Security offices, §117
Inspection, periodic, as material farm participation by landlord, §1228
Institution, resident, SSI, §2121
Institutions, nonprofit religious, charitable, educational, etc., coverage, §931
Instrumentality, State and local employment, §1003
Insured status, §200:
   See Also Fully insured status currently insured, §206
- deemed fully insured, §205 determining, §200, §201, §202
- disability insured status, §207, §208, §209, §508, §509, §510 fully insured status, §202, §203, §204, §205
- lump-sum death payment, §428
- period of disability, §207, §208, §209, §508, §509, §510 provisions for the blind, §208
- quarters of coverage, §212 requirements, §200, §201, §202, §211
- special age 72 payments, §119, §211, §346, §347, §348 special status, before age 31, §208

- survivors insurance benefits, §400 totalization coordination, §216
Interest or dividends as earnings, §1206
Interim assistance, cash or vendor payments, SSI, §2186
Intern for hospital, coverage, §923
Internal Revenue Service (IRS):
- employer tax payment publications, §1413 exclusions, Section 911 code, §1246
- self-employment tax payment publications, §1200, §1418
- Social Security numbers, §101
- Taxpayer Identification Number (TIN), §1246
International Operations, Office of, §114
International Operations, Office of, claimants residing abroad, §114
International Social Security Agreements, §107
Interstate instrumentality defined, §1003
Investigative responsibilities, §142

J
Japanese internees during WWII, wage credits, §1336
Job Corps program, §944
Joint ventures:
- determination factors, §1108
- trade or business partnerships, §1107, §1108, §1109, §1110, §1111, §1112, §1121

K
Keogh Plans, and IRA's, §1338
Kidney disease
  See Hospital insurance benefits

L
Landlord defined, §1221
Landlord distinguished from business operator, §1118
Landlord, gross farm income, §1239
Landlords, material participation (farm), §1221
Lay evidence, defined, §1607

Legal guardian, representative payee, §1605
Legal representative defined, §1903
Legal representative, underpayments, §1903
Legality or illegality of trade or business, §1104
Legitimacy of child:
- acknowledgment or recognition, §327 conceived or born during valid marriage, §326
- State laws, §326, §411
- void marriage statutes, §326
Length of time engaged in business, §1103
Levy or attachment, benefit exemptions, §129
Liability for repayment of overpayment, §1906
Life changing events, §2507
Life insurance salespersons:
- full-time, §828
- renewal commissions, §1310
Life insurance, excluded from countable resources, SSI, §2159
Limitation of State's contribution liability, §1019
Limitations on use of certain exceptions, alien nonpayment provisions, §1846
Limited partner, coverage, §1102
Liquid resources and nonliquid resources, SSI, §2150
Listing of Impairments, §607
Living in household of another, reduction of benefits, SSI, §2143
Living in household of another, SSI, §2142
Living in the same household, lump-sum death payments, §119
Living outside U.S., alien beneficiary, auxiliaries or survivors, §1843
Loans to employees, wages, §1321
Local college club defined, §920
Local college club, domestic service by student, §919
Lodging and meals as wages, §1343

Lord Mansfield Rule, child's legal status, §326
Lost checks, §123
Lump-sum death payment: alien outside U.S., §1847 appeal rights, §106
- application, filing period, §433, §1517, §1518, §1519 child entitled, §432, §433
- child or children, choose not to apply, §432 deported worker, §1842
- distribution, §428
- equal shares paid to children of deceased worker, §432 extension of time limit for good cause, §1519
- filing period, §1517 insured status, §428
- listing of insured status requirement for Social Security benefits, §211 living in same household, widow(er), §430
- no spouse payable, §432 nonpayment situations, §429
- overpayment, §1909 relationship requirements, §430
- reporting events affecting eligibility, §106 requirements, §211
- subversive activities conviction, §1839
- surviving spouse not living in same household, §431 surviving widow(er), §430
- widow(er)'s, §430, §431, §432, §433

M
Magazine distribution, §929
Maintenance services by landlords, rental income under Social Security, §1217
Mandatory payment, State supplement, SSI, §2181
Marketing of farm commodities, agricultural labor, §913
Marriage:
- ceremonial, proof, §1716 common-law, §307, §1717 divorce, effect, §308
- duration, 9-month requirement, §404 restrictions on remarriage, State-imposed, §309 spouse, defined, §306

- SSI benefit affect, §2122
- State-imposed restrictions on remarriage, §309 terminating events, benefit summary chart, §1851 termination evidence, §1718, §1719
- validity of prior marriage, §310
- voidable and annulled, benefits reinstated, §1853 widower's entitlement to benefits, §401

Material participation by landlord (farm):
- advice and consultation, periodic inspections, §1228, §1229 decisions affecting success of enterprise, §1230 determination criteria, §1223, §1224, §1230, §1231, §1232 periodic inspection, §1228
- production costs, §1226, §1227
- rental agreements, §1225 rental arrangement, §1222
- total activities, consideration, Test I-III, §1232

Maximum yearly earnings:
- computation of average monthly earnings, §714 quarters of coverage, crediting, §212
- self-employment income, §1201

Meals and lodging as wages, §1343
Medicaid application, Medicare Savings Programs, §2601
Medicaid application, SSI, §2107
Medicaid, extended eligibility, SSI, §2179
Medical evidence of disability: condition does not meet a listing, §608 consultative examinations, §616 furnished by claimant, §614, §615
- impairments or combination of impairments is not severe, §606 improvement in the individual's impairment(s), §623
- inclusions, §615
- listing of impairments, §607 medical evidence inclusive, §615

Medical evidence of incapability, §1604
Medical insurance benefits: disability, under age 65, §500 enrollment, §2400
- funding sources, §138

INDEX **685**

- Income-Related Monthly Adjustment Amount, §2500, §2501, §2502, §2503, §2504, §2505, §2506, §2507, §2508 overpayment, §1909
- premium collection, §127, §138
- reporting events affecting eligibility, §106

Medically determinable physical or mental impairments, §601

Medicare, §2400:
  See Also Extra Help with Medicare Prescription Drug Costs
  See Also Hospital insurance benefits
  See Also Income-Related Monthly Adjustment Amount
  See Also Medical insurance benefits
  See Also Medicare Advantage
  See Also Medicare prescription drug benefit
- appeals process, Extra Help with prescription drug cost, §2614
- appeals process, Income-Related Monthly Adjustment Amount, §2508 application for benefits, §103
- defined, §127
- health insurance, §127
- prescription drug cost Extra Help with, §2600, §2601, §2602, §2603, §2604, §2605, §2606, §2607, §2608, §2609, §2610, §2611, §2612, §2613, §2614, §2615
- tax rates, §1405

Medicare Advantage, §127

Medicare prescription drug benefit:
- application, §2400 benefit, §2400 defined, §128
- Extra Help with, §2600, §2601, §2602, §2603, §2604, §2605, §2606, §2607, §2608, §2609, §2610, §2611, §2612, §2613, §2614, §2615
- financing the program, §139

Members of uniformed services, coverage, §948

Mental impairments, §601

Military service:
- active duty defined, §950 active duty for training, §951
- active duty, after 1956, §1305
- allied countries, service with wage credits, §957, §1307 armed services components listed, §949, §955
- auxiliary organizations, §955 chaplains, §1133
- Coast and Geodetic Survey, commissioned officers, §958 coverage after 1956, §948, §1305
- coverage before 1957, §948, §954, §1307
- death, presumptive findings of armed services department, §1720 deemed insured status of deceased veteran, §960
- deemed wage credits, §953, §954, §955, §956, §957, §958, §959, §960, §1306 defined, §955
- dishonorable or conditional discharge, §956
- earnings record corrections, time limit suspension, §1426 incorrect report of death, overpayment, §1923
- member defined, §949
- noncontributory wage credits, §953, §954, §955, §956, §957, §958, §959, §960, §1306
- Public Health Service, commissioned officers, §958 quarters of coverage, period of disability, §210 special wage credits, §212
- wage credits, §948
- wage credits after 1956, §948, §953, §1305 wage credits before 1957, §954, §1307 wage credits not payable, §959
- work creditable for Social Security purposes, §952 work performed, amount of member's wages, §952

Minimum benefits, §716

Minimum pay test
  See Cash-pay test

Minimum PIA provisions, §716

Ministers and members of religious orders:
- covered employment, §932
- exercise of the ministry defined, §935

- minister, definition of ordained, licensed or commissioned, §934 net earnings inclusions, §1212
- self-employment, §1100, §1130, §1131, §1132, §1133 work not in exercise of the order, §933

Misrepresentation of material fact, criminal prosecution and penalties, §143

Missing person, evidence of death, §1720

Missing reports of earnings, §1420

Modification to Federal-State agreements, §1000

Modified adjusted gross income, §2500

Money gifts and bequests, §140

Monthly exempt amount, §1807

Monthly premiums for medical benefits, general, §138

Mother's insurance benefits, §416: *See Also* Parent's insurance benefits benefit rate, §418
- entitlement requirements, §415, §421 non-payment situations, §419, §426 reduction, family maximum applies, §418 remarriage, effect, §417
- terminating events, §420

Moving expenses as wages, §1333

Multiple enterprises as trade or business, §1105

Murder of worker, claimant involved, §400

N

Name change on Social Security records, §101

National Oceanic and Atmospheric Administration, commissioned officers, §958

Natural child, §324

Naturally or legally adopting parent of child beneficiary, §333

Naval service of the U.S., §955

Needs and maintenance of beneficiary, current, §1617

Net earnings from self-employment: advice and consultation, defined, §1229 business expenses, computing, §1205 calculation process, §1200

- computation methods, optional, §1233 credits earned, §215
- criteria for Test I, §1224 criteria for Test II, §1230 criteria for Test III, §1231
- dealer in stocks or securities, §1207, §1209
- death of partner before end of taxable year, §1204 defined, §1200
- exclusions applicable to ministers, §1246 farm and nonfarm self-employment, §1244
- farm rental income, material participation, §1221, §1222, §1223, §1224, §1225 farm timber sales, §1240
- farmers, optional methods of computation, §1233, §1234, §1235, §1236, §1237, §1238, §1239, §1240, §1241, §1242, §1243, §1244
- Federal agricultural program payments, §1238
- Form 1040 (U.S. Individual Income Tax Return), §1416
- Form 1065 (Partnership Return of Income), §1417 gains or losses, exclusion, §1211
- grazing land, income from, §1236 gross business income defined, §1202
- gross income, optional method reporting, §1234 income earned outside the U.S., §1245
- income included in applying the earnings test, §1813 landlord services, defined, §1217
- minimum creditable in year, §215 ministers, rental allowance, §1212 nonfarm income, §1242, §1243, §1244 partnership, filing requirements, §1417
- payments for use/occupancy of space, §1219 production cost, §1226, §1227
- real estate rental and sales, §1213, §1214, §1215, §1216, §1217, §1218, §1219, §1220 rental income from multiple properties, §1220
- reporting requirements, §1416

- retirement payments from partnerships, §1203 sale of prior year farm products, §1237
- Schedule C (Profit (or Loss) from Business or Profession), §1416
- Schedule SE (Computation of Social Security Self-Employment Tax), §1416 self-employment income defined, §1201
- stock dividends and interest on bonds, §1206 stockbrokers, interest and dividends, §1207, §1209
- Test I - III not met, §1232
- trader or investor in stocks and bonds, §1208

New Initial Determination, §2506
Newspaper delivery or distribution, coverage, §929
Newspaper vendors, §930
Nonbusiness work, §924
Nonbusiness work on farm, agricultural labor, §915
Noncontributory military wage credits, §953
Noncovered employment, modified formula for determining PIA, §718
Noncovered remunerative activity, §1825
Noncovered work, State and local employment, §1006
Nonfarm earnings, optional method of computing, §1242
Nonliquid resources, SSI, §2150
Nonmedical institutions, SSI, §2144
Nonpayment of benefits:
- alien provisions, §303, §429, §505, §1843, §1844, §1845, §1846, §1847
- annual report of earnings, §1814, §1815, §1816, §1817, §1818, §1819, §1820, §1821, §1822 child's, §339, §413
- child-in-care requirement, §1829, §1831
- convicted of subversive activities, §1837, §1838, §1839, §1840 deported worker, §303, §429, §505, §1841, §1842
- events summarized, §1800
- foreign work test, §1823, §1824, §1825, §1826, §1827, §1828 good cause for failure to file required reports, §1832, §1833 lump-sum death payment, §429
- mother's or father's, §419 parent's, §426
- receipt of periodic workers' compensation payment, §1835 refusal of VR services, §505
- religious reasons, §303
- retirement insurance benefits, §303 spouse's, §321
- treasury restrictions, §1847, §1848, §1849 widow(er)'s, §408

Nonprofit organizations:
- pay for work, §1304
- Volunteers in Service to America (VISTA), §947

Notice of changes in earnings record, §1427
Notice of time and place of hearing, §2009
Notification by Appeals Council, review of case, §2014
Number of penalty deductions imposed for failing to file timely annual report of earnings, §1820
Number of years selected as computation years, §703
Nurse, student, §922

O

Occupations not covered by Social Security programs, §108
Occupations under self-employment coverage, §1100
Offset:
- child's benefits, §339
- disability benefits, §503, §504 father's benefits, §419 governmental pension, §1836 mother's benefits, §419
- special age 72 payments, §348 spouse's benefits, §321 widow(er)'s benefits, §408 windfall, SSI, §2185
- workers' compensation, §1835

Old-age insurance benefits (retirement insurance benefits), §300
On-the-job training pay for veterans, §1328
One-half support situations, §329
One-half support, filing time limit, §1520
One-third reduction rule, §2143
Optional exclusions, State and local employment, §1008
Optional methods of computing self-employment farm income:
- combined farm and nonfarm earnings, §1244 grazing land income, §1236
- gross income, §1234, §1235, §1237, §1238, §1239, §1240, §1241 income from sale of timber, §1240
- nonfarm earnings, §1242
- nonfarm earnings, table summarizing effect, §1243 purpose, §1233, §1235
- sharefarmer's gross receipts, §1239 summary table, §1241

Ordained, commissioned, or licensed minister defined, §934

Overpayment of benefits:
- adjustment against current and future benefits, §1909 adjustment of benefit recovery, §1909
- against equity and good conscience, defined, §1919 civil suit by recovery, §1912
- compromise settlement of recovery, §1911 definition, §1904
- determinations, revised, §1922
- DOD erroneous reports of death, §1923 fault provisions, §1917
- impede effective or efficient administration, SSI, defined, §1920 incorrect report of death by service department, §1923
- liability of beneficiary, §1906
- non-entitlement to payments, §135 notices, §1905
- ordinary and necessary living expenses, defined, §1918 partial withholding of benefits, §1910, §1911
- person at fault, §1917
- rate of withholding, RSDI, §1910 recovery by civil suit, §1912 recovery efforts, §1913
- recovery methods, §1907
- refunds of incorrect payments, §1908
- repayment liability, §1906
- revised prior determination, §1922
- RSI recovery, §1918
- unpaid benefit, written request, §1901 waiver factors, §1918
- waiver of recovery, §1914, §1915, §1916, §1917, §1918, §1919, §1920, §1921 without fault provisions, §1915, §1916
- written request of unpaid benefit requirements, §1901

Overpayment of contributions, State and local employment, §1019

P

Pamphlets and instructions:
- employer's tax guides, §1413
- self-employment tax guides, §1200, §1418
- Social Security office facilities, §117

Parent defined, §422

Parent's insurance benefits, §421: *See Also* Father's insurance benefits *See Also* Mother's insurance benefits amount, §418, §425
- benefit rate, §418, §425 entitlement requirements, §421
- in-care requirements, not met, §315 multiple benefit entitlement, §733 non-payment situations, §419, §426 parent defined, §422
- remarriage effect, §417
- separation from child, §316, §317, §318, §319 support requirements, §423, §424
- terminating events, §420, §427 widower's entitlement, §415

Parent-child relationship:
- birth or baptismal records, §1707 child defined, SS purpose, §411 child-in-care, defined, §312

- court decree as proof, §1710 court order for support, §1711 deemed stepchild of worker, §332
- dependency of child, §333, §334, §335, §336, §337 domestic services by parents, §926, §927
- evidence required, §1707, §1708, §1709, §1710, §1711, §1712, §1713, §1714 family employment, types, §926
- in-care requirements, not met, §315 legitimacy of child, §326, §327 parental control, defined, §313 parental control/responsibility, §313
- paternity decree and support order, §1710, §1711, §1712 personal services, defined, §314
- proof, §1707
- separation from child, §316, §317, §318, §319 stepchild, §331, §332
- stepchild/stepparent, written acknowledgement, §1709

Parental control and responsibility, child-in-care, §312
Parking lot rentals, §1219
Partial adjustment, overpayment of benefits, §1909
Partial withholding of benefits due to overpayment, §1910
Partnerships:
- association taxable as corporation, §1112 corporations, §825
- death of partner, effect on taxable year, §1204 defined, §1107
- determining factors, §1108
- distributive share of net income (or loss), §1200, §1204, §1736 evidence, §1110
- family, §1109
- family employment exclusion not applicable, §928 farm, §1234
- joint ventures, §1107, §1108, §1121

Partnership Return of Income, Form 1065, §1417, §1421, §1736 retirement payments, exclusions, §1203
- silent partners, coverage, §1102

- stock dividends and interest on bonds as income, §1210 transfer of capital interest, family, §1111

Past debts of beneficiaries, §1619
Paternity evidence, parent-child relationship, §1710
Pay envelopes, vouchers, and unsigned wage statements as evidence, §1728
Pay period defined (included-excluded rule), §968
Payment dates, §121
Payments and government pensions, §348
Payments or items received, not income, SSI, §2113
Payments, SVB, §2612
Payments-in-kind, cash-pay test, §1303
Peace Corps volunteers, §943
Penal institution, student beneficiary, §344
Penal provision, §143
Penalties for fraud, false statements, misrepresentation, SSI, §2127
Penalty deductions:
- child no longer in care, §1831
- failure to file timely annual report, §1820, §1821 foreign work reports, failure to file, §1828 unreported tip income, §1408

Pension, governmental, §1836
Pensions and retirement pay, §1317
Period of absence from U.S., alien outside the U.S., §1844
Period of coverage that a worker completed under the social security system of a foreign country, §216
Period of disability:
- application, §509
- computation of benefits, exclusions, §711 continuing reviews, §622
- date of entitlement, §510 defined, §508
- earnings, §620, §621
- evaluation of disability, §608, §609 filing requirements, §1502
- medical evidence, §606, §607 military service before 1957, §210 performance

of work, §618 protection types, under SS, §500
- quarters of coverage, military service, §210 special insured status requirements, §208 substantial gainful activity, §618 termination of disability, §511
- trial work period, §522

Periodic inspection, material participation, §1228

Periodic workers' compensation payments, §1835

Personal records of worker as evidence, §1733

Personal services not required, trade or business, §1102

Personal services, child-in-care, defined, §314

Physical or mental impairments, §507

Physicians' signed statement of disability, §615

Plan or system (wages):
- annuity or bond purchase plans, §1316 cafeteria plan, defined, §1341
- Federal thrift savings fund, §1315
- nonqualified deferred compensation plans, §1318 pensions and retirement pay, §1317
- profit-sharing plan, §1313
- relation to wages explained, §1311
- sick and accident disability pay, §1312 trust fund, payments under or to, §1314

Plan to Achieve Self-Support (PASS), SSI, §2177

Political subdivision defined, §1003

Postal service contract workers, §1117

Power of attorney, representative payee, §1609

Prehearing or posthearing conferences, §2010

Premiums (medical insurance benefits):
- payment of, §127, §138

Prescription drug funding, §139

Presumed maximum value rule (PMV), §2144

Presumption of death, unexplained absence, §1721

Presumptive blindness/disability payments, SSI, §2188

Primary insurance amount (PIA):
- 1990 old-start method, §712 average monthly earnings, §701 basic figure, §700
- child's benefit rate, §338 computation formula, §702 cost-of-living increase, §719 defined, §700
- determination, §706
- disabled worker's benefit rate, §503
- figuring PIA under 1990 consolidated methods, §712 first eligibility, §700, §706
- minimum SS benefit, elimination, §716 mother's or father's benefit rate, §418 old-start formula yields, §706
- parent's benefit rate, §425
- primary insurance benefit computation, §710 principal business activity, defined, §828 recomputation, §721, §722
- simplified old-start formula, §707, §708, §709, §710 special minimum, §717
- spouse's benefit rate, §320 totalization, effect, §216 widow(er)'s benefit rate, §407
- Windfall Elimination Provision, (WEP), §718 worker dies before age 62, §700

Privacy Act, disclosure of information, §117

Private home defined, domestic service, §917

Prizes and awards as wages, §1330

Probation and parole violators, SSI, §2120

Processing or packaging of agricultural commodities, §913

Producing a crop or livestock, §1120

Professionals, self-employed, §1100

Profit-sharing plan, §1313

Program service center: benefit payments, §110 functions, §111, §114

INDEX **691**

- locations, §110 processing claims, §111
- review and final processing of claims, §105

Programs in foreign countries, international agreements, §970
Programs, Social Security, §100
Proof
  See Evidence or proof
Proper use of benefits by representative payee, §1616
Property held for personal use or as investment, §1214
Property necessary for self-support, SSI, §2158
Property, exclusions, SSI, §2163
Proprietary functions, State and local employment, §1003
Proration of benefits, SSI, §2184
Public assistance programs (Federal and/or State): State supplementation of SSI, §2106, §2181
Public Health Service, commissioned officers, §958
Public information, availability, §117
Public institutions, residents, SSI, §2121
Public office holders, self-employment, §1126
Public record of birth, established before age 5, §1705
Public transportation systems, §1013
Public transportation systems, State and local employment, §1007

Q

Qualified employee discount, §1342
Quarters of coverage: agricultural employment, §214 currently insured status, §206 disability insured status, §207
- fully insured status, §202, §203, §204, §205 military service, special wage credits, §205, §210 minimum pay test, §1304
- restrictions, §213
- self-employment income after 1977, and before 1978, §215 self-employment income, allocating, §715

- special age 72 payments, §211, §346 wages paid after 1936, §214

R

Railroad compensation, §1308
Railroad recomputation of PIA, §721
Railroad Retirement Board (RRB):
- application for Social Security benefits, §1506 coverage under Social Security, §967, §1308 included-excluded rule, §969
- wages and quarters of coverage, §212

Railroad work, §967
Raising of crop, agricultural labor, §906
Re-entitlement of benefits: childhood disability, §341, §517 extended period of eligibility, §506 student beneficiary, §341
Real estate agents and direct sellers, self-employment income, §1135
Real estate broker, net earnings from self-employment, §1215
Real estate dealer, profit from sale of stock in trade, §1214
Real estate, income from rental, §1213
Real property, excluded resources, SSI, §2163
Recomputation of PIA, §721
Reconsideration disability report, §533
Reconsideration of determinations: beneficiaries residing abroad, §114 disability hearing, §2006
- disability, DDS responsibilities, §115
- extension of time for filing request, §2196
- filing requirements, §531, §532, §533, §534, §535, §536, §537
- hearing or review, §2007, §2008, §2009, §2010, §2011, §2012, §2013 representative payees, selection process, §1611
- request process, §2004, §2005, §2192
- SVB process, §2723
- time limits, review request, §2001

Record of birth, evidence established before age 5, §1705

Recovery of overpaid benefits:
- adjustment against overpayment, §1908, §1909 against equity and good conscience, §1919
- civil suit, §1912
- compromise settlement, §1911 defeat the purpose defined, §1918
- estate of a deceased overpaid person, §1921
- Federal Claims Collection Act, §1913 partial withholding of benefits, §1910
- refund of overpayment, §1907, §1908, §1909, §1910 representative payee, §1905
- revised prior determination, §1922
- waiver, §1914, §1915, §1916, §1917, §1918, §1919, §1920, §1921 withholding part of monthly benefit, §1909, §1910, §1911, §1912 reduced, §723

Reduced benefits:
- age, §302, §723, §726, §727, §728 basic formulas, §724
- child's benefits, §338 computations, §727
- disability insurance benefits reduced for age, §726
- disabled worker's rate after reduced widow(er)'s or retirement benefit, §503 factors, §723
- family maximum, §731, §732 general, §723
- governmental pension offset, §1836 husband's or wife's, §729
- mother's or father's, family maximum applies, §418 periodic workers' compensation offset, §1835
- rate factors, §723
- reduction factor adjustment, §728 reduction months, computation, §725 restriction of retroactive period, §1514 retroactivity restrictions, §1514
- saving clauses, §731
- special payments/government pensions, §348 spouse, §320, §1514
- widow(er)'s, §407

- worker's compensation offset, reduction, §504

Referendum, State and local coverage, §1010

Referrals to other governmental or community agencies, §118

Refund of overpaid benefits, §135

Refunds of excess tax contributions, §1019

Regional offices, SSA, §110

Regular or reserve components of Armed Forces, §948

Relatives, deemed available income, eligible individual, SSI, §2167

Relief from obligation to repay overpayment, §1914

Religious groups:
- exemptions, §1128
- self-employment tax exemptions, §1128, §1129, §1130, §1131, §1132

Religious record of birth or baptism established before age 5, §1705

Remarriage:
- benefits affected, chart, §1851 divorce decree effect, §308
- father's or mother's benefits, §417 prior spouse, effect on, §1853
- restrictions, decree of divorce, §308, §309 validity, §309, §310
- widow(er)'s benefits, §406

Renewal commissions, §1310

Rental income:
- commercial or business properties, §1216 exclusion from Social Security, §1213
- farmland, §1221, §1222, §1223, §1224, §1225, §1226, §1227, §1228, §1229, §1230, §1231, §1232 parking lots, warehouses, etc., §1219
- real estate broker, §1215
- real estate held by dealer and investment property, §1214 rooms or apartments, §1216
- services provided by landlords, §1217, §1218 two or more property operations, §1220

Reopening and revision of determination or decision, SSI, §2197
Repayment of overpaid benefits, §1905
Report of Casualty, Form DD-1300, used as intent to claim benefits, §1509
Report of foreign work activity, §1827
Report of work activity by beneficiary, §522
Reporting domestic service wages, §918
Reporting responsibilities, §106
Representative of claimant during review process, §2017
Representative payee:
- accounting responsibility, §1623
- advance notice of proposed action, §1612 agents, SSI, §2146
- appointment policy, §1600 beneficiaries competency, §1601 beneficiary over age 18, §1603, §1610 beneficiary under age 18, §1602, §1609 benefit disbursements, §1617
- categories of payees, §1607, §1608, §1609, §1610 civil suit, overpayment of benefits, §1912
- claims of beneficiary's creditors, §1619
- conservation and investment of surplus funds, §1620 conserved benefits savings, §1622
- evidence of appointment, §1611
- evidence of capability, §1615, §1616, §1617, §1618, §1619, §1620, §1621, §1622 fee agreements, §2018
- funds transferred to successor payee, §1622 needs and maintenance of beneficiary, §1617 new payee selection, §1613
- objection to selection, §1612 overpayment liability, §1905
- payment made directly to beneficiary over age 18, §1603 proper use of benefits, §1617
- repayment of overpayment, §1906 repayments, liability, §1906 responsibilities, §1616
- State mental institutions serving as, §1624

- usual order of preference, §1608, §1609
Representative's fees, §2018
Request for extension of time for filing annual report of earnings, §1817
Request for withdrawal of application for benefits, §1516
Request to expedite payment of monthly benefits, §130
Resources:
- burial spaces/funds, §2160, §2161 conditional payments, §2164 converted recipient provisions, §2172 countable, §2153
- deeming, §2167, §2168, §2169, §2170, §2171 disaster affect, §2162
- exclusions, §2130, §2151, §2156, §2157 life insurance, §2159
- liquid/non-liquid, §2150 non-qualified items, §2151 ownership, §2152
- real property, §2163 statutory limits, §2166
- Supplemental Security Income (SSI), §2148, §2149, §2165, §2167 value, §2154, §2155
Resources not counted as income, SSI, §2130
Responsibilities of representative payees, §1615
Responsibility to prove claim, §104
Restricted countries defined, §1847
Retirement Insurance Benefits (RIB): adjustment of reduction factors at FRA, §728 amount, §302
- application, §1502
- computations, §300
- delayed retirement credits, §720 deported worker, §1841 entitlement requirements, §301 entitlement to other benefits, §734 financing the program, §136 insured status requirements, §211 monthly benefits, eligibility, §300 non-coverage, §108
- nonpayment or partial payment situations, §303 overpayment liability, §1905, §1906 overpayment,

adjustment, §1908, §1909, §1910 partnership rules, §1203
- rate of withholding, §1910
- reduced, §302, §723, §724, §725, §726, §727, §728, §729 special minimum, §302, §717
- spousal entitlement, §305 termination of entitlement, §304
- unpaid amount due a deceased person, persons entitled to the underpayment, §1902 when to file, §1503
- without fault situations, overpayment, §1915, §1916

Retirement systems, Federal employee, §937

Retirement test
See Earnings test

Retroactive coverage, State and local employment, §1011

Retroactive effect of application, §301

Review by Appeals Council of decision by ALJ, §2013

Review of assessment disallowance or allowance of credit or refund FICA taxes, §1019

Reviewing offices, §111

Rounding of benefit rates, §738

Rounding of domestic service wages for reporting purposes, §918

Royalties received by writers, §1113

S

Salespersons, §828

Savings account of beneficiary, former representative payee, §1622

Savings clauses, §731

Schedule C (Profit (or Loss) from Business or Profession), §1416

Schedule F (Schedule of Farm Income and Expenses), §1416

Schedule H (Household Employment Taxes), §1409

Schedule SE, Computation of Social Security Self-Employment Tax, §1416

School attendance, evidence, §1715

School, college, or university, student employed in, §921

School, educational institution defined, §343

Scope of application, expanded or restricted, §1510

Secondary evidence of wages, §1727

Secretaries, Board of Trustees for the Social Security Trust Funds Labor, Treasury, HHS, §141

Section 218 agreements:
- effective date, §1010 non-coverage, §1012
- public transportation systems, §1013 purpose, §1002

Social Security and Medicare coverage, §1003 termination of agreement, §1020
- terms, defined, §1002

Section 911 exclusions, §1246

Securities, dividends and interest, §1206

Selection of representative payee, §1607

Self-employment coverage, §1100:
See Also Self-employment income allocation, §715
- association as a corporation, §1112
- Christian Science practitioners, §1130 church employees, §1136
- court reporters, §1127 crew leaders, farm, §831 defined, §1100
- estate income, §1116
- exemption from self-employment tax contribution, §303, §1128, §1129, §1130, §1131, §1132 farm partnerships and joint ventures, §1121
- fee-compensated positions, State and local employment, §1009, §1122, §1125 fiduciaries, §1114, §1115, §1116
- fishing boat crews, §936, §1134 foreign government employees, §1124 hobbies, §1106
- illegal activity, §1104 landowner/operator of business, §1118 mail carriers, §1117
- ministers and members of religious orders, §932, §1130, §1131, §1132, §1133 multiple enterprises, §1105

INDEX 695

- newspaper or magazine vendors, §930, §1123 partnerships, §1107, §1108, §1109, §1110, §1111, §1112 public office holders, §1126
- real estate agents and direct sellers, §1135 real estate broker, net earnings, §1215
- religious group, tax exemption, §1128, §1129, §1130, §1131, §1132 retirement benefits, non-payable, §303
- sharefarmer, §1119, §1120, §1121
- Social Security and effective dates, §1100 trade or business defined, §1101
- writers, royalties, §1113

Self-employment income, §1414: *See Also* Self-employment coverage allocated to taxable year, §715 association as a corporation, §1112 beneficiary of a trust, §1115 business expense deductions, §1205 capital interest, §1111

- church employees, §1136 corrections, time limit, §1424 court reporters, §1127
- crews on fishing boats, §1134 defined, §1100, §1201
- earnings counted as wages, §1811 earnings records, revisions, §1424
- evidence of unrecorded earnings, §1734, §1735, §1736 executors of deceased estate, §1116
- exemptions, §1129
- foreign work test, §1823, §1824, §1825, §1826, §1827, §1828 hobbies, §1106
- illegal activity, §1104
- Internal Revenue Service tax guides, §1418 landlord, §1118
- limits, §1201
- mail carriers, §1117
- ministers and religious orders, §1130 multiple businesses, §1105
- net earnings, net loss, for taxable year, §1809 newspaper vendors, §1123
- non-professional fiduciaries, §1114, §1115, §1116 noncovered remunerative activity, outside the U.S., §1825 not counted in determining earnings for earnings test, §1812 notice of changes in earnings record, §1427
- optional methods of computing net earnings from self-employment income on farm, §1233, §1234, §1235, §1236, §1237, §1238, §1239, §1240, §1241, §1242, §1243, §1244
- partnership filing, Form 1065, Partnership Return of Income, §1417 partnerships or joint ventures, §1108, §1109, §1110, §1111
- personal services, §1102 public office holders, §1126 quarters of coverage, §215
- quarters of coverage, maximum creditable in year, §212 real estate agents, §1136
- real estate agents and direct sellers, §1135 religious group tax exemptions, §1128 reporting, §1414
- sale or exchange of a capital asset, §1211 sale or rental of properties, §1215 sharefarmer, §1119, §1120, §1121
- social security coverage, §1100 special minimum PIA, §717
- state and local government employees, §1125 substantial gainful activity, §621
- tax exemption, §1129 tax rates, §1415
- taxable net earnings, §1416
- time period in trade or business, §1103 trade or business, defined, §1100
- U.S. citizens working in U.S. for foreign governments, §938 writer's royalties, §1113

Separation of parent and child, child-in-care, §315
Service member, wages, §1305
Sharefarmer, gross farm income, §1239
Sharefarmer, trade or business, §1119
Sick pay plan, wages, §1312
Signature by mark on application, §1511
Signature by mark on check, §124
Signature by mark on statement of evidence, §1702

Simplified old-start formula, §707
Simultaneous entitlement:
- child entitled on more than one earnings record, §735, §736, §737 family maximum, child's benefits, §737
- multiple benefit allowances, §733, §734
- retirement or disability and another higher benefit, §734

Sliding Scale Tables, §2503
Social Security Act: disability protection, §500 program administration, §109 programs, §100
- purpose, §100

Social Security Administration, structure, §109
Social Security benefits, issuance, §120
Social Security Earnings Information, Form SSA-L987, §1726
Social Security information program and rights, §117
Social Security numbers: application, §101, §1401 definition, §101, §1401 lost, §101
- obtaining a card, §101
- penalty for falsifying information, §142 precautions, §1402
- purpose, §101, §1401 replacement, §101 updating records, §101

Social Security office functions, §110
Social Security program service centers, §110
Social Security systems, coordination between U.S. and foreign country, §216
Social Security taxes, §136
Special age 72 payments: application requirements, §347 cost-of-living increases, §719
- entitlement requirements, §211, §346 reduced, other governmental pension, §348

Special minimum PIA, §717
Special occupations of employees, §827
Special Veterans Benefits (SVB):
- appeal process, general, §2722

- appeals council review, process, §2725 appeals, extension of time for filing, §2727 appeals, good cause for not filing timely, §2727 definition and purpose, §2700, §2701 disqualification, §2708
- entitlement, §2702, §2710 filing an application, §2710 filing for, §2709, §2710
- final determinations, reopening, §2728 hearing, defined, §2724
- hearing, location, §2724 hearing, request for, §2724 hearing, result after, §2724
- initial determinations, appeal of, §2721 initial determinations, defined, §2721 initial determinations, notification, §2721
- initial determinations, scope of appeal, §2721 other benefit income, §2707
- payment computation, §2712 payment restricted countries, §2715 payment, date, §2713
- qualifications, §2703 reconsideration, defined, §2723 reconsideration, options, §2723 reconsideration, request for, §2723 residing outside the United States, §2711 return to U.S. to live, §2720
- SSI, eligibility, §2705
- SSI, non-eligibility, §2706
- State supplementary payments- (California), §2714
- Treasury Department regulations, §2715
- U.S. District Court, actions, §2726
- U.S. District Court, filing for civil action, §2726 visit to the U.S., §2717, §2718, §2719
- World War II veteran, §2704

Special wage credits, military service, §212
Spouse's insurance benefits:
- adjustment of reduction factor at ages 62 and FRA, §728 amount, §320
- child-in-care, §312, §1829, §1831 defined, §306

- divorced, §308, §311, §320 entitlement requirements, §119, §305 nonpayment or partial payment situations, §321
- reduced, §320, §723, §724, §725, §726, §727, §728, §729 separate payments, §131
- simultaneously entitled to another benefit, §733 support, evidence, §1724
- terminating events, benefit summary chart, §1851 termination, §322

Star route mail carriers and contract postal service workers, §1117

State and local employment:
- agreement by State may not be terminated, §1020 chaplains, §1133
- compulsory coverage, retirement system, §1005 contributions, reporting, and payment, §1019 court reporters, §1127
- coverage agreements, §1000 coverage groups, §1000
- divided coverage, retirement system, §1008, §1015 effectuation of Federal-State coverage agreements, §1017 employees covered by a State or local retirement system, §1010
- employees transferred from one retirement system to another, §1015 employees whose positions are not covered by a retirement system, §1010 fee-compensated positions, §1009, §1125
- governmental functions, §1003 hospital, employee coverage, §1002 ineligibles, §1015
- interns, hospital, §923
- optional coverage, retirement systems, §1015 optional exclusions, §1008
- pension offset, §1836
- police officers' and firefighters' positions under a retirement system, §1012, §1013 police officers/firefighters retirement systems, §1007
- proprietary and governmental functions, §1003 public office holders, §1126

- public transportation system, §1007
- referendum, retirement system, §1010, §1012, §1015, §1016 retirement system coverage group, §1006
- retirement systems defined, §1011 retroactive coverage, §1018
- second chance coverage, §1015
- Social Security coverage, §1000

States request for review of assessment, disallowance, credit, or refund, §1019 termination of agreement by State prohibited, §1020
- Volunteers in Service to America (VISTA), §947

State and local governments provide services to older Americans, §945

State court reporters, coverage, §1127

State data exchange system, SSI, §2107

State DDS, §115

State liability for FICA contribution, State and local employment, §1019

State plans, SSI, §2172

State Social Security Administrator, defined, §1018

State supplementation of SSI payments, §2181

Statement of Agricultural Employer, Form SSA-1002, §1726

Statement of Claimant or Other Person, Form SSA-795, §1732

Statement of Corrected Income and Tax Amounts, Form W-2c, §1409

Statement of Employer, Form SSA-7011, §1726

Statements by persons knowing about employment and wages, §1732

States authorized to extend coverage to employees under a retirement system, §1013

Statutory resources limitations, SSI, §2166

Step-child:
- deemed, §320
- termination of benefits, effect of divorce, §340

Stepchild-stepparent relationships, §311

Stepgrandchild, dependent, §325
Stepparent, benefits, §421
Stockbrokers, net earnings from self-employment, §1207
Stocks and bonds, dividends and interest, §1206
Stolen checks, §123
Strike benefits as wages, §1325
Student beneficiary:
- confined in a jail, prison, or other penal institution, §344 full-time student defined, §344
- nonattendance up to 4 months' duration, §345
- paid by employer to attend an educational institution, §344 period of absence, §345
- proof of full-time attendance, §1715 reentitlement, §341
- terminating events, §413, §414

Student employment:
- District of Columbia work, §941
- domestic service, §919, §920, §921, §922
- foreign exchange students, visitors and their families, §939 local college club, §919, §920
- nonprofit auxiliary organization of school, §921 nurses in training, §922
- work-study programs, §946

Substantial gainful activity:
- ability to perform, §617, §618, §619, §620, §621 continuing disability reviews, §622
- defined, §603
- earnings amount during period of disability, §620
- effect on disabled worker's benefits, §505, §617, §618, §619, §620, §621 evaluation of disability, §608, §609
- exceptions to effect of substantial gainful activity, §617 medically determinable physical or mental impairment(s), §507 self-employment income, §621
- special cash benefits, SSI, §2178

- work availability, disability evaluation, §610, §611

Subversive activities conviction: additional penalty imposed, §1839 benefit forfeiture, §1837
- dependents' benefits, effect on, §1839 lump-sum death payment, §1839 military wage credits not payable, §959 pardon of convicted person, §1840

Supplemental Security Income (SSI):
- administration and funding, §2100, §2101 administration fees, §2106
- administration of program, §121 administrative actions, §2190 affidavit of support, §2170
- aged, blind or disabled, §2112 agents, §2146
- alien, §2115
- Appeals Council review, §2194
- appeals process, §2191, §2192, §2193, §2194, §2195, §2196 application, where to file, §1505, §1507, §1513
- applications, §2111, §2114 areas of operation, §2103 basic principles, §2102
- benefits financed from general funds, §136, §2105 benefits paid at different rates, §2180
- blind, disabled, 12-month duration requirement, §602 blind/disabled work incentives, §2173
- burial funds, §2161
- burial spaces, resource exclusion, §2160 categories of eligibility, §2112
- change in circumstances affecting eligibility, §2126 check receipt, §123
- child under age 18, application, §607 child under age 18, disabled, §517
- child under age 18, subject to deeming, §2169 citizenship status, §2115
- civil action in a Federal district court, §2195
- claimants residing abroad, §115
- COLA coordination, §2183 computation of payments, §2182 conditional payments, §2164 continuing eligibility, §2125

INDEX 699

- conversions, Federal/State matching grant programs, §2109 converted recipient, §2172
- countable income, §2131, §2132
- countable resources, §2153, §2154, §2155 day of the month benefits are payable, §2104
- deeming of income and resources, §2167, §2168, §2169, §2170, §2171 defined, §126, §2100
- definitions, §2110
- determinations, appeals and reopenings, §2189, §2190, §2191, §2192, §2193, §2194, §2195, §2196, §2197 determinations, reopened or revised, §2197
- direct payments, §2187 disability determinations, §600 disability reviews, §622 disabled, §500
- disaster assistance excluded from income, §2138 disaster assistance excluded from resources, §2162 disaster, defined, §2138
- disposal of resources at less than fair market value, §2165 earned income, §2133
- eligibility, §2111, §2112, §2113, §2114, §2115, §2116, §2117, §2119, §2120, §2121, §2122, §2123, §2124, §2125 eligibility based on need, §2113
- eligibility requirements, §126, §2114 eligibility, absent from the U.S., §2116 eligible couple, §2110, §2122, §2123
- eligible individual, §2110 eligible spouse, §2110
- emergency advance payments (EAP), §2187 essential person, §2110, §2172
- evaluation of disability, §608
- excluded resources, §2151, §2156, §2157, §2158, §2159, §2160, §2161, §2162, §2163 exclusions, earned income, §2135
- exclusions, unearned income, §2137
- Federal benefit rates, §2113, §2147
- Federal program administered by SSA, §126, §2100, §2101 filing extension, reconsideration, §2196

- filing requirements, §2117
- Food stamp eligibility, §2108
- Fugitive felons, §2119 hearing request, §2193 hearing, appeal, §2193, §2196
- home energy or support and maintenance, §2139 how resources are counted, §2154
- immediate payments, §2187
- impairment related work expenses, §2175 impairments, 12-month duration, §602
- impede effective or efficient administration, recovery of overpayment, §1914, §1920 in-kind income, §2140
- in-kind income defined, §2129
- in-kind support and maintenance, §2141
- income and resource limits for eligible couples, §2123
- income, effect, §2128, §2129, §2130, §2131, §2132, §2133, §2134, §2135, §2136, §2137, §2138, §2139, §2140, §2141, §2142, §2143, §2144, §2145, §2146, §2147
- ineligible spouse, §2110
- initial determinations, §2189 institutionalization affects, §2121 institutionalized resident, SSI, §2121 interim assistance reimbursement, §2186 life insurance, §2159
- liquid and nonliquid resources, §2150, §2154 marriage, eligible couple, §2122
- matching grant programs, §2109
- Medicaid application, §2107
- Medicaid, eligibility, §2107, §2179 medical evidence of disability, §614, §615 month of payment, §2104
- one-third reduction rule, value on in-kind support and maintenance, §2142, §2143, §2144, §2145, §2146, §2147 other benefit effects, §2117
- overpayment, adjustment, §1909, §1910 overpayment, liability, §1906 overpayment, waiver, §1914
- ownership of resources, §2152 payment amount, §2180 penalties for

- fraud, §2127 persons outside the U.S., §2116
- Plan to Achieve Self-Support (PASS), §2177
- presumed maximum value rule, §2142, §2143, §2144, §2145, §2146, §2147 presumptive blindness/disability payments, §2188
- principles of program, §2102 probation and parole violators, §2120 program of last resort, §2117
- program operation, §2103
- proration of benefits, §2184 purpose of program, §2102
- qualifies under more than one of the three eligibility categories, §2124 rate of withholding, §1910
- real property as resources, §2163 recipient reporting requirements, §2126 reconsideration, §2192 redeterminations, periodic, §2125
- reduced, living in household of another, §2143, §2144 reduction rule value, §2147
- referral to State VR agencies, §518 reopening determinations, §2197
- reopening determinations, "at any time", rule, §2016 repayment liability, §1906
- reporting responsibilities, §106 residents of public institutions, §2121
- resource exclusions, §2156, §2157, §2158, §2159, §2160, §2161, §2162, §2163 resource limitations, §2164, §2165, §2166
- resources, §2148, §2149, §2150, §2151, §2152, §2153, §2154, §2155, §2156, §2157, §2158, §2159, §2160, §2161, §2162, §2163, §2164, §2165, §2166
- resources defined, §2149
- retrospective monthly accounting, §2183 role of income, §2128
- services and resources not counted as income, §2130 special cash benefits, substantial gainful activity, §2178 special provisions for converted recipients, §2172 sponsor, §2110

State supplementary payments, §2106, §2181 statutory resource limits, §2166
Substantial Gainful Activity (SGA), §2178
- temporary absences and in-kind support and maintenance, §2145 timely reports, penalty reduction, §2126
- unearned income, §2136, §2137
- unpaid amount due a deceased person, persons entitled to the underpayment, §1902 valuation of in-kind support and maintenance, §2142
- VR programs, §518, §2174 windfall offset, §2185
- without fault situations, overpayment, §1915, §1916 work expenses of the blind, §2176
- work incentives, §2173

Support and maintenance, SSI, §2139
Support requirement:
- child, §335 evidence, §1724 grandchild, §325
- parent's benefits, §423, §424

Support, evidence, §1724
Surviving divorced spouse:
- 10-year marriage requirement, §119, §403 child-in-care, §1829, §1831
- defined, §403
- disabled widow(er)'s benefits, §513 entitlement requirements, §403
- lump-sum death payment, application, §433
- lump-sum death payment, not living in the same household, §431 mother's or father's benefits, entitlement, §416
- mother's or father's benefits, remarriage, §417 remarriage, §406
- termination of benefits, §409, §420 widow(er)'s benefits, remarriage, §406

Survivor's insurance benefits:
- 9-month duration of marriage, exception, §404 administration of program, §125
- applicable law, defined, §402 application, §1502

- auxiliaries or survivors of deported worker, §1842 benefit rates, §400
- child's, §410, §411, §412, §413, §414 felonious and intentional homicide, §1722 financing the program, §136
- insured status requirements, §211 legal representatives, §1903
- lump-sum death payment, §428, §429, §430, §431, §432, §433, §1842 mother's or father's benefits, §416, §417
- overpayment adjustment, §1908, §1909 overpayment liability, §1905, §1906
- parent's benefits, §421, §422, §423, §424, §425, §426, §427 payable to survivors, §304, §400
- stepchildren qualifying, §331 support requirements, §423, §424 underpayments, entitlement, §1902
- wages paid in a year after worker's death, §1334
- widow(er)'s, §401, §402, §403, §404, §405, §406, §407, §408, §409 without fault situations, overpayment, §1915, §1916

T
Tables and charts:
- annual exempt amounts, §1803 credits, fully insured status, §204 deemed fully insured status, §205
- farm income, methods of computing, §1241
- Federal Benefit Rates/One-third Reduction Values/Presumed Maximum Values, §2147 insured status requirements, Social Security benefits, §211
- marriage of one beneficiary to another, benefit effect, §1852 maximum wages, limitation, §1301
- monthly benefits/lump-sum death payments, evidence, §1700
- non-farm self-employment income, methods of computing, §1243 payment of benefits conditions, §1800

- self-employment tax rates, §1415 sliding scale tables, §2503
- Social Security/Medicare tax rates, §1405 statutory resources limitations, SSI, §2166 termination of benefits, §1851
- time limit for correcting earnings records, §1423

Tax exemption claims, §1129
Tax Guide for Small Business, Internal Revenue Service Publication No. 334, §1200
Tax Payer Identification Number (TIN), §101
Tax reports:
- due dates, §1410
- employer forms for reporting, §1409
- employer records, §1412
- self-employment, §1414, §1415, §1416, §1417, §1418 self-employment tax guides, §1418
- tip income, §1408

Tax-Sheltered Annuity Plan, payments, §1340
Taxes:
- deduction from wages, §1331, §1406 deductions by employers, §1406 disposition of, §1403
- excess deductions, credit against employee's income tax, §1407 exemptions, §1131
- filing due dates, §1410 forms, §1409
- multiple employers, §1407
- religious groups, exemptions, §1128, §1129, §1130, §1131, §1132 self-employment, §1414
- self-employment income, §1414, §1415
- Social Security benefits, §125 trust funds, §141
- wages paid before January 1, 1987, State contributions, §1019

Teleservice centers, SSA, §110
Temporary absences and in-kind support and maintenance, SSI, §2145
Temporary separation of parent and child-in-care, §315

Termination of agreement, foreign subsidiary of domestic corporation, §965
Termination of entitlement: child's, §340, §341, §342, §414 disabled worker's, §506, §511 mother's or father's, §420 parent's, §427
- retirement insurance benefits, §304 spouse's, §322
- student beneficiary, §344 summary of events chart, §1851 widow(er)'s, §409
Termination of marriage, proof, §1718
Termination of State agreements prohibited, §1020
Ticket to Work and Self-Sufficiency Program, §519
Timber sales, farm income computation, §1240
Time limit:
- administrative review process, §2001 annual report of earnings, §1815
- Appeals Council review, §2013 appeals process, §2014
- conditional payments, excess resources, §2164 earnings record corrections, §1423, §1424, §1425 evidence of support, §424
- exemptions, IRS, §1132
- extension for earnings record corrections, §1425
- extension of time limit for filing for reconsideration, SSI, §2196 filing extension, reconsideration, hearing, or review, §2015 hearing by ALJ, §2007
- reconsideration appeal, §2192 reopening determinations, §2016
- request for reconsideration of determination, §2004, §2192
- State request for review, §1019 suspension, military service, §1426
Tips, §1303
Totalization
    See International Social Security Agreements
Totalization Agreements: coverage affect, §970 defined, §107

- foreign countries, coverage, §216 limitations on exceptions, §1846
- U.S. and foreign country agreements, §107, §216, §970, §1845, §1846
Trade or business: absentee owners, §1102 beneficiary of a trust, §1115
- beneficiary working outside U.S., deductions, §1823, §1824, §1825, §1826, §1827, §1828 defined, §1101
- excluded work and services, §1122, §1123, §1124, §1125, §1126, §1127 exclusions, §1122
- family partnerships, §1109 fiduciaries, §1114, §1115, §1116 fishing boat crews, §936, §1134 hobbies, §1106
- income earned outside U.S. by a citizen or resident alien, §1245 landowner distinguished from business operator, §1118
- legal or illegal activity, §1104
- length of time engaged in business, §1103 multiple enterprises, §1105
- nonbusiness work, coverage, §924, §925 operation of an estate, §1116
- partnerships, §1107, §1108, §1109, §1110, §1111, §1112 personal services not a factor, §1102
- sharefarmer, §1119, §1120, §1121
- star route mail carriers and contract postal service workers, §1117 writers, royalties, §1113
Trader or investor in stocks and bonds, net earnings from self-employment, §1208
Training pay for veterans, §1328
Transfer of capital interest in family partnerships, §1111
Transmittal of Corrected Wage and Tax Statement, Form W-3C, §1409
Transmittal of Wage and Tax Statement, Form W-3, §1409
Traveling expenses paid to employee, §1332
Traveling or city salespersons, §829
Treason and similar crimes, benefit forfeiture, §1837

Treasury Department: checks reissued, §122, §130 combined check returned, §131
- countries restricted from payments, §1848 mailing of checks, §123
- return of checks to, §134

Trial Work Period (TWP):
- beginning/ending period, §522
- extended period of eligibility for re-entitlement to benefits, §506 ineligible, §521
- purpose, §520

Trust beneficiary, trade or business, §1115

Trust fund profit-sharing payments, §1313

Trust fund, money gifts and bequests to Social Security, §140

Trust funds:
- application, §433
- extension of time limit for good cause, §1518, §1519 management of, §141
- Social Security tax amounts, §141

Types of employment in the U.S. covered by Social Security, §900

Types of farm work covered as agricultural labor, §904

U

U.S. Savings Bonds, conservation of benefits by representative payee, §1619

Underpayment defined, §1900

Undertakes to produce a crop, defined, §1120

Unearned income, SSI, §2136

Unemployment compensation agencies, findings as evidence, §1731

Uniformed service member, defined, §949

Union records as evidence, §1729

United States:
- citizens working outside U.S., in ministry, §1246 citizenship, evidence, §1725
- income earned outside U.S. from a trade or business, §1245 non-payment provisions, alien, §1845, §1846
- totalization agreements, §107, §216

- work outside, §961, §962, §963, §964, §965, §966, §1823, §1824, §1825, §1826, §1827, §1828

United States Citizen Identification Card, Form I-197, §1725

Unnegotiated checks, underpayment, §1900

Unpaid amount due a living person, §1901

Unpaid benefits, §1900

Use of benefits by representative payee, §1615

V

VA-filed application for Social Security benefits, §1506

Vacation pay as wages, §1327

Vehicle exclusions, §2157

Vendor or cash payments, SSI, §2186

Veteran's benefits:
- allied countries, service with, wage credits, §957, §1307 dishonorable discharge, §956
- insured status, §960
- noncontributory wage credits, §953, §954, §955, §956, §957, §958, §959
- special, §2700

Veterans pay for on-the-job training, §1328

VISTA program, §947

Vocational rehabilitation services:
- continuation of disabled worker's benefits, certain situations, §506 continuing disability reviews, §622
- cost, §518
- disabled worker, §505
- programs, work incentives, SSI, §2173 referral to State VR agencies, §500, §518 trial work period, incentive, §519

Volunteers, Peace Corps, §943

W

Wage and Tax Statement, Form W-2, §1404

Wages:
- actual or constructive payments, §1302 advance payments, §1309, §1320 agricultural, §214, §901, §902

- annual report of earnings, §1814 annuity or bond purchase plans, §1316 back pay, §1323
- bonuses and dividends, §1322 cafeteria plan, §1341
- cash-pay test, §902, §1303 commissions, §1309, §1310 constructively paid, defined, §1302 counted as earnings, §1811
- credits for military service, §953, §954, §955, §956, §957, §958, §959, §960 defined, §212, §1300
- dependent care assistance payments, §1339 disability payments of former employees, §1335 disabled beneficiary, §1335
- dismissal pay, §1324
- domestic service, §915, §916, §917, §918, §919 earnings test, exclusions, §1812
- earnings test, inclusions, §1811 employee tax deductions, §1406
- employee's estate after death, §1334
- employer cost (premiums) of group-term life insurance, §1337 employer records required, §1412
- employer records, not available, §1727 employer-employee conflict, §1422
- evidence, §1421, §1726, §1727, §1728, §1729, §1730, §1731, §1732, §1733, §1734, §1735, §1736 exclusions, employee awards, §1330
- farm rental income, §1221
- Federal Thrift Savings Plan, §1315 fringe benefits, §1342
- group term life insurance, §1337 homeworkers, §830
- idle time pay, §1326
- included in applying the earnings test, §1813 included-excluded rule, §968, §969
- insurance or annuities, §1311
- Japanese internees during WWII, §1336
- life insurance renewal commissions, §1310 loans, §1321

- maximum creditable in 1-year, §1301 maximum, taxable in year, §212, §1301 meals and lodging, §1343
- military service, §952, §953, §954, §955, §956, §957, §958, §959, §960, §1305, §1306, §1307 minimum pay test, §1304
- moving expenses, §1333 multiple employers, §1407 nonprofit organizations, §1304
- nonqualified deferred compensation plan, §1318 occupancy of space payments, §1219
- paid after worker's death to survivor or estate, §1334 paid before January 1, 1987, §1019
- payments from IRA's and Keogh Plans, §1338 payments not intended as wages, §1344 payments other than from employment, §1344
- payments received from insurance plans, pensions, etc., §1311, §1312, §1313, §1314, §1315, §1316, §1317, §1318, §1319
- pension and retirement payments, §1317 personal records, as evidence, §1733 prizes and awards, §1330
- profit-sharing plan, §1313 quarters of coverage, §212 railroad compensation, §1308 retired beneficiary, §1826
- sales commissions, §1309, §1310 self-employment, §1414, §1810 sick pay, §1312
- Social Security purposes, §1300
- statute of limitations, State liability, §1019 strike benefits, §1325
- supplemental retirement plan payments, §1319 tax exempt annuity plan, §1316
- tax exempt trust fund, §1314 tax forms for reporting, §1409 tax payments, §1331, §1405
- tax-sheltered annuity plan, payments, §1340 tips, §1329, §1408
- traveling expenses, §1332 trust funds, §1314

INDEX 705

- type of income counted for earnings test purposes, §1811 types, §1300
- unsigned employer wage statements, §1728 vacation pay, §1327
- veteran's training pay, §1328

Waiting period, disabled worker's benefits, §502

Waiver Certificate to Elect Social Security Coverage for Use by Ministers, Certain Members of Religious Orders, and Christian Science Practitioners, Form 2031, §1130

Waiver of overpayment recovery:
- against equity and good conscience, §1919 defeat purpose of program, §1918
- estate of deceased person, §1921 person at fault, §1917
- relief from repayment, §1914 without fault, §1915, §1916

Warehouse and storage garage rentals, §1219

Warrants: SSI, §2119
- Title II, §1854

Waterways, ditches, etc., maintenance, agricultural labor, §912

Widow(er)'s entitled to mother's or father's insurance benefits, §415

Widow(er)'s insurance benefits:
- adjustment of reduction factor at ages 62 and FRA, §728 amount, §407
- application, §405
- application not required, §405 benefit rate, §407
- certificate of election, §405 defined, §402
- entitlement requirements, §401 entitlement to parents benefits, §415
- listing of insured status requirements, §211
- lump-sum death payment application, §430, §433 mother's or father's, §415, §416, §417, §418, §419, §420 nonpayment situations, §408

- reduced, §723, §724, §725, §726, §727, §728, §729 remarriage, effect, §406
- surviving divorced spouse, §403 terminating events, §409, §420

Windfall eliminated, §718
Windfall offset, SSI, §2185
Withdrawal of application, §1515
Within the U.S. defined, §961
Without fault, overpayment, §1915
Work activity defined, §603
Work activity report by beneficiary, §522
Work activity, disability evaluation, §617
Work availability factor, substantial gainful activity determination, §507
Work excluded from mandatory full Social Security coverage, §1002
Work excluded from mandatory hospital insurance only coverage, §1002
Work incentives, SSI, §2173
Work not in course of employer's trade or business, coverage, §914
Work outside U.S., §961
Work-study programs, students, §946
Workers' compensation:
- disability insurance benefits, effect, §503, §504, §1835 events to report, §522
- lump-sum settlement, §504
- reduction in disabled worker's benefits, §504

Writers, trade or business, §1113
Written decision on reconsideration determination and notice, §2012
Written request for an extension of time for filing an annual report of earnings, §1816
Written statement by beneficiary, acceptable if enough information is given, annual report of earnings, §1818
Written statement in lieu of application for benefits, §1509
Written statements of earnings, §1411

EAST NORTHPORT PUBLIC LIBRARY

3 0602 00342 1077

APR 2024